Forensic Art
and Illustration

Forensic Art
and Illustration

Karen T. Taylor

CRC Press
Boca Raton   London   New York   Washington, D.C.

COVER ART

Front Cover: Two-dimensional facial reconstruction over the skull of "Daisy Jane Doe" by Karen T. Taylor (see Chapter 11).

Back Cover: Drawings by Karen T. Taylor of skull-to-face relationship of the three major racial/ancestral groups (see Chapter 3).

Library of Congress Cataloging-in-Publication Data

Catalog record is available from the Library of Congress.

© 2001 by CRC Press LLC

No claim to original U.S. Government works
International Standard Book Number 0-8493-8118-5
Printed in the United States of America 1 2 3 4 5 6 7 8 9 0
Printed on acid-free paper

Preface

The need for a comprehensive text examining the multifaceted field of forensic art became apparent to me some 20 years ago. As a trained artist new to the realm of law enforcement art, I quickly found a library search on the subject to be futile. Today, many forensic art cases later, I feel both prepared and compelled for a variety of reasons to share information about this highly specific and challenging field. Years of service in a large state police agency provided a never-ending succession of interesting and intriguing cases. My position with the Texas Department of Public Safety often led me into different fields of study related to forensic art. More than a decade of conducting workshops has necessitated the thoughtful evaluation and assessment of the methods and procedures currently in use. As an instructor, I have encountered hundreds of individuals anxious to learn more about forensic art and desperately seeking sources of information. Virtually every time I have appeared in court, it has been necessary to educate the prosecutor as well as the jury about police art.

Since the inception of forensic art, there has been debate about who is best trained to perform various aspects of this activity. Some have contended that an academic background in psychology, anatomy, biology, or anthropology is necessary to maximize the accuracy of the forensic rendering. Others argue that training as a medical illustrator or fine artist is essential. **The author and contributors are committed to a collaborative effort that involves the multidisciplinary expertise of professionals in various fields.** The foundation is the artist, who calls upon the appropriate expertise of psychologists, anthropologists, medical examiners, and others to provide a set of descriptive data that can be interpreted into the forensic rendering.

This book provides an expansive and practical guide to the various aspects of the field of forensic art and attempts to aid in the standardization of some of the methods and terminology being used. Hopefully, it will prevent others from making some of the avoidable mistakes sometimes caused by inexperience or lack of information. My goal is to organize case experience and training materials into one cohesive work and to present them in a comprehensive, usable form for the practicing police artist and others seeking information on the subject.

Because forensic art cases often present challenges that require the artist to have knowledge of a variety of subjects, this text provides an "A to Z" reference covering each of the applicable topic areas. This book is divided into four parts:

Part I   **Forensic Art: The Foundation**
Part II   **Forensic Art: Finding and Identifying the Living**
Part III **Forensic Art: Identifying the Dead**
Part IV   **Forensic Art: Additional Responsibilities**

Part I introduces forensic art, defines pertinent terminology, and traces more than **100 years of forensic art** as an aid to law enforcement. Also examined are fundamental particulars of the ever-fascinating **human face** and ways to use this knowledge in forensic art applications with an emphasis on **drawing the human face**.

Part II describes methods of locating and identifying living individuals through forensic art. **Composite drawings** and the associated **interviewing process** required to achieve accurate and useful composites are covered in depth. Of particular significance are the complexities of **victim trauma** and their effects on **memory retrieval**. Information is provided on how **facial growth** can be used to project the possible appearance of a child missing over a period of years. As growth ceases, **facial aging** begins, and knowledge of this process, too, is essential to the forensic artist for preparation of age progression updates of the faces of fugitives or long-term missing adults. **Part II** concludes with methods of **assessing and modifying images** of various types to make them more useful in criminal investigations.

Part III addresses the rather unpleasant but necessary methods of forensic art used to identify human physical remains. Information is given for use in preparing **post-mortem drawings** that are produced to help identify bodies on which facial features are still intact. These cases require the use of crime scene or morgue photos of the deceased or the viewing of the actual body itself. In cases of semi-skeletal or skeletal remains, **two- or three-dimensional** skull reconstruction methods are used. **Betty Pat. Gatliff** and I discuss specifics of each method in depth and offer important information on **skull protection and preparation for reconstruction.** Forensic anthropologist **David M. Glassman, Ph.D.,** contributes general information on methods of **superimposition for comparison of unidentified skeletal remains with photos of missing persons.**

Part IV outlines additional responsibilities of the forensic artist, including **professional ethics,** knowledge of **printing and graphics reproduction,** ways to deal with the **news media,** and information about **testifying in court**. Demonstrative evidence (trial displays) is a related topic, but because it involves an entirely different and additional range of knowledge and expertise, it is not addressed in depth in this book.

A final function of this book is to provide law enforcement personnel — often faced with an urgent need to identify both criminals and victims *without* the availability of a comprehensive team — a training guide to assist in their work. It is likely that, in pressure situations, these individuals will **need** to do the forensic art procedures whether or not they have had adequate training. Certainly there is no legal mechanism to prevent them from doing so. It is my desire, therefore, to **assist** them in performing these very important tasks by providing a model of instruction as well as the inducement to produce optimum quality work. In light of the more than 17,000 law enforcement agencies in the U.S. handling one violent crime every 21 seconds, this attitude is appropriate.*

The potential importance of high quality forensic art cannot be underestimated. It is the obligation of all those who do this work to constantly strive to improve their skills. One image can literally be responsible for the recovery of a precious stolen child, stopping a serial rapist or murderer, or providing closure for the family who has lost a loved one to homicide. It is my fervent hope that these pages might provide help to better achieve such aims.

— **Karen T. Taylor**

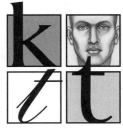

Karen T. Taylor
Facial Images

---

* United States Department of Justice, Federal Bureau of Investigation, *Crime in the United States, Uniform Crime Reports*. Washington, D.C.: U.S. Goverment Printing Office, 1998.

The Author and Contributors

Karen T. Taylor is a freelance portrait artist who worked for 18 years as a forensic artist at the Texas Department of Public Safety in Austin, Texas. She attended the School of Fine Arts at the University of Texas and the Chelsea School of Fine Art in London, where she was also a freelance portrait sculptor for Madame Tussaud's Wax Museum. Her crime-fighting artwork for law enforcement agencies and FOX Television's "America's Most Wanted" has involved a variety of art services to aid in the apprehension and conviction of criminal offenders or to promote the identification of unknown deceased persons. The success of her forensic art led to Ms. Taylor being named one of the "Texas Women of the Century."

A forensic art instructor for many years at the FBI Academy and other law enforcement academies, universities, and medical schools in the U.S. and Canada, Ms. Taylor now

Betty Pat. Gatliff (left) and **Karen T. Taylor** (right). (Photo by Missey Micheletti.)

also trains fine artists. Her specialty is highly realistic and expressive portraits in bronze. She accepts both forensic art and fine art commissions through her studio, Facial Images, in Austin. She is currently working on a book entitled *Understanding the Human Face.*

Betty Pat. Gatliff, B.A., is a retired medical illustrator who develops, teaches, and practices forensic sculpture at her freelance studio, SKULLpture Lab, in Norman, Oklahoma. She is a Fellow of the American Academy of Forensic Sciences, an Emeritus Member of the Association of Medical Illustrators, and an Associate Member of the International Association for Identification. She is internationally recognized for her expertise in this specialized field; the *Wall Street Journal* has called her "a forensic legend."

David M. Glassman, Ph.D., is Chair and Professor of Anthropology at Southwest Texas State University, and Director of the Human Skeletal Identification Laboratory, a private consulting service. He is board certified by the American Board of Forensic Anthropology and is the past Chairman of the Physical Anthropology Section of the American Academy of Forensic Sciences. Dr. Glassman has 20 years experience in forensic anthropology and skeletal biology and an active record of scholarly publication and presented papers. He has consulted in more than 250 skeletal identification cases. Dr. Glassman conducts workshops in forensic anthropology for medical examiners, forensic dentists, and law enforcement agencies.

Dr. David M. Glassman (left) and **Karen T. Taylor** (right). (Photo by Lt. Lisa Sheppard.)

Acknowledgments

I am indebted to my husband, **David,** without whose support this book could never have been written. His example in thought and action provides continuous inspiration.

For chapters that contributed greatly to the training value of the book and especially for their friendship and encouragement during this project, I fondly thank:

> **Betty Pat. Gatliff,** SKULLpture Lab, Norman, Oklahoma
> **Dr. David M. Glassman,** Chair, Department of Anthropology, Southwest Texas State University, San Marcos, Texas

Special thanks go to **Missey Micheletti,** forensic photographer and imaging specialist, Texas Department of Public Safety, whose careful documentation of many of the techniques presented in the text enriched the finished product tremendously. She also reviewed the sections related to photography.

For their generous offers to read and review portions of the text, and for the insight and improvement that resulted in every case, I wish to thank the following individuals:

> **David M. Griffith,** Commander, Motor Vehicle Theft Service, Texas Department of Public Safety
> **Mike Cox,** Chief of Media Relations, Texas Department of Public Safety
> **Dr. Fran Belmont,** Psychological Services, Texas Department of Public Safety
> **Patricia Linebarger,** Crime Analyst, Texas Department of Public Safety
> **Jennifer Wakefield Land,** Texas Department of Public Safety, for her "yuk" or "cool" notes in the margins of the text
> **Glenn Miller,** National Center for Missing and Exploited Children

To **Angie McCown,** Victim Services Director, Texas Department of Public Safety, I am indebted not only for reviewing the text, but also for providing valuable resource material dealing with memory, trauma, and crime victims' issues.

To **Dr. Ron Fisher,** Florida International University, Department of Psychology, Miami, Florida go my particular thanks for the immeasurable contribution of his knowledge of the workings of the human mind. His reviews of the material on memory, interviewing, and victims' issues greatly strengthened the text.

To **Colonel Dudley Thomas,** Director, Texas Department of Public Safety (retired), I am indebted for the use of numerous case examples that greatly aid in the instruction of this material. I thank him, too, for the opportunity to serve the citizens of Texas in the capacity of forensic artist at the DPS.

My appreciation also extends to:

> **Richard Berry** and **Myke Taister** of The Federal Bureau of Investigation for use of case examples
>
> **John Moriarty** and **Louis Fawcett** of the Texas Department of Criminal Justice for assistance with photographs
>
> **Detective Michael Streed,** Orange, California Police Department, for friendship, support, and helpful information
>
> **Detective Frank Domingo,** New York City Police Department (retired), for many insightful training ideas

Special thanks to the following forensic art colleagues who contributed examples of their composite drawings:

> **Deputy Chief Mike Deal,** Altamonte Springs, Florida Police Department
> **Detective Kevin Richlin,** Sunnyvale, California Department of Public Safety
> **Lieutenant David Graves,** Maryville, Tennessee Police Department
> **Lieutenant Roy Paschal,** South Carolina Law Enforcement Division
> **Sergeant Will Beechinor,** Austin, Texas Police Department
> **Marla Lawson,** Georgia Bureau of Investigation
> **Lois Gibson,** Houston, Texas Police Department

To **Lieutenant Lisa Sheppard,** Texas Department of Public Safety, who (with only a little arm-twisting) selflessly allowed me to show her early drawings ("Oh, my gosh, you must be kidding! Swear you won't use my name.") in the hope that they would encourage other budding forensic artists.

To **Mary Griffith** for the photographic series showing facial growth in Chapter 7 and for the guy that it depicts.

Thanks also to:

> **William Boone,** formerly of CRC Press, who encouraged the idea of writing this book in the first place, by dragging Robert Stern to my 1994 lecture in Boca Raton, Florida
>
> **Becky McEldowney,** for her skill, kindness, patience, and good humor as my editor
>
> **Chris Andreasen,** CRC project editor, for the many hours and long weekends spent helping me pull together my thoughts
>
> **Brenda Craytor,** for skillful administrative assistance
>
> **Bonnie and Pansy,** for their faithful middle-of-the-night vigils
>
> **Juanita Taylor,** my mother, who always encouraged me to work hard and follow my heart

There are no words to thank all of the **victims and survivors of violent crime** from whom I have learned so much. May you find peace.

— **Karen T. Taylor**

Contents

4   Drawing the Human Face

PART II   FORENSIC ART: Finding and Identifying the Living

5   The Interview

9 Image Assessment and Modification

PART III FORENSIC ART: Identifying the Dead

10 Postmortem Drawing

11 Skull Protection and Preparation for Reconstruction

12 Two-Dimensional Facial Reconstruction from the Skull

PART IV   FORENSIC ART: Additional Responsibilities

15   Professional Ethics and Conduct

16   Printing and Graphics Reproduction

FORENSIC ART:
The Foundation

Chapter 1

Introduction to Forensic Art and Illustration

Many law enforcement officers have come to know the power of forensic art. They have seen a composite drawing lead to the perpetrator they seek, or a facial reconstruction help reveal the identity of a homicide victim. Age progressions help officers recover abducted children and locate fugitives who have been at large for many years. Many have witnessed the profound impact and clarity that forensic art can bring to court proceedings.

While not every forensic art attempt is successful and not every case lends itself to the use of forensic art, this work does contribute significantly to many criminal investigations. The increasing options for image enhancement and modification that computers allow mean this role is likely to escalate in the future. **It is incumbent upon all who bear the responsibilities of criminal investigations and prosecutions to understand more about forensic art.**

What Is Forensic Art?

Forensic art is "any art that is of a forensic nature; that is, art used in conjunction with legal procedures." A working definition of **forensic art is any art that aids in the identification, apprehension, or conviction of criminal offenders, or that aids in the location of victims or identification of unknown deceased persons.** When applied to a particular profession, "forensic" implies that the contributions of the respective occupation pertain to the administration of justice during a case investigation or its presentation in court.[1] Hence, any art used in conjunction with a case investigation or court presentation can be considered "forensic."[2]

Forensic art is often multimedia in nature; its primary purpose is to present visual information. A suspect composite image enables officers and the public to better focus on a suspect's appearance based on the witness' description rather than on an erroneous image in their own minds based solely on a verbal or written description. Age progressions or appearance updates of missing children or fugitives encourage the viewer to visualize a present-day likeness of a given face rather than an outdated facial image. Art for court presentation aids both judge and jury in the visualization and understanding of crime scenes or events. Facial reconstructions, whether drawn, sculpted, or computer-generated from skeletonized remains, give face to the faceless. Although the art media may vary, these examples all share one common feature: the presentation of visual information.[2]

Four Categories of Forensic Art

Forensic art generally can be divided into four areas of concentration, each of which encompasses several subcategories:

1. **Composite Imagery.** Graphic images made up from the combination of individually described component parts (may include full body drawings or object/evidence drawings) (Figure 1.1).
2. **Image Modification and Image Identification.** Methods of manipulation, enhancement, comparison, and categorization of photographic images (Figure 1.2).
3. **Demonstrative Evidence.** Visual information for case presentation in court as trial displays (Figure 1.3).
4. **Reconstruction and Postmortem Identification Aids.** Methods to aid in the identification of human physical remains in various conditions (Figures 1.4, 1.5, and 1.6).

Figure 1.1 Composite Imagery. Composite drawing by KTT based on a victim's verbal description (left) and photo of subject identified (right). (Courtesy of Texas Department of Public Safety.)

Figure 1.2   Image Modification. Early photograph of fugitive (left), fugitive update drawing by KTT (center), and later photograph of subject (right). (Courtesy of "America's Most Wanted.")

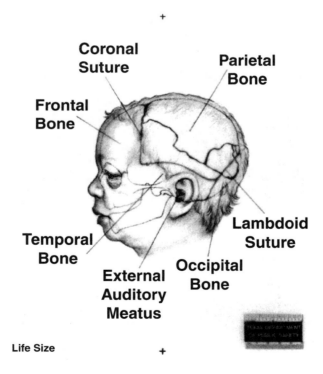

Figure 1.3   Demonstrative Evidence. Trial display by KTT used in infant murder case to depict fatal injuries in contrast to natural suture lines of the skull. (Courtesy of Texas Department of Public Safety.)

Figure 1.4 Two-Dimensional Facial Reconstruction from the Skull. Skull of homicide victim (left), facial reconstruction from the skull by KTT (center), and photograph of victim identified (right). (Courtesy of Texas Department of Public Safety.)

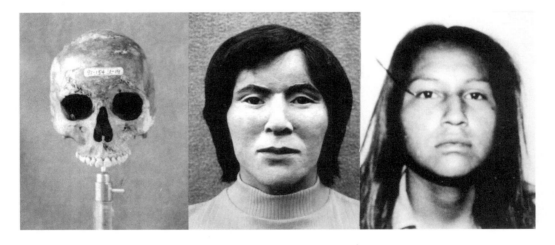

Figure 1.5 Three-Dimensional Facial Reconstruction on the Skull. Skull of homicide victim, missing mandible (left), facial reconstruction on the skull by Betty Pat. Gatliff (center), and photograph of victim identified (right). (Courtesy of Betty Pat. Gatliff.)

Art or Science?

Forensic art is a blend of art and science. This art/science relationship occurs because forensic art can present scientific information or use scientific principles in a visual format rather than a verbal one. Practical examples of the art/science blend may include:

- Knowledge of cognitive psychology, behavioral science, interview techniques, and facial anatomy used during composite imagery sessions.

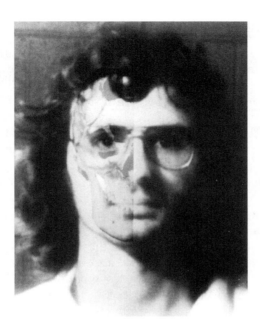

Figure 1.6 Skull-to-Photo Superimposition Comparison. Right side of skull of deceased person compared to a photograph in life. (Courtesy of Missey Micheletti and Texas Department of Public Safety.)

- Application of craniofacial growth data in the preparation of child age progressions.
- Pathology, fingerprint, trace evidence, or other scientific findings incorporated into illustrations for court presentations.
- Taphonomic, anthropological, or odontological data used by the artist when creating postmortem drawings or two- and three-dimensional facial reconstructions from the skull.

Forensic artists combine their artistic skills with science to assist criminal investigations and case prosecutions in a variety of ways. In many instances they work in conjunction with other specialists. For example, forensic pathologists advise and guide artists by providing information about unidentified homicide victims for the preparation of postmortem drawings based on intact or relatively intact bodies.

Similarly, forensic anthropologists offer their expertise when facial reconstructions from the skull are needed from skeletal bodies. Other experts in odontology, radiology, craniofacial or maxillofacial surgery, cosmetology, opthamology, or other specialists may be consulted depending on the nature of the project. Yet, the forensic artist is a specialist in his or her own right. Dr. William G. Eckert, in his book *Introduction to Forensic Sciences*, defines a "forensic scientist" as "a specially trained individual who applies scientific knowledge to the administration of justice during the investigation of a case or during its presentation in court."[3] Similarly, a "forensic artist" is a specially trained individual who applies artistic knowledge to the administration of justice during the investigation of a case or during its presentation in court.[2]

Who Is the Forensic Artist?

Today's forensic artist is capable of performing a wide spectrum of art functions to assist in criminal investigations and case presentations. Some artists specialize almost exclusively in one aspect of forensic art such as composite imagery, skull reconstruction, or child age progression. My many years of work for a large state police agency on an ever-changing array of cases required different areas of study and expertise. Thus, it seems that I have never been able to stop learning to prepare myself for the next challenge, and I continue to strive to be a "jack of all trades" in forensic art.

Most police agencies in the U.S. utilize a forensic artist on an "as needed" basis, either using someone employed on staff in another capacity or hiring a freelancer. Certain agencies employ a full-time forensic artist, but such instances are rare and usually occur in federal or state agencies or in very large cities.

Practitioners in this business tend to enter the field from various directions. Many are police officers who began doing forensic art out of necessity on cases within their own agencies. Others are civilian employees working within police agencies who demonstrated artistic talent and were recruited by detectives to help with their investigations. Some are trained artists who contract with law enforcement agencies on a freelance basis.

Depending upon which forensic art specialty practitioners choose, their education should be geared accordingly, with the intention being to "fill in the gaps" of their own training and experience. For example, experienced police officers who have spent many years conducting interviews and testifying in court may require additional art training. Civilian artists, either employed in law enforcement or freelancers, must learn about functioning within the proper constraints of the laws of the jurisdiction within which they work.

Training for artists should also facilitate the specific area of forensic art to be done. Anyone who prepares composite images should have training in interview techniques and sensitivity to crime victims. I firmly believe that serious composite artists should consider this an area for career-long improvement. Such artists can never have too much knowledge about memory-enhancing interview techniques, and they should feel compelled to constantly read literature involving research in this area.

Those artists who work with image modification, particularly by computer methods, should seek training and expertise in softwares that allow the manipulations and enhancements they require. Image modifications such as age progressions that project growth in a child's face require study of the complex patterns of craniofacial growth. Age progressions of the faces of long-term missing fugitives require a knowledge of facial aging. Both types of age progressions can be enhanced by an understanding of human dentition and the associated patterns of dental eruption in children as well as modifications that occur in the forms around the mouth with aging and dental attrition.

Artists who prepare demonstrative evidence or trial displays must have a wide array of skills. This field has become so complex that many have chosen to specialize in a particular category. Displays can be graphic art, photographic, computer-generated, three-dimensional, or animated. They may be as simple as an enlargement of two side-by-side fingerprints for comparison or as complex as elaborately animated reenactments of an event.

Those who do postmortem drawing or facial reconstruction from the skull must delve into an entirely different base of learning. Postmortem drawings require a working knowledge of taphonomic changes that occur with death and their effects on the face. Facial reconstructionists work very closely with physical or forensic anthropologists and often gain knowledge in that field that directly benefits their work. Trained medical illustrators are "naturals" for going into facial reconstruction because of their strong foundation in facial anatomy.

Methods of superimposition of skulls to photographs of missing persons are generally best approached as a team effort. The forensic artist, as one member of the team, provides knowledge of the morphological structures of the face that aids in the orientation of the skull into the correct position for overlay comparisons. The scientifically trained experts make the assessments that can lead to identification.

In some cases, fortunate individuals trained in various areas of science possess the artistic skills to do the artwork themselves rather than advising an artist.

A recurring theme throughout this text is the benefit of collaboration between the artist and scientist in forensic art, particularly in unidentified deceased cases.

The purpose of this text is to lay a historical foundation of knowledge of the entire field of forensic art and to provide specific data for use in the areas of composite drawing/imagery, image modification, postmortem drawing, facial reconstruction from the skull, and skull-to-photo superimposition. The fields of cognitive psychology, behavioral science, kinesics, anatomy, pathology, anthropology, odontology, computer science, jurisprudence, and others offer a great deal of beneficial research information. Unfortunately, much of the material is quite technical, cumbersome, and time-consuming for the average working police artist to sort through. My intention is to interpret some of the data in an effort to present a synopsis of the literature that is current and readily useful for the forensic artist "in the trenches."

Those who seek to do forensic art should accept the responsibility with seriousness and be prepared to acquire the fundamental knowledge required to properly perform these tasks. Depending on your specific function, solid foundations and information bases *must* be acquired in facial anatomy, art skills, interview skills, and other specific studies as needed. As with any worthwhile field of endeavor, it is simply not good enough to expect a computer program to "take you there" or look for ways to "cut corners." **The victims of violent crimes and the citizens whose lives your work may help to safeguard deserve your full efforts.**

References

1. Domingo, F. J., *Composite Art Manual*. New York: The International Association for Identification and John Jay College of Criminal Justice, 1986.
2. Stewart, K. T. (Karen Taylor) and Richlin, K. R., "Forensic art: defining the International Association for Identification's ninth discipline," *Journal of Forensic Identification*, 39, 215–216, 1989.
3. Eckert, W. G., *Introduction to Forensic Sciences*. New York: C.V. Mosby, 1980, 233.

Chapter 2

A History of Forensic Art

More Than 100 Years of Aid to Law Enforcement

Forensic art is not a new phenomenon. It has been used for decades as a tool by law enforcement professionals. From the case of "Jack the Ripper" to the Oklahoma City bombing, forensic art has documented crime-related information and boosted the quest for justice. Composite sketches from eyewitness descriptions, for the purpose of identification and apprehension of a particular suspect, comprise some of the earliest and best-known examples of police art.

Other early drawings that portrayed the accused criminal's appearance as he or she sat in the courtroom were used to delight curious readers in newspapers across the country. Over time, as another branch of the identification process, systems were developed that measured and classified humans to help track their paths through the criminal justice system.

Crime scene diagrams came to be used to document, clarify, and reconstruct the action at the scene of an incident. Eventually, science professionals began to seek assistance from artists to identify bodies. More recently, artwork has been instrumental in projecting growth of the faces of missing children, sometimes helping to locate them after several years have passed. Similarly, projecting facial aging to depict a more recent appearance in cases of dangerous long-term fugitives has proven effective in nabbing many elusive characters.

Over the years, motivated by curiosity and interest, I have collected information on cases and events that have contributed to the field of forensic art. Particular attention has been paid to successfully solved cases in which forensic art techniques have played a major role in the resolution of the case. Of special interest are "high-profile" cases that have received national or international notice as well as those cases in which technical advances have been achieved.

The information is presented in chronological order to follow the evolution of the field. **Cases examined fall into the discipline's four general areas of concentration:**

1. **Composite Imagery** — composite drawings, mechanically generated composites, and object or evidence drawings.
2. **Image Modification and Image Identification** — methods of manipulation, enhancement, comparison, and categorization of photographic images.
3. **Demonstrative Evidence** — visual information for case presentation in court.
4. **Reconstruction and Postmortem Identification Aids** — methods to aid in the identification of human physical remains in various conditions.

The 1800s

An early example of a composite drawing appeared on an 1881 **Scotland Yard** "wanted" poster that depicted **Percy Lefroy Mapleton**, who was sought on a murder charge (Figure 2.1). The drawing is basically a caricature, as were many of the earliest composite drawings. The Old West also produced "wanted" posters with facial drawings; one example, which concerns outlaw train robber **Cole Younger**, is located at the **Texas**

Figure 2.1 Composite drawing of **Percy Lefroy Mapleton** by an unknown artist, 1881.

Figure 2.2   Postmortem drawing of **"Jack the Ripper"** victim made by Dr. F. Gordon Brown at the crime scene, 1888.

Rangers Archives in Waco, Texas. These are two examples of drawings of known individuals used because of the lack of photographs; thus, they are perhaps not composite drawings by strict definition. In both cases the sources of the drawings, either photo references or witness description, are unknown.

Also documented from this time period is a postmortem drawing of a victim of **"Jack the Ripper,"** who terrorized London's Whitechapel district for a period of approximately 3 months during 1888 (Figure 2.2). He is known to have killed at least five women, and some criminologists credit him with as many as 11 murders. Although numerous theories as to his identity have been proposed, all that is known about him is that he had some rudimentary medical knowledge and that he was possibly left-handed, based on the examination of the victims' wounds by police surgeons. The postmortem drawing, done by pathologist Dr. F. Gordon Brown, shows Catherine Eddowes, the fourth victim. It was used to indicate the location and extent of the wounds to the body.[1]

A courtroom sketch from the 1893 trial of accused murderess **Lizzie Borden** of Fall River, Massachusetts was prepared by a newspaper artist (Figure 2.3). Lizzie, a 32-year-old spinster, lived with her father Andrew, stepmother Abby, and older sister Emma. Andrew Borden, a shrewd businessman, amassed a considerable fortune, but was miserly with his family. Lizzie and Emma felt great resentment toward their

Figure 2.3   Courtroom sketch by an unknown artist of **Lizzie Borden** (left) and Emma Borden (right), 1893.

stepmother and despised the austere way in which they were forced to live despite the family's wealth. On August 4, 1892, Andrew and Abby Borden were found brutally murdered in their home, their skulls smashed with an axe. Two weeks later, Lizzie was arrested for the crimes. She went to trial in June 1893. Former Massachusetts governor George Robinson handled her defense. Courtroom sketches of Lizzie from the *Illustrated American* depict her seated beside her older sister Emma during the 13-day trial. Lizzie was acquitted of all charges, although many questions about the case still remain unanswered today.[2] Courtroom drawings are included here because of their related interest and historical value. However, they do not fall within the strictest definitions of forensic art since they generally play no role as investigative or prosecutorial aids; rather, they were prepared for use by the news media.

Image identification or the recording and indexing of a person's facial features for future identification purposes was greatly advanced in the late 1800s by **Dr. Alphonse Bertillon**, an anthropologist and records clerk at the French Sureté in Paris (Figure 2.4). "Le Portrait Parlé" or "The Word Picture" was Bertillon's system of classification of incoming prisoners based on various measurements of the face and body. A major intent of his system was documentation of individual prisoners to ensure future

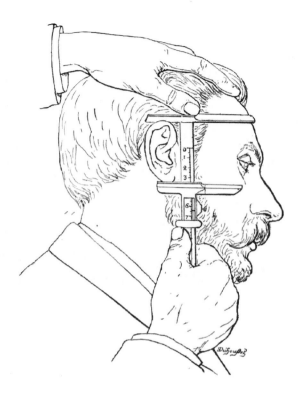

Figure 2.4 Drawing by Duprec demonstrating **Bertillon's system** of measuring the ear for "**Le Portrait Parlé**," late 1800s.

recognition of recidivists and proof of their identity. Taught to detectives and identification technicians in Europe and America, the system flourished for about 20 years until fingerprint classification replaced it (Figure 2.5). Bertillon's 1896 book entitled *The Bertillon System of Identification: Signeletic Instructions, including the Theory and Practice of Anthropometrical Identification* with illustrations by Duprec has provided a basis for future composite kits, catalogues, and even computer-generated recall systems.[3] Forensic artists and other facial identification specialists are particularly indebted to Bertillon for his insights into the importance of examining the unique qualities of ear configurations for identification purposes.

The Early 1900s

The coming of the new century brought many advances in technology that would also boost the efforts of law enforcement. A new invention by Guglielmo Marconi, known as the "wireless telegraph," was first used in crime detection in the pursuit of the notorious murderer **Dr. Crippen**. Born in Coldwater, Michigan, Hawley Harvey Crippen married Cora Turner, an aspiring opera singer and later a music-hall entertainer. The couple moved to London, where they resided at No. 39 Hilldrop Crescent. When Mrs. Crippen disappeared in early 1910, Dr. Crippen maintained that she had left him and returned to America. Her friends became suspicious and made a report to Scotland

Figure 2.5 Class of detectives learning **Bertillon's system** of classification in Paris during the late 1800s.

Yard when Dr. Crippen's secretary, Ethel le Neve, moved into No. 39 and began wearing Mrs. Crippen's clothes and jewelry. In July, Chief Inspector Walter Drew visited the flat, found no sign of Dr. Crippen or le Neve, and conducted a search of the premises. Underneath the floor of the coal cellar, he found the dismembered remains of Mrs. Crippen; she had been poisoned. Warrants were issued for the arrests of the two lovers and bulletins with detailed descriptions of Dr. Crippen and le Neve were distributed.

A British police artist attempted to assist in the hunt by preparing what was essentially an early fugitive update drawing based on old photos of Dr. Crippen (Figure 2.6). Unfortunately, the image was a highly romanticized representation and actually flattered the suspect more than it provided useful information about him.

A captain aboard a ship traveling from Antwerp to Quebec, aware of the search for the fugitives, became suspicious of two passengers — a father and son. He sent a message to the authorities on the newly invented Marconi wireless telegraph, relaying his suspicions. Upon docking, authorities arrested the man and his "son," who were actually Dr. Crippen and le Neve, dressed as a boy. Ethel le Neve was acquitted and freed and Dr. Crippen was hanged in November 1910.[4]

Amazingly, the examples above show that all **four major types of forensic art** — were used before 1915. The Scotland Yard wanted poster (Figure 2.1) uses **composite image**. Bertillon's work (Figures 2.4 and 2.5) is an example of **image identification**. The sketch of Crippen (Figure 2.6) is an early **image modification**. The Lizzie Borden trial (Figure 2.3) included **demonstrative evidence**. The Jack the Ripper investigation (Figure 2.2) utilized **postmortem drawing**.

The years just following the turn of the century were a time of great interest in the various ways in which humans could be measured and classified. Phrenology is the study of the bumps on a person's head, once believed to indicate mental faculties and character. It was popular as a parlor game and even utilized, for a time, for law enforcement purposes. A phrenological diagram was done of the head of **Nathan Leopold** who,

Figure 2.6 Outdated photograph of Dr. Crippen as he appeared on police posters headed "Wanted: For Murder and Mutilation" (left) and highly romanticized version of Crippen with a beard drawn by an unknown police artist — an **early fugitive update example** (right), 1910.

along with **Richard Loeb**, kidnapped and murdered a 14-year-old boy in Chicago in 1924. The intent of the phrenological examination was to prove that Leopold was an intellectual slave to Loeb and therefore less responsibile for the crime. These two wealthy, intelligent young men admitted they had killed the boy for the "fun of it" and, despite the efforts of attorney Clarence Darrow, both were sentenced to life imprisonment.[5]

A composite sketch was done in the early 1920s as part of the investigation of a bombing incident at an office on Wall Street in New York (Figure 2.7). Police located a witness from a nearby blacksmith shop who had shod the horse of a stranger observed carrying a covered object in the back of his wagon. Subsequent interview of the blacksmith provided sufficient facial detail to help an artist prepare a drawing of the **Wall Street Bomber**. A commercial artist hired by the Federal Bureau of Investigation made a sketch that led to the identification of a suspect who was eventually apprehended.[6]

The 1930s

Charles Lindbergh earned the admiration of the world when he flew the Atlantic solo in 1927. The nation was shocked when his only son, 20-month-old **Charles Lindbergh, Jr.**, was kidnapped from his bed in the family home in Sourlands, New Jersey on March 1, 1932. A crudely written ransom note left on the nursery window sill demanded cash for the child's return. Dr. John F. Condon, a physician, was chosen to act as go-between with the kidnapper. A composite sketch was prepared from Condon's description of the abductor as given to Jim Berryman, a political cartoonist with the *Evening Star* newspaper in Washington, D.C. (Figure 2.8). Tragically, the child's decomposed body was found only a few miles from the Lindbergh home. The composite sketch did not directly lead to a perpetrator, but $2\frac{1}{2}$ years later, when

Figure 2.7 Composite drawing of the "**Wall Street Bomber**" by an unknown artist for the Federal Bureau of Investigation in the early 1920s.

Figure 2.8 Composite drawing by Jim Berryman, political cartoonist for the *Evening Star,* of the **kidnapper of the infant son of Charles Lindbergh** (left), 1932, and subject Bruno Hauptman (right).

Bruno Hauptman was arrested, there was noticeable resemblance. Hauptman was tried and found guilty of the Lindbergh murder and was electrocuted on April 3, 1936 in the New Jersey State Prison.[7]

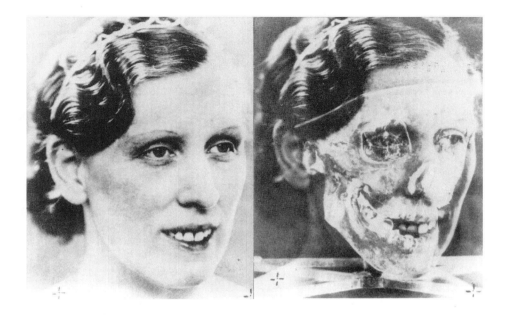

Figure 2.9   Photograph of murder victim **Mrs. Buck Ruxton** (Isabella) (left) and **superimposition comparison** of an enlarged life-photo of her face with the negative from the photograph of her skull by Glaister, Smith, and Brash (right), 1935.

The 1930s saw some significant events in the development of forensic art. An intriguing early study in superimposition comparison for identification is the 1935 case of **Dr. Buck Ruxton**. Dr. Ruxton and Isabella, his common-law wife, quarreled regularly, and he frequently accused her of infidelity. When Isabella and her 20-year-old maid disappeared from their home in Lancaster, England, Ruxton reported that his wife had left him for another man. Approximately 2 weeks later, grisly remains were found near the Scottish border. Police recovered two human heads and about 70 human body parts wrapped in newspaper. The newspaper was from a special edition dated September 15 and distributed only in the area where the Ruxtons lived. Investigation revealed that Mrs. Ruxton and her maid Mary Rogerson had been missing since mid-September. Mrs. Ruxton was identified with the aid of a superimposition comparison of an enlarged life-photo of her face with the negative from the photograph of her skull (Figure 2.9). This procedure, performed by Glaister, Smith, and Brash in Edinburgh, marked the first documented use of this technique in a medicolegal identification case. Dr. Ruxton was tried and found guilty of murder and hanged on May 12, 1936.[7]

In 1938, **The Federal Bureau of Investigation** established its Cartographic Section, later called the Exhibits Section and, still later, the Graphic Design Unit. This unit, now known as the Investigative and Prosecutive Graphics Unit, is the current location for the Bureau's forensic artists.[8]

The 1940s

A 1945 case underscores the importance of the role of the anthropologist in determining the skull/facial relationship. As part of a then-secret project ordered by President Harry

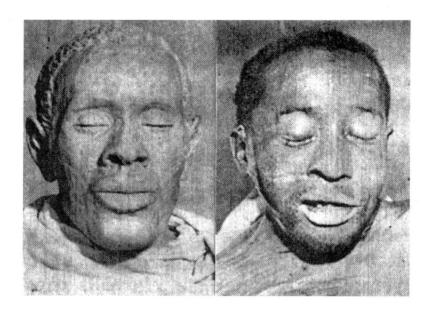

Figure 2.10 Experiment in three-dimensional facial reconstruction on the skull by **Dr. Wilton Krogman** and sculptor Mary Jane McCue, showing reconstruction sculpture based on the skull only (left) and subject (right), 1946. (Courtesy of Federal Bureau of Investigation.)

Truman, anthropologist **Dr. Wilton Krogman** prepared outline drawings to attempt to predict the probable skull morphology of **Adolf Hitler** because of rumors that he might still be alive. The drawings were intended for use by the Allies for comparison and verification purposes should a skeleton ever be found.[9]

The post-war years brought an interest in both superimposition and facial reconstruction techniques, especially among the Russians, as a possible means of identification of concentration camp victims. While an associate professor of anatomy and anthropology at the University of Chicago in 1946, Dr. Wilton Krogman conducted a landmark experiment in three-dimensional soft-tissue facial reconstruction from the skull (Figure 2.10). He selected a cadaver head and photographed it. Then it was macerated and permitted to dry for one month. The skull was turned over to a sculptor, Mary Jane McCue, along with data on average tissue thicknesses at different facial landmarks for the appropriate racial group. With other information provided by Krogman concerning sex, race, and age, McCue prepared a reconstruction sculpture that was then compared to the initial photos of the head. Krogman concluded that this technique was in fact useful as an aid in determining the identity from the skull, and published his results in the July 1946 issue of the *FBI Law Enforcement Bulletin*.[10] Much of the work done years later in the field of three-dimensional reconstruction from the skull by Betty Pat. Gatliff and Dr. Clyde Snow was predicated on the early experiments of Krogman.

The 1950s

The **Sam Sheppard** murder case was one of the most high profile cases and trials of the early 1950s. It proved to be an early example of the ways in which media attention can affect the criminal justice system in the U.S. On July 4, 1954, Marilyn

Figure 2.11 Photograph of murder victim **Mrs. Sam Sheppard** (Marilyn) (left) and **composite drawing** by an unknown artist of suspect as described by neighbors near the Sheppard home (right), 1954. (From *Mockery of Justice: The True Story of the Sheppard Case* by Cynthia L. Cooper and Sam Reese Sheppard. Copyright 1995 by Cynthia L. Cooper and Sam Reese Sheppard. Reproduced with permission of Northeastern University Press.)

Reese Sheppard, who was 4 months pregnant, was beaten to death in her home in Bay Village, a suburb of Cleveland, Ohio. Her husband, Dr. Sam Sheppard, claimed that he had arrived at their home during the assault and struggled with a bushy-haired intruder. A police artist prepared a composite sketch of a man seen by neighbors walking in the vicinity of the Sheppard home near the time of the murder (Figure 2.11).

After repeated media attacks, Dr. Sheppard was charged with his wife's murder, convicted, and sentenced to life in prison. In 1964, with the assistance of attorney F. Lee Bailey, Dr. Sheppard was released from prison after serving 10 years, when a federal district court ruled that he had not received a fair trial. He was retried and found not guilty in 1966, and died in 1970 at the age of 46. The popular 1960s television series "The Fugitive" was based on the Sheppard case, as was the 1993 movie of the same name starring Harrison Ford.[11]

During the 1950s, the notion of a hand-assembled system of building facial composites appeared. Several people have claimed credit for originating the composite assemblage concept, including:

- **Detective Constable Albert Simpson**, Nottingham City Police, England[12]
- **Patrick Dunlevy**, Royal Canadian Mounted Police
- **Hugh MacDonald**, Los Angeles Police Department

This idea led to the commercial production of the assemblage system known as **Identi-KIT** in the U.S., patented by Smith & Wesson. The earliest Identi-KIT was composed of clear sheets called "foils," which were printed with various individual facial features. At the direction of a witness, these foils could be stacked one on top of the other to create a face. The early kits were made from hand-drawn component features and the resulting composites had a "sketch" quality. Updated kits were later manufactured from photographic component features.

Conceptually, a very similar procedure was developed at about the same time by **Corporal Reg Abbott** of the **Royal Canadian Mounted Police**. Abbott's system involved the creation of three-dimensional plaster masks of criminal faces based on witness descriptions. Abbott had a list of 115 questions and seven facial masks that were shown to each witness, with the belief that practically all the variations of the human face were represented in these particular masks. The witness would select individual characteristics from the seven masks and explain how the suspect's face, hair, and complexion differed. They then discussed other subtleties such as tissue development above the eyes and the ear angle. A notable use of Abbott's method was in the case of the murder of RCMP Constable Gammon in Montreal in 1950. A sculpted plaster mask of the killer based on eyewitness descriptions bore a strong resemblance to the suspect who was apprehended. The success of this case led to the installation of the mask-making capability in all Canadian provinces. However, the use of the **mask identification system** decreased over time and the method is not used today.[13]

The Identi-KIT was so simple for the average police detective to use that it may well have overshadowed Abbott's system. Although it was a good idea, it is likely that the cumbersome, messy process of making plaster casts caused its downfall. During the 1950s, Identi-KITs swept into police agencies across the U.S. and resulted in the decline in use of hand-drawn sketches over the next 25 years.

An early success story of use of a kit-generated composite is the case of **Harvey Glatman** in Los Angeles, California. Glatman was an amateur photographer who lured attractive young women with the promise of modeling jobs. Pretending to photograph them for the covers of detective magazines, he explained that his assignment was to photograph a woman in distress, therefore he had to tie and gag them to get the desired shot. Once the women were under his control, he raped and strangled them. A composite, developed from the description of a victim who escaped, showed a strong resemblance to Glatman (Figure 2.12). He was tried and convicted of murder and was put to death in the gas chamber at San Quentin on August 18, 1959.

The 1960s

Although Identi-KITs greatly diminished the use of hand-drawn sketches in the 1960s, the **FBI** continued to use them in the Exhibits Section (formerly the Cartographic Section) and employed the considerable art skills of **Roy Rose, Pat Nobles, and Horace Heafner**. A rather distinct "style" evolved among the FBI artists during this time, with the production of highly rendered drawings involving many hours of work (Figure 2.13). These drawings, called "artist's conceptions," were generally produced from written descriptions and photographic "look-alikes" provided to headquarters artists by FBI field agents, rather than from direct witness interviews. A 1960s FBI publication entitled *Visual Aids for Investigative and Prosecutive Use* states:

> ... we will consider artist's conceptions to be limited to portraits prepared
> by artists using descriptions, *FBI Facial Identification Catalog* selections, and

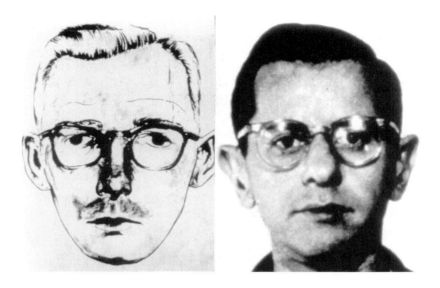

Figure 2.12 Early **Identi-KIT composite** of homicide suspect in Los Angeles (left) and subject **Harvey Glatman** (right), 1958. (Courtesy of Los Angeles Police Department.)

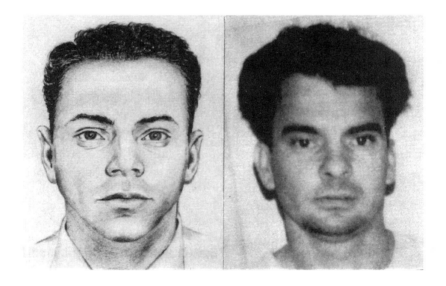

Figure 2.13 **Composite drawing** by an FBI artist of a **1960s bank robber** (left) and subject identified (right). (Courtesy of Federal Bureau of Investigation.)

available "look-alike" photographs as sources of information. Experience has shown that it is possible to prepare effective artist's conceptions without direct contact between the artist and the witness.

... Our use of "look-alike" photographs and detailed descriptions, although not publicized to any great extent outside the Bureau, is considered by us to be the best system in use.

Several devices are on the market which utilize outline drawings and overlays bearing likenesses of typical facial characteristics of human males and females. With these devices the witness and the investigator are required to make a composite portrait from the outlines and overlays. However, we can provide a more detailed likeness by using the services of our staff of artists and employing descriptive and "look-alike" information.[14]

In the introduction to the aforementioned publication, **J. Edgar Hoover** made the following statement: "These aids are valuable investigative tools with which each Special Agent should be familiar."[14]

Thus, in a time when facial assemblage kits were very popular with law enforcement agencies in the U.S., the FBI continued its use of the hand-drawn sketch. Additionally, because of the logistical difficulty of providing art services to the entire nation, the FBI used the method of "long-distance" interviews, relying on agents to gain pertinent descriptive information from witnesses.

The assassination of **President John F. Kennedy** in 1963 led to the production of medical drawings by a Navy artist documenting the alleged trajectory of the fatal bullets through the back of the President's head. In the years that followed, the accuracy of these drawings would be questioned.

The summer of 1966 was a particularly eventful one in the history of modern crime. The term "mass murder" entered the American vocabulary. On the night of July 14, 1966, in a middle-class Chicago neighborhood, a young man knocked on the door of the residence of several student nurses. The young nurse who answered the door found that in one hand he had a gun and in the other, a knife. Before the night was over, **Richard Franklin Speck** had killed eight student nurses and raped one, in what was then called the "crime of the century." A hand-drawn composite sketch was done by Chicago Police Department artist **Otis Rathel**, based on the description of Corazon Amurao, a young exchange student from the Philippines (Figure 2.14). Miss Amurao, a witness to the horror of the killings, had hidden from the confused and drunken Speck by rolling under a bunk bed, thereby escaping detection. After murdering the women, the 24-year-old Speck spent the night in a skid-row hotel and attempted suicide by cutting his wrists with a broken wine bottle. An emergency room surgeon recognized Speck from the composite sketch that had been distributed along with the description of a tattoo that read "Born to Raise Hell." Speck was tried and sentenced to death, but when the Supreme Court struck down the death penalty, he was re-sentenced to serve eight consecutive terms of 50 to 150 years each. He was confined to the Illinois State Penitentiary until his death.[15]

Less than a month after the Speck murders in Chicago, an equally shocking crime occurred in Austin, Texas. In the early morning hours of August 1, 1966, 25-year-old student **Charles Whitman** stabbed and shot his mother, then stabbed his young wife. Taking several weapons, a radio, and sandwiches, he climbed to the top of the observation tower of the University of Texas, clubbed a receptionist to death, and barricaded the stairway. An ex-Marine and expert marksman, Whitman began shooting indiscriminately at people below. He killed 16 people and wounded 31 others in the next 90 minutes, defying the attempts of police and low-flying aircraft to stop him. Eventually police stormed the barricade he had erected and fatally shot him. A note from him was found, saying: "Life is not worth living."[16] Detailed diagrams of the top of the university tower were drawn by **Ken Conoley** of the Texas Department of Public Safety, Graphic Art Department. Conoley's drawings aided in the follow-up

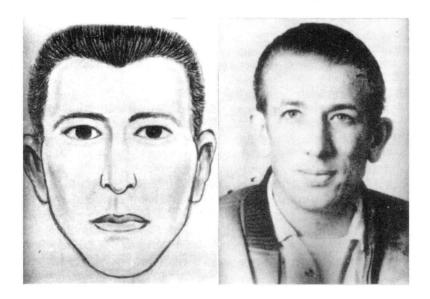

Figure 2.14 **Composite drawing** by Otis Rathel for the Chicago Police Department of the suspect in the murders of eight student nurses in Chicago in 1966 (left) and subject **Richard Franklin Speck** (right). (Courtesy of Chicago Police Department.)

investigation and assessment of the incident by clarifying the positions of Whitman, his victims, and the officers involved in his demise.

Betty Pat. Gatliff of Oklahoma, now internationally recognized as a pioneer in the area of three-dimensional facial reconstruction from the skull, attempted her first reconstruction case in January 1967 (Figure 2.15). Anthropologist **Dr. Clyde Snow**, with whom Gatliff worked at the Federal Aviation Administration in Oklahoma City, had reviewed the technique suggested by **Krogman** in both the 1946 article and

Figure 2.15 **First facial reconstruction** on the skull done by Betty Pat. Gatliff in 1967 (left) and victim identified (right). (Courtesy of Betty Pat. Gatliff.)

Krogman's textbook *The Human Skeleton in Forensic Medicine,* published in 1962. As a consultant on the Medical Examiner's staff for the State of Oklahoma, Snow was confronted with a case of unidentified skeletal remains of a young man. At his prompting, Gatliff developed a sculpture directly on the skull, according to the guidelines set forth by Krogman. After media distribution, the facial reconstruction led to the positive identification of a young Native American. Interestingly, Gatliff sculpted only one side of the face in this and other early cases, photographically "flopping" it to provide the other side. Eventually, she came to realize the importance of the subtle assymetries that exist in most faces and began developing both sides of the face.[17] This early successful collaboration of Gatliff and Snow formed the foundation in the U.S. for the use of facial reconstruction from the skull.

The 1970s

In the early 1970s in Britain, **Jacquer Penry** developed and implemented a hand-assembled, facial composite system known as **PHOTO-FIT**. In 1971, Penry published *Looking at Faces and Remembering Them: A Guide to Facial Identification,* in which he sought to systematize the process of gaining facial descriptions for use by British police forces. He states:

> Often even the best possible intentions cannot bridge the gap between the *recollection and description* of raw material for face-building which the witness may be able to produce, and the *mechanics* of picture-making in which the interviewer has been trained. Such a bridge can only be built by a better understanding — both by the official and the man on the street — of the human face as a subject: that is, as something which can be definitely and profitably learned.
>
> … The answer to the problem of the "gap" must surely lie in a completely fresh and far better approach to the whole subject of facial identification, both in the field of the professional interrogator and the wider area of the man on the street.
>
> … This kind of *preparedness* is vital: knowing how to look at a face according to certain simple rules, and practising these rules in the ordinary course of duty and leisure until a far more expert kind of observation, recollection and description becomes automatic.[18]

Penry's feature-by-feature analysis of the face indicates a familiarity with the earlier work of Bertillon.

Although the United Kingdom and countries of continental Europe adopted Penry's PHOTO-FIT for standard use at this time, police agencies in the U.S. began to move away from assemblage systems, with many returning to the hand-drawn sketch. In fact, in the early 1970s there was a sort of renaissance in forensic art in America. Police artists throughout the country successfully assisted in solving cases with composite sketches. It was a time when high profile cases began to thrust the work of police artists into the limelight like never before, for better or worse.

Training courses for police artists were presented at several locations in the U.S. during the 1970s. **George Homa** of the New Jersey State Police taught a number of aspiring sketch artists on the east coast, and published a book entitled *The Law*

Enforcement Composite Sketch Artist in 1983.[19] **Fernando Poncé** of the Los Angeles Police Department conducted classes for artists on the west coast. Beginning in 1972 **J.A. Cormack** taught workshops for police artists at the Waukesha County Technical Institute in Waukesha, Wisconsin, and published an in-depth guide for artists entitled *The Police Artist's Reference* in 1979.[20] In 1978, Cormack patented a system for assembling symbols for facial features called **MEMOPIX**, intended to be a sort of shorthand "memo" of a facial description done to promptly record a perpetrator's face based on a witness' description. The MEMOPIX would then serve as a guide for the sketch artist to prepare a more detailed facial drawing. While an organized, clever, and well-intentioned concept, Cormack's system never came into common use.

The west coast of the U.S. was the setting for two particularly enigmatic cases at about this time, both of which remain unsolved today. In each case forensic art was attempted, but proved fruitless. A sexual sadist, the killer known in the San Francisco area as **"The Zodiac,"** took pleasure from torture and murder. The official police tally of his victims was 6, although in mocking and sometimes cryptic notes to authorities he claimed to have killed 37. Composite sketches were prepared by both Napa and San Francisco police, as was a full-body drawing of the killer in a hooded costume he was known to wear. This killer, who was never captured, was the likely inspiration for the character "Scorpio" in the Clint Eastwood film "Dirty Harry."

In 1971 **D.B. ("Dan") Cooper** hijacked a 727 airliner at 10,000 feet over western Washington State and demanded that the plane land to pick up a $200,000 ransom and four parachutes. When again airborne, Cooper jumped with the cash from the rear stairwell of the jet in 200-mile-per-hour winds and was never seen or heard from again. FBI artist **Roy Rose** produced a hand-drawn sketch of Cooper based on the description given by a stewardess who had remained on board the plane for a time with the hijacker (Figure 2.16).

Figure 2.16 Composite drawing by FBI artist Roy Rose of 1971 airline hijacker known as "**D.B. Cooper**," with and without glasses. (Courtesy of Federal Bureau of Investigation.)

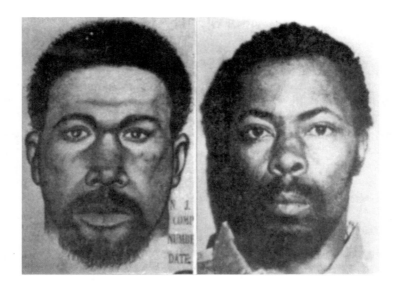

Figure 2.17 Composite drawing by George Homa of suspect in the 1973 murder of a New Jersey State Trooper (left) and subject **Clark E. Squire** (right). (Courtesy of New Jersey State Police.)

A routine traffic stop on the New Jersey Turnpike in 1973 led to the death of a New Jersey State Trooper. The vehicle was occupied by two males and a female later found to be members of a black militant organization. Two troopers were involved. One was overpowered in a struggle and shot to death, the other was wounded and survived. Within 5 hours, New Jersey State Police artist **George Homa** was dispatched to the hospital to interview the surviving officer. A composite sketch prepared from the trooper's description was widely distributed (Figure 2.17). Within 40 hours of the shooting, the man in the sketch was identified as **Clark E. Squire** and was found hiding in a drainage ditch.

The female involved in the incident was **Joanne Chesimard**, the leader of the Black Liberation Army. Both Squire and Chesimard were tried, found guilty of murder, and sentenced to life imprisonment.[19]

Theodore Robert Bundy, a handsome, articulate, all-American law student, is also believed to be one of the most notorious serial murderers in American history, responsible for the rapes and murders of at least 30 young women in at least five states from 1974 to 1978. Several composite drawings of the suspect "Ted" were prepared, but none led directly to his identification (Figure 2.18). For the police artist, he was a difficult subject to "capture" because he had a chameleon-like quality and was adept at altering his appearance.

After years of undetected killing Bundy was arrested on a fluke, suspected of residential burglary. He received several death sentences in different trials, and resided on death row in Florida until his execution in 1989.[21]

For a full year from summer 1976 to summer 1977, a gunman with a .44-caliber weapon who came to be known as the **"Son of Sam"** terrorized New York City. A 300-man task force investigated the case, but the killer continued to stalk his victims, who ultimately numbered 13. None of the various composite drawings of the shooter prepared by the NYPD Artist Unit resembled the others very closely (see Chapter 15,

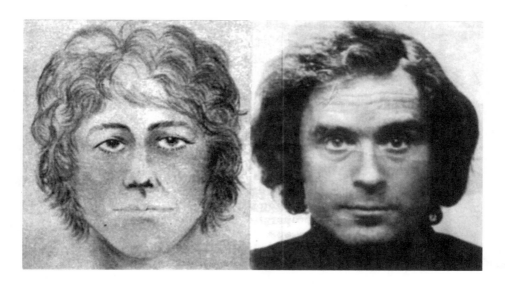

Figure 2.18   Composite drawing by an unknown artist of 1970s serial murder suspect "Ted" (left) and subject **Theodore Bundy** (right).

Figure 15.2). Like Bundy, the killer was finally apprehended on a fluke. A parking ticket he had received near one of the murder scenes was eventually traced to him. **David Berkowitz**, a quiet 24-year-old postal worker from Yonkers, was accused and convicted of the crimes.[22]

The Berkowitz case taught a critical lesson in the field of forensic art regarding the circumstances in which a composite sketch could be done. Public, political, and media outrage surrounding this case were so great that NYPD officials came under tremendous pressure to produce results in the investigation. Unfortunately, several sketches were prepared from descriptions by witnesses who probably had not seen the killer well, hence the discrepancy among the composites. This variance in the drawings has led many to speculate that Berkowitz did not act alone. In 1987, a book by Maury Terry entitled *The Ultimate Evil* put forth the theory that, as a member of a ritualistic cult, Berkowitz "took the fall" for the multiple cult members responsible for the murders. Terry's theory was based in part on the fact that the composites had so many varied looks.[23]

More composite drawings were probably done in the **Atlanta Child Murders** case than in any other serial murder case in recent memory. **Marla Lawson** prepared sketches based on multiple witness interviews. In 1978 George Homa of New Jersey made a sketch from the description of psychic Dorothy Allison. Before subsiding, the death toll in Atlanta reached 28. According to Lawson, as many as 50 composite drawings were prepared for the investigation, none of which played a significant role in the arrest of **Wayne Williams**, who was later charged in some of the crimes.[24]

California was the 1977 and 1978 site of another series of horrific murders perpetrated by a killer called **"The Hillside Strangler."** At least ten young women were raped, tortured, and strangled. Their bodies were then dumped on hillsides northeast of Los Angeles. Several composite drawings were done of the suspect, who actually turned out to be two men, Kenneth Bianchi and cousin Angelo Buono. In another 1978 California case, the **Lawrence Singleton** investigation, a 16-year-old girl was picked up while hitchhiking, sexually assaulted, and left for dead in a rural area near Modesto. The attacker sought to obscure any identification of the victim so he hacked off both her arms just below the elbows. Amazingly, the victim survived and gave a description to artist **Tom Macris** of the San Jose Police Department.[25] Singleton was identified within 48 hours after the sketch was disseminated and convicted based on evidence found in his vehicle. Singleton received a 14-year sentence for this crime and was released after serving approximately 7 years in the penitentiary.

Also in 1978, the U.S. House of Representatives Select Committee on Assassinations convened to investigate the murders of **Reverend Martin Luther King, Jr., President John F. Kennedy, and Senator Robert Kennedy**. Several items of forensic art were examined as part of the committee's investigation. **Horace Heafner** of the FBI had produced a composite drawing from witness descriptions of the murderer of Reverend Martin Luther King, Jr. in Memphis, Tennessee in 1968.[26] Detailed illustrations based on autopsy photographs of President Kennedy were drawn by medical illustrator **Ida Dox**. At the request of the committee, **Betty Pat. Gatliff** prepared three-dimensional life-size models of the President's head to be used for trajectory tests. She was given access to tracings of skull radiographs taken of the President in life as well as various known measurements to aid in the accuracy of the models[27] (see Chapter 13, Figure 13.60).

In December 1978, **John Wayne Gacy** was arrested in Des Plaines, Illinois, after approximately 6 years of torturing and murdering young men and boys. Gacy was a successful businessman, active in Democratic politics, with photographs of himself taken with the mayor of Chicago and First Lady Rosalynn Carter. He frequently entertained children at local hospitals dressed as "Pogo" the clown.

Thirty-three deaths are attributed to Gacy, with the remains of 29 teenage boys found primarily in the crawl-space beneath his suburban home. Nine clay facial reconstructions from the skulls of unidentified victims were done by **Betty Pat. Gatliff**. One boy was positively identified and five others were tentatively identified. The process proved to be particularly difficult because some of the boys were transients and others were male prostitutes whose families were reluctant to come forward and identify them.[27]

The 1980s

During the early 1980s, composite drawings prepared by **Detective Frank Domingo** of the NYPD aided in the resolution of several high profile cases. In July 1980, a 31-year-old violinist was murdered at the Metropolitan Opera in Lincoln Center. She had mysteriously disappeared during a performance intermission. Her nude body, bound, gagged, and thrown from a sixth-floor roof, was later discovered in a ventilation shaft. Domingo prepared a composite drawing based on the description of a ballerina who had seen the suspect for only a few seconds in an elevator. **Craig Crimmons**, a stagehand, was identified and charged with the **"Murder at the Met"** after identification card photographs of hundreds of Lincoln Center employees were compared to the sketch.[28]

Another tragic New York case in 1981 involved a nun in an East Harlem convent. She was brutally attacked by two youths who sexually assaulted her and then cut more than 25 crosses into her skin. Domingo prepared a sketch in the victim's hospital room, which led to the identification of **Harold Wells** (Figure 2.19). A $10,000 reward had been offered, but the man who led police to Wells refused the money.[28]

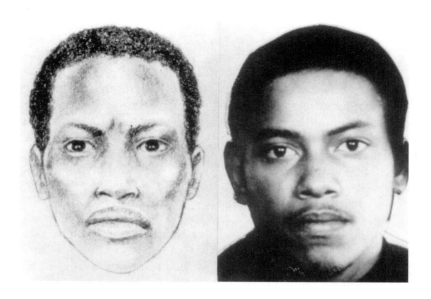

Figure 2.19 Composite drawing by Frank Domingo for the NYPD of suspect in the 1981 sexual assault of a nun (left) and subject **Harold Wells** (right). (Courtesy of New York City Police Department.)

An early 1980s case that demonstrated the use of photographic manipulation to aid an investigation involved **Claude Dallas**, a self-styled mountain man from Idaho who was convicted of killing two Fish and Game Conservation officers in 1981. **Mike Malloy** prepared drawings for wanted posters, tracing over known photos of Dallas and adding dark glasses and a hat to update his appearance.[29]

A composite drawing done for a 1981 murder case in Philadelphia is noteworthy because of a gross procedural error. After a known mobster and his female companion were murdered gangland style outside a restaurant, witnesses were brought to the **Philadelphia Police Department** to prepare a composite drawing (see Chapter 15, Figure 15.3). The frontal facial drawing was eventually used in court as evidence against **Neil Ferber**, a petty thief and forger. Based in part on strong resemblance to the frontal composite drawing, Ferber was found guilty of murder and sentenced to death. Eventually, evidence surfaced that suggested Ferber was wrongfully convicted. Witnesses who gave input for the composite drawing, when re-interviewed, indicated that they had only seen the killer from the profile view, although a frontal view had been drawn. Ultimately, Ferber was released from prison after serving 4 years, 16 months of which were on death row, and he was cleared of the charges.[30]

An ingenious swindle at the Perth, Australia Royal Mint resulted in the theft of a fortune in gold bullion in 1982. Three brothers named Mickelberg were charged with the crime. A book entitled ***The Mickelberg Stitch*** by Avon Lovell later accused police of fabrication of evidence, namely, a fingerprint and a composite drawing. It was alleged that a passport photo of Peter Mickelberg was reversed, and then traced to produce a falsely incriminating composite drawing (see Chapter 15, Figure 15.4). At a 1987 appeal trial, several American and British experts testified for the defense, but the convictions were unanimously upheld.[31]

Since 1982, the bodies of approximately 40 young women have surfaced in the Seattle area. Their deaths are attributed to a murderer known as the **"Green River**

Killer." Several composite drawings were generated in repeatedly unsuccessful attempts to determine his identity. The most widely distributed sketch, done by **Robert Exter** in 1985, showed the face of a man who was last seen with a murder victim just before her disappearance. **Harvey Pratt** and **Dr. Robert George** prepared reconstruction or postmortem drawings based on the remains of victims and **Betty Pat. Gatliff** developed three clay reconstructions from skulls, two of which were identified.[32]

In summer 1983, I attended the first training class in facial reconstruction from the skull offered by Betty Pat. Gatliff. Betty Pat. and I developed a bond that has benefited me both personally and professionally. She has given generously to me, and to many others, of her tremendous knowledge of the human face. Since the mid-1980s, we have taught forensic art courses in sculpture and drawing, primarily at the **Scottsdale Artists' School** in Scottsdale, Arizona. Because of the courses we teach there, as well as those previously taught by Frank Domingo, the school has become known as a major training site for forensic artists. We have enjoyed meeting hundreds of students from the U.S., Canada, and several foreign countries. Our students come from city, county, state, and federal law enforcement agencies, including the FBI, CIA, and the U.S. Secret Service. They include professional artists, art teachers, medical and scientific illustrators, museum preparators, dentists, pathologists, plastic surgeons, anaplastologists, anthropologists, animators, and even doll makers.

"Gorky Park," a 1983 film released by Orion Pictures and based on the 1981 novel of the same name by Martin Cruz Smith, demonstrated clay reconstruction over the skull, thus familiarizing thousands of moviegoers with a forensic technique that had previously been rather obscure.[33] The film was set in Moscow, although the skull reconstruction method shown was the American version rather than the Russian method attributed to **Mikhail Gerasimov** (see Chapter 11), a technical error.

The mid-1980s saw significant advancement in the organization and training aspects of forensic art. A group of practitioners of facial reconstruction from the skull began to have an informal evening seminar as part of the annual conference of the **American Academy of Forensic Sciences**.[27] Attendees shared technical information and case studies.

In 1984, I attended the **First National Composite Art Symposium**, a 3-day program sponsored by the NYPD and held at the World Trade Center. Organized by Frank Domingo, the conference brought together, for the first time, police artists from the U.S. and Canada. The decision was made to form the first professional organization, which resulted in the forensic art discipline that exists today under the auspices of the **International Association for Identification (IAI)**. The founding group of artists met at the IAI conference in Savannah, Georgia in 1985. At the IAI conference in London, England in 1986, a vote officially confirmed the forensic art discipline as a part of the parent organization. It was decided to use the more generic term "forensic art" rather than "composite art" to encourage membership of those who were involved in other forensic art endeavors such as skull reconstruction or demonstrative evidence preparation. The goals for the organization were set forth at the symposium in New York by Domingo with his discussion of the importance of communication, education, standardization, and perhaps eventual certification in the police art field. Domingo also wrote the *Composite Art Manual*, printed in 1986 by the IAI, which laid a foundation of standards and guidelines for composite artists.

In response to Domingo's written request that the FBI consider offering training for police artists, the first artists' training course was held at the **FBI Academy** in Quantico, Virginia in fall 1984. A form was placed in the *FBI Law Enforcement Bulletin* to

Figure 2.20   Composite drawing by Bill McCormack for the NYPD of suspect in the contro-versial 1984 subway shooting in New York City (left) and subject **Bernard Goetz** (right). (Courtesy of New York Police Department.)

determine if there was sufficient interest to organize a course. A small group of the artists who responded to the form was invited to meet and discuss the possible curriculum for the future program. Thus, the first class was organized. I was invited to participate as an attendee in that first 2-week class, and I am proud to be a guest instructor in the current program. The now 3-week course continues to be offered by invitation, usually once or twice annually, and provides consistent, high quality training for law enforcement artists. The original FBI training program was set up by **Horace Heafner**, who has shared his years of expertise with dozens of police artists.

As hand-drawn forensic artwork began to come into its own in the U.S., the British and continental European police forces continued to use the PHOTO-FIT system for most composites; hand-drawn sketches were relatively rare. During this period, hand-drawn sketches derived from witness interviews were considered to be the **"North American Style."** The **"English Style"** sometimes involved preparation of sketches or assemblages with little or no direct contact with the victim or witness, and with descriptive input from the investigating officer's notes.

More and more high profile cases in the U.S. in the mid-1980s involved forensic art. In 1984, NYPD artist **Bill McCormack** made a sketch of the controversial subway gunman who shot two black youths who were allegedly attempting to rob him (Figure 2.20). The gunman was later identified as **Bernard Goetz**.[34]

During a 7-month period in 1985, a serial killer who came to be known as the **"Night Stalker"** paralyzed Los Angeles with fear. During the investigation several composites, both drawn and Identi-KIT, were prepared from the descriptions of witnesses (Figure 2.21). California's newly installed automated fingerprint identification system (AFIS) was credited with the identification of the killer as **Richard Ramirez.** The 25-year-old drifter from El Paso, Texas was captured and beaten by a group of angry citizens and eventually charged with 14 murders in Los Angeles and 1 murder in San Francisco.[35]

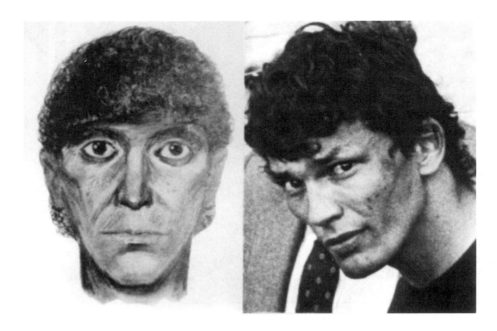

Figure 2.21 Composite drawing by Fernando Poncé of the 1985 Los Angeles serial killer known as the "**Night Stalker**" (left) and subject **Richard Ramirez** (right). (Courtesy of Los Angeles Police Department.)

In the tradition established in the 1930s Ruxton case, work continued with various superimposition methods to aid in the identification of skeletal remains, with the forensic artist often working as part of a team of medical and science professionals. A group of the world's top forensic specialists, including Oklahoma forensic anthropologist **Dr. Clyde Snow** and **Dr. Richard Helmer** of Germany, traveled to Brazil in 1985 to study the skeletal remains thought to be those of Hitler's "Angel of Death," **Josef Mengele**. Known photographs of Mengele were compared with those of a man buried as "Wolfgang Gerhard" after a drowning incident in 1979, and with the skull removed from "Gerhard's" grave (Figure 2.22). Various photographic, video, computer, and drawn superimposition techniques were employed, resulting in 24 points of similarity.[36]

Throughout the 1980s, composites of various types figured prominently in cases of international significance. In the 1986 assassination of Sweden's Prime Minister **Olof Palma**, police in Stockholm used a West German electronic assemblage system to produce a facial image. Because of insufficient preliminary interviews, the facial image distributed worldwide actually depicted an innocent bystander rather than the assassin.

Turkish police developed hand-drawn composite sketches of two terrorists who were responsible for a massacre at a synagogue in Istanbul in 1986. The two men had attempted to blow themselves up with grenades to prevent their own identification once their mission was accomplished. Both witness descriptions and the terrorists' bodies were used to prepare the drawings.

In the 1980s, there was an increased emphasis on the problem of missing and endangered children in the U.S. In October 1982, Congress passed the Missing Children Act, largely as a result of the tireless work of **John and Revé Walsh**. Their 6-year-old son, **Adam Walsh**, was abducted from a shopping mall in Hollywood, Florida and murdered in 1981. At the time of Adam's disappearance, there was no system for

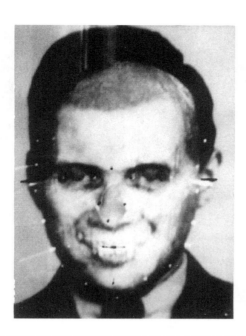

Figure 2.22 **Superimposition comparison** of skull found in Brazil with photograph of **Josef Mengele**. (Courtesy of Dr. Richard Helmer.)

tracking missing children nationally. John's effort to remedy this situation on behalf of all crime victims was also instrumental in the creation of the **National Center for Missing and Exploited Children** (NCMEC) in 1984.[37] As the host of the television program **"America's Most Wanted"** since 1987, John and the show's staff have provided perhaps the strongest vehicle to date for the use of forensic art as a powerful crime-fighting tool on a grand scale. Placing a person's face on national television, be it a composite sketch or a fugitive update, makes it very difficult for that person to hide. This national exposure usually provides the greatest likelihood for locating of missing children and identification of victims depicted in postmortem drawings or facial reconstructions from the skull.

My work was presented as a feature segment of "America's Most Wanted" in 1990, and I have been proud to be associated with the show as a freelance forensic artist ever since. Knowing John Walsh, America's most important victim's advocate, continues to be an inspiration.

By this point in the 1980s, not only did forensic artists update photos of perpetrators/fugitives as in the case of Claude Dallas, but several also began to do work to update victim photographs, particularly children (see Chapter 7). **Scott Barrows** and **Lewis Sadler** of the University of Illinois first put into practice the use of "age progressions" based on the photographs of long-term missing children using craniofacial growth data. Using the method, they successfully aided in the recovery of children as early as 1985.

Upon his retirement from the FBI, **Horace Heafner** went to work at the **National Center for Missing and Exploited Children** in Arlington, Virginia, primarily doing child age-progressions. He and partner **Glenn Miller** continued development and refinement of the child age-progression method, incorporating greater use of familial traits in the images, resulting in the recovery of numerous children. They began with hand-drawn sketches and then went to computer-generated enhancements of available

Figure 2.23 Compusketch composite of the author by Tom Macris (left) and photograph of the author (right). (Courtesy of Tom Macris.)

photographs. Heafner, Miller, and the NCMEC have also trained numerous forensic artists in the child age-progression process.

In addition to the computer software used at the NCMEC in the 1980s, several companies began marketing systems for production of facial composites. One of the earliest, **Compusketch**, was developed with the assistance of veteran police artist **Tom Macris** of San Jose, California (Figure 2.23). Macris prepared the hand-drawn component facial features that comprise the system and provided insight into the importance of the interview process. Today, computer softwares for facial composites are a routinely accepted part of the forensic art field. Most are very user friendly and enable law enforcement agencies to produce and distribute facial composite images in a timely manner — a tremendous asset.

In summary, in the late 1980s traditional methods of forensic art were more fully utilized and new methods were developed. One innovator was photographer and sculptor **Frank Bender** of Philadelphia. Bender chose to use sculpture rather than drawing or computer imaging when asked to update the "look" of long-term missing fugitive **John List** (Figure 2.24). List was an accountant and Sunday school teacher who murdered his mother, his wife, and their three children in New Jersey in 1971. When Bender's updated sculpture of List appeared on "America's Most Wanted" in 1989, List was located and captured in Virginia after 18 years as a fugitive (see also Chapter 15, Figure 15.1). The resemblance to the sculpture was striking and helped pave the way for greater use of fugitive updates in the years that followed.[38]

The International Symposium, "Advances in Skull Identification via Video Superimposition," held in Kiel, Germany in August 1988, formed the foundation for the **International Association for Craniofacial Identification**. This organization is composed predominantly of those conducting research in the varied factors affecting human skeletal identification, and some members also practice facial reconstruction from the skull. Notable founding members are **Dr. Richard Helmer** of Germany and **Richard Neave** of England.

My position at the **Texas Department of Public Safety** in Austin carried a heavy workload, especially in the area of unidentified deceased cases. My training in the facial

Figure 2.24 Photograph of New Jersey multiple murderer **John List** (left), **age progression sculpture** by Frank Bender (center), and List when apprehended (right). (Courtesy of "America's Most Wanted.")

reconstruction method used by Betty Pat. Gatliff and my tremendous case load prompted me to consider a more expeditious method of determining a face based on the skull. In 1985, I devised a method of **two-dimensional facial reconstruction from the skull** that utilized all the available scientific data in a way that had not been done previously (see Chapter 12). For the next 5 years, I drew frontal and lateral facial images based on the skulls of unidentified deceased persons, usually victims of homicide, and I was continually amazed at the number of successful identifications.

The 1990s

In June 1990, I was invited to present this new method at the **"International Symposium on the Forensic Aspects of Mass Disasters and Crime Scene Reconstruction"** at the FBI Academy in Quantico, Virginia (Figure 2.25).[39] I showed multiple case examples of identifications made with this simple and direct method and I was very pleased with the response. I began to receive requests for instruction in the procedure. I taught the technique for the first time to **Royal Canadian Mounted Police** artists **Cameron Pye** and **Ron Morier**. Pye achieved an identification on his first attempt with the newly learned method, when he used it on the skeletal body of a young male who was found in Nanaimo, British Columbia. Eventually, two-dimensional reconstruction became a part of the advanced course I teach at Scottsdale and elsewhere. I still feel elated whenever I receive a call from a former student relating a successful skull identification using this approach.

In late summer 1990, I traveled to **Moscow** at the invitation of the government of the former USSR to familiarize researchers with the new two-dimensional reconstruction technique. I worked primarily with **Boris Fedosyutkin** and **Oleg Korovyanskiy** at the Scientific Research Laboratory of the Criminalistics Center, which was part of the Russian Ministry of Internal Affairs. I also met **Alexander Zinin** and saw his very fine drawings of the ethnic peoples of the USSR. I visited **Galina Lebedinskaya** and **Tatiana**

Figure 2.25 Forensic anthropologist Dr. Clyde Snow and the author at the 1990 **International Symposium on the Forensic Aspects of Mass Disasters and Crime Scene Reconstruction** at the FBI Academy. (Courtesy of Ivan Futtrell.)

Balueva at the Laboratory of Anthropological Reconstruction at the Institute of Ethnography and Anthropology of the Russian Academy of Sciences, University of Moscow. Lebedinskaya had been a protégé of **Mikhail Gerasimov**, by then deceased for a number of years. The meetings were facilitated by the very skilled scientific translator, Lily Burova, and the unprecedented information exchange proved mutually beneficial.

In 1990, I also began doing **fugitive update drawings** at the request of "America's Most Wanted." I have enjoyed watching each and every capture that the program facilitates (see Chapter 8). A 1991 case that was particularly rewarding involved a Cuban national who was a conspirator in the political assassination of former Chilean ambassador to the U.S., **Orlondo Letelier**, and Letelier's young aide. The car bombing incident occurred in Washington, D.C. in 1976 and led to strained relations between the U.S. and Chile for over a decade. I produced a fugitive update drawing, based on poor quality photocopies, to project the possible appearance of **Virgilio Paz Romero**, aging him more than a decade (see Chapter 8, Figure 8.24). The drawing was aired on "America's Most Wanted" and Paz was captured 3 days later in South Florida after eluding authorities for over 15 years. In developing such fugitive updates, I read all available information on a subject from police intelligence files, such as health and lifestyle data; I also use a bit of intuition. The producers of "America's Most Wanted" allowed me to determine the clothing and hairstyle for this and other update drawings. In the case of Paz, I chose to show him in a red shirt, and he was captured wearing an identical red shirt!

An innovative technique for facial reconstruction from the skull, conceived by anthropologist **Dr. Emily Craig**, was presented by Dr. Craig and Dr. Karen Burns at a meeting of the International Association for Identification Conference in Nashville, Tennessee in summer 1990. The method involved preparation of a three-dimensional reconstruction on the skull in the tissue-depth manner practiced by Gatliff and others.

Before final completion of the facial details, the sculpture was scanned into a computer system and features were selected from a database of eyes, noses, ears, and so forth. Features were then merged into the appropriate positions on the scanned sculpted facial outline. The resulting image bore a different "look" from clay reconstructions and offered a satisfactory alternative means to achieve a polished end product for those artists lacking strong sculptural talents.

On October 1, 1993 in Petaluma, California, **Polly Klaas** was abducted from her home while two terrified schoolmates looked on. The two witnesses described the abductor to artist **Ralph Pata**, who prepared a composite sketch that was very widely distributed. Pata's drawing included a yellow bandanna tied around the suspect's head, a detail later confirmed by review of the verbal descriptions given by the young girls during the initial "911" call.[40] **Jeanne Boylan** later drew a second composite after re-interviewing the young witnesses. **Richard Allen Davis** was ultimately identified and arrested because of a matched palm print.[41] He was charged with Polly's kidnapping and murder and convicted in June 1996.

In late October 1994, 23-year-old **Susan Smith** of Union, South Carolina claimed that a black gunman in a knit cap had stolen her car and kidnapped her sons, Michael, age 3, and Alex, age 14 months. Smith described the fictitious abductor to forensic artist **Roy Paschal** of the South Carolina Law Enforcement Division, who prepared a profile composite drawing (Figure 2.26). During the composite interview, Paschal sensed inconsistencies in Smith's story and an inappropriate demeanor, which he reported to investigators. Subsequently, Smith confessed and was convicted of the drowning deaths of her two sons.[42]

The elusive serial bomber known as the **Unabomber** evaded police for almost 18 years. Starting in 1978, he killed 3 persons and injured or maimed 29 others in a campaign of terror directed at airlines and techno-industries across the U.S. A composite sketch was prepared by an unknown FBI artist in February 1987. A second sketch was

Figure 2.26 1994 **composite drawing** by Roy Paschal of the **alleged abductor** of Michael and Alex Smith, sons of Susan Smith. (Courtesy of South Carolina Law Enforcement Division.)

Figure 2.27   Composite drawing by Robert Exter of serial bomber known as the "**Unabomber**," 1987. (Courtesy of Robert Exter.)

done in watercolors by **Robert Exter** in March 1987. After the release of the second drawing, the bomber ceased all activity for 7 years. Both drawings showed an eerie hooded figure with sunglasses (Figure 2.27). The same witness who helped with the 1987 sketches was re-interviewed, and a third sketch was done in 1994 by **Jeanne Boylan**, although most of the bomber's face remained obscured by the hood and glasses. The latter sketch came to function as a sort of logo for the investigation. Eventually, **Theodore Kaczynski**, a former University of California, Berkeley math professor, was captured in April 1996 after his brother recognized the writing style of a published manifesto as a product of his brother's mind.[43] Kaczynski pled guilty to the bombings in January 1998.

The April 19, 1995 bombing of the Alfred P. Murrah Federal Building in Oklahoma City was the nation's worst terrorist action to date; 168 people lost their lives, many of them small children at a daycare center. Composite drawings prepared by FBI artist **Ray Rozycki** of suspects **John Doe 1** and **John Doe 2** were perhaps the most widely distributed in history. A profile sketch of John Doe 2 was later drawn by **Jeanne Boylan** and released. Rozycki's sketch of John Doe 1 was soon identified as **Timothy McVeigh** (Figure 2.28), an ex-Army enlisted man who served in the Desert Storm conflict. McVeigh, an anti-government activist, bore a strong resemblance to the sketch and has been tried, convicted, and sentenced to death.[44]

In January 1997, **Ennis Cosby**, only son of comedian Bill Cosby, was shot and killed on the side of a Los Angeles freeway as he changed a flat tire. A composite sketch was prepared by freelance artist **Marilyn Droz** for the Los Angeles Police Department, based on the description by a woman who briefly saw a young white male leaving the area (Figure 2.29).[45] Following a tip to police, subject **Mikail**

Figure 2.28   Composite drawing by FBI artist Ray Rozycki of the suspect in the 1995 bombing in Oklahoma City (left) and subject **Timothy McVeigh** (right). (Courtesy of Federal Bureau of Investigation.)

Figure 2.29   Composite drawing by Marilyn Droz of the suspected killer of Ennis Cosby, 1997 (left) and suspect **Mikail Markhasev** (right). (Courtesy of Los Angeles Police Department.)

Markhasev, a Russian immigrant, was arrested and convicted of the murder. He was sentenced to life imprisonment in August 1998.[46]

In summer 1997, the **First National Conference on Craniofacial Identification** for forensic artists, held at Windsor, **England**, brought together individuals from the United Kingdom and several other countries.[47]

Clearly, the last two decades have demonstrated a greater use of forensic art as well as ventures into other areas of assistance to law enforcement. A 1997 *USA Today* article states:

> ... police sketch artists' sinister portraits have become as recognizable as the Mona Lisa while evolving into the crime-fighting tools *du jour*. Once relegated to dusty, yellowed "wanted" posters on post office walls, police sketches now pop up on TVs and computer screens in seconds ... Now you push a button and it's all over the nation and the world.[48]

2000 and Beyond

Psychological and physiological research constantly provides forensic artists with new revelations about human cognition and perception, and hopefully improves our abilities to retrieve dim memories of faces seen at a mere glance. At various locations around the country, studies are being conducted to increase our knowledge of soft tissue depths on morphological landmarks on the skull. This information, together with vast improvements in imaging capabilities, will perhaps lead to greater accuracy of predictions of faces from skulls.

I sincerely hope that all those who undertake this important work will strive to constantly improve and never stop learning.

References

1. Rumbelow, D., *Jack the Ripper, the Complete Casebook*. Chicago: Contemporary Books, 1988.
2. Sullivan, R., *Goodbye, Lizzie Borden*. London: Penguin Books, 1989.
3. Bertillon, A., *The Bertillon System of Identification: Signeletic Instructions, including the Theory and Practice of Anthropometrical Identification*, McClaughry, R.W., Ed. Chicago: The Werner Company, 1896.
4. Honeycombe, G., *The Murders of the Black Museum*. London: Hutchison & Co., 1982.
5. Keating, H. R. F., *Great Crimes*. London: Treasure Press, 1987.
6. Heafner, H., FBI (retired), personal communication, 1990.
7. Evans, C., *The Casebook of Forensic Detection*. New York: John Wiley & Sons, 1996.
8. Taister, M., FBI, personal communication, 1997.
9. Sognnaes, R., "Hitler and Bormann identifications compared by postmortem craniofacial and dental characteristics," *The American Journal of Forensic Medicine and Pathology*, 1(2), 105–115, June 1980.
10. Krogman, W. M., "The reconstruction of the living head from the skull," *FBI Law Enforcement Bulletin,* July 1946.
11. Cooper, C. and Sheppard, S. R., *Mockery of Justice*. New York: Penguin Books, 1997.
12. Kind, S., Criminal identification, in *Science Against Crime*. New York: Exeter Books, 1982.
13. Pye, C., Royal Canadian Mounted Police, personal communication, 1994.
14. U.S. Department of Justice, Federal Bureau of Investigation, *Visual Aids for Investigative and Prosecutive Use*, 2nd ed. Washington, D.C.: U.S. Goverment Printing Office.
15. Altman, J. and Ziporyn, M., M.D., *Born to Raise Hell: The Untold Story of Richard Speck*. New York: Grove Press, 1967.
16. Lavergne, G. M., *A Sniper in the Tower*. Denton, TX: University of North Texas Press, 1997.
17. Gatliff, B. P., SKULLpture Lab, personal communication, 1996.

18. Penry, J., *Looking at Faces and Remembering Them: A Guide to Facial Identification*. London: Elek Books, 1971.

19. Homa, G., *The Law Enforcement Composite Sketch Artist*. Berlin, NJ: Community Graphics, 1983.

20. Cormack, J. A., *The Police Artist's Reference*. Pewaukee, WI: Waukesha County Technical Institute, 1979.

21. Rule, A., *The Stranger Beside Me*. New York: Signet, 1980.

22. Klausner, L. D., *Son of Sam*. New York: McGraw-Hill, 1981.

23. Terry, M., *The Ultimate Evil*. New York: Dolphin Doubleday, 1987.

24. Lawson, M., Georgia Bureau of Investigation, personal communication, 1987.

25. Macris, T., San Jose Police Department (retired), personal communication, 1987.

26. Berry, R., FBI, personal communication, 1997.

27. Gatliff, B. P., SKULLpture Lab, personal communication, 1997.

28. Domingo, F., New York City Police Department (retired), personal communication, 1989.

29. Olsen, J., *Give a Boy a Gun: A True Story of Law and Disorder in the American West*. New York: Dell, 1985.

30. "A Good Cop," *60 Minutes*, produced by Ira Rosen, CBS, January 11, 1987.

31. Lovell, A., personal communication, 1987.

32. Smith, C. and Guillen, T., *The Search for the Green River Killer*. New York: Onyx, 1991.

33. Smith, M. C., *Gorky Park*. New York: Random House, 1981.

34. Domingo, F., New York City Police Department (retired), personal communication, 1997.

35. Linedecker, C. L., *Night Stalker*. New York: St. Martin's, 1991.

36. Teixeira, W. R., "The Mengele report," *The Journal of Forensic Medicine and Pathology*, 6(4), 279–283, 1985.

37. Walsh, J. and Schindehette, S., *Tears of Rage*. New York: Pocket Books, 1997.

38. De Leon, D., "Sculptor's fulfillment: art of crime-busting," *USA Today*, June 6, 1989.

39. Taylor, K., Technique of facial reconstruction drawing, in *Proceedings of the International Symposium on the Forensic Aspects of Mass Disasters and Crime Scene Reconstruction*, FBI, 1990.

40. Meese, M., Sonoma County, California Office of the District Attorney, personal communication, 1997.

41. Bortnick, B., *Polly Klaas: The Murder of America's Child*. New York: Pinnacle Books, 1995.

42. Paschal, R., South Carolina Law Enforcement Division, personal communication, 1996.

43. Gibbs, N.. "Tracking down the unabomber," *Time-Special Report*, April 15, 1996, 38–46.

44. Rozycki, R., FBI, personal communication, 1998.

45. Chua-Eoan, H., "Crime: A death in the family, " *Time*, January 27, 1997, 22–27.

46. Corwin, M. and Lait, M., "Suspect in Cosby slaying identified," *L.A. Times*, March 14, 1997, 44 and 46.

47. Cullington, D., National Missing Persons Helpline, London, England, personal communication, 1997.

48. Holland, G., "Sketch artists drawn into growing debate," *USA Today*, March 14, 1997.

Chapter 3

The Human Face

Our faces do many things. They provide our sense of identity. They reflect our age. They indicate our sexuality and provide our emotional display system. Simply put, they represent who we are and act as our tools for recognizing others. The pattern of facial features of each human face is truly individual. With criminals, the face can be the key to identification and apprehension. With victims, the face can be the triggering factor that leads to recovery or identification. Historically, man has sought to gain greater understanding of himself and others through study of the face and head.

Physiognomy or "face reading" has been practiced since ancient times. It was once believed that when human faces were compared to animals, shared resemblance indicated shared qualities (Figure 3.1). Thus a face could indicate a temperament that was strong like the horse, fearless like the lion, or stupid like the goat. In her paper

Figure 3.1 Physiognomy or "face-reading" example from a 1586 text comparing a man and a goat.

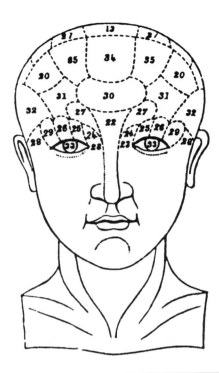

Figure 3.2 Phrenological head diagrams were once used to assess a person's character from the topography of the skull.

"Face Facts: A History of Physiognomy from Ancient Mesopotamia to the End of the 19th Century," Jodie Jenkinson fully explores the topic:

> The history of physiognomy is both lengthy and turbulent. It has fallen in and out of popularity, at times being associated with the development of medicine, and at times having been outlawed for its association with astrology. Although physiognomy is now considered a pseudo-science at best, it has without a doubt influenced our visual and written depiction of facial features as they relate to our interpretation of character.[1]

Phrenology, or the belief that a person's human character could be determined from the topography of the skull, was popularized in the 19th century (Figure 3.2). Itinerant phrenologists traveled across America practicing their trade of feeling the bumps on people's heads to learn about their personalities. Famous citizens who had phrenological readings done include President James Garfield, abolitionist John Brown, and poet Walt Whitman.

At the end of the 19th century and the beginning of the 20th century, individuals who practiced **criminal anthropology** believed that certain facial features were indicative of particular criminal behaviors. Perhaps the best known of the criminal anthropologists was Italian physician **Cesare Lombroso**, who perceived the criminal as an anomaly, organically and physiologically. He studied criminals by weighing them, measuring them, and observing their facial features.

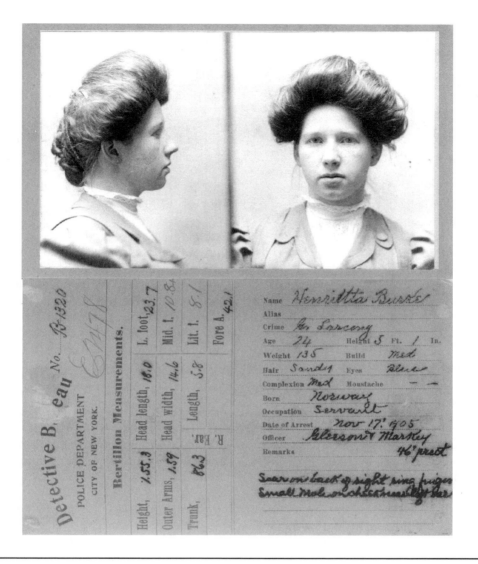

Figure 3.3 An early arrest record showing both mug shots and **Bertillon measurements**.

At about the same time **Alphonse Bertillon**, a French anthropologist, established a system for distinguishing one individual from another based on measurement and assessment of the facial features as well as certain bodily measurements. Bertillon used what he called **Le Portrait Parlé**, or the word picture, to describe an individual with great detail and specificity. His purpose was to create files of documentation on criminals while he worked as a records clerk at the French Sureté in Paris (Figure 3.3). He described his system in his 1896 book, *The Bertillon System of Identification: Signaletic Instructions, The Theory and Practice of Anthropometrical Identification*, as "a new form of applied science which has for its object the description of any human being in a manner so complete, certain and characteristic that he can by no possibility ever be permanently confused with any other."[2] Although his method was somewhat successful in both Europe and the U.S., identification by fingerprints replaced it within 20 years. Bertillon's work remains more useful and valid today, however, than that of the physiognomists, phrenologists, and criminal anthropologists because it was a system for observation, study, and documentation of the features of the face and body rather than a method that presumed to determine character traits.

John Liggett, in his book *The Human Face,* explores the mysteries of the human face:

> Today we may no longer believe that people with small foreheads are fickle, or that large ears are the sign of a tendency to chatter. Yet we are still inclined to like people — even fall in love with them — because of their faces, and we may dislike them just as readily and irrationally. We are as fascinated as our ancestors with that most human of all our features: the face.[3]

Over the years, our ideals of perfect beauty and proportion have changed considerably. It is human nature to assess people unfairly according to their appearance. In recent times, *New Republic* columnist Michael Kinsley wrote, "We are all traumatized to varying degrees about our appearance. Facial discrimination is far more overt and shameless than racial discrimination. Our culture doesn't even attempt to hide its preference for certain arrangements of facial and bodily parts over others."[4]

Clearly, our attitudes about ideal beauty are linked to idealized proportions. The ancient Greeks developed **canons of facial proportion** that they reflected in their art. Discussing the Greeks, Dr. Robert George noted,

> … they constructed the first artistic canons of facial proportion, subjectively guided by their own finely tuned concepts of aesthetics. It must be noted that these so-called canons are not true laws in the scientific sense but merely guidelines for the spacing of facial features in a symmetrical, harmonious, and balanced pattern.[5]

Modification of the face is a universal pursuit done for reasons as varied as changing identity, declaring status, and enhancing sexual attractiveness. Attempts at proportional changes for aesthetic reasons have been made by various cultures, with some methods actually altering the bony structure. Binding of the skull to artificially reshape it has been practiced by the Egyptians, African tribes, Native Americans, and others worldwide. Women of the Padaung tribe in Burma have produced elongated necks by wearing heavy brass rings around the neck and shoulders. Over time the rings press the clavicles downward, creating the appearance of a longer neck. Today, plastic and craniofacial surgeons and orthodontists routinely alter faces to achieve more "perfect" symmetries.

Efforts to augment personal beauty and appeal have often taken other bizarre forms. Both medieval and Elizabethan beauties shaved their hairlines upward to produce what was considered to be a more charming and dignified look. African people have worn uncomfortable lip disks or labrets to enlarge and reshape the lips as a mark of honor. Facial scarification, which dates back to Paleolithic times and continues today in parts of Africa, is most often practiced by dark-skinned people, and tattooing is more popular with light-skinned people. Tattoos, body piercing, and use of makeup are customs practiced by many cultural groups.

Alteration of the teeth is another way to change the face. The technique of filing of the teeth, usually to a point, has been done in Africa, Southeast Asia, Mesoamerica, and the Philippines. The Ibans of Borneo drilled holes in the front six teeth and inserted brass plugs. This is not unlike today's relatively popular practice of placing precious stones into the central incisors or applying gold crowns with cut-out shapes. The film star Marlene Dietrich had several upper molars extracted to enhance her hollow-cheeked look.

Today, as throughout history, the human visage remains a source of both vanity and intrigue and study continues into the ways of deciphering its many secrets. There are multiple potential applications for this research and knowledge in the fields of art, psychology, law enforcement, and jurisprudence. **As forensic artists we seek to document that which is most individual about a given countenance with the intent of identifying the owner of that face.** We work to document facial individuality through composite drawings from witness descriptions, interpretation of outdated or unclear photographs, or by rebuilding a face from the skull.

Although capturing individuality is our goal, the forensic artist must first understand certain fundamental standards about human faces. In this chapter, we cover facial anatomy, distinctions of racial groups and ethnicity, distinctions of male vs. female faces, and the effects of expressions on the face. Each topic is discussed from the perspective of forensic art.

Betty Pat. Gatliff and I have found Louise Gordon's book *How to Draw the Human Head* to be extremely valuable in teaching basic facial anatomy to police artists. The book is clear, concise, and easy to understand, and we recommend it to our students. Much of the content of the following section on facial anatomy is based on Gordon's book.

Facial Anatomy

The forensic artist benefits from a solid foundation in facial anatomy and should strive to understand the intricacies of its functions. While fine artists can simply view and replicate the facial aspects, forensic artists need a greater anatomical understanding. We do not work from models, but instead we must draw or sculpt from descriptions or limited facial information. Therefore, we must possess a more technical knowledge of the face to accomplish our tasks. A working vocabulary of terminology also allows the artist to communicate fully with scientific professionals and forensic specialists such as pathologists, odontologists, and anthropologists, a skill particularly important for work in the area of unidentified deceased cases. Knowledge of the workings of facial anatomy facilitates the ability of the composite artist to make quick, skillful adjustments to drawings in an interview situation.

As forensic artists we must adjust our thinking from that which is traditional in fine art. Most art books teach the structures of the face from the standpoint of "idealized" facial features and "standard proportions." While this is valuable information, the forensic artist must also be aware that the nature of the job requires he or she to assess things differently. Facial recognition is the ultimate goal of most forensic art. Capturing individuality in a face is the key to facial recognition. Therefore, **it is the ability to discern that which deviates from the idealized or standard that establishes individuality and may well lead to recognition and identification.**

In forensic art, we must first learn that every human head has a certain sameness anatomically. Each head is made up of the same general component bones and muscles. However, each component part can have a different size and form that individualizes the face. We must recognize that which is standard in order to become sensitive to the subtle variations of individuality.

Bones of the Skull

The skull creates the architectural form of the head and provides the basic structure for the face (Figure 3.4). Louise Gordon, in *How to Draw the Human Head*, states: "The bones are living substance, supplied with nerves and blood vessels, reactive to the conditions within the whole body, and capable of repair."[6] Bone is everchanging. We grow to a certain point and then begin adult-related changes. The skull and other bones can be altered by nutrition, illness, or injury.

A skull generally is viewed as representing two regions: the **neurocranium** or braincase and the **splanchnocranium** or face. Both regions are comprised of multiple bones joined together, much like a jigsaw puzzle, by interlocking **sutures** or seams. We commonly refer to the skull as the two compounds: the **cranium** and the **mandible**.

The **frontal** bone forms the forehead and the upper portion of the orbital cavity surrounding the eyes. A feature of the frontal bone is the **supraorbital ridge** or **superciliary arch**, the prominence above the orbits that is often more noticeable in males. The **parietal** bones are curved plates that compose part of the top and the sides of the cranium. In most people, the protrusions or eminences on the parietal bone behind the ears at each side of the cranium form the widest part of the head. The **occipital** bone forms much of the base and back of the cranium. Important muscles of the neck attach to this occipital bone along a line or ridge of slightly raised bone called the nuchal line or **nuchal crest**. Within the occipital bone another important feature is the **foramen magnum**, which is the round opening at the base of the skull. The function of the foramen magnum is to allow an opening through which the brain is connected to the spinal cord.

Temporal bones (along with the greater wings of the sphenoid) form the lower sides of the cranium and give us the common term "temples" for the area or cavity at the sides of the head behind the eyes. The temporal bone has three important features: the **mastoid process**, the **external auditory meatus** or ear hole, and a zygomatic process that forms half of the **zygomatic arch**. The mastoid process is an extension of bone behind the ear onto which the sterno-cleido-mastoid muscle attaches. The external auditory meatus is an opening in the bone just above and in front of the mastoid process that determines the placement of the ear. The **zygomatic** bones (sometimes called the malar bones) form the cheek bones when joined with the zygomatic processes of the temporal bones. Together they are called the **zygomatic arches**.

The **maxillae** form the upper jaw. The lower margins of the orbital cavities are also part of the maxillae. The teeth that are held in place by the maxillae are referred to as **maxillary teeth**.

The **nasal bones** create the upper part of the nose or the beginning of the bridge. They attach to the frontal bone at the top and the maxillae on the sides.

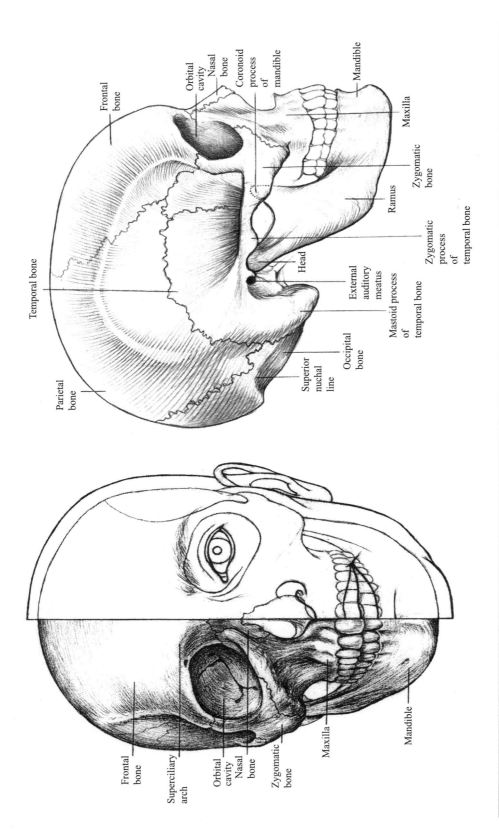

Figure 3.4 **Skull with bones labeled,** frontal (left) and lateral (right). (From *How to Draw the Human Head* by Louise Gordon. Copyright 1977 by Louise Gordon. Used by permission of Viking Penguin, a division of Penguin Putnam Inc.)

The lower jaw or **mandible**, the only truly separate bone of the adult skull, is hinged to the cranium at the **temporomandibular joint (TMJ)**. This movement allows the jaw to open and close the mouth and to rotate in the function of chewing. **Ligaments** or tough bands of fibrous connective material hold the mandible to the cranium. The horseshoe-shaped mandible holds the lower teeth, which are called **mandibular teeth**. The mandible has three other important features: the **ramus**, the **coronoid process**, and the **condyle** of the TMJ. The ramus forms the upright angle of the jaw. The coronoid process is a projection of bone on the upper edge of the ramus acting as a muscle attachment for the temporalis muscle that closes the mouth. The condyle or head of the ramus is the rounded projection on the end of the ramus that articulates the jaw at the TMJ.

Muscles of the Face

Our faces are interesting to observe because they have movement. This movement is made possible by muscles and their ability to contract (Figure 3.5). As John Liggett states: "There are more than a hundred different muscles lying just below the surface of the face. These lie in many different directions, criss-crossing each other in a thousand different ways, making possible a rich variety of complex, subtle and beautiful movements."[3] Facial muscles are divided into two general categories: muscles of mastication (chewing) and muscles of expression, although they sometimes perform both functions.

Muscles exhibit one specific function — contraction. When a muscle contracts, one end (the origin) remains stationary. The bone, muscle, or skin to which the other end is attached (the insertion) is pulled toward the fixed point. To produce movement, muscles must be attached at both ends. Muscles can only pull, they cannot push. A significant phenomenon for the artist to understand is the way in which the action of muscles creates wrinkles. **Wrinkles always occur perpendicular to the stretch of a muscle.** In other words, the wrinkles develop when the skin lying over a muscle bunches up as the muscle contracts. Think of a piece of elastic being stretched and released and the way in which the folds occur. The principle is the same.

A **tendon** is composed of tough fibrous material similar to a ligament and attaches muscle to bone or cartilage, which is often the origin. The insertion can also be attached to bone by a tendon, but is sometimes interwoven with another muscle in a **raphe** fashion.

Orbicularis oculi is a wide flat muscle that encircles the eye, attaching to the inner orbit and the skin of the cheek. It is a sphincter-type muscle that contracts in a pursing manner, similar to the large muscle surrounding the mouth. The eye does not, however, close in the same manner as the mouth because of the cartilaginous **tarsal plates** of the eye, which stiffen the lids. There is a tarsus or tarsal plate running horizontally across both the upper and lower eyelids, with the upper tarsus being larger. The **palpebral ligaments** connect the tarsal plates to the bone at either side. At the medial or inner corner of the eye, the encircling bundles of orbicularis oculi are interrupted by the **medial palpebral ligament**. This ligament anchors the inner corner of the eye to the bones at the sides of the nose on either side of the **lacrimal sac**. The outer attachment of the **lateral palpebral ligament** helps form the outer corner of the eye. The ligament attaches on a tiny tubercle or bump on the bone just inside the lateral orbit. When orbicularis oculi contracts, it forms the small wrinkles at the outer corners of the eye known as "crow's feet." With advancing age the wrinkles radiate around the eye, perpendicular to the stretch of orbicularis oculi.

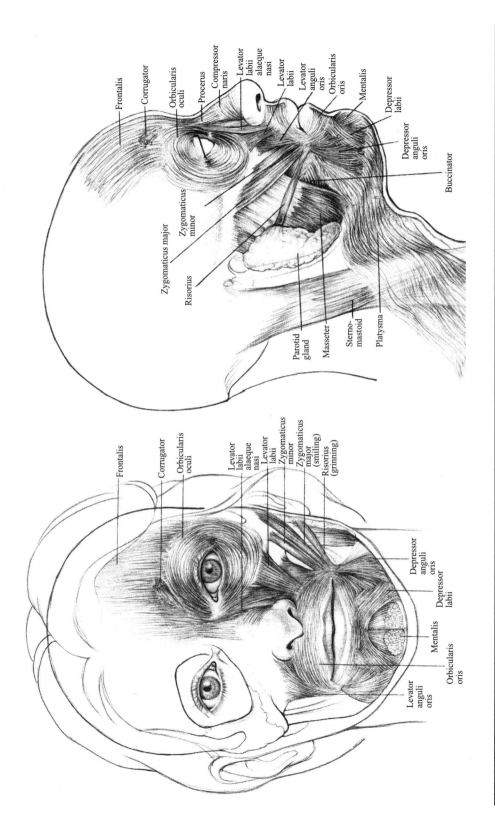

Figure 3.5 Skull with muscles labeled, frontal (left) and lateral (right). (From *How to Draw the Human Head* by Louise Gordon. Copyright 1977 by Louise Gordon. Used by permission of Viking Penguin, a division of Penguin Putnam Inc.)

The **lacrimal gland** is located at the outer side of the upper eyelid and helps create the roundness there.

Levator palpebrae originates deep inside the conical portion of the bony orbit and attaches to the upper eyelid. It serves the purpose of opening the eye by raising the upper eyelid, causing the lid to fold back on itself like an overhead garage door opening.

Frontalis is the flat muscle that covers the forehead on the frontal bone. Its vertical fibers originate approximately at the hairline and insert in the skin under the eyebrows. The frontalis can raise the eyebrows straight up and creates horizontal wrinkles or furrows across the forehead.

Procerus is a small thin-shaped muscle that covers the nasal bones running in the same vertical direction as frontalis. When it contracts, pulling down the inner corner of the eyebrow area, small horizontal wrinkles are created across the upper bridge of the nose.

A related frowning expression is created by the cone-shaped muscle **corrugator**, which pulls the inner corners of the eyebrows together and downward, causing small vertical creases in the skin at the top of the nose. Procerus and corrugator act in concert.

Compressor naris originates on the maxilla at the side of the nose and inserts at the bridge of the nose. Its function is to close down the nostril as the muscle contracts to protect the inner structures.

The primary muscle encircling the mouth is **orbicularis oris**, which is a sphincter muscle extending from approximately the bottom of the nose to about halfway down the chin. It blends with other muscles of the mouth that insert and weave into it. Its function is to close the mouth. Because it actually has three layers of muscle bundles that act differently, it can perform in three ways. It can protrude the lips, purse the lips, or pull the lips tightly against the teeth.

Other muscles around the mouth are antagonistic to orbicularis oris and cause pulling in different directions. **Levator labii alaque nasi** runs from the maxilla beside the nasal bone to blend with orbicularis oris. It lifts the lip and the wing of the nose. **Levator labii superioris** also blends with orbicularis oris, originating from the maxilla under the orbit of the eye, and, as the name indicates, lifts the upper lip, squaring it slightly. Elvis Presley used both of these muscles to great effect (Figure 3.6).

Levator anguli oris originates on the lower margin of the maxilla and inserts into the orbicularis oris at the corner of the mouth. It also helps lift the mouth into a smiling position.

Mentalis (plural: mentales) rests on the chin. It originates just below the teeth and inserts in the skin on the ball of the chin. Mentalis pushes the lower lip up, creating a pouting expression. A dimple or cleft may be created by a noticeable separation between the two mentales. The muscles may also appear as two small mounds on the chin.

Two depressor muscles pull the lower lip downward. **Depressor labii** originates on the lower border of the mandible and inserts into the orbicularis oris and the skin below the lower lip. **Depressor anguli** also originates on the lower border of the mandible and inserts at the corner or angle of the mouth.

The **buccinator** is a flat strap-like muscle that runs along the cheek to the corner of the mouth. It actually originates inside the mandible, attaching at three points, and inserts into the orbicularis oris in the raphe at the corner of the mouth. An important function of the buccinator is to aid in chewing by keeping the cheek close to the teeth, forcing food up on the occlusal or chewing surface of the teeth. It also creates the action of sucking when contracted and blowing when stretched. A flaw or separation in this muscle can create a dimple in the cheek.

The **masseter** muscle is the powerful chewing muscle that runs diagonally downward across the cheek. It originates along the lower margin of the zygomatic arch, and

Figure 3.6   Elvis Presley demonstrating the use of the left **levator labii**. (Used with permission, Elvis Presley Enterprises, Inc.)

it inserts at the angle of the jaw along the mandible. It is used for tightly clenching the teeth.

Temporalis is a fan-shaped muscle that originates on the temporal bone at the side of the cranium and passes under the zygomatic arch and inserts at the coronoid process of the mandible. Its function is to close the mouth.

Although not a muscle, the **parotid gland** is a structure worth learning because it contributes to the curved fullness of the cheek. It surrounds the angle of the jaw and lies partly on the surface of the masseter muscle. Its purpose is to produce saliva. Some people react to the sight of a sour lemon with a little twinge in the parotid gland.

Two muscles that aid in smiling originate on the zygomatic bone. **Zygomaticus major** runs from the zygomatic bone to the orbicularis oris muscle at the corner of the mouth. **Zygomaticus minor** runs from the zygomatic bone to the orbicularis oris muscle at the upper lip.

Risorius acts to pull the corner of the mouth straight back. It originates in the fascia or tough covering of the masseter muscle and inserts in the skin at the corner of the mouth.

The **submandibular gland** lies along the lower edge of the mandible and produces a soft contour there.

Three Types of Heads

Anatomists have classified people into three major groups according to head or skull shape. The forensic artist should be familiar with this terminology. The **cephalic index**, the term for measurement of the head, is used to determine these head types:

   Brachycephalic refers to relatively broad heads.
   Mesocephalic refers to medium heads.
   Dolichocephalic refers to relatively long heads.

Anatomy of the Facial Features

To establish a consistent terminology for use throughout the text, we present the following descriptions of the individual facial features eye, nose, mouth, and ear, in diagrammatic form (Figures 3.7–3.10). The labels represent a compilation of the terms from multiple anatomy texts. Where the anatomy books have conflicting terms, we have chosen the most commonly appearing names. Note that there are multiple other structures, mostly apparent in the aging face, that have commonly used names as well. This nomenclature is presented in Chapter 8.

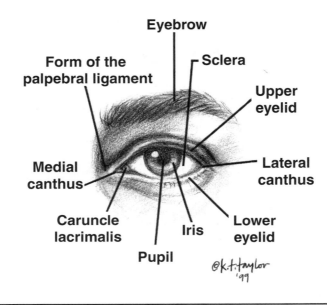

Figure 3.7   Anatomy of the eye. (Illustration by KTT.)

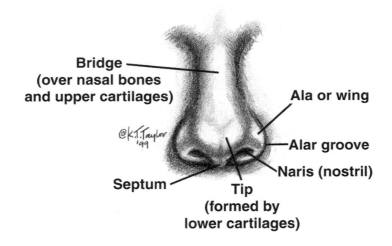

Figure 3.8   Anatomy of the nose. (Illustration by KTT.)

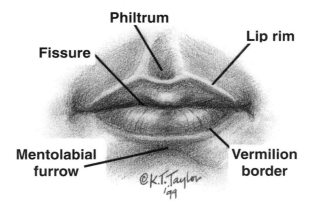

Figure 3.9   Anatomy of the mouth. (Illustration by KTT.)

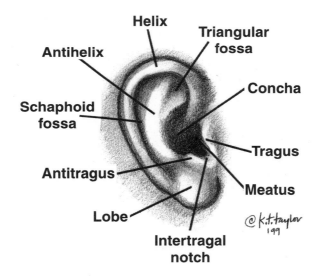

Figure 3.10   Anatomy of the ear. (Illustration by KTT.)

Basic Orientation Terms

A few basic terms used in anatomy will help the forensic artist understand scientific reports and the location of specific structures. These basic reference terms help explain the relationship of one part to another.

Median — the midline of the head or body
Medial — toward the midline, away from the side of the body
Lateral — away from the midline, toward the side of the body
Anterior — toward the front of the body
Posterior — toward the back of the body
Superior — toward the top; above; ascending
Inferior — toward the bottom; below; descending

The Dentition

In addition, it is beneficial to know a few terms with regard to the dentition (Figure 3.11). Each tooth has five surfaces:

Occlusal — the chewing surface
Buccal — the cheek surface
Lingual — the tongue surface
Mesial — toward the midline
Distal — away from the midline

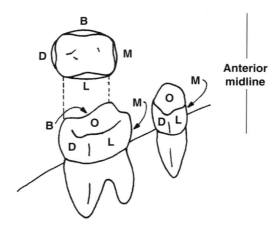

Figure 3.11 Diagram of the lower left molar area illustrates the various **tooth surfaces**. (Illustration by KTT.)

Correct terminology for the specific teeth as they are arranged in the dental arch facilitates the forensic artist's communication with various scientists, particularly with regard to unidentified deceased cases. The diagram shows the names for the upper or maxillary teeth as seen from below (Figure 3.12). The upper teeth are named comparably to the lower teeth.

While efforts are continually being made to standardize dental charts and numbering systems, their formats do vary. A dental specialist should always be consulted for any interpretation of charted information.

Racial/Ancestral Groups and Ethnicity

The forensic artist must understand the complexity of human diversity. In depicting the faces of both victims and offenders, the forensic artist may be called upon to draw or sculpt any sort of face. Often there is difficulty understanding the distinction between race/ancestry and ethnicity. **Race** is defined by Funk and Wagnalls as "one of the major zoological subdivisions of mankind, regarded as having a common origin and exhibiting a relatively constant set of physical traits, such as pigmentation, hair form, and facial and bodily proportions."[7] Race implies a group within a species such as a family, tribe,

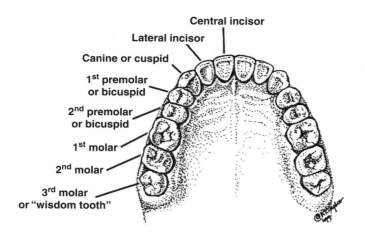

Central incisor
Lateral incisor
Canine or cuspid
1st premolar or bicuspid
2nd premolar or bicuspid
1st molar
2nd molar
3rd molar or "wisdom tooth"

Figure 3.12   Diagram showing the **names of the upper teeth** in the dental arch. (Illustration by KTT.)

people, or nation belonging to the same stock. **Ethnicity** in today's world means a cultural group or affiliation that usually speaks the same language.

In the book *The Use of Forensic Anthropology*, Dr. Robert Pickering and Dr. David Bachman state:

> Race is both a cultural and a biological term. For more than a century scientists and philosophers have tried to define race and describe races. Some scientists define only three races: caucasoid, mongoloid, and negroid, while other scientists have defined more than ten. In our current climate of multicultural sensitivity some scholars, not forensic anthropologists, suggest that race does not exist, or at least it should not be talked about.
>
> The dictionary gives several definitions for race. One definition is a local human population distinguished as a more or less distinct group by genetically transmitted physical characteristics. A second definition is any group of people united or classified together on the basis of a common history, nationality, or geographic distribution. In this definition, common history, religion, and other cultural characteristics supersede genetics. In any case, throughout the history of humanity there have been genetic patterns that vary in time and place. Even if one accepts the categorization defined by "race," there probably never was any such thing as a "pure" race. Wherever humans have gone, they have managed to successfully interbreed with any other group of humans encountered. Today, the ease and cheapness of travel mean that there are more people moving around the globe with greater genetic mixing that ever before.[8]

"Race" is a traditionally used term, though "ancestry" is the more appropriate term for the populations of today's world.

In the workshop setting, I often pose the question to students, "What is Hispanic?" to start a discussion of this issue. Someone usually will answer, "A Latin person from Mexico or South America." Another person may respond, "A person who speaks

Spanish." "How about Puerto Ricans or Cubans?" I then ask, "What race is a Hispanic person?" Students fire back remarks like, "They're considered whites, aren't they?" "Well, Puerto Ricans can look black or Negro." "How about the blue-eyed blond Castilian Spanish?" "I thought that people in Mexico were mixed with the Indians." I then go on to explain that we must consider race as distinguished from ethnicity.

It is important to note that it is not the job of the forensic artist to label people racially/ancestrally or ethnically. It is our job to draw or sculpt their likenesses to aid in their identification. Determination of ancestry is the task of the anthropologist, and it is a very complex one. In the U.S., and in fact worldwide, we are more and more a mixed people. Although it is not the artist's responsibility to categorize or label, a sound understanding of certain racial or ancestral traits is useful. As we will discuss further in the chapters on interviewing and composite drawing, the artist must also distinguish certain factors of description with regard to race or ancestry. For example, skin color description may vary greatly in meaning, dependent upon the skin tone of the person giving the description. **The artist/interviewer must grasp the potential stereotype descriptions, sometimes based on prejudices, that a witness may use even if the artist would not personally use these descriptions or terminology.**

In this section, we offer an overview of the traditionally accepted **three major racial groups: Caucasoid, Negroid, and Mongoloid** (Figures 3.13 and 3.14). The terminology for these groups changes over time. **Currently, terms preferable to most anthropologists when discussing these population groups are European-derived, African-derived, and Asian-derived.** Of course, multiple looks exist within each of the major racial groups. Each description is meant as a general guideline only. This knowledge can be useful for the forensic artist in various ways. The composite artist, with a basic idea of the different racial looks, can better communicate with a witness to do a drawing. The reconstruction artist with this knowledge will be better able to depict the individual features for a given racial or ancestral group, based on the advice of the anthropologist.

Often in workshops, when asked to draw a Negro face, students who lack experience in drawing black or African American faces produce a face that looks like a person from India. This is because they have merely drawn a face with white or Caucasoid proportions, adding dark skin. This shows why we must learn the basic underlying skull structure differences between racial looks.

In class, I sometimes ask the question, "What if your witness describes a face that looked Negro but had light skin?" The artist must understand how to draw the structures of a Negro face, even though the skin is light.

In addition, I always stress to students the importance of everyday observation of people around them. **Forensic artists should become especially familiar with the predominant racial/ancestral and ethnic groups in their particular geographical areas.**

The following descriptions from Dr. Henry Field help lay a foundation of information about the traditionally discussed major groups. We must remember that more than 50 years have passed since Dr. Field made these observations concerning race. Today even greater homogenization of peoples has occurred and will continue to occur. Dr. Field's comments are primarily of historical interest and add to the forensic artist's knowledge base.

Such classifications are antiquated, and **most anthropologists today choose to use the term ancestry rather than race.** Dr. Field's observations cannot be taken as

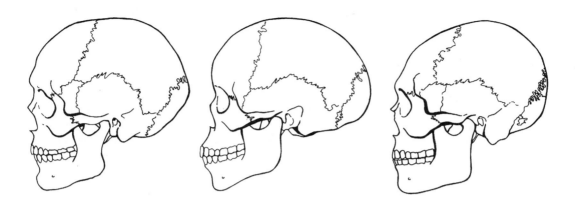

Figure 3.13 Lateral views of the traditional three racial/ancestral groups: **European-derived** (left), **African-derived** (center), and **Asian-derived** (right). (Illustrations by KTT after Betty Pat. Gatliff.)

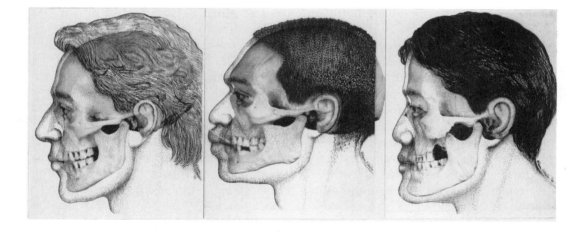

Figure 3.14 Relationship of face to skull in the three major racial/ancestral groups: **European-derived** (left), **African-derived** (center), and **Asian-derived** (right). (Illustrations by KTT.)

a modern guide, and it is no longer acceptable to categorize individuals to this degree. Obviously, people today rarely fall into tidy categories but the general classifications, descriptions, and impressions are helpful.

Caucasoid

The Caucasoids are the group we generally refer to as "white," although certainly not all light-skinned people are Caucasoid, nor are all Caucasoids light skinned. In profile, many Caucasoid skulls exhibit a somewhat flat face with zygomatic bones that retreat or slant back. Frontally, the nasal openings tend to be longer and narrower than in Mongoloids and Negroids. In the 1946 book, *The Races of Mankind,* Dr. Henry Field describes European Caucasoids as falling into three general groups.

The **Mediterranean** race is exemplified by a Sicilian, who is short in stature and stocky in build, with an olive complexion, dark hair and eyes, long head, narrow oval face, and a small mouth. This group is now confined to the Iberian Peninsula, western Mediterranean islands, southern France and Italy, and the western parts of Wales and Ireland.

The **Alpine** race comprises the majority of the round-headed peoples of Europe. They extend from the central plateau of France, Switzerland, and Czechoslovakia southward into the Balkans and eastward into the Soviet Union. A typical member of this group possesses a fairly dark complexion, brown wavy hair, thick eyebrows over brown eyes, heavy body hair, a broad face, sometimes a thick neck, and a medium to heavy build.

The **Nordic** peoples inhabit Scandinavia, northern Germany, and a part of Holland and Belgium. There is also a strong Nordic element in Great Britain. A tall Swede, with light complexion and hair, blue eyes, long head, and a face with a prominent nose and chin, is a typical member of this group.[9]

Dr. Field describes Caucasoid peoples of Africa as follows:

The **Hamites** who inhabit north and northeast Africa … possess dark brown or black hair, which is either curly or wavy in form, and the skin varies in color from reddish brown to dark brown. Their average stature varies from very tall to medium and their build is slender. The typical Hamite possesses a long head, an oval, elongated face with no forward protrusion, thin lips, pointed chin, and a prominent, well-shaped nose.

Semites … in a measure the physical traits of Hamites resemble those of Semites. Members of the Semitic group now living chiefly in the extreme north of Africa migrated from Arabia at early dates. The Arabs, who are typical Semites in both physique and language, are usually medium in stature, are dark-haired, and generally have oval faces with long, narrow, straight noses. There are two typical head forms among the Arabs — one is long, and the other broad.[9]

Negroid

The **Negroid** peoples are often referred to as "black," even though their skin color actually varies on a continuum from light to rather dark brown. In profile, the Negroid skull often exhibits alveolar prognathism, which is expressed as a projection of the lower face. Frontally, the nasal openings tend to be wider and shorter than in Caucasoids and Mongoloids, with a bridge that is broader and flatter. Negroid mouths tend to be broader with fuller everted lips. Many Negro people also have wider set eyes than the other groups. Dr. Field also describes the derivation of various Negro peoples:

The **West African** coastal Negro is long-headed, of medium stature, extremely well developed, with a heavy torso and massive limbs. The arms are long and the legs short in comparison with the length of the trunk. In all Negroes the face is usually broad and massive, sometimes with a projecting chin. The nose is broad, and the lips are thick and everted. Dark eyes and wooly hair likewise are constant Negro features.

The **Nilotic** Negroes (of the upper Nile), if compared with typical Negroes of West Africa, show greater stature, a far more slender build, and heads longer in relation to their breadth.

There are groups of true **Pygmies**, the most typical of which are the Wambuti of the Ituri Forest in the northern Congo. Their dark brown hair is usually short. Their skin color varies from light brown with a yellow tinge to a very dark chocolate color. The average male stature is four feet six inches, and both body and legs are short .... In shape the head is typically round and there is some protrusion of the face. The lips are full, and the root of the nose is flat and broad.

The **Bushmen** possess short, frizzy hair which grows in separate tufts ... there is very little hair on the face and body. The skin ranges in color from yellow to olive, and becomes markedly wrinkled at an early age. The head is extremely small, low in the crown, and in shape intermediate between long and round. The forehead is slightly protruding, and the nose is broader and flatter than in any other race. The dark eyes are often narrow and slightly oblique. The average male is below five feet in stature.[9]

Mongoloid

Mongoloid peoples have been variously described as "red" or "yellow." In truth, the Mongoloid category includes Native Americans, American Eskimos, and the various Asian groups, with many varying skin colors and features. In profile, the Mongoloid skull indicates an often flattened face with a short cranial vault or distance from front to back. Frontally, the cheek area is usually quite wide with projecting zygomatic bones. The width of the nose opening or nasal aperture is usually somewhere between the Caucasoid and the Negroid. Mongoloid mouths may also be of a size somewhere between the Caucasoid and the Negroid.

Dr. Field describes certain Mongoloid groups as follows:

The **Chinese** represent a single racial unit, which has had sufficient strength to maintain its culture and traditions in the face of numerous invaders. The Chinese as a whole are medium in stature. The shape of the head is intermediate between long and round, the skin yellowish brown in color, eyes oblique with the Mongolian fold, and hair straight and black.

There are two distinct types of modern **Japanese**, one of which possesses relatively fine features, while the other is more coarse in type. Both possess certain traits in common .... The fine or aristocratic type is taller and more slender, with an elongated face, and a prominent, narrow, arched nose. The eyes are either straight or oblique, and the epicanthic fold may be present. The coarse type, which may represent immigrants from southeastern Asia, is short and stocky, with a broad face, short, concave nose, and rounded nostrils, oblique eyes, usually an epicanthic fold and a darker complexion than the other group.

The constant physical characteristics of the **American Indians** consist of a brown skin which frequently bears a reddish or yellowish tinge; dark eyes; straight, coarse black hair; a minimum of beard and body hair; and a broad face with high and prominent cheekbones. The head is usually round, although there are certain groups in which long heads predominate. The stature also varies in different groups. The nose varies from flat to aquiline.

The **Eskimos** form a definite group, clearly of Asiatic origin. In many respects they are the most Mongoloid of all Americans. They are distinguished by a short, stocky build, markedly long heads combined with very broad faces, massive jaws, and moderately narrow noses. The sides of the head are often flat, and a ridge may be present along the dome of the skull. The eyes frequently show the Mongoloid fold.[9]

Australian Aboriginals

Some anthropology texts include the Australian Aboriginal as a separate and distinct race. Dr. Field describes this group as follows:

> The physical characteristics of the aboriginal Australian are jet black, wavy or curly hair, which is often heavy on the face; dark chocolate brown skin; medium stature with slim limbs; and a long head with a flat, retreating forehead, prominent brow ridges, projecting face, and a deeply set, broad nose.[9]

It should be noted that many of today's Aboriginals often have much lighter hair. **Dr. Field's descriptions of the peoples of the world are of general interest, but they are not intended to be used as a realistic guide for modern individuals.**

Terminology used for race, ancestry, and ethnicity is a sensitive matter that should be a consideration for the forensic artist. Historically, population groups have been given various names and the "political correctness" of such terms tends to change from time to time. Examples of variations in terminology include "Black" or "African-American," "American Indian" or "Native American," and "Asian" or "Oriental."

Perhaps the most ambitious and thorough artistic study of the peoples of the world was undertaken during the late 1920s and early 1930s by Malvina Hoffman (Figure 3.15). Hoffman, an American, studied with Auguste Rodin in Paris and with Gutzon Borglum, who sculpted the faces on Mount Rushmore. Commissioned by the Field Museum in Chicago, Hoffman traveled throughout the continents of the world observing its people. She drew and sculpted at least 100 different faces. Her phenomenal work was displayed for many years in the Hall of Man at the Field Museum. A few of the pieces can still be seen there today.

Male and Female

In addition to requests to draw various racial and ethnic looks, the forensic artist may be called upon to draw or sculpt both male and female faces. In my experience, a greater percentage of composite drawings requested are of male faces, while more of the victim faces drawn are female, although I have certainly drawn both female suspects and male victims. As with race, the structure of the skull is important for assessment of sex (Figure 3.16). For anthropologists examining skeletal remains, the skull is probably second only to the pelvis to help determine sex.

Structural differences between male and female skulls are sometimes subtle and at other times more pronounced, depending upon the individual. Generally speaking,

Figure 3.15 Artist **Malvina Hoffman** studies the face of a Papuan man.

anthropologists expect male skulls to be more robust with more pronounced muscle attachment indicators.

Male

The male face is more angular overall and usually larger than the female face. The lower half of the face is proportionately larger than that of a female because the male mandible is larger and stronger. The angle of the jaw is usually more acute and defined and the chin is more square and pronounced. The male forehead usually is more sloping and has a projecting brow ridge area. In many instances the teeth are a bit larger. There is often less fat in the facial area, which allows the musculature to be

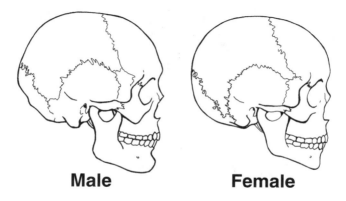

Male **Female**

Figure 3.16 Lateral views showing variations in the **male and female skulls.** (Illustrations by KTT after Betty Pat. Gatliff.)

more visible. The skin appears more coarse. A male face has facial hair, and the eyebrows are more noticeable.

An additional feature in drawing males is depiction of facial hair. Composite artists must learn to realistically draw variations of male facial hair. They may wish to use reference files to help the witness select the correct style. Artists who prepare fugitive updates must make judgments about addition of facial hair based on each individual case. Artists who do postmortem drawings or facial reconstructions must assess the information recovered from the crime scene regarding possibility of facial hair in life. There may be no such information available.

Female

The female face is softer in appearance and is usually smaller overall than the male face. The lower half of the face is proportionately smaller than the male face because the mandible is smaller and weaker. The angle of the jaw is usually more obtuse and less well defined and the chin is more pointed. The female forehead is generally more upright and smooth in appearance. The teeth are often smaller, and there may be more fat covering the muscles of the face, making the face appear softer and more curvilinear. The skin may appear smoother, and there is an absence of facial hair on the cheeks and chin.

Additional considerations in drawing female faces may be makeup and more complicated hairstyles. The composite artist should learn to draw these features from a description and develop good reference files. The artist who does postmortem drawings, fugitive updates, or facial reconstruction may need to make conservative judgment calls regarding makeup and hairstyle on a case-by-case basis.

As is true with regard to race, individuals can sometimes be difficult to visually categorize as male or female (Figure 3.17). A general understanding of the facial differences between the sexes provides another tool for the forensic artist. For

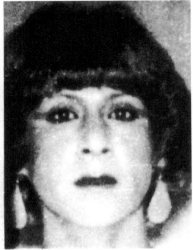

Figure 3.17 Sexual ambiguity in a face: male face (left) and the same male face with makeup to appear female (right). (Courtesy of Texas Department of Criminal Justice.)

example, the composite artist may encounter a witness who, while reviewing the composite, states: "That's close, but the face needs to look more effeminate (or more masculine)." By understanding the differences described above, the artist is better equipped to determine how to correct the drawing to the witness' satisfaction. Again, it is not so much the job of the artist to categorize, but rather to draw what is being described.

Facial Expressions

Because each face acts as an important mechanism for communication and display of emotions, forensic artists benefit greatly from studying expressions and interpretations of those expressions. Facial expressions are such an integral part of the human face that their observation can become second nature if we attempt to scrutinize those around us. In 1872, in *The Expression of the Emotions in Man and Animals*, Charles Darwin wrote:

> It has often struck me as a curious fact that so many shades of expression are instantly recognized without any conscious process of analysis on our part. No one, I believe, can clearly describe a sullen or sly expression; yet many observers are unanimous that these expressions can be recognized in the various races of man.[10]

In his wonderful book *Facial Expression*, Gary Faigin provides a comprehensive and entertaining look at the subject of expression:

> … facial expressions can have such great significance. The slightest suggestion of a smile can start a conversation between strangers; the slightest suggestion of a frown can start an argument between friends.
> … Most experts believe that the fundamental facial expressions — fear, joy, sadness, surprise, disgust, and anger — are common to all human societies and have remained unchanged for thousands for years.[11]

This premise of **universal expressions** has been effectively demonstrated by Dr. Paul Ekman. Ekman, an experimental psychologist, studied expressions on faces of literate people in Europe, South America, Africa, and Japan during the 1970s, and found the same expressive responses in each location. His research with the tribespeople of Borneo and New Guinea, who did not read or write and had never been exposed to the media, indicates universal expressions were used.

The forensic artist can employ a knowledge of expression in many ways. Witnesses request composite artists to incorporate particular expressions in facial drawings. The accurate rendition of an expression as remembered by the witness may be crucial to replicating the face the witness recalls. The witness will probably not be satisfied with the composite until he or she feels that the expression is right. Indeed, it may be the expression that triggers an identification, since some people display certain expressions very characteristically (see Chapter 1, Figure 1.1). The sketch artist must therefore have a good understanding of how to readily convey a given expression in a drawing.

Of great significance to the composite artist, or perhaps to anyone conducting an interview, is the use of expressions as a gauge of the feelings of the person being interviewed. I have often sensed the need for a break in an interview with a traumatized crime victim by closely observing signs of stress in his or her face. Flushing, blanching, perspiration, dryness of the throat, or changes in pupil size may be signs of increased stress or arousal.

Particularly useful in interviewing is Dr. Ekman's discovery of what he calls **microexpressions**, or fleeting expressions that flash across a person's face in a fraction of a second. In his book *Telling Lies*, he explains that these microexpressions are fully formed expressions, usually at odds with the general expression on a person's face. They occur very rapidly and seem to be made totally unconsciously. Ekman describes his discovery of these microexpressions while viewing hundreds of videotaped interviews of facial expressions. With a sensitivity to microexpressions, the trained interviewer will learn not only to be aware of the stresses on a victim, but also to detect indicators of false allegations.[12]

Specialists in jury selection may use this approach along with knowledge of kinesics or body language to advise their clients as to the most potentially favorable jurors for their side.

An understanding of expressions and how to form them is also useful to the forensic artist who does two- or three-dimensional facial reconstructions from the skull. If the frontal teeth are recovered with a skeletal body, it is usually advisable to show a version of the reconstructed face with the teeth displayed. The reconstruction artist must be able to show the opened mouth with a natural-looking expression.

The creation of most expressions involves the areas of the eyebrows and the mouth. Even simplistic "happy faces" show marked variability when changes are made in the brows or corners of the mouth (Figure 3.18). A series of French postcards from the early 1900s shows another example of the importance of eyebrows in the creation of expression (Figure 3.19). Faigin notes:

> The whole face does not participate equally in most expressions. The burden of getting the message across usually falls most heavily on the brow in combination with the eyes, and the mouth and its surroundings. These two locations are the areas of the greatest muscular development

| Pleasant | Mischievous | Angry | Bewildered |

Figure 3.18 Simplistic faces show the **importance of eyebrows and mouth corners in the creation of facial expressions.** (Illustrations by KTT.)

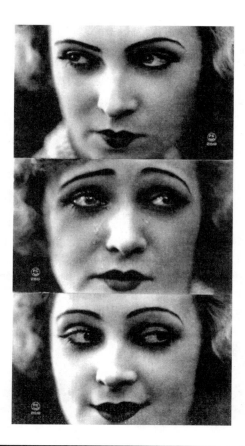

Figure 3.19 French postcards from the early 1900s show the **importance of eyebrows in facial expressions**.

and so are capable of undergoing the greatest changes. They are also, not coincidentally, the parts of the face we always respond to most strongly.[11]

This may explain why Leonardo da Vinci's Mona Lisa wears such an ambiguous expression (Figure 3.20). One of the most potentially expressive features has been omitted from her face: she has no eyebrows!

Witnesses seem to describe certain expressions with frequency. Forensic artists are asked to depict certain expressions more frequently than others (Figure 3.21). Composite artists are often asked to draw an angry or threatening look, a smirk or a sneer, or to make a face appear sleepy, drunk, or drugged. Reconstruction artists are primarily concerned with depicting the rather expressionless face at rest with the lips closed, or the open-mouthed smile. Some useful expressions for the forensic artist include:

Anger or threat — lowered eyebrows, pulled together in the middle with a dark shadow under the brow; eyes narrowed; lips tightened with possible down-turned corners.

Figure 3.20 Lack of eyebrows may explain the **ambiguous expression** on the face of Leonardo da Vinci's Mona Lisa.

Figure 3.21 Several **common expressions**: anger, threat, or irritation shown by furrowed brows (would appear angrier if the lips were tightened) (upper left); sneer formed by pulling up one side of the mouth (upper right); distress shown by eyebrows pulled upward in the center (lower left); stupid or perplexed look formed by lowered brows and relaxed gaping mouth (lower right). (Courtesy of Texas Department of Criminal Justice.)

Sneer — one side of the lip pulled up possibly creating a furrow beside the nose; less frequently, can occur on both sides of the mouth at once, creating a look of disdain.

Sleepy, drunk, or drugged appearance — eyelids lowered, obscuring the upper part of the iris and part of the pupil; eyelids can be drawn lower and lower to progressively exaggerate the look; eyes may also exhibit more white (sclera) below the iris.

Smile, closed mouth — corners of the mouth pulled back and slightly upward; teeth not revealed; eyes may be slightly narrowed with "puffs" beginning to form underneath; cheeks may lift a bit.

Smile, open mouth — corners of the mouth pulled back and upward; eight to ten teeth exposed; rounded "puffs" formed under the eyes; cheeks displaced upward.

Occasionally faces bear expressions that somehow do not seem quite right. For example, a smiling mouth paired with eyebrows having the inner corners lifted in distress may appear very confusing (Figure 3.22). This is known as a **discordant expression**. Such expressions may appear on the faces of beauty queens or members of royalty who must smile for great lengths of time. They appear to be smiling with their mouths only, not their eyes. Discordant expressions may appear in mugshots, and they have also been seen in the photographs of people held captive who are told to smile as they are photographed. Whatever the situation, a discordant expression is a clue that something is amiss.

Gary Faigin offers insightful comments about the human face:

> There is no landscape that we know as well as the human face. The twenty-five-odd square inches containing the features is the most scrutinized piece of territory in existence, examined constantly, and carefully, with far more than an intellectual interest. Every detail of the nose, eyes, and mouth, every regularity in proportion, every variation from one individual to the next, are matters about which we are all authorities.[11]

Figure 3.22 A **discordant expression** due to a smiling mouth combined with distress in the eyebrow area. (Courtesy of Texas Department of Criminal Justice.)

References

1. Jenkinson, J., "Face facts: a history of physiognomy from ancient Mesopotamia to the end of the 19th century," *The Journal of Biomedical Communication*, 24(3), 2–7, 1997.
2. Bertillon, A., *The Bertillon System of Identification: Signeletic Instructions, The Theory and Practice of Anthropometrical Identification*, McClaughry, R. W., Ed. Chicago: The Werner Company, 1896.
3. Liggett, J., *The Human Face*. New York: Stein and Day, 1974.
4. Landau, T., *About Faces: The Evolution of the Human Face*. New York: Doubleday, 1989.
5. George, R. M., Anatomical and artistic guidelines for forensic facial reconstruction, in *Forensic Analysis of the Skull*, Iscan, M. Y. and Helmer, R. P., Eds. New York: Wiley–Liss, 1993.
6. Gordon, L., *How to Draw the Human Head*. New York: Viking Press, 1977.
7. Landau, S. I., Brantley, S. C., et al., *Funk and Wagnalls Standard Encyclopedic Dictionary*. Chicago: J. G. Ferguson Publishing Co., 1968.
8. Pickering, R. B. and Bachman, D. C., *The Use of Forensic Anthropology*. Boca Raton: CRC Press, 1996, 79–80.
9. Field, H., *The Races of Mankind*. New York: C. S. Hammond and Co., 1946.
10. Darwin, C., *The Expression of the Emotions in Man and Animals* (1872). Chicago: University of Chicago Press, 1965.
11. Faigin, G., *Facial Expression*. New York: Watson-Guptill, 1990.
12. Ekman, P., *Telling Lies*. New York: Berkley Books, 1986.

Chapter 4

Drawing the Human Face

Studying the complexity of the human face better prepares us to depict this multifaceted subject in a realistic way. In Chapter 3 we discussed basic information about faces that helps us draw, paint, and sculpt them in a realistic fashion. We explored human facial anatomy, variations in faces due to sex or ancestry, and the element of expression. Here we learn how to apply this information to the process of drawing faces in a way that may prove useful in forensic art.

Michelangelo Buonnaroti, painter of the Sistine Chapel ceiling and sculptor of the *David*, was once asked to name the greatest art — painting or sculpture. He replied, "Drawing." Drawing is fundamental to all other artistic endeavors. **As forensic artists, drawing the human face forms the basis for most of our work.** Even if your work is done entirely on the computer, you must grasp some of the basics about the human face to create high quality facial imaging. In this chapter, we discuss the nuts and bolts of facial drawing with the goal of lifelike, efficient depictions that convey useful, accurate information.

Forensic artists are presented with a particularly challenging task. We do not have the luxury of drawing composite images from models as do fine artists who create portraits. Although we may have photographs from which to work, they are rarely ideal or pleasant because they were taken at morgues or crime scenes. Nor does forensic art possess the element of creative expression. Our more sober job is to represent faces through sound draftsmanship. We must understand our tools and materials, use of light on form to attain perspective, importance of facial proportions, and anatomical facts concerning individual facial features. The forensic artist must be able to readily use his or her artistic "bag of tricks" as needed to perform tasks, and it is only through study and practice that this happens.

Drawing undoubtedly comes more effortlessly to some than others. As an instructor of many years, I have seen remarkable improvement in students who listened to instruction, tried hard, and practiced (see Figures 4.1 and 4.2). In workshops, I have seen dramatic advancement by some in only a week's time.

Figure 4.1   Composite drawing of a black male by a beginning artist (left) and drawing showing greatly improved style (right) achieved after attending a workshop and practicing. (Courtesy of Texas Department of Public Safety.)

Figure 4.2   Composite drawing of a white male by a beginning artist (left) and drawing showing greatly improved style (right) achieved after attending a workshop and practicing. (Courtesy of Texas Department of Public Safety.)

Like physical fitness, drawing skills are developed only through repeated practice. If neglected, your "fitness" for drawing diminishes. This is often a problem for police artists who draw only on an "as-needed" basis. Effort should be made to practice drawing on a regular basis, since the next sketch you are called upon to make may literally become a matter of life or death.

Tools and Materials

As with any discipline, knowledge of the "tools of the trade" enhances one's ability to perform effectively. The tools and materials the forensic artist uses should promote top-quality work of an archival nature.

Each item of forensic art should be prepared with the notion that it is potential evidence for court presentation and that it may not actually be needed for years in advance. Materials used should ensure the archival nature of the art because it may not be needed as a court exhibit for years.

This is especially true in homicide investigations. Years ago, I drew a composite sketch of the perpetrator of a sexual assault and attempted homicide in a case that remained unsolved for 14 years. Thanks to the capabilities of today's automated fingerprint identification systems, the suspect was identified when a latent print from the crime scene was searched by an operator entering information on old, unsolved cases.

A composite drawing course I attended years ago had recommended the use of newsprint paper and vine charcoal sticks for drawing, and I used this combination of non-archival materials for a short time. After 14 years, one such drawing was yellow and crumbling, but the face bore a resemblance to the suspect, so I was subpoenaed in order to get my drawing admitted as evidence. Hopefully, others will learn from my experience and **always use materials that withstand the test of time.**

Papers

Basic Drawing Papers

A forensic art colleague and friend had an experience similar to mine with the newsprint and charcoal, but in his case he had the embarrassing experience of presenting in court a drawing done on photocopy paper with a ball-point pen. **Proper paper for forensic art use should not only be archival in nature, but it should also be substantial enough to withstand numerous erasures without tearing.** I use a **Bristol paper** with a rough rather than a smooth surface, but you should choose paper based on your drawing style. I prefer Bristol because of its texture, durability, and ability to withstand vigorous erasures.

Size — Choose size of pads of paper based on your particular scale of drawing a face and your requirements for convenient filing of your work. I tend to make rather large drawings, so I use 11″ × 14″ Bristol pads. After I complete a composite, I trim the sides so the original drawing can be filed in a legal-size file folder. Others prefer to use smaller pads of paper, usually 8½″ × 11″, and letter-size file folders.

Surface Texture — Artists who do finely detailed drawing using harder pencil leads and very sharp pencil points often prefer smoother textured papers that allow them to achieve more detail. Artists who use softer pencil leads, charcoal pencils, vine charcoal, or chalks for drawing usually prefer rougher papers with more "tooth." The rougher surface of the paper grasps the graphite or chalk and holds it to the surface.

The Bristol paper surface I prefer is called "regular" as opposed to "smooth." Papers are manufactured in surface textures ranging from very smooth, sometimes called "plate-finished," to highly textured. Textured papers designed for charcoal or watercolor work can also be used for pencil drawing, but pencil drawings will reveal the strong textures or patterns inherent in the particular paper.

Color — While most forensic artists choose white or off-white drawing paper, tinted papers may sometimes be useful. I have found softly tinted papers such as **Canson Mi-Tientes** are beneficial when preparing color drawings such as child age progressions, postmortem drawings, or fugitive updates. By beginning with a slight tint, it is easier to layer the pastels or colored pencils to get a natural skin tone. I choose various tints depending upon the lightness or darkness of the skin tone of the person drawn.

Use of colored paper as a base suggests an approach to drawing in which "darks" and "lights" are both drawn in, as in pastel work or painting. When drawing on white paper, you achieve highlights simply by erasing an area to reveal the paper itself. But when drawing on tinted paper, the drawing begins on a middle ground, rather than on white; thus, both lights and darks are added as the drawing develops.

Papers and Boards for Other Uses

General — Several other types of papers may be useful in forensic art. Large pads of fairly inexpensive paper may be kept on hand for use by children who are interviewed or accompany a witness. **Newsprint** or **white butcher-type paper** is good for this purpose. These inexpensive papers may also be used for wrapping or covering artwork such as trial displays, which must be transported carefully.

If you become involved in the preparation of trial displays or demonstrative evidence, you should familiarize yourself with the latest graphic art supplies on the market. **Matte board** and **foam core board** are generally used for mounting trial display projects; however, numerous other special-use materials such as magnetic vinyl may be useful.

Overlays — For years I have used various transparent papers to facilitate my work, particularly **matte acetate**. Matte acetate has a nonglare frosted surface and may be placed on top of a drawing in progress. The artist can then continue drawing in pencil on the overlay. This allows for the addition of items such as glasses, facial hair, or alternate hairstyles without changing the original drawing. Photographs for reproduction can be made through the matte acetate overlay, showing both the underlying drawing and the drawing done on the overlay (see "Alternate Looks" in Chapter 6 for an example of such use when adding a beard). This method may be particularly useful when there are varying opinions among witnesses. Use of such overlays makes it possible to document and separate clearly just what is described by each witness. For example, one witness remembers seeing a mustache and another does not, although both describe the face very similarly.

When preparing an overlay of any type over one of your drawings, whether it is a simple addition of facial hair to a composite or a more elaborate "second look" overlay for a fugitive update, you should include **registration marks**. Commercial art supply stores carry various types of registration marks that usually have a small circle with an "x" or cross in the center. They are available as rub-off films or rolls of peel-off tape. These marks need not be fancy or even store bought. Marks for **registration or correct alignment** may be simply small "x's" drawn at two or three places to indicate the accurate placement for the overlay. The registration marks should be placed first on the original art. Then the overlay should be laid on top and the marks placed or drawn on the overlay, exactly on top of the underlying marks on the original. This ensures that the feature drawn on acetate ends up in "register" or exactly where it should be. For example, it would be possible to determine if glasses drawn on acetate should ride low on the nose of the face in a drawing or be high up on the bridge.

Clear acetate is useful for some types of overlays, especially when preparing trial displays. Items may be cut out and spray-glued to the acetate to present the needed information on overlays. Clear acetate is sturdy and provides an excellent transparent covering for artwork. The surface of another material called **wet media acetate** accepts watercolor, ink, or paint.

Another overlay material I find indispensable is **vellum**, which some manufacturers call **layout paper** or **tracing paper**. (Note that some manufacturers use the term "vellum" to designate a type of paper texture.) I use semi-transparent vellum exclusively for preparing skull reconstruction drawings because it is substantial enough for pencil drawing and erasures. It is also transparent enough that the skull photograph may be clearly seen underneath the reconstruction drawing in progress. Vellums or tracing papers vary considerably in degree of opacity or transparency, so you should check various brands before purchasing them.

Drawing and Blending Tools

Pencils

Because pencils are the first drawing and writing tools most of us use, they tend to be the artist's most fundamental, comfortable, and useful tools. In general, **hard leads produce lighter marks and soft leads produce darker marks.** Any good art supply store offers a wide variety of pencil types and accompanying charts for determining hardness. It is a good idea to have lighter pencils for blocking out proportions in the early stages of a drawing and darker ones for refinement.

Most pencils are cylinders of graphite encased in wood. There are also "woodless" pencils composed of compressed graphite wrapped in a plastic jacket. Figure 4.3 shows a variety of types of pencils taken directly from the box I use to do forensic art on a regular basis, including **woodless pencils, chisel-point pencils** for quick, broad marks, **Design® Ebony pencils** for dark "darks," and various H's, F's, and B's.

You should maintain both very sharp and rounded, dull pencil tips for different areas of your drawings. Blunted or chisel points can be used to quickly block out proportions or lay in areas of hair. Sharper points are needed for tight details such as finishing areas within the eyes.

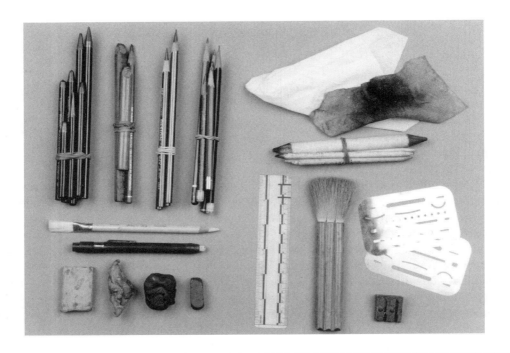

Figure 4.3 Basic drawing tools and materials. Pencils: woodless pencils, chisel-points, Design® Ebony types, and assorted H's, F's, and B's (upper left). **Blending tools:** facial tissue, chamois cloth, and tortillions (upper right). **Erasers:** ink or typewriter type, cylindrical vinyl eraser in a plastic holder, kneaded rubber erasers in various stages of use, and small vinyl eraser in block form (lower left). **Other assorted supplies:** ruler or scale, small bamboo brush for wiping away erasures, eraser shields, and a small pencil sharpener (lower right). (Courtesy of Missey Micheletti.)

Charcoal

Charcoal, another potential medium for drawing, is available in several forms. **Vine or stick charcoal**, often used in life drawing classes in art school, is very good for quick gestural drawing or for obtaining dark skin tones. It is less desirable, however, for archiving as evidence, because of its tendency to smear. **Charcoal pencils**, which are harder and slightly less messy, may be used for tighter details. However, even when sprayed with a fixative, charcoal drawings will suffer a loss of detail over time if handled or repeatedly placed in and taken out of files.

Colors

If you are asked to do color artwork, you must determine which medium is best suited for your purpose. In general, media that are difficult to control and alter such as water colors, acrylic, or oil paints are not used in forensic art, especially not in composite drawings. That is not to say that if you have a particular mastery over a certain medium that you should not use it. You must evaluate the particular needs of each case.

Colored pencils are perhaps the most commonly used medium for color work in forensic art. Although I do not consider myself a very skilled colorist, I have achieved functional results by using a combination of **pastel chalks** and **colored pencils** (see the color figures following p. 266). For most color jobs, I develop a light drawing in graphite, lay a base of pastel tones over that, and then add details with colored pencils. This method, which must be done in layers, takes considerable time. Colored pencils must be used with a light touch or there may be a waxy buildup that prevents addition of more layers of color.

Pastels are available as individual sticks or in sets with a range of colors needed for facial drawing. Quality and price vary. Colored pencils may be purchased individually or in sets of different sizes. Water-soluble watercolor pencils may be used for drawing and then blended by adding water with a brush.

Blending Tools

The blending tools that I like include a small piece of chamois, a facial tissue, and several sizes of tortillions (see Figure 4.3).

Tortillions or stumps are sticks made from cone-shaped, rolled bits of compressed paper, used for blending areas of graphite. Use of tortillions usually produces a very distinctive "look" in a drawing with very smooth-looking skin. Skillful use of tortillions can produce a very realistic skin texture for small children or other young or smooth faces. When tortillions are applied, however, the graphite may be pressed deeply into the paper, making it difficult to erase highlights or to make needed changes. While some artists swear by these blenders, I choose to use them only very sparingly. I find them particularly helpful for laying in large areas of dark hair very quickly.

The tool I use most for blending is the **tip of my finger**. Again, this is a matter of personal choice and style. Some artists consider use of the fingers inappropriate. If you have oily or sweaty hands, fingertip blending probably will not work well for you.

As with pencils and other drawing tools, think of the size of the "mark" that is needed. The tips of tortillions produce small marks, fingertips produce medium-sized marks, and tissue or chamois cloths produce large sweeping blended areas.

Each of these tools may be used to soften contrast and create areas of transition. They are tools for drawing selectively, rather than just smearing around graphite or charcoal.

Erasers

Erasers, too, should be thought of as more than just tools for removal of unwanted graphite. When used with a delicate touch, they become important implements for enhancing your drawings. Figure 4.3 shows several types of erasers including **kneaded rubber erasers**, an **ink or typewriter eraser** with brush, a **vinyl eraser in block form**, and a **cylindrical vinyl eraser** in a plastic holder. Kneaded rubber erasers are soft and may be formed into shapes for lifting out highlights in small areas.

Other Tools and Supplies

General Art Supplies

You will need some type of **carrying case for your art supplies**, particularly if you must travel to remote locations away from your office. You should select supplies keeping in mind the size and dimensions of your case.

You should use some sort of **drawing board** for support of your paper even if you choose to leave the sheet in the pad. A wooden or masonite drawing board may be used to rest on the edge of a table to angle the top of the drawing upward rather than flat on the table. By drawing flat on a surface, you risk distortion of the image. A small **table-top easel** can be very useful for this same purpose and facilitates the viewing of the drawing by the witness.

Other useful supplies include **masking tape** for taping your paper to the drawing board, **spray fixative** for finishing and preserving the drawing, and a **stamp or seal** for marking your drawings as evidence. Some forensic artists have special rubber stamps made that include information such as policy agency logo, date, drawing number, and detective's name.

Other general art supplies useful for forensic art purposes, shown in Figure 4.3, include a small **pencil sharpener**, a **ruler or scale**, a small bamboo **brush** for wiping away erasures, and an **eraser shield**.

An **eraser shield** is a thin metal rectangle with small holes of varying sizes and shapes cut into it. It is useful for placing over an area of your drawing to "shield" it while you selectively erase with a cylindrical vinyl eraser. I find it helpful to use the small dots or holes to erase out the highlights in the eyes. It is possible to draw a dark brown eye and then use the eraser shield to pull out the small highlights that give the eyes "life." The gently curved opening can be used to erase light areas on the surface of upper or lower eyelids. The teardrop shapes are good for getting into small areas such as the "whites" of the eyes.

You need a small **pencil sharpener** to maintain sharp pencil points. Some artists are content with the old-fashioned type while others prefer the electric styles. Battery-operated sharpeners can be carried in a small briefcase or kit for field work. **Sandpaper blocks** for sharpening graphite pencils or charcoals are also available in art supply stores.

Drafting Tools

If you become involved in two-dimensional skull reconstruction, you will need some basic drafting instruments, such as a **T-square** and a **triangle**. The triangle may be either 45° or 30/60°.

Drafting brushes can be used to brush away excess rubber or vinyl from erasures. If these are too large for your purposes, smaller makeup brushes can be used.

"People" Supplies

In addition to the required art supplies, other items can help in the performance of your duties. As discussed in Chapter 5, certain "small comforts" may help a person under stress. **"Fidget toys"** to occupy nervous hands may be placed within easy reach of witnesses to calm and comfort them. Jars containing **candy or**

chewing gum may serve the same purpose by anchoring the witnesses in the safety of the present.

Large pads of **inexpensive paper, crayons, teddy bears, or other small toys** can help occupy children for prolonged periods. Many law enforcement agencies have programs that provide teddy bears to traumatized children.

Tools for Enlargement, Reduction, and Projection

Certain types of forensic art may be enhanced by the use of tools for "cheating." Our purpose as forensic artists is to produce accurate drawings based on the information provided. Any appropriate method to obtain greater accuracy should be used. In other words, **"cheating" is permitted in some types of forensic art, if it produces better quality and more effective results.**

If you are preparing a drawing based on an available photograph, such as a postmortem drawing or fugitive update, it is acceptable to use a mechanical device to start the drawing with accuracy. Even the "Old Masters" used such tools. Figure 4.4 shows an early 16th-century Albrecht Dürer woodcut demonstrating a draftsman's use of a grid device to reduce a life-size reclining figure to a drawing surface.

Enlargement and Reduction

Traditionally, artists have used a **simple grid system** to enlarge or reduce their preliminary sketches. If you work in a situation with limited facilities and equipment, this time-tested method may be useful. A drawing or photograph may be enlarged or reduced by placing tracing paper over the image and drawing a grid at measured intervals. To enlarge a small photograph, such as a morgue shot, so that you can draw it on a larger piece of paper, place tracing paper over the photograph, then draw a grid of squares at small measured intervals. Then trace the facial features on the grid in a linear fashion. Next, move to another sheet of paper and lightly draw another grid, several times larger than the one used over the photograph. Then redraw the face on the largest grid by referring to the grid lines on the sketch. For example, a grid of 1/2″ squares used over the photograph and transferred to a larger

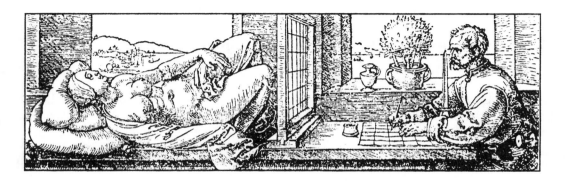

Figure 4.4 A 1525 woodcut by Albrecht Dürer showing a draftsman using a **grid device** for accurate reduction of a reclining figure.

piece of paper with a grid of 1″ squares could be used to enlarge the face 400%, or four times larger. This is a simple way to enlarge a face and start a drawing with accurate placement of features and proportions.

An engineering device called a **pantograph** may be used to mechanically duplicate, enlarge, or reduce drawings. A pantograph looks like four rulers attached together. While the pantograph stylus is used by the artist to trace over the lines of the original image, the pantograph tool simultaneously redraws the lines (either enlarged or reduced) with a pencil held by an extended arm.

Proportional dividers are somewhat expensive tools, but they may prove a good investment. They look like two crossed metal sticks attached in the center like scissors. By using incremental marks on the tool, it is possible to measure a detail of a small photograph of a face, say the width of an eye, with one end of the divider. Then the other end of the "X"-shaped device is placed on the paper where the enlargement will be done and the enlarged measurement of the eye width noted.

A very simple, readily available method is enlargement on a **photocopier**. Such an enlargement may then be traced onto transparent paper.

Projectors

A **projector** is probably the best method for enlargement of a small facial photo-graph to produce a larger drawing. Facial images may be projected and traced at the scale desired. **The three primary types of projectors are opaque, slide, and transparency.**

Opaque projectors may project either vertically or horizontally. They must be operated in a darkened room. When purchasing an opaque projector, you should consider the copy area or the maximum size available for the original image being projected. Also consider the projection range of enlargement or reduction capabilities.

Slide projectors may be used to project and enlarge a face, especially if the original facial image was provided to the artist in slide form. The slide is projected onto paper taped on the wall and then traced. Care should be taken to project directly in a line perpendicular to the floor, otherwise there is risk of distortion.

If **transparency projectors** are used, the original image must be converted to a transparency. Distortion is a frequent problem.

Tools for Copying with No Size Change

Light Boxes

A particularly useful tool for tracing is a **light box**. These boxes may be purchased in art or drafting supplies stores or constructed by the artist. Basically, the device is a simple box, with lights inside and glass or plexiglass on top. I prefer light boxes with glass rather than plastic surfaces because glass allows for cutting with an X-acto knife without damage. A drawing or photograph is placed on top of the glass and the box is illuminated. Tracing paper is then placed over the backlit original. The light box is useful for other purposes such as overlay comparisons of facial photographs at the same scale or for viewing slides or radiographs.

Transfer Paper

A type of carbon-backed paper called **transfer paper** may be used to copy an image onto another surface without a change in scale. Simply place a piece of paper on a drawing board. Then place the transfer paper (color side down) on top of the paper. Place the original image on top and trace it. The transfer paper will "deposit" the tracing on the paper below.

"Style" in Forensic Art

Each forensic artist must settle upon a style that is his or her own. As an instructor, I never attempt to impose my personal style or any particular style on students. Since forensic art, unlike fine art, is done strictly for the purpose of conveying information that may be useful in a criminal investigation, a style should be developed that is capable of fulfilling this primary purpose. **A forensic artist should have a style that is efficient, both in time spent drawing and in the accurate representation of facial features.** The style used should not detract from the information conveyed.

Degree of Facial Detail

A professional style should fall somewhere between portrait art, which would be overly detailed for use as forensic art, and crudely drawn childlike drawings showing too little information to be useful.

Composite drawings, by nature, should only contain a given amount of detail, based on the limits of the human memory. I am always suspicious when I see a composite drawing in which there is a tremendous amount of very specific detail. Something is not right. Either a photograph has been used for copying or the artist has embellished the image, going beyond what the witness was actually able to recall. **Too many hours spent on a composite drawing indicates that artistic ego may have taken over**, with the artist indulging in the overly detailed rendering of a drawing outside the presence of the witness.

Faces drawn as forensic art should exhibit a good knowledge of lighting, using it to convey forms and suggest perspective. Individual features should be anatomically feasible and drawn with an understanding of their diverse forms. **The artist should be able to draw in a style with enough flexibility and speed to make quick changes without losing the witness' attention.**

Scale of the Facial Drawing

In workshops, I have noticed that students become comfortable with a particular scale of facial drawing. I have seen successful composite drawings that were only 3 or 4 inches high, and others as large as life size. An average facial height is approximately 6 to 7 inches.

If you draw small sketches, you must use very sharp pencils, while large-scale drawings necessitate broad strokes with larger drawing tools for rapid coverage.

I tend to draw on the large side, probably because I often do life-sized skull reconstruction drawings, and thus I have become comfortable with this scale. Each artist should find a size that is practical and efficient. Consider the sort of case files in which your drawings will be kept as evidence. Will your original drawing fit comfortably into those files?

A problem common among many artists is lack of speed. If you draw too slowly, you might benefit from reducing the scale of the faces you draw, since it literally takes more time to cover a larger surface with graphite. Choosing broader-edged drawing tools can also help.

On the other hand, if you finish a drawing very quickly and the witness appears to have more to say, you may need to increase the scale of the faces you draw. A drawing that is too small may not allow enough room to include the full amount of descriptive detail available from the witness.

How Long Should It Take?

A composite drawing should simply take as long as it takes. It is far too variable a task to dictate a specific time frame or limitation. There should, however, be certain practical considerations. A witness, the witness' family, and the officer benefit from having at least an approximate idea, prior to the interview, of how long they will be with the artist. **Police composite artists average from 1 to 3 hours to develop a composite drawing.**

It is physically possible for me to complete a satisfactory drawing in one half hour to 1 hour, but the session may require far more time. **When giving an estimate to an officer, I always try to consider the nature of the offense and the general description of the person to be drawn.**

Both victims of violent crime and witnesses who have come forward to aid the police deserve to feel that they are not being rushed. If the person to be interviewed is highly traumatized, we may spend a full hour or more just talking and getting to know one another before the actual drawing process even begins. This is not wasted time. Not until the interviewee is calm and emotionally ready to undertake the process will there be any measure of success. In extreme cases, it may be necessary to conduct a second interview at a later time.

My second consideration in time estimation is the description itself. I need additional time to draw numerous details such as hats, glasses, or jewelry. It is also more time consuming for me to draw dark-skinned people and people with long wavy hair. Such factors must be taken into account when estimating the time involved in the drawing.

Each artist must strive to draw with enough speed so that the witness does not become frustrated, bored, or lose interest. This is a particular problem with younger witnesses. **When the interview session drags on for hours, the risk increases that the witness will make changes detrimental to the resemblance in the drawing.** The fatigued witness may lose confidence in the drawing and in his or her own initial impressions upon seeing the drawing. Overexposure to the facial image may cause the witness to make confused changes that actually diminish the drawing's potential effectiveness. **It is better to produce a generalized drawing with fresh impressions that are correct than to labor over an overly detailed drawing that has begun to veer away from the image in memory.**

Whether or Not to "Neck"!

Successful composite artists differ in the amount of area below the chin they draw. Some years ago, Frank Domingo, now retired from the New York City Police Department, and I discussed this issue when we taught workshops together. The NYPD has had an artist unit since the 1960s and numerous artists with varying styles have worked there. Frank observed that the drawings evolved over time from faces with a small amount of neck to faces with complete necks and shoulders. Eventually, everyone involved determined that the primary identification value did lie with the face, so artists eliminated the shoulders and usually the necks.

I find that identifications can occur with or without necks. Generally, I draw some suggestion of a neck even if it is very slight. If a witness gives a description of a neck that is an integral part of the person's look, it should probably be included. A "football player neck" or a "giraffe neck" may contribute to the identification. Although composite drawings are usually made with the head looking straight forward the artist may choose to manipulate the neck to reflect a gesture of the head.

The Ideal Face

Although we may not want to admit it, for each of us the ideal face is the one we have seen in the mirror all our lives. **It is an age-old struggle for artists to avoid incorporation of their own features in their work.** A few years ago, while teaching at the Scottsdale Artists' School, I took a break from my class to visit the beginning forensic sculpture class taught by Betty Pat. Gatliff. Students were doing a reconstruction based on identical skull castings, yet each sculpture looked a bit like its creator's face! One woman with a lovely Roman nose was busily putting the bump in her own nose on the nose of her sculpture, quite unaware that the skull casting had very straight nasal bones (Figure 4.5). It was a charming example of what each of us as artists and humans may be inclined to do.

Figure 4.5 **Artist unconsciously incorporating her own features into her work** as photographed by Senior Agent Billy Aiken. (Courtesy of South Carolina Law Enforcement Division.)

Figure 4.6   Split-face comparison of the facial proportions of the Mona Lisa with artist Leonardo da Vinci.

Drawings by some forensic artists readily reveal this tendency. All their facial drawings usually exhibit the exact same proportional arrangement of features. The problem is even more likely to occur if you do not use reference photographs as described in Chapter 6.

Even Leonardo da Vinci may have struggled with this dilemma. Figure 4.6 shows a split-face comparison of Leonardo's own facial proportions compared to his painting of the Mona Lisa. As artists committed to achieving specific likeness from either the verbal descriptions of witnesses or from distorted photographs, this is part of the battle!

Drawing Style

Forensic art colleagues around the country have shared with me copies of their drawings for use in showing various styles. I have chosen to use black male faces because the additional rendering of dark skin reveals a little more about the artist's personal style. Each example was created by a successful forensic artist and each style, though slightly variable, has "worked" for its intended purpose. **It is not my intention to recommend one style over another but rather to show that multiple different styles can be effective in forensic art.** Note, too, the variation from no neck at all to neck and shoulders included in these examples.

Each of these drawings was done within an approximate 2-hour interview time frame or less. Generally speaking, however, tighter styles tend to be more time consuming to render than sketchy or painterly styles.

The look or style of a drawing is determined in great part by the way in which the marks are actually applied to the paper. With blended styles, the pencil marks usually are not visible at all. Sketchy styles often allow for the individual marks to be seen, particularly when done as "cross-hatching." More painterly or loose styles freely allow the marks to show.

Tight

Figures 4.7 and 4.8 are fairly "tight" and controlled in nature with crisp, sharp details. There is considerable blending and individual marks are not obvious.

Figure 4.7 shows the smooth-skinned look that can be achieved by blending the graphite using one of the tools discussed in the "Tools and Materials" section. Note that the graphite has been pressed into the paper creating the marked distinction between the white or sclera of the eyes and the skin. The artist has carefully blended the area of the skin, without getting graphite into the eyes themselves. This is an effective way to make the eyes look really bright. The facial highlights have been erased out, but they are not as light as the areas in the eye where the white color of the paper shows through.

Figure 4.8 is also done in a somewhat smooth style with careful blending. This artist prefers to use Design® Ebony pencils with very sharp points, which results in the carefully defined edges around the facial forms. Compared with Figure 4.7 there is less distinction between the highlights that have been erased out and the whites of the eyes.

Figure 4.7 A **smoothly blended style** drawn without a neck by Deputy Chief Mike Deal. (Courtesy of Altamonte Springs, Florida Police Department.)

Figure 4.8 A **smooth controlled style** drawn with sharp Design® Ebony pencils by Detective Kevin Richlin. (Courtesy of Sunnyvale, California Department of Public Safety.)

Figure 4.9 A **sketchy controlled style**, drawn with both sharp and dull pencils by KTT. (Courtesy of Texas Department of Public Safety.)

"Sketchy"

These three examples are "sketchy" and appear slightly more loosely drawn than the previous two, with the marks made by the drawing instruments more visible.

Figure 4.9 is one of my drawings, which I would classify as still rather "tight," but sketchier than the two previous ones. Design® Ebony pencils and woodless pencils have been used with variation in sharpness or dullness of pencil points. Highlights are pulled out with a large blob of kneaded eraser used in a smooth sweeping stroke to indicate smooth skin. The hair was done by using broad marks made at varying pressures with the side of a dark pencil, suggesting the texture. Highlights in the hair were then "lifted" out with a kneaded eraser. The highlights in the eyes were done with an eraser shield and a stick-type vinyl eraser. Fingertip blending softens the marks themselves so that they are not obvious.

Figure 4.10 demonstrates a style in which "hatching" or "cross-hatching" is used. The marks are made with sharp pencil points and are visible, generally following the facial contours to help define them. Note the use of the contoured marks to create a rounded forehead and fullness in the neck area. The hair is drawn in small coils, which effectively suggest the texture although it can be time consuming to do. Note how pencil marks are also used to suggest the ribbed collar of the T-shirt. (It is no surprise that this artist likes to do fine art in the form of detailed ink drawings.) A real plus with this type of method is the high quality of reproduction that is possible.

Figure 4.11 also makes use of a sort of hatching, although it is done primarily in one direction. It has a looser quality than the previous styles and was done by an artist who

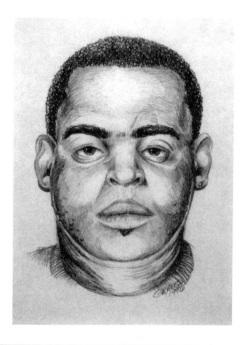

Figure 4.10 A **sketchy hatching style** drawn with sharp pencil marks following the facial contours by Lt. David Graves. (Courtesy of Maryville, Tennessee Police Department.)

Figure 4.11 A **sketchy hatching style** drawn with thick pencil marks, mostly in the same direction, by Lt. Roy Paschal. (Courtesy of South Carolina Law Enforcement Division.)

Figure 4.12 A **loose painterly style** drawn with charcoal pencils by Marla Lawson. (Courtesy of Georgia Bureau of Investigation.)

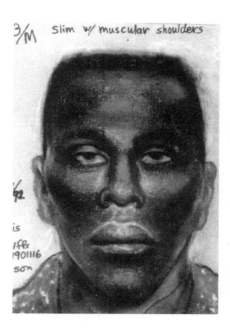

Figure 4.13 A **very painterly style** drawn with pastel chalks by Lois Gibson. (Courtesy of Houston, Texas Police Department.)

likes to do fine art painting. Less sharp pencil points were used than in Figure 4.10. Here the dark collar is used as a device to define the neck and frame a necklace described by the witness. Both Figures 4.10 and 4.11 use pencils to create gradations in tone rather than using a tool for blending. This promotes excellent reproduction with less likelihood that the delicately shaded details will disappear in the printing process.

"Loose/Painterly"

I would describe Figures 4.12 and 4.13 as more "loose and painterly" because the drawing instruments used are broad tipped and the marks are applied in rapid sweeping strokes, similar to painting. This approach can be done very rapidly and is excellent for conveying dark skin tones. Both artists represented here worked as "sidewalk" artists early in their careers. This experience taught them to capture the essence of a face quickly and to make good use of light.

Figure 4.12 was done with charcoal pencils. Note that the artist is unconcerned that the individual marks show in the area of the jacket and tie, thus giving the sketch a more "fine-art look." In those areas, it is possible to see the broad nature of the marks produced by the charcoal pencils. This style can be achieved at great speed, since the dark areas can be applied far more quickly than with a sharpened pencil. Highlights are lifted out with a kneaded eraser.

Figure 4.13 was done with pastel chalks in shades of gray. This artist likes to start with a tinted paper and add both lights and darks, a very painterly approach. Large areas of tone are applied with broad pieces of chalk and details are added with the edge of the chalks. Pastel pencils, which are simply pastel chalks encased in wood like a graphite pencil, are also used for details. This artist used a light chalk the same color as the paper background to in effect "erase" by actually applying more chalk.

This clever trick works well for defining and cleaning up the perimeter of the face. This method is very fast but requires skill and lots of practice. It is not a method for beginners. Drawings must be carefully handled since they are subject to smearing easily even after spraying with a fixative.

In general, loose, sketchy styles are fast and well suited to composite drawing. Tighter styles are more time consuming and work well for very "studied" drawing applications such as child age progressions, fugitive updates, or postmortem drawings.

While graphite pencil drawing is by far the most commonly used method in forensic art, you may wish to experiment to see the variations possible with other approaches. **The most important aspect of style is to do what is comfortable and effective for you.** In an interview situation, you will be under stress, so you should be drawing in a style that will allow you to make the quick changes and adjustments that are always needed. Experimentation with styles should be done as practice or in a classroom setting, not while working on an actual case.

Color vs. Black-and-White Drawing

Most forensic art is done in the form of black-and-white drawing. Occasionally cases can benefit from the use of color. **A good rule is that color drawing should be done only when there is some legitimate basis for it.**

The pros and cons of use of color composite images are discussed in Chapter 6. For most artists, preparation of color drawings is more time consuming and difficult than black-and-white drawings. Research has indicated that the recognition value of color is fairly low when compared with the structural elements of the face. Yet, there may be the rare witness who will only be satisfied by seeing the facial image in color. Some perpetrators may possess color descriptors that are so pronounced that they should be used and not wasted in black and white. So, "never say 'never.'"

It is far more likely, however, that any color forensic artwork you are called upon to do will be other than composite drawings. Types of forensic art that are based on photographs, such as child age progressions, fugitive updates, or postmortem drawings, are logical situations for use of color artwork. If good quality color photographs are available from which you may obtain the color information, it is reasonable to make use of this added dimension.

Lighting to Attain Perspective

In fine art portraiture, flattering or dramatic lighting is often the goal. **The function of the forensic artist is to describe as much facial detail as possible using lighting as a tool.** Lighting that illuminates a face from the left or the right side lends an attractive, sometimes intriguing look to a drawing. This is a traditional approach in fine art that some police artists have used successfully.

Contrived Lighting

You may be comfortable with the use of a side lighting system or you may prefer an approach that many police artists use. **A contrived system of lighting that fully**

illuminates all of the features helps convey even more information about the entire face. Maximum view of the features is revealed when lighting comes simultaneously from above and slightly in front of the head, as well as from above and from each side.

If you use the method of composite drawing that incorporates features derived from various reference photographs, the ability to "think" lighting becomes essential. The photo reference method, discussed in detail in Chapters 5 and 6, involves incorporation of individual features, hairstyles, expressions, etc., that come from reference photographs chosen by the witness. The lighting in each photo used will be different, so it is not possible merely to copy the light and shadows from the photos. Because you are merging multiple component parts from different reference photographs, it becomes necessary to "think" a contrived system of lighting for the drawing to pull together. Light is the tool you need to make the features blend in a way that "reads" as a believable face.

Try to think of a face as a topographical map, learning which parts advance or protrude and which areas recede. **A constant rule is that light hits on the raised or protruding areas, while the receding areas are in shadow.**

Light Basics

Light on form reveals and defines it, be it a sphere, a cone, a box, or a human face. In art, especially drawing, **light is a fundamental tool for describing form and making it appear to have depth and occupy space, albeit on a flat surface.** The process of creating a three-dimensional illusion on a two-dimensional surface is called **perspective**.

A simple but effective exercise I always incorporate into composite drawing workshops is the drawing of a lighted sphere. The artist should learn to modulate form shapes with subtle graduations in shading from light to dark. Use of **tonal variations** or **contrast** will make an object, in this case the sphere, appear to have **volume**. This exercise also forces the artist to think about the way in which the marks are actually applied to the paper and blended to create contours.

Figure 4.14 shows a spherical form, drawn and shaded, with the types of light labeled. The **highlight** is the area of brightest light on the form. The **halftone** is the area of graduated shading. **Cast shadow** refers to the shadow beneath the form, falling opposite the area of brightest light. Note that the cast shadow becomes lighter the further away it is from the object that casts it. **Reflected light** is light that bounces back up onto the form, coming from the surface upon which it rests.

By reviewing each of the composite drawing examples shown in Figures 4.7 through 4.13 you will find that, although different in style, each drawing demonstrates an understanding of these aspects of light. Highlights usually occur on foreheads, noses, cheeks, lower lips, and chins, dependent upon the structure of the individual drawn. Cast shadows may be seen under noses and under chins. Reflected light around the perimeter of the face helps to define form, especially in dark-skinned people.

By understanding how light falls on a simple spherical form, we learn how to convey perspective through use of light on all types of objects. Since the face can actually be simplified into a series of rounded forms, these lessons may be directly applied. Figure 4.15 shows a face drawn with and without an understanding of light. Use of highlights, halftones, cast shadows, and reflected light in the drawing on the

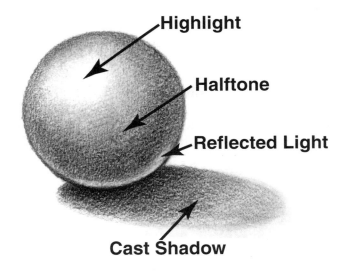

Figure 4.14 A spherical form, drawn and shaded, with the **types of light** labeled. (Illustration by KTT.)

Figure 4.15 **Importance of light in facial drawing;** the drawing at left appears flat while the drawing at right, using contrasting values and tonal variations, appears three dimensional and lifelike; a **contrived lighting scheme** implies that light comes from slightly above and from each side. (Illustration by KTT.)

right suggests a lifelike face, while the drawing on the left appears flat. **Try to apply the principles of light in an "overall" sense as you draw a face as well as when you draw each individual feature.**

Facial Proportions

Proportion in Forensic Art

After many years as a forensic artist, I have come to believe that the single most important factor for capturing likeness and individuality, thus leading to facial recognition, is **proportion**. Since it is identification, triggered by likeness recognition that is the purpose of most types of forensic art, we must pursue this phenomenon of the importance of proportion. Basically, **proportion** means the relationship of one part to another or to the whole; some dictionaries include the terms "balance" and "symmetry" in definitions.

Both experience and psychological research indicate that, as humans, we grasp the spatial relationships of the face in memory more readily than the individual features. I like to use the term **gestalt of a face** when referring to the key to its essence. **The image in its entirety is more important for identification than any of its individual parts.** Figure 5.1 in Chapter 5 shows an example of a witness' ability to grasp the gestalt of a face, particularly the proportional arrangement of features, even during a very brief glance.

Anatomist Dr. Robert George discusses the importance of proportions for recognition in skull to face predictions in "Anatomical and Artistic Guidelines for Forensic Facial Reconstructions":

> It is obviously impossible to precisely predict the intricate details of the eye from the bony orbital outline, the nose from the nasal aperture, the ear from the external auditory meatus, or the lips from the anterior dentition, but it is possible to accurately position theses features within and around their bony substrates. Such positioning alone may be sufficient to create the desired approximation. Portrait artists, and especially caricaturists, are well aware of the significance of facial proportions in determining an individual countenance. To quote the distinguished caricaturist Mort Drucker, "We all have the same features, it's the space between them, their proportions and relationships to one another that distinguish one face from another."[1]

The element of proportion is basically provided to the reconstruction artist, since the bony architecture of the skull dictates where each feature will be placed. Composite drawing poses a more difficult task, since the proportions must be ascertained from a verbal description.

Sadly, the factor that many composite sketch artists fail to capture is proportion. Beginners in composite drawing often use facial templates, which makes all their drawings look alike. Police artists who are formally trained in art sometimes adhere to canons of idealized facial proportions learned in art school, which also makes their drawings all look similar as well as overly attractive.

Canons of Proportion

Most art instruction books offer diagrams of the "ideal" proportions, usually based on the faces of white males. Most artists have seen such drawings suggesting standard proportions: "the face is five eye-widths wide," "the eyes are one eye-width apart," "the eyes should fall half way down the face," "the ears are the same height as the nose," etc. **Few faces encountered by the forensic artist are perfectly proportioned.** Therefore, such "ideals" should be viewed only as very general guides. **The composite artist should seek to capture the deviation from idealized proportions.**

Such canons of idealized proportion may be found throughout art history. The ancient Greeks used certain ideals in their artwork as did the Romans. Over time, attitudes about ideal beauty of face and body change. Consider the differences in the physical appearance of actress Marilyn Monroe and fashion model Twiggy, each of whom was viewed as an ideal of physical beauty at different points in time.

Plastic surgeons sometimes strive to create perfectly balanced, symmetrical faces that fit into certain quantifiable patterns of proportion. Yet, the truly skilled surgeons realize that this should not be the ultimate goal, since overly perfect and symmetrical faces may appear unnatural and uninteresting. As Francis Bacon observed, "There is no excellent beauty that hath not some strangeness in the proportion."[2]

Symmetry/Asymmetry

It is possible to study the subtle asymmetries in a face photographically as shown in Figure 4.16. The unaltered face of the author is shown at the top. The facial photograph

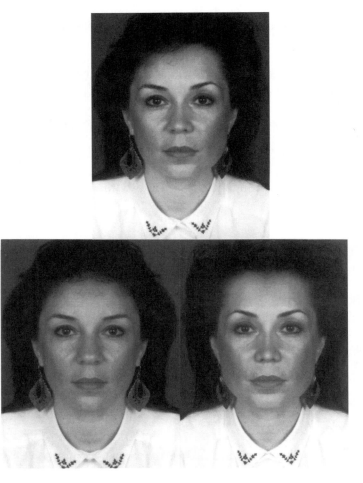

Figure 4.16 **Asymmetry** of the author's face is studied, with the unaltered face shown at top. Two right halves spliced together create the face at bottom left, and two left halves spliced together create the face at bottom right. (Courtesy of Missey Micheletti.)

is split down the center vertically and two left sides are spliced together and two right sides are spliced together. The two resulting symmetrical faces are quite different in appearance from the original, with one a rather triangular shape and the other more square.

It can be beneficial for the forensic artist to observe such specificity of symmetry or asymmetry when studying faces in photographs, particularly when comparing photographs to other photographs or photographs to skulls.

Use of Templates

A questionable practice in composite art is the use of templates to establish the proportions in a facial drawing. This risks giving each drawing a similar look and fails to establish correct proportions, thus failing to utilize one of the most important aspects of recognition and facial uniqueness. **The way a face *differs* from the idealized proportions laid out in a template is what makes it unique and recognizable.**

Some artists use patterns intended to represent faces of differing shapes. They start drawings with templates that are "oval," "round," "triangular," "square," or "oblong," each with eyes, nose, and mouth placement indicated (see Figure 4.17). The problem here is that **faces do occur with unusual proportions**, quite unlike the ones marked on the templates. There *are* broad-faced people with close-set eyes and there *are* narrow-faced people with wide-set eyes. By using such a template, you might miss such distinctive proportions altogether.

Template of Facial Proportions

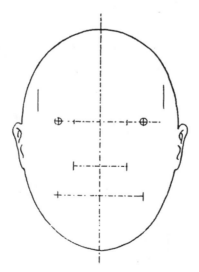

...can make all your drawings look alike.

Figure 4.17 Use of a **template** for facial proportions to begin your drawings can make all of your drawings look very similar, potentially lowering their effectiveness for identification.

Others have created several separate templates for the various racial groups, believing that this overcomes the problem of the use of templates. This fails to take into account the great variation possible within each specific group. Even in the 1880s, Alphonse Bertillon emphasized that, within each particular racial or ethnic group, there is great diversity of proportions, as in the white male faces shown in Figure 4.18. Figure 4.19 shows similar variance in proportions in the faces of multiple black males. Just because a person is a member of a certain race or group does *not* mean that his or her proportions will conform to any preconceived "norm." **The distinctiveness of the proportional arrangement of features within an individual face forms its "look" and triggers recognition** (Figure 4.20). The spatial arrangement of features should come from the witness' description, not from a template.

Figure 4.18 Faces of white males from *The Bertillon System of Identification*, 1896, showing **proportional variations.**

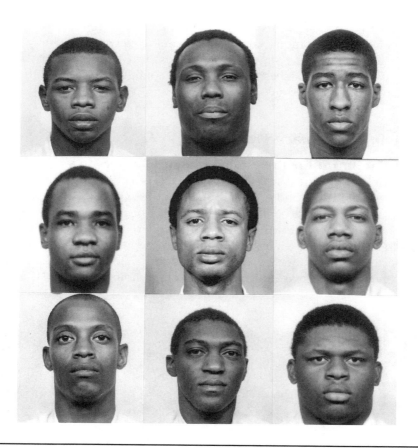

Figure 4.19 **Proportional diversity** in black male faces. (Courtesy of Texas Department of Criminal Justice.)

Figure 4.20 Composite drawing by KTT (left) and subject identified (right), bearing very **similar proportional arrangement of features**. (Courtesy of Texas Department of Public Safety.)

If you feel you absolutely *must* use a template, always remember that you must only *begin* with the proportions laid out, remaining very flexible to changing the arrangement of features as the drawing progresses. If a template is to be used, it is probably best to use one that has only a "cross" configuration to aid in leveling the eyes and aligning the features side to side.

Importance of the Midface Proportions

Particularly significant for the establishment of a person's "look" in a facial drawing is the correctness of the proportions of the features within the midface area. Figures 4.21 and 4.22 demonstrate this with two composite drawings. In each case, the area in the center of the face has been altered in scale and, thus, in proportion. The center drawings are as they were originally done based on a witness' description. The drawings on the left have had the midface features reduced but otherwise totally unchanged. The drawings on the right have had the midface features enlarged but otherwise unchanged. Each combination "reads" as a possibly real face.

Figure 4.21 Composite drawing of a black male as originally done from a witness' description (center), with **midface features reduced** (left) and **midface features enlarged** (right). (Illustration by KTT.)

In other words, a witness could select features from the photographic reference files that were exactly correct. Yet, if the artist did not place the features correctly and at the correct scale, there would be very different results and a likeness could be missed. **The artist must learn to correctly establish the proportion and scale of the individual features in addition to simply drawing the features correctly.**

Younger and Older Proportions

A natural pattern in human craniofacial growth involves gradual alteration in the facial proportions. Observe the two simplified faces represented in Figure 4.23. Which is the adult and which is the child? Instinctively, we know that the face

Figure 4.22 Composite drawing of a Hispanic male as originally done from a witness' description (center), with **midface features reduced** (left), and with **midface features enlarged** (right). (Illustration by KTT.)

on the right is the younger face because of the proportional arrangement of the features. As we grow from infancy through childhood and become young adults, our lower faces push downward and outward. While the child's head appears to be mostly cranium, the adult head appears more balanced between its upper and lower parts. The features seem to rise higher on the face due to the growth of the lower face.

This is not to say that adults cannot possess childlike proportions. An understanding of the proportional differences between the child's face and the adult's face may serve the composite artist well during an interview situation. What if the witness said, "He wasn't really all that young, but there was something youthful about the way he looked." Perhaps a childlike proportional arrangement of features triggered that impression. Craniofacial growth is discussed in more detail in Chapter 7.

As we age, our facial proportions may change to a greater or lesser extent depending upon the individual. **Natural effects of aging may also change the appearance of the proportional relationships of the facial features.** Logically, for example, with

Figure 4.23 Simplified faces showing **proportions of an adult** (left) **and a child** (right). (Illustration by KTT.)

receding hairlines in some men, there develops the impression of a higher, and possibly wider, forehead (see Chapter 8, Figure 8.12). In very advanced age, with accompanying loss of the dentition and bone resorption, the jaw becomes increasingly smaller. This is so pronounced in some individuals that the spatial arrangement of features actually seems to revert from adult back to childlike proportions because the face is again mostly cranium with a small jaw as it was in childhood (see Chapter 8, Figure 8.15). For an in-depth discussion of facial aging, see Chapter 8.

Male and Female Proportions

Chapter 3 provides information about the general comparative anatomy of male and female faces, beginning with the skull. **Proportions are distinct to each individual face regardless of sex or gender, with no hard, fast rules.** Figure 4.24 shows a composite drawing of a female face. In my experience, a far greater percentage of composite drawings requested are of male faces, while more of the victim faces drawn are female.

When drawing faces of females, certain very general proportional observations may be made. Female faces are usually smaller overall than male faces. The lower half of the female face is often proportionately smaller than the male face because the mandible is smaller and weaker. The angle of the female jaw is likely to be more obtuse and less defined and the chin may be more pointed.

Male faces are usually larger overall than female faces, with the lower half of the face proportionately larger due to a stronger mandible. The angle of the jaw is often more acute and defined and the chin more square and pronounced.

Figure 4.24   Composite drawing by KTT of a **female** (left) and the subject identified (right). (Courtesy of Texas Department of Public Safety.)

Temporary Proportional Changes

The forensic artist who does composite drawings should be aware of other factors that might affect the perception of the facial proportions given in a description.

Point of View of the Witness

The point of view of the witness may greatly alter the impression of the face. If the person was viewed by a witness looking down a flight of stairs, the face might appear foreshortened, with a smaller lower face. If the person was viewed from the ground looking up, the face would be distorted in a different way. In general, the artist's job is to draw the face as described, distorted or not. The issue of whether to adjust the face to a different angle must be decided on a case-by-case basis. Consideration should be given as to whether the face was seen at various angles by the witness or exclusively at one angle.

Expression

Expression is another element that sometimes alters the impression of the facial proportions. In a smiling face, for example, the mouth is spread wider than normal, the cheeks are displaced upward, and the size of the eyes is diminished. Again, a determination must be made according to the individual case whether to draw the face with a pronounced expression, even though it might distort the proportions. As a rule, the witness' view of best recollection should be used. If the witness recalls a particular expression, it should be included in the drawing.

Long-Term Proportional Changes

Long-term proportional changes to the face may occur for many reasons, such as maxillofacial surgery, progressive diseases or conditions, weight gain or loss, or dental changes. These factors come into play when the forensic artist doing age progression studies potential changes to a face over time, but they are not usually considerations for the composite artist. These changes are discussed and illustrated in Chapter 8.

How to Capture Proportions in Your Drawings

In workshops, we discuss several ways to better capture the correct proportions in composite drawings.

Avoid the Use of Templates

For the reasons previously mentioned, avoiding the use of templates may actually increase the likelihood of capturing accurate and distinctive proportions.

Block Out the Proportions Lightly

It is good practice to develop a system of facial drawing in which you lightly block out the proportions in the beginning stages of the drawing process. The features should remain free to be adjusted and moved until you are well into the drawing. It is beneficial to maintain the same degree of "finish" overall in your drawings rather than indulge yourself in detailing one area such as the eyes. By prematurely completing one area, you hesitate to make corrections and the witness hesitates to ask you to, even though proportional changes might still be needed.

"Happy Faces"

For years, I have found it helpful to explain what I mean by "proportions" to witnesses, often without even using the word "proportion." I do this with quick doodles of "happy faces" similar to the two in Figure 4.23. I sketch out a couple of these simple faces, each with a different arrangement of the same features. I try to convey that I need the witness to help me with the *spacing* of features as well as describing the look of each separate feature.

Using Your Hands to Determine Proportions

In addition to the "happy faces," I find it helpful to use my hands to demonstrate an area or space on the face I want the witness to think about. For example, I can hold my thumb and index finger up to my upper lip and ask, "Should there be a lot of space here or just a little bit," while gesturing vertically. This simple method helps the witness understand the exact nature of the information you seek.

Using Matte Acetate

If during the course of the drawing there appears to be a problem area for determining the proportions, I sometimes use matte acetate to help work out the spacing. For example, there may be difficulty in assessing the distance from the base of the nose to the lips (or length of the upper lip). By laying acetate over the drawing in progress, you can draw a sketchy outline of the mouth, then move it up or down to allow the witness several views. This has helped witnesses accurately determine spacing because they can quickly see several options for feature placement. Obviously, it is better to try a method such as this prior to getting very detailed in the drawing. Once the proportions are correctly established, then the drawing can become more and more refined.

Computer Composite-Generating Systems

Some computer composite-generating systems offer a real "plus" in determination of the proportions. Unfortunately, many operators of these systems do not receive enough training in facial anatomy or facial memory encoding to effectively utilize this advantage.

With many systems, it is possible to efficiently move features around to correctly establish proportions in a manner similar to the use of matte acetate. The knowledgeable operator can easily make subtle incremental adjustments until the witness is satisfied that the features are spaced correctly.

Individual Facial Features

Although the overall **gestalt** of a face and the correctness of the proportional arrangement of the features seem to trigger recognition, individual features are also very important. **A unique feature may act in conjunction with the overall proportional "look" to further enhance the likeness of a drawing to a perpetrator.**

Figure 4.25 shows a composite drawing done in a child abduction and murder case. When I was given a description of "over 300 pounds with fangs," I was taken aback. Yet, it was my responsibility to draw what the witness indicated, so the fangs appeared in the drawing although they seemed improbable to me. The drawing generated the name of a suspect whose face generally matched the composite drawing. Of particular significance were the teeth of the suspect, or rather the lack of teeth. When the suspect was questioned, it was observed that he was missing the maxillary central and lateral incisors. When he spoke, he appeared to have fangs! Ultimately, he was convicted of the murder of a 9-year-old girl and sentenced to death.

As forensic artists, we must gain expertise in drawing numerous different types of facial features, representative of old and young faces and male and female faces for all races and ancestries. Chapter 3 provides illustrations of the eye, the nose, the mouth, and the ear, and anatomical names for the specific parts of each feature. Many excellent art instruction books include pointers for drawing the face and its features. I have found several books to be particularly useful over the years. The classic *Drawing the Human Head* by Burne Hogarth, first published in 1965, is still very useful today, although the correct anatomical terminology is not always used.[3] I also recommend *How to Draw the Human Head: Techniques and Anatomy* by Louise Gordon[4] and *The Artist's Complete Guide to Facial Expression* by Gary Faigin.[5] *Human Anatomy for Artists: The Elements of Form* by Eliot Goldfinger[6] is also a good reference guide for forensic artists.

The following are some considerations when drawing individual features, particularly from descriptions.

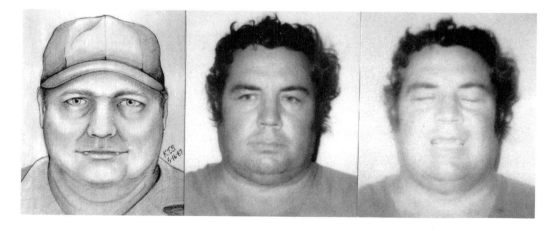

Figure 4.25   Composite drawing by KTT (left) and the subject identified (center). The **subject was missing several anterior teeth** (right), giving the impression of "fangs" as described by the witness. (Courtesy of Texas Department of Public Safety.)

The Eyes

Figure 4.26 is an ink illustration of an eye done by my friend, the very skilled medical illustrator Gerald Hodge. His drawing clearly shows the various structures of the eye that should appear in your drawings, as well as **light falling on the eye area**. Note that light hits on the area under the brow, on the upper eyelid, and on the rim of the lower eyelid. Light also shows in the iris in the form of a highlight. The eyelid casts a small shadow underneath it and onto the eyeball. There may also be shadow cast under the brow bone in males if the brow ridge is pronounced. Figure 4.27 shows the same aspects of light on the eye structures in a pencil drawing.

When drawing eyes, it is necessary to **develop the structures surrounding the eye** for a realistic look. Because our eyeballs are rounded, there is fullness above and below, conforming to the rounded form of the eyeball itself. Depending upon the age and expression of the person drawn, there may also be small pouches below the eyes or sagging tissue above the eyes. The area beside the nasal bones, or each side of the bridge of the nose, is likely to be darkly shadowed. Apply the principles for the use of light to accentuate these forms around the eyes.

Be attentive to the **shape of the iris** as you draw it, taking care to make it very smoothly rounded rather than ragged or lumpy. Common mistakes include drawing the iris too large for the aperture and drawing the iris as if it were U-shaped rather than rounded. Think of the iris as a round circle even though a portion of the top of the circle is obscured by the eyelid. In some cases, a bit of the bottom of the circular iris may also be covered by the lower lid.

Highlights may be drawn at the left or the right side of the iris. Some artists choose to add two highlights to add "life" to the eyes. Highlights placed directly in the center of the iris usually do not look natural, since we are accustomed to seeing the darkness of the **pupil** in that position.

Observe the shape of the **aperture or opening of the eye, also called the eye fissure**. The upper and lower eyelids are not symmetrical curves, a common

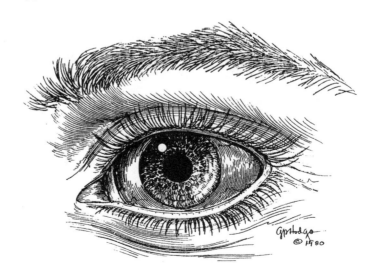

Figure 4.26 Ink drawing of the **structures of the eye** and light falling on the eye area. (Courtesy of Gerald P. Hodge.)

Figure 4.27   Pencil drawing of the **eye**. Note the definition between the medial edge of the eyeball and the caruncle lacrimalis and the slight shadow cast on the eyeball by the upper eyelid. (Illustration by KTT.)

misconception. **The lower eyelid is less curved than the upper eyelid, which is more arched.** In most eyes, the *highest* point in the *upper* lid is toward the inside and the *lowest* point in the *lower* lid is toward the outside.

Remember that **the eyelids have thickness** and are not paper thin, a common error in drawings. The lower lids should show enough thickness to catch light. The skin that forms the eyelids of elderly people will usually be thinner, but younger people and dark-skinned people may have very thick eyelids.

The eyeball is a *ball* with sides that are sometimes evident, especially at the medial side. There should be definition between the edge of the eyeball and the **caruncle lacrimalis**. The **form of the medial palpebral ligament** gently rises up and often catches light, making it visible just above the **medial canthus**. The **lateral canthus** or outer corner should also show clear definition and be different in appearance from the inner corner.

It is possible to have a vertical fold of skin on either side of the nose which may cover the inner canthus, known as an **epicanthus**, or **epicanthic fold**. This extra skin of the eye is often associated with individuals of Asian descent although it may occur in persons of any ancestry. I have observed this eye tissue in European-derived and African-derived individuals and it is often seen on the eyes of infants.

Take care as you draw the **growth pattern of the individual hairs of the eyebrow**. While there is variation from person to person, the pattern shown in the illustration by Gerald Hodge (Figure 4.26) is the one that occurs naturally for most people. A common mistake is to draw eyebrows with the hairs straight up and down or all directed to the side. In reality, they usually grow upward from below and downward from above, merging and blending at a peak somewhere slightly lateral of the middle of the eye. For many faces, this eyebrow peak often rests in alignment with the lateral side of the iris. In other words, if you drew an imaginary line upward from the outside of the iris, the highest point of the brow could be located. This average is useful in skull reconstruction, but the witness' description should determine it in composite drawing. Also, remember that if the person's hair is very curly or kinky, the eyebrow hair will probably be curly. If the witness says, "The eyebrows were thin," try and distinguish between "sparse" and a "thin" line.

In a composite interview, the witness should first be allowed to give impressions of the face, including the eyes, in the manner described in Chapters 5 and 6. The suggestions given in those chapters regarding the *phrasing* of questions should be noted. Do *not* be content with only generalized description of the eyes. Once the artist introduces reference photographs for use in fine-tuning the drawing, **the witness should be asked specific questions in layman's terminology about aspects of the eye area:**

- Did the spacing between the eyes appear to be wide, medium, or narrow?
- Do the eyebrows rest high above the eyes, down low over the eyes, or in-between?
- Are the eyebrows rather straight across or are they noticeably arched?
- Is the upper eyelid visible or is it obscured by fullness above the eye? How much of it is visible? Is it visible all across or only at the inner side? Is there an epicanthic fold?

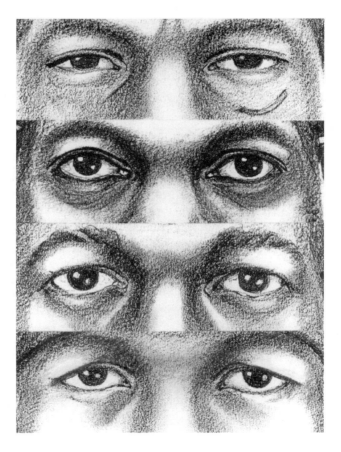

Figure 4.28   Various eyes from composite drawings. (Illustrations by KTT.)

- How do the eyelids rest over the iris? Is the "look" alert and wide open or sleepy and semi-closed? Pay special attention to the amount of iris revealed by the lid.
- Is there sclera visible under the iris?
- Is the sclera very white, or is it yellow or reddish?
- What is the area around the eyes like? Is it puffy or dark or wrinkled?
- Were the lashes very visible? Was there makeup?
- What was the expression in the eyes?

When copying eyes from a photograph, such as for a child age progression or fugitive update, pay particular attention to the **"negative shapes"** created by the two small triangles of **sclera** or "white" at each side of the iris. These shapes help give an eye its individual character.

Study the structures of the eye as shown in Chapter 3, Figure 3.9, so that drawing them becomes second nature. Figures 4.28, 4.29, and 4.30 show various eyes taken from composite drawings, giving just a small sample of the great variety of eye forms possible. Notice that the eye openings have not been drawn as hard lines, but rather as lines that vary in "weight" or thickness as they traverse around the eyeball.

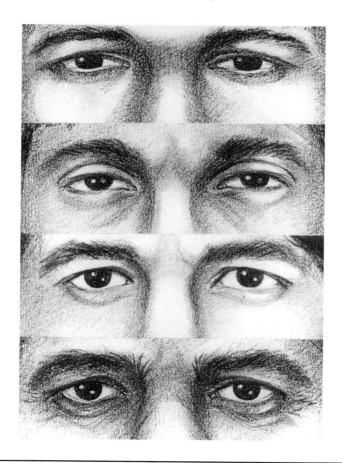

Figure 4.29 **Various eyes** from composite drawings. (Illustrations by KTT.)

Figure 4.30   Various eyes from composite drawings. (Illustrations by KTT.)

The Nose

Noses seem to hold less interest for artists than do eyes. They are certainly more subtle features and descriptions of them in composite interviews may be somewhat vague. The variety of nose shapes seems almost endless, yet they all have a basically triangular form, narrower at the top and wider at the bottom. The nose is made up of a pair of rather saddle-shaped **upper cartilages** coming off the **nasal bones** and a pair of **lower cartilages** that form the tip. In the area where the upper cartilages attach to the nasal bones, there may be a plane change and a bump occurs in some people, as in Figure 4.8. The lower cartilages create the various bulbous forms on the ends of noses and may also show a distinct split down the middle when the two cartilages do not meet closely.

Figure 4.31 shows a rather blunt nose with subtle definition of the forms. Light runs down the **bridge** of the nose and illuminates the **tip**, and is usually seen on the **ala** or **wing** at each side of the nose as well. Some shadow will be cast beneath the base of the nose itself and onto the upper lip. The darkest shadow will be inside the **nostrils** or **nares**. Dark lines should also designate the **alar groove** at the lateral side of each wing or ala. Figure 4.32 shows three noses: upturned tip, straight out, and downturned

Figure 4.31 Pencil drawing of a blunt **nose**, showing light on the different forms. (Illustration by KTT.)

tip. In a very upturned nose, such as the one on the left, light may be caught on the **septum** underneath the tip or on the lower forms of the nostrils where they rest on the upper lip.

In a lateral view of an upturned nose, the septum and the nasal openings may be visible. In a more downturned nose, the nostrils will appear closed or not be visible.

As with the eyes, we must **develop the structures surrounding the nose** in order for the "look" to become realistic. The darkness at each side of the **nasal bones** forming

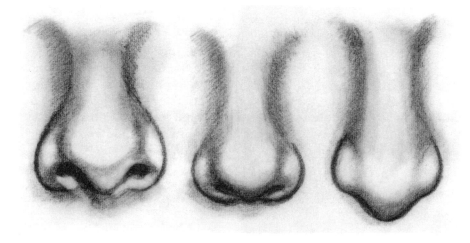

Figure 4.32 Pencil drawings of three **noses**: upturned (left), straight out (center), and down-turned (right). (Illustrations by KTT.)

the **bridge** of the nose defines the upright structure. Note that the bridge is not cut straight back into the face. The sides taper in a tent fashion from the most protruding, raised center ridge down the bridge, angling out to the cheeks. The **tip** will have a highlight or possibly two distinct ones if the lower cartilages are clearly separate.

Many artists tend to draw noses that are too long. Try to carefully work out the nose length with a witness, perhaps by drawing the base lightly on matte acetate and moving it up and down as previously described.

Starting for many people in the twenties and advancing throughout life is the indication of the **nasolabial furrow**, at either side of the nose. A common mistake is to misplace this line or fold. It **should start at the top of the alar groove and proceed diagonally away from the nose and toward the lower face**. I have seen drawings that place the nasolabial furrow at various locations up and down the alar groove, with some even starting it from the bottom of the groove. Because of this confusion, Chapter 8 includes an illustration showing placement for the various age lines of the face with names labeled (Figure 8.11).

In a composite interview, after the witness has given an initial description of the nose, photographic references are introduced for fine tuning, and **certain inquiries should be made about the specific aspects of the nose.**

- Was the distance between the eyes wide, medium, or narrow? This will determine in part the bridge of the nose.
- Did the bridge seem wide, medium, or narrow?
- Could you see up into the nose? Was it upturned, straight out, or downturned?
- What was the shape of the tip of the nose? Rounded? Squarish? Triangular?
- Was the nose ever viewed from the side? Was the side view of the bridge straight, concave, or convex? Was there a hump?

The Mouth

While eyes and noses are closely associated with and anchored to the bony skull architecture beneath them, the mouth is more free floating and moveable. The numerous muscles involved in the workings of the mouth make it a highly variable feature. Of course, our **teeth** and the bony **maxilla** and **mandible** into which they are affixed do determine to a great extent our mouth shapes, particularly when the mouth is at rest. One only needs to see an older person after he removes his dentures to see how important the teeth are to the formation of the mouth.

The angle at which the **dental arch** or **mouth barrel** rests on the face may incline the angle of the mouth downward or upward, causing the middle line between the lips to go either slightly up or down at the corners.

The upper lip is composed of three forms, and the lower lip has two forms. When the two lips are closed, the convexities of one lip lie in the hollows of the other. The darkest part of the mouth is the **parting line of the aperture or fissure** itself.

The upper lip has a small mounded form in the center and two, more elongated forms on either side. Although both lips contain more color than the surrounding skin of the face, the upper lip may appear darker because it is set on a downward plane and is in shadow.

The lower lip is generally more rounded in structure and exhibits two slighted mounded forms on each side, meeting in the midline, where there is sometimes a noticeable vertical depression or crease. The lower lip is set at a more upward plane; thus, it usually catches more light than the upper lip and appears lighter in color.

The **vermilion border** of the lips describes the edge of the reddish area. There may be a raised **lip rim** around this border which catches light and becomes visible as in Figures 4.33 and 4.34. A common mistake in drawing the mouth is to outline the lips with hard, dark lines of equal "weight." Instead, the lines surrounding the mouth should have subtle variation.

Some witnesses describe distinctive **dentition** and the composite drawing should be developed with the teeth showing. Or, in doing two-dimensional facial reconstruction from the skull, the anterior teeth may be recovered and distinctive; thus, they should

Figure 4.33   Pencil drawing of a **closed mouth** and light falling on the structures. (Illustration by KTT.)

Figure 4.34   Pencil drawing of an **open mouth revealing the teeth**. (Illustration by KTT.)

be shown. The artist should be prepared to draw an open mouth if necessary (see Figures 4.25 and 4.52.). Do not be content to draw "picket-fence" teeth. Study the structures of teeth to gain an understanding of the subtle shapes of each. Notice that the **central incisors** are wider than the **lateral incisors** beside them. The **canine** teeth or **cuspids** should be rather pointed (see Figures 3.11 and 3.12 in Chapter 3). The teeth should be gradually more shaded as they recede back at each side of the mouth. In other words, more light should be shown on the front teeth than on the teeth at the sides. As you will learn in the chapters on facial reconstruction from the skull, our mouths usually cover the front six teeth when relaxed. **A fully smiling mouth may reveal as many as ten teeth or more.** Some people exhibit a slack-jawed expression that reveals the lower teeth as well. It is a good idea to practice drawing open mouths, since it can be difficult to achieve a natural look.

As with the other features, **development of the surrounding areas makes the mouth start to "read" correctly.** It is difficult to draw a mouth in isolation, without the shapes around it. The **philtrum** or scooped area on the upper lip may contain more or less shadow. Usually a **depression at each corner of the mouth** catches shadow. Further out beyond the depression is a small mound on each side. The curvy distinction between this depression and mound at the mouth corners helps to create the look of a "youthful" or "sexy" mouth.

Beneath the lower lip is a depression called the **mentolabial furrow**, which may be more or less pronounced according to the individual. Attention should be paid to the **"shadow shapes" below the lower lip.**

After gaining an initial description of the mouth, **references may be introduced in a composite interview to further fine-tune it, as with the other features.** Specific questions might include:

- Did the mouth seem wide, medium, or narrow? Since such quantitative judgments are difficult for people to make, clarify your meaning using references. It is also helpful to use your hands to gesture horizontally.
- How about the vertical thickness? Gesture vertically.
- Were the lips about the same thickness as each other or was one thicker? Top? Bottom?
- Were the teeth visible? What can be determined about them? Are they distinctive enough to be included in the composite?
- Were the lips darkly colored? Were they pale? Was there makeup?
- What about facial hair?

Since the mouth is an area where a great deal of the facial expression occurs, witnesses may also describe aspects of the mouth that reflect this. See Chapter 3 regarding common expressions or consult Gary Faigin's excellent book *The Artist's Complete Guide to Facial Expression.*

The Ears

Ears terrify some artists, who employ every possible method to avoid drawing or sculpting them. Yet, a careful look at the anatomy of ears can demystify them considerably. Review the ear illustration Figure 3.10 in Chapter 3 which clearly shows and names each form. Forensic artists usually draw only frontal views of ears. You must

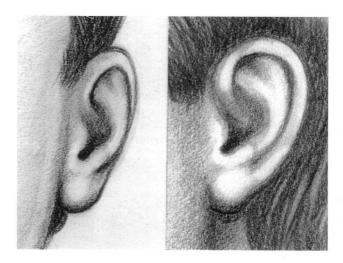

Figure 4.35 Pencil drawing of the **frontal ear** (left) and the **lateral ear** (right) showing the structures. (Illustrations by KTT.)

be prepared, however, to accurately draw the ears in the lateral or profile view, for either a profile composite drawing or for two-dimensional skull reconstruction. In **drawing ears, either frontally or laterally, you should think of the "highs and lows" or "peaks and valleys" as you apply the light.**

Figure 4.35 shows pencil drawings of both frontal and lateral views of the ear. The frontal view shows some of the perimeter of the **helix** and varying degrees of the **antihelix**, depending on the individual. The **tragus, intertragal notch, antitragus,** and the **lobe** should be defined.

In the lateral view, the external ear must rest over the bony **auditory meatus** or ear hole in the skull, which is above and behind the angle of the bony jaw. Therefore, the ear must be placed slightly **posterior** or behind the angle of the jaw, not on top of the cheek. The **helix** winds around the outer perimeter of the ear until it blends with the lobe. The **antihelix** gives the appearance of a Y-shaped form, and the **triangular fossa** is the depression between the two "arms" of the "Y." The **schaphoid fossa** divides the helix and the antihelix, forming a distinct groove. The **concha** is the cup-shaped area forming the inside of the ear. Study of the anatomy of the ear and use of photographic references can help demystify these structures and eliminate potential anatomical errors.

Witnesses being interviewed should be asked questions about the ears in the frontal view, such as:

- Was there anything distinctive about the ears?
- Were the ears protruding away from the head, sitting close to the head, or in-between? Could you see inside the ears a bit?
- Did the ears stick out more at the top or at the bottom?

Figure 6.7 in Chapter 6 shows a composite drawing of a subject who had a small piece of his left ear missing. The addition of that detail to the drawing helped identify him.

Scars, Marks, Tattoos, or Anomalies

Witnesses may describe a virtually infinite number of types of scars, marks, tattoos, or physical anomalies. Maintaining good reference files is very important for discerning the precise type of facial feature or blemish being described. If the witness says, "He had a scar," do not draw just a generic scar. **Determine as much as possible about the scar and draw it with accuracy, correct placement, and at the correct scale.**

Ask about the overall shape, texture, color, and scale of a scar, and if the scar was flat or raised. A type of scar known as a keloid is noticeably raised, often lighter in color than the surrounding skin, and seems to occur most commonly in dark-skinned

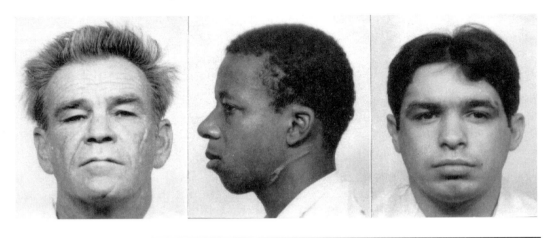

Figure 4.36   Scars: incised or depressed scars (left), raised keloid scar (center), and a scar crossing over the eyebrow (right). (Courtesy of Texas Department of Criminal Justice.)

Figure 4.37   Composite drawing by KTT of a subject with a **distinctive scar.** (Courtesy of Texas Department of Public Safety.)

people. Figure 4.36 shows incised scars, a keloid scar, and a scar that crosses over the eyebrow, interrupting the growth of the hair. The composite drawing in Figure 4.37 includes a distinctive curving scar below the eye.

Use the principles of light to draw scars, moles, or other blemishes. If the scar or mole is highly raised, it will be highlighted with light and cast shadow, just like the sphere in Figure 4.14.

The Profile

From time to time, the forensic artist is asked to prepare a drawing of a face in the lateral view. Occasionally, there are case situations in which a witness was only able to view the subject from one side or the other. Thus, as part of the composite drawing interview process, the artist must elicit a description of the side view. In my experience, witnesses doing a profile composite usually place more importance on the description of the nose.

When preparing two-dimensional skull reconstruction drawings, the artist should produce a lateral drawing in addition to the frontal one so that morphological details of the skull will be fully conveyed. Other cases, such as drawings from surveillance videos, child age progressions, or fugitive updates may call for profile drawings if the original photographic image is a profile one.

The artist must consider most of the same factors in developing both profile and frontal sketches. **The knowledge of drawing techniques, light on form to show perspective, facial proportions, male and female distinctions, race or ancestry distinctions, and facial expressions may all be incorporated into a profile drawing.**

Figure 4.38 shows various photographs used to analyze the highly diverse profile shapes of the head and skull from Alphonse Bertillon's 1886 book on categorizing faces. Reference photographs may become particularly important to the forensic artist when drawing the profile view, since it is usually less familiar.

When utilizing photos for copying, I find it helpful to consider the arrangement of profile features in terms of a **"plumb line,"** or true vertical. In other words, using a clear ruler placed "north and south," or at a 90° angle, each feature can be studied in relation to the other features. It becomes easy to determine where the features advance or recede, the essence of the look of the profile face. It may also be helpful to observe the **"negative shapes"** formed by the space *around* the profile features. By observing the negative shapes as well as the positive shapes, there is even greater accuracy in copying profile features from photographs.

If an invisible line is dropped from the inner corner of the eye, for example, straight downward, where does it fall in relation to the corner of the mouth? In a flattened face, the eye corner and the mouth corner may *align* perfectly. In a very prognathic or projecting lower face, the mouth corner may fall in *front* of the eye corner. In a face with a very receding chin and lower face, the eye corner may fall *behind* the eye corner. The same sort of evaluation can be done for other features or landmarks. Where does the eye corner fall in relation to the chin projection? The alar groove? Or how does the projection of the brow bone relate to the upper lip? The chin? Figure 4.39 shows a profile composite drawing with two "plumb lines," allowing assessment of the relative protrusion or recession of the features. The shapes formed between the two vertical lines are "negative shapes," which can be used to further assess the positive forms, especially when copying a photograph.

Figure 4.38 Analysis of various **profile head shapes** from *The Bertillon System of Identification*, 1886.

Hair and Other Textures

Drawing hair, facial hair, and other textures requires that the artist learn to observe, analyze, and interpret these details. Again, well-organized reference files are of tremendous benefit. A good photograph of a particular skin texture or hair style can be a tremendous plus that facilitates an efficient and accurate drawing.

Hair

Drawing hair requires the artist to incorporate the principles of light while also including shapes and textures. The basic steps for drawing hair are generally the

Figure 4.39 Profile composite drawing over which "plumb lines" have been laid to evaluate which features advance or recede. The shapes seen between the two vertical lines on the lower face are **"negative shapes."** (Courtesy of Texas Department of Public Safety.)

same regardless of hair texture. It is helpful to think of drawing hair as a three-step process (Figure 4.40).

First, the overall head and hair shape should be drawn. Second, the smaller or "sub-shapes" are developed within the large overall shape and tone is added. Third, light and dark tones are blended, directional lines of movement are added, and highlights are lifted out, creating contrast.

Figure 4.40 Drawing hair in three steps: overall shape is drawn (left); "sub-shapes" are developed and tone is added (center); directional lines and highlights are added (right). (Illustration by KTT.)

Figure 4.41 Composite drawing with **very thin hair**, with the outline of the top of the head visible through the hair. (Courtesy of Texas Department of Public Safety.)

If the hair is very short or pulled back, the shape of the head will be emphasized, and the light should be added in such a way that the roundness of the head is shown. If the hair is very thin on top, the outline of the top of the head must show, with the thin strands of hair drawn over it, as in Figure 4.41.

Figure 4.42 shows a composite drawing with very straight hair, with some sheen on top suggested by highlights. It was drawn with long continuous strokes using a broad-tipped pencil. Highlights were lifted with a vinyl eraser.

Figure 4.42 Composite drawing with **straight hair**. (Courtesy of Texas Department of Public Safety.)

Figure 4.43 Composite drawing with **curly hair.** (Courtesy of Texas Department of Public Safety.)

If the hair falls into large waves or smaller curls, each wave or curl must receive individual lighting. This accounts for the added time required to draw long, wavy, or curly hair. Forms of hair must be developed individually to an extent, although it is also possible to suggest large areas of curl with light and shadow as in Figure 4.43. As suggested for drawing ears, **think "peaks and valleys" when applying light to drawings of curly hair.**

Figure 4.44 shows two composite drawings of subjects with very curly or kinky hair. This type of hair is very textural and may be easily drawn with the side of a dark Design® Ebony or woodless pencil, using varied pressure.

Figure 4.44 Composite drawings with **very curly** (left) or **kinky hair** (right). (Courtesy of Texas Department of Public Safety.)

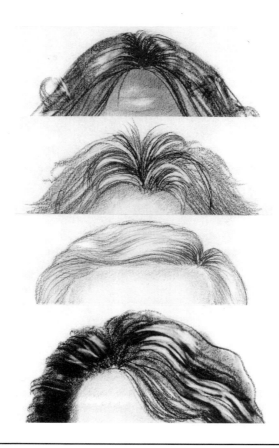

Figure 4.45 Drawing **"parts" in hair** of different colors and textures. (Illustration by KTT.)

In workshops, I have observed that some people have difficulty showing the top of the hair, to convey whether it is "parted" or not. Figures 4.45 and 4.46 show ways of drawing hair of various colors and textures with and without a "part." Again, light is the key.

When the hair is straight and pulled back, as in the top example of Figure 4.46, or worn in bangs across the forehead, there is a **"band of light"** that runs perpendicular to the strands of hair.

Facial Hair

Lighting principles also apply when drawing facial hair. Remember that facial hair must lie on *top* of the facial structures beneath it. Sometimes it further defines the facial shapes and other times it obscures them. Figure 4.47 shows the use of light on a **mustache** to give it fullness and the appearance of volume.

When drawing a **beard**, you should determine whether the hairs were long or short or straight or curly. Was the beard short or thin enough that the skin shone through or was there total coverage? With a **sparse beard**, it is essential to first define the jaw and chin. Then the beard hair should be added as if it were just a texture, as in the left drawing in Figure 4.44. With a **full or heavy beard**, the form of the beard should be treated as a shape rather than a texture, using the same three-step approach as for drawing head hair.

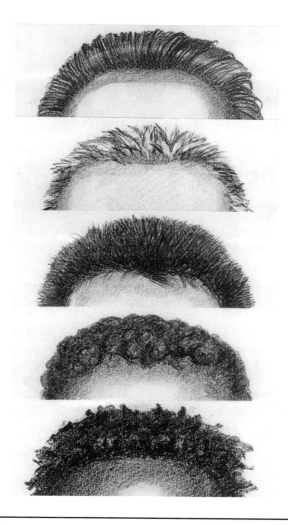

Figure 4.46   Hair with no "part," shown in various textures and colors. (Illustration by KTT.)

Textures

Most textures drawn by the forensic artist fall into the categories of soft or hard. Soft textures include skin, hair, and fabric. Hard textures include metal, plastic, or glass.

Use of skin texture to augment the likeness of a composite drawing is demonstrated in Figure 4.48.

A basic rule in drawing textures is that highlights are needed to produce shine. The more pronounced the highlight, the stronger the shine. **If a very "light light" is placed directly beside a very "dark dark," the effect is strong shine,** such as that needed for lip gloss or metal glasses frames. Figure 4.49 shows two composite drawings of dark-haired males. The subject to the left has hair without highlights, thus without shine. The subject to the right has bright highlights placed directly against dark hair, producing the look of wetness or oiliness. Figure 4.50 shows the same principle used to produce glossy or shiny lips in a composite of a female.

Figure 4.47 Drawing of a **mustache** using light to give it the appearance of volume. (Courtesy of Texas Department of Public Safety.)

Figure 4.48 Composite drawing by KTT of subject with noticeable **skin texture** (left) and subject identified (right). (Courtesy of Texas Department of Public Safety.)

Accessories

Hats and Headgear

Forensic artists are often called upon to draw hats or other types of headgear. **Ideally the artist has built a photo file of the types of hats, caps, or other headgear most commonly worn in his or her area.** Good reference photos of hats can

Figure 4.49 Composite drawings by KTT. Subject (left) has hair without highlights, thus **without shine**. Subject (right) has hair with bright highlights placed directly against dark hair, producing the look of **wetness or oiliness**. (Courtesy of Texas Department of Public Safety.)

Figure 4.50 Composite drawing by KTT in which bright highlights against "dark darks" produce the look of **glossy or shiny lips**. (Courtesy of Texas Department of Public Safety.)

promote efficient communication between the artist and the witness, and usually result in greater accuracy of the drawing. Some hats, such as cowboy hats, can be quite tricky to draw, and a photograph greatly facilitates the process.

In Texas and other western states, a cowboy hat is often a very personal item. Among those who participate in rodeos, the crease of the hat may even be so specific as to identify the rodeo event in which the wearer participates, such as calf-roping or bull-riding.

Perhaps the most common mistake in the drawing of any type of hat is the failure to allow for the cranium. Many drawings depict a hat that appears to cut into the skull. **A hat must be drawn outside of the skull.** To appear to fit naturally, it must *wrap around* the head, occupying space *outside* of that needed for the upper portion of the head, including both bony cranium and the appropriate volume of hair.

Brimmed Hats

Figure 4.51 shows three different hats with brims of different lengths. Note that brims may be turned downward, be rather level, or be turned upward, and they should be shaded slightly differently. Note, too, that **a brimmed hat should cast some shadow on the face to a degree consistent with the length of the brim.**

Figure 4.51 Drawings of **hats with brims of different lengths**. (Courtesy of Texas Department of Public Safety.)

Caps

Caps are extremely popular and are often drawn by forensic artists in various locations. Figure 4.52 shows three different caps with bills. A cap drawing may also include a very important bit of information if there is a name, design, or logo on the front that the witness can describe.

Individuals who routinely wear caps tend to crease the bill in a particular way and rest the cap on the head in a characteristic manner. Care should be taken by the artist to capture these traits in the drawing if the witness can describe them. For example, some baseball players bend three neat creases in a cap's bill, carefully folding it until it is just so. Some individuals habitually wear caps backward; others wear them cocked back on the head. Still others wear them pulled very low over the eyes. **Do not be content to draw a simple generic cap if your witness can give you greater detail.**

Figure 4.52 Drawings of **caps with bills of various lengths.** (Courtesy of Texas Department of Public Safety.)

Having a styrofoam wig head and several caps in my office has proven very helpful. By physically manipulating a cap on the head form, the witness can convey just the right sort of positioning for the cap. This makes it much easier to draw the cap while actually observing it. Remember that caps with bills of some length should also cast a bit of shadow on the face, but not as much as brimmed hats.

Close-Fitting Headgear

Figure 4.53 shows drawings of close-fitting headgear. It is especially important with this type of hat that the artist allow for the full size of the upper area of the head and

Figure 4.53 Drawings of **close-fitting headgear.** (Courtesy of Texas Department of Public Safety.)

for the described volume of hair, and then add the hat *around* these. It is not anatomically possible for the hat to be inside of the skull no matter how tightly it fits!

Glasses

The forensic artist may be asked to draw any of an almost endless variety of eyeglasses styles. As with other accessories, the photographic reference file is very beneficial. Such photographs help facilitate rapid, accurate communication between artist and witness, and provide handy drawing aids for the artist. Even if the precise style cannot be found in the reference file, the scale of the glasses and the general shape of the lenses can usually be determined. As with hats or other accessory details, do not be satisfied to draw *just* a pair of glasses. Attempt to draw the *specific* glasses as remembered by the witness. Remember that if the glasses worn by the perpetrator were of the prescription type, he will likely be wearing them all the time, and they become a very important part of his "look."

Placement

In addition to determining the right type of glasses to draw, be sure that you place them correctly on the face. Were they worn down low on the tip of the nose or pushed up high on the bridge? A rough drawing of the glasses on matte acetate may be used to shift up or down over the facial drawing to aid in accurate placement.

Scale

Pay attention, too, to the correct scale of the glasses. Were they "fly eyes," like Jackie Kennedy's 1960s style, or more like those of Benjamin Franklin or John Lennon in scale?

Lenses

Ask about the lenses. Were they tinted? Was it an overall tint or graduated from top to bottom? Were they visible bifocals? Were the bifocals semicircular in fashion or straight across? Were the lenses strong enough in magnification that they distorted the eyes of the person wearing them? Did they make the irises appear larger or smaller?

Figure 4.54 shows a composite drawing in which the lenses described were thick enough to magnify and enlarge the iris size.

Frame Material

Figure 4.55 shows a composite drawing in which the glasses described were of dark plastic and placed on top of the head. It was necessary to erase linear highlights with an eraser shield and vinyl stick eraser so the glasses would show up in the dark hair.

Use the light principle of placing "light lights" directly against "dark darks" to get the shine of both metal- and plastic-framed glasses.

Figure 4.54 Drawing with glasses in which there were **thick lenses**, causing some magnification and enlargement of the iris size. (Illustration by KTT.)

Figure 4.55 Drawing with dark **plastic-framed glasses**, placed on top of the head. (Courtesy of Texas Department of Public Safety.)

Figure 4.56 Drawing with metal-framed glasses, using **highlights** to partially obscure the eyes. (Courtesy of Texas Department of Public Safety.)

Highlights

Most artists have a personal preference as to the way they place highlights in glasses. This may be done elaborately or simply. Figure 4.56 shows a composite drawing in which highlights in the lenses of metal-framed glasses were erased in broad streaks with a kneaded eraser. The highlights were also used as a device to obscure the eyes, which were not well seen by the witness.

Other Details

Small side drawings of details added to a composite drawing help provide additional information. Figure 4.57 uses a small drawing to further explain a hairstyle.

Figure 4.58 uses a side drawing to express a detail about the front of the clothing. Figure 4.59 shows a detail of the back of the clothing.

Improving Your Drawing Skills

Practice is, of course, simply the very best way to improve your drawing skills.

Try to **think three dimensionally** as you draw the head. A common mistake in composites is the flat, mask-like approach to facial drawing, which is very one dimensional. Figure 4.60 shows a flat way of thinking about a face at the left vs. a three-dimensional attitude at the right. You should develop a drawing from the very beginning with the knowledge that there is a skull inside the head that produces the rounded volumes. Think of the temples as being in a different plane from the sides of the back of the skull.

Simple exercises, routinely used in art schools, can really improve your drawing skills.

Figure 4.57 Small side drawing used to further explain a hairstyle. (Courtesy of Texas Department of Public Safety.)

Figure 4.58 Small side drawing used to express a detail about the front of the clothing. (Courtesy of Texas Department of Public Safety.)

Figure 4.59   Small side drawing used to express a detail about the back of the clothing. (Courtesy of Texas Department of Public Safety.)

Figure 4.60   A **flat approach** to facial drawing (left) vs. a **three-dimensional approach** (right). (Illustration by KTT.)

Gesture Drawing

Gesture drawing is an exercise done by looking at a model or people around you and very quickly drawing an image. This should involve only a minute or two of drawing. The idea is to capture the essence of the image without paying much attention to the details. You should try to think about what is happening in the interior of the figure, sensing the volumes and not worrying about the edges. **This type of exercise helps you learn to block out forms quickly and accurately, sensing the general and the large more than the specific and the small.**

Contour Drawing

Contour drawing is an exercise that is done slowly while looking at a model and not looking at your paper. It is best to set up your drawing paper on an easel and position yourself so that you can see the model. Place your pencil or charcoal on the paper to start, then look at the model and do not move your eyes away from the model as you draw. Allow your eyes to follow the model's form and draw with sensitivity to the details. **This exercise teaches attention to line and subtle detail. It also improves hand–eye coordination, forcing you to be observant and think about what you are drawing.**

Experiment with Styles and Materials

I often recommend to students in forensic art workshops that they experiment with new drawing materials or styles in an effort to improve their skills. While each of us is reluctant to step outside our "comfort zones" and try something unfamiliar, this awkwardness sometimes allows us to make advances. Constantly doing something in a way that is comfortable and familiar may mean that you are not improving as much as you could be.

If you feel, for example, that you are drawing too slowly, you may need to try several things to see improvement. Perhaps you are drawing too large and you should try diminishing the scale of the faces you draw. Or your style may be encumbering you, slowing you down. If you are using cross-hatching, you may wish to try bolder, looser strokes to build up speed. If you use only very sharp pencils, you should try chisel-point pencils and woodless pencils with broad, dull leads.

In any case, it is only by experimenting with new methods of drawing that you will see a real breakthrough. In drawing as in life, the adage applies: **You cannot discover new oceans unless you have the courage to lose sight of the shore.**

References

1. George, R. M., Anatomical and artistic guidelines for forensic facial reconstruction, in *Forensic Analysis of the Skull*, Iscan, M. Y. and Helmer, R. P., Eds. New York: Wiley–Liss, 1993.
2. Landau, T., *About Faces: The Evolution of the Human Face.* New York: Doubleday, 1989.
3. Hogarth, B., *Drawing the Human Head.* New York: Watson-Guptill Publications, 1965.
4. Gordon, L., *How to Draw the Human Head: Techniques and Anatomy.* New York: Penguin Books, 1986.
5. Faigin, G., *The Artist's Complete Guide to Facial Expression.* New York: Watson-Guptill Publications, 1990.
6. Goldfinger, E., *Human Anatomy for Artists: The Elements of Form.* New York: Oxford University Press, 1991.

FORENSIC ART:
Finding and Identifying the Living

Chapter 5

The Interview

In preparing a high-quality composite image, the interview is everything. The skill and care taken to interview individuals for the purpose of developing composite images, whether by hand-drawn, mechanically assembled, or computer-generated methods, cannot be overestimated.

The psychological and medicolegal literature provides a wealth of studies and articles about cognition and perception, memory and trauma, victimology, facial recognition, eyewitness identification, and interviewing methods.

It is difficult for the forensic artist who does composite drawing to sort through this plethora of research and information and find the substantive material that can be readily applied to his or her own work.

This chapter reviews some of the pertinent ideas and concepts in the literature and conveys their potential usefulness to the practicing composite artist during an interview situation. While it is not possible to include every study related to this subject area, effort has been made to present a practical review of some of the most notable and applicable findings. Special attention is paid to the presentation of results of research in which multiple professionals arrive at similar conclusions.

In his paper, "Forensic Art: Practical Considerations of Witness Memory," veteran New York City Police Department composite artist Frank Domingo states:

> Since it is virtually impossible for "real life" situations to be duplicated in the laboratory (particularly in the duplication of trauma), **it is necessary for the composite artist to balance common-sense practical experience with relevant theories about the memory.**[1]

Hopefully, future studies will continually add to our knowledge base to aid in considerate, knowledgeable, and productive interviewing of crime victims and witnesses. The wise composite artist will stay abreast of such research.

The composite artist is obliged to constantly strive to attain the best possible interviewing skills. This effort should continue throughout every stage in one's career.

Unfortunately, I have known long-time sketch artists who were complacent in this regard; they believed minimal interview skills were adequate for their purpose. This is an unfortunate and unwise attitude, because **the method and quality of the interview is key to the success of the composite drawing process.**

Some artists and police agencies make the mistake of believing that strong drawing skills are the only criteria for productive composite drawing. In fact, if required to make a choice of composite artists, I would probably choose a mediocre artist with great interviewing and "people" skills over a great artist with mediocre interviewing skills.

As an instructor of many years, I have seen numerous individuals with only rudimentary drawing skills persevere and greatly improve their drawing abilities. It is somewhat more difficult for a person who simply does not relate well to others to become a great interviewer. This is not to say that good interviewing skills cannot be learned; to a large extent, they can. Clearly, **the ideal composite artist possesses strong drawing skills as well as strong interviewing skills.**

A noteworthy misconception is what I call **"The Good Art Phenomenon."** Over the years, I have realized that certain individuals who do not understand the full spectrum of the composite drawing process accept a "good" drawing as a "good" item of forensic art. This may not always be the case.

Sometimes a police agency hires a commercial artist who is skilled in facial drawing but has no interviewing experience. **The finished product may be a good-looking drawing, but it may not be an accurate representation of the perpetrator.**

Similarly, some vendors of computer softwares used for the production of composite facial images stress their belief that the strength of their product is the fact that "anyone can use it." While it may be true that anyone can easily put together a face with most facial imaging softwares, it may be a face that is a far cry from being the *correct* face. **By whatever method the composite image is to be developed, an understanding of memory function and good interviewing skills must be an integral part of the process.**

This chapter dicusses various topics related to effective interviewing for composite imagery. It is fundamental to the process that the artist have a general understanding of the **processes by which our minds encode memories**. Essential, too, is a working knowledge of some of the **effects of trauma on memory**.

The interviewing process will be explored from the perspective of the **victim or witness** to help the artist gain additional insights that will promote sensitive, effective communication.

The method of **cognitive interviewing** will be outlined as a recommended approach to successful composite interviews. More specifically described will be a **composite-specific method of interviewing**, in which cognitive interviewing is incorporated with **use of reference cues** in the form of facial photographs to trigger recognition ability. Situations in which it may or may not be feasible and beneficial to interview **multiple witnesses** at the same time will also be examined.

The special consideration that must be employed in conducting **child interviews** and **hospital interviews** will be discussed. Situations in which **false allegations** are made will be discussed, providing insights into possible determination of such claims and some of the complex reasons behind them.

Finally, **other psychological factors** that may affect our memories of events will be reviewed.

Functions of Memory and Trauma

The police composite artist, whose function it is to develop an image based on an observer's recollection of a person or event, must have a strong knowledge of the dynamics of human memory. This will enable the artist to more effectively retrieve the information needed to perform his task.

What Is Memory?

Merriam-Webster's Medical Dictionary defines memory as **"the power or process of reproducing or recalling what has been learned and retained especially through associative mechanisms ... the store of things learned and retained form an organism's activity or experience as indicated by ... *recall and recognition.*"**[2]

Ideas regarding memory and its function have evolved considerably over time. The Greek philosopher Aristotle believed that thinking took place in the head, but memory was stored in the heart! In the 21st century, thoughts about memory continue to be altered and reshaped. Dr. Joan Menninger makes the following observations in her book *Total Recall*:

> Memory research is subject to as many fashions and fads as any other science. Before the 1950s, memory was thought of as one system. Then a two-system theory became popular — a short-term memory for our immediate environment and a long-term memory for 'facts': language, history, arithmetic and the like.
>
> In the '60s memory was regarded as a storage system. In the '70s it was looked on as a component in a larger information-processing system that included perception, comprehension, and reasoning. The '80s have brought new interest in nonverbal memory: visual, auditory, and kinesthetic.[3]

Many researchers have tried to define memory and its multiple aspects. In an attempt to explain memory in easy-to-understand terms, Dr. Elizabeth F. Loftus writes: **"Memory is a fragile, elusive thing that is less like a videotape recorder that can capture an event for repeated playback than an interpretive process of putting together information when it is called for."**[4] Graham Davies drew a similar analogy years earlier: **"The brain is not a video recorder and we do not take into permanent storage all the information that reaches our senses."**[5]

According to Dr. Bruce Perry of the Department of Psychiatry and Behavioral Sciences at the Baylor College of Medicine in Houston, **memory is "the capacity to bring elements of an experience from one moment in time to another."**[6] A renowned specialist in memory, especially as it is associated with traumatic events, Dr. Perry offers numerous insights useful to the composite artist in his paper, "Memories of Fear, How the Brain Stores and Retrieves Physiologic States, Feelings, Behaviors and Thoughts from Traumatic Events."[6]

How Does Memory Work?

For survival purposes, the human brain has developed the sophisticated capacity to create internal representations of the external world. Some researchers use the term

schema to describe such representations. In *Memory: Current Issues*, Cohen, Kiss, and Le Voi state:

> According to *schema theory*, the knowledge we have stored in memory is organized as a set of schemas or mental representations, each of which incorporates all the knowledge of a given type of object or event that we have acquired from past experience. ... New experiences are not just passively copied or recorded in memory. A memory representation is actively constructed by processes that are strongly influenced by schema.[7]

Dr. Perry explains that these internal representations are done by complex neuro-molecular processes, but "simply stated — the brain changes with experience — **all** experience, good and bad."[6]

Significantly, Dr. Perry states:

> ... the brain makes and stores associations between the sensory information (e.g., the sounds, smells, positions, and emotions) from that specific event (e.g., the pairing of the growl of the sabertooth tiger and danger) allowing the individual to generalize to sensory information present in current or future events.
>
> ... The prime "directive" of the human brain is to promote survival and procreation. Therefore, the brain is "over-determined" to sense, process, store, perceive, and mobilize in response to threatening information from the external and internal environments. This total neurobiological participa-tion in the threat response is important in understanding how a traumatic experience can impact and alter functioning in such a pervasive fashion. Cognitive, emotional, social, behavioral, and physiological residue of a trauma may impact an individual for years — even a lifetime.[6]

Dr. Perry explains that "in order for any experience, traumatic or not, to become part of memory, it must be 'sensed.'"[6] **The fundamental premise that the memories of events are encoded in correlation with related sensory experiences is poten-tially very useful in the retrieval of a particular memory. The composite artist can employ this knowledge of memory encoding to better obtain the descriptive characteristics held within the witness' mind.**

As humans, we utilize this brain function to protect ourselves against future threat-ening events. The more primitive portions of the brain are the sites for the storage of previous sensory memories, which explains the immediate reaction responses to some potential threats. Dr. Perry calls these types of memories **"state memories,"** defining them as **"memories of previous patterns of sensory input which are connected with a bad experience** — the combat veteran from Vietnam will have an automatic response to the sound of a helicopter."[6]

A well-known example of "state memories" is the **"fight or flight" reaction**, a stress hormone response. Perry writes:

> The classic "response" to the threatening cues involves activation of the autonomic nervous system. ... this "fight or flight" reaction involves the physiological manifestations of alarm, arousal and the emotion of anxiety ... an adaptive response to the impending threat.[6]

These "state memories" are, in part, the reason for experiencing some of the symptoms associated with **post-traumatic stress disorder**, such as exaggerated startle response or the sudden feeling that the event is recurring. Perry explains that "the brain has taken a pattern of neuronal activation previously associated with fear and now, will 'act' in response to this false signal."[6]

According to Perry, all parts of the brain "store" information and have, in some sense, "memory." The **types of memory employed by our brains are use-dependent** and fall into four categories:

1. **Cognitive Memories** — learning names, phone numbers, language, etc.
2. **Motor Vestibular Memories** — riding a bicycle, playing the piano, typing, dancing, etc.
3. **Emotional or Affect Memories** — grief, fear, anger, etc.
4. **State Memories** — sight, sound, smell, touch, etc.[6]

While these four memory categories are present in most people, composite interviews may benefit from emphasis on state memories by using questions geared to the modality of encoding as needed for each individual interviewed.

It is now recognized that for learning to occur, the modality of teaching should match the modality of reception. Skilled educators employ this knowledge by providing instruction in multiple forms, such as visual, auditory, and "hands-on," in order to reach each student. Similarly, the composite artist can use this knowledge to aid in memory retrieval, adapting the mode of questioning to the individual situation being recalled, invoking certain use-dependent memories.

Adrenalin may be a key factor in the encoding of emotional memories. Psychobiologist Dr. James McGough of the University of California at Irvine and his colleagues theorize that hormones such as adrenalin act as "fixatives," locking memories of exciting, stimulating, or shocking events in the brain.[3]

Dr. Larry Cahill, also of the University of California at Irvine, presented some of his views on memory in a lecture before a group of forensic artists at the International Association for Identification's 80th Annual Educational Conference and Training Seminar in Costa Mesa, California in July 1995. His research into the neurobiology of emotion and the critical role of the amygdala for emotional arousal led him to conclude that he does not believe in "flashbulb" memory, although he believes an experience may be so exciting emotionally as to leave a "scar" on a person's memory. He also states that we have a greater memory for emotionally charged events.[8]

Stages of Memory

Short- and Long-Term Memory

Numerous experts discuss the division of memory function into two distinct stages: short-term memory and long-term memory. A few add a third stage: immediate memory. Some believe that information must first pass through the short-term stage to enter into the long-term stage, while others say it can go directly into long-term storage.

Short-term memory or working memory deals with present events; it holds the information we are presently processing.[9] Its capacity is limited. It screens out unwanted information and selects information to be stored in long-term memory.

Long-term or permanent memory is the part of memory that people usually refer to when they speak of "memory." Its capacity for storage appears limitless, although not all stored information is retrievable.[10]

Episodic and Semantic Memory

Some psychologists describe long-term memory in terms of **episodic memory** and **semantic memory. Episodic memory** refers to remembering events or episodes in our lives: the when, where, and how an item occurred. **Semantic memory** is a person's organized knowledge about words, meanings, relations, concepts, symbols, rules, etc. Inputs into the semantic memory system are referred to and absorbed within preexisting cognitive structures.[11]

Acquisition, Retention, and Retrieval

Other experts describe the memory process as divided into **three major stages: the acquisition stage, the retention stage, and the retrieval stage**. In *Eyewitness Testimony: Civil and Criminal*, Dr. Elizabeth Loftus and James M. Doyle state:

> Most theoretical analyses of the process divide it into three major stages. First, the event is perceived by a witness, and information is entered into the memory system. This is called the acquisition stage. Next, some time passes before a witness tries to remember the event, and this is called the retention stage. Finally, the witness tries to recall the stored information, and this is called the retrieval stage.[12]

Memory and the Composite Artist

The information presented above provides a basic foundation for the understanding of the extremely complex and sometimes controversial theories about memory. Certain aspects of memory function and the potential retrieval of memories may hold particular significance for the composite sketch artist. Knowledge of some of these factors may be useful in the composite drawing process. Other factors may be totally out of the control of the artist, but they may provide insight into the process.

*All Faces Are **Not** Created Equal*

An issue fundamental to the composite drawing process has been observed in several studies. **Some faces are simply easier to describe and recognize than others.**

During the 1980s, as part of his extensive work in the area of face perception and recognition at the University of Houston, Kenneth R. Laughery stated, "It seems likely that faces vary in terms of the ease or difficulty with which accurate representations can be created for them."[13]

Similarly, a 1985 study by Wells that used a large selection of faces indicated that certain faces are simply easier to describe, remember, and identify than other faces.[14]

In general, such studies seem to indicate that faces that are either particularly attractive or particularly unattractive better capture our attention. This appears to suggest that **distinctiveness rather than typicality is what makes faces more recognizable.**

My observation, after many years of interviewing victims of sexual assault, is that another phenomenon may occur. The minds of some victims deal with the struggle of coming to terms with the event that has occurred by altering the perpetrator's face somewhat to make it more attractive. The perpetrator's face may have been quite ugly, yet the victim's description often somewhat diminishes the ugliness, apparently in an effort to better cope.

All Witnesses Are <u>Not</u> Created Equal

In a perfect world of forensic art, every witness would observe the suspect under excellent conditions, for the needed period of time, and be able to describe the face in exquisite detail. Of course, this does not happen. To further complicate matters, studies have determined that **a witness who appears to be giving a good description may, in fact, not be as good at recognizing.** The witness may simply be *fluent or confident* in describing a face, yet the description may turn out to be less than accurate.

Goldstein, Johnson, and Chance examined this question in 1979 in their article, "Does Fluency of Face Description Imply Superior Face Recognition?" They determined:

> The results of this and the two preliminary investigations offer little evidence for believing the level of ability to verbally describe faces is predictive of the level of ability to recognize faces.
>
> … Correlational analysis revealed no association between describing ability and recognition memory performance.[15]

A 1985 study by Pigott and Brigham found that test subjects who gave relatively accurate descriptions of a target "suspect" were not necessarily more likely to make a correct identification of the "suspect" than others who had given less accurate descriptions.[16]

Results derived from my own case experience seem to underscore the practical demonstration of some of these controlled studies. Over the years, I have found a lack of constant predictability of the results of my composite drawing likenesses to described faces which, in some instances, may relate to the above-mentioned studies. Occasionally, drawings produced from witnesses who gave highly detailed, confident descriptions seemed to bear less likeness to the subject than drawings based on descriptions of less confident witnesses. I have learned to expect surprises!

Holistic Encoding

Some years ago, it became apparent to me that the identifications that resulted from composite sketches I had done seemed to exhibit a particular recurring element. When comparing sketches to photos of subjects apprehended, the best likenesses could be observed when both sketch and photo bore similar proportions. Even if the individual features were somewhat "off," the resemblance was there if the proportions were there (Figure 5.1). Over time, I have become convinced that while individual features are certainly important, **the single most important factor for attaining likeness and individuality, thus hopefully leading to facial recognition, is *proportion*. I call this capturing the *gestalt* of a face.** By this I mean

Figure 5.1 Composite drawing by KTT based on the description of a victim of sexual assault (left), and subject identified (right). The subject's face was viewed for only a few seconds in dim lighting, yet the victim's memory encoded the proportional arrangement of features to establish the **gestalt of the face.** (Courtesy of Texas Department of Public Safety.)

that the image of the face as a whole is more important, and probably more recognizable, than any of its individual parts.

This phenomenon is reinforced by neuropsychologist Dr. Nancy Etcoff, who indicates that the key to facial recognition is spatial relationships rather than individual features. Her work with prosopagnosics, individuals who have lost the ability to recognize faces, has determined that **we encode faces into memory holistically rather than as individual component parts.**[17]

Findings such as Dr. Etcoff's suggest that preparation of the facial composite sketch should be done by a method of interviewing that is compatible with the way in which the facial memory was initially encoded. To do this, **the facial composite drawing should be as complete a face as possible before the witness sees it, so that the witness views it *holistically*.**

The composite artist should carefully consider the way in which the drawn image is first presented to the witness. It is beneficial to do a rough, but complete facial drawing first, based on the witness' initial description. The proportions should be established as correctly as possible in this early rendition. Then the drawing may be shown to the witness for the additional work of making adjustments, corrections, and "fine tuning" using the reference photos.

Because our minds tend to grasp and encode an overall impression of a face, rather than the bits and pieces of individual features, it is *not* a good idea to show the witness photographic references with facial features displayed in isolation. Instead, in the reference phase of the composite interview, photographs of complete faces would be preferable. (This approach will be discussed in more detail in the section on **composite-specific interviewing** later in this chapter.) A 1993 study by Tanaka and Farah further emphasizes this concept. Their experiment showed that people could more accurately select a feature, say, the nose, if the correct nose were presented in the context of a whole face rather than as one of a group of isolated features.[18]

Importance of Specific Features

Important research on facial recognition was pioneered in the 1980s at the Department of Psychology, University of Aberdeen, Scotland by Graham Davies, John Shepherd, and Hadyn Ellis. Some of their tests dealt with facial descriptions and the importance placed on different components of the face. They assess their studies of facial descriptions as follows:

> By examining the frequency with which features are mentioned and the characteristic qualities associated with them (i.e., narrow eyes, red hair), a measure of the relative importance of different elements of the face can be obtained.
>
> **... It seems that we do not accord equal priority to all aspects of the face when we remember it, certain features are more dominant and habitually employed for recognition.**
>
> ... It will be observed that some features of the face are mentioned many more times than others. Hair was the feature most frequently employed (in particular colour, length, texture, and parting), followed, at some distance, by eyes and eyebrows, nose and general facial structure. By contrast, the cheeks, mouth and forehead area were rarely used as a means of discriminating one face from another. These results appeared to illustrate that, in general, upper features of the face were more important to our subjects in describing photographed faces than lower features.[19]

Additional studies at Aberdeen University confirmed the particular importance of age, facial shape, and hair. Discussing the Scottish study, Loftus comments:

> Subjects looked at photographs of up to ten faces and then tried to identify the ones they had seen from a large array of alternatives. Where a face was similar with respect to the three key criteria, they often misidentified a face, despite the fact that the new face was very different with respect to other features such as mouth or eyes. These results are clearly contrary to the intuitive belief that the eyes are very important for recognition. The researchers suggested that celebrities who did not want to be identified should spend their money on wigs rather than dark glasses.[12]

Importance of the Upper Face

Clearly, both holistic and individual feature information are important for the recognition of faces. A noteworthy observation in this regard may be made about faces with a particularly unusual or distinctive feature. While encoding of a face is usually done as an overall "grasp," when looking at certain faces, we may quickly focus our attention on odd features such as huge ears, crooked noses, or crossed eyes rather than the "overall." Good examples would be the face (and nose) of comedian Bob Hope and the face (and birthmark) of former Soviet premier Mikhail Gorbachev.

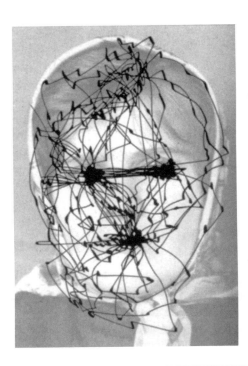

Figure 5.2   Experiment tracking the eye movements of a subject viewing a face for 3 minutes, indicating **specific areas of attention**. (From Yarbus, A.L., Experiment tracking the eye movements of a subject viewing a face for three minutes, indicating specific areas of attention, in *Eye Movement and Vision*, Plenum Publishing, New York, 1967.)

Certain studies have been done using devices that can track the eye movements of test subjects as they stare at facial images. Figure 5.2 shows the results of such a study, with black tracings indicating the viewer's areas of attention while staring at a photograph of a young woman for 3 minutes. The mind's attempts to grasp the arrangement of the mid-face features are shown. Also indicated is a greater interest in the upper face than the lower face. If the hair were not covered, this feature would also, I believe, demand noticeable attention and even more viewing time on the upper face.

Andy Young and colleagues conducted a 1987 experiment regarding the importance of the upper face.[20] When shown isolated upper halves of faces of famous individuals, people identified them quite accurately. When an incorrect lower face was combined with the upper faces recognition ability became extremely difficult.

Figure 5.3 shows a composite drawing of a suspect in a triple homicide case based on the description of a witness who got only a superficial glance at the face. It demonstrates the tendency to recall the upper half of the face better than the lower half. As a predictable result, the drawing shows more detail in the upper half of the face.

Recall vs. Recognition

A review of the psychological literature reveals a recurrent theme regarding the **superiority of our abilities to recognize more than we can recall.** This fact makes a strong case for the use by composite artists of an interview methodology that integrates both cognitive interviewing for free recall and use of photo references as triggers to recognition.

Figure 5.3 Composite drawing by KTT based on the description of a witness in a triple homicide case who got only a superficial glance at the face (left), and subject identified (right). The drawing demonstrates the **tendency to recall the upper half of the face better than the lower half.** (Courtesy of Texas Department of Public Safety.)

Ann Brown of the University of Illinois has stated: "Thus, recall is the most difficult process, as it demands regeneration in the absence of the stimulus, whereas reconstruction and recognition take place in the presence of the actual stimulus or its disarranged elements."[11]

A commonsense example of this is the realization that most of us would have difficulty if asked to recall and describe the facial details of someone we know well. We could, however, recognize that person instantly if shown a photograph.

Although reference photographs may act as effective retrieval cues, they should not be used indiscriminately. Witnesses should not be shown a large number of facial photographs, nor should they be shown photographs that are without pertinence to a specific facial description. This is the reason for the recommendation that a complete face be drawn first, based on the recall elicited during the cognitive interview. Then, in a very controlled manner, a witness may be shown photographs to trigger more detailed recollections of specific details.

In his article, "Forensic Art: Practical Considerations of Witness Memory," Frank Domingo writes:

> Laboratory tests indicate that the use of cues will aid in reviving a witness's memory. Therefore, it would be in the composite artist's best interest to make use of the stronger portion of the retrieval process (recognition), by having witnesses refresh their memories through the use of cues. The use of reference material, such as facial cues, will aid in the recognition of shapes, proportions, or unusual facial characteristics. Since recall is a verbal skill, the mental processing of a visual image can be a difficult procedure, especially when the description utilizes words alone. Even familiar faces,

such as family members, friends and associates, may be difficult to recall and describe verbally. The verbal description of a stranger is even more difficult for a witness. However, using photographic cues, to enhance memory, may make the task easier.[1]

On rare occasions a witness might be confused by the use of reference photographs. At the first sign that this seems to be the case, the artist should discontinue the use of the photographs. Indications of such confusion might be frowning or pushing away the photographs. In my personal experience while doing thousands of drawings over almost two decades, only a handful of people have demonstrated this confusion. In fact, most people seem anxious to view the reference photos so that they can better communicate the subtle aspects of the face that may elude their verbal description.

There is no known legal restriction that prohibits the use of reference cue photographs. If they are used judiciously, they only serve to enhance the potential accuracy of the finished composite. Similarly, **there is no documented research to indicate that witnesses or victims are psychologically harmed in any way by use of this method.** The benefits of use of photographic references as memory cues appear to outweigh any risks.

In fact, the human mind has an amazing capacity to sort and recognize facial images. Leon Harmon commented on this ability in his 1973 article in *Scientific American* entitled "The Recognition of Faces":

> Faces, like fingerprints and snowflakes, come in virtually infinite variety. There is little chance of encountering two so similar they cannot be distinguished, even on casual inspection. Unlike fingerprints and snowflakes, however, faces can be recognized as well as discriminated. It is possible not only to tell one person from another but also to pick one from a large population and absolutely identify it ...[21]

Not everyone shares Harmon's enthusiasm about the abilities of eyewitnesses to describe or identify faces. However, most psychologists do agree that recall is weaker than recognition. In reality, the police composite artist must make use of the most productive method of interviewing the witness to achieve a facial drawing, however imperfect the process.

When asked about the use of reference photographs by composite artists as a cue to recollection, **memory specialist Dr. Larry Cahill indicated, "Composite artists should definitely make use of recognition memory, since it is much easier than free recall for individuals of all ages."** He cited a study in which 10,000 photographs were shown to individuals and 70 to 80% were recognized by the test subjects, pointing up the amazing capacity of the human brain to sort visual images.[8] Such studies suggest that while witnesses are not actually recognizing the complete faces in the reference photographs, they **are** recognizing some aspect of similarity between the reference face and the face in memory.

Similarly, when questioned by the author regarding his views on the use of photographic reference cues to facilitate recognition, renowned **cognitive psychologist Dr. Ron Fisher stated: "While not a perfect process, it is likely the best possible process for composite sketch artists."**[22]

What about Hypnosis?

In the early years of my composite drawing career, I was often asked to produce composite drawings while a witness was in a hypnotic state. I sat in on the hypnosis session while the hypnotist asked questions regarding facial description, and I produced the drawing. I soon came to realize that perhaps this was not the optimal method, because I believed I needed to be allowed to ask more specific questions of the witness as I felt necessary. After a period of time, our working process evolved. I was then allowed to ask the questions and drawings were produced that *did* aid in successful identifications of suspects.

However, in 1984, two events occurred that altered the method I used to prepare drawings in the context of hypnosis sessions. After attending both the First National Composite Art Symposium in New York and the first artists' training course held at the FBI Academy, I realized that my approach was different from that of most others in the field. I found that virtually all of the experienced and successful sketch artists in the country used reference photographs to facilitate their interviews. This was a new concept to me. I tried this method and experienced a quantum leap in the likenesses depicted in my composite drawings; I therefore adopted the process for regular use.

Because the showing of photographic references would be impossible in a hypnotic interview due to the potential for influencing witnesses in the highly suggestible state of hypnosis, a compromise method came to be utilized. Today, in the very rare instances in which an investigator chooses to use hypnosis, I sit in on the hypnosis interview to observe. The hypnotist requests the perpetrator's facial description and suggests that the witness will remember it well when the session is complete. Then the witness is awakened so that I can interview him or her in a refreshed waking state. I thus produce a composite drawing utilizing a cognitive interview method, reference photographs, and the potentially beneficial effects of hypnosis-refreshed memory.

In my experience, a witness whose recollection of an event is so scant as to require hypnosis actually may not have encoded enough information to effectively produce a composite image. **It may be a serious mistake to expect hypnosis to produce a memory when the memory simply is not there.**

Peter Bennett, formerly of the Metropolitan Police in London, comments:

> Although hypnosis has met with some measure of success, its use is now largely discredited as a viable means of enhancing memory retrieval, as research has demonstrated that it can, in reality, cause more problems than it can solve.[10]

Regarding the ban by more than 20 states of testimony from witnesses who have been hypnotized, memory specialist Dr. Martin Orne notes:

> Ninety-five percent of the population believes that hypnosis increases memory, but the data don't support that … Only the likelihood of distortion increases. People tell you more things that they remember under hypnosis, but the accuracy of those memories are not as good.[4]

Well-known memory researcher Roy Malpass of the University of Texas at El Paso discusses hypnosis as an aid to memory retrieval, stating:

… in contrast to the anecdotal evidence favoring hypnosis as a memory enhancement strategy, controlled studies fail to reveal an enhancement effect.

… Most researchers examining this body of evidence raise the possibility that hypnosis induces a more relaxed decision standard for reporting recollections. This would lead to more false reports — higher levels of confabulation — than non-hypnotic techniques.

… A decade ago one might have been able to make a case that hypnosis is at least a promising approach to enhancing witness memory. The promise has evaporated. It is likely that whatever actual effectiveness hypnosis might possess results from the degree to which hypnotic interviews contain context reinstatement techniques.[23]

Obstacles to Perception and Memory

As previously noted, for an event to be encoded into memory, it must first be perceived and experienced. Unfortunately, numerous factors may interfere or distort this process and influence the quality of information that is accepted into memory. While the composite artist deals primarily with the retrieval process of memory, interference can actually occur during any of the three stages: acquisition, retention, or retrieval. Some issues concern the victim/witness as an individual; they will be discussed in the next section. Other factors are inherent in the event itself and are simply physical and environmental obstacles, sometimes called **situational factors** in the psychological literature.

Duration of View

Loftus notes: "It seems obvious that **the longer a person has to look at something, the better his memory will be.** This has been confirmed in many psychological studies …"[12] Obviously, a view of extended duration is ideal; however, results from certain composite drawings I have done over the years indicate that it is possible to produce a useful sketch that will result in a reasonable likeness based on the description of a witness with a view duration of only a few seconds (see also Figure 5.1).

Point of View

As a routine part of the preliminary information gathering process, the composite artist should acertain the angle or point of view at which the witness saw a perpetrator. This angle of view is critical since it may bear directly on the perception of the face encoded in the witness' mind. **The primary point of view by the witness should dictate the view of the facial drawing done by the composite artist.** For example, a perpetrator viewed exclusively or almost exclusively in a profile view should be drawn in a profile view. (Difficulties that resulted from failure to follow this rule in a specific case are discussed in Chapter 15.) Frank Domingo discusses viewpoint, explaining:

> For identification purposes, the optimum viewpoint is at eye level. As the angle changes and the viewpoint diverges from eye level, the problem of foreshortening becomes a concern. The term "foreshortening" refers to

visual distortions that occur when people or objects are viewed at extreme angles — that is, as the angle increases, the amount of distortion becomes more acute. Two examples of a distorted viewpoint may be when a perpetrator is viewed: (a) above eye level (e.g., when the witness views the perpetrator who is standing at the top of a flight of stairs) or (b) below eye level (e.g., when the witness sees the perpetrator while looking out of a second story window).[1]

Obstructions to View

Obviously, **any object that interferes with the witness' sight of the subject can pose serious difficulty.** A well-documented problematic case is the "Son of Sam" investigation in New York City in the late 1970s (see Chapter 15). In that investigation, the pressure on the Police Department to stop the serial killer was so great that a sketch artist was forced to develop composite drawings from witnesses whose observations simply were not good enough. A primary complication was the trees and shrubbery that obstructed a witness' view of the shooter.

Lighting Conditions

As with other physical and environmental factors, **the artist must determine the lighting conditions under which the target suspect's face was viewed.** Dramatic alterations in appearance can result from variables in lighting. Consider the strange effects of stage lighting projected from below onto the faces of actors. Similarly, a child holding a flashlight under his chin looks quite different from a child in normal daylight conditions.

In addition to the direction of a light source on a face, the artist should consider the type of light. Color is especially variable when viewed under artificial lights. Many people have experienced this phenomenon when trying to find their cars in the artificial lights of an unfamiliar parking garage. Thus caution is advised when considering descriptions of skin tones or clothing colors, etc., which have been viewed under certain lighting conditions. Night views of colors may also be less than accurate.

Did the incident occur during daylight hours or at night? Was the sun shining or was the sky cloudy? Was it raining, foggy, or snowing? All of these weather issues can affect the available light on a subject and potentially cause alterations to vision and perception.

Such complications of lighting with regard to a witness' view are out of the control of the artist, yet they should be considered when obtaining the description.

Distance from Subject

Common sense tells us that **subjects viewed at closer distances are better perceived than those viewed at long distances.** However, extremes in distance viewing can hinder perception in various ways.

Victims of sexual assault often view perpetrators at very close distances, which can distort the appearance of the facial features. For example, when the face is seen at a distance of only a few inches, the eyes of the perpetrator are viewed while crossed. Alterations in the perception of facial proportions can also occur at close distances.

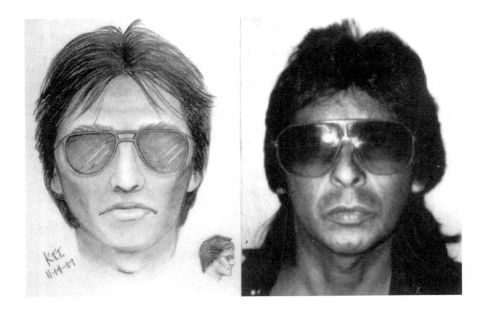

Figure 5.4 Composite drawing by KTT based on the description of a witness in a child homicide case who viewed the subject at some **distance** (left), and the subject identified (right). Note that while the overall proportions were recalled correctly, other details such as hair length were missed. (Courtesy of Texas Department of Public Safety.)

An optimum distance seems to be a range of 2 to 12 feet, depending on the vision capabilities of the viewer, although I know of no empirical data regarding this. Beyond that distance, distinction of details suffers (Figure 5.4). Domingo suggests: "Normally, vision can become obscured at distances beyond 35 feet, even under good lighting conditions."[1]

Occasionally the artist encounters an especially observant witness who may also happen to have excellent eyesight. Horace Heafner, a retired artist with the FBI in Washington, D.C., described such a witness to a bank robbery:

> The tellers were unaware that a robbery was in progress. ... Fortunately, a teller who had been approximately thirty-five to forty feet from the robber had looked at the robber's face out of curiosity. Her description was remarkably accurate. With the sketch, an investigator was able to identify the subject in a bar and the subject was subsequently arrested.[24]

Movement or Motion

A witness who sees the target subject while constant movement is taking place will likely have some diminished capability of observation. Movement can involve the suspect, who may be seen while walking, running, or driving away, or the movement can involve the witness. **Motion can diminish the time that the witness is allowed to view the face and blurring of the features may occur.**

These are not necessarily insurmountable difficulties, but factors that the artist nevertheless should consider. It may or may not be possible to complete a composite drawing from the description of a face in motion. Before committing to do a sketch the artist should obtain a preliminary description of the viewing circumstances and assess the witness' ability to describe details.

I once interviewed an elderly gentleman who saw two men and a car as he drove down a country road. One man was standing beside the car and the other was behind the wheel. As rural residents often do, he slowed and asked if the men needed assistance. They motioned him on, and he never actually stopped his vehicle. He described the standing man, a murderer, to me. Despite the movement involved, the resulting likeness was striking when compared to the perpetrator.

Time since Event

A number of researchers have assessed the effects of time elapsed in relation to the retrieval aspect of memory. They have attempted to define variables based on both accuracy of verbal facial descriptions and facial identification success. Results have varied according to the type of material studied, such as visual vs. verbal, and according to the form of the memory test.

Such tests have been conducted by Chance et al.,[25] Laughery et al.,[26] Shepherd and Ellis,[27] Lindsey et al.,[28] and Deffenbacher et al.,[29] to name only a few.

In "The Effects of Witness, Target, and Situational Factors on Eyewitness Identification," Narby, Cutler, and Penrod address retention period duration:

> A quite common finding in human memory research is that both recall and recognition accuracy decline over time. **Eyewitness recall and identification accuracy can also be expected to suffer over long retention intervals.**
>
> … Experiments that manipulate time delay have shown inconsistent results. Although most found that correct identifications decline over time, there is considerable debate over whether false identifications increase over time.[30]

As a *very* general guideline, it is better to do composite interviews with less traumatized victim/witnesses promptly after an event. "Promptly" may mean an hour, a day, or a week. Severely traumatized victims or witnesses may require time to regain their bearings and be emotionally ready to do a composite interview. The time required for trauma victims to be prepared to do a composite interview may vary considerably from days to many weeks or even longer, depending on their physical or emotional injuries.

It is important to acknowledge that memories held regarding a situation of severe trauma may be lifelong and quite vivid. Several researchers illustrate this concept of extended retention. Most people, when asked to recall their circumstances upon hearing of certain tragedies, found that their memories were quite clear. Where were you when you found out that President Kennedy had been assassinated? Or that the Space Shuttle had crashed? Or that Princess Diana had died? Or that John F. Kennedy, Jr.'s plane was missing?

Certainly, law enforcement officials are often faced with situations that present great urgency, usually matters of life or death, requiring prompt preparation of composite images. Hopefully, in such cases, a balance can be struck between the need to protect the public and consideration for the victim who must relive a recent trauma to prepare a composite.

The Victim/Witness

While it is not the function of the police composite artist to be psychologist or counselor to the victim, **it is the artist's professional responsibility to achieve the best drawing possible without risking psychological or other harm to the victim.**

Some witnesses interviewed by police artists are less traumatized than others, yet the complexities of memory and eyewitness recall must still come into play. Although not personally threatened during a crime, a person may be stressed by the mere knowledge that he is an important witness to a critical event, or a witness may be a totally uninvolved observer with no knowledge of the significance of the event at the time he or she made the observation.

Many witnesses interviewed by police artists have been victims of violent crime and have experienced the detrimental effects of a life-threatening situation. Special attention must be paid to the handling of such victims, with great care taken to avoid further traumatizing them.

Involvement in the Crime

Clearly, the degree of involvement by the witness/victim may have a marked effect on his or her abilities during the acquisition stage of memory and on ability to convey information after the crime has occurred.

Witnesses tend to fall into three categories with regard to involvement in an event: active, passive, and inactive.[1]

1. **Active witnesses** may be actual victims of crime, or close observers who have felt personally threatened (Figure 5.5).
2. **Passive witnesses** are usually impartial observers who view an incident from a safe distance and feel no personal threat (Figure 5.6).
3. **Inactive witnesses** generally have no knowledge that a crime has taken place or that something they have seen may be significant (Figure 5.7).

Interviews of active, passive, or inactive witnesses may vary considerably with regard to the subject's behavior during the session. Active witnesses may demonstrate more stress and emotion in the recollection of the event. Inactive witnesses may also demonstrate stress, although it may result from difficulty in remembering the event. Passive witnesses may indicate aspects of each type of stress.

Stress, Arousal, and Violence

Siegfried Sporer used the same three general witness divisions in his studies. He called them victims, bystanders, and incidental witnesses. He noted:

> Involvement had a very strong effect … with the "incidental witness" condition leading to particularly poor performance as opposed to the descriptions rendered by victims and bystanders.[31]

Sporer expected to notice a deterioration of witness recall for high levels of stress, but this did not occur:

Figure 5.5 Composite drawing by KTT based on the description of an **active witness** (left), and subject identified (right). The college-age victim was abducted at knife point, sexually assaulted, tied to a tree, and had her throat cut. The victim was interviewed in the hospital, unable to speak. The sketch was prepared totally from use of reference photos and brief written descriptions. (Courtesy of Texas Department of Public Safety.)

Figure 5.6 Composite drawing by KTT based on the description of a **passive witness** (left), and subject identified (right). The witness observed a bank robbery in progress but did not feel personally threatened. (Courtesy of Texas Department of Public Safety.)

Figure 5.7 Composite drawing by KTT based on the description of a totally **inactive witness** (left), and subject identified (right). The witness worked at a gasoline station and saw dozens of people during the work shift period. The subject purchased gasoline in a can but was otherwise unremarkable. Within an hour of the purchase, he participated in the murder of a family of six and the arson of their home. (Courtesy of Texas Department of Public Safety.)

> In fact, there seems to be even a linear increase in descriptive details as a function of some of these stress-related variables. For example, even in the highest category of (self-reported or inferred) anxiety ("frightened to death") a higher number of details, longer descriptions, and more precise descriptions were provided.[31]

Elizabeth Loftus and James Doyle discuss the correlation between violence, stress, and fear:

> ... memory is usually worse for details of the more emotional type of event. ... a highly emotional event is accompanied by attentional narrowing. This restricted range of viewing, induced by high arousal associated with an emotional event, means that fewer details are attended to. The process of attentional selectivity could conceivably improve memory for the main theme of the event, and perhaps some of the central details. But the encoding of peripheral details will consequently suffer.
>
> ... The term weapon focus refers to the concentration of a crime witness's attention on a weapon — the barrel of a gun or the blade of a knife — and the resultant reduction in ability to remember other details of the crime.
>
> ... A violent event can be expected to induce stress in a witness, among its other consequences. Thus, violence and stress are inextricably entwined. Whether the event is extremely violent or less violent, the degree of stress it produces in one witness may not be exactly the same as the degree of stress it produces in another.[12]

In a related assessment of arousal and stress, Dr. Ron Fisher has stated to this author in correspondence:

> Most psychologists would agree that heightened arousal causes a narrowing of focus, which serves to increase accuracy for central details, but to decrease accuracy for peripheral details. In the case of a perpetrator's face, assuming that is central to their visual field, I'd expect arousal to lead to improved accuracy.[22]

Personal Fluency of Description

As previously stated, do not assume that the most confident witness is necessarily the best witness. Various controlled tests have indicated that there may not be a direct correlation between witness confidence in a description and the accuracy of that description.

For personal reasons some individuals may have difficulty giving descriptions freely, but they should not be discounted as potentially strong witnesses. Such difficulties might include shyness, limited personal language skills due to educational level, speech impediments, or lack of language fluency.

Perceived Credibility of Members of Certain Professions

Jack Lipton of Pepperdine University, in discussing some of the legal aspects of eyewitness identification,[32] notes:

> As a general rule, courts seem to place more weight on eyewitnesses who have particular occupations. Specifically, identifications made by college professors (*Plummer v. State*, 1980),[33] lawyers (*Robinson v. State*),[34] and security guards (*Royce v. Moore*, 1972)[35] are given high esteem. Furthermore, not only do police commonly testify as eyewitnesses in criminal trials, they are also considered to be excellent witnesses (*United States v. Bothwell*, 1972).[36]

My experience over the years is that two other groups, teenagers and prostitutes, have proven to be particularly skilled observers, capable of giving detailed, accurate descriptions, but I have not formally studied or documented this. It is possible that peer pressure during the teenage years to project a certain personal appearance leads to keen perception of facial appearance of others and specific clothing details. Prostitutes may have especially keen powers of observation because of the nature of their business dealings and concern for personal safety.

Individual Witness Factors

Sex

The question often arises: Who makes a better witness — a man or a woman? The results of the psychological studies have been equivocal. Some tests indicate that men and women pay attention to different things. Most research suggests that **both men**

and women pay more attention to items that catch their interest. Consequently, they store more and better information in memory about items of interest.

Sex of the witness is another factor that is beyond the control of the artist/interviewer. It is best to think of people, men or women, as individuals.

Age

Numerous studies have been conducted on age-related witness performance. Some studies offer rather specific age breakdowns for specific types of memory function. **Overall, young children make less reliable witnesses than young adults and elderly individuals are less reliable than young to middle-aged adults.** With regard to children as witnesses, Dr. Ron Fisher has said:

> The research on children shows that they are not so much less accurate than adults, but rather that they convey less information. In response to open-ended questions, children convey less information, although at equivalent accuracy rates. For lineup (ID) tests, kids are certainly less accurate than adults, but facial composites are probably more like a description task than a recognition task. Actually, they are some combination of both.[22]

Children must always be assessed in terms of developmental age rather than chronological age. Similarly, older citizens demonstrate the effects of aging at highly variable times. Deficiencies of eyesight, hearing, or mental "quickness" obviously might affect a witness' performance, although these conditions may exist at any age.

Of course, these are averages or generalizations; people must be viewed as individuals. As previously mentioned, in my experience teenagers often make very strong witnesses. They notice small details that a distracted, busy, older adult might disregard.

Race

Certain studies have shown a tendency toward "own-race bias" in *recognition* when black and white subjects were shown photographs of both black faces and white faces.[37] **In other words, people may be able to better *recognize* individuals of their own racial group.**

Dr. Siegfried Sporer indicates that more than a dozen studies have investigated the ability to recognize own vs. other-race faces. Referring to a 1975 study by Ellis, Deregowski, and Shepherd, he discusses "Black" and "White" subjects describing faces of their own and the other race:

> ...there were some interesting differences in the frequency with which each group mentioned certain features that may help us understand why we are better able to recognize people of our own race. In particular, White subjects more frequently mentioned hair color and texture as well as the color of the iris. Presumably, due to the White subjects' greater familiarity with other Whites they have learned to pay greater attention to these features as specifically useful cues for discriminating among individual members of their race. In contrast, Black subjects gave more descriptions

of ears, chin, eyebrows, size, and whites of eyes, position of hair (e.g., direction of combing), and face outline. If we combine the categories of "nose" and "nostrils" into a single one, these features are also more likely to be mentioned by Black subjects.[31]

People who frequently interact with individuals of various racial and ethnic appearances in personal or business dealings may be far more adept at describing other-race faces because of greater familiarity with them.

It is also a personal observation that individual prejudices with regard to race may come into play in the description of perpetrators or in the composite drawing process. A strongly bigoted person may sometimes exaggerate the features of a person of another race, providing a "stereotype" description.

As a composite artist/interviewer, there may also be other factors of concern with regard to race or ancestry. In some Asian cultures, it is considered a "loss of face" to be a victim of crime, particularly sexual assault. Interviewing Asian victims and witnesses, particularly those who are recent immigrants, can be highly specialized. It is a good idea to consult a person knowledgeable about the cultural group of the interviewee prior to conducting the interview so that you do not risk inadvertently offending. For example, in some cultures, it is considered proper to approach the oldest male member of the family first, even if he does not speak English, before interviewing another family member.

Use of Drugs or Alcohol

Certainly the use of drugs and alcohol may affect the functions of memory. The degree of impairment depends on the amount used as well as the physiological makeup of the individual.

Handicaps

Robert Royal and Steven Schutt, in their manual *The Gentle Art of Interviewing and Interrogation*, make the following observations:

> Most human behavior is in response to impressions received through the sensory organs, and any distortion of those impressions may affect the nature of the behavior. Defective eyesight, hearing, etc., may result in faulty interception of impressions. Pain, emotion, severe discomfort, exhaustion, etc., may distract the individual so that he becomes preoccupied and inattentive to ordinary impressions received through the eyes, ears, and other senses. Mental impairment may cause the senses to function abnormally and produce delusions or hallucinations.[38]

With regard to physical injury, Royal and Schutt state:

> Individuals who have suffered a *head injury* or have been temporarily knocked unconscious may not be able to remember what occurred only a few minutes or hours prior to the injury.[38]

The Cognitive Interview vs. the Standard Police Interview

For many years the police officer's method of eliciting information from victims or witnesses has usually involved a straightforward question-and-answer approach known as the **standard police interview**. Unfortunately, some have confused *interviewing* with *interrogation* and used an overly forceful attitude even with cooperative witnesses. Today we know that there are far more appropriate and successful methods for retrieval of information. For the forensic artist attempting to produce a facial image, a working knowledge of the **cognitive interview** is strongly advised. While the method of interviewing for developing composite images may not be done *exactly* as outlined in the cognitive interview approach, the general principles will prove very beneficial.

The Standard Police Interview: "Just the facts, ma'am"

The traditional method for gaining information used by police is commonly referred to as the standard police interview. **In the standard police interview there is a question-and-answer approach, seeking primarily the "who, what, when, where, why, and how."** The interviewer develops a rhythym that makes the interviewee feel that his role is strictly to respond to the questions asked, no more, no less. Unfortunately, this may make the person interviewed feel intimidated or reluctant to offer small details from his or her recollection, because the interviewee feels those details are of no importance. As a result, pertinent specifics potentially valuable to an investigation may be overlooked and not recovered, with the interviewer gaining only superficial information.

The Cognitive Interview

During the 1980s, cognitive psychologists Dr. R. Edward Geiselman and Dr. Ronald P. Fisher accomplished ground-breaking work in the area of investigative interviewing. Geiselman notes:

> There are thousands of studies on witness testimony, most of them negative, dealing with the variety of ways witnesses can be inaccurate. … It's easy to do experiments showing the many things that can throw off a witness. Finding ways to improve the accuracy of what people remember is more difficult.[4]

Geiselman and Fisher should be commended for their contribution to practical interviewing for information retrieval in real law enforcement situations. Funded by a National Institute of Justice grant, Geiselman and Fisher devised interview methods to enhance the completeness and accuracy of eyewitness reports. Laboratory and field experiments using real crime victims and witnesses were conducted in the U.S., England, Canada, and Germany. Experiments showed the cognitive interview elicited 30 to 70% more information than the conventional police interview.

Cognitive interview procedures are easy to learn and can be readily adopted for use in routine police interview procedures or as part of the composite-specific interview process for forensic artists.

As interviewers, we must realize that the memories witnesses store in their minds will not be perfect. **There is no such thing as a photograph in your mind.** Even in an ideal situation, it may be difficult to remember correctly. Even cooperative witnesses have limitations of memory and perception, but we do not want to compound these problems by not eliciting the information correctly. Ideally, we develop a procedure for interviewing that includes specific steps and techniques and we practice this procedure to gain expertise in its use.

In "Interviewing Victims and Witnesses of Crime," Geiselman and Fisher state:

> The theoretical underpinnings of the research are based on two generally accepted principles of memory. First, a memory is composed of a collection of several elements. The more elements a memory retrieval aid has in common with the memory of the event, the more effective the aid is. Second, a memory has several access routes, so information that is not accessible with one retrieval cue may be accessible with a different cue.[39]

The cognitive interview approach is based on principles of how the mind works, our memory and cognition/perception, as well as the social dynamics of how people communicate. The following description was compiled from information from journal articles, personal communication with Dr. Ron Fisher, and the text *Memory-Enhancing Techniques for Investigative Interviewing* by Fisher and Geiselman.[40] Anyone who conducts interviews with cooperating victims and witnesses should use this book as a foundation for interviewing procedures. All of the procedures described in this section are attributable to Dr. Fisher and Dr. Geiselman.

Primary Techniques of the Cognitive Interview

Social Dynamics of the Interview

1. **Develop rapport and personalize the interview.**
   Don't underestimate the value of this step, since it is an important investment in a better overall interview.
   - **Treat the witness as an individual** and try to relate to the witness and his or her situation.
   - **Allow the witness to talk about his or her feelings** and validate them.

2. Encourage the witness to be an active participant in the interview.
   The witness is the primary *source* of the information that the interviewer seeks. Establish appropriate expectations that the witness will *provide* the information if possible, without placing the witness under undue stress.
   - **Make an explicit statement that you *want* the witness to participate.** You will find that the witness provides more detailed responses, and you will obtain much more unsolicited information. The witness will probably reveal the information in his or her order of importance. Let the witness know that no detail is unimportant to you.
   - **Make the witness feel "in charge."** This encourages active participation in the interview and helps start the recovery process for victims of trauma.

3. **Guide the witness to the crime-relevant information.**
The witness possesses the needed information, but the interviewer knows which aspects of the information are most relevant to the investigation.

4. **Promote extensive and detailed responses.**
   - **Ask mainly open-ended questions.**   This encourages lengthy, detailed responses. The questions should be framed but open-ended in nature. For example, "Can you tell me about the face?" The interviewer should direct the witness to the needed information without dominating the interview. If needed, more specific questions can follow strategically to complete responses first given to the more open-ended questions.
   - **Don't interrupt.**   An interruption may indicate that you expect only a brief response.
   - **Allow for long silences.**   When the witness stops speaking and you don't interrupt the silence, the witness will go back and search his memory for additional information. Encourage the witness with nods or brief comments, if necessary.

5. **Allow non-verbal responses.**
Allow a witness who has difficulty giving verbal responses or who has vocabulary limitations to use nonverbal methods of expression. For example, a witness may wish to get up and move around or draw a picture to demonstrate a descriptive point.

Memory and Cognition

1. **Recreate the original context of the event.**
Context includes environment, thoughts, feelings, perceptions, and emotions. Consider external conditions such as lighting, physiological conditions, cognitive context, and emotional context, all of which facilitate the recovery of an event.
   - **Ask the witness to act out the event or just think about it.**   Using the various sensory modes encourages a strongly refreshed recollection, since memories and mental images are usually multi-modal. Tests show that odor is a particularly potent sense for reinstating context, and it is uniquely associated with emotion.
   - **What about an overly aroused/distressed witness?**   *Always give the witness the choice whether to attempt context reinstatement.* Suggest psychological ways to deal with hyperarousal, such as use of a third-person viewpoint or viewing the event on a mental videotape that the witness can stop at will. Tell the witness he or she may call "time out" whenever he or she chooses. Reassure the witness that he or she is safe and in control.

Note: Reinstatement of the context of an event may prove very successful with witnesses who were not physically threatened or harmed during an event. Extreme care should be taken, however, in using this method with victims who were physically threatened or injured. **This method should be avoided in cases of victims of highly traumatic events.** Although psychologists believe that mentally and emotionally "facing" an event are the first steps toward gaining mastery over it, this method clearly is not appropriate for some situations. **For**

the forensic artist, the process of creating a facial sketch *necessitates* reinstatement of the event to a certain extent. Realistically, this is simply unavoidable. The face *must* be remembered and the event *is* associated with the face in memory. For legal purposes, it is necessary to establish that the face being drawn is, in fact, the face of the perpetrator of the crime, so the incident must be discussed at some level.

2. **Encourage partial information.**
   Since memories of events are complex and contain multiple elements, a witness may recall only a portion of the information. By encouraging the witness to convey the bits that are recalled, more information may be obtained. For example, a name was spoken during the crime but the witness cannot remember it. Mentally reciting the alphabet may help the witness recall the first letter of the name or the number of syllables.

3. **Use varied retrieval approaches.**
   There may be several paths to a stored bit of information. It may be helpful to encourage witnesses to think of the event in terms of different dimensions, e.g., color, sound, apparel, voice, etc.
   • **Conduct second interviews if necessary.**   Studies indicate that in some cases you may be more likely to obtain additional information from successive interviews.

4. **Keep in mind that people have limited mental resources.**
   Reduce distractions such as extraneous noises or interruptions, if possible.
   • **Fatigue may affect mental resources.**   The witness may need to take a break and continue the interview later.
   • **Direct eye contact breaks concentration.**   Obviously, you look at and speak directly with the witness in the rapport-building stage, but as the witness attempts to concentrate, you should avoid direct eye contact. Some witnesses close their eyes to block out external stimuli and facilitate concentration. Since this requires trust, you should encourage them to close their eyes if they wish to, closing *your* eyes at the same time.

5. **Use guided imagery.**
   • **Use varied sensory properties — visual, tactile, auditory, and olfactory.**   The interviewer can then make use of guided imagery to elicit more specific, less global descriptions of details. For example, a description of "ugly" is a generalized interpretive statement. You may obtain more specific descriptors such as "rough skin" or "bad breath and yellow teeth" if you encourage the witness to concentrate on other sensory systems to guide his or her search of memory. Remember that people are naturally suggestible after trauma. Take care to avoid suggesting specifics.

6. **Use witness-compatible questioning.**
   Because each witness has a unique mental representation of an event, the interviewer should tailor the questions to the particular mental representation of the person being interviewed. For example, if a witness reports seeing a subject from the profile view only, the questions should be geared toward that orientation.

Review of the Stages of the Cognitive Interview

Introduction and Rapport-Building Stage — This stage establishes the essential interpersonal dynamics necessary to promote memory retrieval and good communication throughout the remainder of the interview.

Beginning of an Open-Ended Narrative — This stage is necessary for determination of the witness' mental representation of the crime and how the mental files are organized. The interviewer then can develop an effective strategy for probing the witness' knowledge.

Probing Stage — This is the primary information-gathering stage when the interviewer guides the witness to the stored mental files and attempts to exhaust their contents.

Review Stage — The interviewer reviews the information obtained from the witness to ensure its accuracy, providing the witness the opportunity to recall additional information.

Close of the Interview — The interviewer closes the interview and tells the witness to contact the interviewer in the future if he or she recalls any additional facts.

Cognitive interviewing provides members of law enforcement and others who require effective, detailed information-gathering procedures with a systematic approach to increase the information elicited. Based on known principles of memory and communication, this method works hand in hand with the ways the mind processes information.

The cognitive interviewing approach is also a more victim-sensitive approach for law enforcement personnel to use. Victims/witnesses are allowed to be "fully heard" rather than subjected to the frustrations of the standard police interview.

The police composite artist can gain a great deal from utilizing the basic tenets of cognitive interviewing. Certain adjustments must be made to do a **composite-specific interview**.

The Composite-Specific Interview

Knowledge of the functions of memory and trauma and an understanding of cognitive interviewing techniques form a solid foundation for the composite-specific interview. The interview process is rather personal and each interviewer tends to develop a "style" that is his or her own, just as artists develop personal styles of drawing, painting, or sculpting. Because the production of composite images is done within the context of law enforcement, efforts should be made to standardize procedures within loosely structured guidelines. This promotes professionalism and helps ensure that composite images will be acceptable as evidence for use in the prosecutorial process in court.

The method recommended here has evolved over time. It represents a compilation of the thoughts, methods, and proven experience of the most respected and successful police sketch artists in the world. The outlined composite-specific process also encourages the thoughtful and studied use of applicable research by psychology specialists pertaining to cognition, perception, memory retrieval, eyewitness identification, and the victims' issues. This method is not known to cause harm to traumatized victims or witnesses; it has gone unchallenged in the courts of law.

Pre-Interview

Chapter 6 outlines the circumstances for drawing a composite image, and includes a discussion of issues that should be reviewed with the requesting officer *before* the actual interview. Chapter 6 also addresses **practical considerations** such as location and choice of time of day for the interview. Before the interview, there should be an understanding of situational factors such as duration of view, point of view and distance, lighting conditions, and time since the event. The artist should have an overview knowledge of the crime itself and general information about the victim, particularly physical and psychological conditions. Other **victim/emotional considerations** are discussed in Chapter 6.

Obviously, the **artist should *not* view or be shown any photographs of possible suspects before conducting the interview.** The artist may be given a copy of the victim's statement that includes certain descriptive information about the perpetrator.

Clearly, as a matter of practicality, officers must obtain prompt descriptions for quick distribution in an attempt to locate the suspect. Sometimes, however, descriptions obtained from witnesses immediately following an incident are flawed. This may be due to the physical or emotional condition of the witness or to the lack of experience of a first-responding officer at obtaining descriptive information. Discrepancy between the initial description and the version given to the composite artist sometimes occurs.

The composite drawing should incorporate descriptive information gained directly from the witness at the time of the composite interview, particularly if there is a slight deviation from the verbal description immediately following the event. This is further basis for allowing a victim a reasonable amount of time to "regroup" and rest before conducting the composite interview.

Recent research indicates that **sleep** may play an important role in the traumatized witness' ability to provide accurate information following an event. In their paper, "Critical Incident Amnesia: The Psychological Basis and the Implications of Memory Loss During Extreme Survival Stress Situations," Lt. Col. Dave Grossman and Bruce K. Siddle maintain:

> … it can be observed that immediately after experiencing a critical incident, individuals have not had an opportunity to mentally process and refine what they have experienced. But after a night's sleep there should be significant memory recovery. If an individual has been kept isolated from other sources of information, the memories at this point (approximately 24 hours after the incident) should be the most "pure" since they have not yet integrated data from other sources.[41]

Introduction/Rapport-Building Stage

Some officers choose to accompany the victim/witness to the composite interview; others direct the witness to the artist's office or other setting, allowing the witness to go alone or with a friend or family member. The artist should greet the witness and those who accompany the witness in a warm and courteous manner. **The significance of the initial greeting and rapport-building portion of the interview should not be underestimated because it sets the tone for the entire process.**

Hopefully, a comfortable and reassuring environment for interviewing is available to you. Dingy, cramped quarters are unfavorable for memory enhancement while cheerful lighting and plants may help create a pleasant setting, encouraging relaxation and recall. The goal should be to make the witness feel physically comfortable and emotionally safe.

Walls in the interview room should be free of facial images in the form of photographs or wanted posters, which may influence or confuse the witness.

A somewhat routine, yet flexible structure should be developed for handling this stage of the interview. Certain "business" matters must be addressed, for the benefit of the witness, the family members, and even the officer.

The interviewer's primary focus at this stage is to be pleasant, encouraging, and nonthreatening. The interviewer's clothing and demeanor should be relaxed but professional. **Wearing of police uniforms is not recommended, since this automatically establishes an attitude of authority rather than friendliness.**

Some artists are sworn police officers; others are civilian employees. If the person to be interviewed clearly appears uncomfortable dealing with the police, it may prove advantageous for the artist to emphasize he or she is "just an artist," not a police officer.

Dispel fears, anxieties, and potential psychological blockages.

Act immediately against the natural fears that any witness or victim has upon arrival. Standard reassurances should include:

- **"This is *not* a test."**   Convey to the witness in the presence of family members and officers that the composite process is not a test that he or she will pass or fail. **Explain that you will work *together* to see what you can come up with and that no one expects miracles.** Immediately begin to take the pressure onto *yourself* and away from the witness.
  On occasion, inexperienced officers, under pressure in high profile investigations, state emphatically to a witness: "You're all we've got. You've got to produce a good drawing." This unfortunate blunder sometimes results in a witness who is so stressed that he or she is unable to remember anything by the time of the interview. Officers should seek instead to converse about other topics and allow the witness to arrive without the undue stress that such conversations cause.
- **"Composites are *not* portraits."**   Explain that while the goal is to achieve an accurate likeness of the offender, the witness should not be disappointed if a portrait-standard likeness is not achieved. Composites are investigative tools, not meant to be exact photographic likenesses, despite what the witness might have seen on television or in the movies. Convey that you may ask questions for which the witness has no answers and that is all right. You are simply trying to trigger the witness' thoughts with the questions.
- **"Brief flashes of the face in memory are normal."**   Explain that the witness should not expect to have a constant, clear, or still "snapshot" of the subject's face in his or her mind's eye. The image will likely be more brief, pulsating, and flickering.

- **"Composites do *not* get innocent people in trouble."** A surprising number of witnesses are concerned that their inability to produce an accurate enough composite image will result in the arrest of an innocent person.
- **"We only need to discuss the facial description, *not* all of the details of what happened."** By the time the witness arrives to work with the artist, the witness may be quite weary of the retelling of the events surrounding the crime. It is extremely comforting, particularly to victims of sexual assault, to know that they will not be required to again endure another recitation of the events. Often you see them sigh and visibly relax after making this simple statement.

Discuss the small comforts that may be very important to the witness.

Handling the most fundamental human comforts will go a long way toward relaxation of the witness and the person who accompanied the witness to the interview. It may also increase their concentration on the task at hand.

- **Explain the smoking policy.** For smokers under stress, the reassurance that they will be allowed to take breaks and smoke will be a great comfort.
- **Give the location of the restrooms and refreshment areas.** The witness will be reassured and know that the friend or family member is comfortable.
- **Offer coffee, sodas, gum, or candy.** These small creature comforts may mean a lot at times of stress. Candy jars with free access in the office are usually very popular with nervous witnesses or their friends/relatives.
- **Mention use of the telephone.** Inform the witness and anyone who accompanies the witness about the availability of telephones during the interview. This small reassurance may help avoid interruptions and maintain focus during the interview.
- **Check physical comforts, particularly room temperature.** As discussed in Chapter 6, traumatized people often are cold, although some people under stress become hot. Attend to such needs as much as is reasonably practical.
- **"Fidget toys" may be helpful.** For years, I have found it beneficial to have various items for handling and fidgeting within easy reach of those being interviewed. These items may have the calming effect of maintaining the reality of the present while discussing a traumatic past event. Such items might include any small hand-held toys designed to occupy the hands.

Let the witness know he or she can request a break if needed.

Such information will also help calm family members present who may be concerned that their loved one will be overly taxed by the upcoming interview.

Explain briefly the composite drawing process you will use.

At this stage, you may wish to show the parties examples of successful composites you prepared previously. This instills confidence in the technique and encourages the witness to try the process. You should attempt to give everyone an approximate idea of the duration of the interview. Officers and family or friends may opt to leave at this point and return at a later time.

This is a good point at which to allow the witness to visit the restroom and get something to drink in preparation for a focused interview.

Initial Drawing Stage

Get the witness alone if at all possible.

At this juncture you should shift to a private interview area with the witness or tactfully indicate that it is time for everyone but the interviewee to leave.

There are rare exceptions when a supportive person is allowed to remain during the interview. Traumatized or emotionally upset victims may need friends, relatives, or victim services personnel with them. In such cases, care should be taken not to allow any disruptions or interference to occur as a result of their presence.

A side-by-side interview position is suggested so that the witness does not directly face the interviewer (see Chapter 6, Figure 6.10). By facing the interviewer, or any photographs or other drawings, the witness may inadvertently include features of that face in his or her description.

Do an initial "run-through" to gain the facial description.

During this portion of the composite-specific interview, the witness should be prompted to begin a "free recall" or "free narrative" of the physical and facial descriptions. Remember that the witness has been told it is not necessary to describe specifics of the event itself, although many details will likely be included. This format parallels the cognitive interview and should include open-ended, yet structured, questions. **The interviewer should listen extremely carefully at this stage, to assess what aspects of the description are most emphasized by the witness.**

As previously suggested, it may be beneficial to look away or down at a notepad to avoid eye contact with the witness. The witness is at a point of highly intense recollection and requires optimum mental focus and concentration.

Excessive note-taking may be a distraction to the witness, but you may jot down brief notes occasionally if required. Some law enforcement entities require detailed reporting procedures following such interviews, while others use only synopses (see Chapter 18).

Guide the witness with statements such as "Tell me about his face." Avoid interrupting the witness. Allow for long silences. Prompt the witness as needed with more focused questions, as if continuing the open-ended narrative stage of the cognitive interview.

Block out the proportions and establish the basic facial character.

During the initial stages of establishing the face, it is very important that the witness does not constantly stare at the image in progress. Introduction of this new face into the mind may create confusion.

As the artist begins to draw the face based on the information obtained by free recall of the witness, it is recommended that the sketching be done while turned slightly away from the witness' view. In this way, the artist can block out the proportions of the face and begin to establish the basic facial character before the witness looks at the image.

Some slightly more specific questions will need to be asked at this stage such as: "What was the widest area of the face: the forehead, the cheekbones or the jaw?" **Especially important at this point is the establishment of the proportional arrangement of the features, determining the spacing between the features themselves.** The artist may use his hands to describe "eyes that are wide apart vs. eyes that are close together." Similarly, the thumb and forefinger, held up to the artist's own face, may be useful to elicit information about the distance from the bottom of the nose to the mouth.

Have the witness look at the initial drawing.

Once the face has coalesced somewhat and the proportions are established, the witness should be briefly shown the drawing and allowed to give first impressions. Before showing the drawing to the witness, advise the witness that the first version of the drawing might not be very close to what the witness saw. This may combat any sense of discouragement that the witness might feel. It is important for the witness to know that this early generalization is a normal part of the process.

Then, again turning away from the witness, the artist should begin adjustments based on the first impressions of the witness. At this stage, the witness likely will feel some frustration, yet begin to show interest in resolving the incorrect aspects of the drawing. This initial process of briefly showing the drawing, getting input, then turning away to make changes may be repeated several times.

Fine-Tuning Drawing Stage

Use multiple-choice questions to fine tune.

The witness continues to explain the needed changes. A transitional type of question (not too open, not too specific) might come next, such as, "Tell me more about the tip of the nose." The artist should then be more specific with the framing of questions, using a multiple-choice style rather than totally open-ended questions as done earlier. For example, "Does the nose need to be flatter, fuller, more pointed, or more bulbous?" This stage of the interview begins to parallel the probing stage of the cognitive interview.

Selectively introduce photographic references.

What happens during the composite preparation process is a unique cognitive process. **The witness must transform a visual experience into a verbal description for the artist, who in turn translates the verbal information back into visual terms. It makes sense that the use of the visual mechanism of photo references might serve to make the process more straightforward and direct.** Thus, the process of mental conversion from one "format" to another may be made less difficult for the witness.

Siegfried Sporer's descriptions of this process underscore the **value of using whole or complete faces as references rather than isolated features as in most hand-assembled or computer systems.**

For effective communication between the original perceiver (the witness) and the recognition of the target by another person (the successful identification of the criminal by the police) to take place, the demarcation between the visual and verbal mode has to be transgressed twice: first, to transform a visual impression of the criminal into a description. One of the problems encountered here is that faces are best encoded holistically (viz. as a "gestalt"), whereas a verbal description requires a piecemeal approach in labeling individual features. To the extent that the visual, holistic processing is disturbed, memory for a face is likely to suffer.[31]

A 1990 study by Dr. Graham Davies and Melissa Little in England, documented in "Drawing on memory: exploring the expertise of a police artist," makes a very similar observation. Davies and Little address a 1986 study by Laughery and their own findings and conclude:

> … the inflexibilities of the composite (kit) system which permit the witness to provide information only on feature detail rather than on the relationship between features: the parts rather than the whole. Support for this view comes from a subsequent study by Laughery who examined in detail the differing strategies employed by witness subjects when working on the two rival methods of face reconstruction (hand-drawn vs. kit-generated composites). Witnesses working with a sketch artist were led more frequently to a strategy of progressive refinement whereby witnesses worked on groups of features. The Identi-KIT on the other hand encouraged a feature-by-feature approach where single features were selected in turn and little effort was extended in reconsideration of the overall integration of the examples selected. **Techniques of face recall based on progressive refinement in turn produced more successful likenesses than did attempts at a feature-by-feature approach.**[42]

In another study that supports the use of reference photographs in general, Shepherd of the University of Aberdeen and Ellis of the University of Wales state: "The task of face recall is generally much more difficult than that of recognizing faces …"[43]
Virtually all practicing composite artists in the law enforcement environment agree that photographic references may be beneficial for augmenting and clarifying a facial composite image. They do not necessarily agree concerning the stage at which such reference photos are introduced. **The psychological literature seems to indicate that a facial image should first be established without the use of reference photographs, based on the holistic imagery of the face as described by the witness. References may later be used to fine-tune the initial facial impression.**
Showing of facial reference photographs prior to the composite interview or in the early stages of the interview risks cluttering the mental imagery of the witness. The artist should instead follow the general guidelines of the cognitive interview to first establish the primary descriptive information purely from the witness' memory.
By this point most witnesses are more than ready to view references because they wish to more clearly convey to the artist what words alone may fail to do. Some artists choose to use only the *FBI Facial Identification Catalog* for this purpose. Others use the catalog first, then progress to mug shots or other photo references for even more specificity. (For a discussion of types of photographs used in reference files see Chapter 6.)

In either case, **the reference photographs should be introduced judiciously, taking care to direct the witness only to those photos needed to determine the specific feature desired.**

Some witnesses promptly find photos that help in clarifying the information to the artist. Others want to see more and more photos. **The artist should control the viewing of photos and maintain focus on the mental image rather than on any newly introduced images.**

On very rare occasions, a witness may become confused when shown photo references. It is then advisable to remove the references and work strictly with the witness' ability to recall rather than to recognize.

Finishing Touches

Review the individual components of the face.

It is now helpful to "take it from the top" and fully review the composite facial image, point by point, giving the witness full opportunity to make corrections, even at this more advanced stage. **It is a mistake for the artist ever to make the witness feel that it is "too late" to make changes because the drawing is "too finished."** It is a very foolish artist who moans about suggested changes to the drawing, since these last changes often make important "finishing touch" improvements. This stage is roughly equivalent to the review stage of the cognitive interview.

This review stage is also a critical time for the artist to mentally compare and "double-check" that the features or aspects of the face emphasized by the witness at the beginning of the interview correspond with the face at this stage. If they do not, there may be a problem. Either the witness has been allowed to be overly influenced by the references or there may be fabrication.

There are times when a witness struggles to determine a certain "something" that is missing from the drawing. It may be useful to totally remove the drawing from the witness' view. Engage the witness in a conversation totally unrelated to the task at hand, preferably about a topic of interest and comfort. After a few minutes have elapsed and the witness is comletely distracted, reintroduce the drawing and ask about the aspect of frustration or difficulty. **This method of mental diversity frequently results in an improved recall** of the troublesome feature or characteristic.

A specific discussion of the facial expression may also be beneficial in the latter stages of the drawing. At times, the certain "something" that is missing might be an expression.

Experience teaches the ability to distinguish between a witness whose memory is exhausted and one who still has usable information to offer. If overly fatigued and frustrated, a witness may, in fact, become increasingly insecure about the image. This can result in making changes for the worse in the finishing stages. **This is more likely to happen if the witness has viewed the drawing too much or has been exposed to too many photo references.**

The witness should not be allowed to guess. With a witness who is highly motivated to assist the police, the fine line between valid retrieval and unconscious fabrication may be easily crossed. Over time, the experienced artist gains an intuitive sense of when to bring the interview to a close, even if the witness does not realize that he has done all that is possible for him to do.

Reinstate the context of the event if appropriate.

Method of Context Reinstatement with the Composite — For some witnesses, it may be appropriate and beneficial to use the cognitive interview technique of context reinstatement as a means of adding any final details that may have been missed. **You should always explain the process and give the witness the option of choosing not to attempt it.** You should advise the witness that this may be an uncomfortable or frightening experience, although the additional information retrieved may make it worthwhile.

If the witness chooses to do the context reinstatement, you should explain the entire process to the witness in detail before proceeding. Encourage the witness to select the best "viewing" of the face in his or her memory, preferably at a "safe" time for the witness. The positioning of the face at the time of the viewing, in relation to the witness, should be determined (distance, angle, lighting, etc.) and explained to the artist. Then, the witness should be told to be prepared to think about what he was feeling, thinking, hearing, smelling, etc. at the time of best viewing the face.

The witness should always be reassured and reminded that he or she is now in a safe situation. When ready to proceed, the witness should close his eyes, "back up" in his mind, and begin to mentally replay the images at his own pace leading up to the viewing. The artist should be prepared to hold the drawing in the same position as the original viewing allowing the witness to decide when to open his eyes and "flash" on the composite image. Almost without fail, this method produces new or clearer information, often information the witness has been struggling to retrieve but has been previously unable to do.

Expert Opinions on Benefits of "Facing" the Event — Numerous researchers dealing with the detrimental effects of trauma have addressed the benefits of directly recalling the disturbing event. Many indicate that the event *must* be faced in order to gain control over the memory and integrate it into a functionally controllable place in the mind. The consensus is that symptoms of trauma will begin to be diminished once the victim does this.

Dr. George Everly, Jr., a leading authority on human stress and psychological trauma, has made several observations relevant to the potential positive effects of psychologically revisiting a traumatic event. **One could conclude that the recollection of the offender's face to prepare a composite image is a direct form of "facing" the event.** In discussing Posttraumatic Stress Disorder (PTSD), he indicates:

> Perhaps the most powerful therapeutic assault on PTSD resides in some form of "neurocognitive therapy." "Neurocognitive therapy" is defined as an integrated, coordinated psychotherapeutic effort directed at the psychophysiological arousal (neuro-) and the ruminative recollective cognitions (cognitive) virtually simultaneously. Such an effort reflects an appreciation of the inextricable intertwinings of mind and body, and of the duality of dysfunction intrinsic to PTSD.[44]

Or, more simply put, there may be powerful therapeutic benefit from simultaneously recollecting a trauma and its surrounding aspects, such as the memory of the subject's face.

In his paper, "The Effects of Traumatic Disclosure on Physical and Mental Health: The Values of Writing and Talking about Upsetting Events," James W. Pennebaker expresses similar views:

> ... my research program on disclosure began by noting that people who had faced early traumatic experiences and who had not talked about them were much more likely to have a variety of health problems compared to people who had had comparable traumas but who had shared them with others ... Holding back or inhibiting oneself about an important topic is a stressor ... if we can get people to talk about upsetting experiences, the adverse effects of inhibition can be counteracted.[45]

In another study of PTSD in Vietnam veterans, Keane, Fairbank, Caddell, Zimering, and Bender state:

> Perhaps the hallmark symptom of PTSD is the reliving or recollection of the traumatic event in the form of intrusive thoughts or nightmares... Extinction would occur, we believe, when there is exposure to all elements of the memory, so that those components of the memory that are extinguished are not reconditioned by the unexposed components of the traumatic memory. Exposure to the entire memory of the trauma would in fact promote extinction and foster adaptive recovery from the trauma.[46]

The "Victims of Violence" chapter by Ronnie Janoff-Bulman in *Psychotraumatology* presents parallel concepts:

> Coping with violent victimization involves coming to terms with the cognitive disorganization precipitated by the experience ... information from and reactions to the traumatic experience are stored in active memory and account for the intrusive thoughts experienced by victims. These intrusions cease when the information has been integrated and thereby is no longer stored in active memory.[47]

Simply put, these prominent psychological researchers seem to agree that confronting the traumatic event, i.e., preparation of a composite drawing and possibly reinstating the context of the event, may be beneficial to the crime victim. Several point out, too, that while therapy may well be advised, discussions with laypersons, such as the composite artist, may also achieve the desired positive effects.

If context reinstatement is not done, it is often a good idea to take a short break before concluding the interview. This gives the witness time to mentally relax from the stressful process and then take one last look at the drawing before proclaiming it finished.

Sign and/or stamp for identification purposes.

Because the composite image is an item of evidence, it should be marked in such a way that the artist can clearly identify his or her work product if needed at a later date (see Chapter 6).

Spray with a fixative.

Many artists choose to spray their finished drawings with a fixative product to help preserve the image as an item of evidence (see Chapter 6).

Concluding the Interview

As described in the cognitive interview section, it is wise to conclude the interview by suggesting that the witness feel free to re-contact the artist or officer if the witness recalls additional information.

If the witness has expressed anxiety regarding aspects of the investigation, these items should be addressed with the investigating officer near the completion of the interview. **Often witnesses are anxious about the handling of the release of the composite image in the news media.** It is reasonable that the officer give the witness some idea of plans for media distribution, since the witness will likely feel particularly vulnerable and frightened during that time.

The artist should thank the witness for his or her efforts and cooperation and courteously show the witness to the exit to formally conclude the interview.

Multiple Witness Interviews

In rare cases multiple witnesses may be interviewed together to produce one composite drawing (see Figures 6.6 and 6.7 in Chapter 6). In my opinion, use of multiple witnesses is a procedure that should be discussed with a district attorney, if at all possible, before implementing. **Although legal precedent exists for the acceptance of composite drawings produced in this manner in court, the practice should be carefully considered.**

In his paper, "Forensic Art: Concepts and Approaches in Composite Interviewing," Frank Domingo discusses the process of determining whether to do a multiple witness composite interview:

> There is one very important and crucial question the artist, investigator and supervisor (in charge of the investigation) must ask when dealing with a multiple witness situation: should the artist make one or several composite drawings of the perpetrator? If the artist, investigator and/or supervisor decide to make several composites with the multiple witnesses more questions arise that will have to be answered:
>
> 1. If one composite drawing is produced for each witness, which composite or witness will be the most accurate?
> 2. Of all the drawings produced, with multiple witnesses, how will the investigator determine which one to use?
> 3. If several composites are used during the course of the investigation will the result be confusion?
> 4. If weak sketches are produced, might they be used to discredit the witnesses in the future?

An alternative to making multiple drawings with multiple witnesses is to make one drawing with multiple witnesses. An interview handled properly may result in one strong composite rather than several weak drawings.[48]

Pre-Interview Assessment

Of primary importance to multiple witness interviews is a good pre-interview assessment. First determine that the circumstances indicate that each witness did, in fact, view the same person. Each witness should give descriptions of the perpetrator that are reasonably consistent with the descriptions of the other witnesses. If these conditions are not met, a multiple witness interview is not appropriate.

The pre-interview assessment may be in the form of interviews conducted by the investigating officer or the artist or both prior to the actual composite-specific interview. If possible, the artist should review any statements obtained from persons under consideration for a multiple witness interview. **It may be important to later distinguish descriptions given by each witness singly from a jointly agreed-upon composite.**

A case example of the beneficial use of multiple witnesses occurred a few years ago in a jewelry store robbery. I reviewed the witness statements with the officer before the composite-specific interview and found that neither of the two witnesses had a complete description of the robber's face. The perpetrator walked past an unseen witness (a passive witness) in a car parked in front of the business. She viewed the perpetrator from a distance of several yards. His face and hair were uncovered. He caught her attention when he took a ski mask from his pocket and pulled it over his head as he entered jewelry store. The second witness (an active witness), an employee of the jewelry store who was threatened with a weapon, observed the robber at a close distance, but the robber wore a mask. The holes in the mask were large enough for her to see specific aspects of his facial features.

Because both witnesses described the same clothing, interviewing them jointly seemed warranted. By interviewing the two witnesses together, I produced a successful composite drawing. Neither witness alone saw enough to provide sufficient information for me to produce a successful composite drawing.

Procedural Considerations

Once statements and descriptions have been assessed for similarity, legal advisors have been consulted, and a decision has been made to interview one or more witnesses together, the artist must carefully control the interview situation. **One witness must not be allowed to dominate the others. Note that we have previously discussed the potential lack of correlation between *confidence* of description and *accuracy* of description.**

Often, a natural dominance occurs because of situational factors. An example would be a bank robbery in which one witness employee supervises the other witness employee. I find it beneficial to make certain statements during the early rapport-building stages of the interview. I explain that perceptions may vary slightly due to lighting or vantage point. I make a point of stating that each person's description is important to me and I want to hear what every witness saw.

Although each person's descriptive information should be considered, the artist may find that there is a natural tendency to rely on one witness more than another for certain aspects of the description. This may be due to age, ancestry, sex, or profession of the witnesses. Men may describe vehicles better than women, women or teenagers may describe clothing better than other witnesses, and individuals of the same race as the perpetrator may better describe the face. Individuals of a given profession may be trained in observation of details pertinent to their profession. A dental hygienist, for example, will notice teeth. Each witness must be assessed as an individual. A child who says, "He was really old," may mean 20 years old, while a senior citizen who says, "He was just a kid," may mean 50 years old. The same holds true for descriptions of weight, skin color, and the like. Each description should be considered relative to the person making the description. This phenomenon is discussed in Chapter 6.

I have been asked to interview witnesses together when the witnesses actually saw a perpetrator on different days during the commission of different offenses. In these cases the officer believed the offender was the same based on similarities in modus operandi, clothing worn, and so forth. In such cases, I declined to do a multiple witness interview because the process would be potentially questionable in court. **Although only an investigative tool, the composite drawing should always be prepared in such a way that the procedure used can be readily explained in court, demonstrating a "good faith" effort to be fair and objective.**

In cases of serial offenses, numerous composites released to the public may indeed become confusing. If various victims are interviewed and composites produced, it is perhaps advisable that the officer and the artist consult on the quality of the drawings. In some cases, a decision may be made to release only one of several drawings.

Alternatively, I know of instances in which artists have prepared several drawings from different witnesses and then combined them into an altogether new drawing. I have done this only once, when I combined two of my own drawings with a drawing by another artist and merged them in equal parts using computer software. In this case, the decision was made to retain the "composite composite" for investigative use only, with no public release (Figure 5.8). **If such a practice is undertaken, the district attorney should be consulted before any media release of such a composite.**

Legally speaking, composite images prepared by using multiple witnesses, interviewed together, have been accepted into evidence in U.S. courts. In the 1986 case of *Larry Arnold Wilson, Appellant v. The State of Texas*, the contention upon appeal was that because two witnesses collaborated to produce one composite (mechanically generated), their testimony had become tainted. The Court ruled:

> Admission of composite drawing depicting robber was proper, even though two witnesses reviewed composite together and came up with final edition, ... and ... We find no merit in the contention. The witnesses stated that the final drawing accurately depicted the person who robbed the Cutting Company except for the difference in the mustache.[49]

I believe that most psychologists would caution against multiple witness interviews, out of concern that one witness' recollections might interfere with or corrupt those of another. Yet, Siegfried Sporer discusses the empirical question of the potential for multiple descriptive inputs to be more accurate than individual descriptive input:

Figure 5.8 Three separate composite drawings, one by Sgt. Will Beechinor (above center) and two by KTT (above left and right), merged equally on computer to produce a single image (below). A district attorney should be consulted before media release of such a **"composite composite."** (Courtesy of Austin Police Department and Texas Department of Public Safety.)

Considering the errors in estimates of individual witnesses, the question arises whether or not descriptions obtained from multiple witnesses are superior to individual reports (see also Stephenson, 1984). An interesting prediction derived from the social psychological literature on group processes postulates that group performance in judgment tasks (of ill-defined stimuli) should be superior to individual judgments (Hofstaetter, 1971). This should hold for estimates of height, weight, age, distance, time, and speed.[31]

As with so many areas of the complex workings of the human brain, there are conflicts in research results and in expert opinions. In any case, **multiple witness interviews should be given careful consideration, and legal input should be sought. For me, the use of this method is a last resort, and reserved for cases in which a composite might not otherwise be possible.**

Child Interviews

One of the saddest duties of a police composite artist is to interview young children who are crime victims or witnesses. The voluminous psychological literature examines forensic interviewing and therapeutic interviewing, and aspects of both can provide important insights for the composite artist who interviews a child. This section offers only a brief overview of the subject.

Children are sometimes portrayed as unreliable witnesses who are susceptible to suggestive or misleading questions. In reality, **children often prove to be quite strong witnesses capable of accurately and completely recalling details and aiding with the preparation of composite drawings.** For this to occur, however, the artist must learn to be a child-sensitive interviewer, able to adapt interview methods to be compatible with each individual child.

General Guidelines for Supportive Interviewing of Children

From the onset of the interview, the artist/interviewer should be "nice" to the child, as in the rapport-building stage with adult witnesses. There is no shortcut to gaining a child's trust. You must allow time to establish a relationship. The child will immediately begin to assess whether or not he or she can "trust" you.

Greet the child by name and tell the child your name. Give a simple explanation of what your job is. Further general exchange with the child may include information about the child's age, school, pets, or favorite television programs.

Maintain a light-hearted atmosphere, not "pretend" or silly. **Do not act shocked by anything the child might disclose. The child should not be praised for giving information, because this can encourage fabrication of information just to please you.** It is better to praise the child for having courage or patience.

It may be beneficial to discuss something personal about yourself to help establish rapport. I usually discuss my two border collies and show photographs of the dogs at various ages.

As previously recommended with adult victims, it may also be very reassuring to the child to explain that the focus in the interview is on the face. Nothing else about what happened has to be discussed.

Also, as with adult interviews, the artist/interviewer should be prepared beforehand with case information, including the nature of the event, time since the event, distance of viewing, lighting conditions, and other pertinent situational factors.

The child should be clearly told that it is OK to say "I don't know"; otherwise, the child may make up an answer.

Try to assess the child's understanding of truth and reality. Useful questions for assessing veracity might be "Is this teddy bear a real bear?" or "You're 5, aren't you?" when you know the child is only 4. **Unless proven otherwise, you should *believe* the child.**

Developmental Stages as Related to Interviewing

A well-documented issue for those who conduct child interviews revolves around the assessment of the child's developmental level vs. the child's actual chronological age. **For purposes of communication with the child, the determination of the developmental level is far more important than the actual chronological age.** It is important to understand the levels of language, memory ability, cognitive and social skills, and emotional maturity.

Dr. Bruce Perry of Baylor College of Medicine, Department of Psychiatry and Behavioral Sciences in Houston, discusses age and developmental stage:

> One of the most important clinical considerations in working with traumatized children is recognizing that children of different ages think differently, act differently and have different emotional functioning. Children of different ages will experience a traumatic event in different ways.[50]

Some child development studies discuss age with regard to facial recognition. A 1994 National Institute of Standards and Technology report, entitled *Face Recognition Technology for Law Enforcement Applications*, refers to studies by S. Carey, R. Diamond, and B. Woods:

> It appears that children under ten years of age encode unfamiliar faces using isolated features. Recognition of these faces is done using cues derived from paraphernalia, such as clothes, glasses, hairstyle, hats, etc. Ten-year-old children exhibit this behavior less frequently, while children older than twelve years rarely exhibit this behavior. It is postulated that around age ten, children seem to change their recognition mechanisms from one of isolated features and paraphernalia to one of holistic analysis.[51]

Numerous researchers have attempted to define children's developmental capabilities by age groups in the belief that certain commonalities exist within age groups. A compilation of the information from various sources indicates the following *general characteristics* of each group.[52–54]

Under 2 Years

The expert consensus is that it is impossible to interview children under 2 years of age for investigative purposes because they are unable to talk or understand conceptually.

Preschool Age, 2–5 Years

- short attention span
- hardest to interview
- most easily led, wants to please
- needs to focus on an activity, such as drawing
- has limited verbal ability, so your language should be very simple and precise

5–11 Years

- longer attention span
- easiest to interview, lacks teenage hardness or sophistication
- less easily led, but still wants to please
- less need for activity, but still likes to draw
- more emotional than younger children
- beginning to understand time concepts accurately

12–17 Years

- interested in the consequences of talking about an event
- does not like pictures or games
- most able to lie convincingly
- setting of ground rules is very important

There are also indications that some differences exist between the two sexes in the interview setting. Boys are very uncomfortable with their status as victims. They are embarrassed about being unable to protect themselves. They need reassurance.

Under-educated, under-parented, or unattached teenagers may exhibit traits of the developmental levels of younger children.

The interviewer should attempt to determine the existence of any special conditions, such as Attention Deficit Disorder.

Language Adaptation

The interviewer must adjust his or her language to ensure effective communication with the child. Children are very literal, so you be specific. Sentences should be short and simple, with subject, verb, and object, and they must contain only one question or thought. Avoid complicated, multi-part questions or double negatives. Young children simply cannot understand or follow such language use. Pronouns should be clarified or omitted; for example, ask "Where was Uncle John?" or "Where was the bad man?" — not "Where was he?"

Certain techniques may encourage the child to disclose embarrassing or frightening information. Allow the child to whisper answers or cover his or her eyes when talking. Some children will talk while standing behind you rather than looking directly at you.

Procedural Considerations

Time Frame

Children are often at their best in the morning hours. Consider meal times, nap times, and other aspects of the child's routine schedule. Allow the child to visit the bathroom just before the interview session.

The Setting

The "setting" of the interview is extremely important with children so the interview location should be as "child friendly" as possible. Many police or community agencies have specially designed rooms for children. You may wish to use such a special child interviewing area, if available. Brightly colored surroundings and child-size furniture can help relax a child. The location should be safe and neutral and free from distractions, particularly facial photographs.

The interviewer should sit at eye level to the child, perhaps on the floor. There should be no barriers between the two of you. Speak softly, be gentle in speech and movement, and display a nonjudgmental attitude.

If at all possible, the parents should not be present. If this proves impossible, try to position a parent within the child's range of vision, but far enough away so the parent does not participate in the interview.

Toys — Toys such as crayons and markers and large paper pads should be available. As the interview progresses, the child should be encouraged to draw or color. Give guidance about what you wish the child to draw, such as "the man's clothes" or "the car." At some stage, give the child the freedom to draw other items pertaining to the investigation (see Figure 5.9).

Crayons may be particularly beneficial for establishing information such as eye color or vehicle color.

Any toy that is not a necessary part of the interview will only prove distracting.

Figure 5.9 Drawing done by a child, age 7, who accompanied his mother to a composite interview. Although present during the event, the child was previously discounted as a witness, because it was believed he had no information about the perpetrator. When allowed to draw, he produced information about the clothing and shoes the perpetrator wore. (Courtesy of Texas Department of Public Safety.)

Refreshments — If the interview is lengthy, it will be difficult to maintain the child's attention. While the artist works on the drawing, based on the child's initial description, it may be necessary and beneficial to give the child a break. Offer snacks and drinks brought by the parent or obtained at the interview site. After a break or snack, the child will probably be more attentive to reviewing the drawing and discussing adjustments needed.

Cognitive Interviewing of Children

In their experiments documented in the 1992 paper, "Effects of Cognitive Interviewing and Practice on Children's Recall Performance," Saywitz, Geiselman, and Bornstein gained positive results that indicated the value of the use of the cognitive approach with children as well as adults:

> The results showed that questioning techniques based on principles from cognitive psychology significantly increased the number of correct facts recalled by both 7 to 8 year olds and 10 to 11 year olds over that gained with standard interview procedures and without affecting the number of incorrect items generated.[55]

Concluding the Interview

At the conclusion of the interview, thank and praise the child for participation in the interview, even if it was impossible to produce a composite drawing. Tell the parent in the child's presence how well the child did.

Hospital Interviews

Unfortunately, there are times when the composite artist must conduct interviews in hospital settings because the crime victim has been severely injured physically. A crime may be of such a nature that preparation of a composite drawing is so urgent that the artist is brought to the hospital. **The foremost consideration must always be the health and safety of the victim.**

Purpose before Emotion

Over the years, I have conducted numerous hospital interviews with victims, including a wife who had just witnessed her husband's murder, a soldier with three bullets remaining in his body, a woman whose face had been slashed dozens of times with a straight razor, and a 21-year-old girl shot in the spine who had been told she would be permanently paralyzed. These and other hospital interviews were some of the most intense and stressful interviews of my career.

On more than one occasion during such interviews, I have had to turn my head away to regain my composure and to avoid the victim seeing a tear trickle down my cheek. **The artist has to summon the personal strength to put the task at hand above the emotional issues presented by the situation.** The artist should behave in a manner that is sensitive and caring, yet remain focused on his or her purpose.

This is not unlike the demands placed on medical and psychological professionals who deal with patients.

Permission from the Physician

If a hospital interview is to be conducted, the investigating officer should always consult the physician attending the victim for permission. If permission is granted, the officer and artist should discuss the procedure with the nursing staff, so that they will know what to expect. **Both the officer and artist must respect the advice of the nursing staff and adjust to the needs of the patient/victim.** Discuss the timing of medications that will make the patient drowsy. The nurses should be told that the production of a drawing will probably be a highly emotional experience for the victim.

Consider the potential for liability if the victim experiences further complications such as heart attack or stroke as a result of the stress of the composite interview experience. **Do not disregard the critical procedural step of obtaining the doctor's permission for a hospital interview.**

Victim's Attitude

Above all, the victim should be willing to attempt the composite drawing process. I once interviewed a college-age rape victim, abducted on the way to feed her horse, who had been left tied to a tree with her throat cut almost ear to ear. She could not speak. While in the hospital emergency room, she gestured that she wanted a paper and pencil. She wrote two things: "Someone go feed my horse" and "Get me a sketch artist." The motivation of the victim determines the success or failure of the interview.

With all composite drawing efforts, the willingness of the witness to cooperate is essential. It is especially important that the victim who is physically and emotionally injured want to cooperate with the composite artist. This will likely be a tiring, uncomfortable, and even frightening experience that takes place at one of the worst times of a person's life.

Procedural Considerations

The usual interview procedures probably must be altered. The interview will likely be more segmented, and take longer than usual. For example, the artist may get an initial overall description from the victim, and then leave to allow the victim to rest for a time. Breaks may be required for meals, medications, doctor visits, etc.

Restriction of Visitors

Hospital visits by friends or relatives concerned about the victim present complications for the artist. **It may be necessary for the nurses, working in conjunction with officers, to restrict visitations during the interview time frame.** Discuss this beforehand. It may be advisable to post a "No Visitors" sign on the victim's door. Diplomacy is required, since concerned relatives will not appreciate visiting restrictions.

In some instances, as with all stressful interviews, the victim may choose to have one close associate present at all times. It may also be advisable to have a victim's services counselor present.

Security

After gaining an initial overall description, the artist may retire to a different location to begin work on the drawing. I have utilized nurses' break rooms, linen closets, unoccupied rooms, and hospital cafeterias. **The place where the artist works should be away from the eyes of curious onlookers. Be discreet.** Don't forget that the perpetrator is free or you wouldn't be doing a composite. The surviving victim may be at some risk, perhaps requiring a guard at the hospital room door. Members of the media should be avoided. The investigating officer should be available to assist the artist with any eventualities that might arise.

Victim's Reaction

After a rough drawing is established and the patient/victim is available to continue the interview, the process can resume. **Remember the fragile state of the person's condition at all times, the upsetting nature of "seeing" the face again in the composite.** I have found it helpful to allow the victim to "reveal" the drawing to himself or herself. In other words, I hold up the drawing within the victim's reach with a second piece of drawing paper covering it. The victim can grasp the paper cover and move it away to reveal the facial drawing at his or her own pace. This allows the victim to control what he or she sees and at what pace.

After the first viewing of the overall drawing, the needed changes can be discussed. **Some victims will be strong enough to be shown photographic reference information such as the *Facial Identification Catalog* for fine-tuning the features, while others simply will not be able to do this.** The drawing would then be done without use of any reference materials. Then, depending on the situation, the drawing may be completed in the victim's room, as the victim provides input, or at a different location. The process of reviewing the drawing can be repeated as necessary until the best possible version of the drawing is achieved.

Concluding the Interview

Upon completion of the drawing, remember to provide your business card or contact information to the victim or a family member. Let them know that you are available for any future contact, if desired, regarding the description and the sketch.

False Allegations

A discussion of false allegations should begin with certain statements about the forensic artist's role. **While it is not the artist's function to conduct the criminal investigation or evaluate the witness psychologically, the artist is often placed in the position of making certain observations.** As part of the job of conducting interviews with crime witnesses and victims to prepare composite drawings, the artist often elicits in-depth information about the offense. Sometimes the artist learns a great deal of information about the person being interviewed.

During an interview, an artist may encounter a witness whose behavior and responses do not seem to fit the usual pattern. Artists with many years of interviewing experience, and those who possess good intuition, may pick up on the subtle signs early in an interview. Sometimes deviations in the normal "rhythm" of the interview may only become apparent as the session progresses. Over time, the artist develops a standard method of operating, and learns to expect certain standard reactions from witnesses, within a reasonable range. The artist often develops a "sense" that alerts him or her to interviews that are inconsistent with his or her previous experience as a forensic artist.

My friend and forensic art colleague, Lt. Roy Paschal of the South Carolina Law Enforcement Division, has become quite adept at determining false "alligators." Roy has interviewed more than his share of individuals making false claims to law enforcement. (Perhaps forensic artists and police officers are lied to more often than we realize, and Roy's particular expertise at spotting them just makes it *seem* that he encounters such a high number!) Perhaps Roy's best-known interviewee was Susan Smith, the young mother later convicted of drowning her two sons.

The day following his middle-of-the-night composite session with Smith, Roy called me to discuss his apprehensions about her. Although Smith had described an alleged abductor to Roy and he had prepared a profile drawing, he felt strongly that something was wrong (see Figure 2.26 in Chapter 2), and, of course, he was proven to be correct.

For much of the material in this section, I am indebted to Roy Paschal and his excellent insights. In lectures on the subject of false allegations, Roy is fond of quoting Mark Twain: "None of us could live with an habitual truth teller, but thank goodness, none of us has to."[56]

The reality is that in day-to-day life most of us experience some deceit. This "normal" deceit is different from pathological deceit, and the motivations to lie and the levels of complexity and sophistication of lying can vary tremendously. **The artist should not presume to be a psychological analyst, but should become familiar with some general information regarding the types of people who may make false claims, their motivations, and possible indicators of false allegations during an interview and ways of detecting them.**

Reasons for False Allegations

A glaringly obvious reason for claiming that an imaginary perpetrator exists is for the purpose of covering up one's own crimes. However, many false allegations are far more subtle and complex than that.

Precipitating Stressors

Most behavioral analysts agree that people who feel compelled to make false claims are usually motivated by some sort of precipitating stress factor. These vary widely, from an overwhelming need for attention to financial problems, marital problems, and any number of other perceived life stresses. I have interviewed several college girls who made false claims simply because they were unhappy or doing poorly in school and wanted their parents to let them come home. I have encountered women desperately seeking attention from husbands or boyfriends, and women who have had sexual relations and fear venereal disease or pregnancy.

Extreme Need for Attention/Self-Inflicted Injuries

In the most extreme cases, individuals injure themselves, usually superficially but sometimes quite severely. I once interviewed a woman who placed a "911" call, claiming that a man was attacking her. When officers and emergency services personnel arrived, she had a knife with a 9-inch blade fully inserted in her chest, which required 4 hours of surgery to remove. Many of the classic indicators of false allegation were present in this case. The woman claimed that she scarcely saw the man's face so only a very vague drawing was possible. This is sometimes referred to as **"self-handicapping," an element in many false claims.**

Self-Esteem

An excellent source on the subject of false allegations, specifically of sexual assault, is the chapter entitled "False Allegations" by Dr. Charles McDowell and Dr. Neil Hibler in *Practical Aspects of Rape Investigation*, edited by Roy Hazelwood and Dr. Ann Burgess. Although the chapter specifically addresses sexual assault claims, some of the behaviors discussed may be related to other crimes.

McDowell and Hibler explain the importance of self-esteem and the frequent links between maintaining the self-image and the making of false allegations. They explain:

> Perhaps the central feature of human personality is the concept of self-image. How one views oneself colors one's vision of the rest of the world. ... Self-esteem is maintained by behaving in ways that earn the approval of both the individual's "external audience" and his own conscience. ... Defense mechanisms are the methods the mind uses to protect its self-esteem. They do so by allowing the mind to selectively "forget" what happened, deny responsibility, project blame to someone (or something) else, overcompensate, or seek escape in a world of fantasy. ... When a false allegation of rape is made to preserve the individual's self-esteem, the following defense mechanisms are usually involved: ... Denial ... Projection ... Escape ... Rationalization and ... Self-Handicapping.[57]

Indicators

McDowell and Hibler provide a very useful list of factors that might alert the officer that the witness may be making a false claim. One isolated factor may be insignificant, but clusters of factors should be cause to take notice. Some of the **indicators of false claims that are of particular significance to the forensic artist include:**

- Complainant states an inability to describe the assailant because he or she kept his or her eyes closed during the assault.
- Complainant alleges being assaulted by more than one person, but cannot offer descriptions.
- Assailant was a total stranger or a person who can only be described in vague or nondescript terms.
- Damage to the clothing is inconsistent with any injuries reported.
- Complainant reports seemingly painful injuries with an air of indifference.
- Practice or hesitation marks are present at the site of a wound.

- Complainant has previous history of having been assaulted or raped under similar circumstances.
- Allegation was made after a similar crime received publicity.
- Complainant tries to steer the interview into "safe" topics or those that tend to engender sympathy.[57]

Note that instead of claims of multiple attackers, the complainant may claim that the assailant was large, overpowering, and ugly. I refer to this as the **"Godzilla Syndrome,"** and Roy Paschal calls it the **"Quasimodo Effect."**

Procedural Considerations

Over the years, individuals I have personally interviewed who proved to be making false claims tended to provide facial descriptions that fall into one of two distinctive categories. **Some people describe a face that is totally fictitious, making it up as they go along, while others describe a face that actually exists, which they have predetermined to focus upon mentally.**

A Fictitious Face

For me, the description of a totally "fabricated" face is far easier to sense in an interview than the description of an existing, but incorrect, face. In routine interviews, the overall description of the face is obtained first and the drawing progresses toward more and more refinement of the facial details. The initial description does not usually vary much from the finished drawing, although it has become more clarified and refined.

Something subtly different happens in the case of fictitious faces. As is customary, the overall description is obtained and the drawing progresses toward more refinement of details. However, **as the individual becomes more comfortable and confident that he or she is fooling the artist, the description often becomes more and more exquisitely detailed.**

Even though the individual may have even rehearsed the facial description to match the statements given earlier, the temptation to become more and more elaborate may overtake them. The interviewee comes up with freckles, moles, scars, earrings, tattoos and so forth, none of which were in the initial description. (This is not to say that such items do not sometimes emerge from memory as a drawing progresses in a legitimate interview, because they do.) **An obvious reversal of detail from vague to more detailed should send up a red flag for the artist.** In interviews where I sense this reversal of detail, I immediately withdraw all photo references to avoid their use as tools for elaboration.

A Face That Exists

More difficult to distinguish is a false description in which the person describes the face of someone who actually exists. The face being described may come from the person's daily life or be derived from television or films.

In such cases, the drawing session generally goes along in the usual way, but the artist may experience a nagging feeling that something is wrong. Several years ago, as part of a Texas Ranger investigation, I interviewed a woman who described riding in a car with her husband on their large horse ranch. She claimed they had stopped to offer a ride to a man who then proceeded to shoot and kill her husband and attempted to assault her. She said that she struggled, forced him out of the vehicle, and drove away.

We completed a drawing, but I advised the ranger that something "didn't feel right" to me. I later learned that this case presented several classic elements of false allegations. The description of the events simply did not seem feasible. How could she have thrown an armed man from the car as she claimed? Her description of her behavior is often termed **"heroic escape," an element in many false claims.** Upon examination of the physical evidence, the crime laboratory determined that the blood spatters were totally inconsistent with her story. When the Texas Ranger visited the couple's ranch, he located a worker there who strongly resembled the composite. Barely able to speak English and unaware of his situation, he looked at the drawing, smiled, and said, "That's me!" Not only had the woman killed her own husband, but she also planned to implicate this unfortunate employee.

Other Tools for Assessing Deception

Investigators and others have found several other avenues of study useful for detecting lies or dishonesty. Some interviewers use body language or kinesics, neurolinguistics processing, and observation of facial micro-expressions. Practitioners of these methods believe that they may be useful in the assessment and determination of deception. I mention these methods here only briefly. Each field of study is a subject unto itself that those interested in learning more may explore.

Kinesics

Kinesics is the study of "body language." Courses are offered that provide training in its use. Practitioners use the body, rather than words, to assess deception and the stress it causes.

Typical kinesic indicators include:

1. Averting the gaze at inappropriate times
2. Changing of the position of the body
3. "Closing" of the suspect's body space to the interviewer
4. Inappropriate or "nervous" actions with the hands
5. Attempts to symbolically "run" away from the interviewer

It is important to understand that cultural differences exist with regard to body language. For example, many Asian and Hispanic cultures believe that looking an authority figure directly in the eyes is a sign of disrespect. In America, we call that type of behavior "shifty-eyed" and equate it with deception.[58]

Neurolinguistics

Neurolinguistics processing or programming deals with careful assessment of the eye movements as an individual accesses data from the brain in response to questions. It is based on the assumption that most people's minds store information in different areas of the brain. The premise in neurolinguistics is that our eyes move in one direction as we "think" or develop new information. They move in another direction as we access "memory" or stored information. It is a sign of possible deception if the eyes move in a way that indicates the mind is creating new information in response to a question about a crime or description rather than accessing stored information.

Expressions and Micro-Expressions

I have found particularly useful Dr. Paul Ekman's research about the subtlety of facial expressions. His book, *Telling Lies*, provides practical insights for anyone who conducts interviews on a regular basis. Dr. Ekman discusses what he calls "micro expressions" or brief involuntary flashes of expression that "leak" from the face without our control. With practice, it is possible to become skilled at spotting these flashes and interpreting their meanings.

> The face can be a valuable source for the lie catcher, because it can lie and tell the truth and often does both at the same time. The face often contains two messages — what the liar wants to show and what the liar wants to conceal.[59]

The Artist's Role

McDowell and Hibler discuss the plight of rape victims in the criminal justice system:

> As in all reports of violent crimes, investigative, prosecutorial, and medical personnel must, at some point, make a determination as to the veracity of the complaint. These professionals are usually busy and typically depend on "shorthand" cues to help them assess the complaints made to them. The cues are based on experience and conventional wisdom and usually function quite well. However, in the case of a rape report this technique can easily create a tendency to evaluate prematurely.[57]

From the perspective of law enforcement, false allegations represent injustice and wasted man hours that could have been devoted to a legitimate crime. Keep in mind, however, that individuals who make such claims are, in their own ways, suffering and disturbed, and they should be handled with care. At the end of the day, each interviewer must proceed in these matters with great care. None of us is a "human lie-detector." **Never forget that even with the strongest indications of false allegation, a case may turn out to be legitimate.**

The artist's role, in particular, is to conduct the interview, make observations, and report findings to the investigating officer. Greater involvement than this should be done with great caution and awareness of the potential ramifications.

Other Psychological Issues

As part of the literature review for this chapter, several other issues were noted that may bear significantly on the composite production process.

Unconscious Transference

Unconscious transference is potentially very significant to law enforcement investigators in assessing the usefulness of composite drawings. **Unconscious transference occurs when a person actually seen in an unrelated place or context is mistakenly identified as the offender.**[32]

This phenomenon has been observed by composite artists who, on rare occasions, have prepared composite images, only to find that faces they produced strongly resembled individuals such as the first police officer at the crime scene or the ambulance attendant.

Use of reference files, such as celebrity photos, can be quite beneficial. Witnesses seeking a means of conveying a descriptive detail to the artist often relate some aspect of a face to a familiar celebrity face. Yet, the artist should exercise care to see that the celebrity photo is not viewed for a prolonged period (if at all) by the witness and thus avoid unconscious transfer and transposition of the celebrity facial features with the face in memory. Instead, the artist should ask the witness to elaborate on what aspect of the celebrity's face reminds him or her of the offender. The artist should then study the celebrity photo and attempt to ascertain what quality of the face is triggering the connection.

Multiple Retrieval Attempts

Other findings support the suggestion by Geiselman and Fisher that multiple attempts to retrieve information may lead to additional recall. A study by Ellen Scrivner and Martin A. Safer at the Catholic University of America found that net gains in the amount of information were achieved with repeated recall, without increasing memory errors. They concluded: "… that **eyewitness accounts may become more accurate with repeated attempts to recall information**."[60]

Siegfried L. Sporer at the University of Aberdeen in Scotland has speculated that:

> … multiple questioning of witnesses … also repeated thinking (and talking) about a crime one was personally involved in may lead to overt (e.g., telling others about it) and covert rehearsal (e.g., repeated, perhaps even obsessive thinking about the event), which in turn may facilitate recall.[31]

Better Visualizers May Make Better Witnesses

In the early stages of the composite-specific interview, it may be helpful for the artist to try to determine whether a witness is an adept visualizer. In my experience this knowledge helps determine when and if to introduce reference photographs, since poor visualizers may have a greater need for the visual cues. Some insight may be gained by listening carefully to ways in which a witness describes an event. Someone who says, "I can still see his face in my mind when I close my eyes," may require few or no reference photos to convey descriptive information. A witness who says, "I just can't picture him," may need more reference photographs to trigger the memory.

In a 1991 *Journal of Biomedical Communication* article, Dr. Rudolf Arnheim described visualization: "Visualization refers to the cognitive functions of visual perception."[61] In other words, **visualization is a person's ability to see or form a mental**

image. Although not tested formally, I believe that people who are better able to achieve mental images of a perpetrator's face have an easier time of producing a composite drawing.

In a 1986 *New York Times* article Daniel Coleman discusses research on mental images and their role in human thought processes:

> ... "About three percent of people cannot seem to get mental pictures at all, and about three percent are superb at it," said Stephen Kosslyn, a psychologist at Harvard ...
>
> Since the ancient Greeks, techniques have been taught that used images as an aid to memory.
>
> ... Dr. Kosslyn said he believed that this is one of several vastly underused ways in which the use of mental images could be helpful.[62]

If the artist interviews a person who possesses a strong ability to visualize, the interview may be conducted with fewer reference photos and may actually be simpler. A witness who has difficulty visualizing and forming a mental image may require more assistance to bring forth mental images. Some witnesses may be unable to do this at all.

While unable to control the way in which an event is perceived and registered in memory by the witness, **the artist may find it helpful to encourage the development of mental images for facilitating retrieval of the information.**

Post-Event Inputs

Many researchers have suggested that human recollection can be altered, enhanced, or totally reshaped based on suggestions made after an event has occurred. Such changes should be scrupulously avoided by police and police artists as they attempt to get suspect descriptions and identifications.

Of particular significance to composite artists are two issues: the phrasing of questions and the showing of photographs.

Phrasing of Questions

Questions asked by the sketch artist should always be "open-ended" in structure or multiple choice. "Tell me about his eyes" or "Would you describe his eyes as wide open and large, average in size, or small and narrowed?" might be appropriate questions. "Were his eyes brown or hazel?" would *not* be an appropriate question since it implies a rather forced choice. The witness may not have had the opportunity to determine eye color at all, yet might feel compelled to make a color choice based on the limited options given.

Showing of Photographs

As previously discussed, photographic references may be extremely useful tools that enable a witness to recognize when recall is exhausted. This is not to say that unstructured, premature, or prolonged exposure to facial photographs is recommended. On the contrary, witness memory may be potentially contaminated by such viewing of photographs.

If an investigator intends to have a witness participate in producing a composite drawing, viewing photographs such as those in mug books or photographic lineups should be avoided until after the preparation of the composite. This may not always be possible, but it is strongly recommended. Tests have shown that saturation of a witness' memory with more than about 50 full facial photographs can begin to degrade the memory of a face in the witness' mind's eye. While the human mind has an amazing capacity for sorting and distinguishing between faces, unnecessary and avoidable exposure to photographs is unwise.

The police composite artist has only limited control, if any, of a witness' exposure to photographic images prior to the composite interview. **In reality, no crime witness or victim can be held in isolation from the time of the event to the time of the composite interview, so that no faces will be seen to interfere with memory.** As humans, we are exposed at every turn to a world that includes facial images of all types, on television, in newspapers, or simply en route to the interview. In a perfect world this could be avoided. The police artist's world is far from perfect and his or her task is highly complex.

Training in Facial Recognition

Over the years many individuals have tried to improve the abilities of potential witnesses to observe and remember faces. Because of their interest in faces, some forensic artists have even attempted to provide such training. The potential applications of such skills could be numerous.

Yet, most of these training attempts have proved disappointing and ineffective. I believe most of these training programs failed because they were based on feature-by-feature analysis, which is contrary to the holistic way in which we encode faces in memory.

Certain studies specifically addressed the issue of police officers as witnesses and the question of their abilities as witnesses over laypersons. At some point, most police artists are called upon to interview a police officer as a witness. Results seem to suggest that stressful encounters with suspects may actually be less fearful to experienced police officers than other citizens due to the officers' daily experiences. Therefore, due to less stress, memories might be somewhat better for police. However, in general, it has been shown that a police officer is not necessarily any better a witness than the average person.

Other studies suggest a slight potential for increased memory through training or experience since there could be improved likelihood that a witness would make a deliberate effort to remember specific details while the event is occurring.

Psychological Benefits of Composite Images

May Aid in Later Recognition of the Perpetrator

A 1981 study by Michael A. Mauldin and Kenneth R. Laughery at the University of Houston examined the effects of constructing a composite facial image of a target face on the subsequent recognition of that face. They concluded that subjects who produced a composite were more likely to recognize the target face in a subsequent recognition task:

The act of reconstructing the image may increase the probability that a witness will make a correct identification in a subsequent lineup or mugfile search task.[63]

Thus, *if the composite interview was properly conducted*, with the artist guiding the witness through a cognitive style interview and progressive refinement method, an additional bonus *might* be improved ability to make an identification.

Regarding this possibility, Dr. Ronald Fisher, in personal communication with the author, has stated:

> I think the literature is mixed on this issue of whether constructing a composite helps in later recognition. I have just published some results showing that computerized facial composite construction either has no effect or that it hinders later recognition ... I suspect that whether the act of constructing a composite helps or *hinders* depends on the quality of the composite. If the composite is very good, I can imagine that the process helps later recognition, but if the composite is poor/mediocre, it may actually hinder.[21]

Personal Benefits for the Victim

One of the most important potential benefits of generation of composite images to aid in criminal investigations is the very personal benefit to a crime victim. Aiding the police with the production of a composite image allows the victim to participate, most likely for the first time, in a proactive measure to regain control. I sometimes say to victims, "Now we can work together to get back at this guy." The gathering of strength and regaining of confidence becomes almost palpable following this statement.

There seems to be an internal struggle for most victims of traumatic events regarding the "face" of the perpetrator. On the one hand, they hate this face and fight to suppress it from their thoughts. Yet, with the compulsive repetition of the event known to occur in the minds of many victims, the face *won't* go away. A part of the mind strives to hold onto the facial image so that it can be used to identify the person when faced with suspects in a lineup some day.

A beneficial cathartic effect often occurs with the development of the composite, allowing the victim to feel tremendous release of tension and renewed strength. The composite serves to encapsulate or capture the face for the use of the investigators, and the victim can finally relax, knowing that the image is literally down on paper and won't be lost. One of my most treasured possessions is a thick file of letters and notes of thanks from crime victims following composite interviews. Some call the following day to say, "I just had to thank you; I was able to sleep for the first time since this happened."

The complexity of human cognition and perception has been the subject of numerous research projects over the years. No doubt, there will be more and more studies over time. It is the obligation of the police composite artist and indeed of all those who interact with victims of violent crime to continuously review the psychological literature. **We must always attempt to learn more about the nature of the workings of human memory, although some mysteries will always remain.**

References

1. Domingo, F., "Forensic art: practical considerations of witness memory," *Journal of Forensic Identification*, 40(3), 115–125, 1989.
2. Pease, R. W., Ed., *Merriam Webster's Medical Dictionary.* Springfield, MA: Merriam-Webster, Inc., 1995.
3. Menninger, J., *Total Recall.* New York: Pocket Books, 1986.
4. Leary, W., "Novel methods unlock witnesses' memories," *The New York Times*, New York, November 15, 1988.
5. Davies, G. M. et al., "Remembering faces: acknowledging our limitations," *Journal of Forensic Science Society*, 18, 19, 1978.
6. Perry, B. D., "Memories of fear: how the brain stores and retrieves physiological states, feelings, behaviors and thoughts from traumatic events," in *Images of the Body in Trauma*, Goodwin, J. and Attias, R., Eds. New York: Basic Books, 1997.
7. Cohen, G., Kiss, G., and Le Voi, M., "Memory: current issues," *Journal of Forensic Identification*, 46(5), 597–628, 1996.
8. Cahill, L., "Memory," Lecture presented at the International Association for Identification's 80th Annual Educational Conference and Training Seminar, Costa Mesa, CA, July 1995.
9. Anderson, J., "Retrieval of information from long-term memory," *Science,* 220, 25–30, April 1, 1983.
10. Bennett, P., "Memory, Recall and Recognition: the Implications of Psychological Research for Police Identification Systems," Essay by Independent Study: England, November 1990.
11. Brown, A., The development of memory: knowing, knowing about knowing, and knowing how to know, in *Advances in Child Development and Behavior,* Reese, H., Ed. New York: Academic Press, 1975.
12. Loftus, E. and Doyle, J. M., *Eyewitness Testimony; Civil and Criminal.* Charlottesville, VA: Lexis Law Publishing, 1997.
13. Laughery, K. and Fowler, R., "Sketch artist and Identi-KIT procedures for recalling faces," *Journal of Applied Psychology*, 65, 307, 1980.
14. Wells, G. L., "Verbal descriptions of faces from memory: are they diagnostic of identification accuracy?" *Journal of Applied Psychology*, 36, 619–626, 1985.
15. Goldstein, A., Johnson, K., and Chance, J., "Does fluency of face description imply superior face recognition?" *Bulletin of the Psychonomic Society*, 13, 15–18, 1979.
16. Pigott and Brigham, "The relationship between accuracy of prior description and facial recognition," *Journal of Applied Psychology*, 70, 547, 1985.
17. Etcoff, N., "Face Value," *The Nature of Things*, Discovery Channel, Canada, 1993.
18. Tanaka, J. W. and Farah, M. J., "Parts and wholes in face recognition," *Quarterly Journal of Experimental Psychology*, 46A, 225–245, 1993.
19. Davies, G., Ellis, H., and Shepherd, J., *Perceiving and Remembering Faces.* London: Academic Press, 1981.
20. Young, A. W., Hellawell, D. J., and Hay, D. C., "Configural information in face perception," *Perception*, 16, 747–759, 1987.
21. Harmon, L., "The recognition of faces," *Scientific American*, November 1973.
22. Fisher, R., personal communication, 1999.
23. Malpass, R., Enhancing eyewitness memory, in *Psychological Issues in Eyewitness Identification*, Sporer, S., Malpass, R., and Koehnken, G., Eds. Mahwah, NJ: Lawrence Erlbaum Associates, 1996.
24. Heafner, H., "Police composite art, facial reconstruction and other techniques," *Journal of Forensic Identification*, 46, 233, 1986.
25. Chance, J. E., Goldstein, A. G., and McBride, L., "Differential experience and recognition memory for faces," *Journal of Social Psychology*, 97, 243–253, 1975.
26. Laughery, K. R., Fessler, P. K., Lenorovitz, D. R., and Yorlick, D. A., "Time delay and similarity effects in facial recognition," *Journal of Applied Psychology*, 59, 490–496, 1974.

27. Shepherd, J. W. and Ellis, H. D., "The effect of attractiveness on recognition memory for faces," *American Journal of Psychology*, 86, 627–633, 1973.

28. Lindsey, R., Nosworthy, G., Martin, R., and Martynuck, C., "Using mug shots to find suspects," *Journal of Applied Psychology*, 79, 121–130, 1994.

29. Deffenbacher, K., Carr, T., and Leu, J., "Memory for words, pictures and faces: retroactive interference, forgetting and reminiscence," *Journal of Experimental Psychology: Human Learning and Memory*, 7, 299–305, 1981.

30. Narby, D., Cutler, B., and Penrod, S., The effects of witness, target and situational factors on eyewitness identification, in *Psychological Issues in Identification*, Sporer, S., Malpass, R., and Koehnken, G., Eds. Mahwah, NJ: Lawrence Erlbaum Associates, 1996.

31. Sporer, S., Psychological aspects of person descriptions, in *Psychological Issues in Eyewitness Identification*, Sporer, S., Malpass, R., and Koehnken, G., Eds. Mahwah, NJ: Lawrence Erlbaum Associates, 1996.

32. Lipton, J., Legal aspects of eyewitness testimony, in *Psychological Issues in Eyewitness Identification*, Sporer, S., Malpass, R., and Koehnken, G., Eds. Mahwah, NJ: Lawrence Erlbaum Associates, 1996.

33. *Plummer v. State*, 270 Ark.Il, 603 S. W. 2d. 402 (1980).

34. *Robinson v. State*, 473 So. 2d 957 (Miss. 1985).

35. *Royce v. Moore*, 469 F. 2d 808 (1st Cir. 1972).

36. *United States v. Bothwell*, 465 F. 2d 217 (9th Cir. 1972).

37. Malpass, R. and Kravitz, J., "Recognition for faces of own and other race," *Journal of Personality and Social Psychology*, 13, 330–334, 1969.

38. Royal, R. F. and Schutt, S., *The Gentle Art of Interviewing and Interrogation — A Professional Manual and Guide*. Englewood Cliffs, NJ: Prentice-Hall, 1976.

39. Geiselman, R. E. and Fisher, R. P., "Interviewing Victims and Witnesses of Crime," National Institute of Justice — Research in Brief, December 1985.

40. Fisher, R. P. and Geiselman, R. E., *Memory-Enhancing Techniques for Investigative Interviewing — The Cognitive Interview*. Springfield, IL: Charles C Thomas, 1992.

41. Grossman, D. and Siddle, B. K., "Critical incident amnesia: the psychological basis and the implications of memory loss during extreme survival stress situations," In *Research Review*, a publication of PPCT Management Systems, Inc.: Millstadt, IL, March 1998.

42. Davies, G. and Little, M., "Drawing on memory: exploring the expertise of a police artist," in *Medicine, Science and the Law*, 30(4), October 1990.

43. Shepherd, J. and Ellis, H., Face recall — methods and problems, in *Psychological Issues in Eyewitness Identification*, Sporer, S., Malpass, R., and Koehnken, G., Eds. Mahwah, NJ: Lawrence Erlbaum Associates, 1996.

44. Everly, G. S., Neurophysiological considerations in the treatment of post-traumatic stress disorder: a neurocognitive perspective, in *International Handbook for Traumatic Stress Syndromes*, Wilson, J. and Raphael, B., Eds. New York: Plenum Press, 1992.

45. Pennebaker, J. W., "The Effects of Traumatic Disclosure on Physical and Mental Health: The Values of Writing and Talking about Upsetting Events," Paper presented at the Fourth World Congress on Stress, Trauma, and Coping: Baltimore, MD, April 1997.

46. Keane, T., Fairbank, J., Caddell, J., Zimering, R., and Bender, M., A behavioral approach to assessing and treating post traumatic stress disorder in Vietnam veterans, in *Trauma and Its Wake*, Figley, C., Ed. New York: Brunner/Mazel Publishers, 1985.

47. Janoff-Bulman, R., Victims of violence, in *Psychotraumatology — Key Papers and Core Concepts in Post-Traumatic Stress*, Everly, G. and Lating, J., Eds. New York: Plenum Press, 1995.

48. Domingo, F., "Forensic art: concepts and approaches in composite interviewing," *Journal of Forensic Identification*, 38(6), 259–274, 1988.

49. *Larry Arnold Wilson, Appellant v. The State of Texas*, Appellee No. 05-85-01013-CR, Court of Appeals of Texas, Dallas, September 22, 1986, Tex 3–5.

50. Perry, B., *Principles of Working with Maltreated Children II: Special Considerations for Clinicians*, Booklet by CIVITAS Initiative Product, Houston, TX: Baylor College of Medicine, Department of Psychiatry and Behavioral Sciences, 1994.

51. Wilson, C. L., Barnes, C. S., Chellappa, R., and Sirohey, S. A., *Face Recognition Technology for Law Enforcement Applications*. Gaithersburg, MD: National Institute of Standards and Technology, Computer Systems Laboratory, 1994.

52. Walker, A. G., *Handbook on Questioning Children — A Linguistic Perspective*. Washington, D.C.: American Bar Association, Center on Children and the Law, 1994.

53. McCarrell, K., "Child Interviewing," Lecture presented at the International Association for Identification's 80th Annual Educational Conference and Training Seminar, Costa Mesa, CA, July 1995.

54. Caldwell, L., "Child Interviewing," Lecture presented at the International Association for Identification's 81st Annual Educational Conference and Training Seminar, Greensboro, NC, July 1996.

55. Saywitz, K. J., Geiselman, R. E., and Bornstein, G. K., "Effects of cognitive interviewing and practice on children's recall performance," *Journal of Applied Psychology*, 77, 744–756, 1992.

56. Paschal, R., "False Allegations," Lecture presented at the International Association for Identification's 82nd Annual Educational Conference and Training Seminar: Boston, MA, July 1997.

57. McDowell, C. P. and Hibler, N. S., False allegations, in *Practical Aspects of Rape Investigation, a Multidisciplinary Approach*, Hazelwood, R. and Burgess, A., Eds. New York: Elsevier, 199?

58. Dillingham, C., "Deception in law enforcement interrogations, Part II — "Would I lie to you?" *Police and Security News*, 13(5), 46, 1997.

59. Ekman, P., *Telling Lies*. New York: Berkley Books, 1986, 123.

60. Scrivner, E. and Safer, M. A., "Eyewitnesses show hypermnesia for details about a violent event," *Journal of Applied Psychology*, 73, 371–377, 1900.

61. Arnheim, R., "Perception, cognition, and visualization," *Journal of Biomedical Communications*, 18, 2–5, 1991.

62. Coleman, D., "Mental images: new research helps clarify their role," *The New York Times*, August 12, 1986.

63. Mauldin, M. A. and Laughery, K. R., "Composite production effects on subsequent facial recognition," *Journal of Applied Psychology*, 66, 351–357, 1981.

Chapter 6

Composite Imagery

Overview of Composite Imagery

The production of composite imagery is a multifaceted process. Frank Domingo describes it as a hybrid of several fields of study:

> **Three unlikely subjects form the foundation of this discipline: art and psychology are balanced within the constraints of the law.** Each of these areas are important and necessary to the structure of the discipline. If an inordinate emphasis is placed in one of these areas that balance would be upset, perhaps obscuring the discipline's prime function — "identification," "elimination," "corroboration." It is part of the composite artist's job to maintain that balance while providing his services to agency and society. When composite art is working properly it aids law enforcement in its function to protect life and property.[1]

What Is a Composite?

Composite images have been used to identify and apprehend criminals for over 100 years. We have grown accustomed to opening the newspaper or viewing a television news broadcast and seeing a facial image captioned, "Have you seen this person?"

Composite imagery refers to graphic images made up from the combination of individually described component parts. Probably the best known type of composite imagery in police work is the composite drawing of a face (Figure 6.1).

Composite art or composite drawing can be defined as a *freehand drawing* made up by combining various parts into a single graphic image based on the description of a crime victim or witness. Most investigators are accustomed to associating composite art with the rendering of faces from descriptions, but **composite art can also be done to depict full figures.** Composite art may also include **object or evidence drawings** that are produced from witness descriptions.

Figure 6.1   Composite drawing by KTT of suspect as described by a witness (left), and subject identified (right). (Courtesy of Texas Department of Public Safety.)

The terms **composite, composite art, or composite drawing** are sometimes erroneously used to describe child age progressions, fugitive updates, postmortem drawings, or facial reconstructions. **Composite images refer specifically to images produced from component parts with assistance of witness input, not those based on photographs or skulls.**

Composite images may also be developed by using hand-assembled or computer-generated systems. These mechanically developed images are sometimes incorrectly referred to as composite "drawings." Since they are not drawings, the correct terminology for such facial images is **composite images** or simply **composites**. Software is also available for the electronic development of full-body images, vehicles, and crime scenes.

Object or Evidence Images

An observant witness can sometimes describe other details of a crime in addition to the perpetrator's face or physique (Figure 6.2). Written or hand-drawn records of such details can aid in the apprehension of a criminal or can serve as possible corroborative or ancillary evidence later in the case. Examples of some of the types of items that may be documented by hand drawing or on a computer system are

- Vehicles, including aircraft and marinecraft; vehicle interiors; logos of vehicle manufacturers; bumper stickers or decals; exterior painted designs
- Details of interiors of locations
- Weapons
- Articles of clothing or footwear (Figure 6.3); printing on T-shirts; printing or logos on ball caps, footwear, or clothing brands, or other clothing details; monograms, jewelry (Figure 6.4), or watches; and eyeglasses

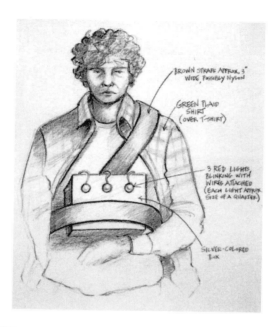

Figure 6.2 **Evidence drawing** by KTT of suspect wearing a **bomb-like device** as described by a witness, drawn in addition to facial composite drawing to document information about the device. (Courtesy of Texas Department of Public Safety.)

Figure 6.3 **Evidence drawing** by KTT of a **unique jacket** worn by a suspect. (Courtesy of Texas Department of Public Safety.)

- Unusual or personalized drug paraphernalia
- Gang- or organized-group-related insignias
- Tattoos, moles, scars, or deformities

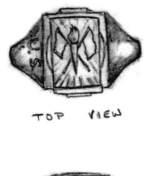

TOP VIEW

SIDE VIEW

Figure 6.4 Evidence drawing of a ring by Lt. Roy B. Paschal based on the description of a victim of a home invasion describing his own stolen property. (Courtesy of South Carolina Law Enforcement Division.)

A sketch artist can document any item of potential future use to the investigation that the witness may be able to describe. The variety of such requests can be very broad. In one case, an artist was asked to draw a distinctive clown mask worn by the assailant during a homicide. This seemed to be a somewhat unusual request, since the assailant's face was not actually seen, but it proved to be very helpful to the investigation. The mask was drawn, and later, when a suspect's residence was searched, a mask matching the drawing was found. This proved to be significant ancillary evidence in the case.

On several occasions, I have sketched physical body parts or unique characteristics of perpetrators, usually sex offenders, which victims were able to describe in great detail. When such traits appear on a suspect, the evidence can be very damaging, particularly when the specific trait would not be observable while the person was clothed.

Facial Composite Images in General

Sketch Quality vs. Photographic Quality in Facial Composite Images

A particularly notable phenomenon is the benefit of "sketch quality" (see Chapter 2, Figure 2.23) vs. "photographic quality" (Figure 6.5) in the production of composite images. Tom Macris, a highly successful police artist formerly with the San Jose, California Police Department, addresses this point in his paper "Composite Art: General Principles for Man and Machine":

Figure 6.5 **"Photographic quality" composite image** produced on a computer system.

Sketch quality in a composite has always offered one key advantage over photo detail. This advantage is that when viewing a completed composite sketch, one is forced to apply a very fruitful margin for interpretation. The accomplished police artist knows how the addition of superfluous detail is an overkill which defeats the purpose of the composite.

In a photographic composite, when such precise details are included and visually totaled, they may result in a product which precisely suggests an absolute identity. This tempts the viewer to interpret what the composite is trying to say very narrowly, thereby leaving many potential stones unturned in the investigation. It is as if twentieth century man, raised on the precise nature of photographic images, maintains a knee-jerk response to expect all photographic images to be precise representations of the subject. This misleading quality is compounded by the fact that much of the detail or subtlety was not even initially requested by the witness. It simply (and unnecessarily) came with the image.[2]

Shaded Drawing vs. Line Drawing

While photographic quality in a composite image may produce *misleading* detail, psychological studies indicate that line drawings may not provide *enough* detail. Graham Davies and colleagues conducted experiments with line drawings of famous faces. Only 47% could be identified when viewed. In comparison, shading and texture information incorporated in shaded artist drawings provide necessary details about shape, tonal variation, and facial topography that encourage facial identification.[3]

Color in Facial Composite Images

In addition to the sketch vs. photographic quality issues and shaded vs. line drawing issues with regard to composite images, an equally significant consideration has to do with use of color.

Some artists who do hand-drawn sketches occasionally do them in color. More commonly, vendors of computer composite-generating systems tout the ability of their particular products to produce color images. **Is color in a composite image really an advantage?**

The actual benefits of the added dimension of color to a composite image are debatable. In an Aberdeen University, Department of Psychology study concerning the importance placed on individual components in a facial description, Davies, Shepherd, and Ellis found that color played a rather insignificant role. Their test subjects allocated only a 2% proportion of their descriptive information to color when describing faces.[4]

This is not to say that a color composite might not be advantageous in certain instances. **If a witness places heavy emphasis on color in the facial description, a color image might be warranted.** It seems that for some population groups, skin color holds particular sociological significance and their descriptions reflect that.

Using color may add confusion to the interview situation. Although the witness actually saw the face in color, the added struggle of describing it in color may be overwhelming. No evidence suggests addition of color to composite images results in a greater recognition value. Proper development of a color drawing by the artist is time consuming and requires skill. Color can be expensive to reproduce and distribute, although this is less problematic than it once was. When a color drawing is copied for distribution, there is nearly always a change in the tonality of the color, which leads to inaccurate reproduction.

These negative considerations may mean **production of color images may *not* be worth the effort for the artist or the risk of confusing the witness.**

Adding color or "colorizing" a composite image without directly receiving the description of the color from the witness is a questionable practice. This is particularly true if you did not generate the original composite (see Chapter 15). Studies indicate that facial recognition seems to be more closely linked to tonal variation in faces rather than in the actual colors. Artistic shading in drawings (even in black and white) preserves the sense of mass needed to trigger identification.

Hand-Assembled Composite Systems

As discussed in Chapter 2, kits have existed since the 1950s for the hand assembly of facial images. Best known and most widely used have been the American Identi-KIT and the British PHOTO-FIT.

The Identi-KIT is composed of individual facial features or components printed on small sheets of acetate. The witness selects the individual features from an index of features and the operator assembles them by stacking them one on top of the other. Adjustments may then be made by either completely changing a particular feature and replacing it with another or by moving the features up or down. Some operators make further adjustments by using a wax pencil to draw on top of the acetate "foils." It is interesting to note that the earliest Identi-KITs were built of hand-drawn or sketch-quality features (see Chapter 2, Figure 2.12) and later changed to use photographic features.

A beneficial aspect built into the Identi-KIT was the numbering or codification of the component features for ease of reproduction of the image by any other person or agency with a copy of the Identi-KIT. However, if the composite were amended by drawing over it with a wax pencil, the accuracy and completeness of the reproduced composite suffered.

PHOTO-FIT is also composed of multiple component features, but the assembly method differs from that of the Identi-KIT. Rather than being stacked one on top of the other, PHOTO-FIT features are arranged in the mid-face or facial triangle with a facial shape surrounding them.

An advantage available to the early PHOTO-FIT operators was use of the 1971 book *Looking at Faces* by Jacques Penry, the inventor of the PHOTO-FIT system. Penry, who called himself a "facial topographer," provided useful insights into facial details and observation and attempted to describe a practical universal method of assessing faces in a methodical way reminiscent of Bertillon.

Computer-Generated Composite Systems

Today, many electronically automated versions of the earlier hand-assembled systems exist, and there are both positive and negative aspects to these computer-generated composite systems. **Some of the most significant factors for consideration deal with computer vendor claims of product superiority due to "photographic quality" and "color." Particularly important in product selection is the quality of the tools for modification that a given system contains.**

Methods of operation and degree of user friendliness vary from system to system. Available feature adjustments in most softwares include both scale changes and options for moving of features in all directions. Some systems, however, require a feature to be totally removed and replaced rather than adjusted. Ideally, a software incorporates a "draw" or "paint" function that allows the operator to subtly adjust individual features in small and precise increments at the direction of the witness. **Ultimately, the usefulness of a computer composite-generating system depends on the system's quality of tools for adjustments.** Vendors strive to expand their feature databases to aid in the variations available to the operator. However, upgrades of the system's adjustment tools and additional training programs would perhaps diminish the constant need for more features.

Disadvantages of Computer Composite Systems

As previously described, the claimed advantages of "photographic quality" and "color" are debatable. Aware of this problem, some manufacturers have attempted to alter the component features in their systems, blurring them so that they appear more "sketchy" and less photographic. On some systems with the "sketch-quality" option, the witness must still initially *select* from an index of component features that are *photographic*, a psychological disadvantage. The sketch option is offered for implementation *after* the photographic components are assembled, as the final touch before completion.

Other manufacturers have offered options for use of photographic or hand-drawn components in their systems, allowing the witness to select from "sketch-quality" features throughout the process. **Perhaps the ideal and most psychologically effective computer composite system would make use of scanned components, well drawn by hand, rather than photographic ones.**

Computers may have an **intimidating psychological effect** on some witnesses, particularly older citizens. In a recent workshop in the upper Midwest, a young, computer-literate state police forensic artist told me he had stopped using his computerized composite system in favor of hand-drawn sketches because he felt that the computerized system had a detrimental effect on some witnesses. Insecure witnesses tended to settle on features that were not totally accurate, simply because they came from a computer. In other words, "If it came from the computer, it must be right," even if it was not. This diminished the identification value of the composite image.

With time, this observation probably will apply to fewer and fewer people as virtually everyone becomes comfortable in front of a computer terminal and recognizes the limitations of the medium.

Another disadvantage is the **inherent limitations of features** within a computer system, while no such limitation exists with an artist. If the correct hat is not in the database, it's just not there, but the artist can draw whatever hat the witness describes. Also, some systems display limited components for females or for certain racial or ethnic groups. This limitation is lessened if the computer operator has some artistic skills and the software incorporates a good "paint" or "draw" function for feature adjustment.

Perhaps the aspect that warrants the greatest consideration regarding computer composite systems should be the approach to the product's use. At police conferences and forensic seminars, salesmen often maintain that "anyone can make a face on this system." While this is certainly true, **the significance of the role of listening and the interview process in the production of a composite should not be underestimated, especially in cases of traumatic events. Similarly, the legal correctness of the procedure is vital.**

The idea that any citizen or rookie patrol officer with little or no training in interview techniques or victimology should be encouraged to prepare composites is unfortunate. **Significant information may be missed, confused, or obscured when a witness is handled by an untrained interviewer.**

Some vendors of computer-generating softwares have even suggested that crime victims prepare their own composite images. Such a practice may be particularly unwise, especially if done outside the oversight of law enforcement.

Sometimes a crime victim or witness is artistically talented and arrives for the composite interview with a drawing of the face that he or she has prepared. In such a case, the drawing should be documented as evidence and the decision made as to whether or not to continue the composite process as scheduled. The artist should make these decisions in consultation with the investigating officer. Most often such a drawing would be used as an additional means of communication between the artist and the witness as they prepare a composite in the usual way.

This is not the same as encouraging witnesses to prepare their own composite images outside of the law enforcement realm. If victims, members of the media, or others prepare composite images and distribute them, who will investigate the tips generated? Would this process stand up in court? Would a guilty criminal be set free because appropriate procedures for probable cause to arrest were not followed? **Is such a risk worth taking?**

In addition to consideration of victims and criminal justice protocols, the experience of the individual accustomed to interviewing specifically for the purpose of preparing facial images should be emphasized. It may be unwise to undervalue the benefit of the "artist's eye" and knowledge of facial anatomy in assembling composites and making subtle adjustments to the facial image.

Obviously, not all departments have resources available to employ a trained forensic artist. Computer systems play an important role in filling that void. **Effort should be made, however, to ensure that sensitive, skilled interviewers operate computer composite systems. Ideally, those who operate computer composite-generating systems should have training in interviewing specifically for the purpose of producing a facial image. Computer-generated composites should be developed according to procedures that are appropriate within the criminal justice system.**

Fortunately, some computer vendors, particularly in the United Kingdom, have made great efforts to incorporate the latest research by cognitive psychologists into their product development and training programs.

Advantages of Computer Composite Systems

Clearly, there is an advantage to having a reasonably priced software operated by a trained interviewer when no artist is available. **Composite systems provide images of uniform quality and style, both of which can be highly variable in hand-drawn sketches.**

Another strong potential plus computer composite systems offer is the capability of **mathematical quantification of the images, allowing for simple storage, accurate reproduction at remote sites, and ease of creation of fliers or posters for distribution.** The completed image produced by most composite-generating softwares may be easily imported into a desktop publishing software for the efficient creation of a pre-designed "wanted" bulletin.

Computer systems have been criticized for lacking specific features for female faces or for certain racial or ethnic looks. However, this lack may be diminished by use of other tools to augment the database of the composite-generating system. With any electronically generated facial image, there exists another option for modification of the final product in addition to the "paint" or "draw" functions the system contains. Images may be imported into other more powerful imaging systems, which possess almost limitless capabilities for modification. **If the operator has knowledge of facial anatomy and art skills, an image originally developed on a composite-generating system may be fine-tuned to an extent, producing specificity to better satisfy a witness.** Subtleties, asymmetries, or facial anomalies not found in a database may be added.

For such a process to flow smoothly with a witness, however, the computer operator should become proficient in the system used. Awkward fumbling with equipment may frustrate the witness and lose the witness' focus. Some of the benefits of using composite-generating softwares in the field on laptop computers may be lost if the more powerful programs required for adjustment are not available on the laptop.

If enhancements are made on a graphics software program other than the composite-generating system, the advantage of mathematical quantification of the image is lost. Since the features have been altered from the original, the composite can no longer be coded and transmitted exactly.

Another option to *manipulation* of features from the original database in a composite-generating system is the *importation and addition* of new features to the composite. The image may be imported into a software that allows for scanned images to be overlayed and merged with a composite face. In other words, the initial composite could be built, then exported or scanned into another graphics program. Then, the artist could search hard-copy photographic reference files for the needed feature, scan it into the system, and merge it or overlay it on the initial composite. This same approach is sometimes useful with hand-drawn sketches, scanned into a system for the production of rapid "multiple-looks," such as adding mustaches, beards, or eyeglasses.

It is even possible, with a digital camera, to capture three-dimensional objects and import them into the software for inclusion in the composite image. For example, with skill, the actual eyeglasses or hat belonging to a perpetrator and dropped at a crime scene can be scanned into the computer and merged with either a hand-drawn or computer-generated composite image.

Long-time computer composite software user and instructor Hayden Baldwin has recommended that those evaluating systems for potential purchase consider the following criteria: image quality, technical support, database, learning curve, graphic compatibility, cost to upgrade, and lease or buy option. I would add to this list: consideration of black and white vs. color, "sketch quality" vs. "photographic quality," and careful evaluation of the "adjustment tools."

With the increased use of digitized images, the practical function of facial database search systems is rapidly approaching. Such systems perform a function that is separate and distinct from the composite production process, but a composite image that is computer-generated vs. hand-drawn may be simpler to integrate and use with these systems in the future. Systems currently exist that can search a target photograph or composite image against a database of known offender faces. This is roughly equivalent to searches by the well-known automated fingerprint identification systems (AFIS), but done by using *faces,* not fingerprints. While very large capacity storage is required for computer graphics files, this difficulty will likely diminish over time, making such systems affordable for police agencies.

Several types of facial database search systems exist. Some were developed to stand alone, and others were developed to work in conjunction with composite-generating systems. To be totally effective, however, such systems must be capable of comparing composite images of various types: hand-drawn, hand-assembled, and computer-generated.

Three-Dimensional Composites

Although rare, three-dimensional composite images have been created by various artists over the years. In Chapter 2 we discussed the method devised in the 1950s by Royal Canadian Mounted Police Corporal Reg Abbott; however, Abbott's method never came into practical use.

In recent decades, other attempts have been made at three-dimensional compositry, most notably by Fernando Poncé of the Los Angeles Police Department.

A news article in the April 22, 1996 issue of *Time* magazine showed a bas-relief-type facial image used by police in Tokyo to depict suspects in a high-profile subway gas attack in 1995.

Other Terminology

While doing composites at the U.S. border with Mexico as part of a triple homicide investigation in 1996, I learned from Mexican authorities that the term used in Mexico for composite images is **"Ritrato Hablato."** This translates as "speaking picture," and parallels the terminology used in the late 1800s by Alphonse Bertillon for his anthropometric analyses of criminals. Bertillon called the photographic records and measurements he compiled on a given individual the **"Portrait Parlé"** or "speaking portrait" (see Chapter 3, Figure 3.3).

So, over time, facial images of wanted criminals have been made in a variety of ways. Therefore, an **outline of composite imagery** would include:

- **Composite Art**
  Drawings of people
  Drawings of objects or evidence
- **Hand-Assembled Composites**
- **Computer-Generated Composites**
  Images of people
  Images of objects or evidence
- **Three-Dimensional Composites**

Facial composite images can be deceptively simple in appearance and not convey the real complexity involved in their preparation. **This chapter deals specifically with composite drawing by hand, although many of the principles described apply equally to both hand-assembled and computer-generated composites. It is strongly recommended that you read the information in Chapter 5 before you attempt to produce a composite image in an actual case situation.** Pertinent information regarding the anatomical aspects of human faces and the ways in which to accurately depict them in drawing form is presented in Chapters 3 and 4.

Only after one begins to understand the complex dynamics of the encoding of memories of events, particularly traumatic events, can fully effective retrieval of those memories take place. **Sensitivity to victims, knowledge of memory function and interview techniques, and some knowledge of the subtlety of facial anatomy are the significant issues in the production of high-quality composite images. Of secondary importance is the choice of method: hand-drawn, hand-assembled, computer-generated, or three-dimensional.**

Circumstances for Doing Composite Images

Most commonly, the request for a composite image is made when a major crime has occurred and police have a witness they believe capable of providing a good description of the perpetrator. Development of full body images or object or evidence images may also be undertaken.

If there are multiple witnesses to an incident, decisions must be made regarding the handling of the interview approach. See the section on multiple witness interviews in Chapter 5. Figure 6.6 shows a composite sketch prepared of a suspect in a homicide case based on descriptive information given by two witnesses interviewed simultaneously. A small profile view was added since one witness saw the "tail" of hair on the subject from the side.

Initial Contact and Request

Whether you are a freelance artist or employed by a police agency, the initial request for a composite sketch is usually made by way of a telephone call from the primary

Figure 6.6   Composite drawing by KTT of suspect in a murder case (left) and subject identified (right). The sketch was based on descriptive information given by **two witnesses interviewed simultaneously.** A small profile view was added because one witness saw the "tail" of hair on the subject from the side. (Courtesy of Texas Department of Public Safety.)

investigating officer to the artist. If an artist employed by a police agency does "on loan" work for other jurisdictions, arrangements should be agreed upon and outlined in advance.

Several decisions usually must be made as part of such agreements. Will the artist be "on duty" and on the payroll of the primary agency that employs the artist? What about potential travel or overtime expenses? Will the artist be required to do drawings on "off-duty" time and be compensated monetarily by the requesting agency? If so, at what rate? Is the artist to be paid per composite or by the hour? What about duty hours that may be required later for court testimony? Which agency pays for those? Who retains the original evidentiary composite drawing? The section on record keeping in Chapter 18 addresses this last point.

In initial contact with the officer, the artist should work out the specific date, time, and place for the interview and discuss the case in general. **The artist should attempt to obtain certain information beforehand from the requesting investigator in order to properly prepare for the composite interview.**

A general description of the crime should be obtained. While the artist need not be privileged to all of the case details, he or she should have some idea of what has transpired. Particularly pertinent are physical details such as time elapsed since the incident, time of day of the incident, weather conditions, lighting, distance, and angle of viewing.

The artist also should know some basic information about the person he will be interviewing, such as sex, age, and race. Knowledge of the person's occupation and general lifestyle factors may also aid in sensitive interviewing. For example, if an officer learns that a witness has recently experienced the death of a spouse or child, he should tell the artist. This would prevent the artist from inadvertently upsetting the witness during the interview by asking, "Do you have children?" or "Are you married?"

It should be determined if the witness has any special needs, such as an interpreter. A specialist in sign language might be required for a hearing impaired witness. While direct communication between the artist and the witness is ideal, assistance is sometimes necessary. In choosing an interpreter for a composite interview, the fluency of the interpreter should be assessed. I learned this lesson the hard way years ago, while struggling through an interview with a well-meaning but inadequate interpreter. These days, I always ask, "Can you distinguish between an eyelash and an eyebrow?" I find that if the interpreter's vocabulary is extensive enough to make this sort of specific distinction, things will work out.

Figure 6.7 shows a composite drawing prepared from the descriptive input of three witnesses *and* aided by a interpreter. Although it was a complex and time-consuming interview, the witnesses were able to accurately describe the subject down to a missing segment from his left ear. Their efforts aided in the recovery of an abducted, sexually assaulted child.

Most important to find out is the physical and emotional condition of the witness. Was the person threatened with a weapon? Was the person physically injured? Is the person hospitalized or on medication? If so, has the doctor approved the interview? How is the witness coping emotionally? Has the witness seen a victim services counselor?

On occasion, an officer may make the artist aware that there are suspicions as to the witness' veracity, or even that the witness is actually a suspect. **While most long-time composite artists become skilled interviewers, the role of interrogator is not the artist's. The artist's function is *never* to confront the witness directly, but rather to assume the witness is truthful until proven otherwise.** If suspicions arise during the course of the composite interview, the artist should

Figure 6.7 Composite drawing by KTT of suspect (left) and subject identified (right). The sketch was based on descriptive input given by **three witnesses interviewed simultaneously with the assistance of an interpreter.** (Courtesy of Texas Department of Public Safety.)

either take a break and discuss the issues with the investigator or wait until the interview is completed to do so.

Rare exceptions to this may occur if the artist is also an investigator, particularly in a smaller agency. In such cases, the responsibility of participation in the investigation may overlap with the duties of composite preparation.

Remember that the amount of information that you are privileged to know about a case may be dependent upon your status as a member of law enforcement or as a civilian freelancer. This may also be determined by the number of times you have previously worked with an agency or officer and the degree of rapport that exists between you and the officer.

If you regularly work together, the officer may fax or send you a copy of the witness' sworn statement and/or police incident reports prior to the interview. Such documents can be very helpful to the artist in preparing for the interview. For example, if the statement included reference to a certain type of eyeglasses worn by the subject, the artist could be sure to have photo references of similar types of eyeglasses on hand for use during the interview.

Saying "No"

There are times, unfortunately, when the appropriate response of a forensic artist to a composite request is "no." If, upon discussing the scenario of the crime, the artist and the investigator determine that the witness simply did not have the opportunity to obtain enough visual information to produce an effective composite, the session should be canceled. It is preferable to assess the case information *prior* to bringing the witness in for an interview, rather than to discover that the witness did not see enough *after* the witness has arrived. Everyone has wasted time and the witness will feel frustrated and ineffectual.

As the "Son of Sam" case (Chapter 15) shows, it is better to produce no composite image at all than to produce an incorrect one by "pushing" a witness. Distribution of a poor quality composite image can cause untold wasted investigative man-hours tracking down false leads.

The best response may be to suggest a delay. Obviously, cases of potential life and death, such as child abductions, should not be delayed for any reason. However, there are sometimes benefits in allowing the witness or victim to have a brief respite before proceeding with the composite interview. Many times, a witness has been subjected to hours of questioning after a crime occurs and has usually missed both meals and sleep. Allowing the witness a reasonable opportunity to rest and recover his or her bearings may dramatically improve the witness' ability to perform in the composite-generating process.

Practical Considerations

Physical Structure of the Interview

The wise interviewer/artist thoughtfully anticipates the variables involved in a successful interview, and attempts to favorably control as many of them as possible in order to produce the best possible results. As with all dealings with people, the unpredictable will occur, but advance preparation and consideration may go a long way toward the effective outcome of a composite interview situation.

Choice of Interviewer/Artist

There may be only one trained sketch artist for miles around to provide needed composite images for a given location. However, some agencies are fortunate enough to have several artists in their area. If that is the case, it may be advantageous to choose one artist over another after assessing the specific case situation.

Some have stated that female victims of sexual assault respond better to female interviewers and artists. In my experience, this assumption should not be made, and some female victims may actually feel safer and more comfortable with a male interviewer, depending on the individual and her background.

Another consideration in making a choice of artist or interviewer may be an individual's ability to relate well to a particular age or ethnic group. For example, some people are particularly good at engaging children in conversation and making them feel comfortable. An artist's ability to speak a particular language may indicate that he or she should be used.

Choice of Location

The choice of the site where the interview is to be conducted is especially important. It may mean the difference in the successful development of a composite sketch or not. Ideally, the place chosen should be safe, pleasant, and comfortable. **Where the victim will be most at ease is likely the place where the most effective interview will be conducted.** If the incident occurred in the victim's home, that may not be the best place to conduct the interview; however, some older victims may actually be comfortable only in the familiar surroundings of their own homes.

Victim/Witness' Home — If the decision is made to go to the victim/witness' home, certain ground rules should be courteously laid out. If at all possible, the distractions of phones, visitors, and family members (especially children) should be avoided. The interview should take place away from potential distractions in the house. The preparation of a drawing often arouses great interest and everyone wants to watch and get involved in the process. The artist needs to be alone with the witness to have the witness' full attention.

Witness' Workplace — Interviews conducted in the workplace, such as banks or businesses where robberies have occurred, may result in the same sort of complications as home interviews. Distractions such as phone calls and work necessities often interfere with a focused interview. A more controlled interview can be achieved at the artist's office or other selected site.

Police Station/Artist's Office — Police agencies sometimes have very comfortable interview rooms designed for the purpose of putting victims at ease. Others have only cramped spaces where interrogations are conducted. **Optimum results will not be achieved if the victim is made to feel he or she is being interrogated.** Some individuals feel uncomfortable simply by setting foot into a police station.

Safety and protection of the victim/witness should always be a concern. In high-profile cases, it is sometimes necessary to "hide" the victim from members of the media who seek an interview. Many times witnesses are brought in quietly through secluded building entrances to protect their identities.

A physically injured victim should also be protected from prying eyes as much as possible. Over the years, I have made it my practice with new employees in the office, particularly the receptionists who greet visitors, to discuss the importance of not staring at victims who come to my office for interviews. Most times, **victims of violent crimes have been embarrassed and humiliated as part of the crime experience and great effort should be made to prevent causing additional feelings of exposure.**

Over the years supervisors at the Texas Department of Public Safety provided me an ideally suited office space for interviewing. A three-room suite allowed for a waiting area for police officers and family members with a separate space for private interviewing. Plants and other furnishings were chosen for comfort. A sink was available if a victim felt nauseous.

The temperature in the interview environment is significant. Victims of trauma often become easily chilled, especially when, in the course of preparation of the composite, the incident again comes to focus in their minds. The effect of being very cold can be totally distracting when it occurs during the interview process.

A few years ago, I was asked by a police agency to re-interview the survivor of a brutal rape, who had been interviewed previously by another artist who was unable to produce a drawing at all. This artist, a male, was someone I knew to be talented and a skilled interviewer, and I felt it unlikely that I could produce a drawing when he could not. After contacting the artist and discussing the case with him, he encouraged me to make the attempt, stating that a female interviewer might have better luck with the young female victim. The second interview resulted in a successful drawing that led to the identification of the assailant (Figure 6.8). At the end of the interview, I asked the young woman what the problem was with the first interview. She stated, "I liked that guy. He was a good artist, but his office was so cold, I just wanted to get up and run out of there. After a while, I couldn't take it any more and just told him I couldn't do a drawing and left." This simple circumstance prevented successful preparation of a sketch.

Hospital — The specifics of interviews conducted in hospitals are discussed in more depth in Chapter 5. Basically, if it is imperative to facilitate the investigation by conducting an interview while the victim is still hospitalized, every effort should be made to consider the victim's comfort and the doctor's wishes.

As with choice of artists, choice of location may not be an option. The situation will vary depending upon whether you work at a police agency or on a freelance basis. I have conducted successful composite drawing interviews in unusual positions at extremely varied locations, including sitting on a dirt floor of a home with no running water and with chickens running through the house. Figure 6.9 shows a composite drawing I did in a broom closet of a back room of a rural Texas grocery store! **Adaptability on the part of the artist/interviewer is a necessity.**

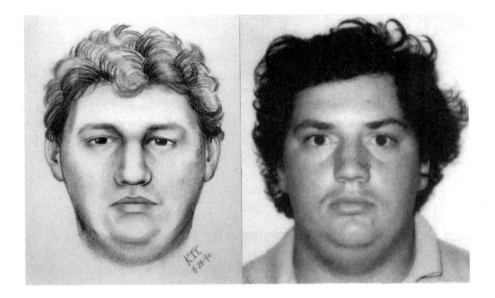

Figure 6.8 Composite drawing by KTT of suspect (left) and subject identified (right). The victim was unable to produce a description or drawing in the first interview, simply because she was placed in a **room that was too cold**. (Courtesy of Texas Department of Public Safety.)

Figure 6.9 Composite drawing by KTT of suspect (left) and subject identified (right). The **sketch was done in a broom closet** in the back room of a rural grocery store. (Courtesy of Texas Department of Public Safety.)

Actual Interview Setup

The actual physical arrangement of witness and artist should be carefully considered. As shown in Figure 6.10, **a good choice is a side-by-side posture.** This ensures that the artist's own face will not be inadvertently focused upon and described. It is also a flexible arrangement that allows the artist to begin the drawing with the drawing board slightly angled away from the witness' view, working until a full face is roughly established. Then the artist can move around so that the drawing is easily viewed by the witness who may give input for progressively refining the face.

Another good working arrangement some artists prefer is achieved through positioning on a corner of a table or desk. The witness sits at one angle and the artist sits at the perpendicular angle.

Drawing with the paper inclined upward rather than flat on the table is advisable for several reasons. In general, facial drawings produced while the paper is flat on a surface may contain distortion or foreshortening. A flat drawing position may cause discomfort to the back during the long hours of drawing often required for composite interviews. Use of a tabletop easel or a hard drawing board angled on the edge of a table to prop up the drawing is recommended. This practice facilitates the composite drawing process because it allows the witness to view the drawing during the fine-tuning stages of the procedure.

I know one artist who works on a large painter's easel and positions the witness slightly behind herself and to the side. This also allows the witness to view the drawing and not the artist's face.

Figure 6.10 The artist interviews the witness in a **side-by-side position** so that her own face is not focused upon. This drawing is in the fine-tuning drawing stage with the witness referring to the *FBI Facial Identification Catalog* and other reference photographs. (Courtesy of Missey Micheletti and Texas Department of Public Safety.)

On rare occasions when two witnesses are interviewed together, I place myself in the center chair with a witness on each side. If a third person is present, I place a witness on each side and the third one slightly behind and above on a high stool. **A face-to-face arrangement in which the witness or witnesses constantly stare at the artist's face is not recommended.**

Time of the Interview

Several factors should be considered when scheduling the time of the interview. Ascertain from the investigator the emotional condition of the witness, the time elapsed since the incident occurred, and the specific witness' lifestyle and time schedule.

Post-Trauma Stages

As a very general guideline, individuals who have experienced traumatic events of various types go through certain stages. In the initial stages of **shock**, the mind protects us by implementing mechanisms of **disbelief** and then **denial**. At some point, there usually follows a period of **anger**. This is highly variable, coming very quickly for some people and taking more time for others. Some experience feelings of **guilt**, usually followed by an attitude of **acceptance**.

In my experience, **the anger phase seems to be a particularly good time to conduct a composite interview.** The shock, disbelief, and denial have passed and the victim is ready to face the event head-on and "get back" at the individual who has caused so much pain and distress. **Preparing a composite drawing often provides the first tangible opportunity control for the victim to regain as well as a constructive step toward recovery.**

Time since the Event

As discussed in Chapter 5, numerous studies have been conducted regarding variables in accuracy of verbal facial descriptions or facial identification success in relation to the retrieval aspect of memory. Although findings vary, **it is generally agreed that both recall and recognition accuracy decline over time.**

As a very general guideline, it is better to do composite interviews with less traumatized victim/witnesses promptly after an event. This may mean an hour, a day, or a week. Severely traumatized victims or witnesses may require time to regain their bearings and be emotionally ready to do a composite drawing. The recovery time trauma victims may need before doing a composite interview may vary considerably from days to many weeks or longer, depending on their physical or emotional injuries.

Certainly, law enforcement officials are often faced with situations that present great urgency, usually matters of life or death, which require prompt preparation of composite images. **Hopefully, a balance can be struck between the need to protect the public and consideration for the victim who must relive a recent trauma to prepare a composite.**

Time of the Day

Consider the hour of the day at which the interview is to be scheduled. Considerations to discuss with the investigators may include:

- Is the witness a "morning person"?
- Is the witness a "night owl"?
- Does the witness normally work nights?
- Is the witness a mother worrying about picking up her children after school?
- Is the witness worried and distracted about an upcoming appointment?

If it is possible to control the scheduling of interviews, use common sense and schedule witnesses at times when they will be most alert and attentive.

Victim Considerations

Put Yourself in the Interviewee's Situation

Perhaps the best way to empathetically approach a victim/witness interview is to try to place yourself mentally and emotionally in that person's situation. Perhaps you think that you have little in common with the person you are interviewing, but we must all be capable of human kindness and compassion.

This does not mean that your treatment of a victim should be condescending or overly emotional. Each of us deals with trauma and stress differently. As an interviewer, you must be able to adapt responsively to the particular individual you are interviewing and express concern for that individual's well-being.

Physical Considerations

Physical Injuries/Pain/Medication

If possible, be aware of the physical needs of the witness before the witness arrives. I once interviewed a sexual assault victim who had jumped from a speeding car to escape her attacker. In the process, she incurred extensive abrasions on one side of her body making it almost impossible for her to sit upright in a chair. The investigator preferred that the interview be done at my office rather than at the victim's residence. After learning of her condition from the officer, I prepared by having quilts for the floor as well as several pillows. Since she was only comfortable while standing or reclining, we conducted the entire interview on the floor.

As discussed in Chapter 5, in the section on hospital interviews, the artist should be aware of any strong medications the witness may be taking. If the medicines cause drowsiness, the composite session might best be delayed. Although the production of a composite drawing with a witness taking a strong medication might be possible, doing so might later provide a point of argument for a defense attorney.

Weaker, "over-the-counter" medications might pose no problem. Figure 6.11 shows a composite drawing done from the description of a man just released from the hospital. Although he had been brutally stabbed and his abdomen was held together by sutures and staples, he managed to produce the composite drawing while taking only mild

Figure 6.11 Composite drawing by KTT of suspect (left) and subject identified (right). The sketch was **based on the description of a severely injured individual, taking only "over-the-counter" medication**. (Courtesy of Texas Department of Public Safety.)

medication. Witnesses, particularly when injured or emotionally upset, should always be made aware in advance by the investigator or the artist of the approximate time frame of the composite interview. It may be wise for the investigator to advise the witness to bring the medication to the interview for use if needed.

Food/Sleep

As with considerations of physical comforts and medications, the witness' need for food and sleep may become important. The artist may suggest that the investigator schedule the witness to be interviewed after a meal, thus preparing the witness for an extended time in the artist's office. The officer should also encourage the witness to try to rest before the interview, although this may be difficult for victims of recent trauma. See also the information in Chapter 5 regarding the importance of sleep.

As a logistical matter for me, working in a state the size of Texas, having lunch with witnesses has proven a practical and useful activity. Officers often travel 2 or 3 hours with a witness to visit me for an interview (or I may travel some time and distance to reach them). Going to lunch with the officer and the witness before the interview is an opportunity to begin building rapport and to dispel anxieties. Time is saved, and the witness is rested and fed, and begins the session more comfortably acquainted with me.

Small Comforts

As discussed in Chapter 5, small comforts can be very important. Explain the smoking policy. Give directions to restrooms to officers, witnesses, and family members. Inquire about the comfort of the room temperature. Explain telephone use procedures. Offer candy or gum from jars in your office. Point out the location of break room facilities or vending machines. Such seemingly small amenities may help ensure the comfort and attentiveness of the witness, and result in a better finished composite.

Emotional Considerations

Choice of Clothing for the Interviewer

I have been accused of dressing in "costumes" for conducting composite interviews. I have learned through experience the real benefit of putting people at ease through my own clothing style. For me, the carefully selected business suits for court testimony usually have no place in the interview situation.

By asking questions of the investigator about the witness prior to the session I gain some idea of how to best put the witness at ease. Certainly, my choice of clothing varies if I interview a small child, a prostitute, a bank president, a teen-age gang member, or a plumber.

While presenting a professional, "together," or "in charge" appearance serves detectives well, the artist may also wish to appear casual and "approachable." **Forensic artists who are also sworn police officers are advised to leave uniforms at home and weapons out of sight.** The idea is to comfort and to avoid intimidation.

Rapport Building

Each interviewer must develop personal ways of calming witnesses and making them comfortable. Relaxing the witness encourages recall and aids in the production of a composite. Flexibility of the interviewer to discuss a variety of topics with many different personality types of various ages is helpful toward this end.

Dispel Fears and Anxieties

Helpful statements to dispel anxieties and potential psychological blockages are outlined in Chapter 5. Particularly in cases of sexual assault it is important to explain that the details of the assault will not have to be repeated.

Language Choice and Voice Intonation

As discussed with regard to child interviews in Chapter 5, adjustments in choice of language and vocabulary may be required to encourage effective communication with some witnesses. The artist should select words or phrases that seem compatible with the particular witness.

The artist's voice may be used to have a calming and soothing effect on witnesses or victims. Careful use of intonation and inflection may help the witness remain stable through difficult portions of the interview. Hypnotists use this method of lulling subjects into a calm, tranquil state. Avoid sudden outbursts or loud statements that might unnerve an "edgy" witness.

"Fidget Toys"

Small, hand-held toys designed to occupy the hands may be helpful for nervous interviewees. Providing them within easy reach allows the witness to handle the toys and maintain the reality of the present while discussing a traumatic past event.

Others Allowed into the Interview

Family members and friends often accompany victims to the composite interview for support. Usually at least one police officer is present and sometimes a victim services counselor is present. **As a general rule, it is best to get the witness alone.** You will be better able to maintain the witness' full attention, focusing on the task at hand.

There are exceptions when a supportive person may be allowed to stay during the interview. Traumatized or emotionally upset victims may need friends, relatives, or victim services personnel with them. In such cases, take care not to allow any disruptions or interference to occur as a result of their presence.

It is not a good idea to allow individuals who are simply curious to be involved in the interview. Similarly, members of the media may seek to have cameras in the interview room to film the rather interesting process of memory retrieval and composite drawing. Although I have been asked on several occasions, my policy is *not* to allow this practice, for protection of the sanctity of the interview procedure. Even though an intimidated victim/witness may be reluctant to say "no" to such a request if asked, the victim probably would rather retain his or her privacy. If showing "an interview in progress" is required for a media production, a simulated interview can be set up, thus sparing the victim the added stress of cameras and avoiding risk to the investigation.

Psychological Considerations

Chapter 5 discusses various psychological issues significant for the composite production process. These include the possibility for unconscious transference and mistaken identification, the potential benefits of multiple memory retrieval attempts, and avoiding postevent inputs.

As a practical matter, I have learned while preparing composite images that certain methods of phrasing questions are more psychologically beneficial. Avoiding terms of direction, for example, lead to greater accuracy. Rather than asking, "Was the scar you are describing on his left cheek or his right cheek?", I avoid the specific terminology. I refer to my own face *or* hold up the drawing and gesture, asking, "Was it on this side or that side as you faced him?" This simple approach helps eliminate the confusion that often occurs when the mind tries to reverse things from left to right. Figure 6.12 shows a composite drawing in which the victim was confused as to which side the hair was parted on, yet an overall resemblance or gestalt was achieved.

Physiological Indicators of Stress

The experienced interviewer learns to become very sensitive to the physiological or autonomic signs exhibited by a witness during the course of the interview. In the case of interrogations by detectives or examinations by polygraphers, such indicators of stress may be clues to guilt.

Figure 6.12   Composite drawing by KTT of suspect (left) and subject identified (right). The **witness was confused as to which side the hair was parted on**, yet an overall resemblance or gestalt was achieved. (Courtesy of Texas Department of Public Safety.)

When interviewing crime victims or witnesses, signs of physiological distress reveal that some of the adrenalin-related changes to the body that originally occurred during the crime event may be revisiting. This may indicate that the interviewer should pull back from a particular line of discussion, thus giving the witness a mental break from the stressor causing the physical arousal.

Numerous signs may indicate stress-related changes in respiration, circulation, or other body processes. Trauma victims often experience chills, but they may also experience increased heart rate, leading to heat and excessive perspiration.

As adrenalin pours into the body, the body prepares itself for action. Blanching of the face may occur as blood leaves the head, sometimes a sign that fainting may be imminent. Facial blanching may also be a sign that the blood has traveled to the muscles of the extremities in preparation for the primitive "fight or flight" reaction. Conversely, the face may redden as blood rushes there from anger or distress.

Visible changes in breathing may be seen and an upset stomach may occur. As digestive processes are affected, saliva production may be reduced, causing dry mouth, usually indicated by licking of the lips or coughing.

More subtly, the pupils of the eyes may visibly change in size despite the lighting in the room. Desmond Morris discusses this phenomenon in *Manwatching: A Field Guide to Human Behavior:*

> …But it is not only light that affects the pupils. They are also affected by emotional changes. And it is because emotional changes can noticeably alter pupil size when the light remains constant that pupil size-change operates as a mood signal. If we see something that excites us, whether with pleasurable anticipation or with fear, our pupils expand more than usual for the existing light conditions.[5]

Sociological Considerations

The sensitive interviewer should be aware of the social variants that may occur within the various cultural groups he or she may be called upon to interview. For example, interviewing an Asian witness or victim may prove quite different from interviewing an African-American witness or a Middle Eastern witness. It is useful to inform yourself about the socially accepted behavior for certain groups so as not to risk offending unconsciously. A gesture or behavior may mean one thing to one group and a totally different thing to another group.

Knowledge of vernacular language may come in very handy for the composite artist. Terminology for descriptions of skin color or hair styles may be very social, cultural, or regional in nature. For example, a soldier from a military base may describe a short hairdo as "high and tight." Descriptions of African-American hairdos may include terms like "corn rows," "dred locks," a "fade," a "jeri curl," or a "freeze."

Over time, the experienced composite artist learns to incorporate subtle changes requested by the witness that are somewhat difficult to quantify in regular language. I have learned to make the face "yukkier," "ickier," "creepier," etc. These terms are sometimes emotional in nature, yet it is important to achieve the look the witness seeks. Since composites may appear somewhat symmetrical or generic, changes described in such terms may be achieved through the addition of slight asymmetries, textures, *or* nebulous expressions (see Chapter 3). In any case, the communication between artist and witness often becomes very sensitive and personal.

Individual Victim/Witness Variants

The interviewer begins the composite interview session with a commonsense assessment of each witness. In addition to the behaviors or descriptions that may be social in nature, other factors of importance affecting descriptions may result from the ancestry, sex, age, or other physical features of the individual witness.

As individuals, we tend to assess things by making comparative assessments using ourselves or our own experiences. That is to say, the child witness describing a person as really "old" may mean 20 years of age. A senior citizen describing a person as "just a kid" may mean 50 years of age. The interviewer/artist must learn to consider factors about the individual being interviewed and then use the information provided in that context.

Parallel statements may be true for descriptions of physical attractiveness, degree of skin lightness or darkness, body weight, etc. The artist must assess such descriptions giving consideration to these factors as seen in the witness. For example, a description of "light skin" would mean something different depending upon whether the witness was a fair-skinned, blue-eyed, blonde Caucasian or a dark-skinned, brown-eyed Negro.

Witnesses who are self-conscious about a particular feature that they consider to be either very good or very bad in themselves may take special note of that feature in others. The classic example of this is small-breasted women, who always notice breast size of other women. A witness who feels he or she has bad teeth or a crooked nose may be especially adept at describing teeth or noses.

Reference Files

The nature and quality of a composite sketch artist's reference files may serve to greatly enhance the artist's ability to do effective work. I will never forget the first time, many years ago, that a witness asked me to draw a cowboy hat and the panic that it struck in my heart! That was the day I began to seriously develop photographic reference files. Good reference files should be cultivated over time. By habitually thinking about file development as you flip through magazines, books or catalogs, your files evolve and improve constantly.

If encumbered by a lack of artistic knowledge of drawing a certain feature such as a cowboy hat, it would be very foolish indeed not to make use of photo references. Commercial illustrators certainly use reference photographs on a regular basis to achieve accuracy. **The police composite artist strives to produce the most accurate facial drawing possible. If correctly used, photographic references can greatly enhance this accuracy.**

Why Use Reference Photographs?

It can sometimes be quite obvious when a particular artist fails to use reference photos. **Without reference photos, all of the faces an artist draws tend to look alike.** Similarly, certain stylistic tendencies show through more heavily than they should, e.g., if the artist tends to draw small ears, all of the faces he or she draws will have small ears. Such unconscious inclusion of personal visions of features should be avoided.

Perhaps the best argument for the use of reference photographs is their ability to produce a clearer, more specific communication between the artist and the witness. For example, if I were an artist who did not use references, and I was asked to draw a round or fat face, I would draw *my* interpretation of a round, fat face. However, if I provided the witness with several photographs of full faces (once the witness had already indicated a full face description), allowing the witness to choose the face shape closest to the one the witness saw, I then would fully understand the witness' meaning. I then draw the **purest version of the witness' memory**, avoiding incorporation of my personal attitudes about what a round, fat face should look like.

My forensic art colleagues Carrie Parks and Lt. Lisa Sheppard have compared the use of photo references to test-taking. Drawing composites from verbal description alone is something akin to answering "essay" questions. Use of reference photos makes it more a matter of "multiple choice," which most people agree is a simpler process.

In Chapter 5, Figure 5.5, the composite drawing was based on input from a victim who had been sexually assaulted and had had her throat cut. During the hospital interview, she was totally unable to speak. Without the use of reference photos the drawing would have been impossible. By writing notes and pointing to reference photos, this victim prepared a composite that led directly to the capture of the offender, a man later convicted of murdering three women.

Recall vs. Recognition

Besides the advantage of a facilitated, more specific communication with the witness produced by the use of reference photographs, there is also a sound psychological basis for their use. **The retrieval aspect of the memory process, the portion dealt with by the composite artist, is composed of two general aspects: (1) recall, a verbal**

skill, and (2) recognition, a visual skill. Most psychologists suggest that recall is a more difficult function than recognition. If information is not easily or automatically recalled, a cue or stimulus may facilitate the recollection, as A.L. Brown describes:

> Thus, recall is the most difficult process, as it demands regeneration in the absence of the stimulus, whereas reconstruction and recognition take place in the presence of the actual stimulus or its disarranged elements.[6]

Frank Domingo refers to the issue of the use of photographic references to enhance memory in his paper, "Forensic Art: Practical Considerations of Witness Memory":

> The terms "cue" and "stimulus" are common expressions used in the field of psychology. In this context, they are synonymous, and refer to abstract or physical hints that can signal the start of another action or thought, and may help retrieve past experiences. A cue may help to restore the memory of an event and to envision the overall situation. It may be abstract mental stimuli that result from recounting the incident, as in the free narrative portion of the interview session or, a cue may be something physical such as an arrest photo.
>
> Laboratory tests indicate that the use of cues will aid in reviving a witness's memory. Therefore, it would be in the composite artist's best interest to make use of the stronger portion of the retrieval process (recognition), by having witnesses refresh their memories through the use of cues. The use of reference material, such as facial cues, will aid in the recognition of shapes, proportions, or unusual facial characteristics.[7]

Correct Use of Photographic References

Reference photographs, while an excellent tool, must be used with thought and deliberate action. It would not be appropriate, for example, to seat a witness in front of a drawer of mug files containing faces of all races and both sexes. This would surely confuse the witness and risk serious contamination of the facial memory.

As outlined in Chapter 5 in the section on composite-specific interviewing, **photographs should be introduced only after the facial drawing has been well established.**

FBI Facial Identification Catalog

The FBI has developed a catalog of facial photographs for the express use by police sketch artists. The booklet, entitled *FBI Facial Identification Catalog*, was prepared by the Graphic Design Unit of the Special Projects Section of the Laboratory Division. Participants invited to attend the artist training workshop at the FBI Academy in Quantico, Virginia are given a copy of the catalog along with instructions for its use.

The booklets are sometimes made available upon request to artists employed by law enforcement agencies, but the availability varies depending upon numbers of copies on hand at a given time.

The original purpose of the catalog was to provide composite images to the FBI field offices all across the U.S. in a timely manner. The field agents interviewed witnesses who then selected features from the catalog that resembled the features of the perpetrator's

Figure 6.13 A page from the *FBI Facial Identification Catalog*, showing "Bulging Eyes," (Courtesy of Federal Bureau of Investigation.)

face. The agent used a form called the Facial Identification Fact Sheet (FD-383), designed to accompany the catalog, to record the features by the key number shown below each photographic feature selection. The form was then forwarded to the Special Projects Section at headquarters in Washington, D.C. for the preparation of a composite drawing based on the selected features. After a drawing was prepared, it was sent to the field agent who showed it to the witness. The witness could request corrections or revisions, which were made at headquarters and faxed to the field office for the witness' review. The process continued until the drawing was satisfactory.

Artists often use the catalog as a reference to facial features. Pages are set up by categories of face shapes, eye types, nose types, mouths types, and so on, with 16 photographs appearing on each page (Figure 6.13). Areas of each face are blocked out, thus focusing attention on the feature of significance in a photo and forcing the viewer to look at the primary area of interest.

I have made several bound copies of the catalog to use during an interview. The witness selects a feature, shows it to me, and then continues looking through the catalog. I may use four or five copies of the catalog as I draw, each turned to the page showing a different feature selected by the witness.

The catalog provides a good basis for the artist's reference files, but it has the disadvantage of obscuring facial proportions with the blocking of certain areas on each face. While it is a useful tool for specific feature selection, it is less useful for the critical establishment of proportions in a drawing. It also lacks photographs of profiles, females, or faces with a wide variety of ethnic looks. Therefore, these areas must be developed in each artist's file of references. As stated in the introduction to the catalog:

> We fully realize that these examples will not provide a "look-alike" for every individual facial feature. They will, however, provide basic categories to serve as a detailed reference source. By using these examples, either in their

entirety or as fragments, likenesses of unknown subjects can be created that will be valuable for investigative use. Briefly, this system is a "mail-order catalog and order blank" which the Agent and the witness can use to clarify the transmittal of thought regarding facial characteristics and which will materially assist in getting good artist's composite drawings made with a minimum of delay and expense.[8]

Mug Shots

Each artist must decide not only whether or not to use reference photos, but also which sort of system will be most useful for the artist's individual style of conducting an interview. Many artists spend years building a system of photographic references that fulfill their needs, while others keep their references quite basic. My personal files are divided rather simply by race, sex, and age. They are then subdivided into "younger" and "older." I have files grouped as "younger Asian females," "older Asian females," and so forth. These photographic files are primarily mug shots. They are stored in small file drawers the same size as the photographs.

Many artists use further subdivisions, often following the general categories used in the *FBI Facial Identification Catalog.* Thus, they develop files of "facial shapes," "types of eyes," "types of noses," etc.

Particularly useful to me is a smaller file I have called "Anomalies." In this photo file drawer, a typical category would be "teeth," subdivided into sections such as "braces" or "protruding teeth." Aspects such as "skin textures" or "prosthetic eyes" are included.

It may be helpful to maintain photo files of both color and black-and-white mug shots, although you may be limited to photographs available to you. Some artists find it easier to use the shading in black and white photos as drawing references for features. The color photos are beneficial for assessing skin tones, particularly in African Americans. Often, I ask a witness to select an appropriate skin tone from color photos even though we are preparing a black and white drawing. I use the photo to aid in drawing the skin tone and also show the color photo selected to the investigator for his insight.

My mug shot files contain photos from the State Department of Corrections and city police agencies. The black and white penitentiary photos are clear and excellent for use of the features, but the subjects lack long hair or facial hair. Therefore, I supplement my files with local arrest photos showing beards, mustaches, and various hairstyles.

Artists who have attended my workshops have assisted one another by exchanging mug shots to help improve their individual reference files. For example, artists who reside in certain areas of the country may have greater access to particular ethnic looks in their mug files.

Certainly, any exchange of mug shots should be done with caution and with a specific understanding of the legal limitations for their use by a given police agency. Some artists even develop photo files that include only photos of deceased subjects to eliminate possible legal difficulties.

A few years ago, a person being interviewed actually found the suspect's photo in the artist's reference files during the composite interview. In this case, the identification was considered sound and there were no problems. It was determined that the suspect had, in fact, been picked from a group of photographs of a far greater number than the number required by law for a photo line-up or photo array. Thus, the identification was legally valid. Perhaps this incident makes a reasonable argument for the benefits of photo exchange by artists from different faraway cities for use in reference files.

Other Reference Sources

The possibilities for photo resources are virtually limitless. Magazines offer all sorts of good quality images for use in the artist's files. I have found that **hairstyle magazines** are especially helpful. For years, I have pestered my hairdresser and friend, Zan Ray, to give me her old stylist catalogs. It is helpful to have books of both older and more current styles. The older styles may be used for reference in cases of skull reconstruction, to select a style appropriate for the approximated year of death of the victim.

Other **catalogs** of various types may be resources for eyeglasses, clothing, hats, weapons, tattoos, jewelry, or just about anything imaginable.

The **Internet** can be searched for very specific information if the artist has advance information about a particular item needed. For example, the artist might be told by the officer requesting a composite that the witness has described a cap with a sports team logo. If known in advance, the artist can probably locate the specific logo on the Internet and arrive at the interview with the precise image needed for accuracy.

After hearing numerous references to likenesses of facial features to celebrities, I began to keep a file of **celebrity photographs**. As previously discussed, the mind tends to seek something familiar and recognizable about a face. As part of encoding a face in memory, many people register, "his eyes remind me of so and so." This associated face may be someone the person knows, but it is often a television, film, music, or sports celebrity. For this reason, it may be useful to maintain files of celebrity photos. It may be necessary to assess the celebrity photo with the witness to ascertain just what it is about the face that is comparable to the offender's face, but the witness should not be allowed to view such a photo for a prolonged period (if at all) because of the potential for unconscious transference and confusion. It is preferable that only the *artist* view the photo and then *discuss* it with the witness to pinpoint the needed simularity.

From time to time, I have borrowed large **catalogs of photos of vehicles** from our Motor Vehicle Theft Service. These books, published by automobile manufacturers, show multiple views of vehicles of different years and models and may be shown to witnesses to aid with vehicle identification. The *Polk Manual,* published annually by a private company, shows photographs of the current license plates for every state in the U.S. Although the composite interview may deal primarily with a facial description, license plate or vehicle descriptions may also be given. Since the memory is emotively and actively refreshed by preparation of the facial composite, it may also be an advantageous time to obtain other descriptive information.

Useful Objects to Have on Hand

In addition to my photographic reference files, I have found it beneficial to have certain items physically on hand. In Texas, as elsewhere, lots of people wear baseball-style caps. It is a simple matter to keep a **styrofoam wig head and a cap** or two in the office. It becomes quite easy for the witness to literally demonstrate the angle at which the cap rested on the suspect's head. The artist can draw in a more precise and naturalistic way by observing the way in which the cap fits the head.

As previously discussed, large pads of **inexpensive drawing paper and crayons** have come in very handy for use in entertaining small children, as well as gaining descriptive information. Figure 5.9 in Chapter 5 shows a useful child's drawing done as part of a composite interview with his mother. Stuffed toys and simple games are also always on hand in my office. Interviewing children is discussed in more detail in

Chapter 5. Crayons, large sets of colored pencils, and graphics product catalogs have also proven useful when trying to establish certain colors of items of clothing or vehicles. For example, descriptions of colors such as "khaki" may mean very different things to different people; it may be described as brown, beige, green, tan, etc. As with other aspects of interviewing for facial drawing, try to clarify specifically by ascertaining just what the witness means by "khaki."

Other Uses for the Photo Reference Files

If you are an artist doing other forensic art functions in addition to preparation of composite drawings, you may need to develop multi-purpose photo files.

If you utilize computer software to enhance facial images, such as morgue photos or fugitive photos, you may have difficulty with scanning of already digitized or half-toned photographs. You may prefer to maintain continuous-tone photographs rather than pixelated ones for this purpose.

If you work with child age progression, you must greatly expand your reference files, as discussed in Chapter 7.

The Composite Drawing

Time Frame for Drawing

Often officers ask how long it will take me to prepare a composite drawing. Of course, this is a difficult question to answer precisely. It is necessary, however, to give the victim/witness, the officer, and family members some reasonable idea of the length of time they will be occupied.

My usual procedure is to tell officers to allow at least 2 hours in my office, with a caveat statement that it could take more or less time. The reality is that I have done drawings in 15 or 20 minutes and I have done drawings that required 4 hours or more. Some drawings have even required a second visit, but this is quite rare.

Figures 6.14 and 6.15 show composite drawings done for use in the same case on separate days. The descriptions came from the victim of a kidnapping and sexual assault who was attacked by three offenders. Because she had to describe three separate faces, it was advantageous for her to come for two different sessions. Although she was able to prepare two drawings in one day, a third would have been quite fatiguing. In two interview sessions, she was better able to separate the subjects in her mind, and she managed to successfully describe all three, leading to their identification. It is interesting to note in the drawings that she described in greater detail the subject whom she considered to be the "leader," and by whom she was most threatened.

The variables in timing should be related to the victim's needs, not to your inabilities as an artist. There are occasions when the victim is so stressed at the mere prospect of reliving the incident by thinking about the person's face, that the artist must take a great deal of time to calm the victim. Stress can be induced by concern over whether or not the victim can successfully accomplish this task of doing a drawing. Recently, a woman came to my office for a composite interview, and twice vomited before we could even discuss the preparation of the drawing. Her husband and I simply comforted her, and allowed her to decide when she was ready to tackle the chore. After about an hour, we finally began the process of doing a drawing and successfully completed it.

Figure 6.14 Composite drawing by KTT of suspect (left) and subject identified (right). This subject was the first of three perpetrators described by a victim of kidnapping and sexual assault. He was considered "the leader" by the victim and his description was more detailed. (Courtesy of Texas Department of Public Safety.)

Workshops or discussions with professional colleagues help the artist to determine whether he or she is drawing at a good pace. If you are in a class, and you are either the first or the last person to finish, you should take note. If you finish too quickly, you may be failing to obtain all of the available descriptive information. If you are too slow, you risk losing the interest and focus of your witnesses and should work to speed up. See Chapter 4 for technical suggestions for enhancing speed.

Figure 6.15 Composite drawing by KTT of suspect (left) and subject identified (right). This subject was the second of three perpetrators described by a victim of kidnapping and sexual assault. (Courtesy of Texas Department of Public Safety.)

Procedure for Composite Drawing

It is with some reluctance that I offer advice for a specific pattern for development for a facial composite sketch, since each witness is an individual and each interview is unique. The following suggestions for drawing should be used only as a general guide, allowing each drawing to unfold in a natural way for you as an interviewer. However, because the production of composite images is done within the context of law enforcement, efforts should be made to standardize procedures within loosely structured guidelines. This promotes professionalism and helps ensure that composite images will be acceptable as evidence for use in the prosecutorial process in court. **Try to find a fairly routine manner of conducting the composite-specific interview and developing the drawing.** You should be prepared to describe this process in court if called upon to do so.

Formal art training courses emphasize first blocking out the face, and then progressively detailing the drawing. All-in-all, I believe this to be good advice for the composite artist. **There is a tendency, particularly with artists who draw slowly or who have done lots of work copying photographs, to overly focus upon and prematurely embellish one area of the face, usually the eyes.** In workshops, I try to discourage this practice, telling students that finishing one area far more than another is permissible in fine art or even when doing child age progressions, fugitive updates, or postmortem drawings in forensic art. In composite art, however, **the witness needs to see the entire face as quickly as possible. Psychological studies indicate that recognition is triggered by the overall face, rather than by specific isolated features,** so I continue to recommend that the entire face be developed to some extent before showing it to the witness for the first time.

It is simply not practical to indulge yourself in detailing one feature, such as the eyes, before establishing the overall proportions. Since establishment of correct proportions is the single most critical aspect of attaining likeness in composite imagery, it must be done as accurately as possible. If you draw highly detailed eyes, only to discover that they must be made wider apart, you will have to erase one and move it. Or, if you moan over the erasure of your beautifully drawn eye and do not move it, your likeness will suffer. This could have been avoided if you had first established the proportional arrangement of features before getting too specific in any one area. **Effort should be made to develop the drawing to the same overall degree of "finish" as you work.**

Even though this approach may be a struggle for you, with discipline it can be adopted, and the resulting likenesses will be improved. If you find yourself overly focusing on a particular area, mentally "pull back" and force your eye to see the overall image.

Over time, I have seen in my own drawings a tendency toward development of the "inner triangle" of the face in somewhat more detail before the perimeter of the facial shape. I like to concentrate on getting the proportions within the eye, nose, and mouth area correct and then firm up the outer shape.

Chapter 4 offers numerous pointers for effectively drawing the human visage in a way that conveys useful, accurate information.

The composite-specific interview section in Chapter 5 should be reviewed in conjunction with the general steps given below. In the four drawings that follow I demonstrate these steps.

1. Initial Drawing Stage: Establishing the Face

Do an Initial "Run-Through" to Gain the Facial Description.

Allow the witness to begin a "free-recall" or "free-narrative" description of the subject. Listen very carefully and assess what aspects of the description are most emphasized. Ask open-ended, yet structured, questions.

Block Out the Proportions and Establish the Basic Facial Character.

Lightly block out the features and proportions of the face to establish the basic facial character. Ask more specific questions regarding spatial relationships of features. Focus on the spatial arrangement of features at this point, not fussy drawing details.

Have the Witness Look Briefly at the Initial Drawing.

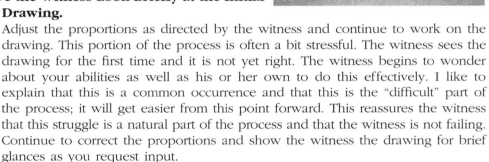

Adjust the proportions as directed by the witness and continue to work on the drawing. This portion of the process is often a bit stressful. The witness sees the drawing for the first time and it is not yet right. The witness begins to wonder about your abilities as well as his or her own to do this effectively. I like to explain that this is a common occurrence and that this is the "difficult" part of the process; it will get easier from this point forward. This reassures the witness that this struggle is a natural part of the process and that the witness is not failing. Continue to correct the proportions and show the witness the drawing for brief glances as you request input.

2. Fine-Tuning Drawing Stage: Refinement of the Face

Use Multiple-Choice Questions to Fine Tune.

Allow the witness to explain the needed changes. Your questions begin to get more and more specific, offering multiple choices.

Selectively Introduce Photographic References to Refine the Face.

With knowledge of the needed changes, introduce photographic references with guidance. Use photos selected to refine the face, defining specific shapes of features. Continue to adjust and define the features at the direction of the witness.

You will find that the apprehension of the earlier stages begins to diminish. Most witnesses seize the opportunity to get actively involved in the process once you introduce the reference photographs. They become more and more enthused as they participate and begin to see improvement and a likeness emerge.

3. Finishing Touches

Review the Individual Components of the Face.

As you correct the features and they become satisfactory to the witness, begin to finish the drawing with contrast, shading, and highlighting.

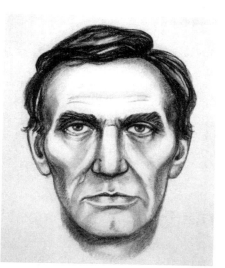

The witness will likely become more and more enthusiastic and feel great satisfaction in providing assistance to the investigation. You should positively reinforce these feelings. Thank the witness for his or her patience throughout the interview.

Sign, Date, and/or Stamp for Identification Purposes.

Document the finished drawing as an item of evidence by signing, dating, and/or stamping. Many artists have a rubber stamp made for this purpose, including the information appropriate for their particular agency, usually a department logo, date, and so forth.

4. Alternate Looks

Occasionally, it is beneficial to prepare an alternate look of a subject's face, such as with or without glasses or facial hair. This may be accomplished by placing matte acetate over the facial drawing and adding the alternate look.

Spray with a Fixative.

Spraying with a fixative promotes the archival quality of the evidentiary drawing. It helps ensure that the drawing will not smear and become altered or diminished when shuffled from file to file. Fixatives can be purchased in a "workable" formula, meaning that it is still possible to erase and alter the drawing to a certain extent. The composite artist's usual intent, however, when spraying a drawing is an acknowledgment of completion of the sketch.

Spraying with a fixative in the presence of the witness and the officer also documents that the drawing was completed during the course of the interview time frame, which can become an important issue in court. (Note that the spraying should be done in a well-ventilated area. The artist may leave for a few moments to spray the drawing and return.) It is never a good idea to continue work on a sketch after the witness has left the interview. If the drawing is changed or amended in any substantial way, it should be re-reviewed and approved by the witness.

Use of a 1 to 10 Evaluation System

Some artists choose to have the witness evaluate each composite drawing on a scale of 1 to 10 and document the witness' assessment in the case file. Others simply have the witness give an evaluation of the drawing's accuracy to the target face and convey this information to the officer.

The purpose of such assessments is to give the officer some idea as to the degree of flexibility that should be applied when making comparisons with suspects' faces. The assessment may also assist later in court if there is a problem with lack of likeness between the composite image and an offender identified by strong evidence such as fingerprints or DNA. If the witness had indicated a weak likeness at the completion of the sketch, the lack of likeness could more easily be explained away.

Distribution of Composite Images

The investigator may utilize the information recorded in the form of composite images of people or objects in a variety of ways. He or she may decide to reserve the composite information for limited distribution to a targeted area, or widespread media coverage may be desired. The investigator may even choose to withhold certain bits of information gained and recorded by the composite or ancillary drawings. Sometimes the officer asks the advice of the experienced composite artist on such matters of distribution.

Once the investigator makes distribution decisions, the artist often assists in the preparation of copies, fliers, or handouts. Many artists not only provide the art for a flier but also do the actual graphic art layout with typography as preparation for printing. **The investigator, not the artist, should determine the strategies for distribution.**

Police composite drawings are potentially powerful tools in law enforcement. Those who undertake the responsibility of preparing them are obligated to do so in the most effective manner possible. The artist should study cognition, perception, memory function, facial anatomy, and art techniques. Care should be demonstrated regarding the appropriateness of any action taken as part of the criminal justice process. And, perhaps most important of all, crime victims should always be treated considerately.

References

1. Domingo, F. J., "Forensic art: concepts and approaches in composite interviewing," *Journal of Forensic Identification*, 38(6), 259, 1988.
2. Macris, T. F., "Composite art, general principles for man and machine," *Identification News*, August 1987.
3. Davies, G., Ellis, H., and Shepherd, J., "Face recognition accuracy as a function of mode of presentation," *Journal of Applied Psychology*, 63, 180–187, 1978.
4. Davies, G., Ellis, H., and Shepherd, J., *Perceiving and Remembering Faces*. London: Academic Press, 1981.
5. Morris, D., *Manwatching: A Field Guide to Human Behavior*. New York: Harry N. Abrams, Inc., 1982.

6. Brown, A. L., The development of memory: knowing, knowing about knowing, and knowing how to know, in *Advances in Child Development and Behavior*, Vol. 10, Reese, H. W., Ed. New York: Academic Press, 1975.

7. Domingo, F. J., "Forensic art: practical considerations of witness memory," *Journal of Forensic Identification*, 40(3), 115, 1989.

8. U.S. Department of Justice, Federal Bureau of Investigation, *FBI Facial Identification Catalog*. Washington, D.C.: U.S. Government Printing Office, 1989.

Chapter 7

Age Progression: Growth

Overview of Child Age Progression

The attention focused on the problem of missing children in the U.S. has increased dramatically since the mid-1980s. America's resource center for child protection, the National Center for Missing and Exploited Children (NCMEC), a private, non-profit U.S. corporation, was established in 1984. Its mission is to help find missing children and to prevent child abduction, molestation, and sexual exploitation.[1]

In 1985 medical illustrators Scott Barrows and Lewis Sadler created the first successful forensic art done specifically to help locate long-term missing children. At the University of Texas Health Science Center at Dallas and later at the University of Illinois, Department of Biocommunication Arts, Sadler collected data on craniofacial growth which was potentially useful for predicting the facial appearance of long-term missing children. Barrows learned about children's craniofacial development while illustrating a major plastic surgery atlas.

The first case in which the technique to age children's faces was used successfully involved two sisters who had been abducted by their noncustodial father in 1977. At the request of NBC, Barrows prepared illustrations for a television documentary called "Missing," which aired on April 29, 1985. The case is described in McQueen's 1989 *Police* article, "Computer Age":

> Using old photographs and this remarkable technology, Scott Barrows and Lewis Sadler developed sketches for a TV program. Within 10 minutes of the televised showing, police officers were getting phone calls on the missing children's hotline from Kettering, Ohio. From the sketches, school officials and neighbors recognized the two little girls they knew as Debbi and Cathy Russo. By 7:30 the next morning, the girls and their father were in custody.[2]

With the results of this exciting early case, the prospect of aging the faces of missing children to aid investigators in finding them suddenly became a reality. The technique attracted the attention of parents, investigators, and the NCMEC. Research and development efforts gained momentum as investigators sought ways to improve and utilize this method in the cases of numerous other children.

Circumstances for Doing Child Age Progression

As parents know, children change and grow so quickly that photographs taken of them become out-of-date after a very short period of time. In the cases of missing and abducted children, the need for an "up-to-date" look of the child is critical. **Child age progression, either hand drawn or computer generated, helps provide a more current and effective facial image for distribution of case information regarding a missing child.**

Children disappear under various circumstances. Lewis Sadler describes the categories of missing children:

> For purposes of categorization, **these children are divided into three groups: those abducted by a non-family member, those abducted by a parent or other family member, and runaways or "throwaways."**[3]

Describing cases in the stranger abduction group, Sadler says:

> … statistically the smallest, but it is the most highly publicized and causes the most anxiety for parents. Children in this category have been abducted by individuals who prey on children, making them victims of sexual abuse, pornography, criminal exploitation, and at times, murder. No crime galvanizes a community more than a stranger abduction.[3]

For the purposes of preparation of a child age progression, the artist may benefit from viewing photographs of the child's family members. The circumstances of the disappearance will affect the availability of family photographs.

Parental Abduction

Cases of abduction by a parent, grandparent, or other family member usually result from a custody dispute. In these cases, photographs of the child will likely be available, but family photographs may be limited. It may be possible to get photos of relatives on one side of the family, but photos from the abducting family's side may be unavailable.

Stranger Abduction

In stranger abduction cases, photographs are more likely to be made available from both sides of the family.

Procedural Considerations

General Approach

There are somewhat differing philosophical approaches to child age progression, and various types have proven to be successful. **Lewis Sadler placed less importance**

on genetic prediction of likeness and more on quantifiable growth data. His work emphasized strict adherence to those cases for which data are available for the particular age range and ancestral background of the child. In "Scientific Art and the Milk Carton Kids," Sadler states:

> …the outcome of predictions based on genetic arguments, when all is said and done, is that your children may or may not look like you and that outcome is not very useful information. Consequently, this technique doesn't invest much emphasis on photos of parents or siblings in producing the aged illustrations unless there is some compelling reason to reconsider that position.[3]

The NCMEC imaging specialists place more importance on incorporation of the features of the siblings and/or parents, in addition to general use of growth principles. The training literature from the NCMEC describing the process used explains:

> The initial step in considering an age progression of a missing child's facial image is the collecting of family photographs and videotapes. When available, they should portray only the biological Mom, Dad, and older siblings, at the missing child's present age. By keeping the selection within the biological family, valuable information is imparted to the computer age-progression specialist that reflects growth, family likeness and unique features and facial patterns influenced by heredity.[4]

Hand-Drawn or Computer-Generated Methods

Effective child age progressions have been done by hand-drawn methods, on computer, or using a combination of both. Because of the volume of work done at the NCMEC, the computer-generated type is best known.

A repetitive theme throughout this text is the emphasis on the foundational study needed to do any type of forensic art. As discussed in Chapter 6, in my opinion it matters less whether an image is hand drawn or computer generated than that the artist is a skilled interviewer with a knowledge of facial anatomy. With child age progressions, the same logic applies with regard to knowledge of how faces grow and mature.

Neither the most technically skilled computer technician nor the finest portrait artist can produce high quality age progressions with no knowledge of craniofacial growth. The importance of this knowledge cannot be overemphasized.

The quality of the available photographs may also play a significant part in the determination of which method to use. If the photographs are of high quality and the needed angles of view are available, then the logical choice would be a computer application. If the photographs are inferior and cannot be scanned effectively, a hand-drawn facial image might be the better choice, using the photos just for reference input. Video images may be of such low resolution that they cannot be effectively used as stills; in such cases, they should be used only for the insights they afford into the child's appearance.

Hand-Drawn Methods

The biggest downside to hand-drawn age progressions is artistic subjectivity. Such images should not be done based strictly on "artistic instinct" or guesswork. **If you have not studied craniofacial growth, you should not attempt child age progression.**

If you are an experienced artist or medical or scientific illustrator and you have the ability to work closely with a growth specialist, such as a pediatrician, it is more reasonable to attempt this aspect of forensic art.

The early work by Barrows and Sadler suggested a combination method in which the computer projected the complex craniofacial growth data onto the original child's photograph, followed by preparation of a drawing by hand using the computer projections.

Ernie Allen of the NCMEC describes the Barrows/Sadler method:

> Barrows and Sadler developed an age progression system based upon anthropometric data of the face and head. Utilizing more than forty anatomical landmarks on the face, they reviewed the photographs of thousands of children and developed a data base of the facial measurements. Programming these data into their system, Barrows and Sadler then generalize from their sample to predict the likely change in the facial measurements to the child to be aged.
>
> The University of Illinois – Chicago process is initiated when a laser scans the photograph to be aged and transfers it to the computer. The data base is queried regarding the degree of change in facial measurements based upon the sample, between the age of the child at the time of the original photo and the current age of the child.
>
> The computer then divides the face into a large number of geometric units and allows the operator to modify each section of the face consistent with the degree of change statistically suggested. The operator, an experienced medical illustrator or sketch artist, then makes appropriate modifications or alterations. An additional software program allows the operator to add cosmetic and less predictable features such as braces, hair styles, eye glasses, etc.[5]

Computer-Generated Methods

Ernie Allen describes the **method used at NCMEC for computer-generated age progressions** from photos that have been scanned into its software:

> Based upon data-based analysis of comparative facial change over specific time intervals, the knowledge, skill and experience of the artist, and utilizing a wide range of software tools, the artist manipulates the facial features to predict basic structural changes in the child's face …
>
> A network of grid lines on the computer screen allows the artist to adjust facial characteristics one section at a time. Additional computer features allow fine detail work, creating a preliminary "aged image."
>
> The artist then utilizes, if necessary and appropriate, the merge feature of the system, in which the child's photo is compared and combined with

comparable photos of the parents, preferably at the same age as the missing child, and/or photos of siblings. The operator is able to manipulate the merge function, selecting varying degrees of merger ... to experiment with various combinations, often with the advise and consultation of the parents, ultimately producing a final "aged" photo of the missing child.[5]

More recently, the NCMEC has worked to develop a system that is as devoid of hand work as possible, with the intent that the computer complete the function. Theoretically, this would allow craniofacial growth specialists who were not artists to produce age progressions.

Pushing the computer technique beyond appropriate limits should be discouraged. Flopping facial images, for example, so that they can be merged with other images in the same view, may not always be wise. **A distinctive asymmetry of a feature or expression may be diminished or lost by placing it on the wrong side of the face.** Forcing two photographic views to fit when the central axis of the face is too far off produces an odd-looking image that requires an extensive amount of cleanup, and risks losing the likeness in the process.

As with so many aspects of forensic art, there are components of both art and science in this process. While it is advantageous to predict electronically as many of the growth factors as possible, the need for the "artist's eye" for fine tuning the process remains significant. In "Image Processing Offers Hope in the Search for Missing Children," Pamela Russell writes:

> While utilization of the system is a process that can be taught without great difficulty, the mechanical expertise required for system operation must be combined with an artistic background and knowledge of facial characteristics to handle subjective aspects of the aging process.[6]

Although the NCMEC has a specially developed software for prediction of growth at various facial landmarks for certain ages, it is not commercially available and other softwares may be used. If you study craniofacial growth and get the input of a growth specialist, it is possible to use any of several "off-the-shelf" imaging softwares for manipulation of the facial features. As long as the software has the capability to warp, merge or layer, and morph, it probably can be used. The ability to fine tune at the pixel level is helpful. It may be advantageous to have both a photo-based program and an illustration-type program.

A "Look" throughout Life

Ultimately, of all the various types of forensic art, child age progression is best done on computer, in order to retain the "look" in the eye area that so often follows us throughout life. As previously stated, this can be done, provided good quality photographs are available and the artist has extensive knowledge of craniofacial growth.

While this "lifelong look" does not absolutely hold true for all people, it is true for a large number of them.

Photographs of President John F. Kennedy taken at various times throughout his life show this quality of retaining a certain lifelong "look." In addition to the strong retention of the look in the eye area, his face continued to have the characteristics of overall broad width, puffy eyelids, wide and low forehead, and large teeth.

It has been my observation that the people who exhibit the most changed looks from childhood to adulthood tend to have noses on the stronger and larger side. If a child is from an ancestral group or of a family lineage that has pronounced noses, the change in look with growth and maturity will probably be more noticeable than in a child who matures to adulthood with a small or "pug" nose.

Information Gathering

Photographs

As preparation for a child age progression procedure, you should attempt to get the best quality photographs available. It is beneficial to have multiple photos of the child in various views, particularly those taken near the time of disappearance.

Still images captured from videotapes are generally of very low resolution and are not ideal, especially for scanning into a computer system. Video stills may be beneficial, however, for viewing to get a sense of the child's characteristic "look" and expressions.

If you use a computer application, you must collect, sort by age, and store photographs of various unrelated children to incorporate into your age progressions as needed. For example, a hairstyle or shirt collar may be pulled from the photo of any child of appropriate age, sex, and ancestry. School photographs of children are ideal for this purpose.

Family Photographs

Good quality photographs of family members from both sides may be beneficial for assessing and gathering facial details. Figure 7.1 shows strong parent-child resemblance

Figure 7.1 A strong **parent–child resemblance** is obvious despite differences in hair and eye coloration.

in facial structure and expression even though the mother is a green-eyed blond and the daughter a brown-eyed brunette. **A child's face should be carefully studied and compared to any available family photos. There may actually be a resemblance of specific features to grandparents or other relatives that is stronger than resemblance to parents.**

Ideally, facial photographs of parents and/or siblings are in the same angle of view as the target photo of the missing child that will be scanned and updated. **Photos of parents and siblings at the age to which the child's face will be progressed are most beneficial.**

Medical History

It is a good idea to inquire whether the child had a medical condition that might be manifested in the face with growth. Seek input from physicians about specialized conditions and incorporate any appropriate effects on the face as directed by the medical specialist.

Parental Input

Some artists seek input from parents of the missing child, but this may produce complications. While parents of a missing child may provide helpful information regarding that child, the production of an age progression will be a very personal and emotionally charged experience for them. They will also be naturally inclined to want to see an idealized, healthy view of the child, when the reality might be different.

Assess each case individually and always treat the parents with respect and consideration.

Craniofacial Growth

General Trends

Figure 7.2 shows a comparison of the fetal skull to the adult skull, with alignment of the orbital cavities of the eyes in the frontal view. **The very obvious proportional change in the amount of lower face is one of the most fundamental aspects of facial growth. Over time, young children's faces grow downward and forward.**

Figure 7.3 shows lateral tracings of the typical growth pattern from 1 month to 6 years and then to 18 years. The forehead transitions from a bulbous look to a more upright and flattened look. The lower half of the face drifts downward and forward or outward.

Medical illustrator Louise Gordon discusses general facial growth trends:

> ... when a child is born the bones of the skull and neck are by no means complete. The process of enlargement goes on, and the ossification is usually not totally completed until the adult reaches twenty-five years of age. In the early years between one and seven, and especially in the first year, there are noticeable changes of which the artist should be aware. The upper and lower jaws are increasing in size and changing form. They

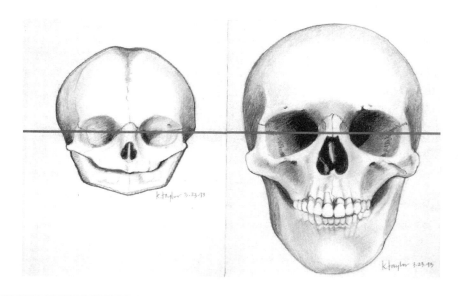

Figure 7.2 **Proportional comparison** of the fetal skull (left) and the adult skull (right). (Illustration by KTT.)

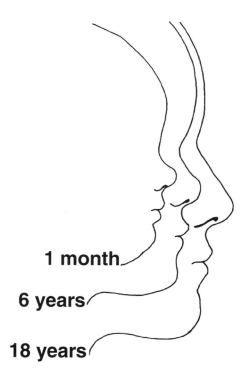

1 month

6 years

18 years

Figure 7.3 Lateral tracings of the **typical growth pattern** from 1 month to 6 years and then to 18 years. (Illustration by KTT after Broadbent and the Bolton Study.)

are becoming more prominent as they grow towards the adult state. The cranium, that part of the skull which encloses the brain and protects it, is enlarging as the brain grows. The margins of the bone of the orbital cavities in which the eyes sit are changing from being round in the baby to becoming more rectangular. It is the time of change from the rounder-eyed look of the baby to the longer-eyed look of the adult. Growth is slow from the seventh year until puberty. Then there is enlargement again, particularly in the face when the permanent teeth begin to form. This is when the lengthening of the face is noticeable and the distance from the eyes to the bottom of the chin becomes so much greater.[7]

Dr. Donald Enlow, in *Handbook of Facial Growth*, discusses the complexity of the general trends in craniofacial growth from an orthodontist's perspective:

The word combination "growth and development" is frequently heard. Why both terms? Growth … is not merely a process of size increases. Rather, progressive facial enlargement is a "differential" growth process in which the many component parts each mature earlier or later than others, to different extents in different facial regions, in a multitude of different directions, and at different rates. It is a gradual maturational process involving a complex of different but functionally interrelated organs and tissues. The growth process also involves a bewildering succession of regional changes in proportions … The child's face is not merely a miniature of the adult …[8]

Dentition

The forensic artist who attempts child age progression must have a general understanding of the eruption patterns of the teeth. Lack of attention to the teeth can produce a very incorrect look in a finished updated image. Information regarding dental terminology is given in Figures 3.11 and 3.12 in Chapter 3.

It is outside the scope of this chapter to attempt to explain the complexities of eruption times for each tooth. Forensic artists should include several good anatomy books in their libraries that explain dental eruption patterns and provide tables for the general prediction of these patterns.

The **primary dentition**, also called the **deciduous teeth** or **"baby teeth,"** serve the child for the first few years of life. They are successively replaced by the **secondary dentition** or **permanent teeth**, the crowns of which have developed inside the bony maxilla and mandible as the child's face grows.

Feik and Glover discuss a few notable tooth eruptions of significance to the forensic artist in *Craniofacial Identification in Forensic Medicine,* in the chapter "Growth of Children's Faces":

The first teeth — the lower central incisors — appear at around 6–7 months of age, and the primary or deciduous dentition is usually complete by 30 months of age … 20 teeth … Little change is evident in the dentition between 2.5 and 6 years of age, when the first permanent teeth begin to erupt … At around 9 years old, when children have eight permanent incisors erupted anteriorly but still have deciduous teeth posteriorly, they typically go through a transitional stage often referred to as the "ugly duckling stage."[9]

When age progressing a child in the time frame of eruption of the front four maxillary teeth (central and lateral incisors), it is possible that those teeth might not have smooth lower surfaces and that should be shown. Alan Segal discusses this dental feature in *Morphology and Anatomy of the Human Dentition:*

> Seen on the incisal, or cutting, edges of newly erupted central and lateral incisors are three rounded prominences, **"mamelons."** These prominences soon disappear with wear.[10]

Ideally the forensic artist consults with a pediatric dentist or orthodontist to obtain information about dental development for the particular child to be age progressed. There may be subtle variations with regard to race and sex of the child which should be factored into the estimated eruption prediction (see Figure 7.4).

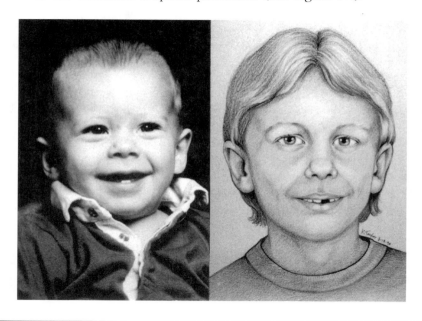

Figure 7.4 Hand-drawn age progression by KTT based on photograph of a male child at about 1½ years of age (left), projecting the appearance to about 6½ years of age (right). The drawing reflects likely changes in the anterior dentition. (Courtesy of Texas Department of Public Safety.)

Photographic Series

The series of photographs on pages 245–247 allows the artist to study the growth that occurs in the face of a young male over a period of more than 20 years. Although this varies by individual, the patterns seen in his face are rather typical for males. The series also gives a good indication of the look of the teeth at the various ages.

Age 1½

- the head is very rounded and the facial contours are full and rounded
- the face occupies the lower portion of the head and there is a lot of cranium
- the bridge of the nose is flattened
- there is the appearance of epicanthic folds and the eyes look large and rounded
- the hair is soft and fine

Age 3

- the cranium expands to accommodate the growing brain
- the eyes are slightly more elongated and less rounded
- the maxilla and mandible have enlarged and widened to allow room for the deciduous dentition
- the interorbital distance is almost established

Age 4

- the nose is still small and buttonlike with small nostrils, but the bridge has begun to form
- the interorbital distance is basically established
- the anterior "baby teeth" are visible
- the ears seem very large and very low on the head
- the chin has taken some shape

Age 5

- the bridge of the nose continues to rise up, lifting some of the excess skin from the medial corners of the eyes
- the face continues to elongate as the nose length and the chin length increase
- growth pattern of the hair seems firmly established, it is less fine, and the color darkens

Age 6½

- the forehead has become less prominent and bulbous looking
- the bridge of the nose continues to rise up and the nostril size and nose width increase slightly
- the nose continues to grow in length, as does the chin
- the forms of the lower cartilages of the nose become apparent and the tip takes shape
- the central and lateral deciduous incisors have been lost and replaced by the permanent maxillary central incisors, thus the dentition is "mixed"
- the mouth has to grow to accommodate the permanent teeth

Age 8

- there is not much proportional change
- the permanent maxillary lateral incisors have appeared but they are not fully down

Age 9½

- the bridge of the nose continues to rise up and the nostril size and nose width still increase slightly
- the face elongates slightly
- the squarish form of the chin becomes obvious
- the permanent maxillary lateral incisors are fully down
- the teeth seem big for the face

Age 11

- the "childlike" face is looking more "juvenile" as some of the facial forms become more apparent due to less "baby fat"
- the bridge of the nose continues to rise up
- the upper lip has remained about the same for several years
- the form of the chin becomes more masculine and square
- the ears still seem large for the face although they do not appear so low on the head

Age 12

- the nose continues to grow, both in the bridge and the nostril size
- the teeth still seem big for the face
- the permanent maxillary canines or cuspids are in
- the mandible and chin continue to grow
- the neck musculature is slightly more masculine

Age 15

- the "juvenile" face is starting to look more "teen-aged" (and would probably be even more noticeable in a female)
- the teeth don't seem so oversized for the face as the mandible continues to grow and become more masculine
- the cheekbones have become relatively more prominent
- the ears don't seem so oversized for the face as it has elongated and they don't seem too low
- the eyebrows have become more masculine
- oops! ... a zit or two!

Age 20

- the nose has grown even more, revealing the nasal bones at the bridge
- the forehead shape has remained consistent though it has grown and risen up at glabella
- the face now looks mature, particularly due to the appearance of facial hair
- the eyebrows are even fuller
- the angle of the mandible is much more squared and masculine
- the neck musculature is mature

Age 25

- the eyebrows are heavier
- the mandible has continued to square and form, looking more masculine and mature
- the neck musculature is more defined and the Adam's apple is visible

Sadler has discussed the lifelong growth and change that occur in our faces:

Although our face undergoes tremendous growth from youth to adulthood and into old age, it is also true that there is a constancy of appearance. The face of a man looks almost the same, regardless of age. Such growth is called "gnomatic," a fact of importance in growth prediction.

Gnomatic growth is a process that leaves the resultant features similar to the original. This unity of the individual's looks cannot be destroyed by growth and decay. The cut pug-nosed, bland face of infancy assumes in turn the expression of youth, the individuality of adulthood, and the character of age. The first 20 years are anabolic, growing and developing; the years after are maturing, catabolic and degenerative.[11]

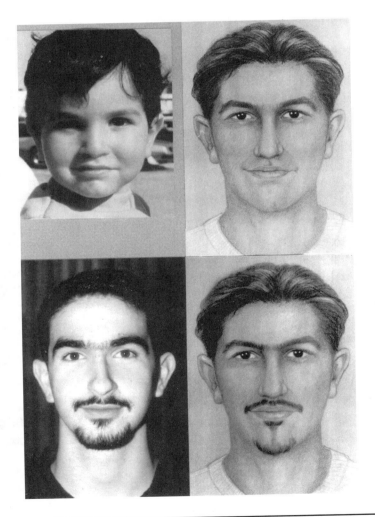

Figure 7.5 Hand-drawn age progression by KTT based on photograph of a male child at 2½ years of age (upper left), projecting the appearance to 18 years of age (upper right), photo of the young man when located at age 18 (lower left), and age progression with facial hair added (lower right). (Courtesy of Texas Department of Public Safety.)

Child Facial Update: Case Example

Figure 7.5 (above left and right) shows a hand-drawn age progression based on photographs of a male child at 2½ years of age, projecting the appearance to 18 years. After his location, photographs of the boy at age 18 were compared to the age progression, adding facial hair to resemble his own (below left and right).

In conclusion, Feik and Glover make the following observations for the future of computer-generated child age progressions:

> At present, prediction of the way in which a particular child's face will age still relies largely on subjective artistic impressions. However, as our anatomical knowledge and understanding improve, the use of scientific and computer modelling techniques should lead to improved results in predicting the growth of faces.[12]

References

1. Allen, E., "Computerized photo aging and the search for missing children," *Interpol International Criminal Police Review*, September–October 1990.
2. McQueen, I., "Computer age," *Police*, June 1989.
3. Sadler, L., "Scientific art and the milk carton kids," *Scientific Illustration — 1986. Selected papers from the 7th Annual Conference of the Guild of Natural Science Illustrators*, Washington, D.C., 1986.
4. Training Materials, National Center for Missing and Exploited Children, 1993.
5. Allen, E., "Computerized photo aging and the search for missing children," *Interpol International Criminal Police Review*, September–October 1990.
6. Russell, P., "Image processing offers hope in the search for missing children," *Advanced Imaging*, 1992.
7. Gordon, L., *How to Draw the Human Head*. New York: Penguin Books, 1986.
8. Enlow, D. H., *Handbook of Facial Growth*. Philadelphia: W. B. Saunders, 1982.
9. Feik, S. A. and Glover, J. E., Growth of children's faces, in *Craniofacial Identification in Forensic Medicine*, Clement, J. and Ranson, D., Eds. New York: Oxford University Press, 1998.
10. Segal, A., *Morphology and Anatomy of the Human Dentition*. Chicago: Year Book Medical Publishers, 1963.
11. Sadler, L., "Scientific art and the milk carton kids," *Scientific Illustration — 1986. Selected papers from the 7th Annual Conference of the Guild of Natural Science Illustrators*, Washington, D.C., 1986.
12. Feik, S. A. and Glover, J. E., Growth of children's faces, in *Craniofacial Identification in Forensic Medicine*, Clement, J. and Ranson, D., Eds. New York: Oxford University Press, 1998.

Chapter 8

Age Progression: Aging

Overview of Adult Age Progression

An age-old problem in the corrections aspect of law enforcement is the reality that incarcerated prisoners sometimes escape. **The concept of "updating" the appearance of long-term missing fugitives has gained popularity in the last two decades or so.** In the U.S. and several other countries, the medium of television has encouraged the production of age progressed images of adult individuals to augment stories of sought-after criminals, usually fugatives. Crime-stopper type programs often feature segments on old cases in which the offender was charged with a crime and either never made it to the courtroom or escaped from a jail or penitentiary.

Adult age progression is sometimes done in cases of long-term absent adults who are classified as missing persons as part of the investigative effort to locate them.

This chapter provides procedural considerations for the forensic artist who does adult age progression and reviews the types of changes that our faces undergo as a result of the passage of time. A nomenclature for the various lines of age on the face is suggested and diagrammed. **Both the terms "adult age progression" and "fugitive update" are used, depending on the status of the target individual.**

Numerous photographs showing faces over a span of time are included as a sort of **reference gallery for the study of facial aging.** Case examples of updated images of adult faces are presented, some in color.

As with all other aspects of forensic art, the artist should carefully **study and assess each case individually rather than assume that every person will have precisely the same indications of age on the face.** The morphological structure of each face is subtly different and must be aged accordingly. Lifestyle, heredity, health, and other factors also must be considered.

Circumstances for Doing Adult Age Progression

Most cases in which adult age progressions or fugitive updates are prepared involve high profile criminals or missing persons sought by members of law

enforcement for many years. The most logical circumstances for use of the method include cases in which there are at least fairly good available photographs of the subject, even though they are out-of-date. It is especially beneficial to produce updates when investigators have gained intelligence information regarding the person's current appearance to include such things as weight changes, and hair or facial hair changes.

In some cases, the production of an age progression is precipitated by an event such as an upcoming anniversary of a major crime or a planned media story about the crime. **The age progression can encourage renewed interest in the investigation and hopefully generate new leads.**

Procedural Considerations

Hand-Drawn or Computer-Generated Methods

As in the cases of projecting growth in child age progressions, projecting aging of adult faces can be done by either hand-drawn or computer-generated methods. In the case of fugitive updates, they have also been done successfully as three-dimensional sculptures, as shown in the John List case discussed in Chapter 2.

It is critical to maintain the characteristic "look" of the individual, especially in the eye area. In this regard, computer methods are especially advantageous. Both in child age progressions and in adult age progressions, the precise look of the eyes can be more easily maintained when the artwork is based on a photograph and the completed image remains photographic. As discussed in Chapter 6, **a photographic composite image is not necessarily advantageous when created from a memory because it is *too* specific. The opposite is true with age progressions since the process is begun with a *known* photograph of the specific individual.**

A theme often repeated in this text also applies to this type of forensic art. **It actually matters less whether an image is hand drawn or computer generated than that the artist has done the preparatory study of facial aging.**

Neither the most technically skilled computer technician nor the finest portrait artist can produce high-quality adult age progressions with no knowledge of the anatomical fundamentals of facial aging.

As is the case with child age progressions, **the quality of the available photographs may also play a significant part in the determination of which method to use.** If the original photographs of the subject are of high quality, the logical choice would be a computer application. If the photographs are inferior and cannot be effectively scanned into an imaging system, a hand-drawn facial image might be the better choice, using the photos just for reference input.

Hand-Drawn Methods

If a hand-drawn approach to age progression is chosen, great care should be taken to maintain the precise look of the individual. It is advantageous to begin the drawing by some sort of tracing or projection method to establish accurate proportions. Methods of projection are discussed in Chapter 4 in the section on tools and materials.

Over-dependence on tracing, however, should be avoided. The drawing should be completed independent of the tracing or projection method, by incorporating a knowledge of the likely physical changes due to aging along with any available intelligence information about the individual.

Computer-Generated Methods

Various "off-the-shelf" graphics imaging softwares are appropriate for the production of adult facial updates. As long as the software has the capability to warp, merge or layer, and morph, it probably can be used.

A "Look" throughout Life

A great advantage to the forensic artist doing age progressions is the tendency of most people to maintain a certain "look" throughout life. **While this "lifelong look" does not absolutely hold true for all people, it is true for a large number of them.** Even with the addition of age to a face, or changes in weight or hair and facial hair, there remains a certain "something" that can be recognized. We experience this when we see childhood friends as adults or when we attend class reunions and observe acquaintances from many years back. The faces have grown older, yet we recognize them. **This quality should be maintained in age progressions.**

Expression may comprise a large part of the lifelong look. Figure 8.1 shows an age progression of the face of a long-term missing person in which the dimples and expression in the mouth area are intentionally retained. In this case, information provided by the family concerning a scar on the neck was also included, as was a slightly offset iris.

Facial Angle

Chapter 10 discusses whether the facial image will be developed in the same angle of view as the original photograph or whether the face will be rotated into a different position. The artist must make the same decisions when preparing an age progression. In postmortem drawing, with less than ideal crime scene and morgue photographs, the artist is more often required to rotate the facial angle. In age progression cases, the original photographs are often good quality frontal view mug shots that can be used as a basis for the update in the same angle.

Color or Black and White

If you are competent with color drawing and have good color photographs of the subject to be aged, color may add a real plus to your age progression. If you are using computer software to do the update and have good quality original color photographs, use of color imaging would also be appropriate. **It is usually not wise, however, to make up the color and risk being incorrect.** If good quality color photographs are not available, a black-and-white image should be produced.

Figure 8.2 shows the aged face of a fugitive in which the production of a color image played a significant role, since his hair was an almost carrot orange-red color.*

---

* Color version of Figure 8.2 follows p. 266.

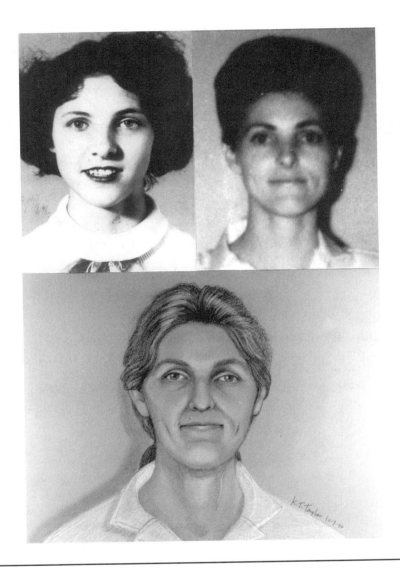

Figure 8.1 Photographs of a long-term missing woman (left and right above) and **age progression** by KTT (below) including dimples and **characteristic expression** in the mouth area. (Courtesy of "Unsolved Mysteries.")

Information Gathering

When investigators have spent many years searching for a particular fugitive, they generally develop a thick file of information on their subject. In age progression cases I have done for the United States Marshals Service or "America's Most Wanted," I am generally provided with a dossier of information to read before attempting the age progression. This furnishes the necessary insights into the "look," history, lifestyle, and habits of the subject, which are all important considerations. The fugitive's case file may include all of the information needed for the update or additional research may be indicated.

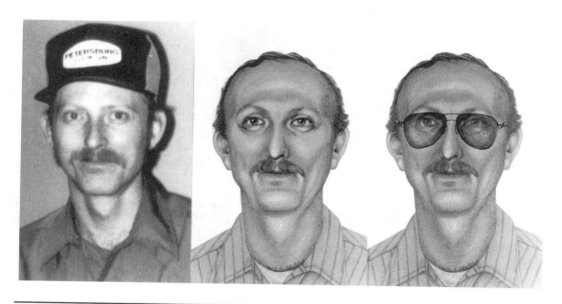

Figure 8.2   Age progression of a fugitive in which the **use of color was important** since he had carrot orange-red hair; original photograph of the subject (left), fugitive update by KTT (center), and with glasses added on matte acetate (right). (Courtesy of Texas Department of Public Safety.)

Photographs of the Subject

It is beneficial and wise to **review any available photographs of a subject to be aged.** Certainly, each of us has different looks in different photographs taken under different circumstances and photographs can be very deceiving. Most people hate to think that they really look like their driver's license photographs!

The more photographs made available to the forensic artist for assessment, the better. Even if a frontal view is to be developed, oblique or lateral views should be studied if provided in the case file.

Family Photographs

As with the projection of craniofacial growth in child age progressions, the **process of projecting age may be made more accurate if the artist has access to photographs of family members.** There are no guarantees that a person will age in the same way that family members have aged, but nevertheless it may be helpful to study them.

It is sometimes possible to discern a trend or tendency within a family that can be incorporated into the age progression. Predictably, fugitives' families may not be cooperative in providing photos of family members. Law enforcement officers may, however, have some access to photos such as those in driver's license or arrest records.

In cases of long-term missing adults, family members will likely be more inclined to provide photographs to aid law enforcement efforts to find their loved one.

Depending upon the age of the target subject, parents' photos or siblings' photos may be assessed. I have found older sibling photos to be particularly useful.

Lifestyle Information

If possible, the artist should seek input from officers who are well acquainted with the target subject. Perceptions regarding the **lifestyle and habits of the person affect the relative harshness or mildness with which the face is aged by the artist.** For example, the face of a health and fitness conscious person should be aged differently from the face of a known drug abuser or alcoholic. Smoking and inclination toward sun exposure should also be considerations.

In some cases, showing a diversity of looks might be indicated by lifestyle information. Figure 8.3 shows the case of female fugitive **Elizabeth Anna Duke**, one of

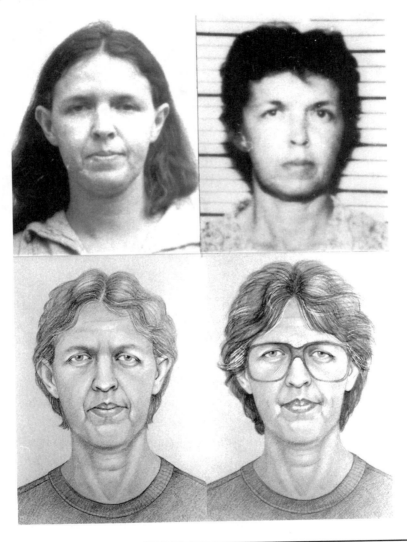

Figure 8.3 Long-time fugitive **Elizabeth Anna Duke**, wanted for the 1983 bombing of the Senate chambers of the U. S. Capitol; early photographs (left and right above) and **age progression** by KTT (below left) with no makeup and **alternate look** with makeup, glasses, and styled hair (below right). (Courtesy of Texas Department of Public Safety.)

three persons involved in the 1983 bombing of the Senate chambers at the U.S. Capitol in Washington, D.C. One version reflects how she might look with a continuation of her earlier "hippie" lifestyle. Because she was highly educated, it was equally possible that, as a mid-50s grandmother, she was leading the sort of life in which she would wear makeup, glasses, and styled hair. A characteristic tight-lipped expression of irritation was also included, with variations prepared using matte acetate.

Medical History

A fugitive or missing person to be aged may have a medical condition that progressively affects the face over the passage of time. Family members or officers might have knowledge of the existence of such conditions and notify the artist. Consultation with a physician for advice on the normal advancement of the particular disease or condition may be worthwhile.

Chapter 9 presents figures that depict various facial changes due to **makeup, disguises, glasses, plastic surgery, weight change, dental change and health conditions.** Any one or more of these changes **may need to be incorporated along with the age-related changes according to information gained about lifestyle and medical history.**

Ancestry

People with darker skin often age more gracefully than lighter skinned people and show less effects of sun exposure. Consider the ever-youthful faces of African-American singers Lena Horne and Tina Turner.

Figure 8.4 shows an age progression of the face of a black fugitive in which the alterations are intentionally gentle due to the ancestry of the individual.

Figure 8.4 Original photograph (left) and **age progression** by KTT (right), in which the age-related changes are minimal due to **ancestry.** (Courtesy of "America's Most Wanted.")

Materials

Many of the age progressions that I am commissioned to do are for use on television broadcasts. For that reason, they are produced with color materials, if appropriate, and in a horizontal format, as in Figure 8.1. Chapter 16 pertains to the copying and distribution of forensic art images in various media, and Chapter 4 includes information on art materials.

Tinted papers for production of color fugitive updates may be used. Choose the color according to the skin tone of the subject. The drawing is first established lightly in graphite pencil, then a base layer of pastel skintone tints is applied and rubbed gently into the paper with a chamois cloth or paper tissue. On top of the pastels, I draw with colored pencils, applied in layers.

Sometimes it is beneficial to cut out the drawing and apply it to a different background of tinted paper. This has the effect of making the image stand out from the background color, and reproduces effectively on television (see Color Figure 4*).

A drawing produced in color may also be distributed in black and white, so the non-color reproduction quality should be checked by photocopying the drawing. Certain lines and forms may need to be further emphasized to ensure good reproduction.

Multiple views of **Joseph Michael Maloney** were achieved on matte acetate using white paint so that white hair could be placed over darker skin. Note that the rounded form of his skull had to be seen and defined through the thinning hair on top of his head. The drawing was cut out and placed on a blue tinted paper background for emphasis and white paint was used to soften the "cut-and-paste" look around the edges. Maloney, of Irish descent, poisoned his wife at her child's birthday party. He has been sighted in Ireland with long white hair and a beard. (Figure 8.5)

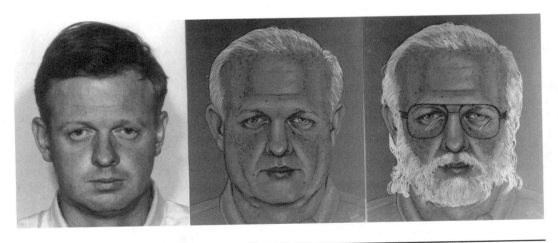

Figure 8.5 Fugitive **Joseph Michael Maloney** (left) and **age progressions** (center and right) by KTT, prepared on matte acetate with white paint. The drawing was cut out and placed on a blue tinted paper background for emphasis, softening the edges with white paint. (Courtesy of "America's Most Wanted.")

---

* Color figures follow p. 266.

Multiple Views

Matte acetate used to produce alterations in hair or facial hair or to add glasses allows photography through the acetate, showing multiple looks without re-drawing the face. It is also a simple matter to scan a completed drawing into an imaging software and add glasses or other small details for alternate looks.

While alternate looks may be indicated, too many variations may confuse the viewer. **Make choices of "multiple looks" selectively, based on intelligence information if available and maintain the primary "look" of the face.**

Figure 8.6 shows the case of **Norman A. Porter**, a Massachusetts fugitive sought for an execution-style murder that sent him to prison and for the murder of a jailer during a subsequent escape. Based on intelligence information that he had shaved his head, versions of the age progression were prepared to alter the hair and facial hair and to add glasses. The clean-shaven, bald version (lower left) was prepared first, then the other versions were prepared with matte acetate overlays.

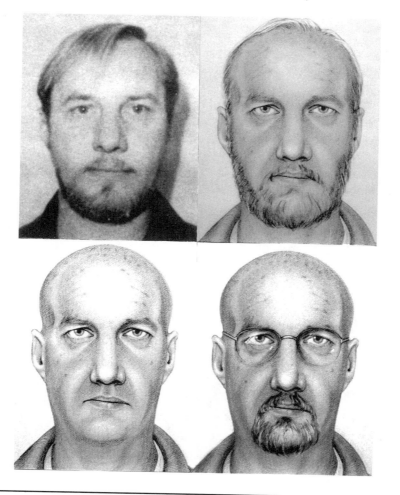

Figure 8.6 Fugitive **Norman A. Porter**, wanted for an execution-style murder in Massachusetts and the murder of a jailer during an escape (upper left), **age progression** by KTT (upper right), and **alternate versions** (below left and right). (Courtesy of "America's Most Wanted.")

Larry Porter Chism, shown in Figure 8.7, was depicted in multiple views like Elizabeth Duke because of the ambiguous lifestyle indicators.* Highly intelligent, Chism was two weeks away from graduating from law school when he got into trouble for drugs. While in prison, he exhibited violent and contradictory behavior. He was editor of the prison newspaper and acted as mediator between prisoners and administrators. Together with three other convicts on a guarded furlough from prison, Chism blasted his way out of a bowling alley in Dixon, Tennessee, kidnapping a young woman employee. He hijacked a small airplane and forced the pilot to fly to Arkansas where he held an elderly couple hostage. Age progressions depict him in demeanors that could reflect both blue-collar and white-collar lifestyles.

Figure 8.7 Fugitive **Larry Porter Chism** (upper left) and **age progressions** by KTT (upper right, lower left and right) showing **multiple looks due to ambiguous lifestyle indicators**. (Courtesy of "America's Most Wanted.")

---

* Color version of Figure 8.7 follows p. 266.

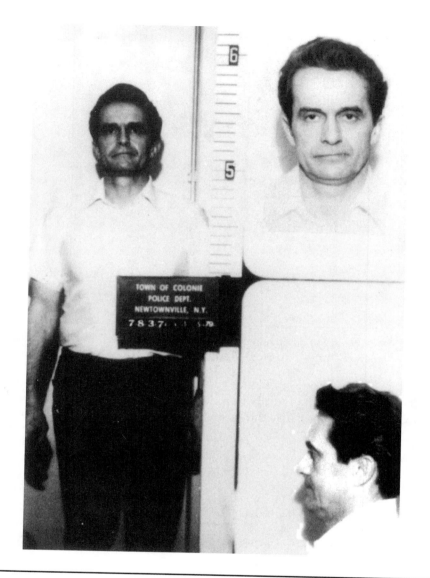

Figure 8.8 Arrest photos of fugitive **Donald Eugene Webb** sought for the murder of a police chief in Pennsylvania. (Courtesy of "America's Most Wanted.")

Procedurally, the case of **Donald Eugene Webb** required a well-planned artistic approach. Webb has been on the FBI's "10 Most Wanted List" and he is sought in connection with the murder of police chief Gregory Adams in Saxonburg, Pennsylvania. Because he specialized in burglaries of jewelry stores and was a master of assumed identities, two distinctly different versions of his "look" were indicated. Figure 8.8 shows arrest photos of Webb.

Behavioral profile information indicated that Webb could be low-key, having aged naturally, or he could have maintained his "slicker" image, perhaps dying his hair. In order to produce both looks, an aged face was drawn first, placing the image high in the format, as shown in Figure 8.9. This allowed for the placement of large matte acetate sheets over the base facial image for the preparation of the "working class"

Figure 8.9 Aged face of **Donald Eugene Webb** by KTT, drawn high in a horizontal format for television. (Courtesy of "America's Most Wanted.")

and "jewel thief" looks shown in Figure 8.10. In the top rendition, the plain shirt was added to the base drawing, and at bottom, a coat and tie and glasses were added and the hair was darkened. Note that the asymmetrical smirking expression of the mouth was carefully maintained.

Facial Aging

Plastic surgeons Dr. David Ellis and Dr. David Ward discuss facial aging, as follows:

> Facial aging is a dynamic process which continues throughout life. Individuals are affected to a variable degree depending on facial motor habits, exposure and susceptibility to damaging ultraviolet radiation, smoking, and the microscopic tissue changes inherent in the aging process. Aside from avoiding smoking and utilizing sunscreens and other solar protection, there is little that can be done to prevent or retard the development of these changes.[1]

Throughout our lives, the changes that occur in our faces are influenced by genetics, environment, and lifestyle. **Forensic artists who attempt to project the advanced appearance of faces must first study the facial morphology of the target face, assess genetic predisposition to the extent possible, and learn what they can about the possible environment and lifestyle of the person.** These factors contribute to the time of onset and the extent of the effects of aging to the face. Guesswork must play a role, but every effort should be made to see that the guesses are educated ones.

A sound understanding of the physical mechanics of the facial aging process helps to promote reasonable judgments and predictions. The procedure is not

Figure 8.10 Two age-progressed versions of **Donald Eugene Webb** by KTT, showing a **"work-ing-class" look** (above) and a **"jewel-thief" look** (below). (Courtesy of "America's Most Wanted.")

an exacting one, but educated predictions generally produce facial images that are far more useful to law enforcement than out-of-date photographs.

The age-related changes to faces occur at variable rates for each individual, yet a fairly predictable series of changes seems to happen in a similar order for most people. Wrinkles begin to occur at certain locations first, then at other locations next, and so forth. This can be predicted in a very general way decade by decade. With this knowledge, the forensic artist can determine placement of the lines of age at certain locations on the face, which one would expect to see for a person of a particular age. This should be adjusted upward or downward according to ancestry, environment, and lifestyle considerations for the individual.

Nomenclature for Facial Lines

With the day-to-day animations of our faces and the accompanying expressions, we inevitably acquire corresponding facial lines or wrinkles over time. In addition, our faces respond to the environment with reactions such as squinting in the sunlight that eventually create permanent lines due to repetition.

A standard guideline for the placement of the facial wrinkles is that **the wrinkles occur perpendicular to the stretch of the underlying muscle fibers.** One example is the transverse or horizontal lines across the forehead that run perpendicular to the vertical pull of the frontalis muscle. Similarly, the sphincter-style muscles orbicularis oculi encircling the eye and orbicularis oris around the mouth create perpendicularly radiating wrinkles due to the repeated contraction of the muscles.

If the forensic artist has learned the musculature of the face, the placement of the lines of age becomes far easier to understand and predict.

A nomenclature for the lines and grooves of the face has been suggested by Dr. Robert George and Dr. Ron Singer and published by the American Society of Plastic and Reconstructive Surgeons. Figure 8.11 shows a facial drawing with the lines of age named, most of which were derived from George and Singer.[2] In the literature, terminology of the lines of age seems to be related to degree of depth of the facial lines. For example, sources include "nasolabial lines," "nasolabial grooves," "nasolabial furrows," and "nasolabial folds," all referring to the etched lines radiating from the ala of the nose downward toward the mouth. It seems reasonable that wrinkles start as "lines," grow into "grooves," and later become deep "furrows" or "folds."

Changes by Decade

After many years of observing faces, it is possible to determine that certain lines occur in a rather predictable fashion with each passing decade.[1,3–5] Such factors as stress, diet, or illness affect the onset of the various lines, as do smoking and sun exposure influences. The upper half of the face tends to exhibit lines earlier than the lower half of the face. **The following decade-by-decade suggestions are offered as a very general guide:**

20s
- fine transverse frontal lines may appear across the forehead
- fine vertical glabellar lines may appear in people who frown frequently
- fine lateral orbital lines or "crow's feet" may appear in people who smile often or spend a lot of time in the sun

30s
- transverse frontal lines deepen
- vertical glabellar lines deepen
- lateral orbital lines increase in number and deepen
- transverse nasal lines may form across the top of the nose
- nasolabial lines or furrows become noticeable

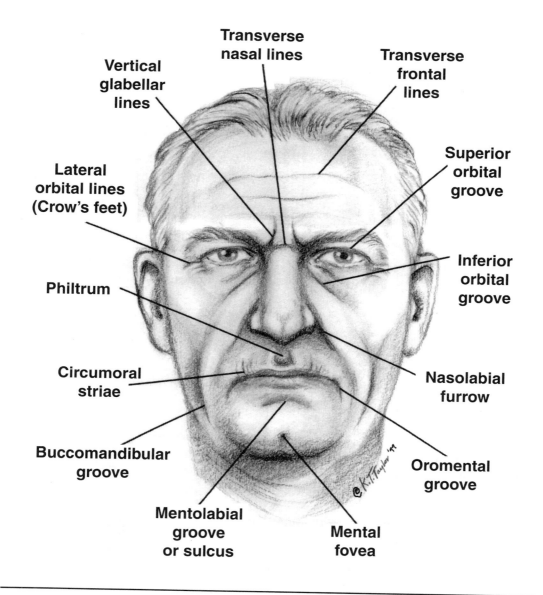

Figure 8.11 **Nomenclature for the lines and grooves of the face.** (Illustration by KTT.)

40s

- inferior orbital groove may become apparent
- the eyebrows may descend slightly
- an excess of upper lid skin may develop and a portion of the superior orbital groove may be obscured at the lateral side
- the jaw line becomes less firm
- circumoral striae become noticeable, especially in smokers
- the lips may begin to thin
- the oromental groove may begin, depending on the facial structure
- the mentolabial groove becomes more apparent, depending on the facial structure
- fine lines in the neck become noticeable

50s

- inferior orbital groove may define a developing pouch under the eyes
- excess upper lid tissue may worsen, obscuring more of the superior orbital groove at the lateral side and creating more lateral orbital lines
- the nasolabial furrow is more noticeable
- the oromental groove deepens
- the lips continue to thin, especially in people with thin lips in youth
- dental changes may become apparent, increasing lines accordingly
- a buccomandibular groove may appear
- the jaw line becomes much less firm
- jowls and a double chin may appear
- lines in the neck are more noticeable

60s

- all of the above-mentioned lines are exaggerated
- the circumoral striae may cross over the vermilion border of the lips
- the ears appear to get larger and wrinkles appear in front of the tragus
- the jaw line is very soft and tissues under the neck sag

70s

- all of the above-described lines become more defined, accompanied by marked loss of elasticity of the skin and sagging of tissues

General Facial Aging

A Reference Gallery

The following figures are presented as a reference guide for the study of the overall effects of facial aging in a variety of individuals. By reviewing these faces, the artist is better able to have a general frame of reference for the prediction of facial changes on other similar faces.

Figure 8.12 shows the dramatic difference that **hair loss** can make in the appearance of age in a male. The loss of hair in this individual is shown over a time interval of only 6 years, yet he appears to have aged considerably more. Weight gain has also smoothed out his facial contours and obscured the squareness of his mandible, considerably diminishing the definition of the jaw line.

In the face of the European-derived or **Caucasian male** in Figure 8.13, various changes can be seen to occur over a span of 29 years. He is shown at age 18 (upper left), age 31 (upper right), age 40 (lower left), and age 47 (lower right). In contrast to the man in Figure 8.12, his facial fat is diminished over time and the structure of his skull becomes increasingly more visible. The youthful, soft contours give way to harder angles. The head hair thins somewhat and grays, but the eyebrow hair thickens; in some men the eyebrow hair thins. The nose drops slightly, the lips thin, and the vertical glabellar lines are pronounced from squinting and frowning.

The **Caucasian male** face series in Figure 8.14, frontal view, and Figure 8.15, lateral view, depicts a multiplicity of age-related changes. He is shown at age 21 (upper left), age 47 (upper right), age 50 (lower left), and age 68 (lower right). The face at 21 is virtually devoid of lines, though it can be observed that the left eye droops, the right ear protrudes more, and he has thick wavy hair. With the head shaved at 47, numerous

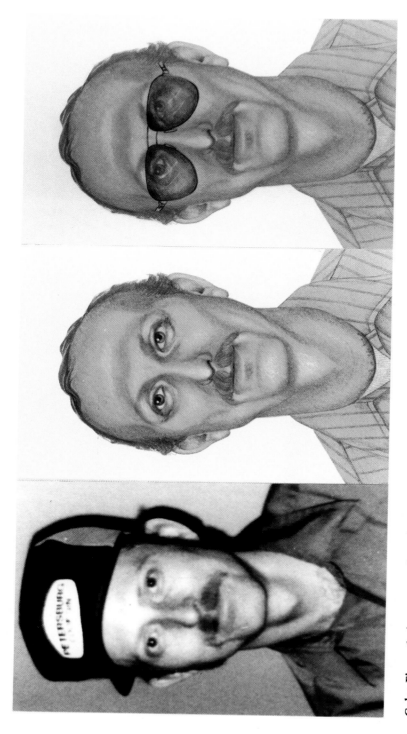

Color Figure 1. Age progression of a fugitive in which the **use of color was important** because he had carrot orange-red hair; original photograph of the subject (left), **fugitive update** by KTT (center), and with glasses added on matte acetate (right). (Courtesy of Texas Department of Public Safety.)

Color Figure 2. Fugitive **Larry Porter Chism** (upper left) and **age progressions** by KTT (upper right, lower left and right) showing **multiple looks due to ambiguous lifestyle indicators.** (Courtesy of "America's Most Wanted.")

Color Figure 3. James Dudley Ashley in early arrest photo (left), **fugitive update** by KTT (center), and actual appearance (right). (Courtesy of "America's Most Wanted.")

Color Figure 4. Roy Wayne Bevan in early penitentiary photo (upper left), **fugitive updates** by KTT (upper right and lower left), and **thin appearance** when captured (lower right). (Courtesy of Texas Department of Public Safety.)

Figure 8.12 Three photos taken over a span of 6 years demonstrate how a slight weight gain and **hair loss** can quickly age the face. (Courtesy of Texas Department of Criminal Justice.)

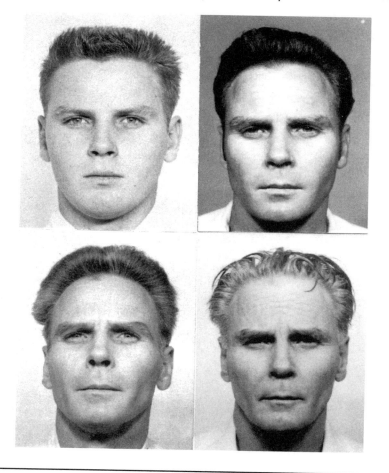

Figure 8.13 Aging in the face of a **Caucasian male**, age 18 (upper left), age 31 (upper right), age 40 (lower left), and age 47 (lower right). (Courtesy of Texas Department of Criminal Justice.)

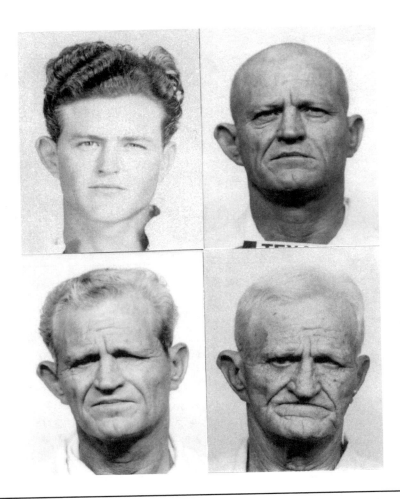

Figure 8.14 Aging in the face of a **Caucasian male**, at age 21 (upper left), age 47 (upper right), age 50 (lower left), and age 68 (lower right). (Courtesy of Texas Department of Criminal Justice.)

facial lines are defined in the face, some prematurely of the norm. Vertical glabellar lines, inferior orbital grooves, lateral orbital lines, transverse frontal lines, nasolabial furrows, buccomandibular grooves, and lines in the neck are all obvious. Note in the lateral view that the **transverse frontal lines cannot come above the natural hairline since they correspond to the pull of the frontalis muscle which stops approximately at the hairline.** His nose tip has dropped, the jaw line has softened, and the protruding ear is more obvious.

At age 50, his squinting is very pronounced and the eyebrows have all but disappeared. The hair has thinned and grayed revealing a much larger forehead. The excess tissue above the eyes creates difficulty in seeing. All of the previously mentioned lines have deepened and the mental fovea has become a vertical line. The skin of the neck has become more sagging and there are wrinkles in front of the tragus. At age 68, there have been obvious dental changes, including tooth loss. The nose has dropped considerably and the lips have rolled inward. In the lateral view, because of tooth loss and the "over-closed" jaw, the chin is thrust forward. The hair has continued to thin

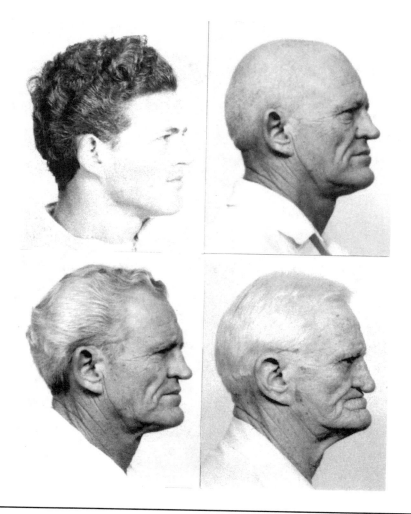

Figure 8.15 Lateral view of the same **Caucasian male** as in Figure 8.14. (Courtesy of Texas Department of Criminal Justice.)

and gray and the skin has become blotchy. The ears appear much larger. Note the change in the distance from the tip of the nose to the midline of the lips from age 21 to age 68.

Figure 8.16 shows the **Caucasian female** face of **Genene Jones**, a nurse who was convicted of killing multiple infants in her care, injecting them with a drug that caused respiratory failure. The time span is about 10 years and several changes are visible in the face. There is weight gain and resultant softening of the jaw line. The fatty area above the eyes has dropped, particularly at the lateral corners. The nose tip has dropped, the lips have thinned, and the oromental groove is pronounced.

Figure 8.17 shows an age progression prepared from photographs of fugitive **Donna Joan Borup**, still sought by the FBI, reflecting some of the same facial changes as with Jones, particularly softening of the jaw line. Note that small moles and blemishes are carefully located and included.

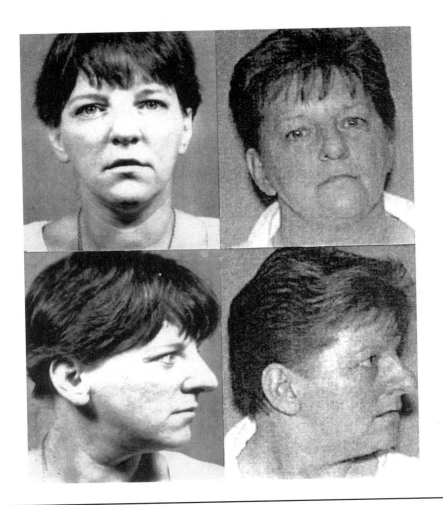

Figure 8.16 Aging in the face of a **Caucasian female**, **Genene Jones**, seen over a span of 10 years in frontal and lateral views. (Courtesy of Texas Department of Criminal Justice.)

Figure 8.18 shows the face of a **Hispanic male** over a span of about 30 years. Notice that his naturally dark and thick hair has changed little. The eyebrows have thickened somewhat. The naturally full lips have thinned only a little bit. The most noticeable changes are in the eyes and at the jaw line. The inferior orbital grooves are very pronounced and the outline of the bony orbits of the skull are clearly visible in the lateral view. There are deep nasolabial furrows and oromental grooves and lines have formed in front of the tragus of the ear. The jaw line is ill-defined and there are jowls. Note that as the lower face has become fuller, the ears have become less visible in the frontal view.

Figure 8.19 shows the face of an African-derived or **Negroid male** spanning a time frame of 30 years. The most noticeable lines are frowning and squinting related. While he eventually develops nasolabial furrows, they are not pronounced due to the alveolar prognathism. The hairline changes little, the skin remains good, and the lips hardly thin at all.

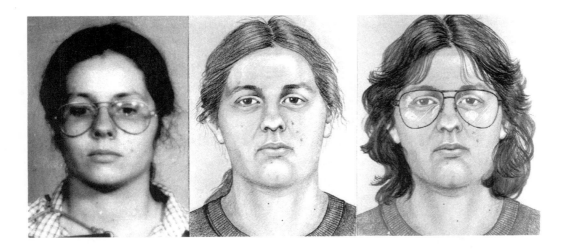

Figure 8.17 Fugitive **Donna Joan Borup** (left) and **age progressions** by KTT (center and right). (Courtesy of Texas Department of Public Safety.)

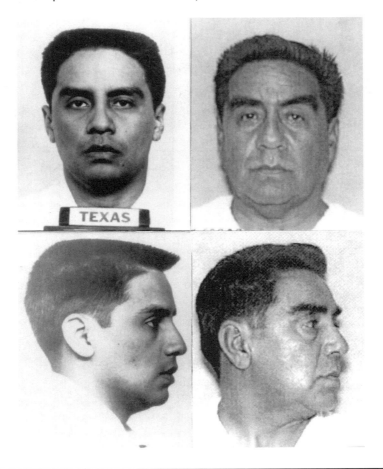

Figure 8.18 Aging in the face of a **Hispanic male** shown over a period of about 30 years, in frontal and lateral views. (Courtesy of Texas Department of Criminal Justice.)

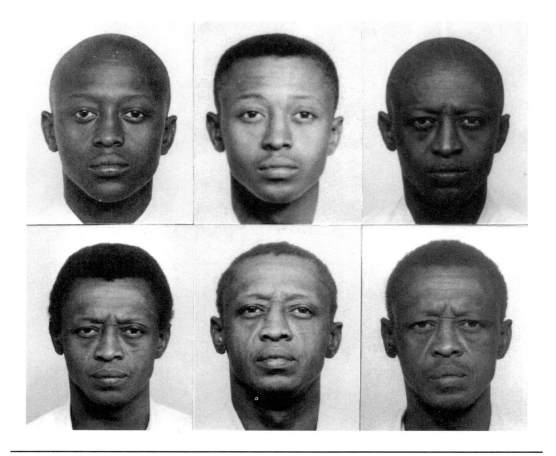

Figure 8.19 Aging in the face of a **Negroid male** over a 30-year period. (Courtesy of Texas Department of Criminal Justice.)

Individual Traits

As previously emphasized, each face must be treated individually. Certain facial structures, habits, or conditions may alter the development of the facial lines.

In Figure 8.20 the face of a **habitual brow lifter** is shown over a span of 13 years. The tissues above the eye are not sagging as in some brow lifters, but it does seem that he must lift his frontalis muscle in order to open his eyes adequately. Over time, his thinning brows rise ever higher and higher, creating deep transverse frontal lines in the forehead.

Figure 8.21 shows the face of convicted serial killer **Henry Lee Lucas**, showing a **prosthetic left eye** since childhood. Lucas is seen as a young boy (upper left), in his mid-20s (upper right), in his mid-40s (lower left), and in his mid-50s (lower right). Over time the upper eyelid becomes less responsive and there is some atrophy of the muscles within and around the orbit.

The structure of the lower face of Figure 8.22 alters the natural formation of the usual lines of age. The subject is shown at age 21 (left), age 33 (center), and age 44 (right). He has a very receding chin and projecting maxilla, which totally prevents any formation of nasolabial furrrows.

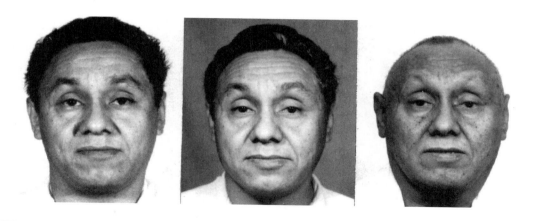

Figure 8.20 Aging in the face of a **habitual brow lifter** seen over a span of 13 years. (Courtesy of Texas Department of Criminal Justice.)

Figure 8.21 Aging in the face of **Henry Lee Lucas** showing a **prosthetic left eye**, seen as a young boy (upper left), in his mid-20s (upper right), mid-40s (lower left), and mid-50s (lower right). (Courtesy of Texas Department of Criminal Justice.)

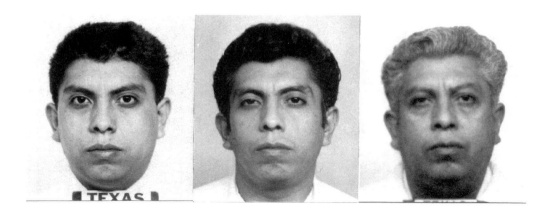

Figure 8.22 Aging in the face of a man with a very receding chin and projecting maxilla, at age 21 (left), age 33 (center), and age 44 (right). Because of the **facial structure**, no nasolabial furrows are formed. (Courtesy of Texas Department of Criminal Justice.)

Fugitives and Adult Facial Update Examples

Case Studies

Virgilio Paz Romero

A Cuban national, Paz was a part of a conspiracy in the political assassination of former Chilean ambassador to the U.S., Orlando Letelier, and a young aide. The murders, resulting from a car bomb in a busy area of Washington, D.C. in 1976, led to strained relations between the U.S. and Chile for over a decade. The fugitive update was prepared from very poor quality photocopies of a photo of Paz from years earlier (Figure 8.23). He was captured after 15 years at large, 3 days after the drawing aired on "America's Most Wanted" in 1991. At the time of his capture, he

Figure 8.23 Virgilio Paz Romero in poor-quality photocopy (left), **fugitive update** by KTT (center), and after capture (right). (Courtesy of "America's Most Wanted.")

was considered one of the most wanted men in the world. There was a lot of teasing because I chose to draw him with a red shirt and he was apprehended wearing an identical red shirt!

Ricardo Caputo

Caputo, an Argentinean serial killer of women, had an exceptional ability to manipulate his victims and was the object of an international FBI manhunt. He was charged with four murders, from New York to California, over a period of 10 years and was a suspect in a fifth. All of the victims were women romantically involved with him. In 1971, he murdered a Long Island, New York girlfriend and was institutionalized for treatment. He proceeded to woo the therapist and, after gaining her trust, killed her as well. Caputo turned himself in to authorities in 1994 after several segments about him, including the fugitive update drawing, were aired on "Unsolved Mysteries" and "America's Most Wanted," calling him the "Ladykiller" (Figure 8.24).

Figure 8.24 Ricardo Caputo in arrest photo (left), **fugitive update** by KTT (center), and in custody (right). (Courtesy of "America's Most Wanted.")

Carmine Esposito

Carmine Esposito, the son of a New York mob figure, was a heavy cocaine user. He entered a restaurant in "Little Italy" and began harassing a young couple by flirting with the girl. He then pulled a gun, saying, "What do you think this is, chocolate?" and murdered the young man. With intelligence information that he was working as a truck driver, fugitive update drawings were prepared of him, showing him both clean-shaven and with facial hair and sunglasses (Figure 8.25). He was captured after a segment about him that televised the drawings was aired on "America's Most Wanted." The accuracy of the pattern of his facial hair growth was determined by assessing the "five-o'clock shadow" in clean-shaven photos.

Figure 8.25 Carmine Esposito in driver's license photo (upper left), **fugitive updates** by KTT (upper right and lower left), and actual appearance (lower right). (Courtesy of "America's Most Wanted.")

Figure 8.26 James Dudley Ashley in early arrest photo (left), **fugitive update** by KTT (center), and actual appearance (right). (Courtesy of "America's Most Wanted.")

James Dudley Ashley

James Dudley Ashley, wanted for loan scams in Oklahoma, systematically poisoned his wife so that he could be with an amateur country and western singer. Leaving behind three young children, he dumped his wife's body in a garbage pit behind their Santa Fe, New Mexico home. He was accidentally released due to a paperwork error by Oklahoma authorities. A fugitive update of him gambled on his continued weight problems and that he liked to wear his hair like Elvis Presley (Figure 8.26).* After the segment about him was aired on "America's Most Wanted," a female acquaintance sent in more recent photos, although he remains at large.

Henrietta Marie Ganote

Henrietta Marie Ganote killed her 15-month-old baby daughter, Jesse Marie, by beating her to death in Lincoln, Nebraska in 1980. She was convicted of manslaughter and sent to Nebraska Center for Women in York, Nebraska. She and another woman escaped in 1984. She was captured after the segment showing the updated drawing was aired on "America's Most Wanted" (Figure 8.27). At the time, she lived in Monroe, Tennessee, and was remarried with two more small children.

Figure 8.27 **Henrietta Marie Ganote** in early arrest photo (left), **fugitive update** by KTT (center), and actual appearance (right). (Courtesy of "America's Most Wanted.")

David Gordon Smith

David Gordon Smith (see Figure 1.2 in Chapter 1) escaped in 1985 from an Oklahoma prison where he was serving a life sentence for murdering Catoosa, Oklahoma Police Chief J. B. Hamby in a 1978 robbery. Smith was arrested in 1993 in Sturgis, South Dakota after a story about him was aired on national television.

Complications

The following case studies present complications in "best guess" predictions of certain factors. In all instances, the overall resemblances are consistent with the capture photos.

---

* Color version of Figure 8.26 follows p. 266.

In each case, however, there was an aspect (hair color or weight) that was impossible to predict.

Roy Wayne Bevan

Roy Wayne Bevan was a Texas child molester convicted of assaulting a 6-year-old girl. Based on his Texas Department of Corrections photograph (upper left), fugitive updates of him were prepared in two versions, clean-cut (upper right) and more "scruffy" (lower left), depicting age changes and an average weight for the projected age (Figure 8.28). When actually captured in Minnesota he was rather thin, due to heavy drug use (lower right).*

Figure 8.28   Roy Wayne Bevan in penitentiary photo (upper left), **fugitive updates** by KTT (upper right and lower left), and **thin appearance** when captured (lower right). (Courtesy of Texas Department of Public Safety.)

---

* Color version of Figure 8.28 follows p. 266.

Enrique Moreno Casas

When Enrique Moreno Casas, at age 19, cold bloodedly murdered Tarrant County, Texas Deputy Frank Howell in 1986, he dropped his wallet with ID at the scene. He was believed to be living the "high life" in Mexico, and family members had a tendency to be on the heavy side, so the fugitive update was made to look "healthy." When captured south of the border, after 10 years at large, he was actually living in squalor, and appeared rather thin (Figure 8.29).

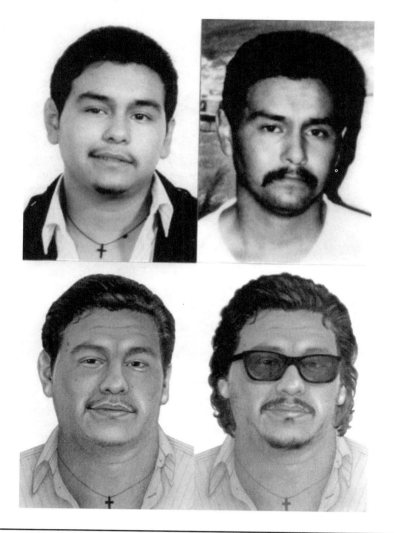

Figure 8.29 **Enrique Moreno Casas** in early arrest photo (upper left), **thin appearance** when captured (upper right), and **fugitive updates** by KTT (lower left and right). (Courtesy of Texas Department of Public Safety.)

William White Graham

In 1972, William White Graham robbed the Arlington Trust Company in Arlington, Virginia and murdered a bank manager and a responding police officer. He fled to

Figure 8.30 **William White Graham** in photos in his youth (upper left and right), **fugitive update** by KTT (lower left), and actual appearance at age 38 with **prematurely gray hair and beard** (lower right). (Courtesy of "America's Most Wanted.")

Houston, Texas, hijacked an Eastern Airlines jet at Houston Intercontinental Airport, killed a ticket agent, and ended up in Cuba for several years.

As Figure 8.30 shows, a fugitive update was prepared of Graham (lower left) based on photographs of him in his 20s (upper left and right). He reentered the U.S. and surrendered after a segment about him aired on "America's Most Wanted," after 20 years at large. The photograph at the time of his surrender (lower right) shows Graham at age 38 with prematurely gray hair and facial hair, which was impossible to predict.

Ultimately, adult age progression is an inexact process, yet as these cases show, it is often worth the attempt. The method has proven that, if done with deliberation and carefully considered inputs, an acceptable degree of accuracy can be achieved. The production of a fugitive update is often the spark of new life that creates enough interest in a "cold case" to successfully result in a capture.

References

1. Ellis, D. and Ward, D., "The aging face," *The Journal of Otolaryngology*, 15, 4, 1986.
2. George, R. and Singer, R., "The lines and grooves of the face — a suggested nomenclature," *Journal of the American Society of Plastic and Reconstructive Surgeons*, 92, 3, 1993.
3. Neave, R., Age changes to the face in adulthood, in *Craniofacial Identification in Forensic Medicine*, Clement, J. G. and Ranson, D. L., Eds. New York: Oxford University Press, 1998.
4. Fedosyutkin, B. A., Korovyanskiy, O. P., Samishchenko, S. S., Usacheva, L. L., and Khokhlov, A. E., *The Combined Graphic Method (CGM) of Cranio-facial Reconstruction.* Moscow, Russia: All-Union Scientific Research Institute, 1985.
5. Stedman, W., "Facial Aging," lecture presented at Scottsdale Artists' School, Scottsdale, Arizona, October 1992.

Chapter 9

Image Assessment and Modification

The Forensic Artist as a "Facial Identification Specialist"

Because of the nature of their work, forensic artists are often considered "facial identification specialists." I realized this slowly over time as, more and more often, I was asked to give opinions regarding facial images even when no drawing was needed.

I do not relish this role, since it is often one of very little certainty, a lot of speculation, and a great risk of being totally wrong. For these reasons, I rarely give a specific or firm opinion regarding arbitrary face-to-face comparisons. A phrase I use is, "I find nothing to indicate it is not this person," rather than "it is this person." I believe the former is a far more appropriate response for a possible match, considering the nature and limitations of such comparisons.

In recent years, I have been asked to assess photographs of people believed to be fugitives, missing children, long-lost relatives, missing-in-action war veterans, celebrities caught topless, literary figures, historical personages from presidents to outlaws of the Wild West, and many others.

I am sometimes asked to modify or enhance facial images to make them more useful in criminal investigations. Today, such modifications can be accomplished by a variety of means and it is necessary to determine the most advantageous method with the greatest likelihood for success.

By whatever method an image is assessed or modified, the most important factor is a solid foundation in anatomical knowledge of the face. This chapter offers suggestions for a methodical approach to comparisons, considerations for evaluation of facial images, and a look at facial changes that might come into play.

What Approach Should Be Used?

Requests for the review of facial or other images come in various forms, involving assessment, comparison, and sometimes enhancement or modification.

Identification pioneer Alphonse Bertillon documented examples of photo-to-photo comparisons in his 1896 book, *The Bertillon System of Identification*. His analyses were done strictly on the basis of morphological comparison and measurement. When comparing faces, Bertillon placed particular importance on the configurations of the structures within the profile ear. His approach is still valid today. I have often referred to Bertillon's suggestions, relying on ears for reliable comparisons. Figure 9.1 shows an early photo-to-photo comparison by Bertillon in which the structure of the ears revealed the identity of a man, although his appearance has changed considerably over a 7-year interval. Figure 9.2 shows a man whose identity was revealed after comparing photographs taken 10 years apart. Although he grew a full beard and lost weight, the ears remain distinctive for comparison.

My job duties routinely include the visual assessment and comparison of facial images. Crime analysts and officers often request assistance in determining whether or not two photographic images could actually be the same person. Fraud cases in which individuals have multiple forms of identification in different names are always prevalent. Fugitive case investigators sometimes ask that known mug photos are compared with surveillance photographs of individuals whom they believe might be the wanted subjects they seek.

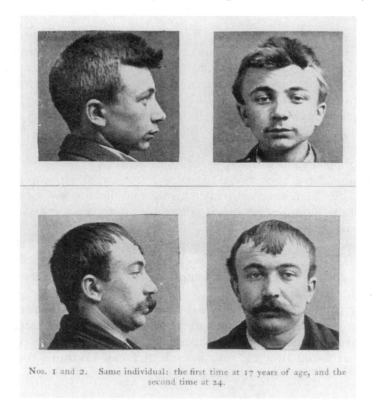

Nos. 1 and 2.   Same individual: the first time at 17 years of age, and the second time at 24.

Figure 9.1 Photo-to-photo comparison by Alphonse Bertillon in which the subject above, aged 17 (top left and right), is revealed to be the same as the subject below, aged 24 (bottom left and right), due to **comparison of the ears**.

FIG. 3. IDENTITY REVEALED (DESPITE BEARD) BY THE SPIRAL LOBE OF THE EAR AND THE FACIAL ANGLE: BERTILLON PHOTOGRAPHS (FULL-FACE AND PROFILE) OF THE SAME MAN AT TEN YEARS' INTERVAL

Figure 9.2   Photo-to-photo comparison by Alphonse Bertillon in which the subject above (top left and right) was revealed to be the same as the subject below (below left and right) due to **comparison of the ears**, even though the man's appearance had changed considerably over the 10-year interval due to aging, weight loss, diminished eyebrows, receding hairline, and facial hair.

Sadly, on occasion I am asked to review child pornography, comparing the faces shown with the facial photos of missing children. In these cases, as was the practice of Bertillon, my evaluations are made almost solely by just looking at the photos. The **anatomical morphological traits of faces are compared to one another, strictly on a visual basis.** This approach may prove accurate if the evaluator is skilled and experienced, but it is **far from being scientific or definitive**. Such comparisons should always be accompanied with a caveat statement of the limitations involved.

As part of certain investigations, I have been asked to simply review photographs to see if there might be something that an "artist's eye" might see that others have missed. A few years ago, I was presented with crime scene photographs from a 2-year-old unsolved homicide case in which police believed that they were seeking a lone assailant. Upon study of the photos, I could see and define three distinctly different sets of footprints, which changed the course of the investigation. So, at times, there are advantages of a "fresh look" at an unsolved case, especially with an "artist's eye."

Many times, it has been advisable and advantageous that I **work jointly with the photography, digital imaging, and video specialists.** When photographs in major cases are assessed, photographers, video technicians, and I examine an image. Each of us applies a different sort of experience when reviewing the image. In case after case, this teamwork approach has paid off.

Concerning enhancement or modification of images, each case must be individually evaluated to determine the best possible approach. For example, Figure 9.3 shows a homicide case in which the Texas Rangers located a surveillance image of the suspect and wanted to improve its quality for distribution. Video, photographic, and electronic methods of enhancement proved unsuccessful, so I was

Figure 9.3 Surveillance image of suspect in a homicide case (top) from which a **facial drawing** was prepared by KTT (lower left) and the subject identified (lower right). (Courtesy of Texas Department of Public Safety.)

Figure 9.4 Surveillance image of suspect in a bank robbery (left), which was **digitally enhanced** by forensic imaging specialist Missey Micheletti (right). (Courtesy of Texas Department of Public Safety.)

asked to do a drawing of the person in the photograph. With some speculation, the frontal drawing was produced, but there was no identification for several years. Subsequently, the case was presented on "America's Most Wanted," and a tip was called in from across the U.S., leading to the positive identification of the murderer through comparison of his fingerprints to latent prints from the crime scene.

Alternatively, the image in Figure 9.4, recovered from the scene of a bank robbery, provided too little information to produce a facial drawing. Forensic photographer and imaging specialist Missey Micheletti digitally enhanced the image to such an extent that it was determined that the perpetrator was female, and she was identified. Digital enhancement of photographic images is an entire field unto itself, practiced by both photographers and artists. It is beyond the scope of this text to discuss it in detail.

Technically, the forensic art methods of child age progression, fugitive updates, postmortem drawing, and skull-to-photo superimposition, all involving use of photographs, could be termed image assessments or modifications. These methods are addressed in separate chapters so we will not discuss them in depth here. Instead, illustrations of various other types of facial changes that the forensic artist may deal with are presented, excluding growth, aging, and postmortem changes. Photo-to-photo comparison is discussed since it is a likely method that forensic artists will be called upon to use.

Photo-to-Photo Comparisons

Once the approach to be used for the assessment or modification of a facial image is determined, the artist may be involved in some capacity. A case may require a team examination with photographic, digital imaging, or video specialists. The most likely assessments asked of a forensic artist involve photo-to-photo comparisons. The following is a general guide for the comparison of facial photos to other facial photos. The procedure suggested is meant for use in assessment of the facial characteristics to determine the possibility that certain photos may or may not depict the same individual. **This approach is not appropriate or legally valid for determination of a positive identification.** In certain rare instances, an experienced facial identification specialist, anatomist, or anthropologist may give an opinion as to a match. However, such visual assessment comparisons **may be useful tools to eliminate an individual as a possible match** or simply **may indicate that further investigation is warranted.**

A methodical step-by-step approach is recommended for evaluation. Multiple factors must be considered when reviewing facial photographs. Some fundamental concerns are the angle of view of the photograph and the age of the subject in the photo. Some elements of the facial "look" are simply natural, such as weight change or expression, while others may be intentional alterations of appearance. It can be beneficial to assess the primary factors first and then consider other aspects and features one at a time.

Photos

For comparison purposes, **gather as many photos as possible.** Check various sources for photos of a particular subject, such as old or out-of-state driver's licenses, passports, school yearbooks, immigration "green card" photos, and so forth.

Get the best possible quality copies of the photos, particularly if they have been duplicated several times. Go back to the "most original" version of the photograph available. An evaluation or comparison of poor quality photographs is usually of little value.

Considerations for Evaluation and Comparison

Angle of View

- Is the head pointing straight forward?
- Is the head tipped up or down?
- Is the head turned side to side?

These factors create potential distortions. Shapes of individual features and the overall facial shape will be affected by the angle of view. For example, the nose may appear much longer if the head is tipped downward. Conversely, if the head is tipped backward, the nose will appear shorter and the nostrils will probably be more visible. **Consider the base of the nose in relation to the placement of the ears.**

Age

If possible, subtract the year of birth from the year that the photo was taken to assess the age of the person (keep in mind that this information may not be accurate). Thus, you have the **age that the person should appear in the photo.**

- Does that age seem consistent with the appearance of the facial photograph?
- If viewing a series of photos, does the progression of age in each photo seem reasonable?

Several **well-known changes occur in our faces as a result of aging.** Gravity affects the tissues over time and causes sagging. Tissues above the eyes drop, the ears appear to get a little longer, and the tip of the nose may drop a bit lower. Long, hook-type noses and very large noses show a more noticeable drop than noses that are naturally small or upturned. Often the lips thin as well, especially in people whose lips were thin when younger. The effects of aging on our faces are discussed in more depth in Chapter 8.

An important point to remember when comparing photographs is that these **aging effects do not go backward**. In other words, as you evaluate a series of photos by date, the aging effects should seem logical and progressive. For example, sagging skin above the eyes should not get less saggy with more eyelid showing in an older photo. Of course, the exception to this could be intervention by plastic surgery.

Other Natural Changes

Growth or removal of **facial hair** may be a change that occurs in a face and obviously does not necessarily mean intentional alteration of appearance for criminal purposes.

Drastic **weight changes**, either gain or loss of weight, can strongly alter the appearance of the face. Weight loss tends to reveal more of the structure of the skull, while weight gain usually obscures facial bones.

Dental conditions such as tooth loss or tooth replacement with dentures can distort or obviously reshape the mouth structures.

A person may have a serious **illness** that has a progressive effect on the face. For example, individuals with AIDS or other serious illnesses may appear to age very rapidly and show pronounced facial changes over a short period of time.

Taking certain **medications**, prescribed or illegal, can produce changes in the appearance in the facial shape, such as sunken cheeks or bloating.

Expressions

Making various facial expressions can noticeably change the face and should be considered when comparing photos.

A **frown** can lower the eyebrows and make them seem closer to the eyes. It may also create vertical furrows between the eyebrows.

A **smile** will stretch the nose and mouth in width, while narrowing the vertical dimension of the lips. The relaxed mouth generally covers about the front six teeth, while a fully smiling mouth reveals ten or more teeth. Also, in smiling, the cheeks are lifted closer to the eyes creating small puffy areas under the eyes. The eye opening or aperture gets more closed down when smiling and less of the iris is revealed.

While the above aspects of expression may distort features for evaluation purposes, they may also be helpful in other ways. **Expressions create lines, creases, and furrows in our faces as we age, which are rather unique to each individual face.** These specific small lines can be compared from photo to photo much like a fingerprint examiner looks for points of comparison between fingerprints. This is especially useful in older faces, although we begin to get some lines of expression as early as the 20s. "Crow's feet" at the outer corners of the eyes come early, as do horizontal lines in the forehead. The lines of facial aging are located and named in Chapter 8. Age and expression lines are often most noticeable in very expressive faces and in people who spend a lot of time in the sun.

Intentional Alteration of Appearance

Those involved in criminal activity sometimes intentionally change their appearance to avoid recognition. These **disguises** may be temporary or more drastic and long term.

Makeup is perhaps the most common and easily done method used to alter the appearance on a short-term basis. A skilled application of makeup can make a person virtually unrecognizable. Career criminals who possess a distinguishing scar or mark may become adept at covering it with makeup, or they may add a distracting scar or mark by use of makeup.

Changes in **hair color or style** can achieve a short-term but dramatic change in a person's "look." Hair may be colored, permed, or straightened/relaxed. Wigs also provide a quick and easy change.

Various **accessories** can disguise a person, including scarves, hats, glasses, or even contact lenses to change eye color. Dark glasses may obscure the eyes altogether. Clear lens glasses may be used to distort the eyes by appearance of enlargement or reduction. Figure 9.5 shows the degree of distortion that eyeglasses can cause, even if the eyeglasses are not an intentional ploy to change the eyes.

Real or false **tattoos** may be added or removed. Tattoos are rarely removed because the removal procedure can be painful, time consuming, and expensive.

Growth or removal of **facial hair** does not necessarily imply deception, but criminals have used hair to change their faces by hiding some of the features. False facial hair is sometimes used.

Figure 9.5   Distortion and reduction of the appearance of the size of the eyes, due to **glasses.** (Courtesy of Texas Department of Criminal Justice.)

In drastic cases, a person may even resort to permanent changes in appearance of the teeth through **dentistry** or facial features through **plastic surgery**.

Individual Features and Traits

It can be beneficial to review the overall face and then consider each individual feature or trait in a more isolated way. Visualize an imaginary vertical line down the midline of the face and assess each feature in relation to that line, observing and noting asymmetries. This can also be done horizontally.

Carefully observe each feature. Then assess them in relation to each other. Remember the **"plumb-line" method of comparison of features** described in Chapter 4 in the section "The Profile."

Head and Face Shape
- Consider the overall shape of the face. Oval? Triangle? Rectangle? Square?
- Where is the widest point on the face?

Hair and Hairline
- Consider the hairline both at the top or the forehead and along the temples.
- Consider the thickness and texture of the hair as well as the style. Has it been permed or straightened/relaxed?
- Remember that style, color, and texture can be easily changed, so place more emphasis on the growth pattern of the hairline.

Eyes
- Are they light or dark?
- In a color photo, what is the color?
- What is the shape of the eye opening or aperture?
- Are the eyes level with each other or is one higher or lower?
- Is the lid showing or partially hidden by tissue above it?
- Is one of the irises slightly askew?
- Remember that if there are glasses, they may distort the scale of the eyes.

Eyebrows
- Are they thick or thin? With age, some thicken and some thin.
- Are they heavy or sparse? Curly or straight?
- Have they been plucked or altered?
- Consider the arch. Observe the highest point of the arch in relation to the lateral side of the iris and the outer corner or lateral canthus of the eye.

Nose
- Look at the bridge of the nose.
- Look at the width of the base of the nose. Remember this will widen when smiling.
- Look at the nostrils. Can you see the openings? Are they symmetrical? Is one nostril lower than the other? Remember that more of the nostril opening will show with the head tilted back.

Mouth

- Consider the width horizontally. Remember that the mouth spreads wider when smiling.
- Consider the mouth vertically. Remember that the lips thin down when smiling.
- Are the lips the same thickness or is one thicker or thinner?
- Is the mouth level or angled up or down at one side?
- Can you compare the teeth?

Chin and Jaw

- What is the shape?
- Is there a cleft or dimple?
- Remember that with age, the jaw line will become less distinct as facial tissue sags. Weight gain will also "soften" the jaw line.

Ears

- The ears are a particularly good feature to observe and compare. Consider them carefully if they are visible. Changing the ear structure is difficult, even with plastic surgery.
- Is one ear higher or lower?
- Does one protrude more than the other?
- Do they protrude more at the top or the bottom?
- Do the inside structures protrude more than the outer rim? Or vice-versa?

Neck Area

- In males particularly, look at the structures of the neck. The Adam's apple may take on a distinct shape worthy of comparison.
- What about chest hair in males? If present, it may grow in a distinctive pattern.

Skin

- Look for any skin irregularities such as acne or blotches.
- Are there scars or any other marks that can be compared?
- Are there freckles? Moles?
- Look for lines of age or expression to compare.

Other

- Don't forget to look for possible items that might be the same in two photos, such as eyeglasses, jewelry, or clothing.
- Is there a characteristic facial asymmetry or expression?

Special Techniques for Comparison

In certain circumstances, it is helpful to employ special evaluation techniques. Generally, these techniques are not necessary when making routine facial comparisons, but special cases may warrant their use. Some such techniques are simple to use while others are more advanced and complex.

Turning Upside Down

Turn the photographs you are assessing upside down to view them. Instead of looking for what you **expect** to see in the facial features, you will be forced to view each shape out of context, and thus view the forms of the face with **greater objectivity**. It becomes easier to consider each facial feature as if it were simply a geometric shape. Subtle asymmetries will likely become more obvious by using this method.

Plumb Lines

Plumb lines are simply **vertical lines** that can be used to assess features in relation to one another. To compare features using plumb lines, use a clear ruler or a plain white piece of paper. This method should only be used on photos in which the face is straight ahead, not tipped up or down or side to side. To assess features, place a plumb or true vertical line at a point on the face, such as the inner corner of the eye. Now consider the placement of other features in relation to the inner corner of the eye. Does the side of the nose line up vertically with the eye corner or does it come out wider? How about the side of the mouth? Now do the same thing on the comparison photo. How does the spacing compare?

Magnification

Simply enlarging a photo on the copier may help you see the features more clearly. Remember, however, that enlarging a digitized photograph beyond a certain point may actually prevent you from seeing details, depending on the resolution of the photo. In general, **enlargement of digitized photos reduces detail, and reduction of digitized photos intensifies detail.**

I often use a vertically mounted video camera, which has proven very helpful in examining small details of photographs and objects. An object or photo is placed under the camera lens and then projected onto a large format computer monitor for evaluation.

Superimposition

Superimposition or the placement of one image directly on top of another may aid in evaluation in some cases. To do this effectively, you must always consider **scale and orientation**. For a useful comparison, the faces in the photos must be the same size and turned at the same angle. **This method may be used only on photos in which the face is angled the same way, preferably straight ahead, in all the photos being evaluated.**

Sophisticated video and computer systems for superimpositions of faces are utilized to compare photographs to unknown skulls. This procedure is covered in Chapter 14. Skull-to-photo superimposition on video is aided by the fact that the skull can be manipulated into the correct orientation using the facial photograph as a guide.

With photo-to-photo superimpositions, the photos cannot be altered in angle of view and they must correspond for a valid comparison. For routine photo-to-photo evaluations of two photos in a very similar facial angle, you can use the interpupillary distance scaling technique, described below.

Scaling Techniques

Interpupillary Distance

Use interpupillary distance to establish approximately the same scale in the photographs being compared (which should have the faces straight forward). Measure from the center of one pupil of the eye to the center of the other pupil to determine this distance.

Enlarge one photograph on a copier to a desired size. For this approach, it is not important that a particular percentage of enlargement or reduction be used, only that the scale be the same in the two photos. Then note the interpupillary distance by measuring with a ruler or by making marks on a piece of white paper. Next, enlarge the second photo until the distance between the pupils is the same as in the first photo.

Once the photos are the same scale, choose one photograph and make a clear version of it using transparency film in a copier machine. Overlay the clear photo on top of the other photo and review the faces feature by feature.

A case report in the *Journal of Forensic Sciences* describes the use of the interpupillary distance of a second party in a photograph to extrapolate the magnification factor in a case from Singapore. An existing photograph of a husband and wife was used to measure the distance from pupil to pupil of the woman. The interpupillary distance of the living woman was then measured in person. The article indicates:

> By a simple division of the true interpupil distance by the photographic interpupil distance, the magnification factor was obtained. The suspect's [deceased] photographic interpupil distance was then measured and multiplied by the magnification factor to obtain the true interpupil distance.[2]

A very clear passport photograph of the man was obtained and used for comparison. Thus, a more accurate superimposition comparison of a life-size photo with an unknown skull could be made since the scale was known.

Iris Size as a Scale to Enlarge to Life Size

In many cases, it is beneficial to enlarge two photos for superimposition or other comparison at life size. Again, the photos to be used for this method should be directly straight on, otherwise the measurements will not be valid. Life-size comparison may be accomplished by **use of an ophthalmological standard** found in various texts, which indicates that the average healthy human iris, or actually the cornea, in healthy eyes is between 11 and 13 mm in diameter. The transparent cornea sits on top of the colored iris, so the two may be considered basically the same width. Adler's *Textbook of Ophthalmology* states that **the diameter of the cornea in the adult eye averages 12 mm.**[3] Thus, the measurement of the iris in each photograph may be taken and the photographs enlarged until the width of the irises reaches 12 mm. Both photos will then be at the same scale, life size.

Other Items Used for Scaling to Life Size

In the historically significant case of the Buck Ruxton murders mentioned in Chapters 2 (Figure 2.9) and 14, a positive version of a photograph was superimposed with a negative to compare a skull and a life photo. The same scale was achieved in the two images by using the measurements of a diamond tiara worn by Mrs. Ruxton in the photograph. **If a photograph is to be compared to another and there is a known object in the photo resting on a plane that is relatively close to that of the face, it may be possible to use that object as a scale.** For example, a surveillance photograph of a bank robber taken while standing at a teller's booth may contain objects in the same plane as the offender's face, which may be later measured for assessing scale. Such items may be helpful for generating life-size photo enlargements of a face, for getting two photos to the same scale, or for approximating the height of the subject.

Many objects may be used to determine scale for enlargement. Such items might appear on the person in the photo or in the environment surrounding the person in the photo. Many objects might be available later for measurement to calculate the correct magnification factor as described above using interpupillary distance in a photo of two people. Such objects include buttons on shirts, articles of jewelry, or headgear.

Making Comparison Photographs

Most of the methodology for photo-to-photo comparison discussed thus far has involved the assessment of two existing photos. Occasionally, it may be possible to create the photographs for comparison, such as when a suspect in custody is to be compared to a questioned photo. In such a situation, it is possible to photographically capture the precise angle needed for comparison. In a 1993 lecture at the International Association for Identification Conference in Orlando, Florida, the late forensic anthropologist Dr. William Maples discussed taking photos for this type of comparison. He recommended moving around the subject and carefully observing the facial structures. He preferred to take approximately 300 photos of a person using a motor drive on the camera. He suggested using the nose to establish a correct camera angle in profile and using the nose in relation to the ear for a correct camera angle in the frontal view.[4]

Each of these special techniques is a tool for better evaluation and assessment of facial photographs, not a means of specifying an individual to the exclusion of all others. It should be noted again that **few visual assessments can lead to a legally valid positive identification.**

Facial Changes Other Than Age

Chapter 8 illustrates the many changes our faces undergo as a result of the passage of time. In this section, we continue to address types of facial alterations that are not necessarily related to the aging process, although age may be an accompanying factor. As noted in the section on photo-to-photo comparisons, criminal offenders and others whose faces forensic artists must draw will most likely experience some **naturally occurring changes**. Other changes may involve **intentional alteration of the appearance**.

This section includes figures intended to visually instruct about some of the changes described in this chapter. These photographic illustrations provide a basis for study and comparison for use when you do either photo-to-photo comparisons or updated representations of faces. The figures are intended as a reference tool for forensic artists and others called upon to compare or alter faces. These figures are a useful guide, but keep in mind when viewing the photos that each face is individual and may be affected differently by a particular condition such as tooth loss or disease.

Intentional Alteration of Appearance

Makeup

Makeup can be used to create a totally alternate persona. Makeup may change the eyelid shapes, nose width, cheekbones, and so forth. We need only to view the magic created by Hollywood makeup artists to realize the astonishing range of facial adjustments made possible by makeup.

Disguises

Figure 9.6 shows three well-known males with disguises of hats and dark glasses added to their faces. Do you recognize singer Elton John? General Colin Powell? Actor Patrick Stewart? Even though the faces are familiar, obscuring portions of the face may greatly deter our ability to immediately recognize them.

Plastic Surgery

Various surgical procedures may cause changes in the proportions of the facial features and even ambiguity of race and sex.

Figure 9.6 Faces of three well-known males with **disguises** added in the form of hats and dark glasses.

Naturally Occurring Changes in Appearance

Weight Changes

Figure 9.7 shows frontal and lateral photographs of a black female taken 5 years apart and after a substantial weight loss. Notice that the fat pads around the eyes within the bony orbits seem to have diminished in addition to the more obvious changes in the cheeks and neck. In the profile view, the angle of the mandible becomes apparent; it had been totally obscured before the weight loss.

Figure 9.8 shows a similar weight loss in a white male after a 5-year interval. Frontally, the temple area is slightly reduced and the loss of bulk in the cheeks makes the ears more obvious (the opposite effect of Figure 8.18). In the lateral view, the general skull structure is more revealed, particularly the angle of the mandible and the base of the skull. Note, too, that the structures of the throat become visible after the weight loss.

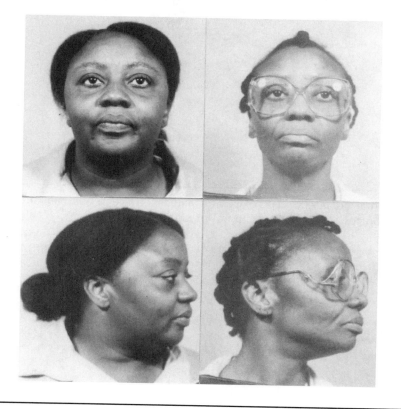

Figure 9.7 Frontal and lateral views of a black female taken 5 years apart and after a substantial **weight loss**. (Courtesy of Texas Department of Criminal Justice.)

Dental Changes

Figure 9.9 shows an individual who has undergone substantial tooth loss particularly of the mandibular (lower) teeth. The result is a change in shape of the lower face, and a "caved-in" appearance.

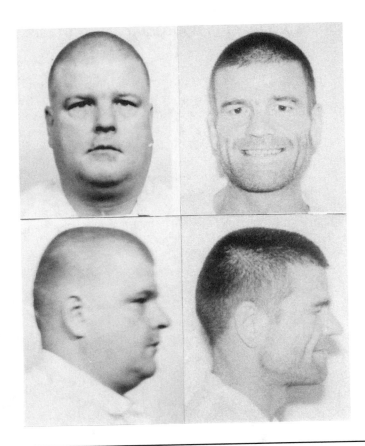

Figure 9.8   Frontal and lateral views of a white male taken 5 years apart and after a substantial **weight loss**. (Courtesy of Texas Department of Criminal Justice.)

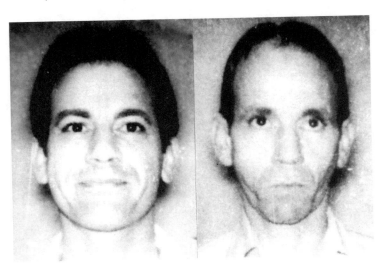

Figure 9.9   Individual who has undergone **tooth loss** in the mandibular dentition, before (left) and after (right). (Courtesy of Texas Department of Criminal Justice.)

Illness-Related Changes

Some health conditions are progressive and the artist should consult a physician for advice when speculating on a particular type of illness or condition. When preparing fugitive updates as discussed in Chapter 8, the forensic artist might be dealing with illness-related changes as well as age-related changes in a face. Each case should be evaluated individually and the appropriate medical input should be sought from a specialist in the type of condition presented.

Figure 9.10 shows a subject with a progressive skin condition. The photo at left shows a loss of pigment primarily on the lower face. The photo at right, taken only 2 years later, shows loss of pigment on the forehead, other areas of the face, and the neck.

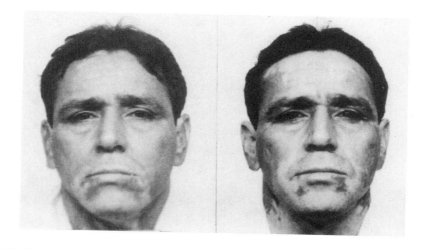

Figure 9.10 Individual who has a **progressive skin condition** (left) as compared to a photo taken only 2 years later (right). (Courtesy of Texas Department of Criminal Justice.)

Figure 9.11 shows a man with a serious illness that has led to great weight loss. The photos, upper and lower right, were taken 12 years after the photos at upper and lower left. As in the previous illustrations of weight loss, the skull is more visible overall. The temples appear reduced, the cheeks are hollowed, the angle of the jaw has become visible, and the structures of the throat have appeared. The eyes appear very hollow and deep set because of the reduction of fat pads surrounding the eyes. Interestingly, the eyelids change from being obscured by fat to being totally visible and the eyebrow hair has diminished.

The method the forensic artist uses to assess, compare, or alter facial images is less important than the artist's knowedge base. The approach may be hand-drawn, photographic retouch, or digital computer alteration. **It is far more important that the necessary anatomical research and study precede the procedure so that the assessment or modification is done from a basis of knowledge, not just speculation.**

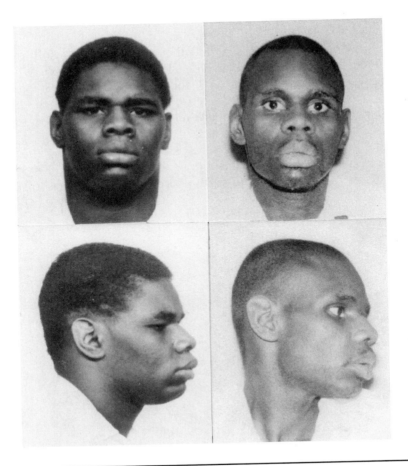

Figure 9.11 Individual who has a **serious illness** and accompanying weight loss shown in photos taken 12 years apart. (Courtesy of Texas Department of Criminal Justice.)

References

1. Bertillon, A., *The Bertillon System of Identification: Signeletic Instructions: The Theory and Practice of Anthropometrical Identification,* McClaughry, R.W., Ed. Chicago: The Werner Company, 1896.
2. Chee, L. F. and Cheng, C. T., "Skull and photographic superimposition: a new approach using a second party's interpupil distance to extrapolate the magnification factor," *Journal of Forensic Sciences,* 34(3), 1989.
3. Adler, F. H., *Textbook of Ophthalmology.* Philadelphia: W. B. Saunders, 1962.
4. Maples, W., "Superimposition in Relation to the Identification Process," Lecture presented at the International Association for Identification's 78th Annual Educational Conference and Training Seminar, Orlando, Florida, July 1993.

FORENSIC ART:
Identifying the Dead

Chapter 10

Postmortem Drawing

Circumstances for Doing Postmortem Drawing

One of the most unpleasant and complicated tasks for law enforcement personnel is dealing with deceased bodies for whom no immediate means of identification can be found. **Postmortem drawing is a method of forensic art done when bodies are in good enough condition for the artist to develop a reasonable facial likeness based on morgue or crime scene photographs or by viewing the actual body.**

The primary purpose of postmortem drawing is to attach a name to the body as a result of someone viewing the facial image, so that medical records of a missing person can be compared to the body and lead to a legally valid positive identification. As with skull reconstructions or even composite drawings, the forensic artist's role is "middle man." The artwork is intended to provide **a link between an unidentified person and the records needed to positively identify him or her.** In and of itself, resemblance of a body to a postmortem drawing is not a means of positively identifying the body.

Although there are jurisdictional variations, **most authorities agree that legally acceptable positive identification is derived by one of the following means: visual identification, fingerprint comparison, dental comparison, comparison of radiographs, or DNA comparison.** When an identification is made by any of the alternative means sometimes used but considered less definitive, such as identification of personal effects, association/exclusion or identifying marks, the official designation may be the term "tentative identification" or "presumptive identification."

While some agencies still identify bodies through visual assessment by family members, this process is not always reliable for a variety of reasons. In "The Horrors of Visual Identification," the following observation is made:

> ... it behooves law enforcement authorities to use visual identification only as an adjunct to more substantive evidence such as fingerprints, dental charting, and DNA typing. In cases of identifications at autopsy where these modalities are absent, it is a *sine qua non* that as much ancillary data as

possible, such as tattoos, old scars, anthropomorphic measurements, miscellaneous X-rays (chest, old fracture sites, etc.), eyeglasses, clothing, jewelry, presence of congenital anomalies, evidence of surgical procedures, etc. be gathered which when taken together may provide statistical significance suitable for burial purposes and insurance settlements.[1]

One of the greatest difficulties for family members asked to identify the corpse of a loved one is the lack of animation in the face. In *Craniofacial Identification in Forensic Medicine*, John Clement and David Ranson discuss this issue:

> ... a dead body may bear much less similarity to the person in life than might be first anticipated. The pallor of death, the unkempt hair or an unrecognizable hairstyle, the lack of expression, make-up or dentures, all make identification more difficult. In life, there is a rich but subtle exchange of signals by means of expressions or gestures between people, which mutually reinforce recognition. These exchanges are obviously entirely lacking, and that too is very disconcerting for someone who may previously never have seen a dead body.[2]

It is the reanimation of the face from a deceased photograph that is one of the most difficult but necessary aspects of postmortem drawing. Adding that look of "life" is a difficult-to-describe, intangible action that the forensic artist must learn to accomplish.

Forensic artists are usually requested to do postmortem drawings in cases that fall into two broad categories. The first group includes unidentified deceased persons whose photographs are inappropriate for media distribution or viewing by possible family members because of trauma or postmortem effects on the face. The second group includes unidentified deceased individuals who have been buried for a period of time before personal identification has taken place and only photographs remain. Postmortem drawings may be done in cases of various types of death and to depict faces in different postmortem stages.

Cases in Which Postmortem Drawing Is Used

- Suicides, natural deaths, or homicides
- Traffic fatalities
- Blunt or sharp trauma fatalities
- Gunshot wound fatalities
- Drowning or boating accidents
- Some other transportation disasters
- Non-extensive conflagrations or fires
- Other miscellaneous types of homicidal violence

Cases in Which Postmortem Drawing Is Generally Not Used

- Extensive conflagrations
- Explosions
- Air disasters

When to Say "No"

For me, postmortem drawing is probably the most difficult type of forensic art, or at least the type about which I feel most tentative. I am far more comfortable with a totally skeletonized case in which I have the skull to study.

Often I receive cases in which very poor quality photographs have been taken and the body has been buried. First, I must decide whether or not the photographs provide enough visual information to be useful. Then, I must decide if the face represented in the photographs is in good enough condition for me to develop a reasonable facsimile in drawing form. I also factor into these decisions the thought that **my drawing may be the only opportunity that this person has ever to be identified and laid to rest.**

Nevertheless, there are times when I must decline to accept a case. In workshops, I use a dramatic example on slides to give artists a shock that, hopefully, they will remember in future cases. I show a slide of the face of a deceased victim of a fire-related homicide. The face seems intact and I request that students comment regarding their visual determinations about this person. Invariably the judgments are very young (even pre-teen), black female with short black curly hair. I then show a slide of the same person in life, revealing that she was an elderly, white female with straight gray hair. It is my intention that the students remember the tentative nature of the facial appearance after death when making decisions about their own cases.

One bad call on a case of this type can seriously damage the artist's professional credibility. **If the photographs do not provide adequate information or the condition of the body is too bad, the case should not be done.**

In declining to do a postmortem drawing, I tell the pathologist or the investigator that the only possibility of my doing any artwork would be from the cleaned skull. This sometimes brings up serious ethical issues for the doctor and the officer. Providing a skull for reconstruction after a body has already been buried requires exhumation and the accompanying legal difficulties and expense.

Perhaps even more complex are cases in which the body has not yet been buried, but the pathologist would have to disarticulate the head for removal of the tissue to extract the skull. Again, such a decision would vary by jurisdiction and by individual pathologist. **The choice must be made between an invasive process which might lead to an identification vs. no alteration of the body and the risk that the person might never be identified.**

Postmortem Changes

Forensic artists who undertake unidentified deceased cases must become familiar with some of the terminology used by pathologists and other forensic scientists. They must gain a general understanding of the physical and biochemical changes that occur after **somatic death** or death of the body. **Both photographs of the deceased and information gained from autopsy or other scientific reports should be used.** This section describes some of the fundamentals needed for case evaluation and for learning to read and understand medicolegal autopsy reports.

Basic Terminology

The terms **forensic taphonomy** or **taphonomic progression** refer to a multiplicity of changes that occur after death. Dr. Joseph H. Davis explains:

> **Taphonomy** concerns the comprehension of multiple factors which play a role in the disintegration and scatter of a body and accoutrements until they have been environmentally recycled and incorporated into the earth, its waters, its air, and its inhabitants.
> ... what happened concerns events remote from and close to the time of death, events that transpired at the time of death, and events in the immediate or long-term period after death.[3]

Dr. Jeffrey Barnard, Chief Medical Examiner for the Dallas County Medical Examiner's Office, lectures to law enforcement personnel in an effort to promote clear communication between police and pathologists and a better understanding of autopsy reports. He defines the following terminology:

- **Cause of death** — injury, disease, or combination of the two, which initiates the sequence of events, however brief or prolonged, that leads to the fatal outcome. Examples of causes of death include gunshot wound of the head, stab wound of the chest, coronary artery atherosclerosis, and AIDS.
- **Manner of death** — refers to the circumstances in which death occurred. Manner of death is broken down into the categories natural and unnatural. Unnatural death is further subdivided into homicide, suicide, accident, or undetermined.
- **Mechanism of death** — is the physiologic derangement or biochemical alteration incompatible with life, which is initiated by the cause of death. Mechanisms do not routinely belong on the death certificate. Examples include hemorrhage, septicemia, and cardiac arrythmia.[4]

Other commonly used terms in autopsy reports with regard to **time** are postmortem, antemortem, and perimortem.

- **Postmortem** — after death
- **Antemortem** — before death
- **Perimortem** — near or around the time of death

Dr. Barnard distinguishes some of the types of external injuries to bodies:

- **Abrasions** — (scrapes) result either from crushing the epidermis or from frictional denuding of the skin.
- **Contusions** — (bruises) caused by blood flowing into the surrounding tissue from traumatically disrupted blood vessels. As contusions age, the color of the bruise changes; however, the rate at which this occurs is variable; darker skin shows bruising less than lighter skin.
- **Lacerations** — (tears) are produced by stretching or splitting of the skin over a hard underlying structure such as bone.[4]

Postmortem Stages

Most forensic scientists agree that the following are the progressive stages of postmortem change undergone by bodies:

- **Fresh**
- **Bloat**
- **Active decay**
- **Advanced decay**
- **Putrid dry remains**
- **Semi-skeletal remains**
- **Skeletal remains**[5]

The determination of whether or not a case can be visually assessed and drawn must be made on an individual basis. **Because of the high variability of the timing of postmortem stages, it is not possible to designate a simple time frame in which postmortem drawings should or should not be done.**

In some climates and conditions, a body may become unrecognizable in a matter of hours or days, making it virtually impossible to draw the face from photographs. In other conditions, months may pass with the face still intact enough to be photographed and drawn.

I had a case from south Texas in which a murdered woman was wrapped in a heavy black plastic tarp and placed in the August sun for only 3 days, baking the body. The face was totally destroyed and skull reconstruction, rather than postmortem drawing, had to be done. In advanced workshops, I use a case from Canada in which a woman was murdered and lay in the snow for many months, yet her face is intact enough that she can be accurately drawn from photographs.

Rigor Mortis

In *Medicolegal Investigation of Death*, Spitz and Fisher define rigor mortis as follows:

> **Rigor mortis** is such a condition in which the muscles of the body become hardened as a result of chemical changes within the muscle fibers. The process is due to the appearance of lactic acid and other by-products of tissue metabolism. As the acid products accumulate in the muscle fibers, the protoplasm, which is in liquid state in life, becomes sufficiently acid that it gels making the muscle rigid. **The process begins at death, usually becomes manifest within two to four hours and advances until approximately twelve hours, when it is generally complete.** It is commonly said to begin in the muscles of the face and neck and then spread downwards over the body. This is not literally true, but the appearance of such a progression results from the fact that the shorter muscle fibers, as in the jaw and neck, develop rigidity sooner than the longer extremity muscle fibers.[6]

Livor Mortis

Spitz and Fisher also describe livor mortis as follows:

> **Livor mortis** appears as a purple discoloration of the skin of the dependent parts of the dead body. It is caused by settling of the blood into the capillaries of the skin as they become dilated after circulation ceases. **Since it depends on gravity, it will be absent in areas of the body where the weight produces pressure and occludes the capillaries.**
>
> ... **livor mortis formation begins immediately after death, but it may not be perceptible for as much as two hours. It is usually well developed within four hours and reaches a maximum between eight and twelve hours.** During this period, if the body is turned over, the lividity that was originally dependent will shift to the newly dependent areas. However, after eight to twelve hours **lividity** becomes "fixed" and will remain where it originally formed.[6]

Algor Mortis

Algor mortis is the term for the normal cooling of the body after death.

Rigor mortis, livor mortis, and algor mortis are processes that are independent of one another, but they generally occur simultaneously.

Decomposition

Spitz and Fisher also discuss changes within the tissues of the body that eventually lead to skeletonization of the remains:

> The time and onset of decompositional changes, like most other elements that shed some light on the time of death, are subject to enormous variation dependent upon the circumstances of the death, the temperature to which the body is subjected and pre-existing conditions within the body. The two principle components of the decomposition process are autolysis and putrefaction.
>
> **Autolysis** refers to the action of digestive enzymes or ferments that breakdown the complex protein and carbohydrate molecules in the body to simpler compounds.
>
> ... **putrefaction** is due to bacterial activity throughout the body ... [and] is the major component of decomposition. As gas is released within the blood vessels and within the tissues, the body becomes distended, the skin changes through green to purple to black, the tongue and eyes protrude ...[6]

In the evaluation of photographs for use in postmortem, it is beneficial to understand the effects of decompositional changes on the skin. As the epidermis softens, the skin readily slips and reveals the underlying layer of skin.

Renowned forensic anthropologist Dr. William Bass developed the University of Tennessee Anthropological Research Facility (ARF), also known as the "Body Farm," for the study of determination of time since death and many other death-related variables.

In a July 1996 lecture to the forensic art group at the International Association for Identification Conference in Greensboro, North Carolina, Dr. Bass offered some helpful insights about decomposition. He described one study case in which the decompositional processes in the body of a black man were documented and the observation was made that once the epidermis slipped away, the underlying skin was white or pinkish in color. In other words, **the color of the skin might be unreliable once it has begun to slip.** Dr. Bass also stated that **the first thing to slough off with decomposition of the skin is the hair.**[7]

Spitz and Fisher make further observations about the importance of environmental temperature in the decomposition process:

> It is not uncommon to see advanced decomposition within twelve to eighteen hours, to the point that facial features are no longer recognizable, most of the hair slips away from the scalp and the entire body becomes swollen to two to three times normal size. External injury of the body enhances the putrefactive process by providing a portal for bacteria. Also, blood provides an excellent medium for bacterial growth, which accounts for more advance putrefaction in areas of injury.
>
> … Conversely, at freezing or near freezing temperatures, putrefaction may be delayed for months.[6]

Spitz and Fisher discuss the effects of drying of the body, leading to **mummification**:

> As the body dries in the hours or first few days after death, the tips of the fingers and toes and the skin of the face shrink with the apparent production of nail or hair growth. This has given rise to the erroneous lay belief that hair and nails grow after death.
>
> In dry atmospheres the body may wither, shrivel, and be converted to a leathery or parchment-like mass of skin and tendons surrounding the bones; the internal organs are often decayed. This process is referred to as mummification.[6]

In cases of **bodies that have been in water** for a prolonged period of time, great distortions of the facial tissues may take place. Even in bodies retrieved after a short interval, **the color of the eyes may be altered and should be considered potentially unreliable.** The opinion of the pathologist should be sought regarding eye color.

Insects and Animals

Insects

Flies are the insects most frequently associated with death scenes. The voracious feeding of their larvae (maggots) dramatically alters the soft issue.[8]

According to Dr. William Bass, **blowflies** lay their eggs on or in the orifices of the body and on wounds. The flies are attracted by the smell of blood and may arrive in just a matter of minutes after death, laying eggs in the eyes, nose, and mouth. The activity of the larvae soon causes distortion of the facial features and distention of the face and is even strong enough to displace dentures.[7]

Sometimes in studying scene or morgue photographs for preparation of a postmortem drawing, I have difficulty distinguishing between insect bites and naturally occurring marks or small moles. In such a case, seek the input of the pathologist who performed the autopsy or a forensic entomologist. In Texas, we have experienced a real invasion of **fire ants** and small dark circular lesions on bodies are often seen as a result of their bites. Bites made by **roaches** seem to have a similar appearance and may be easily confused with antemortem abrasions.

Carrion beetles is the name given to certain beetles that feed on tissue. They are sometimes used to deflesh bones for anthropological or archaeological purposes.

Animals

The faces of victims may be altered to variable extents by the activity of numerous types of aquatic or terrestrial animal life. Postmortem artifacts created by animals such as **mice** may be small. They be much more extensive when caused by **rats, skunks, opossums, dogs, coyotes, wolves, or others.** Small animals tend to attack the lips, eyelids, and the ears. Also subject to animal activity are areas where the skin is broken. Larger animals may go for easy access areas for feeding such as the throat or the stomach.

Effects on the Face

Reanimating the Face

Already mentioned is the necessity of reanimating the face when drawing it from morgue or crime scene photos. There is no simple formula for doing this. The addition of some slight expression sometimes helps as does the action of "lifting" the facial structures somewhat from the way they appear in the death photos.

Unfortunately, most deceased photographs are taken with the subject supine or lying down, with gravity distorting the features. Much better results may be achieved if rigor mortis has left the body and the body is propped up for photography, although this is rarely done. Some morgues have special equipment that allows the photographer to be positioned above and over the body as it lies on a gurney for photography.

Bloating

Many times the face is bloated in morgue photographs, necessitating input from the pathologist. **Height and body weight should be considered when attempting to approximate the amount of facial fullness in life.** I have found it helpful to find either mug shots or a living person of similar height and weight for reference.

Slack Jaw

Figure 10.1 shows a very characteristic type of postmortem change that must be corrected in postmortem drawing — the closing of the mouth. A **slack jaw occurs with the relaxation of the muscles that hold the mandible in suspension** and

Figure 10.1 Morgue photograph (left) and **postmortem drawing** by KTT prepared from the photo, **correcting the slack jaw.** (Courtesy of Texas Department of Public Safety.)

is often seen in photos after death. The decision must be made whether to show the teeth in the drawing, then the mouth must be pulled up and repositioned in a more natural arrangement. Be sure to allow for adjustment of the placement of the chin, pulling it up in a corresponding fashion. This may be done by "eye" or by measuring the distance.

The autopsy report should be consulted for body weight to help determine the amount of fullness beneath the chin, since gravity and positioning also distort this area.

I have seen examples of postmortem forensic art, particularly retouched photographs, which have not included correcting the slack jaw condition. These are not very effective and still retain a look of death even if the eyes have been opened.

Palpebral Changes

Although I have been unable to find a reference in any anatomy or pathology book, there is a condition that I have repeatedly observed in the eyes of deceased persons. **Often the lateral or outer corners of the eyes are noticeably uplifted.** Figure 10.2 shows an early case in which I included this upturned look in the postmortem drawing. Although the victim was identified, I found that I had made this error. Her life photo shows that her eyes were far more level. After this case, I observed this phenomenon many more times and I learned to adjust the eyes accordingly. I have received differing opinions from anthropologists, pathologists, and opthalmologists as to the cause. I suspect that a combination of actions creates this effect. If the photos are taken while the body is supine, gravity pulls the eyes laterally. Rigor mortis may cause the lateral palpebral ligaments to contract and pull slightly upward, possibly releasing the tarsal plates in the lids to become stiffer and straighter and less curving around the eyeballs. If you see this condition in postmortem photographs, you should make some adjustments.

Figure 10.2 Crime scene photograph of unidentified homicide victim (left) showing **uplifted lateral corners of the eyes, postmortem drawing** by KTT (center), and life photo (right). (Courtesy of Texas Department of Public Safety.)

Facial Trauma

Slight

Figure 10.3 shows a case in which the facial trauma is not too pronounced. The features can be readily determined from the morgue photograph. In such a case, the face could actually be projected and traced to avoid any inaccuracies. The primary decision that must be made is the look of the eyes. In this case, an epicanthal fold could be observed, so the eyes have been drawn to reflect that.

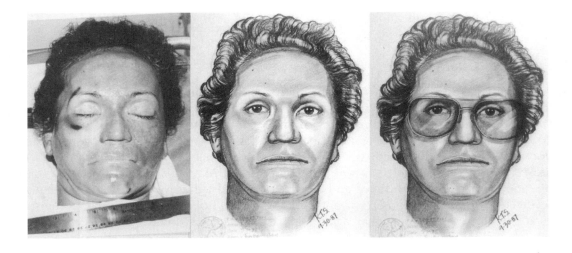

Figure 10.3 Morgue photograph of unidentified **traffic fatality victim** (left), **postmortem drawing** by KTT (center), and with glasses drawn on a matte acetate overlay (right). (Courtesy of Texas Department of Public Safety.)

Matte acetate was used to lay over the original drawing and add the glasses that were found adjacent to the body.

Moderate

Figure 10.4 depicts a victim of stabbing death with numerous superficial wounds to the face. The changes to the face are moderate and the features can still be determined by visual assessment. There is the characteristic slack jaw, and the open mouth reveals unique details of the dentition. A close-up examination reveals a gold-rimmed, "windowpane" crown on the maxillary right central incisor, which is incorporated into the postmortem drawing. His clothing, which is available, is also drawn in an effort to provide all possible clues to his identity.

Figure 10.5 shows the face of an unidentified drowning victim whose body was found face down in shallow water. In a relatively short time, aquatic animals scavenged the face. Crabs produced postmortem artifacts on the lips and one eyelid although the facial damage was moderate. The victim's clothing and religious articles worn around

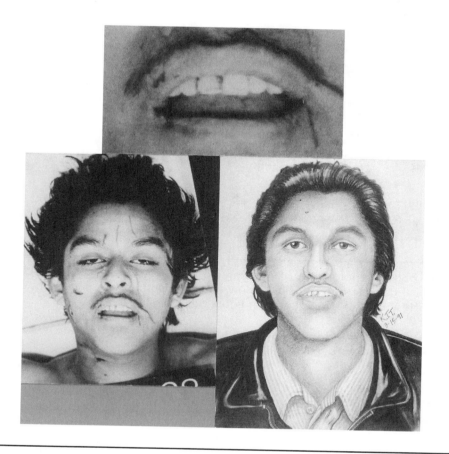

Figure 10.4 Detail of the dentition (above), morgue photograph of unidentified **stabbing victim** (lower left), and **postmortem drawing** by KTT (lower right). (Courtesy of Texas Department of Public Safety.)

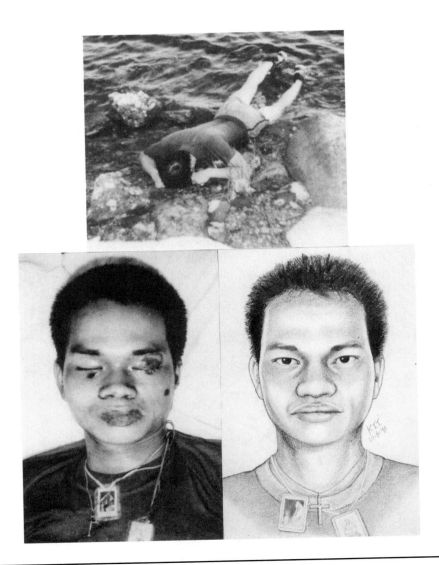

Figure 10.5 Scene photograph of unidentified **drowning victim** (above), morgue photo showing facial damage due to **crabs** (below left), and **postmortem drawing** by KTT (below right). (Courtesy of Texas Department of Public Safety.)

the neck were included in the postmortem drawing. The dental details were unknown so the mouth was drawn closed.

Extensive

Figure 10.6 shows a case of extensive blunt force trauma to the face, rendering it difficult to assess visually. Determination of facial fullness had to be based on body weight from the autopsy report since the tissues were so distorted and displaced. Clothing and jewelry details were included, as was dental detail. Matte acetate was used to show glasses found near the body.

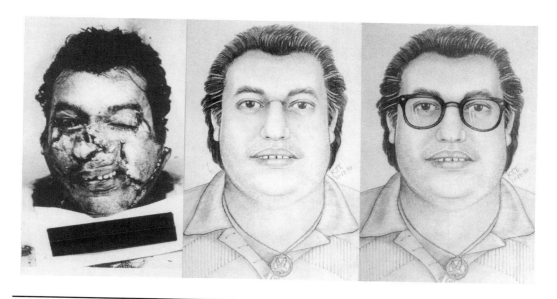

Figure 10.6 Morgue photograph of unidentified victim of **extensive blunt force trauma** (left), **postmortem drawing** by KTT (center), and with glasses drawn on a matte acetate overlay (right). (Courtesy of Texas Department of Public Safety.)

Procedural Considerations

A primary difficulty in postmortem drawing cases is the lack of access to the body for viewing or photography. If a body is available for viewing by the artist, this is recommended. Although not a pleasant experience, the act of personally viewing the body may provide insights into the facial appearance not possible from photos alone.

In some jurisdictions, it may be possible to request that additional photographs be made for the artist's purposes. More than likely, however, the photographs already taken will be the only ones available. The odds, too, are probably better that the body has been buried before the artist ever receives the request to do a postmortem drawing.

Quality of Photography

On more than one occasion over the years, officers have come to my office requesting postmortem drawings, and handed me one or two small poor quality instant photographs. In one case of a person dead less than 1 week, I asked where the body was so we could take some better photographs. I was told, "Oh, he's been cremated." Fortunately, Texas now has stricter laws governing the handling of unidentified deceased persons. Bodies may not be cremated unidentified, but instead must be buried so that they might be exhumed if identified and returned to families. The law now requires that frontal and lateral facial photographs be made, including a scale or ruler.

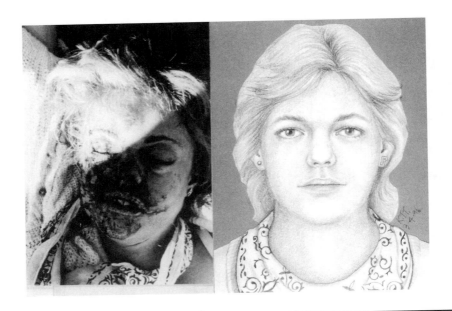

Figure 10.7   Poor quality crime scene photograph of homicide victim (left) and **postmortem drawing** by KTT (right). (Courtesy of Texas Department of Public Safety.)

Perhaps you work in an agency that allows you to coordinate with crime scene photographers and convey to them the types of frontal and lateral facial photographs that you need. For me, this has never been possible since my cases come from all 254 Texas counties as well as other states and vary greatly in quality and style.

Figure 10.7 shows a well-intentioned but poor quality crime scene photograph taken by an officer unaccustomed to taking photos. His own shadow obscures one side of the face and the other side of the face is overexposed, making postmortem drawing difficult.

Use of a Scale

Any photographs of faces, scars, marks, or tatoos should include a scale. **The scale should be placed perpendicular to the camera lens so that it can be accurately read.** In other words, placing a ruler on the ground near a body and stepping back to shoot a photo from an angle will not work. The camera must be positioned so that the lens points straight downward at the face and on top of the scale.

When photographing bodies at the morgue, some photographers place a small paper scale on the forehead. This is better than no scale, but if it is too large it may cover up some useful bit of information. It is, however, a good idea to place the scale in alignment with the facial plane in the frontal view. In a lateral view, a scale is best placed on a stand with a clamp and lined up with the midline of the face or at the nose.

Crime Scene Photographs

It is likely that the artist has no control whatsoever over the way in which the crime scene photographs are taken. The photographer attempts to document all important information, but there may be pressure to quickly photograph the body so that it can be moved. It is important to request scene photographs for viewing, however, since they may provide important information that augments the morgue photos. The scene photographs may also include clothing worn at the time of death.

Often, the scene photographs reflect the most naturalistic representation of hairstyle, especially in women. Once at the morgue, the body is washed, the hair becomes wet, and the style is lost.

Morgue Photographs

Optimum postmortem photographs are taken when rigor has left the face and the body is propped up so that the facial tissues hang naturally according to gravitational pull. This is especially important for corpulent individuals with lots of facial fullness and in the elderly with lots of loose skin.

Figure 10.8 shows a less than ideal morgue photograph in which the face is distorted by the camera angle and lens choice. The photograph is overexposed and taken after the hair is wet, with no scale.

Figure 10.8 Less than ideal morgue photograph of a homicide victim which was taken after the hair was wet, with no scale used — the face was distorted by the camera angle and lens choice and was overexposed (left) — and **postmortem drawing** by KTT (right). (Courtesy of Texas Department of Public Safety.)

Figure 10.9 also shows a typical sort of problematic morgue photograph taken by a photographer standing beside a body on a gurney. The face cannot be completely seen and the features are distorted by the angulation. A scale placed on the shoulder is of no use. Fortunately, in this case, scene photos showed a bit more about the face, including clothing details, and the victim was identified.

Facial Angle

The decision must sometimes be made whether to draw the face at the same angle as the photographs provided or to rotate it to a different angle. There is no strong reason to favor one over the other, although rotation of the face does require more skill and experience by the artist. If good quality photographs are available in multiple views,

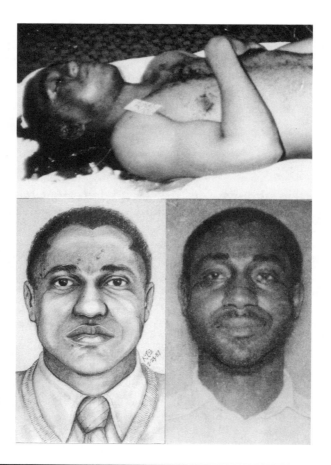

Figure 10.9   Problematic morgue photograph of a gunshot victim, taken from an angle that distorted the features (top), **postmortem drawing** by KTT (lower left), and life photo (lower right). (Courtesy of Texas Department of Public Safety.)

an oblique or three-quarter view might be a good choice. Several psychological studies on face recognition seem to indicate that a three-quarter view reveals more about the way a face is structured in depth than a frontal view.

Same Angle Drawing

Figure 10.10 shows a case in which the face was drawn in the same position as the morgue photographs, an oblique view.

Rotating the Face

Figure 10.11 illustrates a case in which the face of the victim was rotated in the postmortem drawing to produce a straight-on view. A small scar in the victim's left eyebrow interrupting the hair growth was included in the drawing. I suspect that she wore the long bangs to cover the scar.

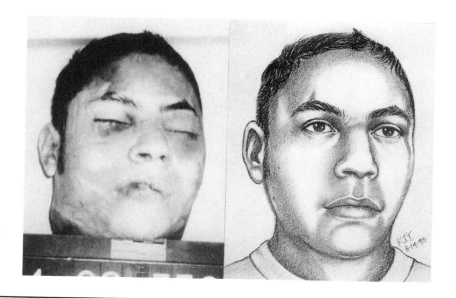

Figure 10.10 Morgue photograph of unidentified victim (left) and **postmortem drawing** by KTT (right) drawn with the **face in the same position as the photograph**. (Courtesy of Texas Department of Public Safety.)

Figure 10.11 Oblique morgue photograph of unidentified homicide victim (left), **postmortem drawing** by KTT drawn by **rotating the face** (center), and life photo (right); the victim had a small **scar** in the left eyebrow which was included in the drawing. (Courtesy of Texas Department of Public Safety.)

The Dentition

As shown in previous examples, including unique dental traits may be beneficial and should be done if possible. Chapters 3 and 4 provide helpful information for understanding and drawing the dentition in a naturalistic way.

Figure 10.12 shows a case with frustrating complications regarding the dentition. In the crime scene photographs, drying of the skin of the lips makes it impossible

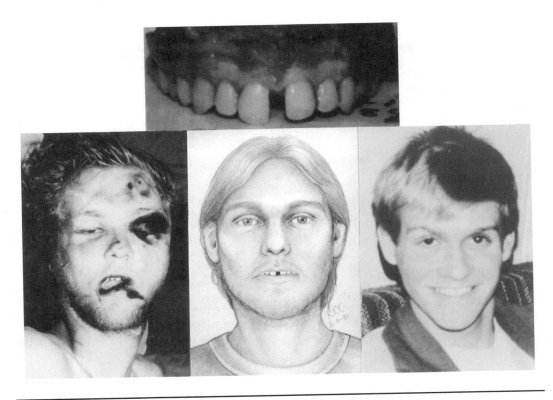

Figure 10.12   Crime scene photograph of an unidentified homicide victim (lower left) with **dental detail** (above), **postmortem drawing** by KTT (below center), and life photo (below right). (Courtesy of Texas Department of Public Safety.)

to clearly see the teeth. (Note that the uplifted outer eye corners previously discussed also appear here.) As part of the autopsy procedure, the teeth were removed and the maxilla was split at the midline for taking radiographs. The teeth were then photographed, giving the misconception of a large diastema or gap between the central incisors, which was included in the postmortem drawing. Fortunately, this did not prevent the identification and the victim was recognized from the drawing despite this error. He did have a diastema in life, but it was much smaller than in the drawing.

Color or Black and White

If you are competent with color drawing and have good color photographs of the unidentified deceased from which to work, color may add a real plus to your postmortem drawing.

However, it is not wise to make up the color and risk being incorrect. If good quality color photographs are not available, a black-and-white drawing should be done.

Using Other Available Details

As shown in many of the case examples in this chapter, it is important to include as many of the available details as possible. Such details may be observable on the

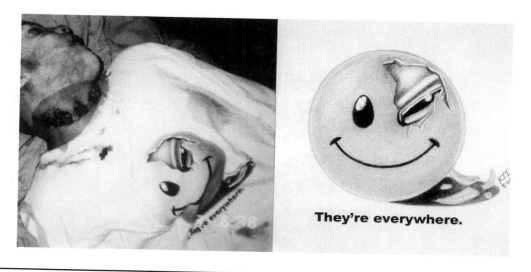

They're everywhere.

Figure 10.13 Crime scene photograph of an unidentified homicide victim (left) and **clothing detail** drawn by KTT (right). (Courtesy of Texas Department of Public Safety.)

photos of the body itself or you may have to ask for additional photographs to obtain the information.

When small scars (Figure 10.11) or marks can be seen on the face, these should be included in the drawing. **If it cannot be determined whether the marks are natural or postmortem artifacts created by injury, insects, or animals, you may wish to indicate their placement lightly, just in case they were there in life.**

Figure 10.13 shows an image on the T-shirt worn by the deceased that I was able to draw in addition to his face. Since the shirt was not straightened out and photographed, the drawing was important for inclusion in crime bulletins along with the postmortem drawing of the victim.

Figure 10.14 shows a case in which it was necessary to obtain additional photographs of the clothing to incorporate in the postmortem drawing. The distinctive pattern and design of the shirt added important additional information.

Complications

Figure 10.15 presents a case in which the alterations to the face incident to funeral home intervention presented complications in the preparation of a postmortem drawing. The morgue photographs were taken in the lateral view only. The only available frontal photograph was taken after the funeral home had performed certain procedures on the face. The eyes were glued or sewn shut and heavy makeup had been applied. It was necessary to combine elements of each photograph to produce the postmortem drawing. A polaroid photograph of a necklace was provided although it had no scale.

As tenuous and imperfect a task as postmortem drawing sometimes seems to be, it is still often worth the effort. If enough accurate descriptive data can be conveyed to the viewer to trigger recognition and lead to identification, it is a job well done.

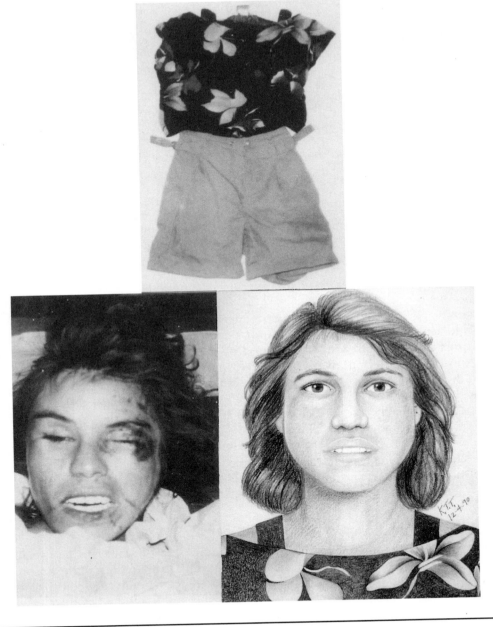

Figure 10.14 Clothing photographs (above) **used with morgue photograph** of unidentified deceased (lower left) to produce **postmortem drawing** by KTT (lower right). (Courtesy of Texas Department of Public Safety.)

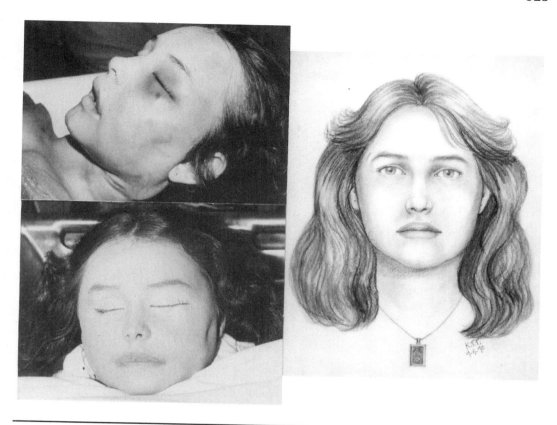

Figure 10.15 Morgue photograph (above left) **and mortuary photograph** (lower left) used to produce postmortem drawing by KTT (right). (Courtesy of Texas Department of Public Safety.)

References

1. Zugibe, F. T., Constello, J., and Segelbacher, J., "The horrors of visual identification," *Journal of Forensic Identification*, 46(4), 1996.
2. Clement, J. G. and Ranson, D. L., *Craniofacial Identification in Forensic Medicine*. New York: Oxford University Press, 1998.
3. Davis, J. H., "Preface," in *Forensic Taphonomy, The Postmortem Fate of Human Remains*, Haglund, W. and Sorg, M., Eds. Boca Raton, FL: CRC Press, 1997.
4. Barnard, J. J., "How to Use and Understand the Autopsy Report," Lecture handout, March, 1993.
5. Craig, E., personal communication, 1991.
6. Spitz, W. U. and Fisher, R. S., *Medicolegal Investigation of Death*, Springfield, IL: Charles C Thomas, 1980.
7. Bass, W., "Forensic Anthropology," Lecture presented at the International Association for Identification's 81st Annual Educational Conference and Training Seminar: Greensboro, NC, July, 1996.
8. Clark, M. A., Worrell, M. B., and Pless, John E., Postmortem changes in soft tissues, in *Forensic Taphonomy, The Postmortem Fate of Human Remains*, Haglund, W. and Sorg, M., Eds. Boca Raton, FL: CRC Press, 1997.

Chapter 11

Skull Protection and Preparation for Reconstruction

Karen T. Taylor and Betty Pat. Gatliff

Specific procedures should be followed to prepare a skull for facial reconstruction, whether the forensic art project will be done two dimensionally or three dimensionally. It is critical that care be taken to protect the integrity of the skull as an item of physical evidence, and to ensure appropriate transferal from person to person or "chain of custody." Equally important is physical protection of the skull since certain parts are extremely fragile. Occasionally, it is necessary to restore missing or incomplete areas of the skull before reconstruction is attempted.

We prefer the term **reconstruction**, the most commonly used term, to designate the procedure of projecting a soft tissue face based on skull architecture. Chapter 12 is entitled "Facial Reconstruction *from* the Skull" and Chapter 13 is entitled "Facial Reconstruction *on* the Skull" because this phraseology is most accurate. As to other names for rebuilding a face from a skull, we believe Dr. Robert George stated it best:

> Regarding terminology, the term *reconstruction* is here considered as preferable to other synonyms such as *reproduction* and *restoration*. The term reproduction implies a perfect replication which is never the case (except in Gorky Park!), and the term restoration more aptly applies to soft tissue repairs on damaged but still intact remains. Facial *approximation* is perhaps a better description of the procedure but this term is not in general use.[1]

Before the artist attempts any skull restoration or facial reconstruction, as much information as possible should be gathered concerning a particular case. Various scientific specialists may need to be consulted, particularly a skilled physical or forensic anthropologist. Only through anthropological evaluation to determine age, sex, and ancestry can the artist select the appropriate tissue depth data as preparation for rebuilding a face on the skull. Generally, in the **anatomical method** of facial reconstruction muscles are defined individually to flesh out the face, and tissue depth data are not utilized. The **tissue depth method** involves use of data gained in anthropological studies as a guide for building up to the facial surfaces. The authors believe that the most advantageous method for use in law enforcement is probably a combination of both the anatomical approach and the tissue depth approach we call the **combination method**.

The Skull as Evidence

A case file should be created and maintained for every skull/facial reconstruction case. Evidentiary skulls are received by various means, including personal transfer by a representative of the investigating police agency (most preferable and reliable), certified mail, and commercial express carriers with a number assigned. Usually the artist receives only the skull, but in some rare instances in which the skull must be maintained with the associated postcranial elements, the artist may receive various parts of the skeleton.

　　Written documentation of the care, custody, and control of a skull or any evidence should be done in the manner prescribed by your jurisdiction. In general, skulls personally delivered should be accompanied by evidence transferal or chain-of-custody forms. Mail or commercial express deliveries often have enclosed paperwork, which should be maintained in the case file. If a delivery of a skull is made with no papers, you should record the date and time of receipt as well as the date and time you later release it.

　　If the police agency or medical examiner did not prepare transfer papers, you should prepare an evidence transferal form yourself. This receipt documents precisely what you received, from whom, and when. You should specify whether you receive a complete skull (cranium and mandible) or the specific portions for incomplete material. **Particularly significant is the inventory of the teeth.** Even if you are not familiar with dental charting, you can at least count and note the number of teeth received. If you have training in dental charting, you may wish to prepare a dental inventory chart for your case file.

　　Other items that might be documented on the receipt form are case photographs, related clothing, jewelry, dentures, hair specimens, eyeglasses, or any other items that may be useful in preparation of the reconstruction.

　　It is important that you get the signature of the person from whom you received the skull, along with the date.

　　Once you have received the evidentiary skull, a case number should be assigned according to the practices of your agency or jurisdiction. If you are a freelance artist, you will need to develop a numbering system that suits your record-keeping requirements. **The skull should be marked promptly with the case number**, placing it on each part of the skull. If the skull is in multiple fragments, however, this may not be practical, and the skull should be restored before it is numbered.

A worksheet may be developed for record keeping of pertinent information about the individual skull. The form could include your forensic art case number, case number of the law enforcement agency, names and contact numbers for investigating officers, age, race, and sex of the individual/skull, medical examiner/coroner case number, any noted anomalies, name of photographer documenting skull with dates, etc.

Your case file might include items such as evidence transferal forms, your worksheet, police reports, crime scene or other photographs, hair specimen, pathology or autopsy report, anthropological report, odontological report and dental chart, related news clippings, or any other items beneficial to the case development.

The skull should be stored in a controlled, secure environment. The artist should be aware of insects or possible health risks. **In many cases, skulls should be handled with protective gloves as a precaution against contamination.** Not only is this practice recommended for the health of the individual handling the skull, but it may act to protect the skull itself as an item of evidence. Although precise testing information is not available, forensic anthropologist Dr. David Glassman advises that there does possibly exist the potential for transmittal of DNA from the hands to the skull. Theoretically, this could alter DNA test findings. Ideally, however, any bony or dental specimens needed for DNA or other purposes should be obtained before the skull is transferred to the artist. An artist preparing a sculptural reconstruction will likely find it extremely difficult to handle clay while wearing gloves. **It is recommended that the artist inquire about any potential need for DNA specimens before handling a skull without gloves.** It is also advisable to request information on the method and degree of cleaning and decontamination done on the skull prior to handling it. Advice on these matters could be sought from pathologists or laboratory personnel. Further, some skulls may retain unpleasant odors and require additional drying in a ventilated or drying cupboard.

Above all, the skull should always be treated with respect. It is what remains of a living, breathing human life and should not be an object for jokes and pranks.

Skull Protection

The skull should always be handled with care. Remember that a skull entrusted to you should never be altered or damaged, nor should any minute bits of possible evidentiary information be lost. Never pick up a skull in the facial area by placing your fingers into the orbits of the eyes or in the nasal aperture. It is not a bowling ball! Cradle the skull with both hands or, if necessary, a good one-handed grip can be made with your thumb in the foramen magnum with the palm of your hand supporting the base of the skull (Figure 11.1).

Always prevent the skull from rolling off a table or hard surface by securing it on a cork ring/donut, bean bag, sand bag, or other stabilizing device.

When you receive a skull, some teeth may have become loose or may have fallen out into the container in transit. Ideally, the artist should seek advice from a trained science professional for proper replacement of teeth, particularly if several are dislodged. Sockets should be cleaned of debris before waxing or gluing teeth in the alveolus. If only one or two teeth are displaced, the artist may be able to correctly replace them without assistance.

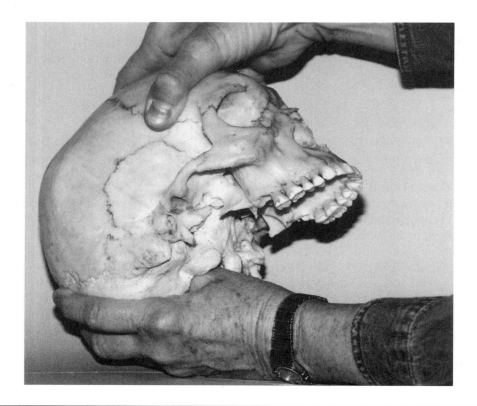

Figure 11.1   Correct handling of a skull. (Photo by Missey Micheletti.)

To protect the inner structures of the nasal aperture from fractures, particularly when doing clay reconstruction, place a cotton ball inside the opening and cover with a small amount of clay (Figure 11.2).

Similarly, the inner orbital bones are thin and fragile and need protection. This may be achieved by placing a small cotton ball deeply into each orbit and covering the cotton with strips of masking tape. This not only protects the bones, but also makes removal of clay easier after three-dimensional reconstructions.

Fractures or bullet wounds may need to be taped with masking tape to avoid being filled with clay.

Gluing the Mandible to the Cranium

General Dental Assessment

Once the teeth are secured in the skull, the artist should carefully evaluate the dentition for potentially useful information before gluing the mandible to the cranium. Ideally a dentist or odontologist is consulted to perform a dental analysis. Assessment of the teeth and bite can provide information not only about the appearance of the mouth area, but in some cases also hints about the socioeconomic status of the individual during life (Figure 11.3). A skull presenting severely neglected dental hygiene might indicate a different demographic background for an individual than one with

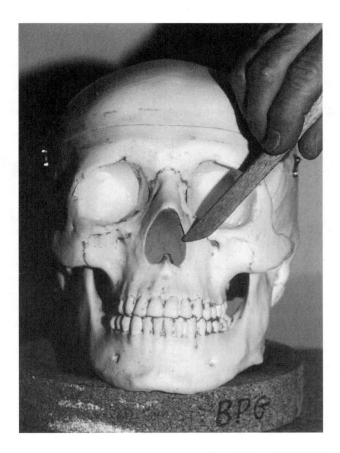

Figure 11.2 Protecting the nasal aperture. (Photo by Missey Micheletti.)

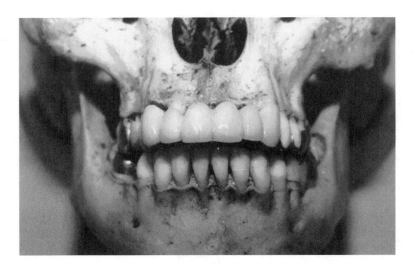

Figure 11.3 Expensive dental work; extensive bridge work spanning several upper teeth and gold crowns. (Photo by Missey Micheletti.)

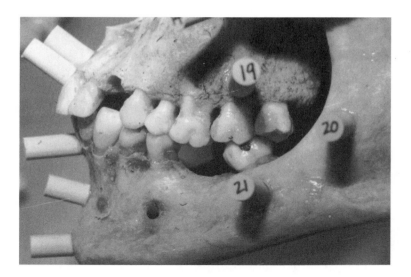

Figure 11.4 Postmortem tooth loss seen in clean open socket in the **maxilla and antemortem tooth loss** seen in healed area of the **mandible.** (Photo by Missey Micheletti.)

perfect teeth or expertly restored teeth. Another dental observation should be made regarding any missing teeth. A clean, open socket usually indicates postmortem loss of a tooth, while a socket filled in with bone may mean that a tooth has been missing for a period of years (Figure 11.4). Partially filled in or healed sockets can be evaluated by dental experts for possible estimates as to the amount of time elapsed since the extraction or tooth loss. Dental anomalies can be good identifiers and therefore should be shown to advantage in a reconstruction by using a smiling or open-mouthed expression to reveal the teeth. Unique traits might include a space between teeth or

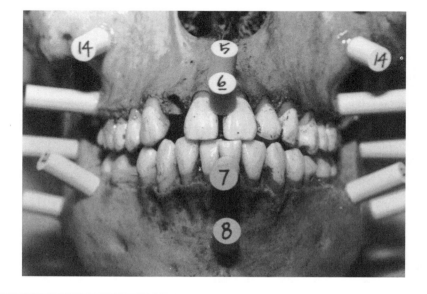

Figure 11.5 Diastema between maxillary central incisors. (Photo by Missey Micheletti.)

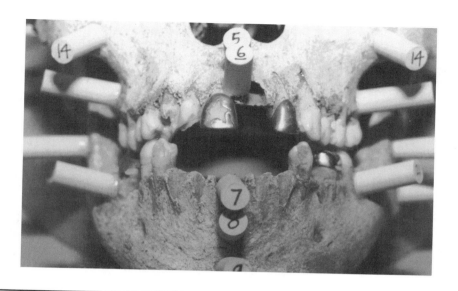

Figure 11.6   Unique gold crowns. (Photo by Missey Micheletti.)

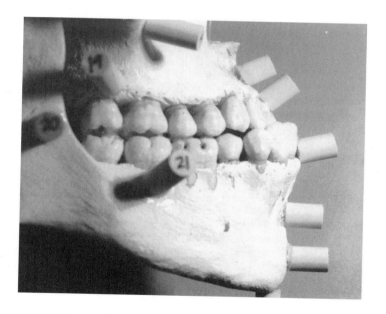

Figure 11.7   Distinctive dental occlusion or bite. (Photo by Missey Micheletti.)

diastema, unusual crowns or chips, tooth rotation, or simply a very distinctive bite (Figures 11.5, 11.6, and 11.7).

Correct Positioning

Once a thorough evaluation of the teeth has been completed, the artist can then proceed to glue the mandible to the cranium. In life, the condyle of the ramus is

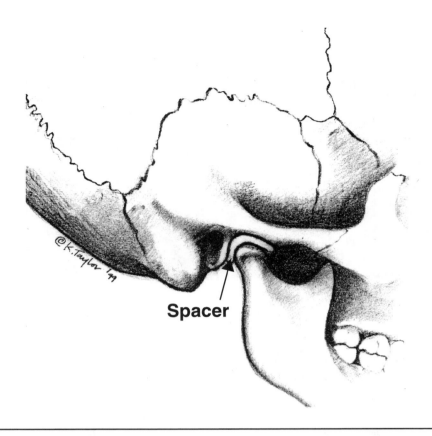

Spacer

Figure 11.8 **Approximate spacing to allow for cartilage and disc within the temperomandibular joint.** (Illustration by KTT.)

covered by cartilage and there is an articular disc within the temperomandibular joint. When gluing the mandible, the spacing of these structures should be simulated to correspond with the living condition; thus a few millimeters should be allowed between the condyle and the fossa (Figure 11.8). Bone-to-bone gluing should be avoided. Spacing can be accomplished with clay, cotton, gauze, or other materials.

In the living face, the jaws are usually relaxed, the teeth are not clenched, and the mandible hangs in a slightly slack fashion. Spacing can be approximated by gluing a portion of a round toothpick on the surface of the molars. You may also further secure the mandible by putting a small amount of glue along the occlusal surface of the teeth.

A cork ring, bean bag, or ring of clay can be used to steady the cranium while gluing the mandible (Figure 11.9).

In some instances the artist might be presented with a skull that is edentulous, totally lacking teeth or dentures. A useful method for positioning the mandible, illustrated in *Grant's Anatomy*, involves use of a pencil or dowel placed through the mandibular notch, behind the pterygoid bones and through the opposite mandibular notch (Figures 11.10 and 11.11).[2] This estimates the proper placement of the mandible in relation to the cranium. If a skull is edentulous, but dentures are located at the crime scene, a dental specialist can advise on correct spacing. Remember that the dentures in life did not sit directly on bone, thus the missing gingival or gum tissue should be simulated with a layer of clay before positioning a denture and gluing the mandible.

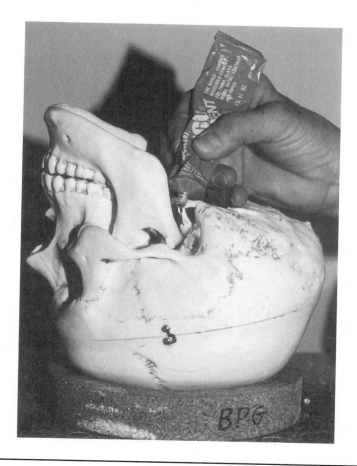

Figure 11.9 **Use of cork ring to stabilize skull while gluing mandible to cranium.** (Photo by Missey Micheletti.)

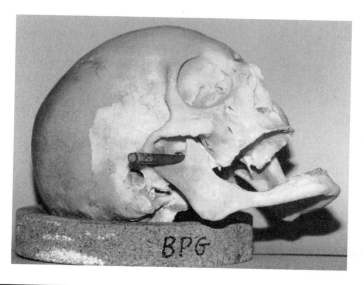

Figure 11.10 **Positioning for the edentulous mandible.** (Photo by Missey Micheletti.)

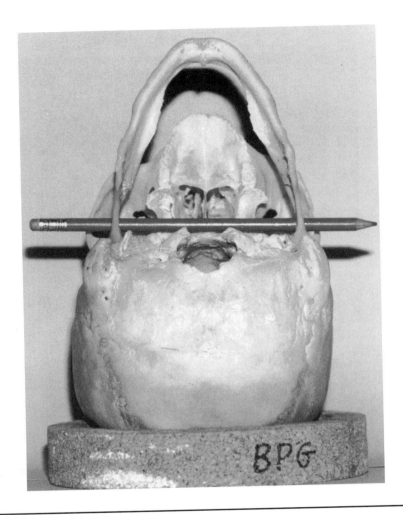

Figure 11.11 Positioning for the edentulous mandible, basal view. Note the location of the foramen magnum in the base of the skull into which the top of the skull stand will later be placed. (Photo by Missey Micheletti.)

Incomplete Skulls

Skulls can be incomplete for various reasons, including animal activity or artifact, perimortem injuries such as gunshot wounds or blunt force trauma, damage due to explosion or conflagration, damage during recovery, or just normal deterioration over time. In some instances, the skull can be restored enough to accomplish a reasonable reconstruction and likeness. However, such **restoration can prove very challenging and is no job for the inexperienced.** Ideally, the artist and anthropologist work jointly to rebuild the skull. An assessment of the missing areas should be made to determine the feasibility of replacing them. **Large areas of cranium can be missing without substantially interfering with the reconstruction process, but most of the facial bones should be present for successful results.**

Occasionally, at autopsy, the pathologist will saw through the skull bones to perform certain examinations, such as cutting the calvarium to expose the brain cavity or other structures of the cranial vault. The saw blade is approximately the thickness of a flat toothpick; therefore, segments of the toothpick can be glued along the cut surface so that the skull cap will fit properly.

Another invasive procedure involves sawing through the lower portion of the maxilla and disarticulating the mandible to examine and chart the teeth. Particularly unfortunate is the fact that this practice sometimes destroys the bony nasal spine. (The nasal spine is a critical indicator for facial reconstructionists to use in development of the nose.) Similarly, flat toothpick segments can be glued along the cut surface to replace the bone lost in sawing.

A common situation regarding incomplete skulls involves cases where the mandible is missing. Obviously, such cases present greater complexity as well as a somewhat diminished likelihood for identification. However, a method that has been used successfully for mandible approximation is outlined by Sassouni and Krogman (Figures 11.12, 11.13, and 11.14). **The method requires the use of frontal and lateral radiographs and is best done with the assistance of an anthropologist, a radiologist, or a dental specialist.** Arcs are drawn to connect important landmarks to reconstruct cranial-facial relationships. Krogman states:

> Obviously this method is not 100% fool-proof. It assumes a "normal," well-proportioned face … in good occlusion. The restoration is admittedly hypothetical. However, I feel that it gives a reasonably acceptable facsimile of cranio–facial proportions that is a useful adjunct in identification work.[3]

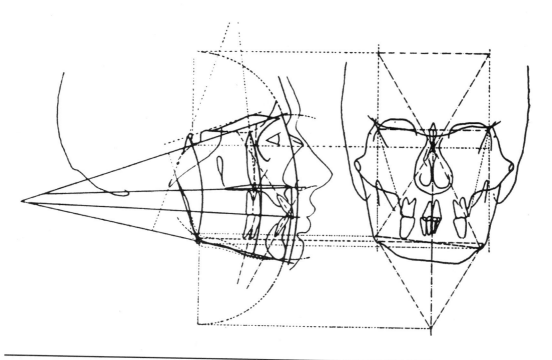

Figure 11.12   Sassouni/Krogman method for approximation of a missing mandible based on the cranium. (From Krogman, W. M., Method for approximation of a missing mandible based on the cranium, in *The Human Skeleton in Forensic Medicine*, Charles C Thomas, Springfield, IL, 1987, chap. 11.)

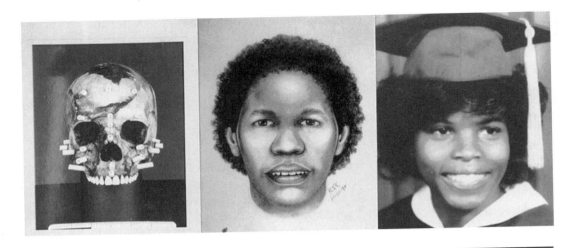

Figure 11.13 Successful identification using the **Sassouni/Krogman method** for mandible approximation; frontal skull, missing mandible (left), **two-dimensional facial reconstruction** by KTT (center), and victim identified (right). (Courtesy of Texas Department of Public Safety.)

Other partial skulls can present tremendous challenges and must be restored on an individual basis. For example, if *only* one side is complete, the opposite side can be sculpted or drawn, mirror-image fashion, for a full-face reconstruction (see Chapter 13, Figures 13.37 and 13.38). If a zygomatic arch is broken or missing, it is possible to predict and replace it by measuring the opposite feature. Damaged condyles of the mandible, often the result of animal chewing, can be restored with clay and wooden splints (Figure 11.15).

One of the most time-consuming and tedious tasks is a complete skull that is fragmented into multiple pieces (Figure 11.16). There is a tendency to start gluing the large pieces of the cranium first. This can be problematic later, when the facial bones fail to fit together properly. It is often preferable to start with the mandible. **In cases of fractured mandibles, glue the mandible together first, then occlude the teeth, and proceed upward with the remainder of the face.** Rebuild the maxilla, then the zygomatic arches, then the frontal and temporal bones, completing the skull with the parietal and occipital bones. Misalignment at the sides and back of the cranium is not as critical since those areas will probably be covered by hair in a reconstruction, and they are not the primary areas for facial identification. Failure to correctly reassemble the facial bones, however, could thwart an identification because of distortions created. **The more precisely the facial bones are assembled, the greater the likelihood of an accurate reconstruction and potential identification.**

Anthropological and Other Scientific Evaluations

Facial reconstruction from the skull is a combination of art and science. It is important that all potentially pertinent data be gathered and reviewed. Usually this is done by the medical examiner/coroner or the primary investigating police agency. Variations exist from state to state as to jurisdiction over unidentified deceased cases. The forensic artist performs a support function and should not overstep boundaries of ethical behavior by demanding confidential information. The artist's accessibility to

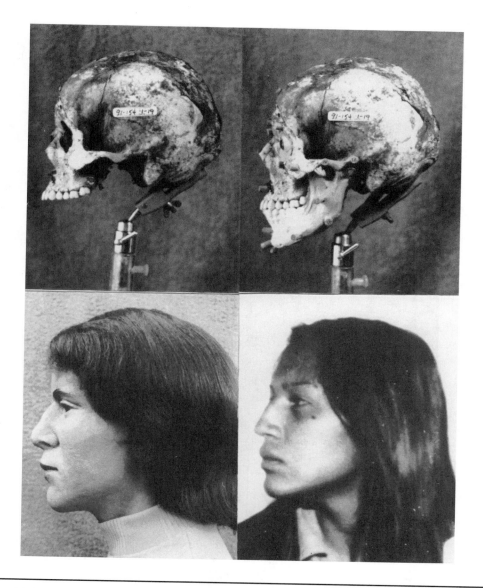

Figure 11.14 Successful identification using the **Sassouni/Krogman method** for mandible approximation; lateral skull, missing mandible (upper left), lateral skull with mandible restored in clay (upper right), **lateral three-dimensional facial reconstruction** by Betty Pat. Gatliff (lower left), and victim identified (lower right). (Courtesy of Betty Pat. Gatliff.)

case-related information may vary depending upon whether he or she is a freelance contractor or a staff member.

Various police and scientific professionals may furnish useful information for the preparation of a facial reconstruction. Crime scene technicians can provide information concerning items found at the recovery scene such as eyeglasses, clothing, jewelry, hair specimens, dentures, etc. Photographs from the scene may suggest helpful hints about hairstyle or facial hair, or appearance of fingernails, particularly in cases of severely decomposed remains. Laboratory personnel can sometimes examine hair microscopically and determine racial characteristics or

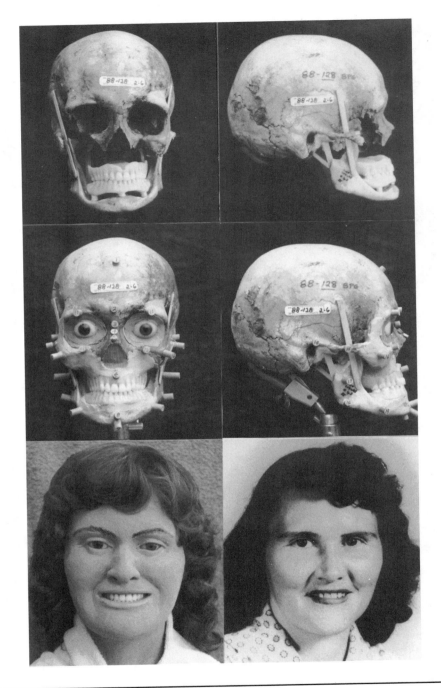

Figure 11.15 Successful identification from a **restored skull**; frontal view of skull before restoration (upper left), lateral view of skull before restoration (upper right), frontal view of skull showing splints for correct spacing, rebuilt clay areas and dentures in place (middle left), lateral view of restored skull (middle right), frontal **three-dimensional facial reconstruction** by Betty Pat. Gatliff (lower left), and victim identified (lower right). (Courtesy of Betty Pat. Gatliff.)

Figure 11.16 Successful identification from a **drastically damaged and restored skull**; frontal skull before restoration (upper left), frontal skull restored (upper right), oblique view of **three-dimensional facial reconstruction** by Betty Pat. Gatliff (lower left), and victim identified (lower right). Note that small fragments of the lacrimal crests and wings of the maxilla allowed nasal width approximation. (Courtesy of Betty Pat. Gatliff.)

evidence of chemical treatment such as perming, straightening/relaxing, or coloring of the hair.

Facial reconstructions from the skull are done on bodies that are severely decomposing, semi-skeletal, or totally skeletonized. In most states, an autopsy is performed in cases of unexplained or unattended deaths and the resulting report might be available to the artist. Sometimes the autopsy is the only procedure done, since some pathologists have extensive expertise in human osteology and are qualified to do skeletal examinations. In other cases, the pathologist or medical examiner may seek further evaluation by a physical or forensic anthropologist and/or a forensic odontologist. The pathologist or the anthropologist should provide the forensic artist with a cleaned skull.

Useful information comes from both the anthropologist and the dental specialist, and in many cases the body is evaluated both skeletally and dentally. As forensic anthropologist Dr. Clyde Snow states:

> As Stewart (1979) points out, the boundary between the domain of the dentist and the anthropologist in skeletal identification is not sharply defined. Many forensic dentists, through training, research, and personal interest, have acquired expertise in assessing the racial, sexual, age, and individual variations in the skeleton — particularly the skull. Some physical anthropologists, on the other hand, have become equally familiar with morphological variations in the dentition. Traditionally, specialists in both fields have been mutually tolerant and respectful of each other's knowledge in this rather shadowy border country between forensic anthropology and dentistry.[4]

Most often, **the dentist's or odontologist's skills are employed to chart the teeth, or again later if a dental comparison between a missing person's dental records and a skull is to be made.** Occasionally, the artist might seek advice from a dentist prior to doing a reconstruction if a skull possesses an unusual dental trait or anomaly.

Anthropologists are the specialists who usually provide the most useful information to the forensic artist as preparation for facial reconstruction from the skull (Figure 11.17). **Ideally, there is a solid working relationship between artist and anthropologist and their work is done as a collaboration.**

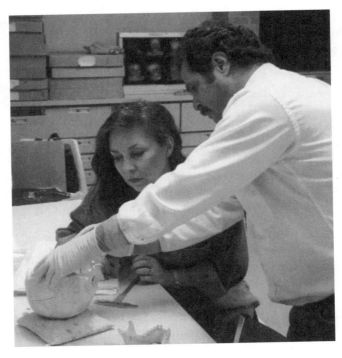

Figure 11.17 Karen T. Taylor and forensic anthropologist Dr. David Glassman jointly examine a skull.

As Iscan and Loth state: "The practice of forensic anthropology centers on the assessment of every aspect of skeletonized human remains in a medicolegal context for the purpose of establishing identity and, where possible, the cause of death and circumstances surrounding this event."[5]

Anthropologists possess varying degrees of training and experience. In 1972, the American Academy of Forensic Sciences established a Physical Anthropology Section. Physical anthropologists who possess a Ph.D. may, through a testing procedure, become Diplomates of the American Board of Forensic Anthropology, thus specializing in medico-legal evaluations and determinations. The forensic artist who has the input of an individual who is board certified (D-ABFA after the name) is indeed fortunate.

The primary information obtained from the anthropologist regarding a skeleton is estimation of age, ancestry/race, sex, and stature. Additionally, he or she may determine factors of individualization such as signs of trauma, surgical procedures or disease, handedness or occupational indicators, or even evidence of childbirth or parturition. The anthropologist may also advise about certain outstanding facial features or give insight into unusual proportions or old healed fractures. Some of this knowledge may not appear to have a direct effect on the development of the face, but it may be useful to give the artist a "feel" for the person he is attempting to depict and identify.

A teamwork approach is ideal. **A tangible image of a face can be the necessary link between the unidentified body and the general public that leads investigators to an identification.** Thus the artist's work can be the factor that helps pull together and put into use all of the diligent work of the various members of the forensic team. The authors believe that best results are achieved and **the greatest likelihood for identification exists when skull reconstruction is done as a team effort.** We strongly suggest that artists do not attempt the process without the proper input from science professionals. Similarly, we believe that scientists without artistic talents greatly reduce the odds of obtaining effective results when they attempt reconstructions without an artist's assistance.

Anatomical Method or Tissue Depth Method

Anatomical Method

After input has been received from the different science and police specialists and the skull has been fully protected, assembled, and evaluated, the artist must then decide which technique or approach of facial reconstruction to utilize.

The **anatomical method**, as described by Michael Anderson:

> ... reconstructs the face by sculpting muscles, glands and cartilage on the skull, in effect "fleshing out" the skull. The skull gives information about the origins and insertions of the facial muscles, or where the muscles begin and end. These parameters, interpreted by a specialist with a thorough knowledge of human and comparative anatomy and biomechanics, provide the information necessary to produce a competent reconstruction from a skull.[6]

The **Russian method** (Figure 11.18) is the method of rebuilding a face, muscle by muscle, generally attributed to renowned Russian anthropologist Mikhail M. Gerasimov. It is likely that Professor Gerasimov studied the concept of rebuilding the face on the

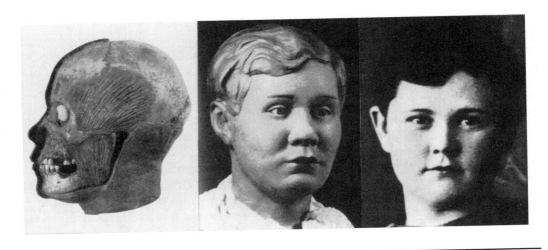

Figure 11.18 Anatomical or Russian method of rebuilding a face from the skull; lateral skull showing muscles in clay (left), reconstruction sculpture by Mikhail Gerasimov (center), and victim identified (right).

skull more thoroughly than anyone. Much of his early work was historical in nature, devoted to reconstruction of the appearance of early humans, but later in his career he did forensic cases. He invented and perfected a specific method for reconstruction of the face with his earliest work on fossil skulls in 1927. After Gerasimov's death in July 1970, his protégé G.V. Lebedinskaya continued and expanded upon his work. Gerasimov felt that application of clay to simulate the facial muscles was a more reliable technique than the tissue depth method suggested by Swiss scientists Kollman and Buchly. Later, Lebedinskaya had access to technologically advanced equipment and did thorough tissue depth studies on multiple population groups.

The general tendency for those involved in rebuilding fossil faces has been to use the anatomical method since there is no possibility to obtain data on very early populations. This method produces very attractive and interesting exhibits in museum applications. In addition to their artistic skills, the practitioners of this method should have considerable knowledge of anatomy. Artists Jay Matternes, John Gurche, Michael Anderson, Dr. Lloyd DuBrul, and others have produced excellent examples of reconstructions using the anatomical method. Depending on the situation in which you work, the anatomical method may be your method of choice. It is, however, very time consuming and therefore more expensive; each project occupies many hundreds of hours. It should be noted that faces built in this manner on fossil skulls offer no possibility for testing or comparison of likeness. However, Richard Helmer of Bonn, Germany says, "Gerasimov (1968) reported that virtually all of approximately 140 court-ordered reconstructions carried out in his laboratory could be identified."[7]

Tissue Depth Method

According to Michael Anderson, the **tissue depth method**:

> … uses average skin-thickness measurements at specific points on the skull to guide the soft-tissue reconstruction. Skin-depth measurements have been

collected on the human face at 21 points for males and females for the three racial groups. These data have been collected using sharp instruments or needles (Kollman and Büchly, 1898; Suzuki, 1948; Rhine and Campbell, 1980), X-rays (George, 1987), and ultrasound techniques (Helmer, 1984) ... Before attempting a skin-depth reconstruction, the sex and the race of the skull must be determined since these characteristics will decide which set of measurements will be used.[8]

The foundational work in tissue depth study was done by His in 1895. About 1898, in addition to publishing tissue depth tables, Kollman and Büchly suggested the first truly scientific procedure for reconstructing the face and proposed a specific technical methodology. The Kollman and Büchly data may remain useful to those who do reconstructions based on historical skulls. Wade and Rhine (1987) have stated that "any rigorous attempt to restore facial features to a skull must unavoidably be based on standardized measurements."[9]

The modern version of the tissue depth method, now known as the **American method**, is **most commonly used by forensic artists working in a law enforcement environment** (Figure 11.19). Because it is more schematic and rapid, thus less expensive, and based on published data that could be referenced in the courtroom setting if necessary, it has become the method of choice for many police artists. Since the average law enforcement artist likely has far less anatomical training than a medical artist, the method is usually more understandable and expeditious. Though lacking in anatomical training, he or she may have strong artistic talent, particularly at drawing, since most police artists have drawn hundreds of human faces as composite sketches. Therefore, those skills can be put to good use by employing this direct approach.

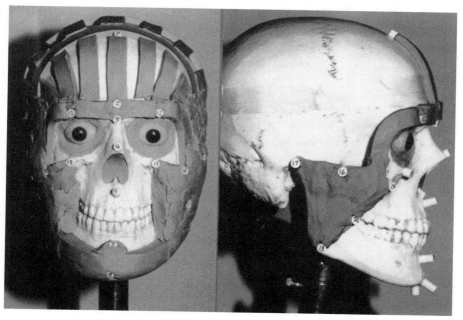

Figure 11.19 Tissue depth or American method of rebuilding a face from the skull; frontal view showing placement of vinyl depth indicators and uniform depth strips of clay (left), and lateral view showing schematic connection of various depth markers (right). (Courtesy of Betty Pat. Gatliff.)

Combination Method

Regarding the choice between the anatomical method and the tissue depth method, Michael Anderson states, "It should be noted that these two methods are not mutually exclusive or contradictory. Many reconstruction practitioners use a combination of both."[6] It is our belief, too, that **the wise reconstruction artist takes advantage of the best aspects of each method. Therefore, a combination approach is likely the best approach.**

English reconstruction artist Richard Neave echoes this sentiment in his book *Making Faces*. Neave is a medical artist, knowledgeable in anatomy, who also makes use of the available tissue depth information (Figure 11.20). His reconstructions are done on plaster castings of human skulls. After preparing the casting, he examines the muscle attachments evident on the skull and, based on their robustness, develops the facial musculature, muscle by muscle (Figure 11.21). Describing the next step of his technique, he states:

> It is the stage where all the precisely calculated anatomical modeling is covered up by a layer of clay, laid over its surface to simulate the outer layers of subcutaneous tissues and skin. … apply this layer as wide strips of clay, allowing them to mirror the form underneath but always using the measurements to guide their thickness. This ensures that the hand of the artist does not and cannot influence the final shape of the head and face. The measurements still rule supreme.[10]

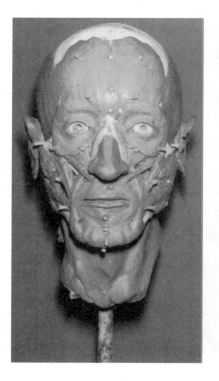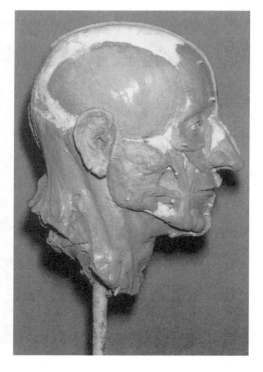

Figure 11.20 Combination method of rebuilding a face from the skull; frontal view showing partly reconstructed face with muscles in place by Richard Neave (left), and lateral view (right). (Courtesy of John Prag and Richard Neave, University of Manchester.)

Figure 11.21   Karen T. Taylor with English artist Richard Neave at the Unit of Art in Medicine at the University of Manchester, England. (Photo by David M. Griffith.)

We believe that it is advantageous for the artist to approach the reconstruction by applying tissue depth markers on the skull as a guide to the contours of the face. Then a careful study of the points of muscle attachment, the subtle asymmetries of the face, and any other visible indicators of individualization should be made prior to connecting the tissue markers. **While perhaps not actually developing each individual muscle, the artist can stylize the muscles in a schematic way and use the "attitude" of the anatomical method.**

As instructors of facial reconstruction, we strive to convey this **combination method** in the most direct, understandable, and repeatable manner possible to our students. We have tried to simplify some of the complicated anatomy to make it more useful to those with a need for practical application in an often very limited time frame, particularly in law enforcement. In addition, we always encourage students to continue to learn more and more facial anatomy, which will provide a basis for increased accuracy in their work.

Discussion of Methods

We have seen favorable results from both the anatomical method and the tissue depth method, and we believe each reconstructionist should use the method most appropriate for the given situation. Obviously, those working in a research environment may have the luxury of time-consuming methods, such as skull casting and building all of the facial muscles. At the Texas Department of Public Safety, the situation has been quite different. With a border with Mexico and a total of 254 counties, Texas has perhaps the highest number of unidentified deceased cases of any state in the U.S. In addition to an endless number of intact or decomposing unidentified deceased cases, there are sometimes two dozen or more skeletal cases in need of work at any given time.

We maintain that facial reconstruction from the skull is composed of two main tasks: first, the technical/mechanical action of applying the soft-tissue data or muscles to the skull to establish a general facial shape, and second, the development of the individual features and the areas of transition. These we will call the **technical phase** and the **artistic phase**.

Certain individuals have become frustrated with facial reconstruction and have developed the attitude of "If I can't do it, it can't be done." They attempt to overly quantify and mechanize the process, which may work well in the first stage. However, in the second phase, artistic talent is required and underestimation of the critical role played by the "artistic eye" produces a stiff, unrealistic mask-like face that may never be recognized. This is why we **strongly suggest a collaboration of artist and scientist**.

We further contend that **both two-dimensional and three-dimensional facial reconstruction work equally well if the techniques are correctly followed.** We agree with the assessment of Dr. Robert George:

> There are advantages and disadvantages to both plastic and graphic methods of reconstruction, but there is no reason why the two methods cannot be integrated to strengthen their weaknesses. For example, **a two-dimensional reconstruction could and probably should be developed as a working "blueprint" for more complex sculptures.** Clay sculptures are complete, take in many more cranial points, and can be photographed from any angle and under varied lighting conditions. But the clay method requires the skull or a cast which often cannot be released, and thus the artist must be "brought to the mountain." And it is tedious and requires considerable artistic skill.
>
> Photographs of the skull can be more easily mailed and graphic reconstructions can then be drawn on tracing paper or frosted acetate directly over the photographs. The views, however, will be limited and calibration of data will be a problem if the photographs are not life size.[11]

We agree, with only one comment of exception. Ideally, with two-dimensional reconstruction, the artist also should receive the skull. A first-person viewing of the structural nuances and control of the photography greatly add to the accuracy of the two-dimensional method. An additional advantage of the drawing method is its potential use in cases of very delicate skulls unable to bear the weight of the clay.

To test consistency of results of facial reconstruction from the same skull, we worked on a case known as "Daisy Jane Doe," which was requested by the television program "America's Most Wanted" (Figure 11.22).

A fisherman found the body of a young woman floating face down in 6 feet of water, entrapped in the limbs of a tree. Tied around her waist was a black cable securing a large concrete block. The unrecognizable young white female was in an advanced stage of putrefactive change. On her left shoulder was a simple yellow and green floral tattoo, hence her nickname, "Daisy Jane Doe."

The cleaned skull was first transported to Texas, where Taylor completed reconstruction drawings based on skull photographs, both frontal and lateral. Then the skull was forwarded to Oklahoma, where Gatliff built a three-dimensional sculpture directly on the skull. The two reconstructions were performed totally independently.

When completed, the images were compared by Stephen Baranovics, the producer of the "America's Most Wanted" segment, and then the forensic artists themselves. All

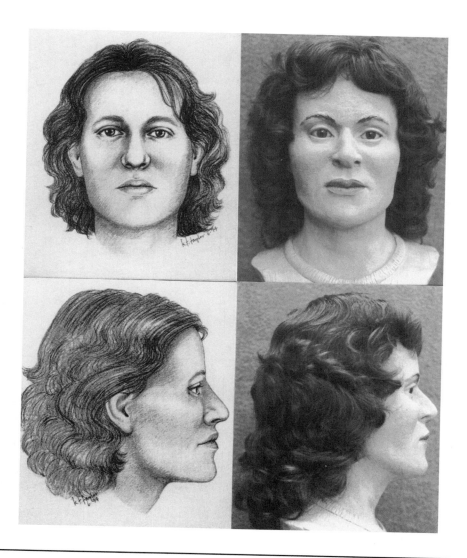

Figure 11.22 "Daisy Jane Doe" case showing comparison of two-dimensional and three-dimensional facial reconstruction; frontal reconstruction by KTT (upper left), frontal reconstruction by Betty Pat. Gatliff (upper right), lateral view by KTT (lower left), and lateral view by Betty Pat. Gatliff (lower right). (Courtesy of "America's Most Wanted.")

agreed that the drawings and the sculpture compared favorably. Realizing that some artists are more at ease with drawing while others prefer sculpture, we believe that both methods can prove equally effective. The key to either approach is accuracy of procedure and attention to detail.

Frankfort Horizontal Plane

A useful orientation for facial reconstruction is the Frankfort Horizontal Plane. **The Frankfort Horizontal Plane is an anthropological standard position that closely approximates the natural position of the head in life.** Keeping the skull in this

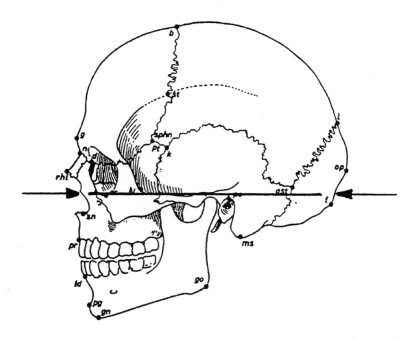

Figure 11.23 Frankfort Horizontal Plane. (From Krogman, W. M., Method for approximation of a missing mandible based on the cranium, in *The Human Skeleton in Forensic Medicine*, Charles C Thomas, Springfield, IL, 1987, chap. 11.)

orientation will limit distortion and produce the best results. To achieve this position, orbitale, the lowest point on the lower margin of the orbit, is horizontally aligned with porion, the most lateral point on the roof of the external auditory meatus (bony ear hole) (Figure 11.23).

Tissue Depths

Tissue Depth Tables

A logical choice for use on skulls as part of museum projects is the 1898 tissue depth data by Kollman and Büchly shown in Figure 11.24.

The tissue depth data most often used by U.S. police artists were developed primarily at the University of New Mexico by Dr. Stanley Rhine and colleagues. **The measurements collected by Rhine take into consideration the thickness of the muscle, fatty and connective tissue, and skin thickness all in one calculated measurement at a particular morphological landmark.**[12]

In 1980, Rhine and Campbell published new tissue depth data on American Negroids, which are shown in Table 11.1.[13] They compared their data with Japanese and European studies previously done. In 1982, Rhine and Moore published the data on American Caucasoids and revised the tables in 1984, as shown in Table 11.2.[14] Rhine has also prepared limited unpublished data on Southwestern American Indians or Native Americans, shown in Table 11.3.[15] All of Rhine's tables are useful, particularly since the data are divided by emaciated or slender, normal, and obese groupings, as well as by sex and race.

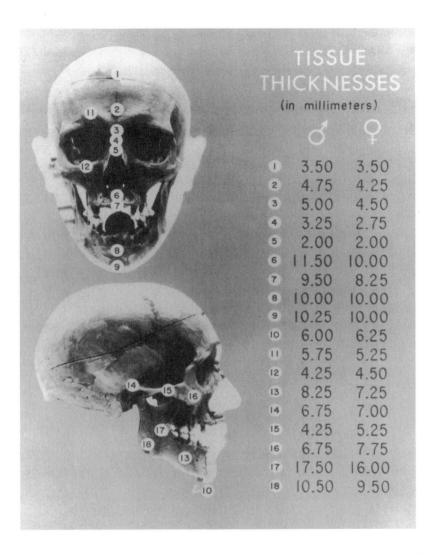

Figure 11.24   Tissue thicknesses (in millimeters) of European Caucasoids by Kollman and Büchly, 1898. (Courtesy of Betty Pat. Gatliff.)

It should be noted that tissue depth data collected by use of ultrasonic probing are in publication by Lebedinskaya in Russia and by Helmer in Germany. Helmer's tables give measurements for 34 anatomic points, while Rhine's material consists of 21 points. Lebedinskaya's tables include measurements taken for the multiple ethnic groups of Russia.[16]

The tissue depth tables developed by Rhine are broken down by numbered location and osteologic landmark name. The locations correspond to specific established bony sites. It is possible for the forensic artist to simply glue the markers by number, according to the numbered locations on the diagram (Figure 11.25). However, **we recommend that the anthropological landmarks be learned and fully understood for accurate placement of the markers.**

Table 11.1   Tissue Thicknesses (in millimeters) of American Negroids (African-derived)

Measurement	Slender Male (24)	Slender Female (5)	Normal Male (27)	Normal Female (10)	Obese Male (1)	Obese Female (2)
Midline						
1. Supraglabella	4.00	5.00	5.00	4.50	5.00	3.50
2. Glabella	5.25	6.00	6.25	6.00	7.50	6.00
3. Nasion	5.25	5.25	6.00	5.25	5.25	4.75
4. End of nasals	3.00	3.25	3.75	3.75	3.25	3.00
5. Mid-philtrum	11.75	10.00	12.25	11.25	11.75	12.00
6. Upper lip margin	12.50	12.00	14.25	12.50	12.50	15.25
7. Lower lip margin	13.75	12.25	15.50	15.00	15.50	12.00
8. Chin–lip fold	11.75	9.50	11.75	12.25	13.00	12.25
9. Mental eminence	11.25	11.00	11.50	12.50	15.25	13.00
10. Beneath chin	8.00	6.50	8.25	8.00	9.50	8.50
Bilateral						
11. Frontal eminence	3.75	3.25	5.00	4.00	5.50	5.00
12. Supraorbital	7.75	7.25	8.50	8.00	11.75	8.50
13. Suborbital	5.75	6.50	7.75	8.25	9.25	9.00
14. Inferior malar	14.00	14.50	16.50	16.75	17.50	18.75
15. Lateral orbit	10.50	12.00	13.25	13.00	20.00	12.75
16. Zygomatic arch, halfway	6.75	8.00	8.25	9.50	13.75	9.25
17. Supraglenoid	9.50	9.75	11.00	11.50	17.50	17.25
18. Gonion	11.50	11.00	13.00	13.50	24.00	17.50
19. Supra M^2	19.00	20.50	23.00	20.25	24.00	23.50
20. Occlusal line	16.75	17.75	19.00	19.25	30.00	20.00
21. Sub M_2	13.50	14.25	16.50	17.00	23.50	20.00

Courtesy of Dr. Stanley Rhine and Dr. H. R. Campbell.

Table 11.2 Tissue Thicknesses (in millimeters) of American Caucasoids (European-derived) by Rhine and Moore[a]

Measurement	Slender Male (3)	Slender Female (3)	Normal Male (37)	Normal Female (19)	Obese Male (8)	Obese Female (3)
Midline						
1. Supraglabella	2.25	2.50	4.25	3.50	5.50	4.25
2. Glabella	2.50	4.00	5.25	4.75	7.50	7.50
3. Nasion	4.25	5.25	6.50	5.50	7.50	7.00
4. End of nasals	2.50	2.25	3.00	2.75	3.50	4.25
5. Mid-philtrum	6.25	5.00	10.00	8.50	11.00	9.00
6. Upper lip margin	9.75[b]	6.25	9.75	9.00	11.00	11.00
7. Lower lip margin	9.50[b]	8.50	11.00	10.00	12.75	12.25
8. Chin–lip fold	8.75	9.25	10.75	9.50	12.25	13.75
9. Mental eminence	7.00	8.50	11.25	10.00	14.00	14.25
10. Beneath chin	4.50	3.75	7.25	5.75	10.75	9.00
Bilateral						
11. Frontal eminence	3.00	2.75	4.25	3.50	5.50	5.00
12. Supraorbital	6.25	5.25	8.25	7.00	10.25	10.00
13. Suborbital	2.75	4.00	5.75	6.00	8.25	8.50
14. Inferior malar	8.50	7.00	13.25	12.75	15.25	14.00
15. Lateral orbit	5.00	6.00	10.00	10.75	13.75	14.75[b]
16. Zygomatic arch, halfway	3.00	3.50	7.25	7.50	11.75	13.00[b]
17. Supraglenoid	4.25	4.25	8.50	8.00	11.25	10.50[b]
18. Gonion	4.50	5.00	11.50	12.00[b]	17.50	17.50
19. Supra M^2	12.00	12.00	19.50	19.25	25.00	23.75
20. Occlusal line	12.00	11.00	18.25	17.00	23.50	20.25
21. Sub M_2	10.00	9.50[b]	16.00	15.50	19.75	18.75

[a] Adapted from Rhine and Moore, 1982; revised 1984. Prepared by J. Stanley Rhine, Ph.D. and C. Elliot Moore II, Ph.D., through the cooperation of J. T. Weston, M.D., Office of the Medical Investigator, State of New Mexico.

[b] Given the small samples, these values have been slightly adjusted from observed to values more in accord with trends in the rest of the data. Other adjustments have been made due to a programming error in the original table.

Table 11.3 Tissue Thicknesses (in millimeters) of Southwestern American Indians (Asian-derived) by Rhine

Measurement	Slender Male (4)	Slender Female (1)	Normal Male (9)	Normal Female (2)	Obese Male (5)	Obese Female (3)
Midline						
1. Supraglabella	5.75	4.00	5.00	4.50	4.50	4.25
2. Glabella	5.75	4.75	5.75	4.50	6.00	4.50
3. Nasion	5.75	6.50	6.86	7.00	6.50	5.00
4. End of nasals	2.75	2.50	3.50	2.50	3.25	3.25
5. Mid-philtrum	7.50	10.00	9.75	10.00	9.25	8.51
6. Upper lip margin	8.25	9.50	9.75	11.00	9.25	10.00
7. Lower lip margin	9.25	12.00	11.00	12.25	8.75	11.25
8. Chin–lip fold	8.50	9.00	11.50	10.00	9.75	11.00
9. Mental eminence	8.00	11.00	12.00	13.00	12.50	13.25
10. Beneath chin	5.25	8.00	8.00	8.00	8.00	7.75
Bilateral						
11. Frontal eminence	4.75	4.75	4.25	4.00	4.50	4.20
12. Supraorbital	6.75	5.00	9.00	8.50	8.50	8.25
13. Suborbital	3.75	3.25	7.50	6.25	7.75	6.75
14. Inferior malar	10.00	9.00	14.00	12.00	15.75	15.00
15. Lateral orbit	8.00	8.25	12.50	11.50	11.75	13.75
16. Zygomatic arch, midway	6.00	5.75	7.50	7.00	8.75	9.00
17. Supraglenoid	5.75	4.50	8.50	6.25	9.75	7.75
18. Gonion	7.75	6.25	13.25	10.50	15.40	12.75
19. Supra M^2	14.25	11.75	21.50	18.00	23.50	19.00
20. Occlusal line	15.50	12.25	20.75	17.50	22.75	19.25
21. Sub M_2	12.50	10.50	19.25	17.00	18.50	15.75

Courtesy of Stanley Rhine, Ph.D., Laboratories of Physical Anthropology, Maxwell Museum of Anthropology, April 1983 (unpublished).

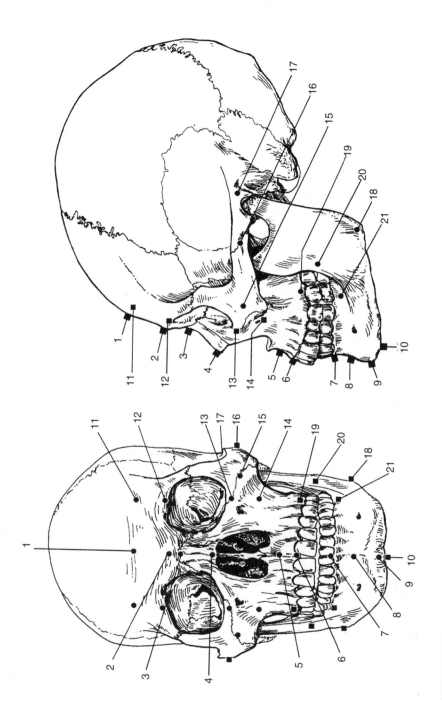

Figure 11.25 Anthropological or craniometric landmarks on the skull for placement of tissue depth markers. (Courtesy of John Prag and Richard Neave, University of Manchester.)

Landmarks for Location of Tissue Depth Markers

The following are the **landmarks for location of tissue depth markers on the skull**, for use of the numbering system by Dr. Stanley Rhine. Alternate names or abbreviations are also given if applicable.

(*Note:* Markers 1 through 10 are glued along the midline of the skull. Cut one marker each for these landmarks.)

1. **Supraglabella** — *Above* glabella
2. **Glabella** (G) — The most prominent point between the supraorbital ridges in the midsagittal plane
3. **Nasion** (N) — The midpoint of the suture between the frontal and the two nasal bones
4. **End of Nasals** (Nasals or Na) — The anterior tip or the farthest point *out* on the nasal bones
5. **Mid-Philtrum** — The midline of the maxilla (east and west), placed as high as possible before the curvature of the anterior nasal spine begins
6. **Upper Lip Margin** (Supradentale or Sd, or Alveolare) — Centered between the maxillary (upper) central incisors at the level of the Cementum Enamel Junction (CEJ)
7. **Lower Lip Margin** (Infradentale or Id) — Centered between the mandibular (lower) central incisors at the level of the Cementum Enamel Junction (CEJ)
8. **Chin–Lip Fold** (Supramentale) — The deepest midline point of indentation on the mandible between the teeth and the chin protrusion
9. **Mental Eminence** (Pogonion or Pog) — The most anterior or projecting point in the midline on the chin
10. **Beneath Chin** (Menton or Me) — The lowest point on the mandible
    (Note: Markers 11 through 21 are glued bilaterally on the skull in a parallel fashion on each side. Cut two markers each for these landmarks.)
11. **Frontal Eminence** — Place on the projections at both sides of the forehead
12. **Supraorbital** — *Above* the orbit, centered on the upper most margin or border
13. **Suborbital** — *Below* the orbit, centered on the lower most margin or border
14. **Inferior Malar** — The lower portion of the maxilla, still on the "cheekbone" (Note: This point is not actually on the malar or zygomatic bone, but rather on the maxilla.)
15. **Lateral Orbit** — Drop a line from the outer margin of the orbit and place the marker about 10 mm below the orbit (Note: According to Dr. Stanley Rhine, the measurements were taken at this location.)
16. **Zygomatic Arch, Midway** — Halfway along the zygomatic arch (*Note:* This is not necessarily correspondent to the suture line. It is generally the most projecting point on the arch when viewed from above.)
17. **Supraglenoid** — Above and slightly forward of the external auditory meatus (ear hole) at the deepest point
18. **Gonion** (Go) — The most lateral point on the mandibular angle
19. **Supra M²** — *Above* the second maxillary molar (Note: If the second molar is missing, the marker should be placed in the approximate area where it *would* have been.)

20. **Occlusal Line** — On the mandible in alignment with the line where the teeth occlude or "bite"
21. **Sub M₂** — *Below* the second mandibular molar (Note: If the second molar is missing, the marker should be placed in the approximate area where it *would* have been.)

Excellent descriptions of both the cranial skeletal or craniometric points as well as their soft tissue counterparts or cephalometric points can be found in George.[17] The illustration explains how the soft tissue landmarks actually correspond to their bony counterpart landmarks in the lateral view (Figure 11.26). This provides the insight for more sensitive placement of the surface sites in the reconstruction drawing or sculpture. Note that while bony angles found in individual skulls may force the gluing of markers at angles somewhat different from the projections shown in Figure 11.26, the illustration is a guide for the correspondences that should be incorporated into the finished reconstruction.

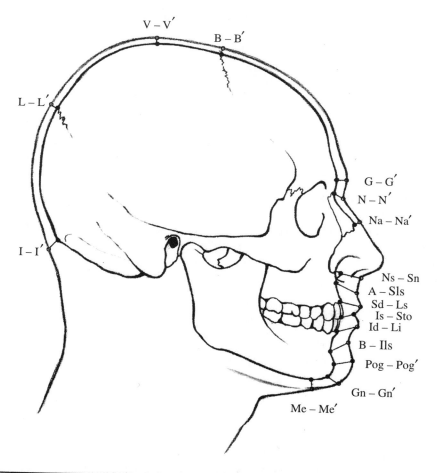

Figure 11.26 Craniofacial correlations, lateral view. (From Iscan, M.Y. and Helmer, R.P., *Forensic Analysis of the Skull*, John Wiley & Sons, New York, 1993, chap. 11.)

Cutting and Placement of Tissue Depth Markers

Since every individual skull presents its own challenges, gluing of the tissue depth markers has to be somewhat tailored to each particular skull. Figure 11.27 shows markers glued to the skull of a white female. Figure 11.28 shows markers on the skull of a very robust black male. In comparing them, certain subtleties become apparent. Laterally, the markers serve to emphasize the flatter face in the profile of this individual female, with cheekbones that are more forward. Compare this profile to the projection of the maxilla in the black male and the more pushed back cheekbones. Tissue markers #5 and #6 are more upward angled in the prognathic male. Tissue marker #17 may need to be moved slightly forward or backward depending on the placement of the glenoid process in the area above the auditory meatus or ear hole.

Individual dentition also necessitates careful placement of markers #19, #20, and #21. Review of Figure 3.12 in Chapter 3 will aid in understanding the teeth. Tissue marker #19 should be placed *above* the second maxillary molar and #21 should be placed *below* the second mandibular molar. But what if those teeth are not present? Note that the female in Figure 11.27 has second molars, but lacks third molars or "wisdom teeth," a fairly common condition. The male in Figure 11.28 has maxillary third molars but lacks both first and second mandibular molars, so marker #21 must be glued in the area where the second molar *would* have been. Marker #20 should be placed on the frontal edge of the ascending ramus of the mandible, in alignment with the teeth in occlusion. Note that markers #6 and #7 may be difficult to glue in place if the anterior teeth are missing. It is possible to add clay to approximate the space once held by the missing teeth and glue the markers to the clay.

We wish to emphasize the need for accurate cutting and placement of the tissue depth markers. According to the table, cut vinyl eraser material to the depths listed for the midline markers on the face, or numbers 1 through 10. Next, cut two each of the bilateral markers, or numbers 11 through 21. As you cut these markers, number each one with a ball-point pen, so you will have the location for gluing. Take care not to cut markers at an angle, but rather straight up and down (Figure 11.29). If this poses difficulty for you, invest in a metal X-acto miter box, which aids in cutting guillotine fashion. It is a good idea to line up markers as you cut them in an orderly fashion, so that there is less chance for inadvertent placement of the wrong marker at the wrong location.

Because the tissue depth information will be used slightly differently depending upon whether you are drawing or sculpting, there will be further discussion of its use in the following two chapters. Certain slight variations in angulations for gluing the markers may be more advantageous depending upon which method you will use. For example, gluing marker #3 so that it tips downward and #8 so that it tips slightly upward can be helpful when preparing a sculpture.

Several organizations are currently involved in new tissue depth research. With the almost limitless technologic capability for assessment and measurement of humans through imaging, the future holds great promise for improved volume and subtlety of tissue depth data for various ages and population groups.

We believe that there are some very practical reasons for use of the tissue depth method over the muscle-by-muscle method, particularly in the law enforcement setting. Mikhail Gerasimov effectively used the muscle method after performing numerous facial dissections, utilizing his personal knowledge of the actual

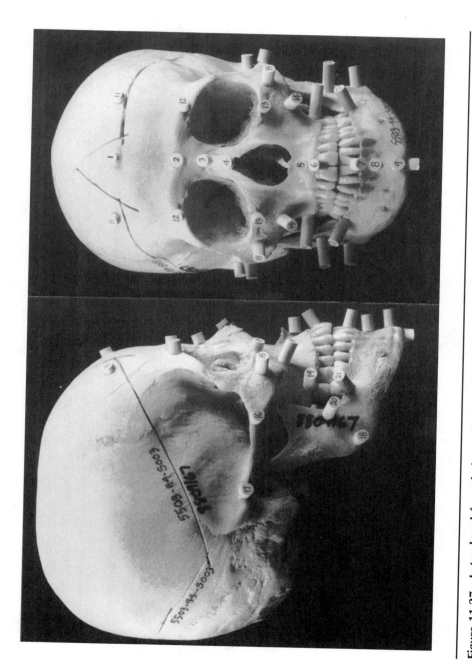

Figure 11.27 Lateral and frontal views of tissue depth markers glued to the skull of a white female. (Courtesy of Kent Kinkade and Texas Department of Public Safety.)

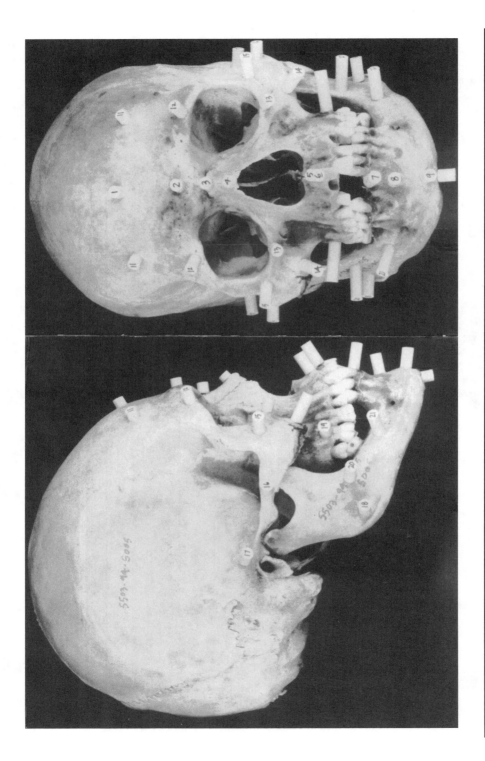

Figure 11.28 **Lateral and frontal views of tissue depth markers glued to the skull of a black male.** (Courtesy of Kent Kinkade and Texas Department of Public Safety.)

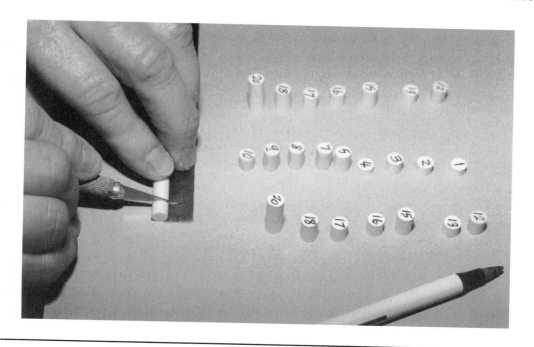

Figure 11.29 Cutting vinyl tissue depth markers. (Photo by Missey Micheletti.)

thicknesses of the various facial muscles. Few in law enforcement have the benefit of such background and experience, or the time or means to acquire it.

A literature search reveals that use of the muscle-building technique does not *totally* allow for the accurate placement and volume of each muscle. Exact size and thickness of each muscle are individual and highly variable. At best, a very *stylized* representation of each muscle must be sculpted because many of the muscles are actually very thin and there is, in fact, often more fat than muscle in the massive area of the cheeks.

While technical accuracy is the desired effect, we believe that in many cases, the use of the tissue depth method combined with knowledge of the facial muscles may actually lead to greater accuracy. The specific thicknesses of the muscles, fatty and connective tissues, and skin can only be speculated upon. Thus, building to an overall depth based on averages determined by repeated studies and research in the literature has validity. In the United States, emphasis is traditionally placed on documented research when a process is evaluated for admissibility into the court system.

Further, we hope that by outlining a simplified, systematized methodology for facial reconstruction from the skull that the artistic subjectivity that has often been a criticized part of the process will be minimized over time.

All in all, we believe that a combination approach is the optimum approach.

References

1. George, R. M., "The lateral craniographic method of facial reconstruction," *Journal of Forensic Sciences*, 32(5), 1305–1330, 1987.
2. Anderson, J. E., *Atlas of Grant's Anatomy*. Baltimore, MD: Williams & Wilkins, 1983.
3. Krogman, W. M., *The Human Skeleton in Forensic Medicine*. Springfield, IL: Charles C Thomas, 1962.

4. Snow, C., "Forensic Anthropology — An Overview," Report prepared for training purposes, Norman, OK.
5. Iscan, M. Y. and Loth, S. R., The scope of forensic anthropology, in *Introduction to Forensic Sciences*, Eckert, W. G., Ed. Boca Raton, FL: CRC Press, 1997, 343.
6. Anderson, M., "Fleshing out the past: reconstructing fossil faces," *Discovery*, 22(1), 1990.
7. Helmer, R. P., Rohricht, S., Peterson, D., and Mohr, F., Assessment of the reliability of facial reconstruction, in *Forensic Analysis of the Skull*, Iscan, M. Y. and Helmer, R. P., Eds. New York: Wiley–Liss, 1993.
8. Anderson, M., "Fleshing out the past: reconstructing fossil faces," *Discovery*, 22, 1, 1990.
9. Wade, W. D. and Rhine, S. J., Ultrasound measurements of soft tissue thickness in living chimpanzees, *Canadian Review of Physical Anthropology*, 6(1), 45, 1987.
10. Prag, J. and Neave, R., *Making Faces*, London: British Museum Press, 1997.
11. George, R. M., "The lateral craniographic method of facial reconstruction," *Journal of Forensic Sciences*, 32(5), 1305–1330, 1987.
12. Rhine, S., formerly with the Maxwell Museum of Anthropology at the University of New Mexico, personal communication with Betty Pat. Gatliff, 1980.
13. Rhine, J. S. and Campbell, H. R., "Thickness of facial tissues in American blacks," *Journal of Forensic Sciences*, 25(4), 847–858, 1980.
14. Rhine, J. S. and Moore, C. E., "Tables of facial tissue thickness of American Caucasoids in forensic anthropology," *Maxwell Museum Technical Series*, No. 1, 1984.
15. Rhine, S., formerly with the Maxwell Museum of Anthropology at the University of New Mexico, personal communication with Betty Pat. Gatliff, 1983.
16. Lebedinskaya, G. V., Balueva, T. S., and Veselovskaya, E. V., Principles of facial reconstruction, in *Forensic Analysis of the Skull*, Iscan, M. Y. and Helmer, R. P., Eds. New York: Wiley–Liss, 1993, 183–198.
17. George, R. M., Anatomical and artistic guidelines for forensic facial reconstruction, in *Forensic Analysis of the Skull*, Iscan, M. Y. and Helmer, P., Eds. New York: Wiley–Liss, 1993.

Chapter 12

Two-Dimensional Facial Reconstruction from the Skull

Consider the situation parents often experience on Christmas Eve. They bring the shiny new bicycle into the house still packed in a cardboard box. They dive into putting it together, only to find when they are finished that they have an ill-fitting mess and leftover parts. Then they decide to read the directions, and they assemble the bike rather easily. Things are assembled step by step for a purpose. Cutting corners does not necessarily save time, and you end up with a bicycle that doesn't look like the picture on the box.

Hopefully, anyone who tackles this not-so-easy job of putting together a face will take time to first read the directions. **As a foundation, review the information contained in Chapters 3, 4, and 11. It is also very beneficial to understand the three-dimensional method of reconstruction in Chapter 13 because the principles are the same.**

Background of the Method

An explanation of the method of two-dimensional facial reconstruction from the skull that I use should be prefaced by a discussion of **skulls in general** and a look at **methods used by others** prior to my development of this method. Skulls have long provided a source of fascination and study for many people in various disciplines.

The Skull

Some have commented that all skulls look alike. But others, who make it their business to study human bones, know that this simply is not true. One only has to compare the heads and bodies of jockey Willy Schumaker and basketball player Wilt Chamberlain

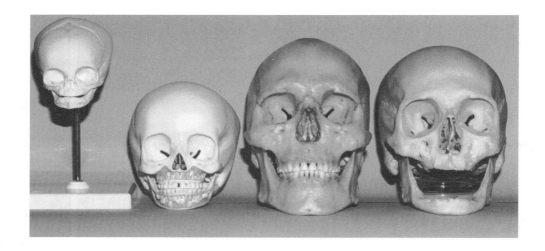

Figure 12.1 **Four human skulls**, left to right: a fetal skull, the skull of a 6-year-old child, a middle-aged adult, and an edendulous elderly person. (Photo by Missey Micheletti.)

to see the dramatic **variability** that can exist. The top of Schumaker's head comes only to Chamberlain's waist!

By comparing one skull to another, we get a much better understanding of the **diversity**. With Schumaker and Chamberlain, the difference in size becomes immediately obvious. A side-by-side look at two skulls of the same size often reveals other more subtle differences. **To the trained eye of the anthropologist or skeletal biologist, the distinctions of race/ancestry, age, and sex are also usually determinable from the skull.** The specific facial looks with regard to **sex** and **race** are described in Chapter 3. Chapters 7 and 8 discuss in detail the factors that affect the face when it comes to **growth** and **aging**. Figure 12.1 shows four skulls (left to right): a fetal skull, the skull of a 6-year-old child, the skull of a middle-aged adult, and the skull of an edentulous elderly person.

Facial **symmetry** is a frequent topic in art instruction books. In the 1920 classic, *Constructive Anatomy*, George Brigman discusses the bilateral symmetry of the head and body:

> A vertical line in the centre divides the head or the trunk into parts equal, opposite, and complemental. The right eye is the counterpart of the left; the two halves of the nose are symmetrical; the limbs, except for changes of position, are exact though reversed duplicates of each other.[1]

While this is a worthwhile general observation for use in fine art, the forensic artist perceives things differently. Perfect symmetry is a component of idealized beauty that plastic surgeons endeavor to achieve for aesthetic reasons. The truth is very few people are perfectly balanced side to side. For those of us who try to discern identity from skulls, it is, in fact, the subtle asymmetry that is of interest.

We can readily see this common facial asymmetry by taking a facial photo and splitting it down the center. Using the negative, make a regular print and then reverse the negative and make a print. Cut the photos down the midline and then combine a left with a reversed left to form a new face. Then combine a right with a reversed right to produce another new face (see Figure 4.16 in Chapter 4). With this emphasis on the asymmetries, you will very likely come up with two facial images that look only like distant relatives of the original face.

I have come to realize that another interesting phenomenon exists in forensic art with regard to **proportion** in the skull and face. This text has emphasized multiple times that **the single most important factor in facial recognition is proportional arrangement of features.** This fact holds true for all the types of forensic art and yet it is more difficult to achieve by some methods than others. For the composite artist, the proportions must be determined from a verbal description provided by the witness. For the skull reconstruction artist, things are much easier in this regard. The proportions of the face in life are revealed to the artist by the arrangement of the bony clues. In other words, placement of the eyes is directly correspondent to the location of the bony orbits. The nose and mouth are similarly located over the underlying bony landmarks, and the shape of the face is dictated by the overall shape of the skull. Thus, this important **proportional essence of a face, although specific details may be off a little, is there for the forensic artist to capture from the skull.**

It has long been acknowledged that **our skulls form the bony architectural understructure for our faces on the surface.** A very dramatic example of this correspondence can be seen by examining the skull of the Victorian era Englishman known as the "Elephant Man." Most experts agree that Joseph Merrick (later known as John Merrick) was afflicted with a genetic disorder called neurofibromatosis, which affected both his skeleton and the soft tissue covering it. (In recent years, some have suggested that his condition was unique and should be called the "Elephant Man's Disease.") Merrick spent most of his sad life as a circus freak, before being rescued by Dr. Frederick Treves, who examined him and treated him with dignity. His skeleton was retained after his death by the Royal London College of Medicine Museum, and a casting or death mask of his face was made. These remarkable relics provide a dramatic example of the strong correspondence of our faces in life to our bony framework.

Dr. William Maples, a leading American forensic anthropologist, traveled to London to study the skeleton of Joseph Merrick. He discusses the case in his book, *Dead Men Do Tell Tales:*

> … I can only declare that this skeleton, perhaps more than any other I have ever beheld, talks to you in very simple, powerful, human terms. It transfers emotions to you in a physical sense, with a directness and immediacy unequaled by any other skeleton I have ever seen.[2]

Dr. Maples also studied the skeletal remains of prominent figures dating back to the 1500s including Spanish explorer Francisco Pizarro, President Zachary Taylor, Czar Nicholas II of Russia and other members of the Romanov family, as well as many forensic cases. His insightful remarks about the human skeleton and the way in which it can literally talk to those who will listen should be considered by all those who investigate the death of another human being. He said, **"Patient and silent while we live, our skeletons shout to heaven and posterity after we die."**[2]

Historical Review of Two-Dimensional Facial Reconstruction

The idea that the skull can be used to predict the face in life has been around for a long while. The anatomist **W. His** is generally credited with being the first to develop a scientific reconstruction, publishing on the subject in 1895. His work included a reconstruction from the purported skull of Johann Sebastian Bach. The Viennese team of anthropologist **J. Kollman** and sculptor **W. Büchly** published important contributions, particularly in the area of tissue depth research in 1898. Others in Europe and Russia sought to recreate faces from skulls, particularly fossil skulls.

The real foundation for facial reconstruction as it is practiced today in the U.S. was laid by anthropologist **Dr. Wilton M. Krogman**. During the 1930s, Krogman was a laboratory assistant to famous crime fighter Elliot Ness when Ness was in Cleveland. In 1946, while Associate Professor of Anatomy and Physical Anthropology at the University of Chicago, Dr. Krogman conducted a test of his hypothesis that a reasonable likeness to the face in life could be predicted from the skull (see Figure 2.10 in Chapter 2). He selected the cadaver head of a 40-year-old Negro male and photographed it. He then defleshed the head and gave the cleaned skull to a sculptress, **Mary Jane McCue**. With only general guidance from Krogman as to sex, race, and tissue depths, McCue sculpted a face based on the skull. In the July 1946 issue of the *FBI Law Enforcement Bulletin*, Krogman discusses the experiment:

> In this report I am, for the first time—as far as I know—reporting an experiment where the procedure has gone from a known head, to the skull, and finally to a restoration in the form of a bust modeled in clay.
> … The problem we have set has, we think, been reasonably well answered. The restoration was readily recognizable. … The entire technique is, we think, useful in the identification, via restoration, of an individual represented by a skull, alone.[3]

In a literature search as part of exploring the background of two-dimensional reconstruction from the skull, I found an illustration by John Adams in Krogman's 1962 book, *The Human Skeleton in Forensic Medicine* (Figure 12.2). Because the method of reconstruction drawing that I currently practice involves full use of both tissue depths and formulae for individual features, this drawing held particular significance. **It is, in fact, the only reference in the early literature to the usage of any tissue depth data affixed to the skull prior to photography for the drawing process.** All other drawn reconstructions found in the literature review were made by simply following the morphological outlines suggested by a given skull. Another observation that can be made from Adams' drawing involves the nose area. He places the nose directly on top of the piriform nasal aperture, which produces a nose that appears to have the same width as the bony opening. We now know that this is not correct because of information from Krogman himself. Inexplicably, this drawing was published in the 1962 book in which the improved formula for determining nose width also appeared. Since the drawing is not dated, we can only assume that it was an early attempt.

Krogman continued to have an interest in this restoration process and worked with several different artists in the years that followed. Other than the pictured drawing with a few clay tissue depth indicators, Krogman seemed to have completely abandoned that approach. He opted instead to do tracings over radiographs of a skull in both frontal and lateral views for the artist's use. He then worked with the

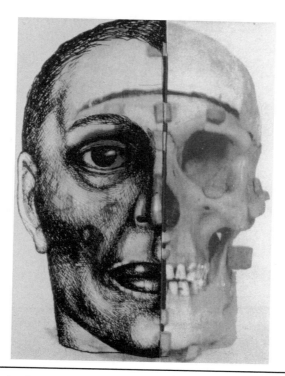

Figure 12.2 Face sketched over the skull by **John Adams**, with a few clay tissue depth indicators, from Krogman, 1962. Note that the sides of the nose erroneously sit directly on top of the piriform nasal aperture, at the same width. (From Krogman, W. M., Method for approximation of a missing mandible based on the cranium, in *The Human Skeleton in Forensic Medicine*, Charles C Thomas, Springfield, IL, 1987, chap. 12.)

artist as they prepared tracings based on his outlines of the skull's structures derived from a radiograph.

A 1975 New Jersey case of a badly decomposed body was solved by the collaboration of Krogman and New Jersey State Police artist **George Homa** (Figure 12.3). The drawing was made by sketching the facial features on an overlay of radiograph tracings of the skull prepared by Krogman.[4] In 1978, Krogman also worked with New York State Police artist **Herb Buckley** to produce drawings based on radiograph tracings of an edentulous skull (Figure 12.4).[5]

The historical review of two-dimensional reconstruction indicates that other prominent anthropologists also worked with artists over the years to predict faces from skulls in drawing form. **Dr. J. Lawrence Angel** of the Smithsonian Institution worked on a 1975 skeletal case from Columbia, Maryland with artist **Don Cherry** of the Metropolitan Police Department in Washington, D.C. An article about the case appeared in the August 1977 *FBI Law Enforcement Bulletin*. Discussing the technique used, Angel and Cherry state:

> Scale front and profile photographs of the victim's skull in standard eye–ear plane orientation were taken. Tracings of the skull were also made. Several meetings between the scientist and the artist insured that the artist remained within the limits established by the anthropological study — mainly, the tissue depths and probable placing of eyes, ears, mouth corners, and nasal tip.[6]

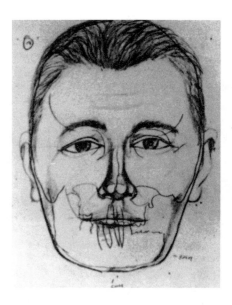

Figure 12.3 Two-dimensional facial drawing by **George Homa** based on the skull, with advice provided by **Dr. Wilton Krogman**.

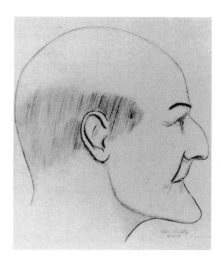

Figure 12.4 Lateral two-dimensional facial drawing by **Herb Buckley** based on an edendulous skull, with advice from **Dr. Wilton Krogman**. (Courtesy of Herb Buckley.)

Tips generated when the likeness was publicized in the news media led to the positive identification of the victim.

There is evidence that Dr. Angel continued with his interest in the potential for such drawings to aid in the identification of unknown remains. For some years, he examined skeletal bodies as a service to law enforcement, sometimes doing drawings himself based on the skulls. Shortly before his death, in a paper published from the proceedings of the 1986 meeting of the Guild of Natural Science Illustrators, he discusses his method and shows two of his drawings:

> None of us have time or technical help enough to make a plastic model either on the skull or a cast, as Krogman (1973) originally recommended in his book. … After standard measurements and observation (Martin and Saller, 1928), the first step is use of standardized profile and front view 35 mm photographs. … As soon as the film is developed, trace accurate outlines and details to exactly 2/3 natural size… There is never enough time to wait for a photographic laboratory's enlarging, which anyway would not get the scale correct. The second step is to put tracing paper over the skull drawings and draw outlines and details of the head and face following the tissue thicknesses of Rhine et al. (1980).[7]

Excellent drawings from skulls were being produced in Russia by **M. M. Gerasimov** starting in the 1920s and continuing for several decades until his death in 1970. Although best known for his sculptures (Figure 12.5), his two-dimensional reconstructions also provide a rich legacy of work, particularly of ancient humans. He prepared drawings as preliminary studies for his sculptures or as studies unto themselves (Figure 12.6). I first became aware that he had done such drawings when I saw them hanging on the wall of his former laboratory in Moscow. In July 1990, I visited the Laboratory of Anthropological Reconstruction at the Institute of Ethnography and Anthropology of the Russian Academy of Sciences. As an invited guest of the government, I was taken to the Institute to meet **Galina Lebedinskaya**, Gerasimov's protégé, who kindly allowed me to personally view their work of many decades. It should be noted that no tissue depth indicators were applied to the skulls in Gerasimov's work, although his drawings reflect his personal anatomical knowledge of the depths.

Figure 12.5 Russian anthropologist and skull reconstructionist **Professor M. M. Gerasimov** working on a sculpture.

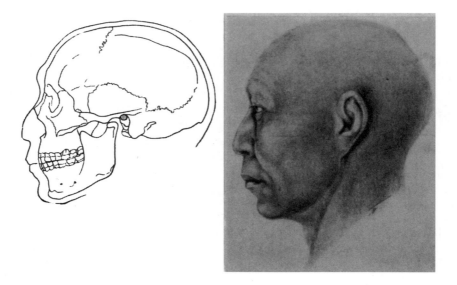

Figure 12.6 Skull tracing (left) and **reconstruction drawing** (right) by **Professor M. M. Gerasimov.**

In the summer of 1983, I attended the first workshop in facial reconstruction taught by **Betty Pat. Gatliff** and **Dr. Clyde Snow**. The week-long course was held at William Carey College in Gulfport, Mississippi. During this class, I learned not only the method of clay or three-dimensional reconstruction, but I also gained a foundation of knowledge that would benefit me throughout my career in forensic art. Betty Pat. Gatliff taught the tissue depth method of rebuilding a face, and included the principles for development of individual features that she had adapted from Krogman, who had published these guidelines as what he called "Rules of Thumb" in his 1962 book.

In the December 1985 issue of *Law and Order*, Florida artist **Ernest Walters** showed an illustration of a face drawn from the skull. He described the technique he used:

> The frontal photograph is placed on the drawing board and a sheet of tracing paper is placed over the photograph. I do use the appropriate previously mentioned skin thickness guide as a reference for the outer outline of the face.[8]

Walters further describes development of the individual features based on the principles taught by Betty Pat. Gatliff as interpreted from Krogman. Walters made general use of the available tissue depth and feature information without actually applying markers to the skull.

During the mid-1980s, anthropologist **Peggy Caldwell**, a protégé of Dr. Angel, taught a method for reconstruction drawing. In a handout she used for a course at the FBI Academy in Quantico, Virginia, she discussed her method:

> ... in creating the two-dimensional facial reproduction ... have a life-size outline drawing of the skull in two views preferably frontal and a right or left lateral. The reason for life-size will become apparent as you work on the sketch — a lot of the data you will using is numerical and will not work

on a drawing that is less than life-size! To prepare life-size outline drawings of a skull, you must have kodachromes/slides of the specimen with a label/scale of some sort actually in the plane of the face that you will be sketching … Once the slides have been processed, put them in a projector one at a time. … Project the image on the slide onto a wall (perpendicular to the projector) and tape a piece of paper there for the outline to be drawn on. Before drawing the outline, focus and move the projector so that the label in the picture is exactly the same size as the actual label used in the picture in the first place … Once the outline drawings of the skull are prepared, add the relevant facial soft tissue thickness depth data from the tables of data provided to you … Also note that since you are working in two-dimensions, and the tables were created for working on three-dimensional facial reproductions, there will be a lot of points which are not relevant to your sketch given in the tables. … I prefer to have my artist work on the frontal view, then go to the lateral view once the frontal is completed.[9]

As she stated, Caldwell's method used a few of the tissue depth points, but many were not used.

During the 1970s and 1980s, excellent work was being done by various medical and scientific illustrators using the anatomical approach to facial reconstruction on ancient and historical skulls. **Jay Matternes** produced painstaking muscle-by-muscle drawings over various skulls to produce drawings that were both informative and beautiful.

When I was an artist with a very large state police agency, my work load was always heavy. In the early years, I used the same small office for interviewing crime victims, preparing trial displays, and working on unidentified deceased cases in varying conditions. After taking the 1983 course with Betty Pat. Gatliff, I used the sculptural method successfully on several cases. I enjoyed sculpting; it was my area of emphasis at the University of Texas and I worked professionally as a sculptor in London prior to working in law enforcement.

However, a complication for me always seemed to be my inability to start a reconstruction and take it to completion without interruption. These interruptions usually meant that a victim of violent crime would come into my office for a composite drawing interview. Since the frightening face of a half-sculpted skull was obviously inappropriate for a victim to view, I had to pack up and hide all evidence of the skeletal case in progress.

I began to consider another method of doing facial reconstruction that would prove more practical for me. I decided to fully utilize *in drawing form* Krogman's "Rules of Thumb," Dr. Stanley Rhine's tissue depth research, and Betty Pat. Gatliff's method of three-dimensional reconstruction. **I glued the tissue depth indicators onto the skull** *before* **it was photographed and drawn.** With this approach, **it became possible to use** *all* **of the tissue depth information because the camera performed the function of foreshortening the depths just as the planes of the face are foreshortened in a life photograph.** In addition, by enlarging the skull photographs to exactly one-to-one or life-size, all of the formulae of Krogman and Gatliff could be applied directly.

I began using this method in early 1985 but considered it somewhat experimental. When skull after skull was identified I worked to refine the procedure. At the invitation of Horace Heafner, starting in 1987, I taught this method to students attending the art course at the FBI Academy in Quantico, Virginia.

In 1987, Robert George's article, "The Lateral Craniographic Method of Facial Reconstruction," published in the *Journal of Forensic Sciences*, contributed greatly to the two-dimensional method.[10] George suggests guidelines for production of lateral drawings and provides very specific diagrams and mathematical suggestions for the calculation and prediction of the individual features in profile.

In June 1990, I was invited to present the new method at the **International Symposium on the Forensic Aspects of Mass Disasters and Crime Scene Reconstruction** at the FBI Academy in Quantico, Virginia, and details were published in the proceedings of the conference.[11]

In response to numerous requests for training in this method I began teaching it to members of the Royal Canadian Mounted Police, at the Scottsdale Artists' School, and elsewhere around the U.S.

In the January 1992 issue of the *Journal of Forensic Sciences*, anthropologist Dr. Douglas Ubelaker of the Smithsonian Institution and Gene O'Donnell of the FBI suggested a method of computer-assisted facial reproduction in which they appear to use the tissue depth markers on the skull.[12]

Circumstances for Doing Two-Dimensional Facial Reconstruction

The technique of two-dimensional facial reconstruction from the skull is a method of forensic art used to aid in identifying skeletal remains. The artist and anthropologist collaborate to construct the facial features of the unknown individual on the basis of the underlying cranial structure.

As discussed, the concept of visualization of the face in life as extrapolated from the bony architecture is not a new one. While much of the early research done in this regard was used to project the looks in life of various illustrious forebears, today's interest leans toward the more recently dead.

Both medical examiners and law enforcement agencies are regularly presented with challenging cases of unidentified deceased persons, victims of homicide, accident, or unexplained death. It is both their statutory and moral obligation to make every attempt to identify these individuals. We automatically think of all of the various scientific methods of identifying bodies today that we have seen used so often on television: fingerprint comparisons, radiograph and dental comparisons, and DNA. Yet the simple fact is that these are all **comparative methods**, which means that **there must first be records in order for them to be compared to a body.**

This is where the forensic artist comes in. I have often categorized my role as that of "middle man." My work in **forensic art provides the needed connection between an unidentified deceased person and the records needed to identify that person.** Placing an item of forensic art in the public media or in police publications may generate a lead or tip that results in a possible name attached to the body. Then science can do its job of comparing the body to a missing person's records and positively identifying the body by any of various available means.

There are numerous reasons why it is so important to make every effort to identify deceased persons. **For every unidentified deceased body, there is someone who cared about that person in life.** Family members should not have to go through life with the painful mystery of never knowing. Missing persons who are never located or identified may leave complicated legal issues such as inheritances and other business matters. Especially significant is the knowledge that **an unidentified**

body likely means that a murder remains unsolved and the murderer is walking free.

As a result of climatic and situational factors, human remains are found in a variety of physical conditions. Postmortem drawings may be prepared from morgue or crime scene photographs of intact or relatively intact bodies as shown in Chapter 10. Such drawings may not be possible, however, in cases of severely damaged bodies or those in advanced stages of decompositional change. In instances of semiskeletal or totally skeletal remains, a method of reconstructing the face from the skull may be indicated.

Both two- and three-dimensional methods have proven successful, but some cases may be better done by either one or the other method. The artist may prefer one method or have greater skill in a particular method.

Extremely fragile skulls, either forensic or historical cases, may not be strong enough to bear the weight of clay for a sculptural reconstruction (Figure 12.7). In such cases, particularly if the damage is in the facial area, a two-dimensional approach may be taken.

Three-dimensional reconstruction offers the advantage of viewing and photographing the sculpture in multiple views. In addition, actual items recovered at the scene with the skeletal body, such as eyeglasses, jewelry, or clothing, may sometimes be placed directly on the finished sculpture for photography.

A plus with the drawing approach is that it is somewhat less expensive, and the skull is left uncovered so that it is available for other types of analyses to be conducted. With the drawing approach it is also easy to alter the hair, the facial hair, or eye color using matte acetate overlays, without purchasing wigs or prosthetic eyes.

It is simple to scan a drawn facial reconstruction into a graphics software and manipulate the hair or facial hair, add glasses, and so forth. It is also possible to convert a three-dimensional reconstruction to a two-dimensional image by scanning or digitally photographing it and importing it into a software for manipulation. As mentioned in Chapter 2, this concept was first suggested in 1990 by Dr. Emily Craig and Dr. Karen Burns.

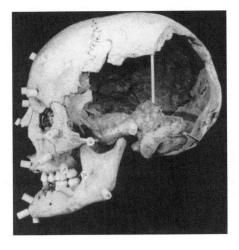

Figure 12.7 Fragile or badly damaged skulls may not hold the weight of clay for a sculpture and may better lend themselves to two-dimensional facial reconstruction.

With any digitization process, care must be taken to avoid distortion of the skull. A digitally photographed or scanned skull should be carefully measured and re-measured on the computer screen to check and correct for distortion alteration. **If a computer application is used for the insertion of features of the face, I would recommend that a feature database composed of drawn components rather than photographic ones be used.** The same principle applies here as is explained in depth in Chapter 6 regarding the diminished likelihood for recognition when an image is overly photographic in nature.

I actually practice both two- and three-dimensional methods of reconstruction on a regular basis, although drawing is more time efficient for me. **I always do a drawn reconstruction as a sort of "blueprint" in preparation for a sculptural reconstruction.** The two-dimensional version, though perhaps not complete or highly rendered in this application, acts as a useful guide for carefully studying the skull. It can also be helpful for the artist who must stop mid-project for interruptions, because it allows constant review of the skull, although clay may cover certain areas on the in-progress sculpture. With excellent frontal and lateral photographs of the skull and my "blueprint," I can continually assess the subtle nuances of each individual skull throughout a three-dimensional process.

I have been asked on several occasions to prepare **reconstructed faces based on available radiographs** in cases where the body has been buried, but I have declined to do this for several reasons. Figure 12.8 shows one case I was asked to do that involved a male who was strangled with wire wrapped multiple times around his neck. **Use of the two-dimensional reconstruction technique described in this chapter is simply not suitable for use over such radiographs.** The technique is based on certain formulae applied to life-size, undistorted photographs of a skull, using discernible bony landmarks. In a radiograph such as this, it cannot be assumed that the image

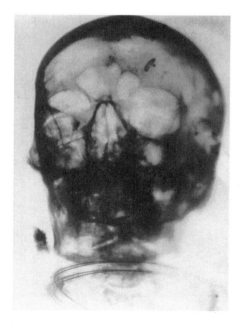

Figure 12.8   Radiograph of the skull of a homicide victim that is not suitable for preparation of two-dimensional facial reconstruction.

is life size, since most equipment produces a variable enlargement factor of an indeterminate percentage. The use of the calculations would therefore be incorrect. Further, it is not possible to measure the nasal spine or the nasal aperture or locate any other landmarks on the skull with any degree of accuracy from the radiograph. The radiograph does reveal the uniquely shaped frontal sinuses of this individual and could be used for comparative purposes if the name of a missing person who had a head X-ray in life were found.

An exception might be if the skull were actually available and the radiographs were made in a controlled manner specifically for the purpose of producing tracings to rebuild the features.

In this text, both two- and three-dimensional facial reconstructions are viewed as two-phase processes. The steps of the phases for **two-dimensional reconstruction** are listed below.

Technical Phase:
- Receipt of skull/evidence transferal/record keeping
- Gathering case information/scientific input
- Preparing and protecting the skull
- Gluing the mandible to the cranium
- Cutting and applying tissue depth markers
- Orientation into the Frankfort Horizontal for photography
- Photographing the skull/preparing one-to-one prints, frontal and lateral
- Setting up drawing boards with photos and tracing paper/reorienting into the Frankfort Horizontal

Artistic Phase:
- Drawing to establish facial contours
- Drawing of the eyes — frontal and lateral views
- Drawing of the nose — frontal and lateral views
- Drawing of the mouth — frontal and lateral views
- Drawing of the ears — frontal and lateral views
- Drawing of the hair based on specimen, if available
- Drawing of other details as appropriate
- Copying with solid sheet of paper between tracing paper and skull photo for distribution

Tools and Materials

The tools and materials for the production of two-dimensional facial reconstruction are, with a few additions, essentially the basic drawing tools that most artists possess. See Chapter 4 for additional information on drawing materials.

- Duco® cement (or other adhesive soluble in acetone)
- X-acto knife and blades
- Three (3) vinyl machine eraser strips (see Figure 13.1 in Chapter 13)
- Matched pair of drawing boards, about 12" × 16"
  (I like to use two boards cut with precisely square corners out of ¼" Masonite, smooth on both sides.)

- T-square
  (The T-square should be long enough to span across both drawing boards when they are lined up side by side, or about 24".)
- Triangle
  (Either 45° or 30/60° will do)
- Masking tape
- Several sheets of 11" × 14" Bristol or other heavy weight drawing paper
- Frontal and lateral "one-to-one" black-and-white photographs of the skull
- Two (2) sheets of 11" × 14" vellum-type paper
  (The paper should be as transparent as possible so that the skull photos below it may be seen, yet sturdy enough to withstand multiple erasures.)
- Small scale or ruler in millimeters
- U.S. quarter to use as a template
- Assorted drawing pencils and erasers
- Soft drafting or other brush for wiping away erasures

Technical Phase

The technical phase deals with information gathering about a case and the application of known quantifiable data by a mechanical process. The first few steps of the technical phase are described in Chapter 11. At this stage, the skull should be received by the reconstructionist and the proper evidence transferal paperwork accomplished. Next, all pertinent case information should be gathered and the necessary scientific input obtained. The skull should be prepared and protected as outlined in Chapter 11, and the mandible should be securely glued to the cranium.

Tissue Depth Markers

Select the appropriate tissue depth data and cut the markers from the vinyl eraser strips. Number each one according to location as pictured in Chapter 11 (Figure 11.25). Glue the markers at the appropriate landmark, using Duco® or similar cement (Figures 11.27 and 11.28). The skull is a very important item of evidence and great care should be taken to prevent damaging it in any way. Duco® cement is an ideal adhesive because it is soluble in acetone, and any glue residue can be removed from the skull without harming the bone.

The skull drawing that accompanies the soft tissue data in Chapter 11 (Figure 11.25) is easy to follow for placement of the landmarks or locations of the markers. It is significant to consider that the tissue depth studies by Rhine, which have been most commonly used for many years, were taken with a needle-type instrument. Consider, too, that the vinyl cylinders are approximately 6 mm in diameter, which means the surface that you are gluing to the skull is larger than the point at which the original measurement was taken. For this reason, some artists have chosen to use small sticks of wood, cork, or other materials to pinpoint a smaller point. The vinyl markers are preferable for accuracy of cutting and gluing. Location numbers can be written on the end of each marker to avoid possible misplacement. Choice of specific vinyl eraser material may affect cutting, since the softer materials are more difficult to cut with accuracy than the firmer materials.

The vinyl tissue depth markers should be glued as closely as possible to the morphological measurement sites shown in Chapter 11 (Figure 11.25). **There is a tendency to rush this part of the procedure and not pay proper attention to the accurate placement of each marker.** Although this step is less exciting for the artist, as are most of the technical phase steps, it should not be slighted. **Errors here can ruin your entire project and cause you to waste many hours of work.**

Dr. Robert George's illustration (Figure 11.26 in Chapter 11) is especially beneficial for the artist doing two-dimensional facial reconstruction. The illustration explains how the soft tissue (cephalometric) landmarks actually correspond to their bony (craniometric) landmarks in the lateral view. This provides insight for more sensitive placement of the surface sites in the reconstruction drawing. Note that while bony angles found in individual skulls may force gluing of markers at angles somewhat different from the projections shown, the illustration is a guide for the correspondences that should be incorporated into the finished reconstruction.

The Frankfort Horizontal Plane for Skull Photography

Texas Department of Public Safety forensic photographer Missey Micheletti provides the following considerations when photographing skulls for two-dimensional reconstruction:

> Since color information is usually absent with skulls, it is preferable to shoot them with a **fine-grain black-and-white film**. This gives the photographer control of the contrast during printing.
>
> For 35-mm photography, a **lens with a focal length of 100 to 200 mm** will avoid distortions. The longer the focal length, however, the narrower the depth of field. A smaller aperture and increased exposure time may be necessary on longer lenses to maintain an adequate range of sharpness.
>
> **Soft, diffuse lighting** works best when shooting skulls. Outdoors, this would mean cloudy-bright light. Indoors, soft box lights would be ideal. If point light sources must be used, a translucent tent built around the skull will diffuse two lights, one on either side, sufficiently to get reasonably even lighting.
>
> Skull alignment in the Frankfort Horizontal Plane should first be **established in the lateral view**. A true horizontal (parallel to the table surface) must be placed to align from the bottom of the orbit of the eye to the top of the external auditory meatus or bony ear hole to achieve this plane of alignment (see Figure 11.23). A ruler or scale is placed at the midline of the face when shooting the side view. The **alignment should be carefully maintained for the frontal view**, placing the ruler at the area of the facial plane.[13]

Figure 12.9 shows the same skull, correctly photographed with a 100-mm lens at left and incorrectly with a 20-mm lens at right, and the resulting **perspective distortion**. Figure 12.10 shows a different sort of potential photographic problem in that the skull has been photographed at varying angles. Although these **angulation problems** are less dramatic than the incorrect lens problem, they could be equally problematic for the reconstruction project. The skull at the top was correctly photographed while placed in the Frankfort Horizontal Plane, with the lens pointed straight toward the skull. At lower

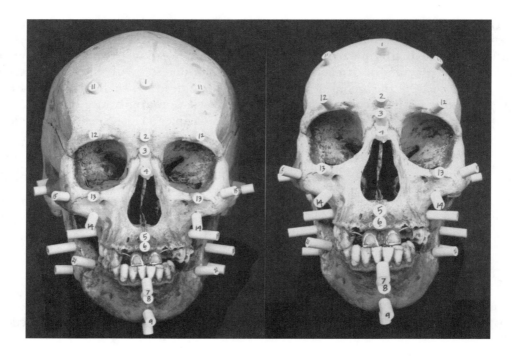

Figure 12.9   The same skull photographed correctly with a 100-mm lens (left) and incorrectly with a 20-mm lens (right), causing **perspective distortion**. (Courtesy of Texas Department of Public Safety.)

left, the lens was pointed upward at the skull. At lower right, the lens was pointed downward at the skull. **Notice that the photographer has glued a small wooden stick to the top of the external auditory meatus to facilitate the correct alignment with the bottom of the orbit of the eye.** In the photographs at lower left and right, the wooden stick is either too high or too low.

Once the skull has been correctly photographed, the photographer prepares one-to-one prints in which the scale used in the photographs is used as a guide for life-size enlargements. **Ideally the same scale is used for photography and in the darkroom for enlargements.**

Either lateral view may be used, unless damage indicates a preference for one over the other. My inclination is to ask for the right side of the skull since most mug photographs are made in this view. A certain percentage of the individuals identified may have had criminal records and their file photos for comparison will reflect the right view. The fact that mug photos are right views also makes it simpler to have a photographic reference file of right profile features, if needed.

Drawing Board Setup

Once the frontal and lateral photographic prints are made, the artist is ready to set up the drawing boards for beginning the reconstruction drawings.

I find it most accurate and efficient to line up the two drawing boards side by side. I then place a sheet of 11" × 14" Bristol paper on each board and tape the four corners with masking tape. The Bristol paper acts as a pad.

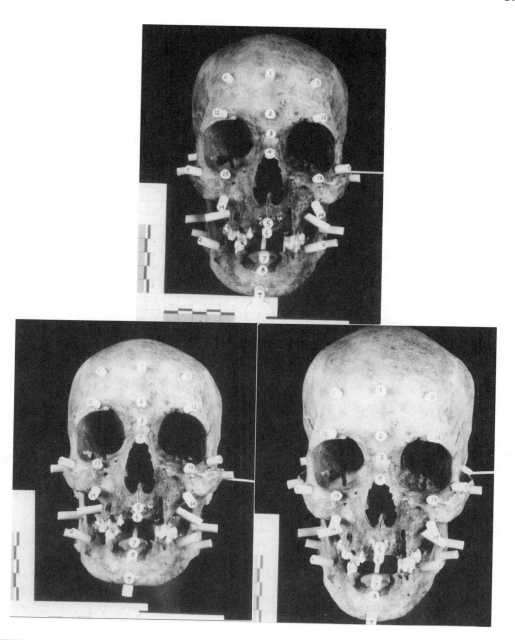

Figure 12.10 The same skull photographed at **varying angles**; with the lens pointed upward at the skull (lower left), correctly photographed in the **Frankfort Horizontal Plane** with the lens pointed straight toward the skull (top), and with the lens pointed downward at the skull (lower right). Note the placement of the small wooden stick in the auditory meatus as related to the bottom of the orbit of the eye. (Courtesy of Texas Department of Public Safety.)

On top of the Bristol paper, I tape the frontal skull photograph to one board and the lateral skull photograph to the other board. At this step, several points should be considered. What was found with this skeletal body? If there was long hair, the skull photos should be placed a little higher on the boards to allow room for drawing long hair. If, on the other hand, a hat was recovered, the skull photos may need to be placed a little lower to allow room to draw the hat.

It is very important to note that **at this stage of taping down the skull photos that the lateral view must be re-oriented into the Frankfort Horizontal Plane.** The frontal view, if properly photographed, is correctly oriented for you. But the lateral view must be aligned with the T-square, placing it so that the bottom of the orbit again lines up with the top of the auditory meatus.

It is a good idea to use the T-square with the triangle placed against it to establish a true vertical. Then use this vertical to place the frontal skull photograph in a straight orientation, by lining up the midline of the face with the vertical line of the triangle. Obviously, there will probably be asymmetries within the skull and this is just a rough vertical alignment.

I have also found it beneficial to align the photographs on the two boards in a rough correspondence to each other. In other words, I use the T-square to span across the two boards and line up the skull photos so the bottoms of the orbits align on both frontal and lateral photos.

Because of depth-of-field issues, it is not possible to exactly project each feature across from board to board, front to side, but it is usually pretty close. Due to depth of field, this differential varies with the individual skulls. For example, a very vertical-profiled, Asian-derived individual with a shallow skull depth front to back may have less difference in front-to-side projection than a very prognathic, long-headed, African-derived individual. This is due to the depth differences when the photographs are made. You must determine where to place the scale to best represent the facial plane when photographing the lateral view.

The four corners of each skull photograph are taped with masking tape on top of the Bristol paper. Then an 11" × 14" sheet of **vellum is placed on top of each skull photograph and taped at the top only.** This allows the artist to lift the paper and re-examine the skull photographs as needed throughout the drawing process. You should have two additional loose sheets of 11" × 14" paper handy. These can be used to slip under the vellum and block the view of the skull to check the drawing from time to time.

Although you will be working from skull photographs, you have the tremendous advantage of simultaneously observing the skull itself as you work. Place the skull on a cork ring or other stabilizing device and put it on the drawing table beside you as you draw. **Everything is now prepared to enter the artistic phase of the process.**

Artistic Phase

The artistic phase deals with the development of the individual features themselves and with the completion of the areas of transition. It is beneficial to review the anatomical structures of the individual features as shown in Chapter 3, in Figures 3.7 (eye), 3.8 (nose), 3.9 (mouth), and 3.10 (ear). Chapter 4 provides more information concerning drawing these and other features of the face.

As discussed in Chapter 11, the **optimum approach to facial reconstruction, whether two or three dimensional, may well lie in a combination method which encompasses aspects of both the anatomical method and the tissue depth method.** It is advantageous for the artist to first apply the tissue depth data as a guide to the contours of the face. Then, a careful study of the points of muscle attachment, the subtle asymmetries of the face, and any other visible indicators of individualization should be made prior to connecting the tissue depth markers.

Remember, too, that while this is the artistic phase of the process, it is beneficial to consult with the anthropologist for input on the individual features. Ideally, the artist and anthropologist work side by side during the preparation of the drawings. Since this is not always possible, I have made it a habit to always **check the completed reconstruction drawings with the advising anthropologist for approval before their release.**

Although others maintain that a reconstruction drawing should be fully developed in the frontal view before starting the lateral view, I strongly encourage the artist to do otherwise. Working out a feature in one view requires that you examine that feature in the other view as well. If you draw them in isolation, you are missing the opportunity to capture subtle distinctions. For example, before the nose can be accurately drawn frontally, you must determine the angulation in profile for tipping the nose upward or downward. **Drawing the reconstructed face by alternating from one view to the other view produces a more accurate drawing.**

The reconstruction drawings, frontal and lateral, are best accomplished by working on one view, switching to the other view, and then back again. **This encourages constant thinking, study, correction, and refinement of the morphological characteristics.**

It is important to **place emphasis on those features that are based on the strongest bony evidence and less emphasis on those that are not.** In some cases, the development of an anatomically correct feature is the best you can hope for.

I often attempt to build in certain **intentional ambiguities** in areas where limited information is determinable about a feature. For instance, since eyelid structure cannot be exactly determined, I might make one lid a bit heavier than the other to "cover all the bases." Similarly, eyebrows can be drawn with some variance, one from the other.

Caution should be taken against the over-rendering of two-dimensional reconstructions. By allowing artistic ego to interfere, **the artist risks adding incorrect information that may actually detract from the correct information and** *discourage* **recognition and identification.**

The following discussion of development of the individual features is based on a thorough search of the literature. Statements made by some sources are far better documented, tested, and proven than others. Some papers were based on small sample sizes, and assumptions were made after examining only a limited number of cadavers. My intent is to offer as many references as possible, although the artist should be aware that they may vary in validity. Hopefully, future anthropologists and anatomists will do dissections and other studies to make additional information available.

Drawing the Facial Contours

The facial outline as dictated by the bony forms of the skull should be observed. Note, too, the tissue depth indicators and simply **"connect the dots," drawing lightly around the contours of the cheeks, jaw, and chin.** Refer to the profile skull photo and note the location of tissue marker #16, midway on the zygomatic arch. Now locate marker #16 on the frontal skull photo. This will usually be the widest part of the face. In rare cases, if the zygomatic arches are very flattened, marker #17 might be the widest point.

Note also the location of tissue markers #19 and #21, above and below the 2nd molars. These indicators can be used as guides for shading the planes of the cheeks in the frontal view, with consideration given to the approximate weight in life if indicated by clothing, etc. In the lateral view, the cheeks should be formed with consideration given to the depth of markers #13 and #14. The **parotid gland** in front of the ear fills up the curve of the mandible. There is generally a **slight dip as you draw the jaw line just in front of the massater muscle.**

The bony forms of the chin and the **jaw at gonion** should be carefully observed, especially in males, since they provide clues to the surface look in life. Pronounced muscle attachments in these areas indicate more visible forms. Experience has taught that even though a chin may have two small projecting bony eminences, it is not possible to determine for sure that it would have appeared cleft in life, although it would probably have appeared squared. A chin with a strong bony mound in the center was probably rounded in life. Structural fat under the chin becomes more visible as the **platysma** relaxes with age.

Drawing of the facial contours as either firm or soft should be assessed based on the sex and age of the individual. Chapter 13 suggests that the sculptural reconstruction be done as if the individual were on the young side, then age it as needed after the sculpture is complete. **In two-dimensional facial reconstruction, it is suggested that you build in elements of age as you go along.** In addition, female faces should be drawn in a softer manner, with less harsh angles than male faces.

Drawing the Eyes

Leonardo da Vinci said of eyes, "Who would believe that so small a space could contain the images of all the universe?" In discerning such an important and individual feature from the skull alone, the forensic artist should make use of all available information and produce an anatomically feasible eye. There is some disagreement in the literature about prediction of eyes. Some believe that, at best, the artist can only draw an anatomically correct eye, properly situated in the bony orbit. Other sources indicate it may be more predictable.

The choice for **"color" of the eye**, which is actually represented as a tonal variation in the black-and-white drawing, must require some educated guesswork, basically "playing the odds." There may be very light blonde or red hair found with a body that suggests that the eyes be drawn on the light side. If there is very dark hair, especially Negroid in nature, the best bet would be darker eyes. Fortunately, with drawing, it is possible to shade the eyes in such a way that they are darker under the overhanging lid and light is caught in the lower part of the iris, and another "built-in ambiguity" can be achieved.

Placement of the Eyeball — Frontal View

In his "Rules of Thumb," Dr. Wilton Krogman specified a method of placement of the eyeball within the orbit:

> The apex of the cornea when viewed from norma frontalis, is at the juncture
> of two lines, one drawn from the medial edge of the orbit (maxillofrontale)

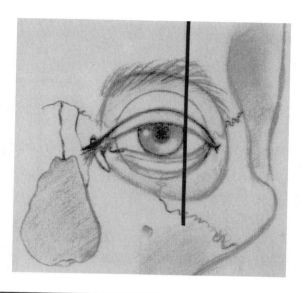

Figure 12.11 The **eyeball and iris** are centered in the bony orbit, with the eyeball measuring 25 mm and the iris 12 mm. A line indicates general correspondence between the lateral iris and the highest point of the **eyebrow**. (Illustration by KTT.)

to the lateral margin of the orbit (ectoconchion); and the other line bisecting the orbit between the superior and inferior margins.[14]

In simpler terms, **the eyeball should basically be centered in the orbit in the frontal view.** The ophthalmology texts indicate that the average adult **human eyeball is approximately 25 mm** or about 1 in. in diameter — the size of a U.S. quarter. Because we are working life-size, the quarter becomes a handy template for drawing the circular eyeball within the orbit. Figure 12.11 shows the placement of the eyeball and iris, centered in the orbit as indicated by Krogman.

Placement of the Eyeball — Lateral View

Referring to the placement of the eye in the lateral view, Krogman states:

The outer point of the cornea is approximately tangent to a centrally located line drawn from the superior and inferior margins of the orbit.[14]

The projection of the eyeball in profile view can be determined by drawing a light line from the top (and center) of the orbit to the bottom (and center) of the orbit. The profile eye should project to about that point. Note that tissue markers #12 and #13 should have been glued at those landmarks. Therefore, if markers #12 and #13 are correctly placed, the line to determine projection can be drawn from the base of marker #12 to the base of marker #13 (where the marker is glued to the bone). The quarter may also be used to trace the correct rounded shape for the lateral eyeball, even though only a small portion of the ball is seen once the lids are drawn (Figure 12.12).

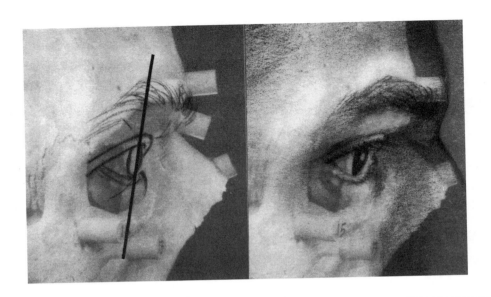

Figure 12.12 Placement of the **eyeball in the lateral view**, projecting tangent to a line drawn from the top of the orbit to the bottom. (Illustration by KTT.)

Consideration should also be given to the age of the person being drawn. The guidelines for the technique of facial reconstruction generally favor an age group from 25 to 35 years. With advancing age, some volume may be lost from the fat pads behind the eyes, so it is reasonable to draw the eyes more deeply set. The eyes of younger people may project a slight bit more than the average suggested by Krogman. These placements should be considered only general guidelines. Disease or medication may alter these placements.

Dr. Boris Fedosyutkin, with whom I worked during a 1990 visit to the Scientific Research Laboratory of the Criminalistics Center of the Ministry of Internal Affairs in Moscow, has stated that there is additional information for placement of the eyeball in profile. He believes that there is a correspondence between the depth of the conical orbit in the lateral view and the depth at which the eyeball rests. This seems logical anatomically, though we lack a standard from which to measure this deviation.[15]

Development of the Eye — Frontal View

The ophthalmology books also tell us that the diameter of the cornea for the average human eye can be considered rather constant. In *Textbook of Ophthalmology*, Dr. Francis Adler states, **"The diameter of the cornea in the adult eye averages 12 mm."**[16] Since the cornea and iris are very close in size, this dimension can be useful for drawing the iris within the eyeball. So, once the 25-mm eyeball itself is placed, pinpoint the center of the circle which is the placement for the pupil. Then draw a 12-mm iris centered in the circle of the eyeball.

Although some have indicated a vertical correspondence between the infraorbital foramen and the location of the pupil, I have checked this on many skulls while doing superimposition comparisons, and I do not believe it to be true. Placing the pupil in alignment with the foramen produces crossed eyes since the foramen occurs medial of the pupil location in most people.

From Chapters 3 and 4, we have an idea of the muscles surrounding the eyeball and the various anatomical structures that should be shown. The lids should be drawn to conform to the shape of the eyeball, clinging closely to it. **In almost all people, the lateral eye corner is a few millimeters higher than the medial corner.** This is a matter of practical design for drainage of tears. Although it may appear otherwise in some eyes, close observation will usually reveal that it is a laxity of overhanging tissue that causes this impression of a lower outer corner and not really the corner itself.

Some information is available to help locate the inner and outer corners of the eye and the resulting angulation of the palpebral opening. In his 1983 article, "The Points of Attachment of the Palpebral Ligaments: Their Use in Facial Reconstructions on the Skull," eminent forensic anthropologist Dr. T. Dale Stewart described sites for use in setting the frontal angle of the eye opening. Stewart quotes H. H. Wilder, who actually attributed the location of the malar or zygomatic tubercle to Samuel Ernest Whitnall, a demonstrator in human anatomy at Oxford in 1911:

> The position of the two canthi (angles, outer and inner, that form the corners of the eyeopening) is almost precisely determined, the inner by the naso-lacrymal duct (sic., lacrimal sac or fossa), and the outer by a slightly but definitely indicated "malar tubercle," to which attention has recently been directed by Whitnall.[17]

Figure 12.13 shows an illustration from this article depicting the two points used for location of the lateral and medial canthi of the eye. Note that while the points do not precisely locate the exact location of the eye corners, they provide an understanding of the general placement and direction of travel (under the skin) of the ligaments at the inner and outer aspects of the upper eyelids that help create the eye corners. In other words, if you actually drew the eye corners at these points, they would be out on the bone at each side of the eye instead of inside the orbit as they must be.

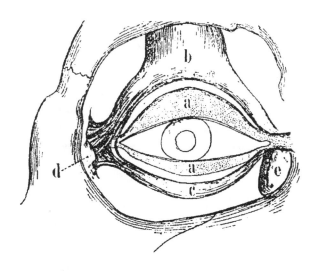

Figure 12.13 Drawing used in an article by **T. Dale Stewart**, locating the lateral and medial canthi of the eye. (Courtesy of T. Dale Stewart.)

Medial or Inner Corner — The suggestion is that the inner corner be located by observing the lacrimal area. **The palpebral ligament that extends from the stiff tarsal plate in the upper lid to help form the inner eye corner attaches to the nasal bones, spreading U-shaped to either side of the lacrimal sac or fossa.** According to Stewart, the inner eye corner should occur approximately 10 mm down from dacryon (Da) which is the point of junction of the frontal, maxillary, and lacrimal bones on the medial wall of the orbit.

Lateral or Outer Corner — The lateral or outer eye corner may be determined in many skulls by first locating the tubercle mentioned by Whitnall and Stewart. This "Whitnall's tubercle" or malar tubercle cannot be located in all skulls, but I have found it in quite a few. It is necessary to gently rub your finger just inside the outer orbital opening, a few millimeters back inside. Many times, this tiny rise or bump can be felt and located. **The palpebral ligament, which extends from the stiff tarsal plate in the upper lid to help form the outer corner of the eye, attaches to this small tubercle** (see Figure 12.14).

Always bear in mind the age, race, and sex of the individual as you draw the eyes and the surrounding area. If you are drawing a face with an open mouth to depict some unique trait of the dentition, the eyes may also need to be adjusted to coincide with degree of smiling expression used on the face.

Development of the Eye — Lateral View

As the eyes are drawn in profile, remember that the lids actually wrap around the eyeball and disappear into the inner corner of the eye where they cannot be seen. **The outer corner of the eye cannot come outside the bony orbital opening.** The bony orbit is designed to protect the eyeball, so the eyeball must therefore rest inside it for this to work. In people with very loose tissue at the outer corners of the eye, the skin may appear to be outside the orbit, but the eyeball itself is inside.

As you develop the profile eye, it will become apparent how deep the eyes are set and the amount of the side of the nasal bones will be obvious.

Drawing the Eyebrows

A very common mistake in both two- and three-dimensional facial reconstructions is the tendency to place the eyebrows much too high above the eyes. In some cases, the brows are placed totally above the superior margins of the bony orbits of the eyes. This produces a surprised, "Lucille Ball" sort of expression.

For both males and females, the brows must bear at least some correspondence to the orbital margins, although this usually varies somewhat by sex. Of course, if the eyebrows were altered in life, such as by plucking, this is impossible to predict.

As with most areas of reconstruction, a reasonable judgment must be made based on a combination of all the known factors. If dark, thick, wavy hair is recovered with the skeletal body, darker, fuller brows would make sense. If thin, blond hair is found, more sparse, light brows would be a logical guess. Negroid eyebrow hair is often curly, corresponding to the head hair.

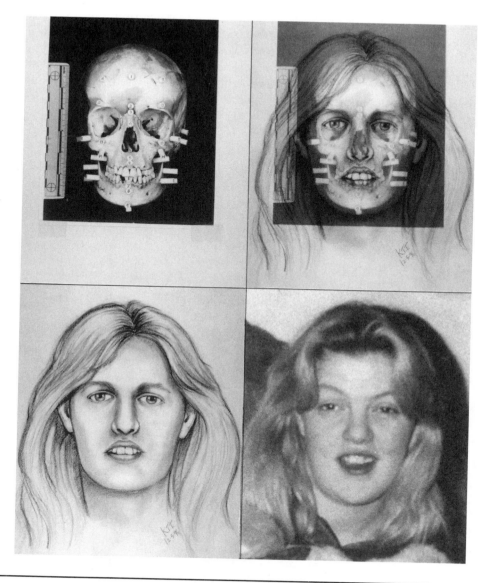

Figure 12.14 Skull (upper left), **two-dimensional facial reconstruction** by KTT with skull visible beneath (upper right), two-dimensional facial reconstruction (lower left), and subject identified (lower right). **Note that because the small tubercles within the bony orbits were rather low, the lateral eye corners were drawn accordingly, which was true of the subject's eyes in life.** (Courtesy of Texas Department of Public Safety.)

Figure 12.11 shows a vertical line drawn from the lateral iris upward. There is some correspondence in many people between the outer side of the iris and the highest point of the eyebrow, although it is variable.

Males

Male eyebrows in general tend to be heavier than female. They also tend to start at the medial side, slightly tucked under the margin or the orbit, then proceed laterally up along the orbital margin and end slightly above and wrapping around the lateral side. Figure 12.15 shows an average pattern for male brows in correspondence to the orbit. (The top photo also shows a small black mark tracing around the malar or "Whitnall's" tubercle.) Figure 12.16 shows an individual with a strongly projecting and masculine brow ridge. In the lateral view, with such an obvious bony element, the structure itself becomes more important than the superficial hair.

Females

The female brows can only be drawn in conjunction with any hair specimens recovered. If no hair specimen is available, the best approach is to downplay the brows rather than make a strong statement.

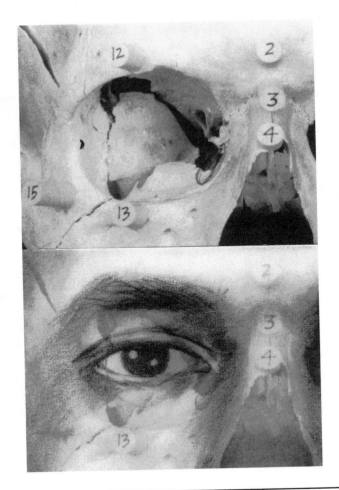

Figure 12.15 Male **eyebrows** as they generally correspond to the superior margin of the bony orbit. (Illustration by KTT.)

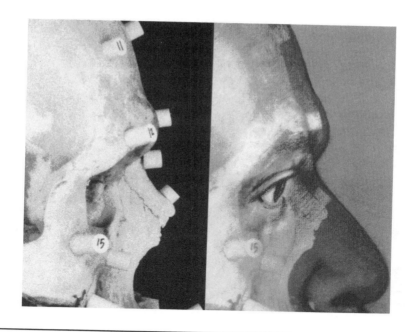

Figure 12.16 Lateral view of a **projecting male brow ridge.** (Illustration by KTT.)

In general, female brows are thinner and more arching than male brows, and often rise a bit higher. There is often a greater distance between the inner corners of the female brows than in the male, but this varies according to the eye width or interorbital breadth of the individual skull. Again, the age of the person should be considered since the brows drop somewhat with age, as shown in the illustrations in Chapter 8.

Drawing the Nose

The nose is based specifically on the individual skull to be reconstructed. While there are certain "rules of thumb" for nose projection, it is the skull itself that dictates the needed information. In observing the "hits" examples in this text, you will note that the nose is usually the most accurate feature. The basis for the method of nose prediction used is derived from Krogman. Hopefully, the nasal spine is intact since it is so important for development of the nose. It is beneficial to look at it with a magnifying glass to see if a portion has been broken off. **If the nasal spine is missing, the prediction of the nose will be far more speculative.**

Frontal View

Krogman gave a simple-to-use formula to predict the soft tissue nasal width based upon the bony piriform aperture. **For Caucasoids, the nasal aperture is measured at its widest point, then 10 mm are added to get the total width** (5 mm should be added to each side of the aperture for a total of 10 mm). **For Negroids, the nasal aperture is measured at its widest point, then 16 mm are added to get the total width** (8 mm should be added to each side of the nasal aperture for a total of 16 mm).

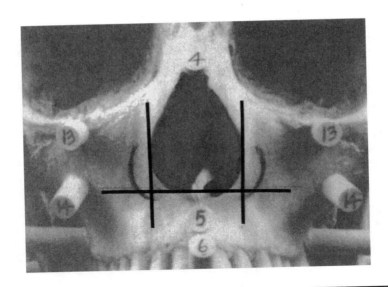

Figure 12.17 Measuring the nasal aperture at its widest point to determine the width of the nose. (Illustration by KTT.)

Since Krogman gave no formula for Mongoloids, the widths for Caucasoids and Negroids can be averaged for a "best guess."

Figure 12.17 shows this simple approach to ascertain nasal width (see also Figure 13.23 in Chapter 13). The overall shape of the piriform opening should be observed including the angulation of the base or nasal sill. **The ala or wing at each side of the nose must attach below the aperture in order for the person to have breathed in life.** This distance is usually approximately 4 or 5 mm.

It has been suggested that there is a rough correspondence between the nasal width and the canine fossa at each side. In other words, if you extended an imaginary line upward from root of each cuspid or canine tooth, you would have the approximate width of the nose.

Figure 12.18 shows three shapes of nasal apertures (below) and the corresponding nose types (above). As previously stated, **it is always necessary to consult the lateral view, particularly the angulation of the anterior nasal spine to determine the placement of the tip in the frontal view.** In Figure 12.18, the nose at the left would have an upturned anterior nasal spine, the nose in the center would have a straight out anterior nasal spine, and the nose at the right would have a downward projecting anterior nasal spine.

Figure 12.19 shows a detail of the nose area in a young homicide female victim identified from the facial reconstruction. Although it is not a perfect likeness, there is a **correspondence between the angulation of the base of the nasal aperture and the attachment of the wings.** Although I have found no anatomical documentation or study of this, I have observed it on several cases that have been identified and compared (see Figure 12.50). In the facial reconstruction of this young girl, her left ala was drawn subtly lower than the right, which is visible in the life photo, even though her face was tilted back in the photo.

Figure 12.20 shows a close-up of the eye–nose complex of another young woman identified from the facial reconstruction. In this case, the nasal sill is relatively level as was the woman's in life (see also Figure 11.13 in Chapter 11).

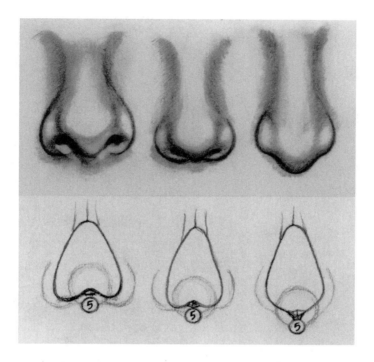

Figure 12.18   Various shapes of nasal apertures (below) and the corresponding nose types (above). (Illustration by KTT.)

My personal observation is that **a reasonable assumption may be made with regard to the shape of the nasal spine in relation to the shape of the tip of the nose.** Although the nose tip is composed of cartilage, it makes sense that a slight, pointed anterior nasal spine was designed to support a slight, pointed soft tissue nasal tip. On the other hand, a very sturdy, broad nasal tip may have been designed to bear the load of a bulkier soft tissue nasal tip. A bifurcated nasal spine may indicate a more visibly dual-lobed soft tissue nasal tip, with a discernible split between the lower cartilages. My own identified cases seem to bear this out, although there has been no formal study (see Figure 12.33).

To determine the lateral view of the nose, the reconstructionist must have a clear understanding of how to measure an anterior nasal spine. Because this is such an issue of misunderstanding and error for many people, effort has been made here to convey this point very clearly. Figure 12.21 shows a simple diagram of the frontal bony nasal aperture and the structures that must be understood to correctly measure the anterior nasal spine. You must first observe the vomer or root of the spine. The vomer inside the nasal cavity is the attachment for the septal cartilage in life. **The point at which the vomer ends is where the nasal spine begins. Measure the nasal spine from the juncture of the vomer to the tip of the spine.** Figure 12.22 shows the measurement of the anterior nasal spines in two different skulls clearly showing this distinction between vomer and nasal spine. Figure 12.23 shows the measurement of the anterior nasal spines in three skulls where the distinction between vomer and nasal spine is more difficult to see.

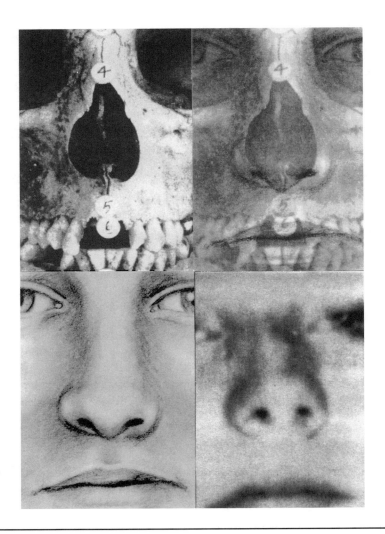

Figure 12.19 Detail of the frontal nose of an identified homicide victim showing correspondence between the **angulation of the base of the nasal aperture** and the attachment of the wings of the nose. Note that the victim's face was angled back in the lower right photo. (Courtesy of Texas Department of Public Safety.)

Lateral View

Krogman also gave a formula for prediction of the soft tissue nose projection laterally based upon measurement of the bony anterior nasal spine. First, **the nasal spine is measured** as described above. **That length is then multiplied by 3 and added to the depth of tissue depth marker #5.** As Krogman stated, **the nose projection is from subnasale to pronasale, approximately three times the length of the nasal spine.**

Figure 12.24 shows three lateral views of anterior nasal spines — one projecting upward (left), one straight outward (center), and one projecting downward (right) — as indicated by the small arrows. This angulation should be carefully observed before drawing the lateral nose.

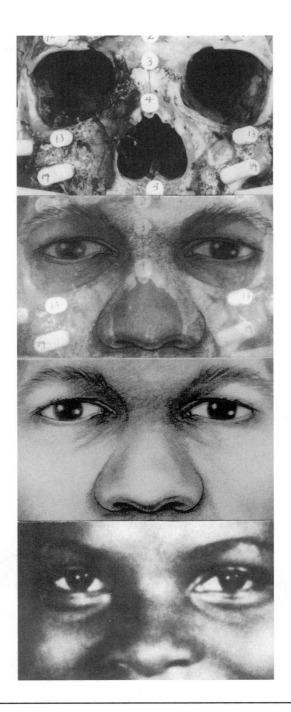

Figure 12.20 Detail of the frontal **eye–nose area** of an identified homicide victim. (Courtesy of Texas Department of Public Safety.)

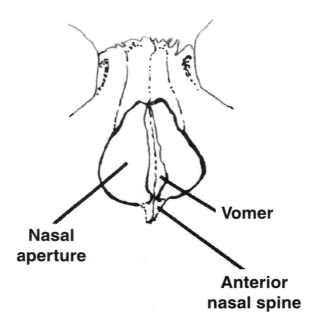

Figure 12.21 Diagram of the frontal bony nasal aperture. (Illustration by KTT.)

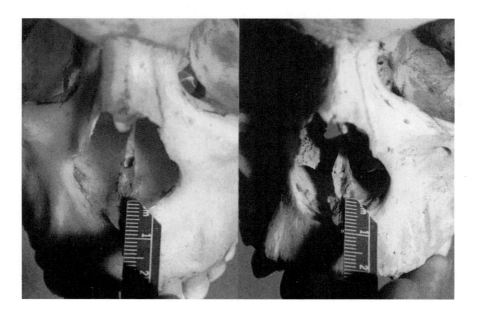

Figure 12.22 Measurement of the anterior nasal spine on two skulls in which the distinction between the vomer and nasal spine is clear. (Photo by Missey Micheletti.)

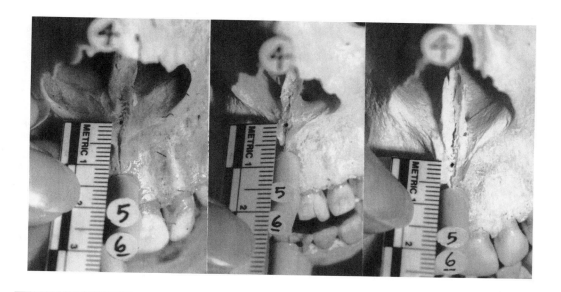

Figure 12.23   Measurement of the anterior nasal spine in three skulls in which the distinction between vomer and nasal spine is less clear. (Photo by Missey Micheletti.)

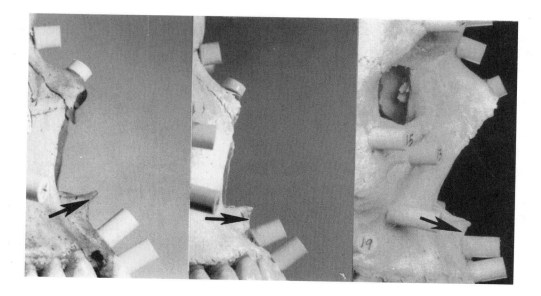

Figure 12.24   Lateral views of **three anterior nasal spines**; projecting upward (left), straight outward (center), and projecting downward (right). (Photo by Missey Micheletti.)

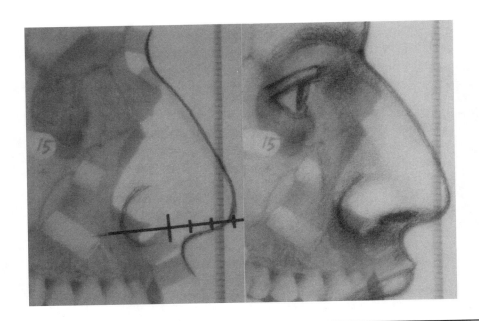

Figure 12.25   Use of Krogman's formula to predict the lateral nose. (Illustration by KTT.)

Figure 12.25 shows the use of Krogman's formula to predict the lateral nose. First, the overall direction of the nasal spine is observed and a line is drawn to show the general angulation. I sometimes think of the lateral nasal spine like an "arrow" pointing in a certain direction. The depth of tissue depth marker #5 is transferred to the line of angulation. Then the measurement of the nasal spine, times 3, is added to come off #5 depth. Depending upon the degree of tipping upward or downward of the spine and the form of the maxillary area to which #5 is glued, it is sometimes a bit tricky to transfer the #5 depth to the projected line, and a best estimate must be used.

A couple of other factors should be considered when developing the lateral nose. **The C-shaped form of the alar groove does not rest directly on top of the side of the nasal aperture,** as is seen in many reconstructions. **It actually sits downward and forward of the C-shape created by the side of the aperture.** I learned this point from Dr. Robert George's 1987 paper, "The Lateral Craniographic Method of Facial Reconstruction."[18]

The reconstruction artist should carefully observe the curved form of the lateral maxilla, just under the anterior nasal spine. It makes sense that, although the soft tissue is full in this upper lip area, it must bear some resemblance in shape to the bony maxillary form underneath.

Figures 12.26 and 12.27 show lateral drawings of two females with upturned nasal spines. Note the distinctively feminine and Negro characteristic of frontal "bossing" of the forehead in Figure 12.26. Figure 12.28 shows a lateral drawing of a male with a down-turned nasal spine.

Reconstructionists in Russia and elsewhere have used a method of lateral nose determination that calls for the projection of two lines, one coming off the nasal bones and the other off the anterior nasal spine, as shown in Figure 12.29. The nose tip is placed according to the convergence of these two lines. With this method it is difficult

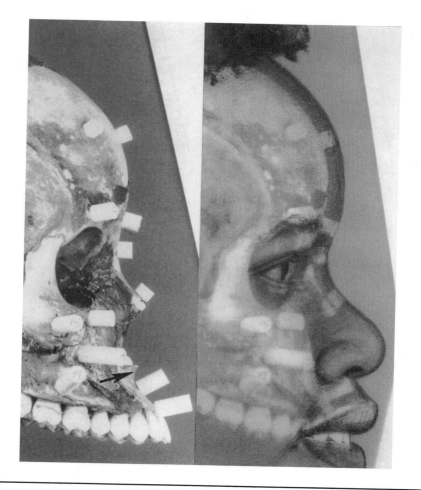

Figure 12.26 Lateral reconstruction drawing of female with **upturned nasal spine** and **frontal bossing** of the forehead. (Illustration by KTT.)

to accurately predict a nose with a hump because this occurs in people with long nasal bones and short nasal spines.

Some have suggested a correspondence between the lateral shape of the nasal aperture and the lateral shape of the tip of the nose, using a sort of mirror image to arrive at the shape of the tip from the aperture shape. I know of no in-depth studies on this, but it does not appear to have any sound basis in anatomy.

Drawing the Mouth

As described in Chapter 11, before gluing the mandible to the cranium, a careful look at the dentition and the occlusion should be the first steps in assessing the mouth. Figure 12.30 shows how varying dental occlusions can greatly affect the shape of the lips and mouth, both in the frontal and the lateral views. **It is advantageous to consult a dental specialist if possible for suggestions as to the type of mouth that might have been created to conform around a particular dentition.**

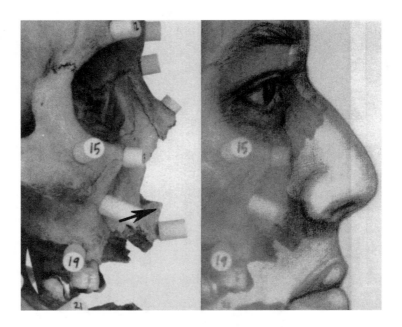

Figure 12.27 Lateral reconstruction drawing of female with an **upturned nasal spine**. (Illustration by KTT.)

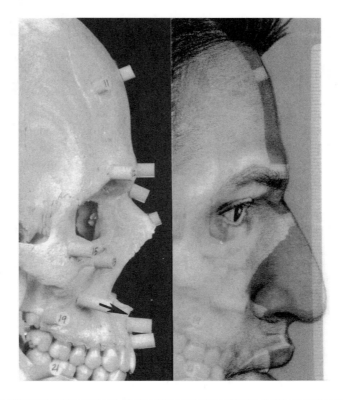

Figure 12.28 Lateral reconstruction drawing of a male with a **downturned nasal spine**. (Illustration by KTT.)

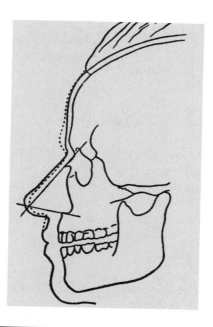

Figure 12.29 Russian method of lateral nose projection determination.

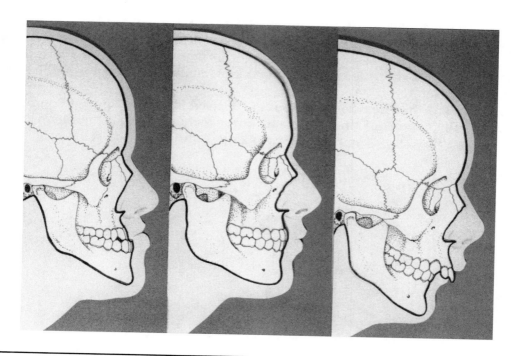

Figure 12.30 Three dental occlusions that produce very different lip and mouth shapes. (Illustration by KTT.)

As previously stated, the mouth is an area that readily conveys facial expression because there are at least seven muscles in that area involved in the production of expressions. In *Facial Expression*, Gary Faigin describes these muscles:

> As a minute or two in front of the mirror will demonstrate, the mouth is capable of being stretched, squeezed, or curled into just about any shape. Obviously, it requires quite a muscular network to allow us to do all those funny things with the mouth.
>
> … zygomatic major, [is] the smiling muscle. There is also levator labii superioris, the sneering muscle; triangularis and mentalis, which work as a team to bend the mouth downward; risorius/platysma, which elongates the lips; depressor labii inferioris, which pulls the lower lip downward; and orbicularis oris, the muscle of the lips, which presses both lips together.[19]

Frontal View

Krogman's "Rule of Thumb" for mouth width was stated as "the distance between two lines radiating out from the junction of the canine and the first premolar on each side."[20] This means that, basically, **the width of the mouth is determined by measuring the front six teeth.** Figure 12.31 shows the application of this formula in drawing form. Two lines indicate the mouth width. Note that Krogman's landmark guides for the mouth corners reside *between* the canines and first premolars. Since the mouth forms an arc over the dental arch, these corners can be interpreted as extending outward a bit in width in the drawing. In workshops, I stress that although we should follow this general formula for drawing the mouth width, it is equally important to **think about the age, race, and sex of the individual as you draw the mouth.** The figure shows two outlines for mouths covering the front six teeth, one drawn conservatively for a Caucasoid person and the other drawn more fully for a Negroid person.

    The vertical thickness for the mouth is derived by measuring the combined height of the enamel of the upper and lower teeth. The distinct textural change between the tooth enamel and the cementum or root area usually causes a slight ridge.

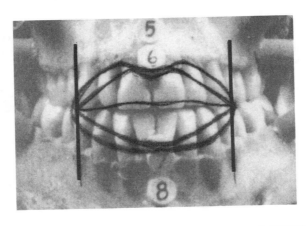

Figure 12.31 The mouth width is determined by measuring the front six teeth. The mouth should also be drawn with the race, sex, and age of the individual in mind. (Illustration by KTT.)

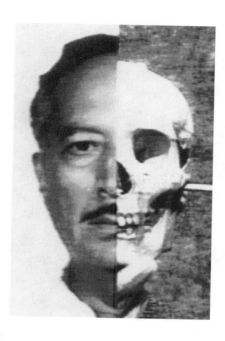

Figure 12.32 Superimposition of face and skull, revealing an average **relationship between the teeth and the parting line of the lips.** (Courtesy of Texas Department of Public Safety.)

Dentists refer to this location as the cementum enamel junction (CEJ). Another way of stating this vertical distance is **upper CEJ to lower CEJ**.

The placement of the parting line of the lips is somewhat variable according to dental structure and age. A pretty good **average placement of the parting line of the lips is slightly above the edges of the upper central incisors.** Figure 12.32 shows a superimposition of face and skull identified to be one and the same. The parting line of the lips is a little bit above the bottoms of the upper incisors. As we age the lip drops and the vermilion area thins a bit, and the central incisors may then be totally covered by the upper lip.

Figure 12.33 is a detailed enlargement of the nose–mouth area of a woman identified from a two-dimensional reconstruction, showing the use of Krogman's formula for prediction of the mouth. Note that it was speculated that due to a broad nasal spine, there might be a bulbous nasal tip, a feature that can be confirmed in the life photograph (see also Figure 1.4 in Chapter 1).

If there is something unique about the anterior dentition and the decision is made to draw an open mouth, **great care should be taken to draw the teeth exactly correctly.** After all, our teeth are the only part of our skulls that people who know us in life have ever actually seen. If you are fortunate enough to get a case in which the frontal teeth have been recovered, be certain to draw them accurately. Figure 12.34 shows a male mouth drawn with teeth showing. Figure 12.35 shows a female mouth (see also Figure 12.14). It is sometimes helpful to go through mug photos, if accessible, and attempt to find a person with dentition similar to that of the skull you are reconstructing. The way in which the lips form around a similar dental structure can then be studied to help with your prediction.

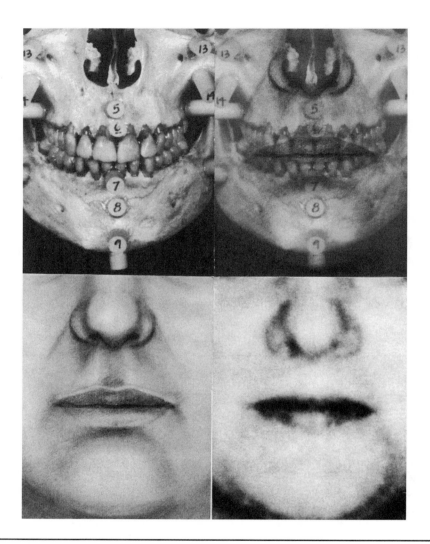

Figure 12.33 Detail of the frontal **nose–mouth area** of an identified homicide victim. (Courtesy of Texas Department of Public Safety.)

The **philtrum** or depressed area above the vermilion upper lip seems to have some correspondence to the angulation of the roots of the maxillary central incisors. If the roots are vertically placed in parallel fashion, the philtrum may be squarish. If the roots are angled medially, the philtrum may be more rectangular.

Lateral View

The lateral mouth should be drawn consistently with the frontal mouth. As with the other features, they should be worked back and forth, from frontal drawing to lateral drawing. Locate the point between the canine and the first premolar for the placement of the lateral corner of the mouth, which is usually dropped a bit. The tissue depths at #5, #6, and #7 indicate the general depth of the lip area. The vertical

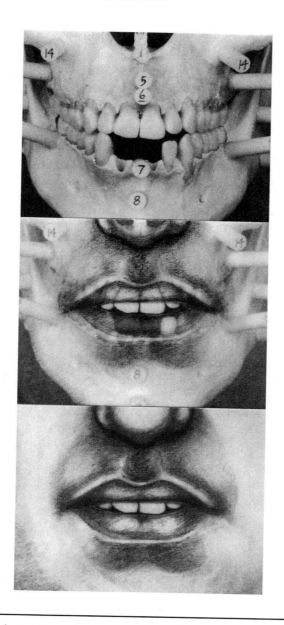

Figure 12.34 Detail of a male mouth drawn with the **teeth** showing. (Illustration by KTT.)

dimension of the lips from CEJ to CEJ can also be used in the lateral view as can the suggestion for placement of the parting line between the lips.

The structure of the individual skull and the accompanying dentition must then determine the "look" of the lateral mouth–chin area (Figure 12.30). Figure 12.36 shows the reconstructed lateral mouth of an elderly individual who wore only an upper denture. A few millimeters of clay were used to allow for the spacing to simulate gum tissue. The "over-closed" condition due to absent mandibular dentition caused the chin to be thrust forward. The lips were drawn as quite thin.

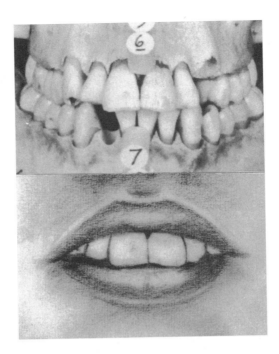

Figure 12.35 Detail of a female mouth with the **teeth** showing. (Illustration by KTT.)

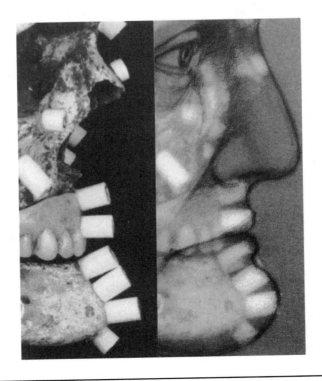

Figure 12.36 Reconstructed lateral mouth of an **elderly individual** who wore only an **upper denture**. (Courtesy of Texas Department of Public Safety.)

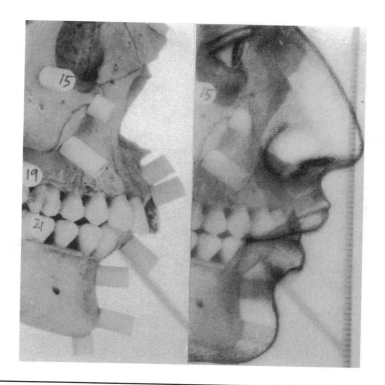

Figure 12.37   Reconstructed lateral mouth of a **young person** with **a problematic overbite**. (Courtesy of Texas Department of Public Safety.)

Figure 12.37 shows the reconstructed lateral mouth of a young person with full dentition and a problematic overbite. The lips were drawn as full and youthful. It was speculated that a bit of the upper dentition would be revealed, due to the nature of the bite.

Drawing the Ears

Since the ears are composed primarily of cartilage, we know little about how they will look. The best bet is to draw an anatomically correct ear structurally, which is correctly placed. Our best guide on the skull, of course, is the external auditory meatus, and the soft tissue ear rests on top of this bony landmark (see Figure 12.38). **The ear must reside behind the angle of the jaw,** although it is surprising how many profile drawings depict an ear up on the cheek! **The average ear sits at an angle, resting backward about 15°.** The ears attach rather closely at the anterior or front portion and tip out or away further from the head at the back portion. In other words, they **should not appear to be glued to the head.** In many people, there is about one "finger" of space between the back of the ear and the head. The tragus rests over the bony auditory meatus blending into the cheek area.

An artistic canon says that ears are roughly equal in length to the nose. With this in mind, you may wish to adjust the ear length to correspond to the finished length of the nose in your reconstruction. Remember, too, that the ears elongate with age and the pull of gravity.

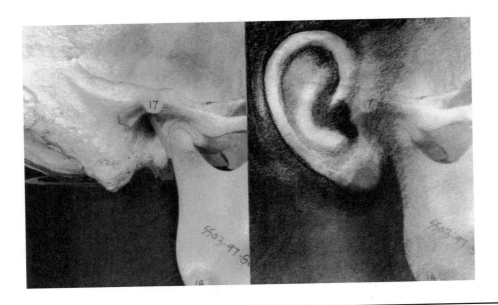

Figure 12.38 Correct placement of the **lateral ear** over the external auditory meatus. (Illustration by KTT.)

A personal observation, though untested, is that **there may be some correspondence between the mastoid processes and the degree of visible projection of the ears.** It seems logical to me that in skulls that are wide across the back and that have pronounced mastoid processes, the ears are more likely to be seen from the front. Conversely, skulls that are wide in the cheek area and narrower across the back would produce ears that are less visible from the front. This is true for many African-American males who have broad zygomatics and strong cheeks, but who are narrow from mastoid process to mastoid process, so their ears hardly show from the front.

Drawing the Hair

It is a real bonus when hair is recovered with a skeletal body at the scene because hair often provides valuable information to the artist. It is just as likely, if not more likely, that no hair at all will be recovered.

As we discussed in Chapter 9, the head hair sloughs off fairly early in the process during which the body becomes skeletal. Sometimes it is found as a large mass at the base of the skull if the body is found after decomposition has occurred and has not been disturbed by scavengers or other natural factors. The hair may also be recovered some distance from the body, displaced by birds, animals, wind, rain, or some other means.

Ideally, any recovered hair is evaluated by laboratory personnel and a report of their findings is made available to the artist. Determinations may be made regarding color, length, and textural quality of the hair. Microscopically, it may be possible to determine if the hair has been chemically altered with color or perms. When an experienced examiner views the hair, it may be possible to make certain assessments about the race of the individual as well. Sometimes the artist is provided with a hair sample to aid in reconstruction.

When I first receive a skull, I always look closely for any possible hairs that might be clinging in any of the sutures. On a couple of occasions, I have found short, thick hairs inside the nasal aperture, which our laboratory personnel determined were mustache hairs. When faced with a skull and a report stating that no hair was found, you are delighted to find just one!

When the scene is processed by an experienced anthropologist, he or she may look in some seemingly peculiar, yet logical places in hopes of finding hair or teeth, depending on the terrain. My friend and colleague Dr. Glassman may check the dwellings of mice or other rodents on the ground or bird nests in trees. Apparently, hair makes great nests.

If no hair is available, artistic decisions then must be made. Many years ago, I had the idea that **showing multiple versions** would be a good idea. It is a very easy matter in two-dimensional reconstruction to use matte acetate to produce multiple varying hairstyles, or variations in facial hair (Figure 12.39). I can also quite easily scan a reconstruction into a computer graphics software and produce multiple looks. Experience revealed that this probably was **not the best approach** and that it **created a great deal of confusion**. Figure 12.40 shows two versions of the same reconstruction that vary, yet are not too confusing.

In cases with no hair, I now feel that it is preferable to produce one primary image with intentional ambiguity built into the look of the hair. An advantage of the two-dimensional method is that the hair may be either downplayed altogether or drawn in such a way that it is a bit straight on one side and a bit wavy on the other (see Figure 12.47). A few strands may fall on the forehead on one side only and the top of the hair is drawn so that there is no strongly distinct part. There is intentional streaking of the gray tones with darks in the underlying areas such as beside the neck. Lighter values are used where the light would naturally fall. By building strong contrast into the values of the hair, the viewer can read it as either light or dark.

Figure 12.39 The same facial reconstruction shown in **two versions of "coloring,"** which may cause confusion. (Courtesy of Texas Department of Public Safety.)

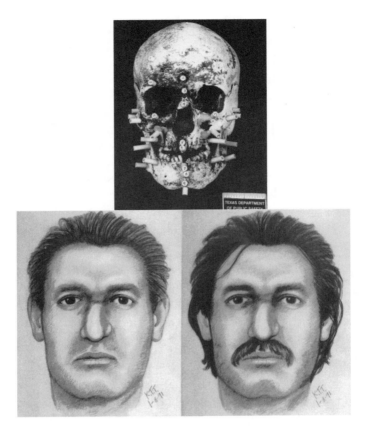

Figure 12.40   The same facial reconstruction shown in **two versions** which are not so different as to create confusion. (Courtesy of Texas Department of Public Safety.)

Drawing the Neck

As with other features, the neck should be developed so that it is consistent with all known information about the individual. Insights from the anthropologist concerning age, stature, and muscular robustness should be included. Clothing recovered with the remains, particularly a shirt with a readable collar size, should be considered.

The size of the mastoid processes should be considered, since the strong sterno-cleidomastoid muscles of the neck come off of these processes. Figure 12.41 shows a strongly drawn male neck due to the robustness of the mastoid processes. Also shown are the strong muscle attachments at gonion, indicating a strongly defined angle of the jaw in the reconstruction.

Other Details

Various other details, if available, may be included in the facial reconstruction drawing, such as glasses, jewelry, hats, or other hair accoutrements. Such details may be included directly as part of the reconstruction or they may be accomplished as additional side

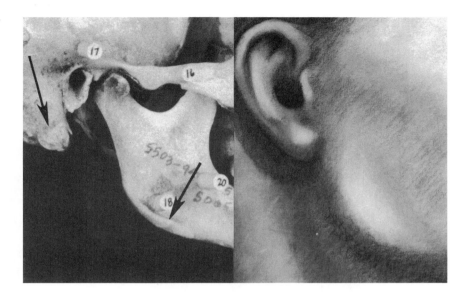

Figure 12.41 Strongly drawn **male neck** due to the robustness of the mastoid processes. Also indicated by muscle attachments at gonion is a strongly defined **angle of the jaw**. (Illustration by KTT.)

drawings. Figure 12.42 shows dresses found with two skeletal bodies, which were drawn and circulated in bulletins along with the facial drawings.

Copying for Distribution

To copy the facial reconstructions for distribution, you must place an 11" × 14" sheet of opaque drawing paper between the skull photograph and the reconstruction drawing on vellum so that the skull does not show through. I also find it helpful to slide a piece of paper in and out in this fashion as the drawings are in progress.

On a good quality copy machine, reproduction may be made *without* an opaque sheet so that the drawing may be studied as it relates to the skull photo below. Both the underlying skull photo and the corresponding reconstruction drawing will reproduce jointly (see Figures 12.14, 12.47, 12.48, and 12.50).

Case Examples

Assessment of the reconstructions with photographs of the person in life teaches the forensic artist a great deal for use in future cases. The artist should attempt to obtain comparison life photographs, in various views if possible, since a study of each individual feature may lead to useful information.

Unfortunately, good quality photographs for comparison may be difficult to obtain. Some comparisons prove astonishingly close while others may be rather disappointing to the artist. It seems, however, that **for the friends or loved ones of a missing person, there is some nebulous quality in a face, represented implicitly in a**

Figure 12.42   Dresses found with two skeletal bodies which were drawn and circulated along with the facial reconstructions. (Courtesy of Texas Department of Public Safety.)

reconstruction, that somehow triggers the inquiry that leads to identification. If this occurs, and the case can be resolved, then the reconstruction was a success.

Figures 12.43 through 12.50 show reconstructions in cases that led to information that allowed victims to be positively identified.

Figures 12.48 and 12.49 show a case in which an anatomical canon derived from Farkas and Munro (as described by Dr. Robert George[20]) was used to replicate the mouth of the woman in life. The mouth area of the skull was so badly damaged that there was no information to predict the mouth. First, the eyes were developed within the bony orbits and the approximate placement of the outer corners of the eyes was established. The anatomical landmark for the outer eye corners is known as Ecto-canthion (Ec). **The facial triangle** canon dictates that an equilateral triangle is created

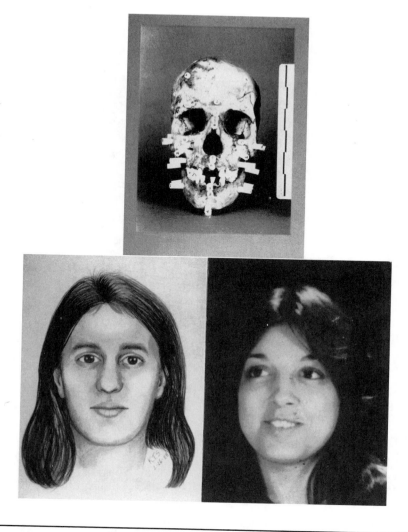

Figure 12.43 Skull (top), **two-dimensional facial reconstruction** by KTT (lower left), and subject identified (lower right). (Courtesy of Texas Department of Public Safety.)

from Ec to Ec to Li, which is the midpoint on the vermilion border of the lower lip.[20] Thus, I was able to place the eyes, then draw the triangle and determine a reasonable placement for the lower lip, even though the bone in that area was missing. When she was identified, the placement was quite accurate (Figure 12.49).

While the process of two-dimensional facial reconstruction from the skull is not an exact or a perfect one, it is a way of visually creating enough of a likeness to identify bodies that might otherwise go unidentified altogether. By leading to the identification of numerous victims of violent death, it has served its intended purpose.

Anyone who has experienced the loss of a loved one, particularly the absolute disappearance without a trace, understands why those of us in identification work make these attempts to determine the identity and fate of each individual.

This process has merit if only a limited number of reconstructions of deceased victims results in families experiencing the relief of knowing what happened to their loved ones.

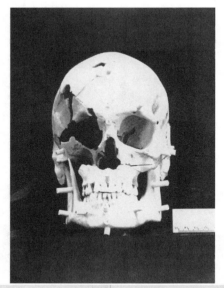

Figure 12.44 Skull (top), **two-dimensional facial reconstruction** by KTT (lower left), and subject identified (lower right); **beard hair was found in decomposing tissue removed from the skull.** (Courtesy of Texas Department of Public Safety.)

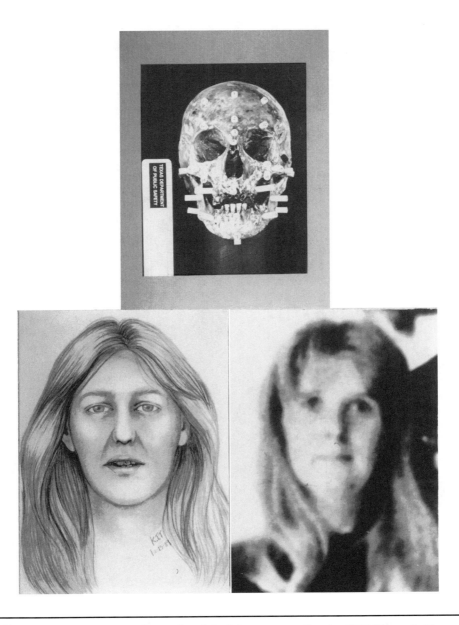

Figure 12.45 Skull (top), **two-dimensional facial reconstruction** by KTT (lower left), and subject identified (lower right); **long blond hair was recovered with the skeletal body.** (Courtesy of Texas Department of Public Safety.)

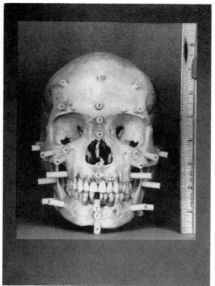

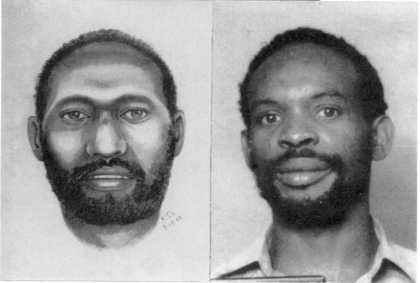

Figure 12.46 Skull (top), **two-dimensional facial reconstruction** by KTT (lower left), and subject identified (lower right); **precisely placed facial hair was recovered from duct tape used to wrap around the victim's head and suffocate him**. (Courtesy of Texas Department of Public Safety.)

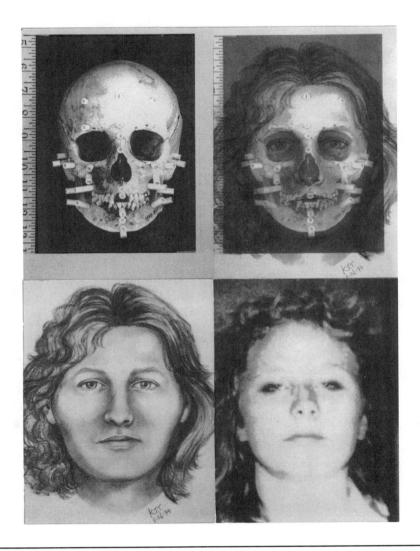

Figure 12.47 Skull (upper left), **two-dimensional facial reconstruction** by KTT with skull visible beneath (upper right), two-dimensional facial reconstruction (lower left), and subject identified (lower right). **No hair was recovered so it was drawn with built-in ambiguity.** (Courtesy of Texas Department of Public Safety.)

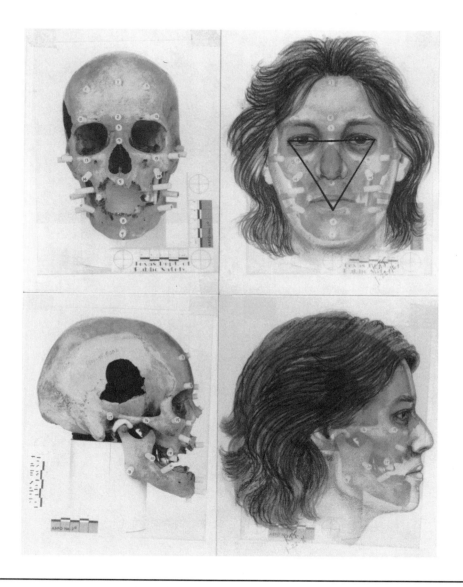

Figure 12.48 Frontal skull (upper left) and lateral skull (lower left), **facial triangle** used to locate the mouth (upper right), and lateral **two-dimensional facial reconstruction** by KTT (lower right). (Courtesy of Texas Department of Public Safety.)

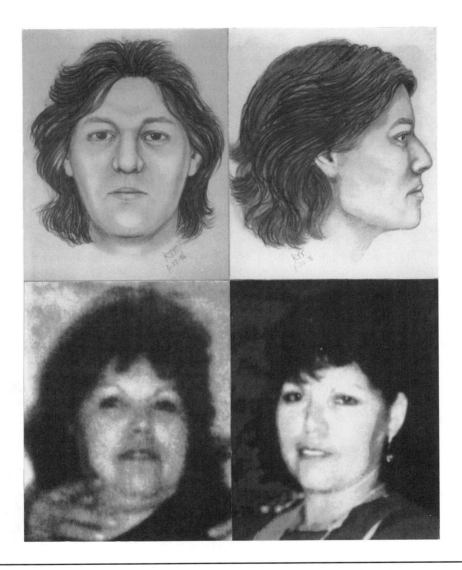

Figure 12.49 Frontal and lateral **two-dimensional facial reconstructions** by KTT (upper left and right), and victim identified shown at different ages and weights (lower left and right). (Courtesy of Texas Department of Public Safety.)

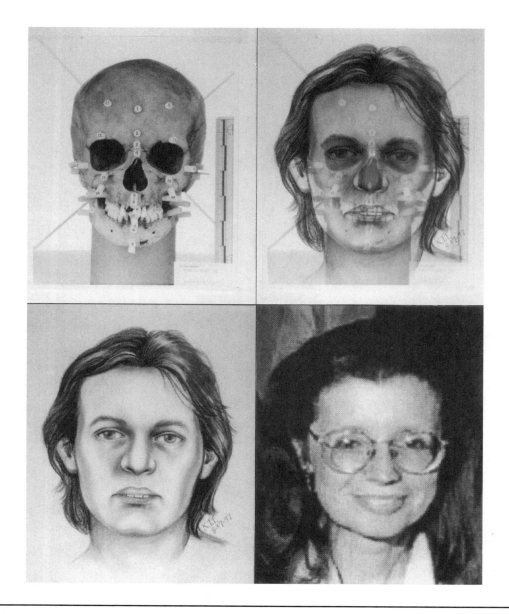

Figure 12.50 Skull (upper left), **two-dimensional facial reconstruction** by KTT with skull visible beneath (upper right), two-dimensional facial reconstruction (lower left), and subject identified (lower right). (Courtesy of Texas Department of Public Safety.)

References

1. Bridgman, G. B., *Constructive Anatomy (1920)*. New York: Dover Publications, 1973.
2. Maples, W. R. and Browning, M., *Dead Men Do Tell Tales*. New York: Doubleday, 1994.
3. Krogman, W. M., "The reconstruction of the living head from the skull," *FBI Law Enforcement Bulletin*, July 1946, 11–18.
4. Homa, G., *The Law Enforcement Composite Sketch Artist*. Berlin, NJ: Community Graphics, 1983.
5. Buckley, H., New York State Police, personal communication, 1987.
6. Angel, J. L. and Cherry, D., "Personality reconstruction from unidentified remains," *FBI Law Enforcement Bulletin*, August 1977, 12–15.
7. Angel, J. L. "Graphic reproduction of head and face from the skull," *Scientific Illustration — 1986, Selected papers from the 7th Annual Conference of the Guild of Natural Science Illustrators*, Washington, D.C., 1986.
8. Walters, E., "Law enforcement art: from bone to recognition," *Law and Order*, December 1985, 40–43.
9. Caldwell, P., "Instructions for Creating Two-Dimensional Facial Reproduction," Handout for Training Purposes.
10. George, R., "The lateral craniographic method of facial reconstruction," *Journal of Forensic Sciences*, 32, 1305–1330, September 1987.
11. Taylor, K., "Technique of facial reconstruction drawing," *Proceedings of the International Symposium on the Forensic Aspects of Mass Disasters and Crime Scene Reconstruction*. Quantico, VA: FBI Academy, 1990, 281–284.
12. Ubelaker, D. and O'Donnell, G., "Computer-assisted facial reproduction," *Journal of Forensic Sciences*, 37(1), 155–162, January 1992.
13. Micheletti, M., personal communication, 1999.
14. Krogman, W. M., *The Human Skeleton in Forensic Medicine*. Springfield, IL: Charles C Thomas, 1962.
15. Fedosyutkin, B., personal communication, 1990.
16. Adler, F., *Textbook of Opthalmology*. Philadelphia: W. B. Saunders, 1962.
17. Stewart, T. D., "The points of attachment of the palpebral ligaments: their use in facial reconstructions on the skull." *Journal of Forensic Sciences*, 28(4), 858–863, October 1983.
18. Faigin, G., *Facial Expression*. New York: Watson-Guptill, 1990.
19. Krogman, W. M., *The Human Skeleton in Forensic Medicine*. Springfield, IL: Charles C Thomas, 1962.
20. George, R. M., Anatomical and artistic guidelines for forensic facial reconstruction, in *Forensic Analysis of the Skull*, Iscan, M. Y. and Helmer, P., Eds. New York: Wiley–Liss, 1993.

Chapter 13

Three-Dimensional Facial Reconstruction on the Skull

Betty Pat. Gatliff with Karen T. Taylor

Betty Pat. Gatliff has described her first venture into the realm of three-dimensional facial reconstruction as detailed below.

Background of the Method (by BPG)

My first attempt at facial reconstruction was on the skull of an unidentified Native American male in January 1967. It was accomplished when I worked as a medical illustrator with physical anthropologist Dr. Clyde Snow at the Civil Aeromedical Research Institute at the Federal Aviation Administration in Oklahoma City. Dr. Snow was a consultant with the Oklahoma State Bureau of Investigation and the Oklahoma State Medical Examiner's Office. The unidentified case came from the Medical Examiner's Office. Dr. Snow asked me to assist by sculpting a face on the skull. As preparation for the assignment, he recommended that I read Chapter IX of Dr. Krogman's book, *The Human Skeleton in Forensic Medicine*. In Chapter IX, "From Skull to Head: Restoration of Physiognomic Details," Krogman writes:

> A skull may tell of age, of sex, of race, and thus in part contribute to cranial identification. But it may do more: it may provide a further individualization, for it may give clues as to cephalic identification. This is to say that the dead skull is, in a sense, the matrix of the living head; it is the bony core of the fleshy head and face in life. Upon the cranial framework (which is really subjacent to all soft tissues) we may build bit by bit, until details of physiognomy take shape, and a reasonably acceptable facsimile of a living human head emerges.

This is a tricky thing to achieve, for the skull doesn't give all the clues it should. We recognize a person by so many little details, so many subtle nuances, that it is hard to recapture precise individuality. Only a rather gross likeness may be achieved. (See Suk, '35.) Furthermore, **the average identification specialist is not gifted in the necessary direction wherein art must supplement science. I refer to the creation of a bust (head and neck) in modelling clay, built upon the nuclear skull. A competent sculptor, working under my direction, using data supplied by me, has been my answer.**[1]

Krogman's remarks encouraged me to try to sculpt the face of the Native American Indian male, to attempt to associate a name with the remains so that authorities could work toward a positive identification. This first case challenged me but it was also a real struggle. Reading Krogman's text, working on the facial sculpture, setting it aside for a while, reading more from Krogman, then struggling further, I eventually completed the project. It seems miraculous that the young man was positively identified, considering my lack of confidence in my ability to utilize this technique and the piecemeal fashion in which the project was completed (see Chapter 2). Our beginner's luck on this first case encouraged us to do the next one, and on and on.

Each new case over the years confirms the wisdom of Krogman's words "art must supplement science." The teamwork situations of an artist working jointly with one or more scientists on reconstruction projects have led to identifications that likely would not have occurred with any member operating in isolation.

Now, some 30 years and over 200 cases later, I feel very confident about the potential for success of the facial reconstruction process in a variety of applications. I retired from Federal service in 1979, and established my freelance studio, SKULLpture Lab, in Norman, Oklahoma. Opportunities to use the technique abound. Because of many favorable results, I began teaching in 1983, and I truly enjoyed witnessing former students' successes. Karen T. Taylor was in my first training course, and our friendship has proven mutually beneficial. I was her teacher in anatomy and clay facial reconstruction and she has kept me apprised of numerous other innovations in forensic art.

As artists, we sometimes unconsciously do things as we work. For me, teaching has necessitated the evaluation of every aspect of the facial reconstruction technique. It has forced me to create the step-by-step approach that is outlined in this chapter.

A point that I strongly emphasize in workshops is that a week-long course provides only a foundation, something akin to one piano lesson. You cannot take only one lesson, nor can you go without repeated, studied practice and expect to become a concert pianist. Nor will the finest grand piano make your playing perfect. The music is written, but to become proficient you must place your hands on the correct keys as you practice. With discipline and experience over time, you can then become qualified to interpret what the music says. Thus, reading books about forensic art, attending workshops about forensic art, or purchasing expensive work-related tools and equipment *will not* "automatically" make your reconstructions perfect. All of this can only provide a basis from which the real study and practice must begin.

In addition to fine-tuning my skills, teaching also affords me the personal benefit of exposure to an intriguing array of students. Surprisingly, although most of my students are involved in law enforcement, many attendees from other professions have benefited from learning this basic process and adapting it to their particular needs.

Fine artists who attend feel that the process of building the face from the inside out refines their abilities to understand the underlying structures and therefore improve their portraiture. Doll makers who study the method say that their dolls become more realistic. In the advanced class, both infant and child skull models are made available for use by the toy makers. Morticians, anaplastologists, medical artists, scientific artists, movie industry special-effects artists, and animators have all attended. Museum exhibit preparators find the method particularly useful. Plastic surgeons and dentists find special enjoyment in the process, having previously studied the head and neck anatomy so thoroughly. Several dentists have commented that they wish they had been taught anatomy in dental school in such a hands-on manner, because they more readily learned and understood it.

In 1987, Karen Taylor and I attended an artist's anatomy workshop at the Scottsdale Artists' School in Arizona, taught by Jon Zahorek, which helped us both gain a greater understanding of craniofacial anatomy. Zahorek teaches a hands-on approach to learning anatomy that involves building the muscles in clay over a skeletal framework. He often states, "The mind cannot forget what the hands have built."

Later, we studied anatomy with Dr. Wilfred Stedman, a sculptor and retired orthopedic surgeon. Dr. Stedman also teaches anatomy through use of a hands-on method, applying muscles to the skeleton. Like Jon Zahorek, Dr. Stedman encouraged us to incorporate more anatomy into our facial reconstruction techniques.

Through exposure to students while teaching and from the challenges presented by each new case, I continue to learn.

I have arrived at the method presented here as a result of knowledge gained working on cases over the years and enrichment from all of the classes, both those I taught and those I took.

Circumstances for Doing Three-Dimensional Facial Reconstruction

Facial sculpture, synonymous with facial or skull reconstruction, restoration, approximation, and reproduction, is a method of forensic art used to help identify skeletal remains. The artist and anthropologist collaborate to construct the facial features of the unknown individual on the basis of the underlying cranial structure.

Law enforcement agencies and medical examiners are regularly presented with difficult cases of unidentified victims of homicide or unexplained death. It is their statutory and moral obligation to make every attempt to identify these individuals. There are numerous very important reasons to identify bodies. Doing a representation of an individual's visage may be the only hope of ever identifying that person. For every life, there is someone somewhere who cares. Missing persons who are never located or identified may leave behind complicated legal issues such as inheritances and other business matters. Especially significant is the knowledge that **an unidentified body likely means a murder unsolved and a murderer walking free.**

Due to situational and climatic factors, human remains may be found in a great variety of physical conditions. Intact bodies may be photographed to use in the preparation of postmortem drawings. In cases of more severely damaged bodies or those in advanced stages of decompositional change, postmortem drawings may not be possible. In instances of semi-skeletal or totally skeletonized remains, a method of reconstructing the face from the skull may be necessary.

The authors have obtained positive identification results from both two- and three-dimensional methods. In some cases, however, one method may be indicated over another. Or the artist may prefer a certain method or have greater skill in a particular method.

Extremely fragile skulls, either forensic or historical cases, may not be strong enough to bear the weight of clay for sculptural reconstruction. To do a three-dimensional approach, a fragile skull would have to be painstakingly molded and cast in a stronger material and then sculpted. Alternatively, two-dimensional reconstruction drawing could be done.

Perhaps one of the greatest advantages of three-dimensional reconstruction is the ability to view and photograph the face in multiple dimensions. Since we look at friends and associates in moving and rotating views in life, this method may provide a real plus in identification. **The third dimension may aid some viewers in making the necessary connection to a missing acquaintance or loved one.**

Another advantage to the three-dimensional approach may be seen in cases in which items such as clothing, jewelry, hair accoutrements, eyeglasses, or dentures are recovered with a body. In some instances, it may be possible to place the actual items directly on the sculpture and photograph them.

Three-dimensional facial reconstruction on the skull has been traditionally used for both forensic and museum/historical applications. Forensically, it aids in the recognition of missing persons, while in the museum setting it allows us to imagine how some of the faces of ancient humans may have appeared. In recent years, special projects have utilized adaptations of the technique, including trial displays, forensic testing, plastic and dental implant design, and television applications.

Facial reconstruction is a two-phase process. The steps of the phases for **three-dimensional reconstruction** are listed below:

Technical Phase:
- Receipt of skull/evidence transferal/record keeping
- Gathering case information/scientific input
- Preparing and protecting the skull
- Gluing the mandible to the cranium
- Placement of skull on an adjustable stand
- Orientation into the Frankfort Horizontal
- Cutting and applying tissue depth markers
- Setting the prosthetic eye
- Connecting tissue depth markers to establish facial contours

Artistic Phase:
- Development of the mouth
- Development of the eyes
- Development of the nose
- Development of the cheeks
- Development of the ears
- Texturing and surface details
- Hair or wig
- Finishing and photography

Tools and Materials

Tools:

- Sculpture tools: a flat wooden spatula, a wire tool, and a pointed wooden stick
- Boley-style gauge (in millimeters)
- Metal scale (in millimeters)
- Plastic brayer or roller
- X-acto knife and blades

Materials:

- Oil-based modeling clay, 10 to 12 lbs
- Duco® cement (or other adhesive soluble in acetone)
- Cotton balls
- Cotton swabs
- Vinyl machine eraser strips
- #40 Grade sand paper
- Aluminum "Gutter Guard" or flexible mesh

This list indicates the minimum tools and materials required (Figure 13.1). Over time, you may find many others you like to use, particularly modeling tools. In reality, few modeling tools are needed to manipulate the clay, and probably the best tools are your fingertips.

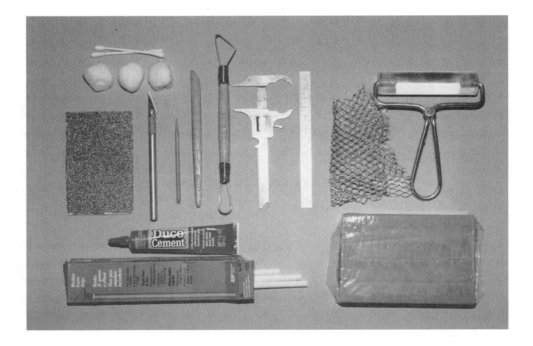

Figure 13.1 Tools and materials for three-dimensional facial reconstruction. (Photo by Missey Micheletti.)

Technical Phase

The technical phase deals with information gathering about a case and the application of known quantifiable data by a mechanical process. The first few steps of the technical phase are described in Chapter 11. At this stage, the skull should be received by the reconstructionist and the proper evidence transferal paperwork accomplished. Next, all pertinent case information should be gathered and the necessary scientific input obtained. The skull should be prepared and protected as outlined in Chapter 11 and the mandible should be securely glued to the cranium.

Adjustable Skull Stand

An adjustable skull stand may be constructed by obtaining the items pictured (Figure 13.2). The PanaVise, pictured lower left, available from the hobby shop or hardware store, acts as a base to hold the upright armature structure of the skull stand. The tripod head may be purchased from a photography supply shop. Most other items are found at a hardware store.

Mount the PanaVise to a board at least 1 ft square to avoid tipping. You may also find it beneficial to purchase a heavy-duty "Lazy Susan" ball-bearing turntable at the hardware store for use under the base. This allows free rotation of the sculpture for viewing as you work. Useful sculpture stands on wheels for standing work, already equipped with rotating tops, are available from art supply stores.

Assemble the stand by stacking the component parts pictured in the upper half of the photo to resemble the lower right half of the photo. Insert this upright armature structure into the mounted Panavise base.

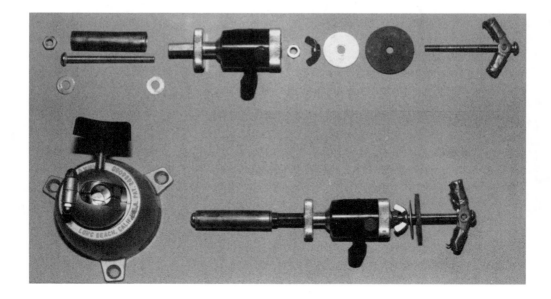

Figure 13.2 Adjustable skull stand. (Photo by Missey Micheletti.)

The pieces to be assembled for the upright armature structure, left to right, are

- $\frac{1}{4}$" Nut and $\frac{1}{4}$" washer, $\frac{1}{2}$" diameter
- $\frac{1}{2}$" Copper tubing, in a 3" length
- $\frac{1}{4}$" Bolt, $3\frac{1}{2}$" long
- $\frac{1}{4}$" Washer, $\frac{1}{2}$" diameter
- $\frac{1}{4}$" Connecting bolt, $\frac{3}{4}$" long
- Heavy-duty tripod head
- $\frac{1}{4}$" Nut
- $\frac{1}{4}$" Wing nut
- $\frac{1}{4}$" Washer, $1\frac{1}{4}$" diameter
- $\frac{1}{4}$" Washer, $1\frac{1}{2}$" diameter (gasket material)
- $\frac{1}{4}$" Toggle bolt, 3" long

To mount the skull onto the adjustable skull stand once it is assembled, you must locate the foramen magnum. The foramen magnum is the large opening in the base of the skull into which the first vertebra of the neck, called the cervical atlas, is attached or articulates.

Insert the spring-opened wings of the toggle bolt against the inside of the skull through this opening. Push the two washers upward against the base of the skull and tighten the wing nuts securely. You are now ready to orient the skull into the Frankfort Horizontal Plane.

The Frankfort Horizontal Plane

After the mandible is glued on the cranium, mount the skull on the adjustable stand in the Frankfort Horizontal Plane. **The Frankfort Horizontal Plane is an anthropological standard position that closely approximates the natural position of the head in life.** Orbitale, the lowest point on the lower margin of the orbit, is horizontally aligned with porion, the most lateral point on the roof of the external auditory meatus (bony ear hole) (see Figure 11.23 in Chapter 11).

This orientation may be achieved using a triangle set upright with a straight edge aligned in a vertical position, and then using the perpendicular side to locate the points on the skull for alignment. Remember that the PanaVise can be adjusted first to get a naturalistic thrust of the neck. The tripod head can then be used to rock the skull into the Frankfort Horizontal. Always keep the head in this orientation for best results and to avoid distortion.

Tissue Depth Markers

Select the appropriate tissue depth data and cut the markers from vinyl eraser strips. Number each one according to location as pictured in Chapter 11 (Figure 11.25). Glue the markers at the appropriate landmark, using Duco® or similar cement (Figure 13.3). The skull is a very important item of evidence and great care should be taken to prevent damaging it in any way. Duco® cement is an ideal adhesive because it is soluble in acetone, and any glue residue can be removed from the skull without harming the bone.

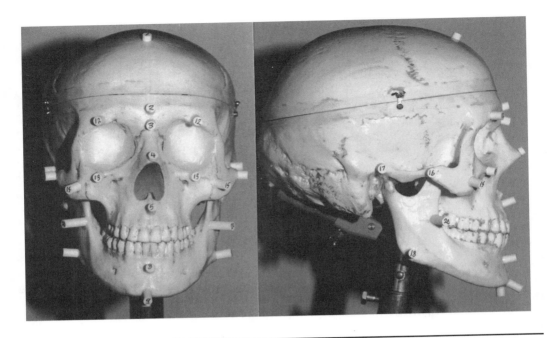

Figure 13.3 Tissue depth markers on the skull, frontal (left) and lateral (right). (Photo by Missey Micheletti.)

The skull drawing that accompanies the soft tissue data in Chapter 11 (Figure 11.25) is easy to follow for determination of the landmarks or locations of the markers. While the method of two-dimensional facial reconstruction described in Chapter 12 makes use of most of the available tissue depth data, certain markers are *not conveniently utilized* when preparing a sculpture. **In the sculptural method, the following tissue markers are not generally used: #6, #11, #14, #19, and #21.**

Marker #7 provides the depth of the closed mouth. By applying both lips together to form the mouth barrel, marker #6 is not needed. The sculpted lips are spread and shaped at a later stage in modeling.

Because marker #11 is the same measurement as marker #1, long strips of clay can be rolled to the depth of marker #1 and placed in strips over the entire forehead and scalp to maintain the bony surface shape, without use of #11 markers.

In the authors' experience, the dimensions in the data tables for #14, #19, or #21 produce cheeks that are too hollow. In other words, the depths seem to be too shallow. It is preferable to develop the cheeks and jaw, by considering the underlying muscles and even the parotid gland as in the anatomical method. The soft tissue changes that occur with facial expression must also be considered. For each case, both open and closed mouth versions are usually prepared, so the cheeks must be altered in each view to reflect changes due to creation of the expression. Also, the age of the person whose face is being reconstructed in each individual skull should determine the amount of fullness added to the cheek area.

The tissue depth studies by Dr. Stanley Rhine, which have been the most commonly used for many years, were taken with a needle-type instrument. Consider, too, that the vinyl cylinders are approximately 6 mm in diameter, so the surface that you glue to the skull is larger than the point at which the original measurement was taken. For this reason, some artists have chosen to use small sticks of wood, cork, or other materials to pinpoint a smaller point. The vinyl markers are preferable for accuracy of cutting and gluing and convenient use in conjunction with the clay. Location numbers can also be written on the end of each marker to avoid possible misplacement. Choice of specific vinyl eraser material may affect cutting, since the softer materials are more difficult to cut with accuracy than the firmer materials.

The anthropological landmark sites should become very familiar to the reconstructionist so that they may be accurately located. Then, the remaining vinyl tissue markers should be glued as closely as possible to the morphological measurement sites as shown in Chapter 11 (Figure 11.25). **There is a tendency to rush this part of the procedure and not pay proper attention to the accurate placement of each marker.** Although this step is less exciting for the artist, as are most of the technical phase steps, it should not be slighted. **Errors here can ruin your entire project and cause you to waste many hours of work.** Additional subtle studies should be made for the midline sites (see Chapter 11, Figure 11.26). As George has stated:

> In many illustrations depicting soft tissue thickness data, the overlying cephalometric points are drawn as perpendiculars from their underlying craniometric points. ... this is not always the case. Thus, in building a face in clay, sculptors should bevel their erasers or cork markers in order to achieve the proper alignment.[2]
>
> [Note: George refers to beveling the placement of the markers, not cutting them at a bevel.]

In addition to the gluing method for accurate craniometric (bone) to cephalometric (soft tissue) correlation, I have developed certain ways of gluing particular markers, simply for advantage in doing the sculpture. For example, marker #3 (nasion) can be glued with the lower margin of the marker on the frontal-nasal suture, so that it will tip downward to predict the proper location of the soft tissue nasion. I choose not to glue marker #7 on the skull, but rather to use it to gauge the depth of the closed mouth barrel. At the chin-lip fold, marker #8 is glued slightly lower than point B as shown on George's diagram in Chapter 11 (Figure 11.26), which will tip the marker upward into a little more natural contour for the chin.

Marker #12 (supraorbital), above the orbit, is located with the lower margin of the marker on the upper crest of the orbit and it is then centered. Marker #13 (suborbital), below the orbit, is located with the upper margin of the marker on the lower crest of the orbit and it is then centered. Marker #15 (lateral orbit) should not actually be placed directly lateral of the orbit as you might expect. Dr. Rhine has indicated that he took the measurements for the tables at a position straight downward from the lateral orbit on the zygomatic (malar) bone. Thus that is where the marker should be glued at the zygomaticus minor muscle attachment. Marker #20 (occlusal line) is glued on the frontal edge of the ascending ramus of the mandible, in alignment with the teeth at occlusion.

Setting the Prosthetic Eye

The human eye is a ball approximately 25 mm in diameter. I prefer to use plastic prosthetic eye caps for their realistic appearance as well as for the ease of modeling the eyelids around them. Some choose to use less expensive doll or taxidermy eyes or to simply model the eyes in clay. I find both these methods provide less than satisfactory results. One exception might be a sculpted reconstruction that is to be totally cast, as with a museum project. In such case, it would be preferable to sculpt the eyes. Artist Frank Bender has produced very successful cast and painted renditions of reconstructions, although this is a very time-consuming, multi-step process. It requires studio space for the messy casting procedures and thus is not practical for most police artists.

Selection of Eye Color

The choice of color of prosthetic eye to be used should be based on the information provided by the anthropologist and may also require some guesswork. This guesswork should, however, be based on logic as much as possible. The *ABC's of the Human Body* discusses the eye color variations in people:

> Two brown-eyed parents usually produce a brown-eyed child, and two blue-eyed parents almost always have blue-eyed offspring. But when one parent has blue eyes and the other has brown eyes, their children are usually brown-eyed. The fact is that brown eyes are a stronger hereditary trait, so that brown-eyed people far outnumber those who have blue eyes throughout the world.[3]

Eye color choice for skulls designated by the anthropologist as being Negroid or Mongoloid would most logically be reconstructed with brown prosthetic eyes. When light blond hair specimens are recovered, a lighter eye choice may be suggested. Hazel eyes are a good all-round choice, however, for Caucasoid skulls. Obviously, any eye color can occur in any group, but eye color choices are best made based on the odds.

Prosthetic eyes, although rather expensive, may be purchased from the same suppliers who provide them to patients who have lost eyes to disease or injury. Sometimes marketed as mannequin eyes, they are sold in pairs that may be less than perfectly matched.

Doll or taxidermy eyes are less expensive and may also be used, but they usually demonstrate one very serious scale flaw. The human iris averages 12 mm in diameter and remains virtually constant throughout life. Generally, both doll and taxidermy eyes have oversized iris diameters and too little sclera (white area) to appear life-like in a reconstruction.

Frontal View Placement

When viewed from the front, the prosthetic eye should basically be centered within the orbit, north and south, east and west (Figure 13.4, left). As Krogman states:

> Relation of eyeball to bony orbit ... The apex of the cornea when viewed from norma frontalis, is at the juncture of two lines, one drawn from the medial edge of the orbit (maxillofrontale) to the lateral margin of the orbit (ectoconchion); and the other line bisecting the orbit between the superior and inferior margins.[1]

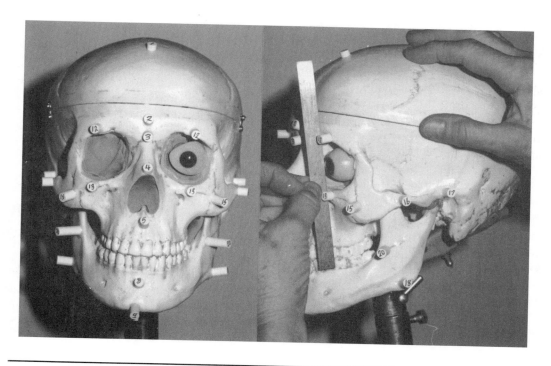

Figure 13.4 **Setting the prosthetic eye**; centering the eye frontally (left) and aligning the eye laterally (right). (Photo by Missey Micheletti.)

Lateral View Placement

Referring to the placement of the eye in the lateral view, Krogman further states:

> The outer point of the cornea is approximately tangent to a centrally located line drawn from the superior and inferior margins of the orbit.[1]

More simply put, the projection of the eyeball in profile should be determined by placing a straight edge against the bone at the top and bottom edges of the orbit. Then, make it project to that point as pictured (Figure 13.4, right). You may also wish to give some consideration to the age of the individual whose skull you have. The basic principles of the method favor a range of 25 to 35 years, but certain adjustments can be made if they seem reasonable and logical. Individuals of advanced age sometimes lose volume in the fat pads behind the eyes, so it is reasonable to push the eyes in a bit deeper when placing them. Much younger people may have eyes that project slightly beyond the tangent discussed by Krogman. Of course, diseases and certain medications can alter these placements in life, but for the most part, they are good guidelines.

After the prosthetic eye is correctly positioned on a small "stem" of clay, small amounts of clay should be modeled in to help secure it in place.

Connecting Tissue Depth Markers

To reiterate, gluing the tissue depth markers in place and then connecting them with clay will provide the general shape of the face, based on the shape of the skull. You will find that using neat, uniform strips of clay to make these connections is most accurate and appropriate. A brayer-type roller or wooden dowel can be useful for rolling strips of uniform thickness. **In other words, by carefully maintaining the accuracy of the thickness of each piece of clay applied, these strips function as large-scale tissue depth markers.** After rolling, start with #1 and go directly down to markers #2 and #3. From there, proceed to marker #12, both right and left (Figure 13.5). Of course, the markers vary in depth, depending on the data for a particular point, so a strip of clay must be devised that will taper from one thickness to the next. From marker #12, bend the strip (which forms part of the orbicularis oculi muscle) around the lateral side of the orbit in such a way that all of the clay is behind the orbital margin, and **a small edge of the outer bony orbit remains visible** (Figure 13.6). The reason for this is to allow room for placement of the outer side or lateral canthus of the eyelid. This outer corner of the eyelid is set further into the face than is the inner corner or medial canthus of the eyelid. In other words, when viewed from above, the eyelid would appear as an "S" curve. Many professional sculptors miss this subtlety and produce flat-looking eyes.

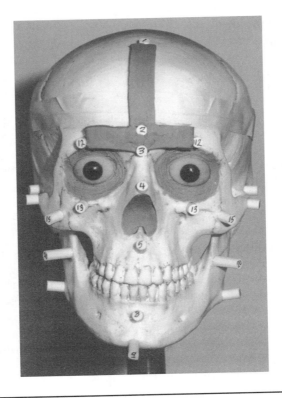

Figure 13.5 Prosthetic eyes are secured in the bony orbits. Tissue depth markers #1 and #2 are connected, then #2 and #3 are connected to #12 on each side. (Photo by Missey Micheletti.)

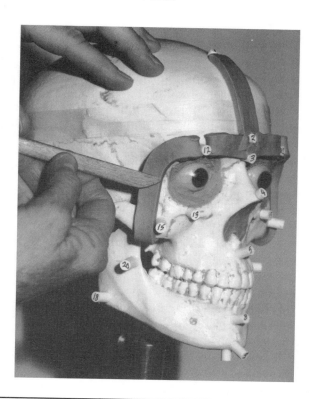

Figure 13.6 Connect tissue depth markers by bending a strip from marker #12 around the lateral side of the orbit to #15. (Photo by Missey Micheletti.)

It is important to note that the tissue at the lateral or outside of the eye is only about 5 mm thick. The clay should therefore taper in at the corner of the eye, clinging close to the bone. In other words, it should not be the same thickness as #12 all the way around the orbit. The wooden tool in Figure 13.6 shows the area that should be thinner. Excess thickness in this area is a common mistake that also makes the eyes look flat. Dr. Stanley Rhine did not take a tissue depth measurement at this point, but Dr. Richard Helmer did.

Some of the tissue marker connections are not necessarily done with strips and it is permissible to fill larger areas. The area we will refer to as the **"back triangle"** is defined by the area of marker #15 (lateral orbit), #16 (zygomatic arch, midway), #17 (supraglenoid) along the zygomatic arch, then downward to #18 (gonion) and diagonally past #20 (occlusal line) and back to #15 (Figure 13.7). As this triangular area of clay is added, the back portion of the masseter muscle and a portion of the parotid gland are being simulated.

The next area covered is the chin. Place a long strip of clay rolled to the depth of marker #10 (beneath chin) all along the lower edge of the mandible (Figure 13.7). Then, on the outer surface, place a long strip of clay using the depth of marker #9 (mental eminence) around the chin and back to connect with marker #18 (gonion) (Figure 13.8). This process ensures that two very different thicknesses, on and below the bony jaw, are maintained. Now make a small coil of clay, approximately 6 to 8 mm in diameter, to fill in the space between the two strips just added. Then model or blend the areas together (Figure 13.9).

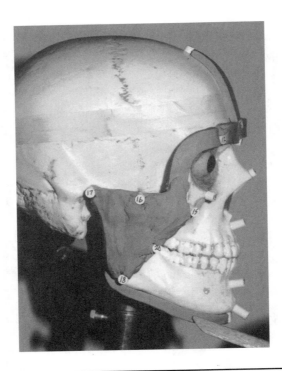

Figure 13.7   Connect tissue depth markers to form the "back triangle" between #15, #16, #17, #18, #20, and back to #15. A uniform layer of clay rolled to the depth of marker #10 is then placed along the underside of the mandible. (Photo by Missey Micheletti.)

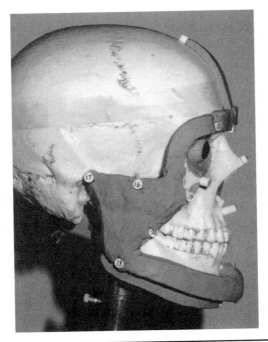

Figure 13.8   A clay strip the depth of #9 is placed on the outer surface of the mandible from #9 to #18 on each side. (Photo by Missey Micheletti.)

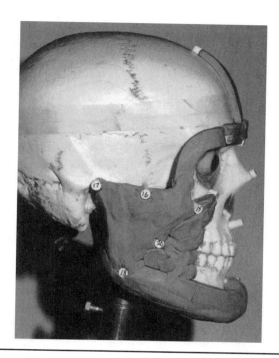

Figure 13.9 **A small coil of clay fills the area between the two jaw strips and is blended. The "front triangle" is formed.** (Photo by Missey Micheletti.)

Make a mark in the clay along the jaw halfway between markers #9 and #18. The "front triangle" of the face is bounded by marker #15 (lateral orbit) over to #13 (suborbital) and down to the "jaw strip," at about halfway between #9 and #18. This area can be filled with larger pieces of clay and smoothed. The addition of the "front triangle" then completes the masseter muscle and extends the orbicularis oculi under the orbit. The mouth region is developed no further at this point.

The top of the head is covered with long strips of clay, approximately 10 to 15 mm in width and the thickness of #1 (supraglabella). This will preserve the shape of the forehead, frontalis muscle, and cranium (Figure 13.10).

The technical phase is now complete. The contours of the face now emerge and begin to become apparent. By applying the vinyl tissue depth markers on the anthropological landmarks and then carefully connecting them with larger strips that represent specific depths, the bony shapes dictated by the skull are maintained.

At this juncture the artistic phase begins. Non-artists seem to have little difficulty completing the process up to this point. The remainder of the procedure will likely be easier for artists to accomplish than for non-artists.

Artistic Phase

The artistic phase deals with the development of the individual features themselves and with the completion of the areas of transition. In the classroom setting, I have found that students with anatomical or scientific backgrounds deal quite comfortably with the technical phase, but become less confident and more frustrated

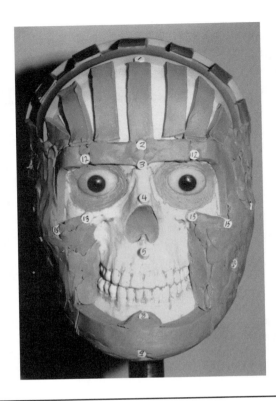

Figure 13.10   Strips of clay rolled to the depth of #1 preserve the shape of the forehead, frontalis muscle, and cranium. (Photo by Missey Micheletti.)

upon entering the artistic phase. On the other hand, students with art backgrounds find the technical phase somewhat boring and really begin to excel in the artistic phase. In addition, I find that this second phase is far more difficult to teach since it is less defined and relies heavily on innate ability.

As you begin development of the individual features, it may be beneficial to refer to the anatomical structures of the eye (Figure 3.7), nose (Figure 3.8), mouth, (Figure 3.9), and ear (Figure 3.10), as shown in the drawings in Chapter 3 as well as the overall diagrams of the facial bones (Figure 3.4) and muscles (Figure 3.5).

Development of the Mouth

The Closed Mouth

To build the mouth barrel for a closed mouth, you need three dimensions: the depth of the lips, the vertical thickness of the vermilion or colored part of the lips, and the width of the mouth side to side.

The depth of the mouth is determined by the depth of #7 tissue marker as taken from the appropriate chart for a particular skull. The #7 location is the lower lip margin, so it provides a guide for rolling out clay to the correct thickness for the lip or mouth depth (Figure 13.11).

The vertical thickness for the mouth is derived by measuring the combined height of the enamel of the upper and lower teeth. There is a distinct textural

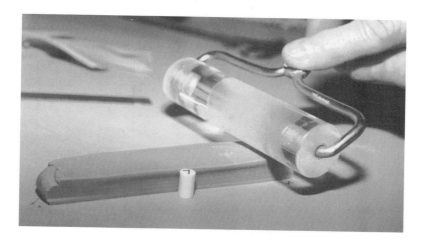

Figure 13.11   Depth of the mouth. Roll the clay to the level of #7 tissue depth marker to establish lip depth. (Photo by Missey Micheletti.)

change between the tooth enamel and the cementum or root area, usually causing a slight ridge. Dentists refer to this location as the cementum enamel junction (CEJ). Another way of stating this vertical distance is **upper CEJ to lower CEJ** (Figure 13.12).

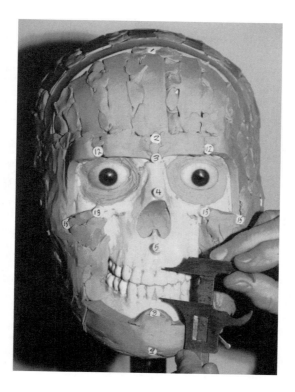

Figure 13.12   Vertical thickness of the mouth. Use the Boley gauge to measure upper CEJ to lower CEJ. (Photo by Missey Micheletti.)

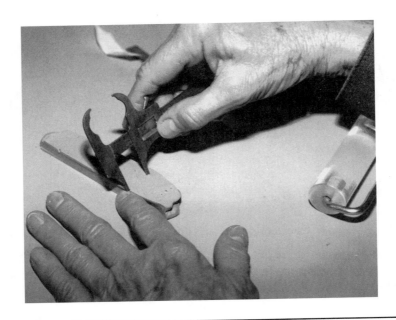

Figure 13.13   Transfer upper CEJ to lower CEJ measurement to the clay strip to establish vertical thickness of the mouth. (Photo by Missey Micheletti.)

The Boley gauge may be used to measure this vertical thickness and then transfer the measurement directly to the strip of clay previously rolled to #7 depth (Figure 13.13). The clay strip should be cut to that vertical dimension.

The width of the mouth is generally determined by measuring the front six teeth. Krogman's "Rule of Thumb" for mouth width was stated as "the distance between two lines radiating out from the junction of the canine and the first premolar on each side."[1] This can be accomplished by bending the prepared strip of clay around the dental arch and then cutting in perpendicularly between the canine and the first premolar (or the third and fourth tooth on each side) (Figure 13.14, left). Krogman also stated that there may be some correspondence between the mouth width and the interpupillary distance. The parting line or fissure of the lips may then be incised at the halfway point of the vertical thickness (Figure 13.14, right).

The orbicularis oris muscle would naturally be contained within the mouth barrel. Around the orbicularis oris, there are some 18 facial muscles inserted that radiate out from their various origins in the lower half of the face. With those muscles in mind, connect the mouth barrel to the chin, down to the jaw, and over to the cheeks. Roll two strips of clay 4 to 5 mm thick, cutting one end of each strip at about a 45° diagonal to fit around the upper mouth barrel, as pictured (Figure 13.15). Place the strips tangent to the nasal aperture, thus connecting between the upper lip and tissue marker #13, below orbitale. This stylizes the levator labii muscle and establishes a base of soft tissue at the sides of the nose so that when the nose is added, it will be at the correct depth in relation to the bony aperture in the maxilla.

Continuing to form the shapes of the lips is optional at this point. You may prefer to leave the mouth barrel dimensioned and in place, then move on to the next feature, the eyes, and come back to the mouth after forming the nose. In doing so, it is easier to fill in the upper lip and connect it to the septum and ala of the nose.

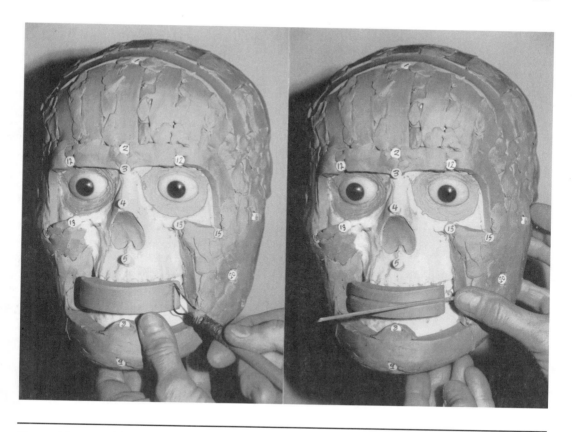

Figure 13.14   Width of the mouth. Bend the prepared strip of clay around the dental arch and cut in between the canine and the first pre-molar. The parting line of the lips is incised at the halfway point. (Photo by Missey Micheletti.)

To continue forming the shapes of the lips, spread the lips from the partition line with a flat wooden tool, pushing the upper lip upward and the lower lip downward. The index finger is used to scoop out the philtrum on the upper lip (Figure 13.16). The vertical dimension is again checked with the Boley gauge (Figure 13.17) and the depressor labii muscles are added on each side beneath the lower lip to give it support (Figure 13.18). Further contours are achieved by placing three small dabs of clay on the upper lip and two small dabs on the lower lip (Figure 13.19). This helps give the lips a more naturalistic shaping. In the finishing stage, consider both the race and the age of the individual whose skull is being reconstructed. Population affinity or youthfulness may dictate fullness or roundness of the lips. Advanced age may hint at the appropriateness of thinner lips. Younger lips often have a slight depression or dimple at the outer corner of the mouth in front of the small roundness created by the bundle or raphe of muscles that insert there. Lips in older people usually develop a line or groove at this location, sometimes called the commissural or oromental groove or furrow. The more highly pigmented lips of some population groups as well as some youthful lips display a distinct edge or lip rim around the colored portion or vermilion border of the lips. This small ridge tends to catch light and cast shadow. You may also wish to add light lines in the clay lips to represent the striations within the lips (Figure 13.20).

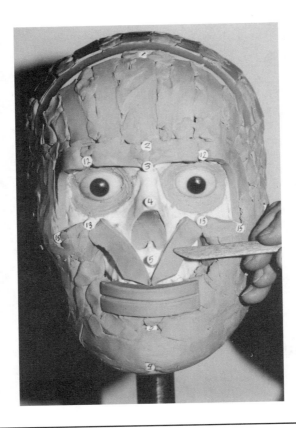

Figure 13.15   Connect the mouth barrel to the chin, jaw, and cheeks. Then use two diagonal strips of clay to stylize the levator labii muscles and create a base for the later addition of the nose. (Photo by Missey Micheletti.)

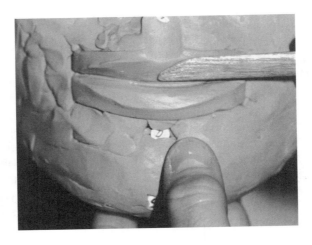

Figure 13.16   From the parting line, the lips are spread with a flat wooden tool and the index finger is used to scoop out the philtrum. (Photo by Missey Micheletti.)

Figure 13.17   The vertical thickness for the mouth is double checked with the Boley gauge to maintain accuracy. (Photo by Missey Micheletti.)

Figure 13.18   The depressor labii muscles are added on each side beneath the lower lip for support. (Photo by Missey Micheletti.)

The Open or Smiling Mouth

When the anterior teeth are recovered and particularly if there exists a distinctive trait or aspect of these frontal teeth, it may be advisable to sculpt a version of the reconstruction with the mouth opened or partially opened. **This exposure of the frontal teeth may be key to recognition and identification since the teeth are the only parts of a person's skull that are actually seen by friends and acquaintances during life.**

To depict the smiling mouth, other areas of the face besides the mouth must be altered as well. Otherwise, a conflicted or ambiguous expression, sometimes called a discordant expression, will result.

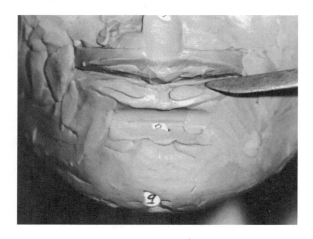

Figure 13.19   Lips are further contoured with five small dabs of clay on the flat vermilion lip surfaces, three upper and two lower. (Photo by Missey Micheletti.)

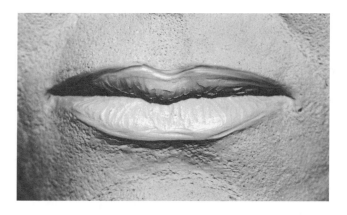

Figure 13.20   The finished, textured lips. (Photo by Missey Micheletti.)

In a smiling mouth, several functions occur simultaneously. The zygomaticus muscles pull the outer corners of the mouth upward and backward, causing them to separate, stretch and thin, thus exposing eight to ten anterior teeth. The upper lip remains more level and the lower lip becomes more curved. So, sculpturally, #7 mouth depth dimension is somewhat diminished while the mouth width is increased to cover more teeth.

As all of this occurs with the mouth, the cheeks displace upward, squinting or narrowing the eyes vertically and creating small puffs under the eyes.

Because the entire face is involved in smiling, the smiling mouth version is usually done after the reconstruction sculpture is completely finished and photographed with a closed mouth first or vice versa. Some people prefer to do the smiling mouth first so that the teeth will remain free of clay, then covering them with clay to close the mouth. Of course, some skulls may only be done in the closed mouth version.

Development of the Eyes

As with the refinement of the mouth, the sculptural development of the eye should be done keeping in mind the race, age, and expression of the individual being reconstructed. By this stage, iris color selection for the prosthetic eyes should have been done, based on the anthropologist's findings regarding race.

Age of the individual must also be considered. Eyes in younger individuals should appear subtly set more forward, while older people usually have more deeply set eyes. In addition, the areas surrounding the eyes should be sculpturally rendered with age in mind. Younger eyes may appear more open and alert, while older eyes often have sagging of the tissues of the upper eyelid or around the eye area. In reality, aging may occur quite unpredictably, yet your reconstruction must include some aging indications (see Chapter 8).

Expression may become a factor if you prepare a smiling version of the reconstruction. Has the mouth been developed in an open or closed manner? This will affect the degree to which the eyes squint as well as cheek formation.

To begin forming the eyelids, roll a section of clay to a depth of about 4 mm. From this clay, cut four small strips for the eyelids which are 7 mm by about 40 mm. The ends of each of these eyelid strips must be angled to form four small trapezoids (Figure 13.21).

The lower eyelid strips are applied first and may require several adjustments to correct the lengths. **Keep in mind that the eyelids must fit inside the bony orbits.** The lids should hug the eyeball as you place them on the lateral side and come around just to the bottom of the iris. Then, as they wrap around toward the medial canthus or inner corner of the eye, they deviate away from the eyeball slightly, creating an S-curve. Thus, **the medial canthus is naturally closer to the frontal plane than the lateral canthus or outer corner.** After the lower lids are in place, a small ball of clay is placed at the medial canthus to represent both the **caruncle lacrimalis**, the pink tissue at the inner corners of the eyes.

The upper lid strips, also started from small trapezoids, should be slightly longer and more arched than the lower lids. The upper lids should hug the eyeball as you place them on the lateral side and then come around to the iris. They should rest at a point about halfway between the pupil and the upper margin of the iris. Then, as they wrap around toward the medial canthus or inner corner of the eye, they deviate away from the eyeball slightly, as with the lower lids, coming over the caruncle.

To fill in the remaining areas around the eyes, you must consider the underlying structures as you connect these areas to the eyelids. The nasal bones should be covered by clay to a thickness of the #4 depth marker, because the flesh is close to the bones in that area. The shape of the nasal bones should be retained as this is done. The clay must then be tapered from the nasal bones to #13 below the eye and around the eye and over to #15.

The lacrimal gland rests above the eye, to the lateral or outer side, to create tears that will bathe the eye and drain out of the lacrimal duct at the medial or inner corner of the eye. These structures should be considered as the upper lid areas are modeled in. The tissue should cling closely to the bone at the inner sides of the upper eyes. At the outer sides of the upper eyes, there should be fullness to represent the forms of the lacrimal gland.

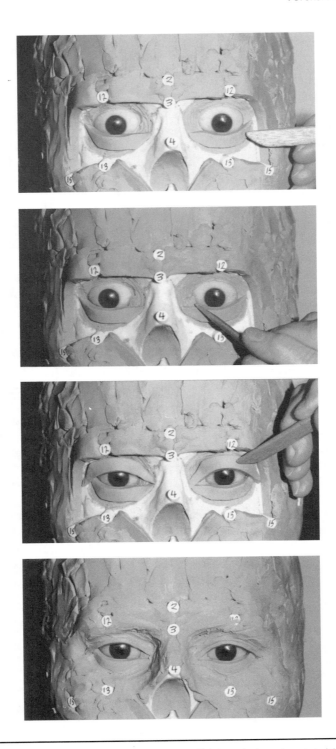

Figure 13.21 Eyes. The lower lids are laid in. Small bits of clay simulate the caruncle forms at the inner corners. The upper lids are laid in. Eyelids are connected to the surrounding structures. (Photos by Missey Micheletti.)

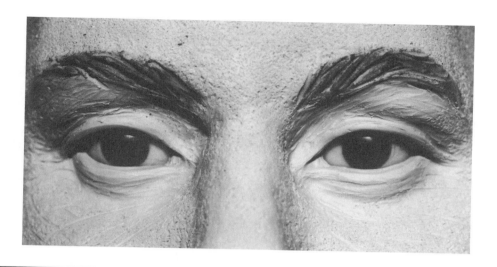

Figure 13.22 The finished, detailed eyes and eyebrows. (Photo by Missey Micheletti.)

As a rule, **the medial canthus of the eye is slightly lower than the lateral canthus** to facilitate the tear drainage process. Occasionally, it may appear that a person has a lower lateral canthus, but closer examination usually indicates that, in reality, it is an area of sagging skin, not truly the eye corner.

The eyebrows may be indicated at this stage, but you will probably choose to detail them more in the finishing stages (Figure 13.22).

Development of the Nose

Dimensioning the Nose from the Skull

The nose will be based specifically on the individual skull you are reconstructing. While there are certain "rules of thumb" for nose projection, it is the skull itself that dictates the needed information. As the "hits" examples are reviewed in this text, both two- and three-dimensional, you will notice that **it is the nose that is usually the most accurate feature.** The basis for the method of nose prediction used by the authors is derived from Dr. Wilton Krogman.[4]

Frontal View — Krogman gave a simple-to-use formula for prediction of the soft tissue nasal width based upon the bony nasal aperture (Figure 13.23). **For Caucasoids, the nasal aperture is measured at its widest point, then 10 mm are added to get the total width** (5 mm should be added to each side of the nasal aperture for a total of 10 mm). **For Negroids, the nasal aperture is measured at its widest point, then 16 mm are added to get the total width** (8 mm should be added to each side of the nasal aperture for a total of 16 mm). Since Krogman gave no formula for Mongoloids, the width for Caucasoids and Negroids can be averaged for a "best guess."

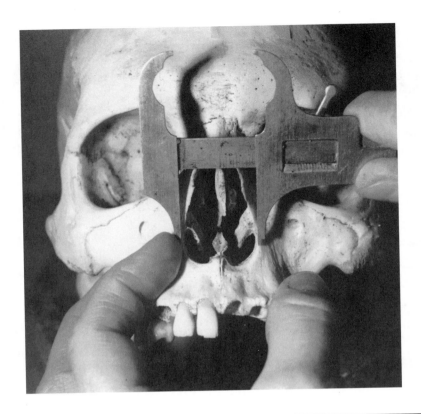

Figure 13.23 Nose width. Measure the width of the bony nasal aperture with the Boley gauge to predict the width of the nose. (Photo by Missey Micheletti.)

Lateral View — Krogman also gave a formula for prediction of the soft tissue nose projection laterally based upon measurement of the bony anterior nasal spine. It is necessary to first measure the length of the bony nasal spine (Figure 13.24). Then, that length is multiplied by 3 and added to the depth of tissue depth marker #5. As Krogman stated, **the nose projection is from subnasale to pronasale, approximately three times the length of the nasal spine.**

We find a high degree of error and misunderstanding occurs in the measurement of nasal spines, so we have tried to illustrate clearly in Chapters 12 and 13 the correct method of measurement of the anterior nasal spine (Figures 12.22 and 12.23). The vomer inside the nasal cavity is the attachment for the septal cartilage in life (Figure 12.24). To correctly measure the nasal spine, you must first observe the vomer or root of the spine. The point at which the vomer ends is where the nasal spine begins. **Measure the nasal spine from the juncture of the vomer to the tip of the spine.** Unfortunately, in some instances the nasal spine is broken or missing. The more accurate the measurement of nasal spine, the greater the accuracy of the nose is likely to be.

Applying the Skull Dimensions to Construct the Nose

Frontal View — **The attachment of the nostrils is generally 4 to 5 mm lower than the bottom or sill of the nasal aperture.** The appropriate nose width

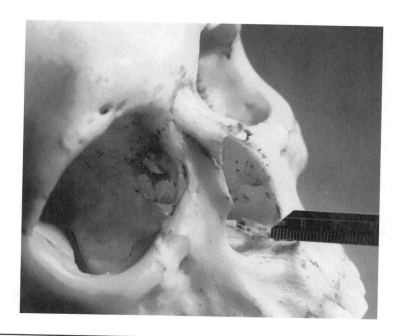

Figure 13.24   Measure the bony nasal spine from the vomer or root of the nasal spine to its tip. (Photo by Missey Micheletti.)

measurement (the measurement of the bony nasal aperture, plus the appropriate addition on each side, according to race) should be applied to the base of the nose by marking the clay with the Boley gauge (Figure 13.25, left). This provides an indication of the total width of the nose. Then the nose is roughly shaped in clay, adhering to this width (Figure 13.25, right).

Lateral View — **The total projection of the lateral nose (#5 plus three times the length of the nasal spine)** must be indicated in the clay profile. A convenient way to accomplish this is by forming a block of clay that is the length of #5, or mid-philtrum tissue marker, plus the projection calculation. The block of clay can then be placed slightly inside the nasal opening and on top of the nasal spine to form the architecture of the nose (Figure 13.26, left). Then the lateral nose is roughly shaped in clay, adhering to this projection (Figure 13.26, right). Figure 13.27 shows the finished, textured nose.

Development of the Cheeks

The cheeks can be made more lifelike with attention to their contours. As with other features, consideration must be given to the race, age, sex, and expression of the individual whose face you are reconstructing. In addition, you should carefully observe the placement of the zygomatic bones, especially in the lateral view. The cheeks should be rounded to conform to their more advancing or receding nature.

In the frontal view, certain features occur. The cheeks actually come off of the bridge of the nose, proceeding to the top edge of marker #13, rounding out and down toward the mouth. The naso-labial furrow at the side of the nose is created with age by the action of the zygomaticus muscles pulling the corner of the mouth up and back.

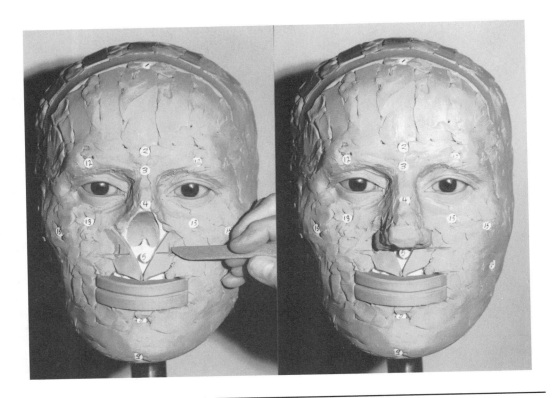

Figure 13.25 Apply the skull dimensions to construct the frontal nose; the correct total width marked in clay (left) and the roughed-in nose (right). (Photos by Missey Micheletti.)

The furrow originates at the top of the alar groove and becomes more pronounced with age as the tissue sags downward and forward from the zygomatic bone (Figure 13.28).

Development of the Ears

Ears seem to strike fear into many artists. Many opt to cover them with hair or omit them all together. You should learn to correctly sculpt an ear, since there will eventually be a case of an individual with short hair and exposed ears. Learning the basic anatomical structures goes a long way toward demystifying the process of making ears. As with any sculptural project, you may choose an additive or a subtractive approach to ears.

Step-by-Step Ear Construction

The ear structures as labeled in Figure 3.10 in Chapter 3 can be easily built by following the steps shown in Figure 13.29. In this method, the ears are first built and then applied to the sculpture. For a right ear, form a cylindrical piece of clay about 2 in. long and 5/8 in. in diameter. This piece is the basis for the **antihelix**. Hold the clay cylinder in your left hand, and press your right thumb into the middle of the cylinder while pushing with your left hand to create a "C" or cup shape, creating the **concha**.

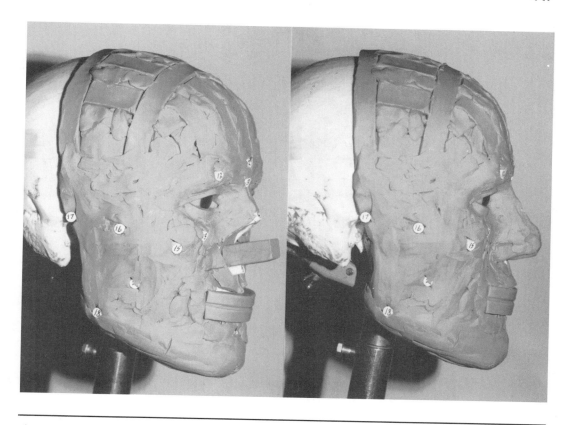

Figure 13.26   Nose projection. Apply the skull dimensions to construct the lateral nose; the correct projection in the form of a clay block (left) and the roughed-in nose (right). (Photos by Missey Micheletti.)

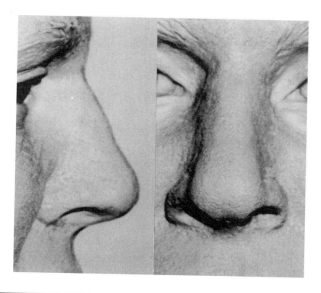

Figure 13.27   The finished, textured nose: lateral view and frontal view. (Photos by Missey Micheletti.)

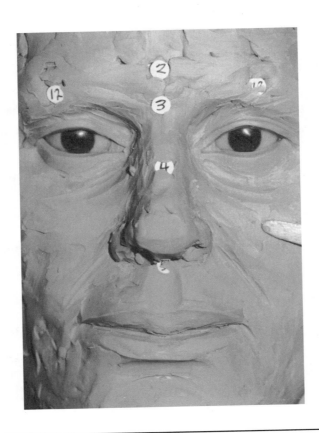

Figure 13.28 Adding roundness to the cheeks and a nasolabial furrow. (Photo by Missey Micheletti.)

Use a wooden tool to develop the top of the Y-shaped form of the antihelix by pressing in the **triangular fossa**. Next roll out a coil of clay about 6 in. long and $1/4$ in. in diameter. This coil should be added below the lower part of the Y-shape, spiraling up, out, and around the perimeter to form the **helix**. Blend this coil around the cup-shaped concha form, creating the **schaphoid fossa** and then merging it in completely near the bottom at the beginning of the lobe. Continue to shape the concha more smoothly and form the **antitragus, intertragal notch,** and **lobe**.

Make a mirror image of the ear you have just built, so that you will have a pair. The ears are ready to be attached to the sculpture adding the final structure, the **tragus**, which comes off of the cheek area.

Attaching the Ears

To attach the ears to the head, the neck should be developed first and then several points must be considered in order to get a naturalistic ear placement. The **auditory meati**, or bony ear holes, dictate specifically where the ears must be positioned. Remember that the **ears usually rest at a backward angle of about 15°.** Particularly important is that the **ears sit behind the angle of the jaw.** The ears should attach

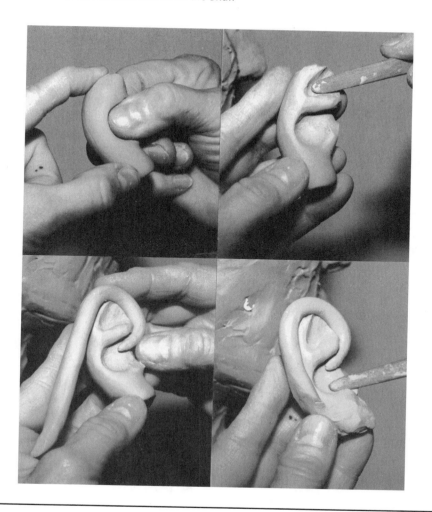

Figure 13.29 Ears. Step-by-step construction of an ear. Forming the antihelix and concha shapes from a clay cylinder (upper left), pressing a tool into the triangular fossa (upper right), a coil spirals round to form the helix (lower left), then intertragal notch and lobe are shaped (lower right). (Photos by Missey Micheletti.)

rather closely to the head at the anterior or front portion and tip out or away further from the head at the back portion. In other words, they should not appear to be "glued" to the head. In many people, there is a width of about one "finger" of space between the back of the ear and the head.

Once the ear is positioned and smoothed into the head, the small triangular form of the **tragus** must be added. The top of the tragus is just below the helix and rests over the bony auditory meatus. The anterior edge of the tragus should be blended into the side of the cheek (Figure 13.30).

Since the external ears are a totally soft tissue feature not based on bone, our best hope is to create anatomically correct, naturalistically placed features. A "rule of thumb" in art states that the ears are roughly equal in length to the nose. With this in mind, you may wish to adjust the finished ears to correspond somewhat to the finished length of the nose in your reconstruction (Figure 13.31).

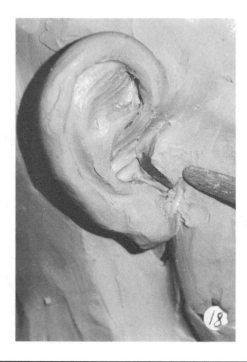

Figure 13.30   The ear is attached and the tragus is blended into the cheek. (Photo by Missey Micheletti.)

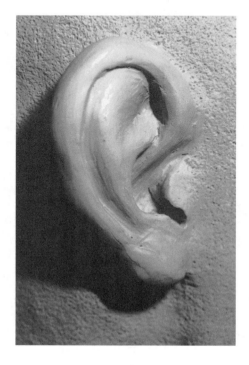

Figure 13.31   The finished, textured ear. (Photo by Missey Micheletti.)

The Neck

As with other aspects of the reconstruction you should review particular known traits of the individual whose face you are reconstructing. Include insights from the anthropologist concerning age, stature, and muscular robustness. Consider clothing recovered with the remains, particularly a shirt with a readable neck size.

Hardware cloth may be used to form an armature for the shape of the shoulders. A connection between the shoulders and the head may be built with either flexible aluminum mesh such as that used for gutters or aluminum foil squeezed around the upright portion of the adjustable stand (Figure 13.32). Remember to make the armature small enough to allow for clay on top of it — otherwise the neck will grow too large.

The neck should not appear as a stiff stovepipe, but rather should tilt forward as it leaves the shoulders due to the curve of the cervical vertebrae. This angle may be more pronounced in a woman than in a man.

The two muscles that most affect the appearance of the neck are the **sternocleidomastoid** and the **trapezius**. The sternocleidomastoid muscles come off the mastoid processes or extending bones behind the ears and are stronger and often more pronounced in men. The trapezius muscle, in the shape of a large trapezoid, provides the gentle angle that connects the neck and the shoulders.

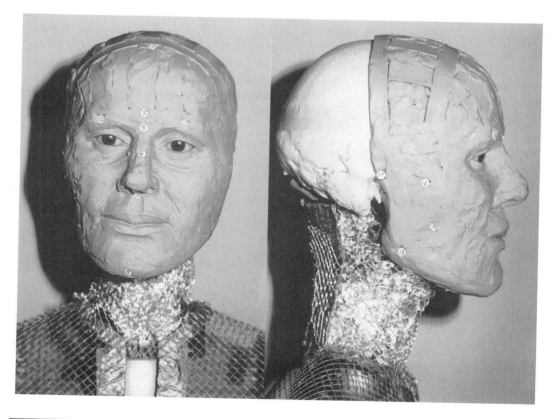

Figure 13.32 Hardware cloth is used to prepare a shoulder armature and aluminum foil forms the basis for the neck. (Photos by Missey Micheletti.)

The **forms of the throat caused by the thyroid cartilage, trachea, and other structures** should be defined in the sculpture as well as the "pit" of the neck or **supra sternal notch**.

Texturing and Finishing Details

Texturing

Once the neck is sculpted onto the shoulders, you are ready to add the finishing details. The tissue depth markers are covered with a thin layer of clay, and #40 grade sandpaper can be torn into small pieces and used to press into the clay surface for a skin-like appearance (Figure 13.33). Hand stippling with various pointed tools or a toothbrush can also be used to produce skin texture. This texture is beneficial in the photography process because it knocks off some of the sheen of the clay that can cause glare problems. Most of the face has some sort of visible skin texture, although the eye area may be more lined, depending on age. The ears should be left smoother. They may be touched up with a cotton swab dipped in petroleum jelly.

Eyebrows

The individual hairs of the eyebrows should be indicated and scratched in the clay with the side of a sculpture tool in a direction that follows the natural growth pattern of the hair (Figure 13.33). We have no real basis for the eyebrow color or configuration other than matching a hair specimen if one is available.

In general, the eyebrows tuck slightly under the bony brow ridge at the medial side (especially in men) and hug the brow bone toward the lateral side, rising above it at the lateral side (especially in women).

Coloration

Some reconstruction artists go to great lengths to produce highly detailed and finished products in lifelike color. Frank Bender casts his sculptures and totally paints them to highlight the colors of the face. For important historical projects, British artist Richard Neave sometimes sends his cast sculptures to the very skilled finishing artists at Madame Tussaud's Waxworks in London for tinting and hair insertion, producing beautiful and elaborate results.

For most law enforcement reconstruction artists, such processes may not be possible, financially feasible, or timely. Simple, though not as attractive, facial coloration may also be accomplished by use of several types of less expensive media. **Clay color choice will set the overall skin tone look for the reconstruction** from the onset. Darker clay choices may be indicated by certain racial characteristics.

Powdered cosmetics are very handy for applying color to the eyebrows, the edge of the eyelids, the cheeks or the lips (Figure 13.34). Experimentation and practice may improve the necessary tinting. A light-handed application of cosmetics usually produces a better appearance than too much makeup, which may detract from the face.

It is likely that you have no clue as to whether or not a woman may have even worn makeup. However, sometimes reasonable judgments can be made based on items

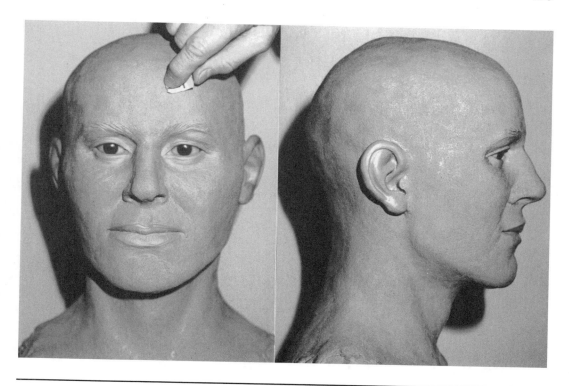

Figure 13.33 Eyebrows are incised in clay and skin-like texture is added with sandpaper. (Photos by Missey Micheletti.)

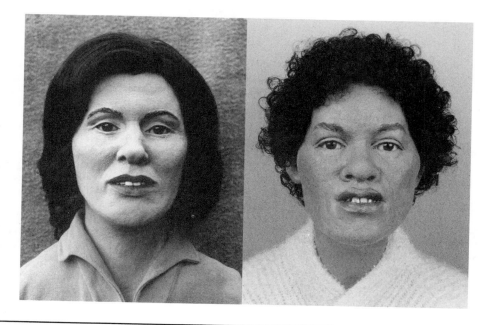

Figure 13.34 Finished reconstructions by Betty Pat. Gatliff (left) and by KTT (right) with wigs and light applications of makeup. (Photos by Betty Pat. Gatliff (left) and KTT (right).)

found with a body. For example, elaborate clothing and jewelry may be better indicators for more makeup than simple jeans and T-shirt.

Psychological research indicates that three-dimensional facial images are more readily recognized with some inclusion of tonal distinction, if not actual color.

Age Indication

The basic facial reconstruction technique favors an age range of 25 to 35 years. You may have built your entire reconstruction with a certain age range in mind or you may choose to adjust the age upward or downward during the finishing stages (Figure 13.35). Refer to Chapter 7 or 8 for more guidance on younger vs. older faces.

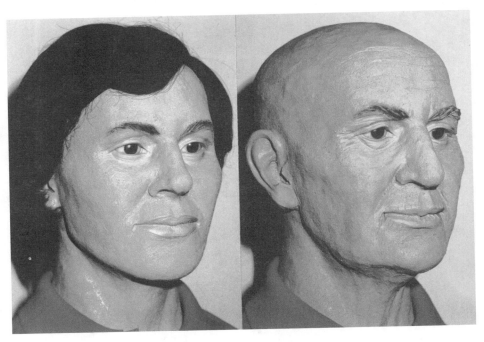

Figure 13.35   The same reconstructed skull by Betty Pat. Gatliff shown at a **younger** (left) **and an older age** (right). (Photos by Missey Micheletti.)

Adding Accessories

If any clothing items or accessories are recovered at the crime scene, they may be evaluated for possible inclusion with the reconstruction. **Clothing is often highly soiled and damaged and not usable even if recovered. Hats, eyeglasses, dentures, jewelry, or other items may, however, greatly contribute to the individualization of the finished product and should be used if possible** (Figure 13.36, right). Assistance and permission should be sought from crime scene investigators for the possible cleaning and use of such items.

If items of jewelry were found arranged or worn in a particular way on the body that was determinable at the crime scene, this same pattern should be adhered to in the reconstruction. In other words, if a decomposed body was found with the ears pierced three times, with each hole holding a different style earring, the earrings should be correctly replaced in the reconstruction.

Hair or Wig

Hopefully, you will be fortunate enough to receive a case for reconstruction in which hair was recovered with the body. Sadly, this is not always the case, and the odds for identification decrease as a result. As humans, we place a lot of recognition value on hair and hairstyle and its absence can interfere with the recognition process.

Figure 13.36 Finished reconstruction from a skull without hair specimen, **showing vaguely suggested sculpted hair** (left), and finished reconstruction with available hair specimen, showing **hair sculpted to match short gray hair sample** and including subject's own **dentures** (right), both by Betty Pat. Gatliff. (Courtesy of Betty Pat. Gatliff.)

The selection of hair and hairstyle for a reconstruction may be based on a recovered hair specimen or may have to be totally vague or speculative. The hair may be added in the form of a wig or it may be modeled in clay and colored in some way (Figure 13.36). If a wig is to be used, it should be selected not only for color, but also for texture, volume, and length if known.

It is reasonable that the hairstyle be consistent with the styles that were popular within the time frame of the time of death estimate.

Some reconstructionists choose to distribute the facial image showing multiple different hair or wig styles. The authors believe that this is not the best approach, since experience has shown that this practice usually creates confusion. We prefer to minimize the importance of the hair altogether. If little is known about the hair, it should probably be downplayed with attention focused on the facial features in the photographs for distribution. **Cropping tightly in on the face in a photo helps draw attention away from the hairstyle.**

Method of Photographing the Sculpture

The photography of the reconstruction sculpture may be as simple or as elaborate as the artist chooses. If you are a skilled photographer, you may place more importance on refinement of this part of the procedure, or you can turn the sculpture over to a professional for the photography work.

One of the greatest benefits of the three-dimensional method is the flexibility of the photography. **The usual five views that are shot are frontal, oblique left, lateral left, oblique right, and lateral right.**

Psychological studies on face recognition indicate that oblique or three-quarter views are advantageous and may provide more information about the way a face is structured in depth rather than frontal views.

Take care to light the sculpture in such a way that the morphological details are shown, not diminished. While dramatic lighting may be desirable in portrait photography, the goal here is to convey information rather than flatter. A backdrop that is solid in color and neutral will also help emphasize the face. Soft, diffuse light is preferable.

It is advisable to photograph any of the variations that have been prepared such as open and closed mouth or with and without wig, etc. In short, any photos of documentation should be made at this time because the sculpture will likely be disassembled and the opportunity for further photos will be lost.

Your situation may vary as to whether you are employed by a law enforcement agency or work as a freelancer. Freelancers are advised to make double copies of negatives, and maintain a copy for themselves and send a set of negatives to the requesting agency along with the cleaned skull.

Some cases require disassembly immediately while others allow for the maintenance of the sculpture for a period of time. **As a freelancer, you will need to disassemble the sculpture in order to retrieve your equipment such as prosthetic eyes, wig, and skull stand soon after the project is photographed.** Return the skull promptly to the investigating agency after doing the appropriate cleaning of the skull and evidence transferal paperwork.

Case Examples

Early Cases

As discussed in Chapter 2, the first attempt by Betty Pat. Gatliff at facial reconstruction was in 1967. The earliest cases in the 1960s and early 1970s were done as spliced or half faces (Figures 13.37 and 13.38). The facial reconstructions were done only on the right side of the skull, which was then photographed frontally. The negative was reversed and printed, and the two right sides were spliced together to form a full-face image.

Although a number of identifications occurred using this split-face method, it became apparent over time that skulls, like faces, are almost always asymmetrical in nature.

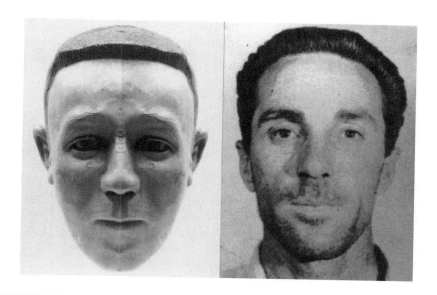

Figure 13.37   Late 1960s case done as a **spliced face** (left) and subject identified (right). (Courtesy of Betty Pat. Gatliff.)

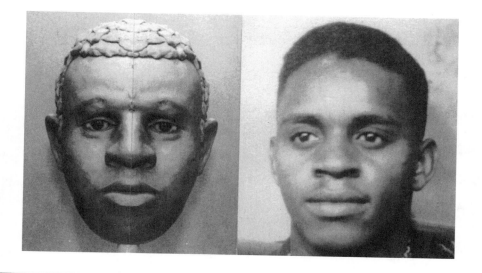

Figure 13.38   Early 1970s case done as a **spliced face** (left) and subject identified (right). (Courtesy of Betty Pat. Gatliff.)

Since this asymmetry is a specific and individual trait, it is important that it be emphasized, so the method was soon altered to do a full-face sculpture rather than only half.

The potential usefulness of this half-faced approach on damaged skulls remains valid. **In cases of skulls from which large sections of the face are missing, it may be useful to reconstruct one half only and then replicate that half onto the other side by a mechanical means.**

As with the earliest cases, this can be done photographically, or it can be easily accomplished by scanning in the half sculpture into a graphics software and reversing the facial image to the opposing side.

Other Case Examples

A collection of cases accompanied by the photographs of the subjects subsequently identified demonstrates that the method herein presented works regardless of age, ancestry, or sex.

The forensic artist can learn much, for use in future cases, from assessment of the reconstruction with photographs of the person in life. The artist should attempt to obtain comparison life photos, in various views if possible, since a study of each individual feature may lead to useful new information. Unfortunately, good quality photographs of victims in the desired view may be difficult to get.

Some comparisons prove astonishingly close while others may be rather disappointing to the artist. It seems, however, that **for the friends or loved ones of a missing person, there is oftentimes a nebulous quality in a face, represented implicitly in a reconstruction, that somehow triggers the inquiry that leads to identification.** If this occurs and the case can be resolved, the reconstruction was a success.

Children, Juveniles, and Young Adults

See Figures 13.39, 13.40, 13.41, 13.42, 13.43, 13.44, and 13.45.

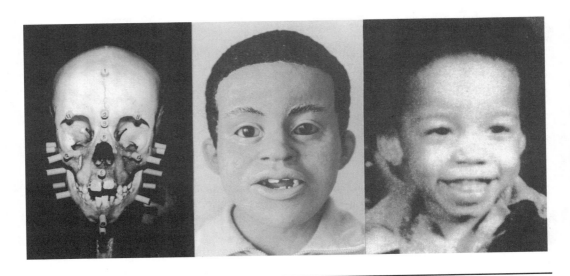

Figure 13.39 Identification of a **young child, approximately 6 years** of age: frontal skull (left), **three-dimensional facial reconstruction** by Betty Pat. Gatliff (center), and victim identified shown in last known photograph taken at 4 years of age with deciduous teeth (right). (Courtesy of Betty Pat. Gatliff.)

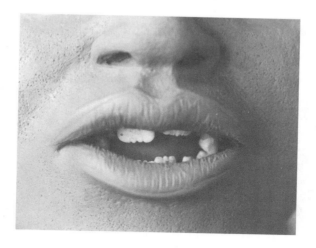

Figure 13.40 Detail of the mouth in child's reconstruction, showing partially erupted permanent teeth. (Courtesy of Betty Pat. Gatliff.)

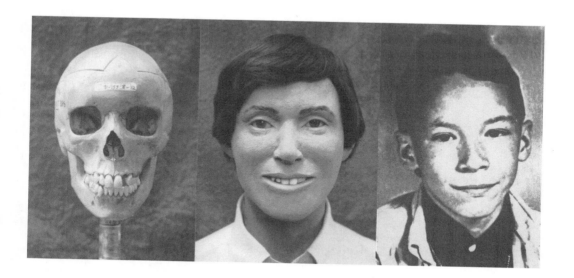

Figure 13.41 Identification of a **teenage boy, 14 years** of age: frontal skull (left), **three-dimensional facial reconstruction** by Betty Pat. Gatliff (center), and victim identified shown in a photograph at a slightly younger age (right). (Courtesy of Betty Pat. Gatliff.)

Figure 13.42 Identification of a **young woman in her late teens**: frontal skull (left), **three-dimensional facial reconstruction** by Betty Pat. Gatliff (center), and victim identified (right). (Courtesy of Betty Pat. Gatliff.)

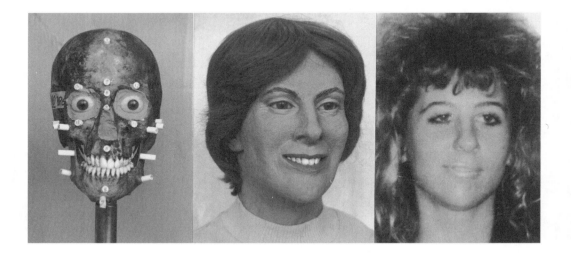

Figure 13.43 Identification of a **young woman approximately 20 years of age**: frontal skull (left), **three-dimensional facial reconstruction** by Betty Pat. Gatliff (center), and victim identified (right). Note the slight asymmetry of the nose and mouth. (Courtesy of Betty Pat. Gatliff.)

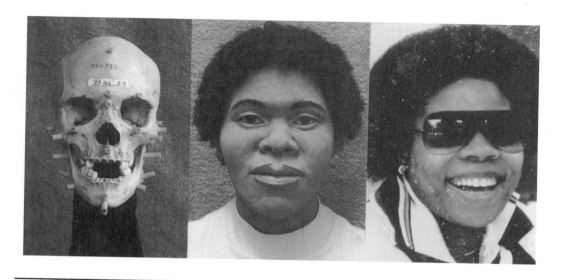

Figure 13.44 Identification of a **woman in her late 20s**: frontal skull (left), **three-dimensional facial reconstruction** by Betty Pat. Gatliff (center), and victim identified (right). (Courtesy of Betty Pat. Gatliff.)

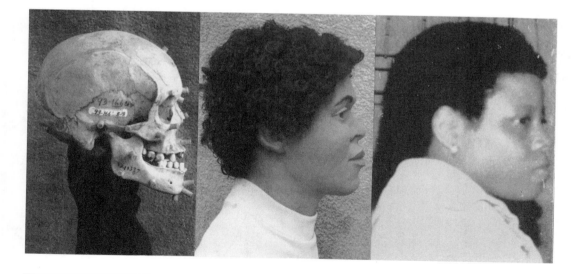

Figure 13.45 Identification of the same **woman in her late 20s** showing lateral views of skull (left), **three-dimensional facial reconstruction** (center), and victim (right). (Courtesy of Betty Pat. Gatliff.)

Middle-Aged Adults

See Figures 13.46, 13.47, 13.48, 13.49, and 13.50.

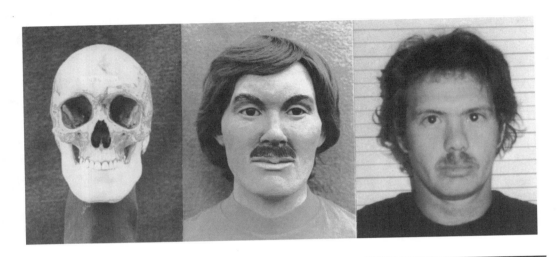

Figure 13.46 Identification of a **man, 30 years of age**: frontal skull with **missing mandible** rebuilt in clay (left), **three-dimensional facial reconstruction** by Betty Pat. Gatliff (center), and victim identified (right). Note that hair and facial hair specimens were provided, but iris misalignment could not be predicted. (Courtesy of Betty Pat. Gatliff.)

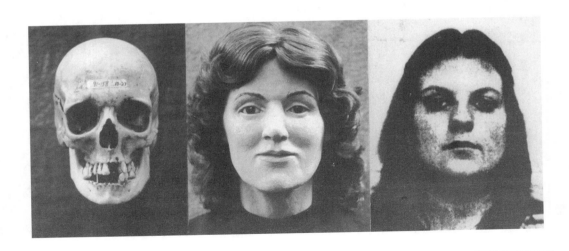

Figure 13.47 Identification of a **woman approximately 30 years of age**: frontal skull (left), **three-dimensional facial reconstruction** by Betty Pat. Gatliff (center), and victim identified (right). (Courtesy of Betty Pat. Gatliff.)

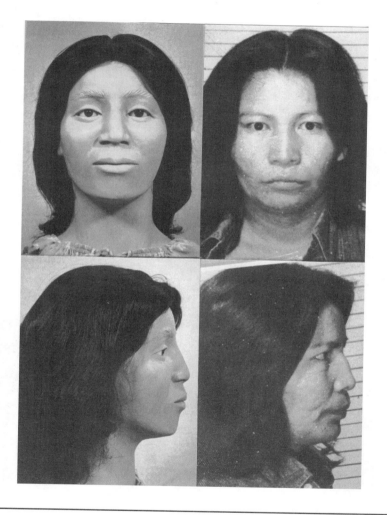

Figure 13.48 Identification of a **woman in her mid-30s**: frontal **three-dimensional facial reconstruction** by Betty Pat. Gatliff (upper left), victim identified (upper right), lateral reconstruction (lower left), and lateral photo of victim (lower right). (Courtesy of Betty Pat. Gatliff.)

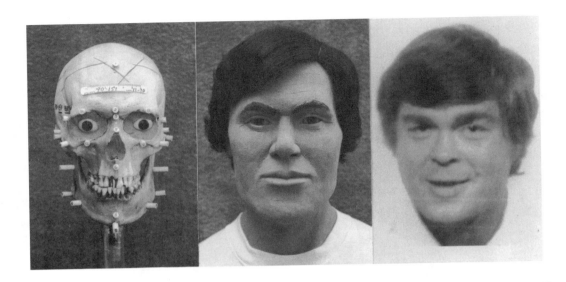

Figure 13.49 Identification of a **man in his early 40s**: frontal skull (left), **three-dimensional facial reconstruction** by Betty Pat. Gatliff (center), and victim identified (right). (Courtesy of Betty Pat. Gatliff.)

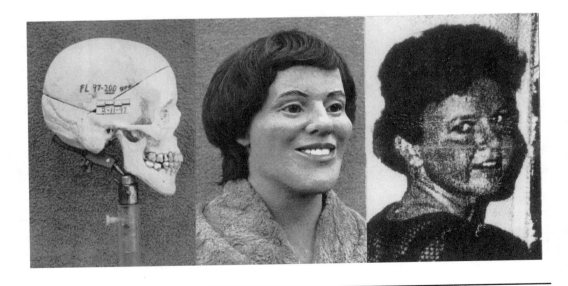

Figure 13.50 Identification of a **woman in her mid-40s**: lateral skull (left), **three-dimensional facial reconstruction** by Betty Pat. Gatliff (center), and victim identified (right). (Courtesy of Betty Pat. Gatliff.)

Older Adults

See Figure 13.51.

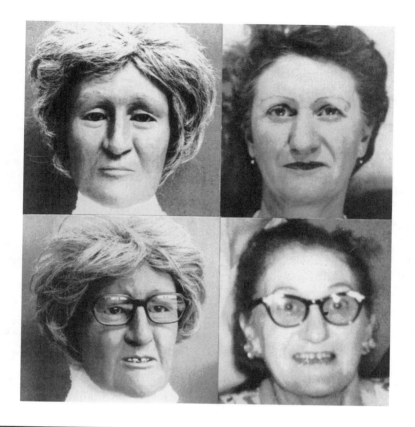

Figure 13.51   Facial reconstruction of a woman photographed in progress at different ages and comparison photos at different ages of victim identified. (Courtesy of Betty Pat. Gatliff.)

Museum and Other Applications

The technique of three-dimensional facial reconstruction on the skull has been useful in forensic cases, museum and historical work, prosthetics, demonstrative evidence, and certain forensic testing procedures.

Some special case projects of interest include mummies, early Americans, soldiers, and historical figures. In recent years, museums around the world have removed hundreds of skeletal remains from public view due to human rights considerations, and many of these remains have been repatriated. This trend has led to the production of a number of facial reconstructions from the skulls, so that these humans of historic interest may be remembered and represented.

Mummies

King Tutankhamen

The boy king Tutankhamen lived in Egypt more than 5000 years ago. His tomb was discovered in 1927 A.D. by English archaeologists. Betty Pat. Gatliff was commissioned by a Miami, Florida orthopedic surgeon to do a facial reconstruction on a plaster skull casting (Figure 13.52). The casting was fabricated from radiographs of the mummy by Joe Young, an Oklahoma physical anthropologist. The completed reconstructed face was unveiled at a meeting of the Egyptology Society of Miami in summer 1983. Photographs and descriptions of the procedure were published in the June 1983 issue of *Life* magazine.

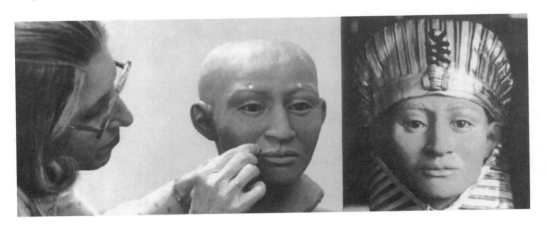

Figure 13.52 Betty Pat. Gatliff finishing the **King Tutankhamen Mummy Project** (left) and the completed reconstruction with headgear (right). (Courtesy of Betty Pat. Gatliff.)

Anniston, Alabama Museum Project

The Anniston, Alabama Reconstruction Project was prepared on an unknown mummy from the museum's permanent collection (Figure 13.53). A benefactor's curiosity regarding the visage of the mummy in life prompted the funding of the project. A skull was fabricated in clay by Joe Young, who sculpted the forms based on radiographs of the mummy. The facial reconstruction was done over a plaster skull casting. The finished sculpture, then cast in bronze, is now on exhibit as part of the Egyptian collection.

Early Americans

Galveston Island Aboriginal Female

An aboriginal female skull, ca. 1500, found on Galveston Island, Texas, was reconstructed for the Harris County Heritage Society Museum in Houston, Texas (Figure 13.54). Three drilled beads made of conch shell columella forms were found at another Texas Gulf Coast burial site, so artistic license was taken in adding them to this

Figure 13.53 The **Anniston, Alabama Mummy Project** showing completed reconstruction with wig typical of the era and Betty Pat. Gatliff. (Courtesy of Betty Pat. Gatliff.)

reconstruction to reflect the type of adornment typical of the period. The beads were possibly strung on leather and worn as a necklace. The original skull was used as a foundation for development of the reconstruction, then the sculpture was cast in bronze and the skull returned to the museum collection.

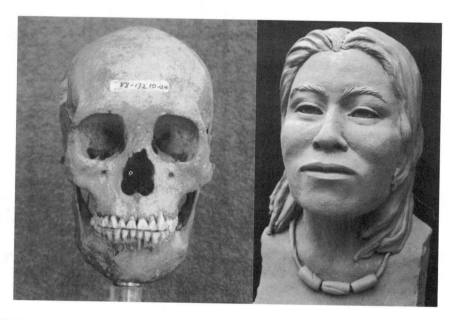

Figure 13.54 Galveston Island aboriginal female: frontal skull (left) and completed reconstruction with conch shell beads (right). (Courtesy of Betty Pat. Gatliff.)

Leanderthal Lady

In 1983, a late prehistoric skull of a female was discovered near Leander, Texas by highway construction crew members as they built a major highway. Construction work was halted on the site 20 miles north of Austin on Brushy Creek, while Texas Department of Highways and Public Transportation archaeologists supervised the recovery of the remains at the Wilson-Leonard site. Termed the "Leanderthal Lady" by the media, the discovery proved to be one of the six most complete Paleoindian skeletons recovered in North America. The facial reconstruction was prepared and cast in bronze for exhibit at the Houston Museum of Natural Science (Figure 13.55).

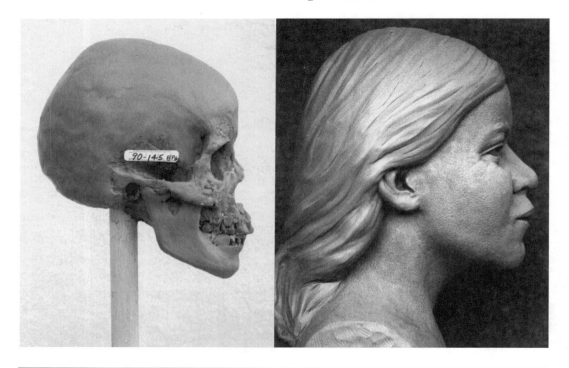

Figure 13.55 Leanderthal Lady: lateral restored skull (left) and lateral reconstruction by Betty Pat. Gatliff (right). (Courtesy of Betty Pat. Gatliff.)

Soldiers from the Custer Battlefield

Remains have been recovered at different time periods over the past 30 or more years from the site of the Custer Battlefield at Little Big Horn, Montana. Three different projects have led to the preparation of seven individual facial reconstructions based on skulls recovered at the battlefield site. Subjects of three of these seven cases have been identified using available photographs, known information about burial sites, and other individualizing descriptive information. The U.S. Parks Service has photographs of approximately 40% of the 7th Cavalry soldiers who participated in the battle, under the leadership of General George Armstrong Custer. If photographs of the remaining 60% were available, it might be possible to provide a name to each of the remaining skeletal cases.

Miles O'Hara — Little Big Horn

As part of the original project, a skull was reconstructed and later identified as Miles O'Hara, an immigrant from Ireland. Considering the visual resemblance of the reconstruction to O'Hara, a superimposition comparison was then done to help determine the identification (Figure 13.56). Based on this favorable comparison, the hat of the period worn by O'Hara in the photograph was then added to the reconstruction. The finished sculpture, complete with appropriate hat, was then cast in plaster for exhibit at the Little Big Horn Museum.

Sgt. Edward Batzer — Little Big Horn

Sgt. Edward Batzer, originally from Germany, was identified in 1990 after a television documentary entitled "Custer's Last Trooper" was aired on the Arts and Entertainment

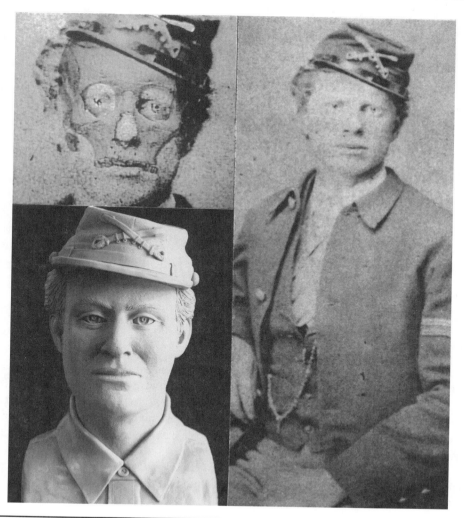

Figure 13.56 Custer Battlefield Project: Miles O'Hara. Frontal skull superimposed over photograph of Miles O'Hara (upper left), completed reconstruction by Betty Pat. Gatliff (lower left), and photograph of Miles O'Hara (right). (Courtesy of Betty Pat. Gatliff.)

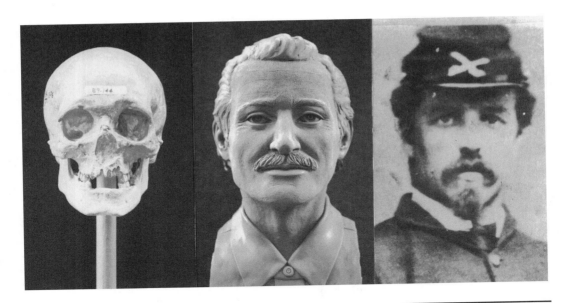

Figure 13.57 Custer Battlefield Project: Sgt. Edward Batzer. Frontal skull (left), completed reconstruction by Betty Pat. Gatliff (center), and photograph of Sgt. Edward Batzer (right). (Courtesy of Betty Pat. Gatliff.)

Network (Figure 13.57). This partial skeleton had been discovered washing out of the bank of the Little Big Horn River during the filming of a documentary concerning other artifacts. As a result of the unexpected recovery of the skeleton, the title of the television project was changed and the reconstruction became a focal point in the episode. After the broadcast, a viewer supplied the comparison photograph of a relative to the U.S. Parks Service. Unlike the case of O'Hara, before the availability of the comparison photograph, the sculpture had already been cast in bronze, which destroyed the clay original. Thus, the hat was not added after the identification of Sgt. Batzer.

Other Projects

Pizarro Project

Francisco Pizarro, the Spanish conquistador who conquered Peru in 1533, was assassinated in 1541. Not until 1977 were his skeletal remains discovered in a cathedral crypt in Lima, Peru. Dr. William Maples and Dr. Robert Benfer authenticated the discovery based in part on the historical account of the injuries inflicted during his assassination. A facial reconstruction from the skull was then developed (Figure 13.58). A bronze casting of the facial sculpture based on his skull is on exhibit at the museum in his hometown of Trujillo, Spain. A plaster casting of the same reconstruction is exhibited at the State Museum of Florida in Gainesville.

Colonial Williamsburg Project

While excavating an area of the Carter's Grove site on the James River, Colonial Williamsburg archaeologist Ivor Noel Hume discovered the long lost settlement of

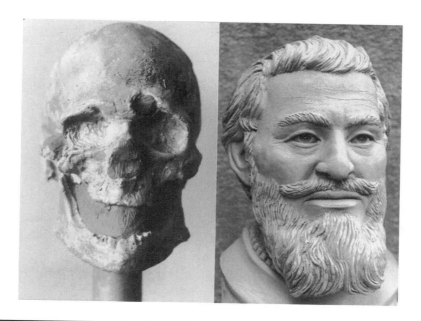

Figure 13.58   Francisco Pizarro Project. Casting of frontal skull (left) and completed reconstruction by Betty Pat. Gatliff (right). (Courtesy of Betty Pat. Gatliff.)

Wolstenholme Towne, dating to about 1620. Betty Pat. Gatliff was asked to sculpt a facial reconstruction based on a skull recovered at the site. Anthropologist Dr. Lawrence Angel of the Smithsonian Institution and Dr. David Wiecking, Medical Examiner for the Commonwealth of Virginia, provided scientific input. The face that was developed on the skull was believed to be perhaps the oldest homicide victim known from colonial America (Figure 13.59). Historians believe that the victim of the 1622 Wolstenholme massacre may, in fact, have been the settlement's military leader, Lt. Kean. The sculpture is on display at the Carter's Grove Plantation Museum.

President Kennedy Assassination Project

The most challenging project of Betty Pat. Gatliff's career came from the U.S. House of Representatives Select Committee on Assassinations in 1978. An important part of the panel's work involved the resolution of controversial issues relating to the number, timing, and source of the shots fired in Dealey Plaza on November 23, 1963. Their inquiry included engineering, medical, and photographic studies to plot the trajectory of the bullets that struck President John Kennedy and Texas Governor John Connolly. To facilitate the trajectory project, a model of President Kennedy's head was sculpted for analysts to use to obtain crucial measurements (Figure 13.60).

Special Project for the FBI

An investigation by the Human Rights Unit of the FBI required an accurate reproduction of the victim's head at the correct scale for forensic testing purposes to determine if an alleged human rights violation had taken place. The question posed to Betty Pat.

Figure 13.59   Colonial Williamsburg Project. Reconstruction by Betty Pat. Gatliff and the skull recovered at Wolstenholme Towne. (Courtesy of Betty Pat. Gatliff.)

Gatliff was, "Can you sculpt a person's head to the actual size?" Her response was, "Possibly, if I have access to the skull."

The primary obstacle was to produce a sculptural head model without performing any invasive procedures on the victim's body. The body was exhumed and available for examination, but the head could only be radiographed and CT scanned. The best procedure at the time for replication of a skull involved use of the CT scans. Oklahoma anthropologist Joe Young fabricated a skull by cutting 115 pieces of cardboard made from the victim's CT scan data and stacking them together.

Using the CT-generated skull as a foundation, the facial reconstruction was done using the tissue depth data from Dr. Stanley Rhine and Dr. H. R. Campbell (Figure 13.61). In addition, autopsy photographs, which included a scale in millimeters, helped determine the details in the face, neck, and clothing. Eventually, the sculpture was used for testing by the FBI Laboratory and as a court exhibit during the sentencing phase of the accused subject's hearing.

In conclusion, the authors hope that the description of this procedure will be useful to others, be it for use in museum or other special projects or for forensic cases.

In the museum setting, the reconstruction sculptures provide respectful alternatives to the displays of human remains. By creating a visual connection with the past, they humanize our ancient ancestors and facilitate our understanding of those who have gone before.

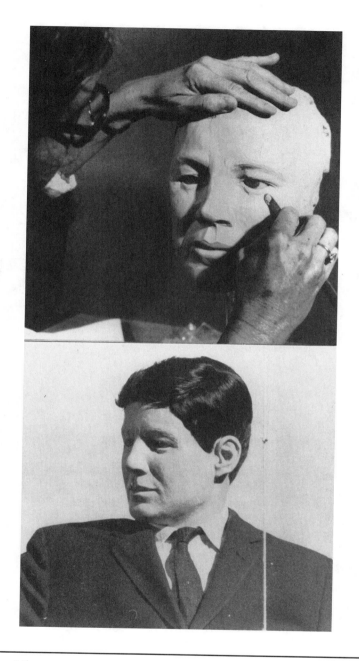

Figure 13.60 President Kennedy Assassination Project. Three-dimensional model of the head of President John F. Kennedy being sculpted by Betty Pat. Gatliff (top) and completed sculpture positioned for use in trajectory tests (bottom). (Courtesy of Betty Pat. Gatliff.)

With regard to the forensic application, the process of three-dimensional facial reconstruction on the skull has led to the identification of numerous victims of violent death. While not a perfect or exacting procedure, it has served its intended purpose, as exemplified in the cases detailed above. Sometimes,

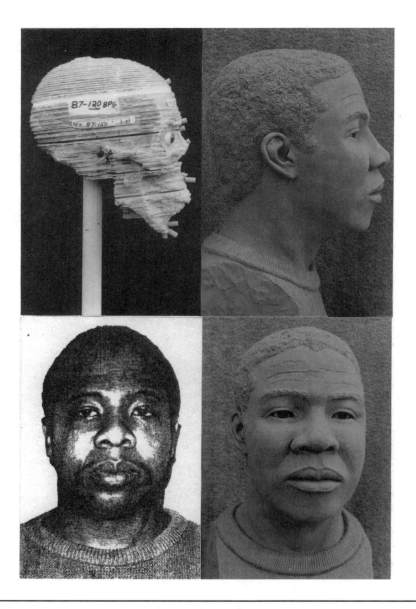

Figure 13.61 Special Project for the Human Rights Unit of the FBI. Lateral skull built from CT scan data (upper left), lateral sculpture by Betty Pat. Gatliff (upper right), deceased subject (lower left), and frontal sculpture (lower right). (Courtesy of Betty Pat. Gatliff.)

through aiding in the identification of victims, it has also aided in the identification of the perpetrators. Although there are no guarantees that each attempt will produce positive results, we believe that all humans deserve the consideration of our devoted efforts to attach a name to them for proper burial.

References

1. Krogman, W. M., *The Human Skeleton in Forensic Medicine.* Springfield, IL: Charles C Thomas, 1962.
2. George, R. M., Anatomical and artistic guidelines for forensic facial reconstruction, in *Forensic Analysis of the Skull*, Iscan, M.Y. and Helmer, R.P., Eds. New York: Wiley–Liss, 1993.
3. Guinness, A. E., Ed., *ABC's of the Human Body.* Pleasantville, NY: The Reader's Digest Association, Inc., 1987.
4. Krogman, W. M., personal communication with Betty Pat. Gatliff, 1969.

Chapter 14

Methods of Superimposition

David M. Glassman, Ph.D.

During the past 130 years, a number of techniques for comparing images of an individual with their skeletal remains by means of superimposition have been developed. Superimposition comparisons have developed into a useful tool for assessing identification of unknown skeletal remains. **These techniques fall into three general categories: photographic, video, and computer aided.** All three have been modified several times since their first appearance in the scientific literature, and several variations within all three categories are used for identification purposes today. There appears to be no agreement as to which category of technique, or which variation within a specific category, yields the most accurate comparisons.

This chapter introduces the uses of superimposition analysis in forensic identification, discusses the critical variables necessary to develop an accurate comparison, and describes the video superimposition procedure and subsequent analysis technique that I have successfully used over the past 15 years. The chapter is not intended to be a comprehensive presentation of the subject, nor does it focus on the technical aspects. Instead, it provides an overview of superimposition studies for forensic artists, law enforcement personnel, and others who collaborate with researchers involved in forensic identification. More detailed accounts of superimposition comparison techniques may be found in texts by Helmer,[1] Helmer and Iscan,[2] and in a number of articles published in the *Journal of Forensic Sciences* over the past decade.

Background of Superimposition Comparisons

Attempts to compare skeletal remains to photographs, paintings, death masks, or other images of an individual to confirm identity have a relatively long history. The earliest comparisons were primarily for scientific purposes of confirming osteometric measurements or morphology of the skulls of historical persons such as J. S. Bach, Immanuel Kant, Robert the Bruce, Oliver Cromwell, and George Buchanan with their preserved images.[3-9] None of these studies was concerned with medico-legal or criminal issues, and results varied as to the reliability of their techniques for an accurate match.

The first documented use of photographic superimposition in a medical-legal context has been attributed to Glaister and Brash[10] for their 1937 analysis of the 1935 Buck Ruxton case. Comparisons were made between photographs of two recovered skulls and antemortem photos of two missing women, Buck Ruxton's wife Isabella, and her housemaid Mary Rogerson (Figure 2.9 in Chapter 2). The superimposition involved the overlay of a negative of one of the skulls over a positive print of a photo of Mrs. Ruxton in life. The skull picture had to be scaled and oriented to the precise size and angle and adjusted so that the angle of the jaw, the chin, and other traits were correctly aligned. A diamond tiara worn by Mrs. Ruxton in the photograph acted as a scaling device for correct enlargement of the photo. When overlaid, there were several morphological areas of concordance. The superimposition evidence in the Buck Ruxton case was allowed by the court as supporting evidence in the identity of the unknown skulls. It was not accepted, however, as a means for determining positive identification in lieu of other supporting data. Today, the issue of reliability in superimposition comparisons for making positive identification is commonly debated among researchers involved in superimposition analyses.[11]

A second early case involving superimposition, which received wide public attention, took place in 1942 in London. The remains of a skeleton found in the cellar of a bombed Baptist church by a workman were initially thought to represent a victim of a German blitz raid. However, after observing the remains, pathologist Keith Simpson concluded that the pattern of the remains was not consistent with a bomb victim. Further anthropologic and dental observations suggested that the skeleton may have belonged to Rachel Dobkin, who had been missing for approximately 15 months. To test this possible match, Simpson superimposed a photograph of the skull with an antemortem photograph of Rachel Dobkin. A convincing similarity was concluded (Figure 14.1). Subsequently, Rachel Dobkin's husband, Harry Dobkin, was arrested and found guilty of the murder of his wife. Apparently, he had placed his wife's body in the cellar of the bombed church, where he had previously served as a fire-watcher, to confuse authorities into thinking she was a bomb casualty.[12]

Following the Ruxton and Dobkin cases, the use of superimposition comparisons gradually increased and new techniques were developed.[13-14] This research remained focused on high profile cases rather than as a routine protocol in the identification of hundreds of unknown skeletal remains recovered each year by law enforcement agencies in the U.S. and abroad. These high profile cases included the famous superimposition comparisons used to aid in identification of the remains of Hitler,[15] Bormann,[15] and Mengele[16] (see Figure 2.22 in Chapter 2).

In 1976, Dr. Clyde Snow[17] became one of the first American forensic scientists to advocate the use of video cameras for superimposition in routine identification cases. Procedural protocols for using video superimposition were already being suggested and others followed shortly thereafter.[13,18-20] The basic protocol included the use of two video cameras, one to project the unknown skull, and the other to project the antemortem photograph. Both images were then electronically interfaced using some type of mixing unit with the superimposed image projected on the monitor. Since first

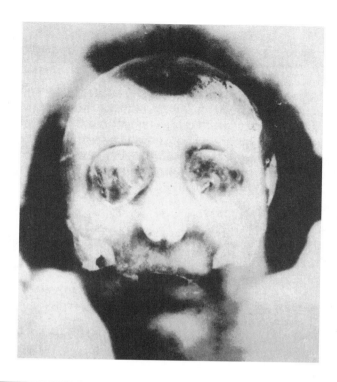

Figure 14.1   World War II era superimposition of Rachel Dobkin.

reported, the technique for video superimposition has been modified by several researchers in efforts to produce the most reliable comparison for assessing the concordance between image and skull.[21-23] In some cases this has included the use of computed-aided assistance.[24-27]

The use of photographic, video, and computer-aided superimpositions has remained a useful tool for assisting in the identification of unknown skeletal remains. More cases than ever are being subjected to this form of analysis. Debate continues as to which technique provides the best indicator of identity. It is likely that each technique has unique advantages and disadvantages. Undoubtedly further technological advances in computer digitization and photographic enhancement will yield a degree of accuracy not yet obtainable by today's methodology.

Procedural Considerations

Regardless of the technique one uses in superimposition cases (i.e., photographic, video, or computer-aided) a few **critical variables** must be considered. These include, but are not limited to, **positioning, size, distortion, features to be used for comparison, and the defining limits for concluding a possible match or exclusion.** The importance of each of these issues for the results and accuracy of superimposition studies has been discussed since the technique was first proposed, and continues to be debated today. Logic dictates that an effective comparison between two images must be controlled for position and size. It is no wonder then that attention in perfecting superimposition comparisons has focused primarily on these two issues.

Orientation

In most cases the antemortem photograph is unalterable in pose and therefore the skull must be rotated to approximate the identical position in the photograph. This has proven to be a difficult task in many cases. From my own experience in video superimposition analyses, I have observed that an extremely slight alteration in skull positions may influence a decision from one of matching to one of poor concordance. Various methodologies have been suggested for skull positioning, ranging from simple rotation on a cork flask ring[11] to motor-driven skull rests[23] and tilt-measuring devices.[28]

Scale

A variety of scaling techniques have been used to correct for size differences between the skull and photographic image. For example, Delfino and colleagues[24] have effectively used a crosshatch generator that superimposes a network of vertical and horizontal lines onto the image and projected onto the video monitor. This represents a technology that expands upon the traditional use of determining lines.[29] In a different approach, Dorion[21] has corrected for size differences by enlarging the antemortem photograph, using reference points of the skull. Similarly, Bellemare[30] measured several dimensions of the skull with a sliding caliper and enlarged the antemortem photograph in accordance with the points measured. More recently, several researchers[27,31] have turned to computer-aided technology using electronic imaging of photographs and crania in the attempt to minimize size distortion. Unfortunately, no matter what techniques are used, some measure of size and optical distortions persist.

A Model of Video Superimposition

The following is a description of the **protocol** that I have employed for **developing superimposition videotapes** and the subsequent **methodology used for analysis to support or reject a match.** I do not contend that my procedure is superior to any other. However, discussion of the technique will yield insight into dealing with the critical variables necessary to make accurate comparison conclusions.

Protocol for Developing Superimposition Videotapes

A Team Approach

I am assisted in conducting superimpositions by Gene Henderson and other members of the Media Productions Unit of the Texas Department of Public Safety and the broadcast-quality video technology utilized there. I am also assisted by forensic artist Karen T. Taylor. **I have found collaboration with a forensic artist to be extremely helpful in both positioning the skull and evaluating video comparisons.** Apparently, an artistic "eye" may visualize aspects of contour, asymmetry, and shape that may be missed by those professionals who are more conventionally trained to assess aspects of size and conformity of specific anatomical structures. This collaborative effort, which views the superimpositions from two differing educational and professional backgrounds, has resulted in an increased number of skeletal identifications.

Camera Placement

The basic procedure for comparison requires two video cameras, one directed at the skull and one directed at the comparison photograph. Positioning the skull for video superimposition involves placing the skull on a sand-filled cushion or cork ring on the floor with the eye orbits facing upward. This allows for manipulation of the skull's orientation while retaining a sturdy positioning of the skull. **The first video camera points directly downward at the skull, perpendicular to the floor.**

The antemortem photographic image is affixed to a vertical bulletin board. **A second video camera points at the photographic image, parallel with the floor.** Both images are projected onto a monitor placed near the skull so that the assistant, usually the forensic artist, can easily view the superimposition in progress while maneuvering the skull. The skull is superimposed and blended with the photographic image, both on the monitor used by the assistant and on monitors in a nearby control room where the anthropologist views them. The anthropologist and assistant communicate by means of conversation broadcast through headsets.

Skull Preparatory Steps

Several preparatory steps have proven helpful during the procedure. If the mandible is recovered, it should be affixed to the cranium with a few millimeters of spacing allowed in the temperomandibular joint. This is often done by the forensic artist, who is familiar with similar procedures used in preparation for facial reconstruction on the skull.

The insertion of small dowels or soft rubber cylinders into and projecting from the auditory meati has been valuable in aligning the skull with the corresponding region of the ear in the photographic image (Figure 14.2). In addition, it is helpful to use determining lines for locating the appropriate position of the skull and to assist in size comparisons. This can be done by laying a piece of matte acetate or other sheer paper material over the facial photograph and drawing lines to clearly indicate the location of certain landmarks such as the base of the nose, midline of the lips, midline of the eyes, occlusal surface of the exposed teeth, and the base of the lower jaw (Figure 14.3). It may also be beneficial to attach a series of tissue depth markers in the fashion used for preparing skulls for facial reconstructions as described in Chapter 11. This may assist in the comparison of superimposed contours as well as the adjustment of the size and orientation of the skull to the photo image, as illustrated in Figure 14.4.

Adjustments for Scale and Orientation

Once the skull has been positioned in a corresponding orientation to the antemortem photograph, the video camera dedicated to the skull manipulates the size of the skull to most closely fit the photograph as indicated by the determining lines, auditory meati markers, and visual inspection. **Within the control room, as second and third video monitors are observed by the anthropologist, instructions are given to the video camera operator for minor skull size adjustments and to the assistant for skull positioning adjustments.** When the closest approximation of size and position are located, the cameras are "locked down."

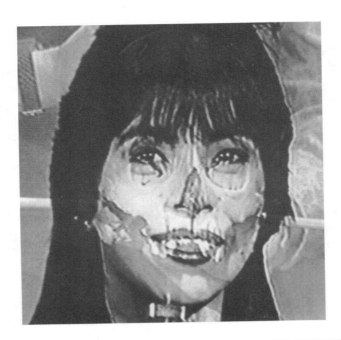

Figure 14.2 Superimposition comparison using dowels in the auditory meati to assist skull/photo positioning. (Courtesy of Texas Department of Public Safety.)

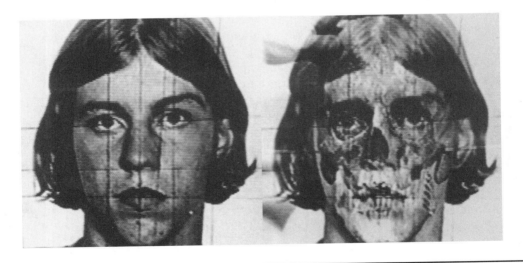

Figure 14.3 Lines drawn on matte acetate over the photographic image indicating specific landmarks to assist in positioning the skull in superimposition comparisons. (Courtesy of Texas Department of Public Safety.)

Blends and Sweeps

Taping of the video superimposition is initiated after correct scale and orientation are determined. The two primary video techniques used for documenting the

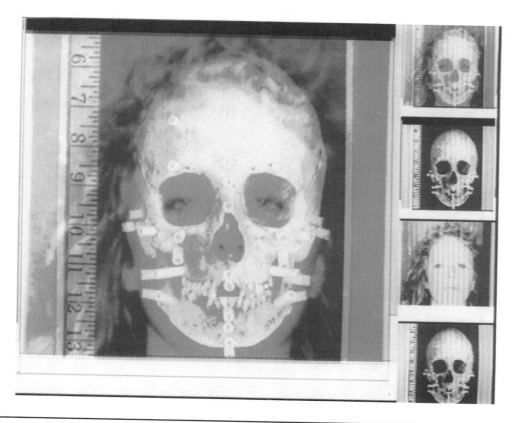

Figure 14.4 **Superimposition comparison in which tissue depth markers have been attached to the skull to assist in skull positioning and size adjustment.** (Courtesy of Texas Department of Public Safety.)

superimposition and for analysis of conformity are **"blending or fading" and "sweeping."** A blending of the photo and skull is manipulated in the control room starting with the photo image only, and then slowly and progressively increasing the superimposed image of the skull (Figure 14.5). The blending progresses until the skull dominates the superimposition and finally terminates with a skull-only image. This procedure is documented several times. While the blending procedure is being taped, the control room monitors are studied to identify any needed correction in size and/or positioning of the skull. If necessary, the skull will be reoriented or size corrected and the blending procedure will be continued.

The technology in the DPS video laboratory allows for several types of **sweeping procedures** that may be used in the superimposition taping. In practice, I prefer to sweep the photo image across the skull. Either way, however, should produce equivalent results. Most frequently, I have relied on a set of **vertical, horizontal, and diagonal sweeps** for use in analyzing the superimposition (Figures 14.6 and 14.7). In some cases, it has been useful to **"box sweep"** from the center of the superimposition, which affords careful comparison of the mouth and lower nasal structures (Figure 14.8). The contrast of a solid blank sweep across a blended image of skull and photo is useful in point-by-point comparisons of specific structures (Figure 14.9).

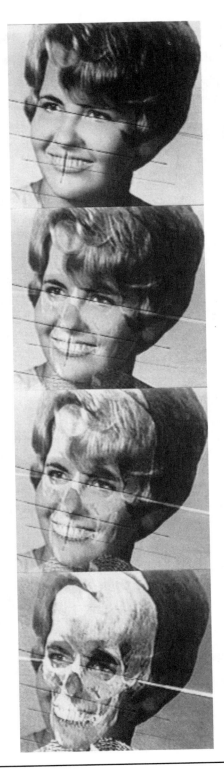

Figure 14.5 The **blending progression** from photographic facial image only (top) to skull (bottom). (Courtesy of Texas Department of Public Safety.)

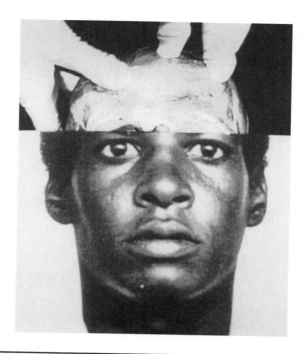

Figure 14.6   Horizontal sweep of photographic image and skull. (Courtesy of Texas Department of Public Safety.)

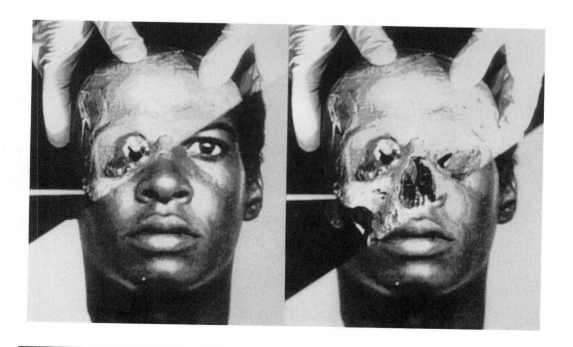

Figure 14.7   Diagonal sweep at two locations of the photographic image and skull. (Courtesy of Texas Department of Public Safety.)

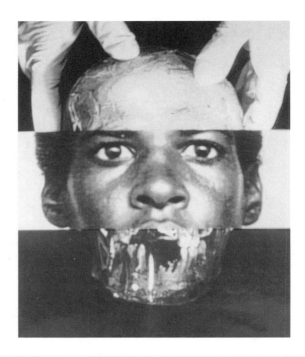

Figure 14.8   Box sweep of photographic image and skull. (Courtesy of Texas Department of Public Safety.)

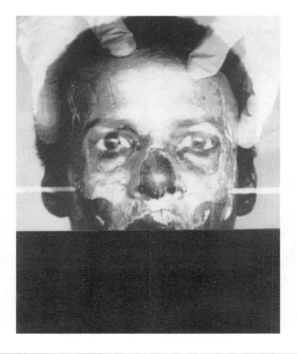

Figure 14.9   Blank sweep across a superimposed image of the skull and photographic image. (Courtesy of Texas Department of Public Safety.)

Methodology for Analysis of Superimposition Videotapes

Analysis of the superimposition videotape is conducted at the osteology laboratory at Southwest Texas State University. **It is not a reasonable practice to attempt to analyze the superimposition in the limited time offered during taping.** Hurried comparisons are apt to result in erroneous conclusions. Even early speculations should be kept to oneself to alleviate any unnecessary follow-up work by law enforcement investigators or inaccurate reporting to the media.

Equipment for Methodical Analysis

For accurate analysis, it is necessary to use a VCR and monitor that produce high resolution, provide for continuous slow-speed viewing, and have single frame advancement and a pause function that maintain the image in a stable format. During the course of analysis, the blending and sets of sweeping images are reviewed several times. This includes, but is not limited to, the overall shape, teeth and dental sockets, chin region, nasal region, interorbital breadth, orbital contours, and forehead. Superimposition comparisons augmented by a close-up overlay comparison of the recovered anterior teeth in a skull and the teeth in a smiling photograph are very beneficial. The teeth will appear larger with the gingeval tissues missing.

Concordance of each feature or region between the antemortem photograph and unknown skull is recorded by degree of similarity. For example, note the degree of similarity that exists between the maxillary central incisors depicted in the smiling photo image and the corresponding alveolar region of the skull in Figure 14.10.

Ranking System

Once completed, all records are reviewed and the comparison is given a ranked score between I and IV. The ranking is based on a qualitative assessment of the number and closeness of anatomically matched areas. **Grade I** represents a close match with strong concordance in all anatomical areas available for comparison, and no area dictates exclusion. **Grade II** reflects a somewhat less convincing comparison and is described as a reasonable match with strong concordance in most anatomical areas and no area dictates exclusion. **Grade III** is used in those cases where the comparison cannot be used to definitively exclude a match, but is judged unlikely due to a number of anatomical areas that exhibit poor concordance. The final stage, **Grade IV**, is assigned when comparison of one or more areas indicates definite exclusion. Figure 14.11 illustrates an example where an exclusionary decision was made from video superimposition analysis. In this case, the profile superimposition clearly shows a disparity in conformity of the overall shape, frontal contour, and mandibular size. Any attempt to correct for size results in either a skull that is too small to accurately compare with the photo or, if enlarged to fit anatomical markers such as the nasal sill, bottom of the eye orbit, and level of the auditory meati, the mandible becomes outside of the image parameter of the photographic jaw. This is one case where the exclusion is obvious due to large differences between the anatomical structure of the skull and the photographic image. Often the differences

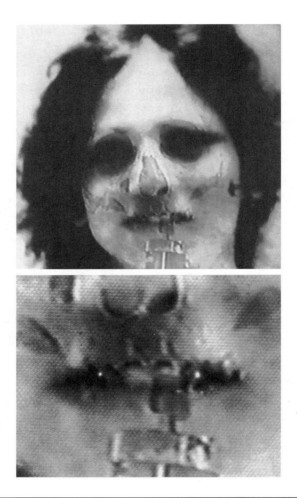

Figure 14.10   Superimposition comparison (top) and **close-up of the alveolar region** (bottom). (Courtesy of Texas Department of Public Safety.)

identified in video superimposition are much more subtle. Occasionally, comparisons result in a mosaic pattern whereby some areas exhibit strong concordance and other areas much less. Here it is more difficult to ascertain what degree of nonconcordance warrants an accurate exclusion decision. We do not know which, if any, anatomical areas are less prone to minor size, position, or distortion error incurred from the superimposition procedure and, therefore, could be more greatly relied upon for an accurate determination.

Additional Issues

Difficult Orientations

Positioning of a skull to match a photographic view that is oriented in a position other than straight forward or in profile is often difficult regardless of the technique used.

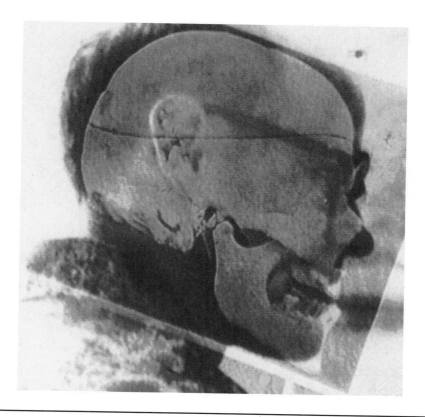

Figure 14.11 Example of an **exclusionary superimposition** with disparity in the overall shape, frontal contour, and mandibular size. (Courtesy of Texas Department of Public Safety.)

Figure 14.12 illustrates an in-progress superimposition of a skull to an oblique photographic view. Given that a small error in positioning of the skull relative to the photo image may result in an inaccurate interpretation, comparisons of this type warrant a conservative conclusion. In this case, the skull is being manipulated to test conformity in the dentition. With an oblique orientation, it may be necessary to reorient the skull several times to assess different facial regions. Even though conformity existed, a Grade II would be assigned to the superimposition to reinforce the possibility of an orientation error factor in the match.

Incomplete Skulls

Skeletal remains do not need to be complete to be useful in superimposition comparisons.

Figure 14.13 illustrates a video superimposition of an antemortem photograph with a partial cranium. The skull is missing the mandible and most of the left side of the face. Strong concordance was documented in the right side of the nasal sill, nasal height, and the right orbital border. Although a high degree of similarity was noted, the superimposition was scored a Grade II due to the number of regions that were unavailable for comparison. Shortly after the analysis was completed, a positive identification was made between the partial skull and the man in the photograph using other evidence.

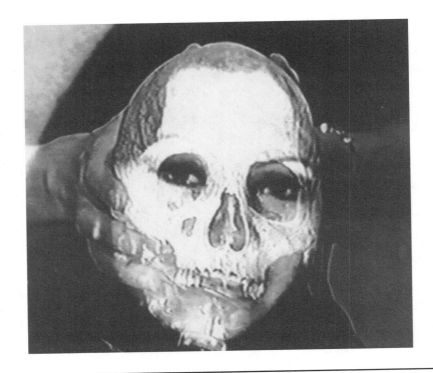

Figure 14.12   In-progress superimposition of a skull to an oblique photographic view. (Courtesy of Texas Department of Public Safety.)

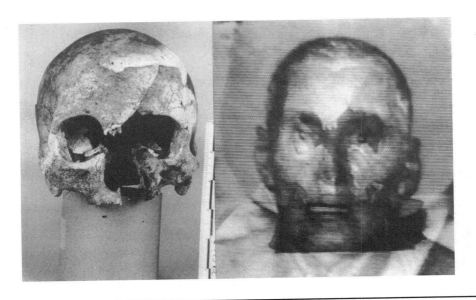

Figure 14.13   Superimposition comparison of a photographic image and a fractured cranium. (Courtesy of Texas Department of Public Safety.)

Ambiguous Indicators of Ancestry or Sex

Occasionally, superimposition analysis may be useful when there are ambiguous morphological indicators of ancestry or sex.

During a routine anthropological analysis of a skull, the ancestry of the victim was difficult to determine. The morphological traits generally used to assess ancestry were split between European ancestry or African ancestry. The majority of characteristics, however, suggested a European ancestry. Furthermore, the diagnostic characteristics for distinguishing Euro-Americans and African-Americans in the mid-facial region including the sharpness of the nasal sill, projection of the anterior nasal spine, shape of the nasal aperture, nasal root structure, and interorbital breadth (Figure 14.14) all followed the Euro-American pattern. The area of the mid-face is considered to be one of the most influential regions for deriving ancestry information. The report was submitted to the law enforcement agency suggesting the ancestry was most likely Euro-American.

After review of my report, the investigating officer contacted me and told me that the only missing person fitting the time and location parameters of this case was African American. Forensic artist Karen T. Taylor viewed photos of this missing subject and saw shapes and forms of the face that were rather consistent with those of the skull.

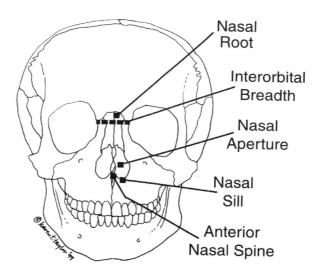

Figure 14.14 Illustration of the skull indicating **features of the mid-facial region.** (Illustration by KTT.)

I was asked if there was any likelihood that the skeleton could be of African ancestry. I was doubtful, but because a few of the morphological traits from the skull suggested an African origin, we decided to conduct a video superimposition of the unknown skull and an image of the missing African American (Figure 14.15). Analysis of the superimposition found no region or structure to qualify exclusion. Surprisingly, the mid-facial region, which was the major basis for suggesting the individual was of European extraction, demonstrated concordance with the photographic image. At the very least, the superimposition indicated that further investigation of the case was warranted.

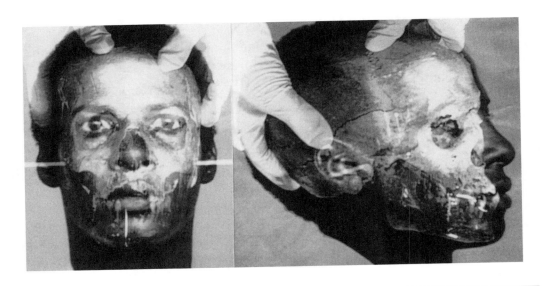

Figure 14.15 Superimposition comparison, frontal and lateral views, of unknown skull and photographic image of missing African-American male. (Courtesy of Texas Department of Public Safety.)

Multiple Views

Different photographic views of the same individual may lead to different conclusions in the superimposition analysis.

Over the past 15 years of working with video superimpositions, I have encountered cases in which different photographic views of the same individual have led to differing conclusions in the superimposition analysis. Of course, this may only be encountered when multiple photographs depicting different views are available for comparison with the unknown skull. Nevertheless, this poses the very real possibility that even when comparisons exhibit strong concordance, the photo and skull may not represent the same individual. Therefore, **it is important to attempt as many comparisons with different photographic views as are available.** I would further suggest that the strength of the superimposition analysis toward assisting in making a presumptive identification increases substantially with the number of comparative views examined. The case discussed below shows how different photographic views resulted in differing interpretations.

Case Studies

Exclusionary Case Study

In 1997, I was contacted by the Mexican Attorney General's Office at the suggestion of Karen T. Taylor of the Texas Department of Public Safety to assist in the identification of skeletal remains recovered from the ranch of Raul Salinas, brother of the former President of Mexico, Carlos Salinas.[32] At the time of the discovery, the Mexican authorities believed the remains to be those of Manual Munoz Rocha, a federal congressman from the State of Tampaulipas, who had been missing for approximately 2 years. Munoz

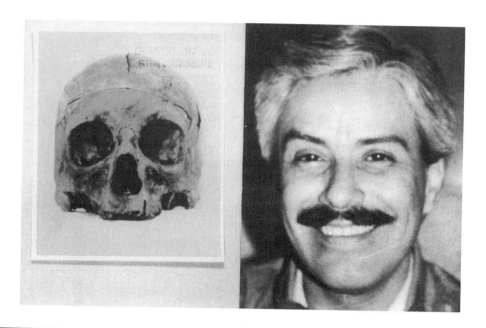

Figure 14.16   Skull found on the Salinas ranch in Mexico (left) and missing person Manual Munoz Rocha (right). (Courtesy of Texas Department of Public Safety.)

Rocha had been implicated as a co-conspirator with Raul Salinas in the political murder of Jose Francisco Ruiz Massieu. My involvement was to conduct a video superimposition analysis between the recovered skull and photos of Manual Munoz Rocha.

Figure 14.16 shows the unknown skull, which was missing the mandible, and a facial view photograph of Manual Munoz Rocha. Figure 14.17 exhibits the superimposed photo and skull revealing close similarities in the size and shape of the eyes, interorbital breadth, facial breadth, nasal sill, lateral cheek dimension, and other areas. This view alone yields a conclusion of strong concordance and consistency with the hypothesis that the remains belonged to Munoz Rocha.

A second superimposition was recorded using a lateral profile photograph producing the merged image illustrated in Figure 14.18. A different interpretation emerges as the frontal contour of the skull and nasal root are poorly matched to the forehead profile of Munoz Rocha. This superimposition concluded that a match was highly unlikely.

Interestingly, Karen T. Taylor produced two-dimensional skull reconstruction drawings in frontal and lateral views, without having seen any photographs of Munoz Rocha. Upon comparison of her drawings to photographs of Munoz Rocha, she felt that a similarity was possible in the frontal view, but not so in the lateral view. Thus, our procedures, conducted independently, illustrated similar findings when compared.

A few weeks after the superimposition was conducted, a DNA comparison determined conclusively that the remains did not belong to Munoz Rocha.

Matching Case Study

Skeletal remains and associated clothing were found in a brushy area and reported to the local law enforcement agency. An investigation commenced to identify the remains

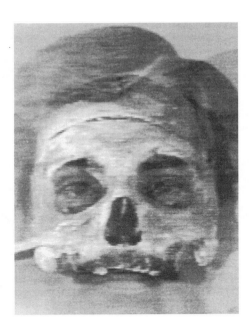

Figure 14.17 Superimposed comparison of unknown Salinas ranch skull and facial view of Manual Munoz Rocha. (Courtesy of Texas Department of Public Safety.)

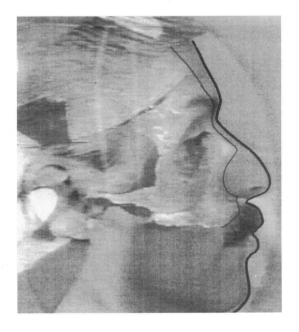

Figure 14.18 Superimposed comparison of unknown Salinas ranch skull and profile view of Manual Munoz Rocha. (Courtesy of Texas Department of Public Safety.)

and determine the cause of death. A belt found with the remains had a man's first name inscribed into the leather. The name, although common in the area, became a starting point for matching the unknown skeleton with local missing person reports. A report was located indicating a missing Chilean national with the same name who fit the parameters of sex, age, ancestry, and stature. Dental records were requested from the individual's country of origin and submitted for comparison with the dentition of the unknown remains. Review of the dental record was cause for excluding the match.

It was not until 2 or 3 years later that an informant provided information as to the identity of the skeletal remains. Curiously, the informant matched the remains with the same individual who had previously been excluded by dental information. It was decided to exhume the remains and review the anthropologic and dental evaluations. As a part of this review, a video superimposition was conducted between the reconstructed skull and antemortem photographs of the missing Chilean.[33] Figures 14.19 and 14.20 illustrate the skull, photo, and superimposed images in facial and oblique views, respectively. The comparisons revealed several areas of strong similarity and no region resulted in

Figure 14.19 Skull (left), **frontal-view** photograph of missing Chilean male (center), and **superimposed comparison** (right). (Courtesy of Texas Department of Public Safety.)

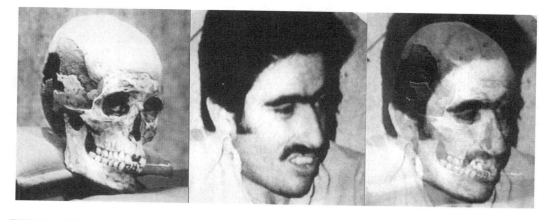

Figure 14.20 Skull (left), **oblique-view** photograph of missing Chilean male (center), and **superimposed comparison** (right). (Courtesy of Texas Department of Public Safety.)

an exclusionary decision. In addition, the right maxillary lateral incisor recovered with the skull exhibited a procumbant position relative to the other anterior teeth. One of the antemortem photographs fortunately depicted the individual in an open-mouthed position, allowing for comparison of the dentition. An identical positioning of the lateral incisor is noted in the photograph and matched in the superimposition. This finding placed suspicion on the accuracy of the dental record. Further study of the dental record indicated that restorations noted on the chart were reversed on the recovered dentition. The chart also indicated extraction notations for all third molar teeth. These teeth, present in the recovered remains, were the major factor in the original exclusion. It now appeared possible that the third molar notations may have indicated an unerupted condition, rather than antemortem extractions. Indeed, the individual was at an adolescent age when the dental charting was done. The superimposition analysis and additional evidence finally led to a presumptive identification and completed the case.

Discussion

The use of superimposition comparisons continues to be valuable in forensic identification. Advanced technology is poised to take superimposition studies to a new level. Even so, a few issues will certainly continue to be debated. For example, how do we correct for distortion error inherent in any photographic image? Will this problem of distortion be worsened as digital images replace traditional silver-based photography? Or, how closely can computer enhancement manipulate a skull and photograph to attain the same precise orientation?

A further consideration involves **how many areas of nonconformity are necessary to make an exclusion decision, and how many points of commonality are necessary to make a match likely.**

A standardized protocol of the number of points or specific areas to be compared in superimposed images has not been adopted. Obviously, the greater the number of areas of nonconformity, the greater the likelihood that the skull and photo belong to different individuals, and vice versa. However, it is not always the number of points that lead to a specific conclusion. Sometimes it is the degree of specific conformity or nonconformity that exists at a single area that indicates a conclusion. Exclusions may be based on a single area or a few areas that exhibit major size variation between the photo and the unknown skull. Conversely, the conformity of a specific anatomic anomaly which may be matched between the skull and photo can provide increased probability that the two represent the same individual.

I have always considered video superimposition to be an exclusionary tool rather than one of positive identification. There are too many variables that contain some measure of error, such as size, position, and distortion inherent in the video superimposition procedure, which preclude the making of a positive identification. Furthermore, for video superimposition techniques to be used as the sole basis of a legally accepted identification, a series of detailed, systematic tests would need to be conducted to calculate the probability of error, that is, the likelihood that a determined match between photo and skull is actually misclassified. **It is more likely that video superimposition and other photo-type comparisons will remain important tools to assist in the identification of unknown remains, but they will not be exacting techniques for making positive identifications in the same way as DNA and antemortem/postmortem radiographic comparisons.**

References

1. Helmer, R. P., *Schadelidentifizierung durch elektronische Bildmischung*, Heidelberg: Kriminalistik-Verlag, 1984.
2. Iscan, M. Y. and Helmer, R. P., Eds., *Forensic Analysis of the Skull*. New York: Wiley–Liss, 1993.
3. His, W., "Anatomische Forschungen über Johann Sebastian Bachs Gebeine und Antlitz nebst Bemerkungen über dessen Bilder," *Abhandlung durch Mathematic und Physik*, 22, 380, 1895.
4. Pearson, K., "The skull of Robert the Bruce, King of Scotland, 1274–1329," *Biometrika*, 16, 18, 1924.
5. Pearson, K., "On the skull and portraits of George Buchanan," *Biometrika*, 18, 16, 1926.
6. Pearson, K., "The skull and portraits of Henry Stewart, Lord Darnley, and their bearing on the tragedy of Mary, Queen of Scots," *Biometrika*, 20, 1, 1928.
7. Pearson, K., "The Wilkinson head of Oliver Cromwell and its relationship to busts, masks and painted portraits," *Biometrika*, 26, 269, 1934.
8. Welker, H., "On the skull of Dante," *Anthropological Review*, 5, 56, 1867.
9. Welker, H., *Schiller's Schadel und Todtenmaske, nebst Mittheilumgen über Schadel und Todtenmaske Kants*. Berlin: F. Viehweg und Sohn, 1883.
10. Glaister, J. and Brash, J. C., *Medico-Legal Aspects of the Ruxton Case*. Edinburg, U.K.: E. & S. Livingstone, 1937.
11. Austin-Smith, D. and Maples, W. R., "The reliability of skull/photograph superimposition in individual identification," *Journal of Forensic Sciences*, 39, 446, 1994.
12. Simpson, K., "The Baptist church cellar murder," *Criminologist*, 5, 93, 1970.
13. Sekharan, P. C., "A scientific method for positioning of the skull for photography in superimposition studies," *Journal of Police Science and Administration*, 1, 232, 1973.
14. Gerasimov, M. M., *The Face Finder*. London: Hutchinson and Co., 1971.
15. Sognnaes, R. F., "Hitler and Bormann identifications compared by postmortem craniofacial and dental characteristics," *The Journal of Forensic Medicine and Pathology*, 1, 105, 1980.
16. Helmer, R. P., "Identification of the cadaver remains of Josef Mengele," *Journal of Forensic Sciences*, 32, 1622, 1987.
17. Snow, C. C., "A video technique for skull-face superimposition," presented at the 28th Annual Meeting of the American Academy of Forensic Sciences, Washington, D.C., 1976.
18. Sekharan, P. C., "A revised superimposition technique for identification of the individual from the skull and photograph," *Journal of Criminal Law, Criminology and Police Science*, 62, 107, 1971.
19. Helmer, R. and Gruner, O., "Schadelidentifizierung durch Superprojektion nach dem Verfahren der elektronischen Bildmischung, modifiziert zum Trickbild-Differenz-Verfahren," *Zeitschrift für Rechtsmedizen*, 80, 189, 1977.
20. Brown, K. A., Hollamby, C., Clarke, B. J., and Reynolds, L. A., "A video technique of cranio-facial photo superimposition," in *Proceedings of the 8th International Meeting of the International Association of Forensic Scientists*, Abstract 119, 1978.
21. Dorian, R. B. J., "Photographic superimposition," *Journal of Forensic Sciences*, 28, 724, 1983.
22. Iten, P. X., "Identification of skulls by video superimposition," *Journal of Forensic Sciences*, 32, 173, 1987.
23. Seta, S. and Yoshino, M., A combined apparatus for photographic and video superimposition, in *Forensic Analysis of the Skull*, Iscan, M. Y. and Helmer, R. P., Eds. New York: Wiley–Liss, 1993.
24. Delfino, V. P., Colonna, M., Vacca, E., Potente, F., and Introna, F. Jr., "Computer-aided skull/face superimposition," *Journal of Forensic Medicine and Pathology*, 7, 201, 1986.
25. Delfino, V.P., Vacca, E., Potente, F., Lettini, T., and Colonna, M., Shape analytical morphometry in computer-aided skull identification via video superimposition, in *Forensic Analysis of the Skull*, Iscan, M. Y. and Helmer, R. P., Eds. New York: Wiley–Liss, 1993.

26. Lambrect, J. T., Brix, F., and Gremmel, H., Three-dimensional skull identification via computed tomographic data and video visualization, in *Forensic Analysis of the Skull*, Iscan, M. Y. and Helmer, R. P., Eds. New York: Wiley–Liss, 1993.

27. Ubelaker, D. H., Bubniak, E., and O'Donnell, G., "Computer-assisted photographic superimposition," *Journal of Forensic Sciences*, 37, 750, 1992.

28. Sekharan, P. C., Positioning the skull for superimposition, in *Forensic Analysis of the Skull*, Iscan, M. Y. and Helmer, R. P., Eds. New York: Wiley–Liss, 1993.

29. Chai, D.-S., Lan, Y.-W., Tao, C., Gui, R.-J., Mu, Y.-C., Feng, J.-H., Wang, W.-D., and Zhu, J., "A study on the standard for forensic anthropological identification of skull-image superimposition," *Journal of Forensic Sciences*, 34, 1343, 1989.

30. Bellemare, J.-F., "Use of photographic superimposition in identification of skeletal remains," *Journal of Evidence Photography*, 7–11, 1985.

31. Nickerson, B. A., Fitzhorn, P. A., Koch, S. K., and Charney, M. A., "A methodology for near-optimum computational superimposition of two-dimensional facial photographs and three-dimensional cranial surface meshes," *Journal of Forensic Sciences*, 36, 480, 1991.

32. Glassman, D. M. and Taylor, K. T., "Facial reconstruction and video superimposition of the Salinas ranch skeletal case from Mexico," presented at the 50th Annual Meeting of the American Academy of Forensic Sciences: San Francisco, CA, 1998.

33. Glassman, D. M., "Sex, drugs, rock and roll, and of course, death: a case study," presented at the 46th Annual Meeting of the American Academy of Forensic Sciences, San Antonio, TX, 1994.

FORENSIC ART: Additional Responsibilities

Chapter 15

Professional Ethics and Conduct

Once you set foot into the realm of forensic art, you have undertaken a serious responsibility. You are no longer creating art for beauty, for pleasure, or even for profit. You have accepted the task of aiding law enforcement with some of the most serious matters possible, at times involving life and death. Your professional behavior becomes subject to scrutiny by the judicial system; it must be above reproach. In a worst case scenario, failure to conduct yourself in an appropriate manner could potentially help a dangerous criminal escape justice.

Codes of Ethics and Conduct

Simply put, ethics means an accepted standard of conduct, particularly within a certain profession, to which all members are expected to conform. Virtually all professional organizations have established written codes of ethics and conduct. These guides are sometimes structured in generalized language that may allow for loose interpretation and adherence to the codes. For those who do not belong to any professional organization, there are no apparent limitations for ethical behavior. However, it is an incumbent obligation upon all individuals, whether members of an organization that assumes certain professional behavior or not, to conduct themselves in an ethical manner. **Ethical conduct helps ensure the administration of justice.**

Don Harper Mills, M.D., discusses **The American Academy of Forensic Sciences Code of Ethics** in his 1986 article, "Comments from the Perspective of the AAFS Ethics Committee Chairman." The code outlines ideas that can be good food for thought for forensic artists, parallel in some respects to conduct appropriate for the forensic art profession. He states:

Section 1(b): "Every member of the AAFS shall refrain from providing any material misrepresentation of education, training, experience or area of expertise." ... An expert who fails to utilize standard scientific techniques and methodology applicable to his area of expertise misrepresents his own expertise.

... Section 1(c) "Every member of the AAFS shall refrain from providing any material misrepresentation of data upon which an expert opinion or conclusion is based."

... Section 1(a): "Every member of the AAFS shall refrain from exercising professional or personal conduct adverse to the best interests and purposes of the Academy."

... Section 1(d): "Every member of the AAFS shall refrain from issuing public statements which appear to represent the position of the Academy without specific authority first obtained from the Board of Directors.

... Concluding, he says ... The Academy's code of ethics has proved efficient and effective. It is neither perfect nor all-encompassing. It has been a good first step. Whether we should go further is open to discussion.[1]

The Association of Medical Illustrators has a somewhat more specific **Code of Ethics** as well as a Code of Fair Practice. The Code of Ethics begins:

... Medical Illustration is a profession dedicated to the advancement of medical education through cooperation with medical and allied professions ... The aim of the medical illustrator is to reveal the truth and make it apprehensible through the visual media, with the fidelity of the scientist and the imagination of the artist ... Plagiarism and piracy of any nature must be avoided. Credit to whomever credit is due in an inherent obligation of the medical illustrator.[2]

Certain standards have also been set forth in the field of forensic art. Guidelines for those who become certified are discussed in part of the **Operations Manual for the Forensic Art Certification Program** under the auspices of the **International Association for Identification**:

This code is intended as a guide to ethical conduct of Certified Forensic Artists. It is not to be construed that these principles are immutable laws nor that they are all inclusive. Instead, they represent general standards which each artist should strive to meet. It is to be realized that each individual case may vary, just as does the information with which the artist is concerned, and no set of guides or rules will precisely fit every occasion. At the same time the fundamentals set forth in this Code are to be regarded as indicating, to a considerable extent, the conduct requirements expected of members of the profession and this Association. A failure to meet or maintain certain of these standards will justifiably cast doubt upon an individual's fitness for this type of work. Infractions of these principles may be regarded as inconsistent with certification as a Forensic Artist.

... It is the duty of practicing Forensic Artists to serve the interests of justice to the best of their ability at all times. In fulfilling this duty, they will use all of the scientific, interviewing and investigative techniques at their command to ascertain all of the significant facts relative to the matters under investigation. ... In carrying out these functions, the artist will be guided by those practices and procedures which are generally recognized within the profession to be consistent with a high level of professional ethics. The motives, methods and actions of the artist shall at all times be above reproach, in good taste, and consistent with proper moral conduct.[3]

Representation of Credentials and Capabilities

Professional Organizations

It is advisable for forensic artists, particularly those who work on a freelance basis, to become members of professional organizations to establish credibility and credentials for court testimony. An additional benefit is the exchange of ideas, techniques, and case information. Learning about procedures followed by colleagues on difficult cases can help artists avoid the same problems later with their own cases. A goal of uniformity of standards and procedures through professional organizations benefits everyone in a given field and can serve to upgrade an entire profession over time. More important, establishment of minimum acceptable standards helps focus a discipline. Members become more proficient at doing their work and giving testimony regarding that work. The escalating trend in all forensic disciplines is toward establishment of uniform protocols leading to certification processes.

Certification

After a workshop in composite drawing that I taught more than 10 years ago, one student returned to his home state and gave media interviews, copies of which he proudly sent to me. In newspaper articles, he discussed his newly gained credentials as a "certified composite artist." I realized that this was a presumption that I could never again allow to take place within my class.

Now, I carefully explain to each class that there is only one "certification" in forensic art, and that is *only* for composite drawing. At this writing, **the certification process administered by the International Association for Identification is the only existing certification process for composite drawing.**

If you attend a workshop, you may receive a "certificate" upon completion of the course. Such a certificate is a "certificate of attendance," and means only that you have attended that workshop for the required time. The certificate may be important documentation of the hours of training you received, useful in court testimony or when applying for certification. **However, a "certificate of attendance" is not a "certification."**

Similarly, **those who attend the forensic art course at the FBI Academy are *not* certified by the FBI.**[4] I have seen multiple business cards and promotional brochures in which artists state that they are "FBI certified" artists. Such a certification simply does not currently exist.

Education and Experience

It would seem obvious that any and all statements of education and experience by a forensic artist should be honest, forthright, and unexaggerated. Unfortunately, this is not always the case. There is a direct correspondence between your personal credibility and how you present yourself on resumes, on Web sites, in media interviews or, most important, in the courtroom.

When qualifying as an "expert witness" in a court of law, most states recognize education and experience equally, provided that they are honestly stated and can be documented or verified. Vague references to "years of training and experience" or "thousands of cases, too many to count" are not appropriate preparation for a statement of credentials in the courtroom setting.

Artists sometimes claim that such numbers or records are not available to them. Clearly, any education or training is verifiable by reference checking. Accredited colleges and universities, law enforcement training facilities, and instructors in forensic art should maintain retrievable records of course information and attendance.

Lack of proper record keeping on case work is unacceptable and opens the artist to being totally discredited in court by a skillful attorney who has done his or her homework.

Proper record keeping (discussed in Chapter 18) is especially important to the artist who contracts as a freelancer, with no departmental affiliation to add to the individual's credibility.

Statements, either on a resume or curriculum vitae, in media interviews, on personal Web sites, or in court must be carefully considered. For example, stating that you have had "extensive experience," when you have done only classroom work and a few cases, is just not true. I have known artists who boast that they have been doing composite drawing for 25 years, when in reality, they have done only one or two drawings per year. Thus, the implication of a lot of experience is less than honest. Consider the actual experience level of such a person vs. a full-time sketch artist who does several hundred drawings per year for multiple years. **Attorneys questioning forensic artists regarding their credentials should ask specifically about verifiable numbers of cases worked rather than about years of experience only.**

Statements that imply you have done work on specific cases in which you have actually had only peripheral involvement or no involvement are inappropriate.

An example of this improper misstatement of experience is a high profile case a few years ago in which a composite drawing was done of a suspected abductor of two small children. A freelance artist from another state, anxious to do a job for a television program, strongly desired to re-do the first drawing, and flew cross-country to the site of the offense. The primary law enforcement agency advised the artist that it was satisfied with the original drawing, and did not wish to have it re-done. The artist refused to accept that investigators were in charge of the case investigation. Ambitiously, she tried to force an interview with the witness, and visited the house where the witness was staying day after day. Finally, in frustration, the artist flew home having done **no interview and no drawing**. Nevertheless, the artist was so anxious to claim involvement in the prominent case that she later stated on resumes and in media interviews that she "worked" on the case as a consultant.

Another example of implication of work not actually done involved a newspaper story about a forensic artist. The artist's photograph appeared in the article, in front of multiple examples of forensic art hanging on the wall. Posing in front of another artist's work implied that the work shown on the walls of his office was his own. Care should be taken to avoid such insinuation, which opens the possibility for misrepresentation.

Statement of Capabilities

It is inappropriate to exaggerate in describing forensic art functions in general or describing your personal capabilities specifically. Because forensic art has the potential to produce prompt, dramatic results, the artist sometimes receives a great deal of attention. Unfortunately, certain forensic artists become so enamored of their own talents that they do self-aggrandizing media interviews, "stretching" their own abilities as well as the limitations of the field as a whole. This self-serving behavior can do harm by implying capabilities that forensic art simply does not offer.

An example would be the implication that the artist can, through interviewing a witness, produce a drawing of "exactly" what the witness saw. Memory simply does not have this kind of "flashbulb" accuracy; it is far more complex (see Chapter 5).

Another misstatement I have heard is that forensic art can produce a "positive identification." At best, *all* forensic art, by its nature, is ancillary information that merely *assists* in leading to a positive identification by some other legally established means. **Forensic art can be the link that leads investigators to the necessary information that will establish positive identification. Forensic art alone does not establish identification.**

Subjects represented in composite drawings must be legally identified by the visual confirmation of the witness who initially described them, by fingerprints, DNA, or other valid methods. Victims depicted in postmortem drawings or skull reconstructions must be legally identified by comparison of fingerprints, dental records, radiographs, DNA, or other accepted means.

In general, an artist should avoid taking undue credit for the favorable resolution of a case. The artist's work, although important, is only an investigative tool used by officers conducting an investigation. **The forensic artist is part of a team.**

Dealings with Other Artists

On occasion, you may be requested to redo artwork that was previously done by another artist. **Any alteration or change of previously done forensic art should be done only after careful consideration of possible ramifications for the investigation.** The integrity of the case is absolutely the primary concern.

There are circumstances in which an update of work previously done might be beneficial for a case, but they are relatively rare. Whether the redo request is for a composite drawing, a fugitive update, a postmortem drawing, or a skull reconstruction, the potential effects on the case must be carefully thought through.

Redoing Composite Drawings

On a few occasions I have been asked to **update or redo my *own* drawings**. These were situations in which more information or a new witness became available who was a potential boost to an investigation. In such a case, it is most important to carefully document in the case file what is being done and why, particularly if a drawing is being altered, not re-drawn.

I would recommend that an interview be conducted, without showing of the original composite, to first determine how close the original description and the new witness' description are. In some instances, the officer may have already shown the sketch to the witness or the witness may have seen the sketch in the media. In either case, **it must be determined whether the original sketch will be altered or a totally new sketch will be drawn.** An example for making that distinction might be a sample scenario such as this:

> A sexual assault has occurred at a residence and the victim has described the suspect to produce a sketch. She saw his face, but his hair was covered by a stocking cap. She could also describe his clothing. A new witness is located who saw a subject near the victim's residence around the time of the incident who was wearing clothing similar to that described by the victim. The witness saw the face and saw the hair because the subject was not wearing a hat.

In such a case, I would first confer with the investigating officer to determine that we concurred on the approach. I would then show the new witness the victim's sketch and, provided he or she felt the facial features were close to his or her recollection, choose *not* to do a totally new drawing. Instead, I would prepare an overlay of some type over the original drawing (see Chapters 6 and 9) to depict the hair described by the new witness along with the facial description from the victim. I use matte acetate whenever possible to alter a drawing because the changes can be made on the overlay film, and the original drawing shows through from underneath without being changed in any way. This method maintains the integrity of the original drawing as evidence, yet updates the information as requested. This would be a good faith effort to prepare the best possible likeness that could be explained in a court of law. The overlay should be initialed and dated by the artist as if it were an original drawing.

If the new witness did not agree with the drawing of the face, of course, this method would not be appropriate. In that case, a totally new drawing would have to be done. The suspect may have had a partner who was wearing similar clothing or there may have been an innocent bystander.

It should be emphasized that you should not undertake to make changes to drawings that are not yours even if you are requested to do so. I know of one case of an abducted child in which the victim's playmates were interviewed to produce a composite black-and-white drawing. Another artist believed that it would be better to have a color composite drawing and set about reproducing the original black-and-white drawing in color. A serious problem lies in the fact that the initial witnesses were not re-interviewed to produce the color version. The artist simply "colorized" the first drawing and did not consult the original artist.[5] Unfortunately, the case has not been resolved, but I believe potential problems could exist if an arrest were to be made through assistance of the color composite. It could be shown that the color composite was made without any witness interview or input and therefore was highly speculative. Although made with good intentions, I suspect such a drawing could harm the case. Such incidents point up the need for communication among artists, membership in professional organizations, and establishment of accepted standards and procedures.

Redoing or updating one's own drawings is a far simpler matter than redoing another artist's drawing. **Ideally, you should never alter or redo another artist's composite drawing.** On rare occasions, there are situations where there was a problem with the preparation of a drawing and a witness simply is not satisfied with the original drawing. Investigators might ask another artist to attempt to produce a drawing that will be more acceptable and accurate to the witness. In this case, the preparation of a new composite would be reasonable.

Far less appropriate are the "ambulance chasing" tactics of certain artists, particularly some freelancers, who seek media publicity in high-profile cases. Encouraging media entities or even bereaved victim family members to hire them, they sometimes operate over the objection of law enforcement agencies leading an investigation. An artist's belief that he or she has superior techniques or skills is not a valid reason to redo a drawing. Actively seeking out case situations and attempting to interject oneself into a case is self-serving and unethical. This behavior can seriously jeopardize investigations. Certainly, the existence of multiple composite sketches creates a prime opportunity for defense attorneys to question the drawings in trial, possibly developing reasonable doubt. A good attorney might ask, "How many composite drawings were necessary in order to produce one that looked like my client?" or state, "Those drawings are different; there was someone else there; my client couldn't be guilty." I can imagine nothing worse than being responsible, through some error of judgment or procedure as an artist, for aiding in a guilty person being freed.

If an investigator determines that a new drawing might benefit his or her case and asks you to redo someone else's work, the professional thing to do would be to contact the first artist, if possible, and explain the request.

In certain circumstances, it would also be advisable to get an opinion from your prosecutor or district attorney before proceeding.

Probably the most common requests for redoing work that I receive regard mechanically generated composites, either hand assembled or computer generated. Many witnesses are not fully satisfied with the completed composites and want some feature or subtlety of expression not available in the kit or database.

Redoing Other Types of Forensic Art

Requests to redo other types of forensic art should also be considered carefully, although these actions do not pose as strong a potential threat to investigations and prosecutions as those inherent in composite redos.

Child age progressions or fugitive updates, by their nature, may need to be redone over time if there are no results. Postmortem drawings or skull reconstructions are sometimes redone in order to try a variation in techniques. An example might be a postmortem drawing first done as an image modification by computer retouching and then redone by hand drawing or vice versa. A skull reconstruction may be done in both two- and three-dimensional versions.

It is generally unpredictable by what means these methods might prove effective, and the truth is sometimes a lot of luck is involved. In other words, one method may produce results when another did not, perhaps merely due to luck, timing, or both. One example is the well-known fugitive update case of John Emil List who murdered his family in New Jersey in 1971 (Figure 15.1). Many people are aware of the dramatic recovery of List in 1989 after a remarkable bust of him, prepared by

Figure 15.1 Images of fugitive John Emil List. Early photograph of List (upper left); fugitive update drawing by Lew Trowbridge of the New Jersey State Police (lower left); photographic fugitive update by Gene O'Donnell at the FBI (lower center), sculptural fugitive update by Frank Bender (lower right), and List when captured after 18 years at large (upper right). (Courtesy of "America's Most Wanted," New Jersey State Police, Federal Bureau of Investigation, and Frank Bender.)

Frank Bender, was aired on "America's Most Wanted." Less known is the fact that two earlier updates were prepared in 1987 and 1988, each using a different method. Lew Trowbridge of New Jersey State Police prepared a hand-drawn fugitive update sketch of List. Gene O'Donnell at the FBI also prepared a two-dimensional photographic update, altering a 16-year-old image. A neighbor of a man known as "Bob Clark" in Denver saw a strong resemblance between Clark and one of the early fugitive updates of List when it appeared in a 1987 issue of the tabloid newspaper *World Weekly*. She was acquainted with Delores, "Clark's" wife of 2 years, and showed her the article about the 1971 murders along with the updated image. Ultimately, Delores dismissed any possible connection to her husband and neither woman took any action at that time. Thus, earlier efforts had triggered recognition, but it was timing, circumstances, and perhaps national television coverage that eventually led to the capture.[6] Ironically, this same neighbor called "America's Most Wanted" in 1989 after seeing the segment with Bender's sculpture and reported the name of "Bob Clark" along with the new location in Virginia where he was captured.

Whatever the situation regarding redoing another artist's work, the case should be considered first. Then, each artist should take into account the position of the artist whose work he is redoing, mentally putting himself in that same situation. Our profession is one of such importance that we should all strive to put aside artists' egos and do whatever will help solve cases. At the same time, we should **remember that criticism of work done by others does not improve our standing. Veteran artists should help newer artists to better perform their important tasks, not criticize and downgrade them.** There has to be a starting place for everyone.

Conduct with Victims and Witnesses

The forensic artist's personal behavior should be professional at all times. Always deal with victims, witnesses, and their families with respect and consideration. Sadly, this is not always the case, as headlined in *The Boston Globe* in March 1994, "Police Artist Suspended for Making Racist Slurs."[7]

As a police sketch artist, you will be called upon to conduct interviews with people from all walks of life, and interview them in a variety of settings. In virtually all situations, you will be dealing with victims or witnesses who are cooperating with a police investigation. Thus, your role varies greatly from that of an officer who is dealing with a suspect or uncooperative witness. **Interviewing is not interrogation.**

Witnesses

The fact that a person is present and participating with the preparation of a composite drawing implies a wish to assist the police. The witness should be afforded the basic courtesy that is standard when conducting other types of business.

From the time an appointment is made, you should attempt to respect the witness' time schedule. Give the witness a general idea of what will occur during the composite session, including the approximate time frame. If you do not directly make the appointments, you should convey the proper information to be given to the witness to the person making the appointments for you.

When a drawing must be prepared in an emergency time frame, make the witness as comfortable as possible under the circumstances. Simple courtesies such as telephone use or providing coffee or sodas can help in these situations. Remember that **even though the witness may not have been physically injured or threatened, he is likely under a tremendous amount of stress just knowing the significance of his role as a witness.**

Victims

Even more significant than the appropriate respect for witnesses is the artist's dealings with victims of violent crime. It is the responsibility of every forensic artist to learn as much as possible about the issues surrounding personal trauma. **You should make it a career-long goal to continuously learn about ways in which you can most effectively interact with victims without re-traumatizing them.**

You should realize that you may be dealing with this person at perhaps the most traumatic time of his or her life, and it is your obligation to do your work while causing as little emotional pain as possible. Specific suggestions for sympathetically dealing with crime victims are offered in Chapters 5 and 6.

Family Members

In stressful and emergency situations, it is perfectly natural for people to want family members or loved ones near them. Ideally, you can comfort the victim or witness by allowing this, while not letting the other person's presence cause a distraction from the forensic art task at hand. Ideally, there are separate rooms, so that the family members can be separated but nearby. I first meet with both the interviewee and family members together, and I explain the process we will use, the approximate time it will take, etc. and encourage everyone to become comfortable with me. It is also important to explain telephone use and smoking policies at your building, location of restroom facilities, and snack machines or break areas.

More specific issues involving the importance of the artist having a one-on-one interview structure with the witness are discussed in Chapter 5.

Taking care of the basic needs of everyone involved will comfort the family member as well as the victim or witness. You are more likely to have the witness' full attention if you reassure the witness that his loved one will be comfortable. After all of this is done, I then move with the witness to a separate room adjoining the room where the family member waits. This assures the witness that the person is nearby, but also gives the witness the privacy of a door in-between to encourage the telling of information he or she might have difficulty stating in front of the loved one.

Such treatment of victims, witnesses, and their families is common courtesy and professionalism and should be a routine method of operating for the forensic artist. Interviewees should never be made to feel rushed, or be treated discourteously. Their cooperation should be appreciated.

Questionable Witnesses

As you become more experienced as a composite artist and interviewer, it is possible that you may encounter a witness whose credibility you feel is questionable. Strictly speaking, it is only your job to prepare the composite drawing; however, sometimes your interview may produce much more. Ethically, your role is to promptly forward information to an investigating officer whose responsibility it is to determine how to act upon such information.

It would be presumptuous of beginning artist/interviewers to make judgments regarding witnesses and their veracity. The veteran interviewer may be in a different position, providing useful insight to detectives.

Consider very cautiously any allegations that you present formally, such as in written documents or reports. Do not forget that you may end up in court, questioned as to what training and experience in psychology you have that qualifies you to make such an accusation.

In my career, I have interviewed numerous perpetrators under the guise of being victims, including at least four murderers. In each case, I indicated verbally and informally to officers that something "didn't feel right," thus allowing the officers to make any further determinations based on investigative means.

Another group of questionable witnesses are those who make false allegations, particularly of sexual assault. It is not the role of the artist to question or confront a victim. Rather, the artist should be courteous and conduct the interview in the usual way, and then notify detectives of any suspicions. Individuals who make such false allegations usually possess deep psychological needs that should be addressed by mental health professionals (see also Chapter 5).

Conduct with Police

When dealing with the law enforcement professionals, always remember your role in the investigative inquiry. You are providing assistance in the form of an investigative tool. The amount of specific information regarding the case which you are privileged to know depends on multiple factors.

It is the responsibility of the officer or detective to protect the integrity of his investigation. Allowing certain information to be known may be a risky matter and he must consider this carefully. If you have often worked with a particular detective or agency, you may receive access to a great deal of information. Remember trust must be earned and developed over time. Do not expect to be given full case information if officers do not know you well.

Another consideration may be your particular status as a forensic artist. Freelance artists with no law enforcement affiliation may not be afforded the same access to cases as those artists who are employed by a police agency. In addition, detectives may view a civilian artist differently from an artist who is a sworn or commissioned officer.

Under no circumstances should you presume as an artist to inject yourself into an investigation. This is especially true if you are not employed by a law enforcement agency and are not a sworn police officer.

Release of Information

You should always remember that you work primarily for members of law enforcement with special consideration for victims and witnesses. It is to them that you are responsible (see Chapter 17).

You should not be the person making determinations about the release of a composite drawing. If you are very experienced, police may seek your advice regarding the drawing's release, but it is the detective's call as to what is to be done with a drawing. The detective should determine when or if to release the drawing to other law enforcement agencies, the news media, or family members.

It is also not normally your role to conduct press conferences in conjunction with a drawing's release to members of the media. Some artists enjoy and seek publicity, and appear in front of a camera at any opportunity. However, most law enforcement agencies have a Public Information Officer (PIO) whose job it is to make such press releases. The PIO and the detective know better than you just what information is to be made public and what information will be safeguarded for the sake of the victim or the investigation or both.

It is particularly important that you do not presume to release copies of your drawing to family members or the victim/witness themselves. Consider the terrible possibility of irate and bereaved family members taking the law into their own hands with your assistance.

If, on a rare occasion, you are hired by a media entity to do a drawing, it is still your moral and ethical responsibility to operate within certain reasonable limitations. When I worked full time in law enforcement, I was hired on a freelance basis for many years to do composite drawings for the FOX television program "America's Most Wanted." Initially, certain producers asked that I allow them to film over my shoulder while interviewing a traumatized victim. After I explained the necessity for privacy for the victim and maintaining the integrity of the interview, they understood. Because they were responsible, ethical journalists, they respected these terms and we accomplished both the preparation of the composite drawing and the development of a story in video form. Both were done without risking further trauma to the victim or jeopardizing the case investigation.

Certain artists contract on a freelance basis to do forensic art directly for family members of victims; thus, release of the drawing is totally up to the family. The artist should carefully consider such a proposal. First of all, **family members should not have to pay for law enforcement services that are generally available free to all citizens.** Taking fees from bereaved family members may be opportunistic and inappropriate. Second, law enforcement officers conducting an investigation should make the strategic investigative choices, such as whether or not to do a sketch or what witness to use, without civilian assistance.

If family members are dissatisfied with the way in which an investigation is being conducted, the situation becomes even more complex. A fundamental problem lies with the fact that a drawing done at the request of a family member then has to be distributed. If the family member successfully distributes the drawing outside law enforcement means, and a suspect is sighted, who will interview or arrest the suspect? It is also questionable as to whether or not such a drawing or identification procedure would be admissible in court.

The bottom line is, **nothing should be done by the artist to jeopardize the potential apprehension and successful prosecution of the perpetrator.**

Questionable Methods

Before proceeding with any forensic art project, you should review the integrity of the method to be used. This applies to composite drawings and interviews, age progressions to predict growth or aging, postmortem drawings, skull reconstruction, preparation of trial displays, or any other art done in the medico-legal environment.

An excellent rule of thumb is to approach any project with the thought that you will later explain your method on the witness stand in a court of law. Although you may never be required to do this, it is best to operate as if you will. You should never do anything that you could not explain effectively in trial if needed.

Insufficient Information

The Unfit Witness

In some instances, you will meet with a witness to do a composite drawing interview and, while assessing the witness' potential to complete a sketch, decide the witness will be unable to do so for some reason. It is your ethical obligation to all concerned to consider this before doing a drawing.

Ideally, the detective should assess witness difficulties before the artist meets with the individual, but this does not always happen. It is a good idea to discuss by telephone with the officer such matters as timing of the offense, nature of the offense, general information about the witness, and the witness' involvement in the crime. This can help prevent premature or unsuccessful interview sessions that must be canceled.

Perhaps the victim/witness is too traumatized to be interviewed at that time and the interview should be delayed. Timing of interviews is discussed in more depth in Chapter 5. I know of several cases in which victims were interviewed too soon after the crime occurred, resulting in an unsuccessful interview. Obviously, certain circumstances merit this kind of rush, such as the abduction of a child, but whenever possible the victim's physical and emotional condition should be the foremost consideration.

As part of the preliminary interview process, the artist may determine that the witness did not actually see enough to complete a sketch. In such a case, the interview should probably be terminated. From time to time, high profile cases place law enforcement agencies under tremendous pressure and mistakes are made. An example of this is the "Son of Sam" investigation in New York City in the late 1970s (Figure 15.2). In a good faith effort to protect the public, composite drawings were made from the descriptions of witnesses who simply had not seen enough. The result was that, when David Berkowitz, the murderer of 13 people, was finally apprehended, there was speculation that he had not acted alone since most of the composite drawings did not particularly look like him.[8]

Sometimes, physical limitations of the witness must cause cancellation of the composite session. Unfortunately, some people who may want to help the police simply do not have the physical or mental capacity to do so. This is not to say that individuals with physical or emotional/mental handicaps cannot make excellent witnesses, because they can. Each witness in a particular circumstance must be evaluated individually. Remember a criminal defense attorney will not hesitate to point up perceived witness inadequacies if the attorney feels it will aid his or her client.

Witnesses may simply be too old or too young to effectively produce a drawing. Physical limitations of advancing age such as visual or hearing impairment may be considerations with older witnesses. It may be significant for the detective or the artist to ask the witness if he or she wore glasses or a hearing aid at the time of the crime.

Another type of physical or perceptual limitation may be drug or alcohol use on the part of the witness. Inquiries about such matters should be made.

Ultimately, **a drawing produced from the description of an unfit witness helps no one.** It can be very difficult to terminate an interview session, but it is sometimes the best thing to do. **Poor drawings can lead to many wasted man hours on the part of the police and can even implicate an innocent person.**

The Incomplete Case

Cases of unidentified deceased individuals may also require judgment calls based on professionally ethical behavior on the part of the artist. No matter how badly you may wish to assist on a case or to get a freelance job, there are times when you must say "no."

Figure 15.2 Composite drawings done in the "Son of Sam" investigation. (Courtesy of New York Police Department.)

Cases in which morgue photographs are to be used for potential preparation of postmortem drawings are especially important to review critically. In the case of a recent death, the photographs are probably adequate for use. Often, however, in cases of decomposing faces, the photographs may not contain adequate information for a drawing to be done. In workshops, I strongly emphasize this issue and attempt to teach "when to say 'no.'" **Postmortem drawings done from poor quality photographs or overly decomposed faces may be far too speculative on the part of the artist.**

In cases of faces too decomposed to be properly studied, the best option is probably to obtain the cleaned skull for reconstruction.

Caution should be taken in doing any type of forensic art in which too much speculation is involved. There is a case, for example, in which an artist developed a two-dimensional reconstruction based on a skull of a young woman in her 20s. She then went on to draw the reconstructed face as it might have looked when the victim was a little girl. Such speculation is extensive and goes beyond what is reasonable. To reverse the age progression process (which is intended to be based on use of *known* photographs), basing it on a speculative skull reconstruction drawing, was quite a stretch! Such behavior only risks your credibility in the long run.

Frontal View vs. Profile

Angle of View

One of the primary aspects of your initial interview is to determine the location of the witness with respect to the crime. At what distance did the witness view the subject? What were the lighting conditions? And, particularly important, what was the angle of the view? **You should produce the composite drawing in the same angle as the primary angle of view of the witness.** Most witnesses observe a face while it is moving, seeing various angles. Allow the witness to tell you which is the angle of primary view, and do the sketch accordingly.

If you prepare composite drawings with the aid of reference photographs, and are asked to draw a profile composite, you must have profile view reference photographs. The *FBI Facial Identification Catalog* will not be adequate for this purpose.[4] Hopefully, such information will have been determined by the detective and you will be prepared with the correct reference materials before your interview begins.

This issue was of great significance in a well-known Philadelphia homicide case a few years ago. A composite drawing was done from the descriptions of a husband and wife who had witnessed two gangland style murders outside a restaurant. Based in part on the strong resemblance to the drawing, a man named Neil Ferber was convicted and received a death sentence. Later, evidence surfaced that seemed to indicate that a mistake had been made. It was determined that **the witnesses had only seen the suspect in the profile view, although the composite drawing depicted a frontal view.** Eventually, the man was cleared of the charges and released from prison after serving 4 years, 16 months of which were on death row.[9]

Frontal to Lateral Projections

Some artists claim that their experience level allows them to easily draw a frontal view based on a lateral view and vice versa. While this is perhaps possible with some faces, it is a mistake to assume that it can be done with all faces. The illustrations shown indicate that such frontal to lateral projection capability is too speculative to be reliable and such assumptions should probably not be made (Figure 15.3).

Inappropriate Requests

There may be times when you receive a request to do something regarding your forensic artwork that you feel is inappropriate. Sadly, I have heard of more than one instance in which an overzealous officer, convinced that he had the "right" suspect, asked an artist to draw a composite drawing of the suspect to help pin the crime on the suspect.

Such an accusation was made in a high profile case in Australia in the 1980s, involving the swindle and robbery of the Royal Mint in Perth. Three brothers named

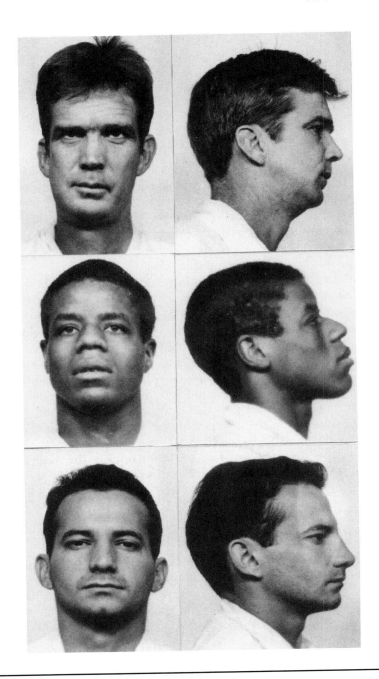

Figure 15.3 Unpredictable frontal to lateral projections. (Courtesy of Texas Department of Criminal Justice.)

Mickelberg were charged with the crime. Allegations were made that the police fabricated evidence, including a composite drawing of one of the brothers. It was alleged that a passport photograph was reversed and traced to produce the composite.[10] An appeal trial was conducted in 1987, with several composite artists from the U.S. giving testimony in Australia, but the convictions were unanimously upheld.

Some years ago, a pathologist appeared at my office with a box containing a skull. He told me that he wanted to request that a facial reconstruction be done based on the skull. He then pulled out an envelope with a photograph of a woman, indicating I should "make it look just like her." He further stated that he felt convinced that it was indeed her but had no records for comparison to prove it. I did not do the reconstruction, explaining to him that since I had seen the photograph, it would be impossible. To this day, I do not know if this request was made out of ignorance or with some other intention; I prefer to think it was the former. Today, DNA comparisons using bone have virtually eliminated the potential for such a situation.

Hopefully, you will never encounter a request to "fake" an item of forensic art, but if it should happen, consider your professional reputation. Consider, too, that it could be you giving testimony in a court of law with regard to your work.

There could be extenuating circumstances in which it might be feasible to develop an item of forensic art for investigative purposes, but such cases would be extremely rare. It is reasonable for you to request that any such work you do be documented in the case file, for your protection.

Forensic Art Language

To enhance your standing as a professional, it is advantageous to develop a sort of "language" of forensic art terminology for use in both written and oral communication. That is not to say a "formal" language should always be used, but rather a "professional" language.

In addition to a correct knowledge of terms, carefully consider the use of terms. A consistent vernacular within the field of forensic art aids in concise and accurate communication, both within and outside the field.

Chapter 1 clarifies many terms commonly used in forensic art.

For example, the term "composite drawing" is commonly misused. For years, I have heard the term used for everything from Identi-KIT composites to postmortem drawings to skull reconstructions. A "composite drawing" is hand drawn, composed of component parts which have been put together, and it has been done at the direction of a witness.

An Identi-KIT composite is not hand drawn, although it is certainly put together from component parts. It is properly called an "Identi-KIT," an "Identi-KIT composite," or even just a "composite."

The potential significance of such a clarification lies in the possible use of such a facial image in court. Calling it a "composite drawing" implies that it has been drawn by an artist, when, in fact, it has been put together by a technician.

Similarly, computer-generated composites are just that — "computer-generated composites." They are properly termed a "composite" or a "computer-generated composite," not a "composite drawing."

While some technicians who prepare mechanically generated or computer-generated composites have some knowledge of the face, their skills are not generally at the same level as the forensic artist who does artwork by hand. Hence, this terminology specifies for the court an implied skill level of the individual who prepared the composite.

Use of anatomically correct terms, which have been used throughout this text in the descriptions of aspects of the human face, further enhances the professionalism of the artist. Correct terms aid in clear and precise communication in dealings with the medical and scientific associates who aid the artist in preparation of postmortem artwork and skull reconstructions.

In addition to the accurate and specific use of forensic art terms, it is important for the artist to choose very carefully the manner in which terms are used. Certainly if you become involved with work as a "facial identification expert," comparing photographs to photographs, you must guardedly choose your words. It is a good idea to adopt a manner of presenting information that parallels language usage in the forensic sciences.

For example, I know of a case in which a forensic artist compared a known photograph and a questioned photograph, stating that he was "99.9%" sure that they were the same individual. It was subsequently determined that they were not and he looked very foolish.

A more appropriate statement could be made regarding the assessment of a comparison in which you simply cannot be certain, although you feel it might be a match. A better phrase might be, "I find nothing to indicate that it is not this person." **Remember forensic art is "soft science," at best. Firm statements of identity only on the basis of visual comparison can only be made in very rare instances, if at all.** In addition, such statements should be made only after years of experience.

Use of overly emphatic expressions only sets you up to be trapped in the courtroom setting. You may be totally discredited based on your poor choice of words.

In conclusion, the issue of professional ethics and conduct should be of foremost importance to all those who practice forensic art. Because of the importance of the tasks you perform, there is no room for laxity in your professional behavior. **Your conduct, language, and demeanor tell everything about you as a professional.**

References

1. Mills, D. H., "Comments from the perspective of the AAFS Ethics Committee Chairperson." *Journal of Forensic Sciences*, 31(3), 798–799, 1986.
2. "Code of Ethics," Association of Medical Illustrators, 40–44.
3. "Code of Ethics for Forensic Artists, Operations Manual for the Forensic Art Certification Program, International Association for Identification," *Journal of Forensic Identification*, 44(6), 698–699, 1994.
4. Taister, M., "Ethical Standards for Composite Artists," unpublished FBI brochure, July 1995.
5. Macris, T., Forensic artist, San Jose, California Police Department (retired), personal communication, 1990.
6. Ryzuk, M., *Thou Shalt Not Kill*. New York: Popular Library Books, 1990.
7. Coakley, T., "Police artist suspended for making racist slurs," *The Boston Globe*, March 31, 1994.
8. Terry, M., *The Ultimate Evil*. New York: Dolphin Doubleday, 1987.
9. "A Good Cop," *60 Minutes*, produced by Ira Rosen, CBS, January 11, 1987.
10. Lovell, A., *The Mickelburg Stitch*. Perth, Australia: Creative Research, 1985.

Chapter 16

Printing and Graphics Reproduction

For most types of forensic artwork to serve their intended purpose, they must first be graphically reproduced by some method that allows for the images to be distributed to a large number of people. With this knowledge, **the forensic artist should prepare his or her artwork in a way that promotes good quality reproduction of the work.**

Forensic artists must have at least a rudimentary understanding of the basic requirements that aid in the true and accurate reproduction of the images prepared as part of a criminal investigation. For the most part, the process of distribution of forensic art images is out of the hands of the artist. Yet, it behooves the artist to strive to avoid some of the possible difficulties that may be presented in the reproduction process. Certainly, there are no absolute guarantees that ensure a great rendition of your artwork. Yet, effort should be made to do your part in the process in such a way that makes reproduction as easy and effective as possible.

Traditionally, **"graphic" means visual or pictorial arts which are of, or related to, the art of printing.** For the purposes of this chapter, I have also included several other methods by which forensic art may be reproduced and distributed. Although it is not within the scope of this chapter to provide detailed technical information, my intent is to provide a practical overview for the use of forensic artists.

General Information

History of Printing

Probably the earliest known visual communication was in the form of pictographs done by cave dwellers in France and Spain, ca. 35,000 to 15,000 B.C. With assistance from the ancient Phoenicians, the Egyptians, and the ancient Greeks and Romans, our system of writing came into being. Since the development of written language, people have attempted to make multiple copies of important documents, forming some of the earliest written records. There were handwritten and illuminated theological works laboriously lettered by scribes, but they were available only to the very rich.[1]

Actual printing had its origins in the Far East where wood block prints were being used in China at least 800 years before the use of printing in Europe. The "father of modern printing" is the title given to Johann Gutenberg. The printing of the *Gutenberg Bible* in about 1450 was the first documented use of movable type and is considered a benchmark in human history. With the invention of movable type, the "graphic arts" were born and printed documents became more and more available. So, historically, the graphic arts have made it possible to make permanent and multiple copies of written communication.[1]

In the 1880s, the halftone processing for reproduction of images was invented, making it possible to print type and photographs together on the same page.[2]

The printing industry made great strides during World War II, becoming more electronic in nature. Typesetting progressed from the old Linotype machines to photo-typesetting. Advancements included the advent of the use of the cathode-ray tube system (CRT) for type composition. Today most newspapers and magazines are typeset and printed using some form of computerized system.

Typography

Since computerized desk-top publishing is quite a simple matter these days, the forensic artist also sometimes becomes the graphic artist preparing posters or fliers for mass distribution of his or her work. A facial image and some form of type presents the pertinent information. A general knowledge of typography is helpful.

The primary intent of a police publication is the dissemination of information. It is not generally the place for use of fancy, flowery type. Choose type for its appropriateness and legibility. **When choosing type, there are two important factors: readability and legibility.** In *Ink on Paper 2, A Handbook of the Graphic Arts,* Edmund Arnold writes:

> Two characteristics of type are often misunderstood because the terms are used interchangeably — and incorrectly. *Readability* is that characteristic which makes it easy and pleasant to read large masses of type. The pages of a book or columns of newspapers must be set in readable type. *Legibility* is that characteristic which brings a few words off the page and into the comprehension of the reader as rapidly and unmistakably as possible. The work STOP on a highway sign is an excellent example of legibility, ... Roman types have the highest readability; Sans Serifs, the highest legibility.[1]

Roman types are those fonts or alphabets that are composed of letter forms with both thick and thin aspects. In other words, the vertical bar or stroke of an "I" will be thick and the horizontal strokes top and bottom are thin. These finishing strokes are called "serifs." There are numerous type faces classified as Roman types, with the variation in thick and thin strokes being more or less obvious.

Sans serif simply means "without serifs." Types that fall into this category possess letter forms in which the entire letter is of equal "weight" without thick or thin variations.

Most typefaces may be used in various forms, such as italicized, bold, or light, and extended or condensed, so that they will better fit the space needed for a particular use. Type may also be "reversed" or made light on a dark background.

People seem to be attracted to script letters, Old English, or other novelty typefaces, but these are not the best choice for official police publications.

Images

Images produced by forensic artists are used in a wide variety of ways from simple photocopying to photography, computer scanning, and video. Some general principles regarding the documentation, acquisition, and printing of images should be understood.

Historically speaking in the printing industry, black-and-white or **monochromatic art** for reproduction is classified as either "line art" or "continuous tone." **Line art** consists of just what the name implies, graphic images that are prepared simply with the use of line only, such as black-and-white inked cartoons. **Continuous-tone art** has traditionally referred to art work that incorporates variations on a gray scale. Shaded facial drawings would be an example of continuous-tone art. These two types of art have to be photographed differently for optimum reproduction. Line art can basically be treated in the same way as text or type. Continuous-tone artwork must be broken down into dot patterns called a **halftone** in order to accurately replicate the variations in grays. Continuous-tone art may be photographic in nature or in the form of shaded drawings. **Color art** to be reproduced must be broken down into halftones as well as by component colors into what are traditionally referred to as color separations.

Photography

Photography has been a valuable tool for the documentation and reproduction of information since its inception. The first known photograph was produced in 1836. By the mid-1880s, the new image-making process of photography became very popular, and virtually every famous person who has lived since that time has been documented on film. Actors and actresses had publicity photos made, war heroes posed for photos, and politicians made photographic campaign buttons. Mathew B. Brady gave us sobering reminders of the devastation and carnage of the American Civil War. Photo-journalism was born and events and places began to be documented for all to see.

Over time, it became apparent that cameras could reveal things that the human eye could not see, and there was great potential for scientific research applications. In the late 1800s, Eadweard Muybridge conducted extensive photographic studies of motion using people and animals, creating in the process a visual dictionary for artists that is still useful today. Photography became an instrument for education as well as personal expression.

In 1888, George Eastman sold his first Kodak box camera, containing rolled film, making cameras available to far more people than ever before. Color photography had become practical enough by the 1930s and 1940s that it could also be used on a fairly wide scale. In *Principles of Visual Perception*, Carolyn Bloomer writes:

In the 150 years since its invention, photography has developed many variations and found many applications, including moving pictures, stop-action photography, stereoscopy, microphotography, holography, and telescopic and space photography. Fixed images like those in photographs are also generated by means of forms of energy other than light: shortwave radiation (X-rays), heat (infrared photography and thermography), and sound (sonograms and radar).[2]

Many of these types of photography have found applications in law enforcement. The mechanics of photography are certainly too complex to be detailed here. If you take your own photographs, you should learn far more specific information about photography than presented in this text. If your agency or department has a professional photographer, you may not need to know much about photography at all.

There are some very basic terms with which you may wish to be familiar to aid in communication with photographers. The following information is provided by Texas Department of Public Safety forensic photographer, Missey Micheletti:

> **Exposure** is equal to intensity × time, or aperture × shutter speed. The **aperture** controls the amount of light hitting the film by a variable opening in the lens. The **shutter speed** controls the time the light is hitting the film by a moving curtain over the film plane. The aperture or **f/stop**, is equal to the diameter of the lens opening over the focal length of the lens. Larger openings let in more light while smaller openings allow less. The aperture also controls the **depth of field**, or range of sharp focus in a photograph. The larger the aperture opening, the narrower the range of sharp focus.
>
> **Shutter speed** is the length of time that light is allowed on the film. Shutter speeds are measured in fractions of a second down to one second, then change to whole seconds which are usually denoted in a different color. The **focal length** of a lens is the distance between the optical center of the lens (when the lens is focused at infinity) and the film. The focal length is usually denoted on the front of the lens in millimeters. The shorter the focal length, the wider the field of vision that is produced. When the focal length of the lens is about the same as the diagonal length on the film size, it is considered a "normal" lens. So, a 50-mm lens would be considered a "normal" lens for a 36-mm film size.[3]

Basic photography of composites and other facial drawings is pretty straightforward. For the accurate photography of three-dimensional objects, particularly skulls as preparation for two-dimensional reconstruction, knowledge and skill are required. The correctness of the photographs directly effects your ability to do high quality forensic artwork, as described in more depth in Chapter 12.

Photography of Two-Dimensional Art

When your drawings are photographed for printing purposes, it is ideal that this be done on a copy stand with balanced lighting. Use of a fine grained film helps ensure good detail. A macro or micro lens will tend to be sharper from edge to edge and is usually best to use.

Photography of Three-Dimensional Art

In photographing three-dimensional items of forensic art such as clay facial reconstructions on the skull, the goals are somewhat different from photographing other sculptures. The purpose here is to convey as much information as possible about the sculptural image, rather than to present it with dramatic or "mood" lighting as in fine art.

One of the greatest benefits of producing three-dimensional work is the opportunity for photographing it in various views. **Usually, the photographic views taken are direct frontal, oblique left, lateral left, oblique right, and lateral right.**

Care should be taken to light the sculpture in such a way that the morphological details are shown, not diminished. A backdrop that is solid in color and neutral will also aid in emphasis of the face.

Digital Imaging

With computers integrated into the everyday lives of most people, we have begun to deal more and more with ways of using images that are conducive to computer applications. Our ways of processing visual images, including both drawings and photographs, have been altered substantially. In today's lingo, some new terms for the breaking down of an image into more easily reproducible and transmittable patterns have emerged.

In more modern computer terms, images are now **digitally encoded** or **digitized** in order for them to become computer processable. In *The Reconfigured Eye, Visual Truth in the Post-Photographic Era*, William Mitchell writes:

> Although a digital image may look just like a photograph when it is published in a newspaper, it actually differs as profoundly from a traditional photograph as does a photograph from a painting. The difference is grounded in fundamental physical characteristics that have logical and cultural consequences.
>
> The basic technical distinction between analog (continuous) and digital (discrete) representations is crucial here. Rolling down a ramp is continuous motion, but walking down stairs is a sequence of discrete steps — so you can count the number of steps, but not the number of levels on the ramp.[4]

Mitchell continues with what is a further description of the often confusing distinction between **analog and digital**:

> A photograph is an analog representation of the differentiation of space in a scene: it varies continuously, both spatially and tonally …
>
> But images are encoded digitally by uniformly subdividing the picture plane into a finite Cartesian grid of cells (known as **pixels**) and specifying the intensity or color of each cell by means of an integer number drawn from some limited range. The resulting two-dimensional array of integers (the raster grid) can be stored in computer memory, transmitted electronically, and interpreted by various devices to produce displays and printed images.
>
> In such images, unlike photographs, fine details and smooth curves are approximated to the grid, and continuous tone gradients are broken up into discrete steps.[4]

So, simply put, if your forensic art work is to be photographed for use on a flier, in a newspaper, or in a magazine, it will probably need to be broken down into a halftone or dot pattern. In most cases, you will probably not be required to do this, since the publisher of your artwork will do it for you.

Acquiring and Printing Images

Scanning drawings, photographs, or other images into a computer will involve the digitization of the artwork. There are two steps in the process: that of acquiring or scanning, and that of retrieving or printing.

DPI and Resolution

The quality of the finished product will depend on both the way in which the art was initially acquired and the way it was retrieved. The term **dpi** or "dots per inch" is used when determining image quality regarding the scanning or capture device and the printer. **The higher the number of dots per inch, the higher the resolution or detail quality of the image.** Good resolution is required from both the scanner (for acquiring the image) and the printer (for retrieving the image). In other words, you can scan a drawing on a very high quality scanner with high dpi, but if you print it on a low dpi printer, it will not have good detail quality or resolution.

Printers

John Russ, in *The Image Processing Handbook*, describes the basic types of printers and how they function:

> Each of the various printing methods produces dots in a different way. **Dot-matrix printers** use small pins to press an inked ribbon against the paper. **Ink-jet printers** produce a stream of fine ink drops, some of which are electrostatically deflected away from the paper. The drops that strike the paper produce dots. **Thermal printers** use a pin to pass an electric current through the coating on a paper. One common kind of paper is coated with a white oxide of zinc that is reduced by the current to deposit a dark spot of metal at the location; ... **Laser printers** work essentially like a xerographic copier. The light from the laser (or in some versions photodiode) falls on a selenium-coated drum and by the photoelectric effect produces a localized electrostatic charge. This in turn picks up carbon particles (the toner or "ink"), which is then transferred to the paper and substantially heated to remain permanently.[5]

Enlargement and Reduction

Once an image has been half-toned or digitized, and the resolution determined by the equipment used, enlargement or reduction may take place. It is a simple fact, however, that the more the enlargement, the more "broken up" the image becomes.

Conversely, reducing a dot-patterned image generally improves the image by intensifying the detail.

Digital Cameras

Use of digital cameras provides a simple method of acquiring images for immediate use in the computer. When photographed with a digital camera, images which are either two- or three-dimensional may be sent directly to the computer for further processing and manipulation.

As with traditional photography, however, the same potential problems of distortion exist. There has been some debate among forensic photographers about the use of digital imaging vs. traditional photography for criminal investigative-related purposes. In traditional photography, distortion inaccuracies must be controlled by lens choice and focal length. With digital photography, the potential exists for distortion in both the acquisition and the retrieval phases. Digital photography and imaging allow for manipulation at the pixel level that may be difficult to detect.

Digital photography does not have nearly the resolution quality and detail as traditional photography.

Video Cameras

Another method sometimes used is the direct capture of images on video. Video cameras may be mounted in a variety of ways for the purpose of "grabbing" an image, either photograph or drawing, and "pulling" it into a computer system. A number of states, including Texas, have converted the driver license systems from traditional photography to video-capture cameras for efficiency.

I have found that video-captured copies of color drawings, particularly those done specifically for use on television, may be useful. By using a video camera to photograph a color drawing, the image may then be sent directly on a videotape for reproduction on television. Keep in mind, however, that **video is very low in resolution when compared to photography or film.**

Evidentiary Documentation

Most professional photographers generally agree that alterations are easily done on either format: traditional/silver-based photography or digital photography. To promote the best possible resolution, several organizations seek to set minimally acceptable standards for dpi and resolution of digitized images for law enforcement purposes.

Most photographers who do forensic work also agree that **the integrity of the individual giving testimony in court regarding a particular piece of photographic information is more important than the choice of medium used.**

Herbert Blitzer, Program Manager for Law Enforcement Programs at Eastman Kodak Company, has stated:

> ... it is the integrity of the witness presenting the image that must be demonstrated. Physical items themselves are not evidence. The testimony of

a witness is evidence, and the image is an exhibit to that testimony. An image, all by itself, is totally unacceptable. A person, testifying under penalty of perjury, must explain what the image represents, why it is relevant, how it was acquired, how it came to be in court and what it implies.

Thus, the issue is greater than the image per se. The key to successful use is in control of the procedures employed.[6]

Methods of Distribution

Print Media

Newspapers

Over the years, my facial drawings have been diminished in most every way imaginable by their inclusion in newspapers. They have been materially altered, reduced to postage stamp size, and noses have been cropped off profile views. Yet, I am always grateful for the appearance of a drawing in the newspaper because of the potential benefits for an investigation.

Some problems with reproductions in newspapers have been technical, as with washed-out or grainy images. Other problems have resulted from a lack of understanding of the purpose of the artwork. Once, a newspaper graphic artist preparing a layout with a two-dimensional reconstruction I had done, actually retraced and changed the profile drawing to make it more "graphically appealing." The profile was made more "classical" in structure, losing the look of the unidentified person in the process. Hopefully, as forensic art becomes better known and understood, such things will not happen.

Newspaper quality in larger cities continues to advance dramatically, with color reproduction and paper quality greatly improved over those of a few years ago. Forensic art, however, is often used in the newspapers of smaller communities that do not have the resources to upgrade the very expensive printing equipment.

Magazines

Since there is often more time and money spent in the production of magazines, greater care is usually taken with the reproduction of the forensic art images. I have experienced far better results with the outcome of my drawings in magazines.

Images are photographed at a much higher resolution and thus reproduced in much finer detail than in most newspapers.

Posters and Fliers

Like other printed documents, police posters, fliers, and bulletins vary considerably in form, content, and quality. In their simplest forms, they may be composite drawings or photographs with headings and typed information cut and pasted and added. Figure 16.1 shows a 1933 "wanted" poster used to help track down Bonnie Parker. A very inexpensively produced flier of a type similar to this may suit the needs of your community. Certainly such simple posters have been known to work.

Figure 16.1 Simply prepared but effective **1933 "wanted" poster for Bonnie Parker** issued by the Dallas County Sheriff's Office. (Courtesy of the Dallas County Sheriff's Office.)

Posters or fliers may include any information that investigators deem important and potentially useful to the case, such as victim photographs, composite drawings, vehicle images, or practically anything of pertinence. Figure 16.2 shows a more expensively produced poster including various bits of information about the case.

Most police agencies of any size do have some sort of computer capability for generating posters. Scanning in the images and adding text is quite easy, and can also be done in color if needed. Developing a format to be repeatedly used by inserting a new image and new text as needed can be very effective.

I have seen some very useful scaled-down wanted posters, approximately 4" × 5", produced by police agencies (Figure 16.3). These were designed with the intent that they be pocket-sized for the officer on patrol — a very wise idea. These small posters are large enough for inclusion of the forensic art image along with other vital information, yet small enough to be pulled out and be viewed conveniently and discreetly by the officer.

In high profile cases, commercial quick-copy printers within a community sometimes volunteer their services and rapidly produce very large numbers of "missing persons" or "wanted" posters. In the Polly Klaas case in California, it was estimated that 8 million copies of the poster showing her photo along with a composite sketch were distributed.

Billboards

While not a common occurrence, billboards are sometimes utilized to present photos, drawings, and information to the community. This is an effective way to generate public interest, most commonly used in high profile investigations. Figure 16.4 shows a billboard used in a Florida case to try and generate leads in a triple homicide case.

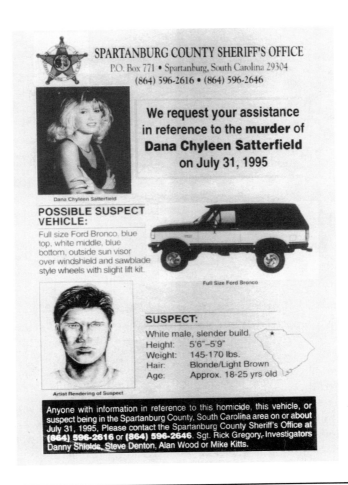

Figure 16.2 A more elaborate and expensively produced **"wanted" poster** showing a photograph of the victim, possible suspect vehicle, as well as a composite drawing. (Courtesy of South Carolina Law Enforcement Division and Spartanburg, South Carolina Sheriff's Office.)

Television

For many years, members of law enforcement have made use of television as a means of mass distribution of forensic art to aid in capturing criminals. As "Little Richard" has so aptly put it, "There's nowhere to run to, baby; nowhere to hide" … for fugitives once their images have appeared on national television.

Horizontal Format

If given a choice, television producers prefer artwork done in a horizontal or "landscape" format, rather than a vertical or "portrait" format. This is, of course, because horizontal formats automatically coincide with the design of the television screen onto which they are placing the images.

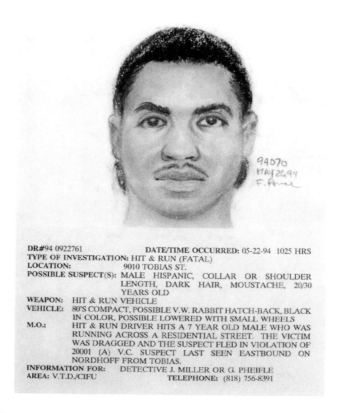

DR#94 0922761   DATE/TIME OCCURRED: 05-22-94 1025 HRS
TYPE OF INVESTIGATION: HIT & RUN (FATAL)
LOCATION: 9010 TOBIAS ST.
POSSIBLE SUSPECT(S): MALE HISPANIC, COLLAR OR SHOULDER
                     LENGTH, DARK HAIR, MOUSTACHE, 20/30
                     YEARS OLD
WEAPON: HIT & RUN VEHICLE
VEHICLE: 80'S COMPACT, POSSIBLE V.W. RABBIT HATCH-BACK, BLACK
          IN COLOR, POSSIBLE LOWERED WITH SMALL WHEELS
M.O.:   HIT & RUN DRIVER HITS A 7 YEAR OLD MALE WHO WAS
          RUNNING ACROSS A RESIDENTIAL STREET. THE VICTIM
          WAS DRAGGED AND THE SUSPECT FLED IN VIOLATION OF
          20001 (A) V.C. SUSPECT LAST SEEN EASTBOUND ON
          NORDHOFF FROM TOBIAS.
INFORMATION FOR: DETECTIVE J. MILLER OR G. PHEIFLE
AREA: V.T.D./CIFU   TELEPHONE: (818) 756-8391

Frame 16.3 A **small-format "wanted" poster**, approximately 4″ × 5″, designed to be carried conveniently by patrol officers. (Courtesy of Fernando Poncé and Los Angeles Police Department.)

Figure 16.4 A **billboard** used to elicit information in a Florida triple homicide case. (Courtesy of St. Petersburg, Florida Police Department.)

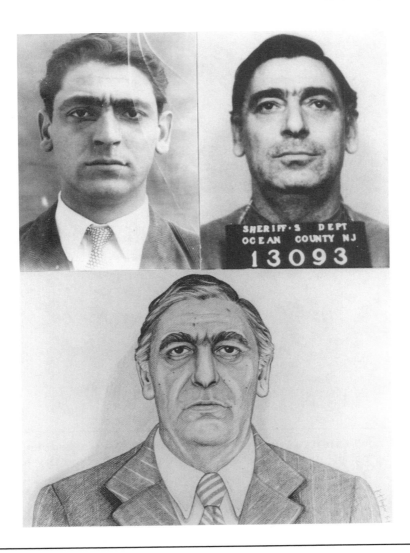

Figure 16.5 A fugitive update case commissioned **for television use**, showing early photographs of the subject (upper left and right), and the fugitive update drawing by Karen T. Taylor (below). The drawing is done in color in a **horizontal format** with full shoulders and a cast shadow "anchoring" the image in the format. (Courtesy of "America's Most Wanted.")

Most of the work which I have been directly commissioned to do for "America's Most Wanted" or other television programs has been done in a horizontal format (Figure 16.5). The request was made that the facial image be "anchored in the format." Thus, I drew downward beyond the face and neck, adding shoulders that spanned across the entire page. This allows the producer to more easily fill the screen with the drawing rather than having to crop it down and place it inside some type of border. If the drawing is done with only a face and suggestion of a neck as in most composite drawings, it may look strange on television, appearing to "float" unfinished at the bottom. In addition, a distinct cast shadow helps to "anchor" the image to the screen.

Color

Television producers also generally choose color over black and white. I have had to explain to more than one of them the downside of color use in preparing composite images, as described in Chapter 6. Some types of forensic art obviously lend themselves far better to color use than others, but, generally speaking, it is my belief that color should not be contrived, especially not because it was requested for television use. If there is a legitimate basis for color, such as with postmortem drawings, child age progressions, or fugitive updates based on original color photographs, then its use is appropriate and potentially advantageous. If color is contrived simply because it looks good on television, it may prove incorrect and actually be detrimental to the identification process.

Technically, for television, color artwork should be as saturated or rich as possible, although enhancement of less strong colors is usually possible. As with other methods of reproduction, the original art should be produced in such a way that it does not require much alteration. That way, you as the artist exert more control over the finished "look" of the image, rather than encouraging someone else to do so because of the inadequacy of your artwork for reproduction.

Electronic

Another method of distribution of forensic art images becoming more and more commonly used is direct electronic dissemination, particularly via the **Internet** or **World Wide Web**. The National Center for Missing and Exploited Children (NCMEC) in Arlington, Virginia has made great strides in developing innovative ways of quickly distributing photographs of abducted children on a massive scale, particularly through use of electronic means. Through technological advances, it has become possible to send abducted child photographs to locations such as special NCMEC kiosks in airports for the greatest potential usefulness in a very timely manner.

In May 1998, Texas Governor George W. Bush formally announced the capability of placing information on Texas missing children directly on the Internet, an important step forward in rapid dissemination of such urgent information (Figure 16.6). The Texas Missing Persons Clearinghouse has held a leadership role nationally in aiding in the recovery of missing persons and identification of the unknown deceased.

Photographs of the FBI's well-known "10 Most Wanted" now appear on the Internet as do the U.S. Marshal Service's most wanted offenders. Many other state, county, and municipal law enforcement agencies have set up Web sites to aid in their work.

Today, a photograph, a computer-generated image, or a drawn image can be scanned into a computer and transmitted easily almost anywhere in the world via the Internet. Sending scanned images through e-mail has become common practice. Hopefully this improved efficiency of information distribution will help save lives.

Primary Considerations for the Artist

Contrast

Nothing is more discouraging for the artist than spending hours producing what he or she thinks is a pretty good drawing, only to have it turned into something

Figure 16.6 Texas Governor George W. Bush announces at a press conference that photographs of Texas missing children may be placed directly on the Internet to give them a better chance for recovery. (Photo by KTT.)

unrecognizable in the newspaper. This often happens because of a lack of contrast in the drawing.

"Punch"

For great reproduction in any media, your drawings should possess a quality known as "punch." This is the term commonly used for a high degree of contrast. As discussed in Chapter 4, it is contrast that makes your drawings look good. **Contrasting values define form and give the illusion of three-dimensional forms on a two-dimensional surface.** It is the degree of contrast that helps your drawings to "jump off the page" with realism. Chapter 4 offers suggestions to achieve this quality in your drawings in the section "Lighting to Attain Perspective."

To develop great contrast in your drawings, you must emphasize the difference in shades of gray, including the lightest "lights" all the way to the darkest "darks." It is the visible difference in variation in these lights and darks that makes a drawing both look great and reproduce well.

Altered Background

On rare occasions, you may be asked to draw the face of a person who is extremely "light," perhaps with light hair, skin, and eyes, and you find it difficult to make the face "show up." One device to aid with this is an altered background. You could take the approach initially of drawing on a tinted paper, drawing in both lights and darks.

A similar effect could be created by darkening the background behind the face in order to make them more visible. If you do not do something to define the face, your drawing will probably disappear in the newspaper.

Definition of Form

In fine art portraiture, the artist may use strong lighting on one side of the face to create a certain mood. One side may be well defined with visible features, while the other side appears faded and shadowy. While a beautiful effect in some drawings and paintings, this does not achieve our purpose in forensic art. The face must be made to "read" in all its parts. Sometimes it is necessary to draw a much firmer outline around the perimeter of the face than would be customary in fine art. Figure 16.7 shows a composite drawing of a bald subject in which a hard line is drawn around the form of the cranium so that the shape will reproduce properly.

Figure 16.7   Composite drawing by KTT of a bald subject in which a **hard line is drawn around the form of the head for definition and proper reproduction.** (Courtesy of Texas Department of Public Safety.)

References

1. Arnold, E. C., *Ink on Paper 2, A Handbook of the Graphic Arts.* New York: Harper & Row, 1972.
2. Bloomer, C. M., *Principles of Visual Perception.* New York: Design Press, 1990.
3. Micheletti, M., personal communication, 1999.
4. Mitchell, W. J., *The Reconfigured Eye, Visual Truth in the Post-Photographic Era.* Cambridge, MA: MIT Press, 1992.
5. Russ, J. C., *The Image Processing Handbook.* Boca Raton, FL: CRC Press, 1995.
6. Blitzer, H. L., "Forensic imaging options: worth a thousand words," *The Police Chief,* October 1996.

Chapter 17

Dealing with the News Media

Not so many years ago, the general public had never heard of this thing called **forensic art**. Over the past decade this situation has changed substantially. More and more people are curious about just what forensic artists do.

Most people have some knowledge of the fact that police artists interview crime victims and witnesses and prepare **composite drawings**. But, in recent years, thanks to public interest and the interest of the various media, other aspects of our work are becoming better known. Forensic art has played an ever-increasing role in high profile cases in the last decade or so, such as the murder of Polly Klaas, the Susan Smith child murders, the Oklahoma City bombing, and the murder of Ennis Cosby.

The issue of missing and abducted children has entered the national psyche and **child age progressions** produced by the NCMEC and others are seen everywhere. These facial images have triggered recognition and aided in the recovery of numerous children.

The successful capture of 18-year fugitive John Emil List in 1989 created an interest in adult age progressions or **fugitive updates**. An appearance update of List, in the form of a three-dimensional bust done by Frank Bender, was broadcast on "America's Most Wanted" and the murderer of five was captured shortly thereafter (see also Chapters 2 and 15).

Nationally broadcast crime-related television programs that communicate information to help solve crimes often include items of forensic art. Internet Web sites have been created to feature the most sought-after criminals wanted by the FBI, the U.S. Marshal's Service, and other law enforcement agencies internationally, and these sources, too, incorporate forensic art.

Forensic art appears more and more frequently in fictional television and film stories about crime. Actors Nick Nolte and Eddie Murphy contemplated a composite in the 1982 Paramount Pictures film, "48 Hours." The 1983 film "Gorky Park," from Orion Pictures, familiarized movie-goers with the forensic art technique of three-dimensional facial reconstruction on the skull. Dozens of television productions during the 1990s have included composite images, age progressions, computer-generated image modifications, or skull reconstructions.

Forensic art is a subject of interest and function in the public media and forensic artists should have some knowledge of the appropriate methods and protocols for dealing with this aspect of their work.

General Information

Undeniably the relationship between members of the media and law enforcement has been stormy on occasion. Each entity has its respective primary function and role, and there are moments when these roles may seem at odds. The article "Officer, Meet the Press," discusses these difficulties:

> At times, some of these relationships may be strained, the problem arising for a variety of reasons. For example, the reporter may have a deadline, the public may be pressing for results, or the police officer may not be the best person to communicate with members of the media. However, most strained relationships are caused by misinformation, a lack of information, or the misinterpretation of existing information. Most of these situations can be avoided.[1]

With effort and professionalism, good relations between police and media can be built and sustained, with members of the public, including crime victims, probably benefiting most of all. The following observations are made in the article "Is No News Really Good News?":

> Such antagonisms do not have to exist. Indeed, police officers and news reporters probably have a great deal more in common than either group would acknowledge. Both professionals are highly inquisitive, somewhat suspicious if not downright cynical, aggressive when on the trail of elusive facts, and hard to intimidate.
>
> Both share what each would describe as a powerful sense of justice and love of fair play. Likewise, both would truthfully claim an interest in sticking up for the downtrodden and the victims of society.[2]

Forensic art has proven to play a somewhat unique role in this arrangement, sometimes landing squarely in an area of middle ground. By their very nature, most types of forensic art are done with the intention of public distribution. Despite distribution in law enforcement bulletins and publications, it is usually a "tip" from a member of the public that makes an item of forensic art useful. Thus, placement of the forensic art before the "eyes" of the public requires media assistance. Few composite drawings, age progressions, or skull reconstructions are of much use if placed in a file somewhere.

It is important that the forensic artist grasp some of the dynamics of the law enforcement/media relationship, understand the limitations of his or her particular role, and learn not to overstep his or her position in the process of dissemination of information.

The Role of the News Media

Responsible journalists are dedicated to accurate reporting of news that they believe that the public has the "right to know." They feel an obligation to provide their readers, viewers, and listeners with information that is interesting, timely, and, sometimes, necessary for their safety.

Members of the media may also play the important role of instructing the public about police matters or soliciting the public's assistance in solving crimes. Crime-stoppers programs across the U.S. have greatly enhanced the ability of the police to solve difficult crimes through cooperative efforts between police, the media, and the public.

The Role of Law Enforcement

The function of law enforcement in media-related matters is also multi-purpose. There is a responsibility to inform the public via the news media regarding matters that may affect the public safety, without jeopardizing the outcome of ongoing investigations.

Most important, police agencies need to be prepared to deal with media inquiries by designating a person to fill the role of communicator. Smaller agencies, unable to employ a full-time person, generally assign an individual to be the **information officer**, sometimes called the **IO**.

Larger agencies often have a complete public information office, with a staff specially trained for the job, called **public information officers** or **PIOs**. Most PIO offices have written policies regarding what kind of information may be released to the news media and under what circumstances. The Chief of Media Relations at the Texas Department of Public Safety, my friend Mike Cox, has assisted me on many occasions over the years.

In his book, *Stand-Off in Texas, "Just Call Me a Spokesperson for the DPS…,"* Mike discusses his job:

> Police officers, especially during the occasional crisis, have enough problems dealing with the situation without having to take time out to talk with the press. That's not their area of expertise. I don't arrest drunk drivers or write search warrants and then go kick in doors with a pistol in my hands. And most police officers I know don't want to write a news release or stand in front of a video camera. Some officers I know would just as soon be involved in a gunfight as to be involved with a reporter … Cops sometimes think of us as reporters. Reporters tend to see us as cops in our black DPS jackets, even though the big white letters on our backs say "PIO" (public information officer).
>
> My staff and I often are caught in the middle — sometimes uncomfortably so. We need the balancing skills of the Flying Wallendas to walk the highwire between the two groups and our dual responsibilities of being forthright while not saying something that would adversely affect the outcome of a high-risk situation, endanger the progress of an ongoing investigation, or interfere with a person's right to a fair trial.[3]

The PIO of a law enforcement agency should be the person making most media releases of forensic art, if the primary investigator so designates.

The Artist's Role

Releasing Forensic Art to the News Media

Items of forensic art are distributed and utilized in a variety of ways. Although we tend to think a composite drawing must immediately hit the newspaper or television for optimum effectiveness, this may not be the case at all. An investigator may plan to discreetly canvas a certain neighborhood with a composite drawing or even to show it to certain key individuals before mass distribution. **The vital thing to understand is that it is the investigator's decision, not the artist's, as to how, when, or even if a drawing will be disseminated.**

You may think because you have some knowledge regarding a case that qualifies you to make media releases on your own — this simply is *not* appropriate. The fact is, you do not have *all* of the information. Your particular position with regard to an investigation will likely affect the degree of insight you have been privileged to have about a case. If you are a long-time employee of a police agency, it stands to reason that you will probably be given more information than if you are a freelancer. With-holding information for the sake of an investigation is only reflective of good investigative technique on the part of the officer and should not be taken personally by the artist.

The investigative-related decision to release forensic art, in some cases, will necessitate a great deal of advance planning. "Tips" received from the general public require that arrangements be made for adequate personnel to handle incoming calls as well as the resulting "follow-up" after the calls.

The investigator may make direct contact with the news media or may arrange for the PIO to handle all contacts, depending upon the nature of an investigation. The PIO may coordinate with the officer to prepare a **press release** in advance to assure that the correct details are given out to the media, such as the basic … who, what, where, when, why, and how. The press release may be the full extent of the information provided to the media or a **press conference** may be arranged, allowing for a question-and-answer session.

Remember that it is the officer who has all of the knowledge regarding his or her investigation, so that informed investigative-related decisions can be made. The artist does not have the knowledge or the right to presume to make such decisions.

Occasionally, in cases involving efforts to identify bodies using forensic art, the **medical examiner** or representatives of his or her staff may make the media releases.

If you are a freelancer making your own media releases, your career as a forensic artist in law enforcement will probably be a short one.

Making Comments to the News Media

The same logic applies when it comes to making comments directly to the media. **It is generally the investigating officer or the PIO, not the artist, who should make any comments regarding a case.** The standard rule when I was an employee of the Texas DPS was that I tell reporters requesting interviews certain things. I always make it clear that, if interviewed, I will discuss *only* generalities about the forensic art techniques I use. I will *not* discuss specific case details. Routinely, I also indicate that I must first speak to the primary investigating officer and obtain his or her permission before any interview may take place.

Fortunately, most requests of this type were routed through our public information office and were not received directly by me. Because of the favorable publicity sometimes generated by the use of forensic artwork during investigations, my agency usually preferred that I consent to conduct requested interviews if they did not seriously interfere with my workload. **Providing an interview about forensic art methods may help keep a case in the "public eye" without actually releasing any new details.**

When a high profile investigation is going on, there may be requests for interviews from various members of the media. In these cases, the PIO will arrange for a joint press conference for simultaneous release of the forensic art-related information to all who are present. This includes newspapers and radio and television stations. Since it is my role in a press conference to describe only the techniques used, the primary officer may choose to be present to step in and answer questions that are specific to his investigation.

I have known freelance forensic artists who gave media interviews that included remarks critical of the primary investigating agency. This practice is self-serving and certainly does little to increase your standing professionally. If you feel you have a legitimate concern about the use of forensic art in an investigation, it should be directed to the officers, not in the public media. It benefits no one to encourage the public, especially the crime victim, to have doubts about the abilities of the police.

Personal Stories

When some item of forensic art you have produced is instrumental in the resolution of a high profile case, you may be approached by members of the media seeking personal interviews. First and foremost, the policies of the agency for whom you work must be respected. As a freelancer, you should discuss the request with the agency that hired you to do the artwork. Equally important, you must consider the status of the particular investigation to be discussed.

Some forensic artists get the idea that they are "stars" and enjoy the media attention to the fullest. Most often, these are freelancers who also are interested in self-promotion in hopes of generating additional business. It is more appropriate that the investigation and the forensic art methods hold center stage, and not the artist.

Hopefully, artists who have spent most of their careers in a law enforcement environment have a more reserved approach in their dealings with the media. Certainly good publicity generated by the effective techniques used by law enforcement in the successful resolution of cases is not a bad thing. A media story that presents a positive picture of forensic art functions stands to benefit the law enforcement agency, the general public, and the artist.

In addition, such stories can potentially generate new information useful to an investigation. For some time, I have made it a habit to try to get something "in return" when agreeing to do personal interviews. Some years ago, when "America's Most Wanted" requested to be allowed to do a feature story about my work, I asked that several drawings of unidentified homicide victims be shown as part of the story, with the permission of the officers whose cases were represented. The program agreed to this condition and one person was eventually identified as a result. Figure 17.1 shows an appearance with John Walsh on "America's Most Wanted."

Figure 17.1   An appearance by KTT with John Walsh on the set of the television crime-fighting program "America's Most Wanted." (Courtesy of "America's Most Wanted.")

Practical Matters

There are certain practical matters that the forensic artist, especially when inexperienced, should learn about from the PIO. If an interview is to be your first, allow the PIO to guide and assist you. Seek advice on choice of words or phrasing if you feel uncomfortable. They will also assist you in the completion of the interview, if reporters linger or become long-winded.

Choice of Location

The PIO or the investigating officer may prefer that an interview or press conference be conducted at a particular location. An agency may have special rooms designated for this purpose, which have extra electrical outlets and phones or other essentials.

There are both advantages and disadvantages to conducting an interview in the artist's office. The materials and props you need use during the interview will be at hand, which is more convenient. Consult supervisors for permission. Be sure to clear your office of any materials that involve active case investigations. Put away any tempting reports, files, and photographs that should not be viewed. The downside may be that it is far more difficult to gracefully finish an interview and get on with business when reporters have been allowed to set up in your office.

Another consideration should certainly be the other employees in the surrounding offices. I have known television crews to request that all paging be stopped over intercom systems and even ask that fans or air conditioning be turned off for sound-recording purposes. Such requests should simply be courteously denied if they interfere with work being done by co-workers.

Appropriate Attire and Demeanor

As when testifying in court as a representative of law enforcement, your appearance and demeanor should always be professional. Your appearance says a lot about you personally and the seriousness with which you approach your work. This is not to say that you should be stuffy or overly formal, but attempting to appear as an "eccentric artist" usually does not come off very well.

Posters May Be Helpful

If a formal press conference is called, it may be helpful to prepare one or more posters for use in conveying information visually. Such posters should be reviewed by both the investigator and the PIO prior to the press conference so that there will be no surprises. Since you would not be present if forensic art was not involved, some item of art likely will be shown as part of the intended purpose of the press conference. Preparing posters in advance will enable you to show these items in exactly the manner you intend. Mounting drawings on poster board stabilizes them, allowing them to be placed on an easel for easier viewing or filming.

With multiple posters to be shown in a particular sequence, it is wise to place large numbers at the top of the back of each poster. You can then be sure that the top is up and you are presenting the posters in the correct sequence. It is also a good idea to glue a business card on the back of each poster for identification.

Be Careful with Skulls

If you do skull reconstruction, you may be involved in an interview or press conference in which a human skull is shown on camera. You will find that skulls create incredible interest and curiosity. Once during a press conference regarding the release of a skull reconstruction, we actually had a television reporter ask if he could borrow the skull for a few minutes. He wanted to go outside and set up a dramatic-looking shot of himself on camera while holding the skull. Needless to say, he was not given the evidentiary skull.

When skulls are involved, great caution should be taken as to the way the skull is presented, especially when it comes to your personal demeanor. **You should avoid being photographed while holding a skull in a joking manner.** Such a thing can happen innocently, but it appears morbid and disrespectful to the homicide victim whose skull you hold as well as to the victim's family. It is not Halloween and the skull entrusted to you once belonged to a living, breathing human and should be treated with professionalism and respect.

Watch Those Cameras and Microphones

During an interview, you will be recorded, and various types of sound recording devices may be present. Newspaper reporters may bring hand-held recorders, while television crews will place a small microphone somewhere on you personally. You will be naturally alert or even nervous during the more formal portion of an interview. If you take a break and go to the restroom, *don't* go with the microphone turned on, or you may suffer one of life's most embarrassing moments!

After the interview appears to be terminated, you will feel more relaxed. You may, however, still be wired for audio. **If there is a video camera nearby, it may be turned on. Don't ever forget this.** Unfortunately, some reporters may sense your inexperience or lack of attentiveness and use it to advantage, capturing a casually spoken, inappropriate phrase. A good rule of thumb is to consider yourself as *always* subject to scrutiny any time a reporter is nearby, even if the reporter is someone you like and trust.

If you have some occasion to be at or near a crime scene or police station where members of the media are seeking information on a breaking story, be equally cautious. Today's microphones and cameras have amazing capabilities for picking up sounds and images from a distance.

On more than one occasion, I have had to cautiously enter a back door of a police station with witnesses in order to protect their identities. If you are a sketch artist who becomes well known in your community, your presence alone may alert local reporters about a witness in a "hot" case. If that witness is the only witness to a recent homicide, revealing that witness' identity may literally endanger his or her life and seriously affect the investigation.

When interviewing victims who are hospitalized, be extremely cautious about your conversations, since reporters could be anywhere in a public building. "Coffee-shop talk" should be very limited in hospitals or courthouses.

All in all, forensic artists can forge a very effective, mutually beneficial working arrangement with members of the news media, provided there is professionalism, respect, and effective communication.

References

1. Gaddis, R. D. and O'Daniel, C. R., "Officer, meet the press," *FBI Law Enforcement Bulletin*, November 1979.
2. Garner, G. W., "Is no news really good news?" *Law and Order*, April 1986.
3. Cox, M., *Stand Off in Texas, "Just Call Me a Spokesperson for the DPS,"* Austin, TX: Eakin Press, 1998.

Chapter 18

The Forensic Artist in Court

The purpose of forensic art is to aid in the identification, apprehension, and conviction of criminal offenders, in addition to helping to locate victims and identify bodies. **A logical "follow-up" to production of the artwork is that appearance by the artist in a court of law may be required.**

Each aspect of the preparation of an item of forensic art should be approached with this possibility in mind. Thus, the artist's **record-keeping** and **evidence-handling** practices should be professional and thoughtfully considered.

The forensic artist should be knowledgeable of appropriate **courtroom demeanor** and be prepared to give **expert testimony** if called upon to do so. This chapter addresses these issues and provides a list of some existing **case law** of pertinence to forensic artists.

Record Keeping

Each law enforcement agency or jurisdiction will have slightly different requirements and guidelines for case documentation and record keeping. **Artists working as full-time employees of municipal, county, state, or federal law enforcement agencies should consult supervisors for advice and abide by departmental regulations.**

Artists who do freelance work may not be *required* to keep case records in a particular way, but they should develop a consistent procedure nevertheless, since they are just as likely to have to appear in court.

All artists who undertake this work must handle records and procedures in a manner that would never place at risk the integrity of a criminal investigation or prosecution.

Case Records

Work Log

A simple log for noting case information such as the times and dates of composite interviews is a basic means of scheduling, documenting, and recording case work. Other information such as detective names, witness names, etc. may also be noted.

Case Files

You should create a case file for each item of forensic art that you prepare, whatever the type. This practice promotes the organized, orderly maintenance of all items related to the particular case, be it artwork, reports, photographs, officer or witness business cards, or other information.

Decisions should be made about what will be held in your case files or folders, considering the requirements for your jurisdiction or agency. For me, a **typical case file for a composite drawing case** usually includes the original composite drawing, associated victim or witness statements, associated offense reports, related news clippings, and a form prepared specifically for the case called a forensic art activity form. **Typical case files for other forensic art cases** such as child age progressions, fugitive updates, postmortem drawings, facial reconstructions, or skull superimpositions may contain original drawings, associated offense reports, related news clippings, photographs, and a forensic art activity form. Some agencies require the artist to write a synopsized report, similar to that written by the investigator, to be included in each case file.

Depending on the nature of the particular case, other items of significance are added as appropriate.

Case Reports

When I worked for a state police entity, I did work for numerous jurisdictions across 254 counties. My purpose in writing a forensic art case report was to enter case information into the intelligence system. These reports included only the most basic information about a case, such as requesting officer's name and agency, victim/witness name and personal descriptors, type of offense and date, and date and location of interview/drawing. The reports I wrote were attached to the forensic art activity form, a copy of the drawing, witness statement, and requesting agency offense report and sent to the agency's computerized intelligence system. The information was coded and entered into the system for cross-referencing with cases from other areas of the state or the country. **Note that the artist should be aware of the victim confidentiality laws regarding the right to use a pseudonym.**

The documentation concerning a composite interview in the form of notes or case reports varies among sketch artists. Frank Domingo, now retired from the New York City Police Department, states that the long-time policy of the NYPD Art Unit dictated a *minimum amount of record keeping*. Their unit kept a log book to document basic information such as date, offense, requesting detective's name, witness' name, and so forth. The only other information retained was the original sketch itself.

Students who attend the FBI Training Course for artists are generally encouraged to keep *far more documentation*. They are trained in filling out the form that accompanies the FBI Facial Identification Catalog and encouraged to record every reference photograph used to produce the drawing.

Use of Forms

Potential ramifications of all case documentation and the use of forms should be carefully considered. Obviously, these vary from agency to agency. In my case, since my department required that I do some documentation of this type, I designed **a form that fulfilled the agency requirements, yet did not potentially work counterproductive to the later prosecution**. Figure 18.1 shows the forensic art activity form that I have used for many years.

If you decide to use a form, careful attention should be paid to the design, with thought to the "pros and cons" of the use of forms. Forms and the information they contain have the potential to be used against a witness in court. Remember that your case file and its contents are subject to subpoena.

The filling out of forms can also create a cold, impersonal feeling at the beginning of an interview when the opposite should be happening during this time of rapport-building.

Some artists who use forms fill them out in the witness' presence, filling in the blanks as they ask question by question. This is not advisable. The same principle applies here as with the standard police interview vs. the cognitive interview, as discussed in Chapter 5. **More correct information is obtained if the witness is allowed to remember in his or her own words what he or she saw, not forcing the recall in an overly structured format.**

If a form is used that contains small "check-off" boxes, the witness may feel forced to make a choice that can be used against him or her later. For example, when referring to eye color, a form that offers only choices of blue, brown, green, or hazel *forces* a choice, even if the witness *does not* remember the exact eye color. Note that the form in Figure 18.1 has large blanks to be filled in, not "check-off" boxes. This allows for writing in information that the witness does remember such as "small, squinty eyes," instead of forcing an unclear, potentially incorrect choice.

Another problem with forms is that the composite drawing process is not a simple matter of choosing features and putting them together. Rather, the drawing is fluid in nature, with subtle changes and adjustments taking place throughout the interview. If a form forces the witness to choose features in the beginning of the process, it is very likely that the finished drawing will contain features that are not precisely the same as they started out. This evolution and refinement of the face is a desirable and natural part of the procedure. Yet the discrepancy between these early choices on a form and the final drawing could be used by a defense attorney in an attempt to confuse or discredit a witness in court. For example, if the witness checks the box for facial shape on the form that says "oval" and the face ends up very round in the finished drawing, an unnecessary problem may have been created.

Incorporated into this problem is the simple fact that terminology on the form may be interpreted differently by each witness. What is an "oval" face to one person may be a "round" face to another.

If you must use a form, it is recommended that you fill it out after the drawing is completed and the witness has left. The information contained in the form then coincides precisely with what the drawing includes.

FORENSIC ART ACTIVITY REPORT
Criminal Law Enforcement Division/Special Crimes Service

APPOINTMENT

TYPE JOB	FORENSIC ART CASE NO.	DATE COMPLETE	DATE	TIME
REQUESTED BY (AGENCY-OFFICER)		AGENCY CASE NO.	LOCATION HQ-SC	ARTIST KTT
TYPE OFFENSE	DATE OF OFFENSE	COUNTRY OF OFFENSE	NUMBER OF ACTORS	

VICTIM/WITNESS NAME	RACE	SEX	DOB	OCCUPATION	OTHER

EXAMINATION/ANALYSIS DONE

TYPE N/A	DONE BY N/A	COMMENTS N/A

SUBJECT DRAWN

RACE	SEX	APPROX. AGE	APPROX. HT.	APPROX. WT.	APPROX. BUILD	GENERAL APPEARANCE

HEAD/FACE SHAPE	HAIR	FACIAL HAIR
FOREHEAD	EYES	EYEBROWS
NOSE	EARS	CHEEKS
CHIN	MOUTH	TEETH
SKIN TEXTURE	SKIN COLOR	FACIAL LINES

CLOTHING
ACCESSORIES
OTHER

COMMENTS:

SUBMITTED BY _____

NUMBER ____5503____ DATE _____

Figure 18.1 Forensic art activity report form. (Courtesy of Texas Department of Public Safety.)

Applying the same logic, I further recommend that you **do not write down the photographs used as references.** Such photos are only a guide, and it is natural for the finished drawing to deviate from them. By writing down which photos were used, you set up an unnecessary basis for challenge and create an opportunity for the defense to raise reasonable doubt. After all, the finished drawing is, in fact, the witness' statement and the documentation of his or her memory. The steps taken to achieve the finished drawing are only a means to arrive at the work product and need not be precisely documented.

On forms or in other notes in the case record, consider very carefully any references made to the witness or his or her abilities to recall the face. If you believe that the witness may be less than truthful, it is advisable to verbally discuss this with the investigating officer rather than putting it in written form as part of the formal written case record.

Evidence Handling

The Composite Drawing as Evidence

Each composite drawing you do should be considered an item of evidence and should be handled accordingly. As discussed in Chapter 4, materials used should be sturdy enough that the evidentiary composite will endure over a prolonged period of time, if necessary. Chapter 5 discusses issues pertaining to interviewing methods, which avoid leading or improperly influencing a witness while producing the sketch.

Who Keeps the Original Composite

If you are employed by a law enforcement agency, the original drawing should be kept in your files, in your "care, custody, and control," preferably in a secure, locked cabinet. This way, you can state later in court, sometimes many years later, that the drawing has been held in your custody and there has been no opportunity for it to be altered. You have acted, therefore, as the "keeper of the record."

If you do work on a freelance basis, a more logical practice might be for the original evidentiary drawing to be held in the case file of the requesting agency. The agency must consider that at the time of trial, perhaps many years later, it might be difficult to even locate the artist.

Sign, Date, Stamp

The composite drawing should be documented as other items of evidence by signing, dating, and possibly stamping. Many artists have a rubber stamp made for this purpose, including the information appropriate for their particular agency, usually a department logo, date, and the like. Figure 18.2 shows a stamp for documentation of drawings.

Figure 18.2   Stamp used for documentation of forensic art as evidence. (Courtesy of Texas Department of Public Safety.)

Fixative

Spraying with a fixative promotes the archival quality of the evidentiary drawing. It helps ensure that the drawing will not smear and become altered or diminished if shuffled from file to file. Fixatives can be purchased in a "workable" formula, meaning that it is still possible to erase and alter the drawing to a certain extent after spraying. The usual intent, however, for the composite artist, when spraying a drawing with a fixative, is an acknowledgment of completion of the sketch. "Nonworkable" fixatives may be used for this purpose.

If fixative spraying is done in the presence of the witness and the officer (in a well-ventilated area), it also documents that the drawing was completed during the course of the interview time frame, which can become an important issue in court. **It is never a good idea to continue work on a sketch after the witness has left the interview.** If the drawing is changed or amended in any substantial way, it should be re-reviewed and approved by the witness.

Use of a 1 to 10 Evaluation System

Some artists choose to have witnesses evaluate each composite drawing on a scale of 1 to 10 and document the witness assessment in the case file. Others simply have the witness evaluate the drawing's accuracy to the target face and convey this information to the officer.

The purpose of such assessments is to aid in composite distribution strategies and to give the officer some idea as to the degree of flexibility that should be applied when making comparisons with suspects' faces. Documentation of the witness appraisal may also assist later in court if there is a problem with a lack of resemblance between the composite image and an offender identified by strong evidence such as DNA or fingerprints. If the witness had indicated a weak likeness at the completion of the sketch, the lack of similarity could more easily be explained away.

Other Types of Evidence

Skulls and Other Physical Evidence

Chapter 11 includes a section on the skull as evidence. If you do facial reconstruction procedures and receive skulls, teeth, clothing, hair specimens, and so forth, you should consult this section.

Photographs

Several types of forensic art require that the artist receive photographs in order to complete the assignment, including child age progressions, fugitive updates, photo-to-photo comparisons, postmortem drawings, and superimposition methods. In any case of a deceased person involving either an intact body or a decomposed or skeletal body it is likely that crime scene and/or morgue photographs may be entrusted to the artist.

Depending upon the agency procedures, a written receipt may be required for such photos. In any case, when receiving photographs, you should count the number of photos in the presence of the person transferring them to you and write it down. If the photographs are "originals," the loss of one photograph could prove critical to a case. Do not treat the receipt of photographs lightly.

Photographs entrusted to you should also be treated with confidentiality and not be carelessly shown around to the curious. Morgue and deceased photographs should be treated respectfully.

If receiving photographs for the preparation of an age progression of a missing child or adult, consider, too, that these may be the only photographs that a family member has of a loved one. To lose them would cause a great deal of distress.

Expert Testimony

For experienced police officers who also happen to be forensic artists, this information is very familiar. For freelance artists unaccustomed to the criminal justice system, it is necessary to gain a basic understanding of the responsibilities and procedures involved, along with some of the terminology.

Court testimony by forensic artists varies in degree and frequency across the U.S. Some artists testify very infrequently, if at all. **In cases where the artist does give testimony, it is almost always with regard to a composite drawing rather than some other type of forensic art.** Many very experienced composite artists never give testimony during their entire careers and others are called to court for virtually every successful drawing they prepare.

In a few states, **artists give testimony infrequently because composite sketches are considered hearsay under both the federal and state court systems.**

All composite artists should be prepared, nevertheless, to give testimony with regard to their drawings. In most cases, your appearance would be required just to aid in getting the composite drawing admitted as evidence. **Because the victim/witness gave you the description, obviously it is the witness who will be making an identification of the accused.**

Generally speaking, composite art is a means to an end. If a suspect can be identified based upon the sketch, law enforcement should view this as a starting point, not the end point. Direct evidence will be needed to secure a conviction.

Definitions

Expert Witness — a witness with a special knowledge of the subject about which he or she is to testify.
- That knowledge must generally be such as is not normally possessed by the average person.
- This expertise may derive from:
  1. Study and education
  2. Experience and observation
- **An expert witness must be qualified by the court to testify as such.** To qualify, he or she need not have formal training, but the court must be satisfied that the testimony presented is of a kind that in fact requires a special knowledge, skill, or experience.

Evidence — all means by which any alleged matter of fact is established or disproved in a judicial proceeding.
- Evidence includes testimony of witnesses, introduction of records, documents, exhibits, or objects, etc.
- **Your composites should be treated as evidence and properly marked. Allow as few people as possible to handle them.**

Voir Dire — literally means to *speak the truth;* the preliminary examination to determine the competency of a witness or juror.
- Questions about the ways in which you have derived your qualifications as an expert witness will be asked during voir dire.
- Be prepared to answer questions about your study, education, experience, and observation.

The Rule — at the request of either party, the witnesses on both sides may be sworn and placed in the custody of an officer of the court and removed from the courtroom to some place where they cannot hear the testimony as delivered by any other witnesses. This is called invoking **the Rule**. If you are to give testimony, and are sworn in by the court and then removed to another area, **you must not discuss issues pertaining to the case or your upcoming testimony.**

Subpoena — a writ issued under court authority that compels the appearance of a witness at a judicial proceeding.

Subpoena Duces Tecum — a type of subpoena issued at the request of one of the parties requiring the witness to bring to court all relevant documents under the witness' control. This is the type of subpoena a forensic artist will most likely be issued. Under this subpoena, you would be required to bring to court several kinds of items:
- Original composite drawing
- Forms, if any
- Notes and files
- Witness notes and drawings
- Basically, everything you have pertaining to the case

Preparation for Testimony

You may do several things to prepare to give testimony in a court of law. Although you may be subpoenaed by either the defense or the prosecution, it is more likely that it will be as part of the prosecution, since your function tends to help get criminals identified and prosecuted.

It is advisable to have a pre-trial conference with the prosecutor, especially if you have not worked together before. You can make the process much easier if you prepare a list of questions about what you do for the attorney to potentially ask you on the stand. Review them with the attorney beforehand.

If you work in law enforcement and are asked to meet with a defense counsel prior to trial, it is appropriate that you notify the prosecutor, who will likely send a representative of his or her office to attend the meeting with you.

You should be prepared to answer questions as to your training and experience. You may be asked the approximate number of composite drawings you have done, the years you have been doing them, and about your formal training. Ideally, you should have an up-to-date resume or curriculum vitae with you in court, which includes academic credentials, experience, associations, or professional organizations to which you belong, and any publications for which you are responsible. All of this information contributes to your "expert qualifications." The preparations you have made and skill with which you answer questions regarding your qualifications may directly affect the weight given to your testimony.

During voir dire, you may be asked certain standard questions. Frank Domingo lists some of these in the International Association for Identification's publication *Standards and Guidelines for Composite Artists*:[1]

- By whom are you employed?
- In what capacity are you employed?
     Sworn officer?
     Civilian employee?
     Freelance artist?
- What percentage of time is spent as a composite artist?
- How long have you been employed in this capacity?
- How long have you been drawing composites in conjunction with criminal investigations?
- Have you received specialized training in this field?
- Have you any certificates, awards, or publications in your particular specialty?
- Is there any other background information in regard to your specialty that may be beneficial for the court to know?
- Have you testified as an expert witness before?
- How many composite drawings have you made?
- What is a composite drawing?
- Is it intended to look exactly like the defendant in the case?
- What is the purpose of a composite drawing?
- How is it prepared?
- Is this the composite drawing you prepared with regard to this case, and if so, how can you identify it?
- How is the drawing protected against alterations?
- Who gave you the information needed to prepare the sketch?

By thinking about these sorts of questions in advance of the court date, you may be better prepared to answer the questions when asked. **Be prepared to clearly and understandably define forensic art and composite drawing** for the court.

It is important that you develop a standard procedure for the development of your composite drawings and be able to explain it. By doing this, the process can be more readily described in court and can be repeated in a similar manner with each interview.

If you have given any pretrial testimony or depositions, go back over them in order to be consistent. When giving a deposition, the testifying environment seems much more casual than in the courtroom, but it should be approached with the same seriousness.

You should review your case file and all of its contents and place them in a clean folder if necessary. When you enter the court, you should carry the case file in your left hand, since you will be raising your right hand to be sworn.

Courtroom Demeanor

Beyond the basic qualifications of knowledge and experience in a particular field, an expert witness must also learn to communicate clearly and objectively and be psychologically prepared to do so. Appearance and demeanor should be reflective of professionalism. They may greatly affect the acceptance and impact of the testimony that is given and influence the court's perception of the expert witness' credibility. For much of the following material on courtroom demeanor, I am indebted to Judge Jan Breland.[2]

Personal Appearance

Very specific studies have been done to ascertain the perceived credibility of individuals in court on the basis of personal appearance. If giving testimony is something that you often do, you may benefit from reading some of these studies.

Wearing of a uniform in court is appropriate if that is your normal attire on duty, although it is usually minus the weapon. Otherwise, you should dress conservatively, so as not to create a distraction. Standard attire is dark blue suits and white shirts. Females should avoid jewelry, hairstyles, and clothing that distract from their testimony. Women are usually perceived as more credible and competent if their hair is pulled back or put up in some way. You should not look sloppy, because a sloppy appearance may imply that you do sloppy work.

Testimony

When testifying, pay attention to your posture, gestures, and eye contact. Try to speak in a loud and clear voice. Avoid covering your mouth with your hand. Do not nod or shake your head for an answer, since the court reporter needs to hear you to record your response. Take the oath seriously, with your right arm held high and your fingers straight. Say "I do" clearly.

You should be serious, sincere, objective, and confident. Use your common sense and avoid signs of nervousness such as hair twisting or knee pumping.

When the Rule is in effect, do not talk to other witnesses — certainly not about the case. If you spend time in an enclosed room with other witnesses, conversation should be kept casual and to a minimum.

Direct examination is when the *prosecutor* questions you. Cross-examination is when the *defense attorney* questions you. Be sure that you understand each question and think before you answer.

Do not volunteer more than you are asked. Attorneys often use the "silent treatment" to make you uncomfortable and make you feel like you must keep talking. Do not try to memorize what you are going to say. Turn to members of the jury and talk to them openly and frankly.

If your answer somehow comes out wrong, correct it immediately. If your answer was not clear, clarify it immediately.

The three most important answers are "yes," "no," and "I don't recall." Try and avoid use of words like "never" or "always." A better term is "under certain circumstances."

Use formal forms of address for all about whom you speak, using "sir" and "m'am," and "Mr." and "Ms. or Mrs." If addressing the judge, say "Your Honor." Avoid use of slang or overly technical language. Your objective is to engage and educate the jury about your work, so try to explain your techniques clearly, but simply, remembering that some members of the jury may not be well educated.

Do not be a smart aleck, because this never comes across well in court. Avoid exaggeration or sarcasm and always keep your temper. If you lose your temper, the opposing attorney will have achieved his or her goal. It is far better to let the opposing attorney come across as arrogant or temperamental to the jury, rather than making those impressions yourself.

You should treat the prosecutor and the defense attorney with the same respect. Be polite and non-argumentative. You should be fair and appear impartial as if the outcome is impersonal, even if it is not.

If the judge speaks or there is an objection, stop speaking immediately.

Upon the completion of your testimony, ask "May I be excused?" at the end if you are uncertain. Then leave the room in a professional, confident manner. **Above all, you should always tell the truth.**

Primary Issues for the Forensic Artist

Defining and Explaining Your Methods

Of primary importance is the development of the ability to define and concisely explain the composite drawing technique you use so that any juror can clearly understand it.

When Asked for an Opinion

In some instances, the artist may be asked to give an opinion about certain issues. Typical questions raised might be, "Do you feel that this drawing really resembles the defendant?" or "Do you feel that _____ was a good witness?" In the case of either of these questions, you should pause slightly and wait for a possible objection before answering.

When answering the question regarding resemblance to the defendant, it may become necessary to elaborate on the more subtle aspects of your craft. On one occasion, for example, I was asked by a defense attorney defending a suspect charged with sexual assault, "Ms. Taylor, do you mean to tell me that you really think that *this drawing* looks like my client?" *"His eyes are different."* My reply had to do with expression. I said,

> The overall facial shape and features do resemble Mr. _____ . His eyes appear different because the expression is different. As he sits looking at me in the courtroom, he is smiling. Ms. _____ (the victim) recalled and described a sinister, threatening expression to me when we prepared the drawing, so his eyebrows are lowered and his eyes are narrowed in the composite drawing to reflect the expression she described.

A good reply when asked whether or not a particular witness was a good witness might be, "The witness seemed to understand the process."

Use of Photographs

Be sure that the prosecutor understands the difference between photographs used as references as opposed to files of mug shots of past offenders who could be suspects. More than likely, you will *not* be called upon to elaborately explain your use of photographic references. If questioned about it, the prosecutor should understand the procedure and be prepared to aid you in explaining it by asking the right questions. It is also a good idea to explain **that the use of references is a standardly accepted method used across the U.S. and taught at the FBI Academy.**

Good Likeness/Bad Likeness

If your sketch proves to bear a strong and accurate likeness to the defendant, be prepared for the defense attorney to attempt to discredit you and the sketch.

If the sketch bears a poor likeness to the defendant, the defense attorney may try to use it to exonerate his or her client.

Court Presentation Artwork

It is not within the scope of this book to cover preparation of trial displays or demonstrative evidence. An entire book could be written on those topics alone. It does behoove the forensic artist to sometimes prepare poster-type presentations of his or her work for its formal presentation in court.

Since anything offered into evidence may be taken into the jury room, your artwork should be sturdily mounted and labeled so that it will not be flimsy or difficult for jurors to handle or understand.

On most occasions, you will explain your own artwork, but in some instances, the artwork is prepared to aid in the testimony of another witness. Figure 18.3 shows

Figure 18.3 Travis County Assistant District Attorney Robert Smith (left) and Medical Examiner Roberto Bayardo (right) use **forensic art posters** to explain anatomical information to the jury in a capital murder case regarding the death of an infant.

Travis County, Texas prosecutor Robert Smith and Medical Examiner Dr. Roberto Bayardo using forensic art to assist in explaining detailed information to the court in a capital murder case regarding the death of an infant.

Forensic Art Case Law

In U.S. courts, certain cases over the years have been of relevance to the forensic artist. In many instances, findings pertaining to the admissibility of photographs or kit-generated composites may also apply to hand-drawn or computer-generated composite images. Although not necessarily a complete reference, the following are legal findings of interest to the forensic artist.

Hearsay Rule Exceptions

As previously stated, composite drawings are generally considered "hearsay." The courts have ruled that, under certain circumstances, hearsay can be admitted.

People v. Coffey (1962) 11 NY2d 142, 227 NYS2d 412,182 NE2d 92

A composite was admitted to refute the theory of *recent fabrication* or the allegation that a composite had been prepared *after* the arrest of a suspect by showing that the composite was actually done soon after the commission of the crime. This admission was to bolster a witness whom the defense was attempting to impeach.

People v. Cooks (1983) 141 CA3d 224

A composite drawing may be admissible as a prior extrajudicial identification by the testifying witness (and as an exception to the hearsay rule as independent evidence of identity),

> IF: The witness admits the prior identification, provided:
> 1. It was made at the time the crime was fresh in the witness' memory, and
> 2. The drawing is offered after the witness testifies he or she made the identification and that it truly reflected the witness' opinion at the time,

> OR IF: The witness denies his prior identification or testifies contrary to it.

Standards for Admitting a Composite

Commonwealth v. Weichell — Massachusetts Supreme Judicial Court 9-23-83

A composite prepared by a police officer and a witness using an "Identi-KIT" may be introduced as substantive evidence of identification if two conditions are met. **Such a composite is admissible if:**

1. **The witness is available for cross-examination, and**
2. **The procedures used in preparing the composite were not unduly suggestive.**

The court ruled that the "composite drawing" was really nothing more than the sum of a series of statements. Thus, the use of such drawings is not limited to corroboration of a witness in court identification, but, in a footnote, the **majority indicated that they were not yet ready to uphold a conviction in which a composite drawing was the only identification evidence.**

The dissent contended that substantial reasons exist to question the reliability of composites. It was suggested that the proponent of a composite should be required to lay a foundation of admissibility by adducing evidence of the reliability of the composite process and also the reliability of the procedures used to produce the composite drawing before offered.

State v. Genardi (1970) 111 NJ Super 435, 268 A2d 534, 42 ALR3d 1168, affd 57 NJ 438, 273 A2d 353

If the prior out-of-court identification of a defendant becomes an issue, the court held that a sketch can be admitted if the witness who made the identification is in court and is available for cross-examination.

Quality and Availability of the Original Composite

People v. Molina (1981) 116 Cal App 3d 223, 224–225

In a prosecution for kidnapping, rape, oral copulation, sodomy, and robbery, no prejudicial error resulted from the trial court's asserted **admission in evidence of a black-and-white photocopy of a composite drawing** of defendant made from the victim's description of him.

Thus, the photocopy was considered to be the "best evidence" available.

State v. Palmer 196 Conn 157 (May 1985)

The court ruled that the loss of the original composite before conviction did not prejudice the conviction and was not basis for an appeal. The original of the composite sketch was lost before the commencement of the defendant's first trial. **A photocopy of the sketch was introduced into evidence by the state in its place.** The defendant claimed that because the witness had described his assailant as dark skinned and the defendant was in fact light skinned, the state's loss of the original sketch deprived him of presumably exculpatory evidence and therefore denied him due process. The court disagreed since the defendant failed to make an objection at the time of the first trial.

The original **court also recognized that the qualifications of the sketch artist who drew the composite sketch were sufficient to justify the trial court's permitting him to compare certain spatial features in the sketch to the defendant himself;** that testimony was proffered not on the issue of the identification of the defendant but rather in an effort to teach the jurors how to view the materials before them.

People v. Garcia (1988) 201 Cal App 3d 324, 325

In a prosecution for first degree murder with a firearm, the trial court properly exercised its discretion in **admitting a color photograph as a duplicate of a sketch of the**

suspect made by a police artist from an eyewitness' description. The defendant failed to make any substantial showing of unfairness in the admission of the photograph rather than the original sketch.

Gardner v. State 745 SW 2d 955 (Tex. App. — Austin 1988)

The court ruled that the destruction of the original composite drawing prepared by a police artist of a last customer of a murdered taxicab driver did not substantially prejudice the defendant.

The defendant failed to establish that the composite drawing would have played a significant role in the defense of the murder conviction or that the destruction of the composite was a conscious effort to suppress exculpatory evidence. The witness identified the defendant in a photographic array and a corporeal lineup as well as at trial.

Multiple Witnesses

Wilson v. State — Texas Court of Criminal Appeals; Sept. 22,1986 Dallas No. 05-85-01013-CR

Admission of a composite was proper, even though two witnesses corroborated in making the composite. The two witnesses reviewed the composite together and came up with the final rendition. The officer who assembled the features was not available for cross-examination. The witnesses stated that the final composite accurately depicted the robber.

Other Related Case Law

Probable Cause to Stop and Identify

Carlos v. State — Texas Court of Criminal Appeals; Feb. 26, 1986 Beaumont No. 09-84-185 CR

The defendant had been convicted of murder and he appealed. The Court of Appeals held that **the close resemblance of the defendant to the composite sketch of a person who had talked with the murder victim a day or two prior to her death warranted the police officer's stopping the defendant and asking his name and address, regardless of whether the intrusion was classified as a stop or arrest.**

To Aid the Defendant

Kostal v. People (1966) 160 Colo 64, 414 P2d 123, cert den 385 US 939, 17 L ED 2d 218, 87 S Ct 305

A sketch was admitted to show that the artist's composite, based upon eyewitness description, depicted a black man, and the defendant was white.

Counsel for a Caucasian defendant offered into evidence a composite "picture," allegedly depicting a Negro, produced by a police officer relying upon verbal descriptions provided by eyewitnesses a few days after the crime had been committed. The police officer who produced the picture was called as a witness and identified his composite.

Right of the Accused to the Production of a Composite Drawing

Several cases in the courts have held that the court's failure to permit an accused criminal to inspect a composite drawing made of the suspect was not error.

United States v. Zurita (1966, CA7 Ind) 369 F2d 474, cert den 386 US 1023, 18 L Ed 2d 462, 87 S Ct 1379

The court held that a composite drawing made by an FBI agent during an interview with two witnesses who identified the defendant during the trial was not discoverable under the Jencks Act. The Jencks Act basically states that statements made by witnesses shall be made available to the defense, but the **composite drawing was not considered to be a "statement" within the meaning of the statute.**

People v. Therriault (1976) 42 Ill App 3d 876, 1 Ill Dec 717, 356 NE2d 999

The court ruled that it was not error for the trial court to deny a motion that the police department be forced to produce a copy of a composite drawing of the defendant.

State v. Fitzpatrick (1975), Mo App 525 SW 2d 342

The court held that a defendant was not entitled to the discovery of a composite drawing, since the **description for the drawing was not given by the victim in the rape case.**

State v. Koch (1983) 138 Ariz 99, 673 P2d 297

In a homicide prosecution, the court held that the failure to provide a copy to the defendant of an Ident-KIT composite did not violate pre-trial disclosure rules since the **defendant was provided with a report which contained the formula from which the composite could have been reproduced.**

People v. Trudo (1982, 3d Dept) 88 App Div 2d 1091, 453 NY S2d 54

The court held that the defendant was not entitled to the production of the composite sketch which led to his arrest, where the **sketch was drawn by a newspaper artist and was not under the control of the District Attorney or the police.**

Hypnosis

People v. Miller (1990) 50 Cal 3d 954, 955

In a prosecution for multiple counts of first degree murder, the witness had stated before the hypnotic session that he could identify the perpetrator. A police artist's drawing, made under the witness' direction, was not to his satisfaction. Under hypnosis, the witness made several changes to the picture. The original composite drawing was ruled not admissible as a memorialization of his prehypnotic recollection of the man he was trying to identify. However, the error was harmless since the hypnotic session did not taint evidence discovered in the ensuing police investigation.

Though the act of giving testimony in a court of law may at first seem stressful and intimidating, it is part of the foundation of the system of justice and a necessary step toward obtaining a conviction. **If your forensic art procedures have been professionally conducted and accurately documented, testifying in court can actually provide a satisfying and rewarding completion to your artistic efforts.**

References

1. Domingo, F., *Composite Art Manual.* New York: The International Association for Identification and John Jay College of Criminal Justice, 1986.
2. Breland, J., Judge, County Court No. 6, Travis County, TX, personal communication.

Summary

In conclusion, there are certain points about forensic art that I wish to emphasize. **It is my hope that there develops a thread of continuity of attitude among all who undertake this work.** It is simply not enough to take a superficial view of any aspect of this important support function for law enforcement. **Each case deserves individual attention, study, and consideration.**

1. Do not just do passable **drawings of faces**: *learn to draw them well and with an understanding of their anatomy.*
2. Do not do superficial **interviews of crime victims**: *interview them with skill, sensitivity, and a solid knowledge of how memory works.*
3. Do not be content to produce **child age progressions** using simple stretches and merges: *really study the subtleties of each child's face, the faces of the child's relatives, and craniofacial aging to make educated predictions.*
4. Do not just throw a few age lines on faces to produce **fugitive updates or adult age progressions**: *carefully evaluate each individual face, use your knowledge of aging, and incorporate any other available information.*
5. Do not make claims regarding **photo-to-photo comparisons** that are not reasonable: *remember the limitations of the method so as not to destroy your professional credibility.*
6. Avoid the injustice of rushing **postmortem drawings** of murder victims: *learn about postmortem changes to the face, study every facial nuance, and really give the victim a chance to be identified.*
7. Produce **facial reconstructions from skulls** with respect for the skulls of homicide victims entrusted to you: *make every effort to get sound scientific input, and follow methodologies carefully to more accurately recreate their faces in life.*
8. Do this work with the **highest ethical conduct**: *be prepared to present your work in a **court of law**.*

It has been said that **the pen is mightier than the sword ... if used correctly, so is the pencil ...**

— KTT

Index